AF823932

Palgrave Studies in Global Entrepreneurship

Series Editor
Vanessa Ratten, La Trobe University, Bundoora, Melbourne, VIC, Australia

This Palgrave Macmillan book series on global entrepreneurship provides an urgently needed platform to focus on issues related to entrepreneurship from a global perspective. It showcases the global nature of entrepreneurship and provides a home for high quality and novel research. These include a broad range of topics related to entrepreneurship that incorporate a global mindset. By focusing on the global aspect of entrepreneurship it combines an international element to how micro, small, medium and large enterprises need to consider international ramifications into their business decisions. In doing so, the series covers new areas including digital technology, crisis management, sport business and sustainability. Each book in the series will encompass a different ground breaking area related to global entrepreneurship. While the series focus is on global entrepreneurship, it is interdisciplinary in nature as it will link global aspects of entrepreneurship to new subject areas. These will contribute to a more global discussion on how entrepreneurship is fundamentally entrepreneurial in nature. The series responds to the need to incorporate global thinking amongst students, practitioners, policy makers and researchers.

Milton Rajaratne

Concepts, Processes and Practice of Entrepreneurship

A Primer on Innovation and Venture Creation

palgrave
macmillan

Milton Rajaratne
Department of Operations
Management, Faculty of Management
University of Peradeniya
Peradeniya, Sri Lanka

Palgrave Studies in Global Entrepreneurship
ISBN 978-981-97-6179-1   ISBN 978-981-97-6180-7 (eBook)
https://doi.org/10.1007/978-981-97-6180-7

© The Editor(s) (if applicable) and The Author(s), under exclusive license to Springer Nature Singapore Pte Ltd. 2024

This work is subject to copyright. All rights are solely and exclusively licensed by the Publisher, whether the whole or part of the material is concerned, specifically the rights of translation, reprinting, reuse of illustrations, recitation, broadcasting, reproduction on microfilms or in any other physical way, and transmission or information storage and retrieval, electronic adaptation, computer software, or by similar or dissimilar methodology now known or hereafter developed.
The use of general descriptive names, registered names, trademarks, service marks, etc. in this publication does not imply, even in the absence of a specific statement, that such names are exempt from the relevant protective laws and regulations and therefore free for general use.
The publisher, the authors and the editors are safe to assume that the advice and information in this book are believed to be true and accurate at the date of publication. Neither the publisher nor the authors or the editors give a warranty, expressed or implied, with respect to the material contained herein or for any errors or omissions that may have been made. The publisher remains neutral with regard to jurisdictional claims in published maps and institutional affiliations.

Cover illustration: © CSA Images/getty images

This Palgrave Macmillan imprint is published by the registered company Springer Nature Singapore Pte Ltd.
The registered company address is: 152 Beach Road, #21-01/04 Gateway East, Singapore 189721, Singapore

If disposing of this product, please recycle the paper.

For my wife—Anula
And Children
Tharo, Shinta, Umeda

Foreword

> "Although, as of today, entrepreneurship is believed to be confined to undertaking of business for private profit, its presence in the society is much broader" (*Concepts*, *Process*, and Practice of Entrepreneurship—Milton Rajaratne).

As the author of this book states in the introduction (see quote), entrepreneurship in practice has a much broader meaning than simply launching a new innovative business for profit. Those entrepreneurs who define their only purpose as making a profit will probably develop their new venture to demonstrate its economic value and then cash out by selling their small startups to the highest bidder.

The vast majority of entrepreneurs strive, however, to grow their small innovative startups with just a few people into a larger enterprise. They typically have two purposes—to build wealth and to impact the world through their innovation. But increasingly entrepreneurs have a third purpose for their entrepreneurial ventures. It is to create social value, that is to contribute to the larger good of society—the well-being of their people, community, and larger society by minimizing the negative impact of their growing venture on the environment and climate.

To achieve all three purposes, entrepreneurs have to learn to organize, manage, and lead the company in a way that creates a collaborative community capable of building high trust and commitment.

Elsewhere I have referred to this as building a high commitment, high-performance organization (Beer, *High Commitment, High Performance*, 2009). Arguably the best examples of this are entrepreneurs David Packard and Bill Hewlett who began their enterprise in 1937 in David Packard's a garage. By the 1990 they had built the global multibillion company Hewlett-Packard (HP) that for five decades was rated as the most "Admired Company in the World."

They did this by believing that people are naturally motivated to make a positive contribution and difference. This belief guided how they organized, managed, and led HP. The company created high trust and commitment through an egalitarian culture that minimized titles and did not provide private offices for anyone regardless of rank. As the company grew, they expected their managers to lead with the same values that the company had adopted.

For example, they expected their leaders to manage by walking around to listen to what people told them about what was going well and what stood in the way of doing better. They created a sense of ownership through profit sharing, wide stock ownership, and a decentralized and semi-autonomous divisional structure in which every division had to earn its own way to growth. They created a transparent and open culture through skip level meetings that allowed them to talk to lower levels without the presence of their bosses. This allowed top managers to hear the truth about what needed to change and what innovations and business opportunities were being missed or mismanaged.

Hewlett-Packard is not the only entrepreneurial venture that grew from its modest beginning into a vibrant large high commitment, high-performance company. For example, Southwest Airlines has outperformed its competitors in profits and service. Nucor, a mini steel corporation, has outperformed its competitors and gets extremely positive reviews from the employees for the team structure and complete support of it. Lincoln Electric has been in the arc welding business for well over 40 years and gets high marks for its development of employee commitment and business performance.

My own research, supported by many other studies, has revealed seven leadership, organizational and management capabilities that entrepreneurs must develop to succeed. I review them briefly here for readers who aspire to grow their startups into high commitment, high-performance business organizations. These seven essential management and leadership capabilities are described below.

1. Leadership and management skills really matter. The entrepreneur who wants to grow his or her startup into a larger successful high commitment, high-performance company must first reflect on whether he or she has the following qualities required to lead and manage:

   a. A desire to be a "servant leader" who empowers those below to lead and manage.
   b. A belief in people's motivation to make a difference.
   c. Value teamwork and collaboration and develop these as central features of the company's culture.
   d. Be motivated to learn from peers and importantly from those below the top about the effectiveness of their organization and leadership of it. Without the readiness to hear feedback and learn they will be unable to become good and effective leaders and managers.

2. Develop a clear direction for the enterprise to be understood by every employee. That direction should include the firm's higher purpose, strategy, and shared values about how people and customers should be treated. Involve people throughout the organization in discussing your direction for the company to enhance understanding and commitment to that direction. That direction must be developed by the whole top team.
3. Develop a strong top team and ensure they work as a team, speaking with one voice about the direction of the whole enterprise. The only way to achieve this is to involve the whole team in the process of setting the direction. Consider how Peter Don the CEO of a fast-food chain developed commitment from his senior team. He met with them in several meetings to discuss what legacy for the enterprise they wanted to leave and what they believed was the right strategic direction. These were open meetings in which he had a voice but did not force his own view. The result was a common understanding of how the company will develop economic, human, and social value.
4. Coordination and collaboration across the organizational internal and external boundaries are essential organizational and cultural qualities on which success rests. Developing this organizational

quality depends on the leaders' values and importantly their willingness to create cross-boundary lower-level teams; product development, business, and project teams, for example, are composed of people with relevant information and skills from all parts of the organization. The designation of a manager with general management capabilities and people skills to lead the teams effectively is critical. They must be coached and supported in this role.

5. Is the entrepreneur must be ready to delegate work, technical and business decisions, to the lower teams even if historically they enjoyed, liked, and were highly capable of doing the work themselves. To empower others to do what you have done is often a very difficult transition for an entrepreneur. Yet unless this transition occurs the entrepreneurial venture will run into difficulties and result in failure to grow. If the entrepreneur is uncomfortable with delegating critical tasks and decision rights to lower levels, he or she should consider hiring an experienced CEO who can.
6. Developing a strong bench of managers capable of leading various teams is discussed in 5 above. This is an essential capability that entrepreneurial organizations require if they are to staff the teams and new businesses discussed in the previous section. And these are the potential successors to the entrepreneur when he or she is ready to or has to step back due to age and health issues. Despite its importance key people in 8 out of 10 companies I worked with and studied identified insufficient leadership development as a barrier to effectiveness.

   Research indicates that the best way to develop management and leadership capabilities is to provide cross-functional experience to high potentials. This enables them to learn what these functions do, a requirement for general management. And moves to areas in which they, the high potentials, have no technical capabilities that test and develop their people and management skills to lead.

   In partnership with their human resources executives, entrepreneurs who want to grow their company must create a systematic system for reviewing high potential people so they can determine their management capabilities and then plan successive moves to develop their capabilities as managers and leaders.

7. Successful high commitment and performance organizations enable key lower-level people to speak truth to power—the top management team—about barriers to implementing the firm's strategy and values. This is not about identifying and firing people who are the problem. It is about learning how the system of organizing, managing, and leading is functioning—what is working and not working and what needs to change.

Growth from a startup to a larger enterprise inevitably demands changes in many aspects of the organization. Unless a process for making it safe for people to tell the CEO and his or her senior management about what needs to change to make the firm better, including the CEO and the senior team, trust, commitment, and performance will suffer. That is why Hewlett-Packard leaders organized skip level meetings to enable lower levels to speak truth to power, then the top management team, l without their bosses present.

Becton Dickinson, a global medical devices company, adopted a structured process my colleagues and I developed called the Strategic Fitness Process. Its structure and guidelines for a constructive conversation about the unvarnished truth facilitated by an external consultant enabled senior management to be non-defensive and learn about the good, bad, and sometimes ugly about their organization and their leadership. And it made it safe for a task force as a group to report honestly what they had learned from 100 confidential interviews they had conducted to learn the truth (Beer, *Fit to Compete*, 2020).

The honest conversations between top management teams and lower levels at Hewlett-Packard and Becton Dickinson are emotionally powerful. That is why it builds trust, commitment, and energy for continuous change and improvement so important given the uncertain and constantly changing competitive and social environment in which we are living.

In conclusion, entrepreneurship has come to mean much more than inventing a new technology, product, or service. Today, as the author of this book noted in the introduction, entrepreneurship involves growing and building an enterprise that contributes to the wellbeing of all its stakeholders—employees, customers, community, the wider society, and of course the shareholders. This high trust, high commitment, and high-performance firm requires entrepreneurs to develop seven essential management and organizational capabilities if the growing company is to prosper and survive in the demanding and constantly changing competitive and social environment of the twenty century and beyond.

Michael Beer
Professor Emeritus, Harvard
Business School, Soldiers Field
Boston, MA 02163 USA
mbeer@hbs.edu

References

Beer, M. (2009), *High Commitment, High Performance: How to Build an Organization Capable of Sustained Advantage.*

Beer, M. (2020), *Fit to Compete: Why Honest Conversations About Your Company's Capabilities is the Key to a Winning Strategy.*

Preface

Aim of the Book

Emphasis

This book emphasizes the concepts, processes, and practices of entrepreneurship with special focus on innovation and venture creation which are the outcomes of entrepreneurship. Value creation and wealth creation also have been brought to the mainstay of the book with the intension to broadly view the socioeconomic role, challenges, social responsibility, and new trends of entrepreneurship. The comprehensiveness of the book has been derived from the decade-long readings, university level teachings, exposure to renowned enterprises, acquaintance with entrepreneur biographies, hands-on experiences, and innovative concepts of the author which the reader can witness in the text.

Intended Readership

This book extensively explores a large number of topics in entrepreneurship with the intension of catering to the needs of academics, teachers, and undergraduate and postgraduate students, in the first place. And then the book aims at identifying the needs of trainers and trainees of Entrepreneurship Development Programs, current and prospective entrepreneurs, and those who have interest in business in general. Also, this book is designed to provide the readership with comprehensive but clear and easy-to-understand content that includes definitions, examples, tools, analyses, and unique styles that many books lack. This book, also, intends to inspire entrepreneurship spirit in the reader's mind and to guide through the path of venture creation.

Entrepreneurship is a highly popular subject at present at postgraduate, undergraduate, and school levels. Entrepreneurship Development Programs (EDPs) are another segment that is widely accepted by every country. They aim at inculcating entrepreneurial skills and business knowledge among the participants. Similarly, both current and prospective entrepreneurs are keen to advance their innovative skills to enter the market, to raise competitiveness, and to stay away from business failure. In this context, this book identifies the importance of development of entrepreneurship education, creation of entrepreneurs, creation of venture, and creation of national wealth and intends to instill the sense of the art of doing business. Accordingly, this book will be equally useful for teaching and learning circles and also for the entrepreneurship careerist circles.

Structure of the Book

Major Themes

This book is organized into five major themes presented in five parts: (1) Facets of Entrepreneurship, (2) History and Theory of Entrepreneurship, (3) Entrepreneurship Process, (4) Entrepreneurship Practice, and (5) New Trends and Topics of Entrepreneurship. While each part has its specific focus, they together compose a consistent body of text that sequentially furthers from fundamentals to advanced level. Part V is quite different from the rest of the book as it advances a few discourses of entrepreneurship. This part is an extension to the subject of entrepreneurship and thus, it is new to the entrepreneurship textbooks. Each part of the book is then divided into 19 comprehensive chapters altogether which present a host of real-world examples, tools, charts, and tables. In addition to the core of the book, a few teacher and learner friendly features are also added. They include Key Learning Points, Chapter Summary, Review Questions, Additional Reading List, and a Subject Index.

Chapters

Part one of the book is organized into three chapters that lay foundation for the subject of entrepreneurship. They provide a lengthy discussion on Introduction to Entrepreneurship, Entrepreneurship Environment, and Perspectives of Entrepreneurs. Then, in part two, two chapters are organized as the History and Evolution of Entrepreneurship and the Theory of Entrepreneurship. They initially explore emergence, evolution, and present state of entrepreneurship and then provide a lengthy discussion on the theory of entrepreneurship. Part three is as big as one-third of the book and it contains six chapters, namely; Opportunity Recognition Process, Invention and Innovation Process, Intellectual Property Rights and Registration, Feasibility Planning Process, Business Modeling and Venture Creation, and the Growth Management Process. They are designed to elaborate the process and sub-processes of entrepreneurship with the view to inspire entrepreneurial ambition in readers. Part four includes four chapters that are designed to elaborate on the Production and Service Ventures, Acquisition and Merger and Franchising and Licensing, Neo-entrepreneurship Models, and Entrepreneurship Development Programs. They explore the venture areas, their unique features, entrepreneurship models, and entrepreneurship development effort. Part five contains four chapters, namely; Comparative Entrepreneurship, International Entrepreneurship, Political Economy of Entrepreneurship, and Entrepreneur Social Responsibility and Ethics. They discuss topics useful for advanced learners and researchers.

Special Features of the Book

Tables and Figures

This book introduces more than 100 tables and figures directly in relation to the content presented. Tables and figures are designed and presented in a manner to immensely improve the readability of the book. These informative and eye-catching portrayals, graphs, flowcharts, and tables help illustrate the content and context as they provide additional explanations and information also. The reader will find the tables and figures very helpful in understanding the logics and arguments advanced in the text. Special care has been taken not to stuff the book with too many tables and figures that can annoy the reader and disturb reading or too few such features that make the reader bored. In essence, the number and the design of tables and figures have been designed in reader friendly manner and thus, to guarantee a pleasant reading of the entire text.

Add-Ons

In addition to the core content of the book, a few essential features are also added-on to make the book more user friendly and an effective learning material. Accordingly, at the beginning of each chapter, a comprehensive list of Key Learning Points is provided. They directly refer to the text of each chapter and thus, instructors and readers can easily embark on the sections of chapters via the learning point chosen. At the end of each chapter, an attractive summary is provided deriving from the chapter content. Chapter summary is helpful for the readers who prefer to read synopses to quickly grasp the main points before exploring details at a later time. Also, this book provides, at the end of every chapter, a long list of review questions aimed at covering every important point deliberated in each chapter. For almost all review questions, texts are assigned and so, the answers can easily be derived and developed from relevant sections. Only a very few questions connected to advanced topics require comprehensive analyses and thus additional enquiry.

Original Works

This book introduces several innovative and original works of the author in the form of concepts, hypotheses, and analytical tools. They elaborate the texts and contexts and help expand the subject of entrepreneurship. The original works, except for the portrayals and illustrations, include the following: (1) Entrepreneurial Opportunity Diagnostic Matrix, (2) Venture Classification Matrix, (3) Intervention Hypothesis, (4) Opportunity Observation Methods, (5) Innovation Path, (6) Innovation Power, (7) Business Model Matrix, (8) Entrepreneurship Process, (9) The 5-C Growth Model, (10) The Venture Growth Scheme, (11) Social Entrepreneurship Model, (12) Political Freedom Assessment Matrix, and (13) The Risk-Return-Matrix. These original works will take the analyses of entrepreneurship to new heights by illuminating relationships between entrepreneurial phenomena and extending avenues of entrepreneurship research.

Attractiveness

Several unique features are added to this book to enhance its quality, standard, and attractiveness to ensure strain-free reading. The content is thus, organized and described in a way as if the reader were taken on hiking that inflicts no affliction regardless of the elevation the reader is taken to. Although the content discussed in each chapter is comprehensive and sometimes technical, it is presented in an attractive manner that the readers frequently meet real-world organizations and practical examples which help unremitting reading. This book furnishes an all-round process of entrepreneurship that is beneficial to learners of all categories. In addition to deliberations of general and essential matters, the advanced learners can find at least four chapters, toward the end of the book, that are extremely useful for academic enquiries.

How to Use the Book

Rudimentary Level

Entrepreneurship courses offered worldwide are normally designed to impart knowledge to a spectrum of students engaged in diploma, graduate, and postgraduate learning. This book, organized in 19 chapters, incrementally builds subject matters to suit learners from rudimentary, intermediate, and to higher level. From among the 19 chapters of this book, instructors are advised to choose chapters to suit the syllabi of their teaching and training programs. In general, chapters belonging to Parts I and III of the book will be more suitable for diploma programs whereas Parts I, II, and III, are recommended for Higher National Diploma level course of entrepreneurship. For an undergraduate level program, Parts I, II, III, and IV are useful to deliver a full course in entrepreneurship.

Postgraduate Level

For a master level program by coursework, suitable chapters from the initial 4 parts and a chapter or two from Part V shall be useful whereas a postgraduate program by research can concentrate more on Part V along with the earlier chapters of higher order. In Part V, all the four chapters illustrate advanced topics of entrepreneurship discourse. So, they are more useful for research students for expanding their thoughts on entrepreneurship and designing a research problem taking into consideration the external spheres of entrepreneurship. The original concepts and tools presented in the book will be more useful for the learners of master level and above.

EDP and Professional Levels

This book is useful for both trainers and trainees of Entrepreneurship Development Programs (EDPs) and professional courses also. Part II of this book alone will be a sufficient teaching and learning material for these programs with an exception that EDP trainers will find Chapter 15 also will be much more useful. The training instructors accordingly can use and recommend for the students the sections as stipulated in the table below. The instructors of rudimentary level programs should refrain from introducing the chapters of Part V and the original works included in this book as they are too advanced for those levels. In conclusion, this book is useful for all levels of learners and instructors because of its resourceful content and chapter arrangement, if used as recommended.

Learning Points and Review Questions

All instructors are urged to select relevant learning points from the Key Learning Points provided at the beginning of each chapter and peruse the exact topics together with the closely related preceding and following sections of that chapter to fully accomplish teaching and learning objectives. Instructors can task the students to examinations giving relevant questions from the section of Review Questions that appear at the end of each chapter. Instructors and students are advised that a few questions, however, require additional knowledge, exposure, and data which require them to peruse additional and specific sources. The table given below guides the instructors and students on how to use this book for different qualifications.

Guide to Use This Book

Qualification	*Chapter number*
Entrepreneurship Development Programs*	1, 2, 6, 7, 8, 9, 10, 11, 15
Diploma*	1, 2, 3, 6, 7, 9, 10
Higher National Diploma*	1, 2, 5, 6, 7, 8, 9, 10, 11, 12, 14
Undergraduate Degree*	1, 2, 3, 5, 6, 7, 8, 9, 10, 11, 12, 13, 14
MBA/MSC by Coursework	1, 5, 6, 7, 8, 9, 10, 11, 12, 13, 14, 15, 19
MPHIL/ MSC/PHD by Research	1, 4, 5, 6, 7, 8, 9, 10, 11, 12, 13, 14, 15, 16, 17, 18, 19

* Instructors may avoid some sub-topics and analytical tools at their discretion

Peradeniya, Sri Lanka

Milton Rajaratne

Acknowledgments

Writing and publication of this voluminous work was a tedious task that consumed a few years. I started writing this book during the "COVID-19 lockdown" in early 2020. At the time this book rolls out from the press, I am obliged to express my sincere gratitude to many who contributed to this work both directly and indirectly.

I largely owe Professor Michael Beer of Harvard Business School (USA) a great deal of thanks for writing an impressive and lengthy foreword that added an enormous value to this book.

Professors Suzuki and Sasaki of Osaka City University and Professors Ohashi, Yano, and Mikita of Wakayama University who taught me business courses and exposed me to large Japanese corporates such as Toyota, Panasonic, Sharp, Kao, and Daikin deserve much appreciation.

The Japanese entrepreneurs, whose name list is too long to carry in here, operating in the district of Wakayama, Japan generously spent time with me in discussing matters relating to business, entrepreneurship, and Japanese Management Thought deserve special and unwavering gratitude.

Palgrave Macmillan Co. deserves a great deal of appreciation for finding value in this work and publishing it; which provided me with a remarkable opportunity to take my insights to international readership.

Back at home, I thank my daughter, Shinta, for proofreading and making initial corrections to the manuscript. My younger son, Umeda deserves many thanks for resolving technical issues I encountered during page making of the manuscript. My heartfelt gratitude goes to my wife, Anula, whose support and sacrifice were immense, immeasurable, and priceless. So, I dedicate this book to her knowing, also, that this cannot recompense her sacrifices.

Milton Rajaratne
University of Peradeniya,
Peradeniya, Sri Lanka

Contents

About the Author

Milton Rajaratne is the Senior Professor in Operations Management and the Founder Dean of the Faculty of Management at the University of Peradeniya, Sri Lanka. In his three decade long academic career he has published 20 books in Management and Economics in addition to numerous research articles, chapters of books, and a few hundreds of articles and interviews in national newspapers on contemporary political economic issues.

Milton's alma maters include: University of Peradeniya, Sri Lanka; Swarthmore College, USA; Osaka University, Japan; Wakayama University, Japan; Osaka City University, Japan where he read for his doctoral degree and enquired into the theory and practice of international industrial location and invented International Specialization and Development hypothesis. He also has served as a Visiting Fellow at the Faculty of Tourism and Entrepreneurship, Hokkaido University, Japan.

Milton started his career as a Central Banker but soon joined the academic career at the University of Peradeniya. He introduced several subjects to the university curricula, co-authored the proposals of Bachelor of Business Administration and Master of Business Administration degree programs and the Master Plan of the Faculty of Management at Peradeniya.

Abbreviations

ADB	Asian Development Bank
B2B	Business to Business
BCE	Before Common Era
BCG	Boston Consultancy Group
BEP	Break-Even Point
BFF	Business Format Franchising
BOI	Board of Investment
BOO	Build Own Operate
BOT	Build Operate Transfer
BREAD	Business Research and Development
C2C	Customers to Customers
CAD	Computer-Aided Design
CAM	Computer-Aided Manufacturing
CE	Common Era
CEO	Chief Executive Officer
CERN	Conseil Européen pour la Recherche Nucléaire
CI	Certificate of Incorporation
CID	Company Identity Card
CNN	Cable News Network
COVID-19	Coronavirus Disease 2019
CRT	Cathode Ray Tube
CSR	Corporate Social Responsibility
CSSI	Cottage and Small-Scale Industries
CT	Certificate of Trading
DCM	Depth of Capital Market
DEF	District Enterprise Forum

DFCC	Development Finance Corporation of Ceylon
EDB	Export Development Board
EDP	Entrepreneurship Development Program
EDU	Entrepreneurship Development Unit
EU	European Union
FAQs	Frequently Asked Questions
FDI	Foreign Direct Investment
FJV	Foreign Joint Ventures
FSSU	Financial and Support Services Unit
FTA	Free Trade Area
GATT	General Agreement on Trade and Tariff
GCEC	Greater Colombo Economic Commission
GDP	Gross Domestic Product
GEDI	Global Entrepreneurship Development Institute
GEDR	Global Entrepreneurship Development Report
GEI	Entrepreneurship Development Index
GEM	Global Entrepreneurship Monitor
GERD	Gross Domestic Expenditure on Research and Development
GmbH	Gesellschaft mit beschränkter Haftung (German)
GMP	Good Manufacturing Practice
GVC	Global Value Chains
HCCP	Hazard Analysis and Critical Control Points
IBM	International Business Machines
IC	Integrated Circuit
ICT	Information and Communication Technology
IDB	Industrial Development Board
IFA	International Franchise Association
IL&F	International Licensing and Franchising
IM&A	International Merger and Acquisition
IMF	International Monetary Fund
IP	Intellectual Property
IPO	Intellectual Property Organization
ISO	International Standard Organization
JAICA	Japan International Cooperation Agency
JIT	Just-In-Time
JPO	Japan Patent Office
KAB	Know About Business
KK	Kabushiki Kaisha (Japanese)
KOICA	Korea International Cooperation Agency
LCD	Liquid Cristal Display
LDC	Less Developed Countries
LED	Light Emitting Diode
LIOC	Lanka Indian Oil Corporation

M&A	Merger and Acquisition
MDU	Market Development Unit
MEP	Micro Enterprise Programs
MFN	Most Favorite Nation
NAITA	National Apprentice and Industrial Training Authority
NASA	National Aeronautics and Space Administration
NDB	National Development Bank
NEDA	National Enterprise Development Authority
NEF	National Enterprise Forum
NGO	Non-Government Organization
NIPO	National Intellectual Property Organization
OECD	Organization for Economic Cooperation and Development
OHSAS	Occupational Health and Safety Assessment Series
OMIS	Overseas Market Introduction Service
OPEC	Petroleum Exporting Countries
OS	Operating System
PDF	Product Distribution Franchise
PERC	Public Enterprise Reforms Commission
PESTEL	Political Economic Social Technological Environmental Legal
PLC	Public Limited Company
PPP	Public–Private Partnership
R&D	Research and Development
RAM	Random Access Memory
RDB	Regional Development Bank
RDU	Research and Development Unit
REF	Regional Enterprise Forum
ROM	Read Only Memory
RRDB	Regional and Rural Development Bank
SEDD	Small Enterprises Development Division
SEDP	State Entrepreneurship Development Programs
SEEDS	Sarvodaya Economic Enterprise Development Services
SLR	Single Lens Reflex
SLSI	Sri Lanka Standards Institute
SMEs	Small and Medium-Sized Enterprises
SWOT	Strengths, Weaknesses, Opportunities, and Threats
TEA	Total Entrepreneurial Activity
TIU	Technology and Innovation Unit
TQM	Total Quality Management
TRIPRA	Trade-Related Intellectual Property Rights Agreement
TVP	Textured Vegetable Protein
UAE	United Arab Emirates
UNCTAD	United Nations Conference on Trade and Development
UN-CTC	United Nations Center for Transnational Corporation

UNDP	United Nations Development Program
UNESCO	United Nations Educational, Scientific and Cultural Organization
USAID	United States Agency for International Development
USPTO	United States Patent and Trademark Office
WB	World Bank
WIPO	World Intellectual Property Organization
WIR	World Investment Report
WTO	World Trade Organization

List of Figures

List of Tables

PART I

Facets of Entrepreneurship

CHAPTER 1

Introduction to Entrepreneurship

Key Learning Points

- Background.
- Undertaking, Entreprendre, and entrepreneurship.
- Evolution of entrepreneurship thought.
- Entrepreneurship as the fourth factor of production.
- Entrepreneurship as a "more than average" skill.
- Productive and unproductive entrepreneurs.
- Definitions of entrepreneurship:
- Richard Cantillon.
- Bernad Belidor.
- Adam Smith.
- J.B. Say.
- J.S. Mill.
- Francis A. Walker.
- Carl Menger.
- Max Weber.
- Joseph A. Schumpeter.
- Frank. H. Knight.
- Harrison Cole.
- Everett E. Hagen.
- John Galbraith.

© The Author(s), under exclusive license to Springer Nature Singapore Pte Ltd. 2024

M. Rajaratne, *Concepts, Processes and Practice of Entrepreneurship*, Palgrave Studies in Global Entrepreneurship,
https://doi.org/10.1007/978-981-97-6180-7_1

- Peter F. Drucker.
- David McClelland.
- Robert Ronstadt.
- Intervention as Entrepreneurship.
- Creation of consumer and producer surplus.
- Entrepreneurship, private, and social profit.
- Economic perspective of entrepreneurship.
- Entrepreneurship and economic development.
- Entrepreneurship as the means of formation of national wealth.
- Significance of international entrepreneurship.

Introduction

The terms entrepreneur and entrepreneurship are believed to have been transliterated by J.B. Say from the French term "entreprendre" *(˜ɑ.tʁə.pʁ˜ɑdʁ)*, in early 1800.[1] The word "entreprendre" has been constructed in the conjugation of "entre" (between) and "prendre" (take) which means "undertaking." As of today, entrepreneurship encompasses key functions such as invention, innovation, intervention, business modeling, venture creation, and growth management. Entrepreneurship creates organizations that are large or small, of government or non-government, public or private, for or not for profit. Every organization, wanting to achieve goals, requires designated administrative system for effective functioning. Organizational effectiveness is achieved through planning, organizing, leading (coordinating), and controlling procedures; which are the functions of general administration according to Henri Fayol; which is presently referred to as General Management.[2] Organizational efficiency is achieved via coordinated techniques of operations as advocated by Scientific Management and Management Science. Efficiency is sought in the organizational functions broadly known as production, marketing, human resource, finance, inventory, technology, and security that help generate profit. Thus, entrepreneurship not only innovates goods and services but also administrative and management systems for organizations.

Although, as of today, entrepreneurship is believed to be confined to the undertaking of business for private profit, its presence in the society is much broader. Individuals or groups of persons that create organizations to earn private profit are identified as private entrepreneurs. Similarly, the bureaucrats who create organizations to generate social profit are bureaucratic entrepreneurs. The aristocrats (noblemen) who create public organizations to generate social profit are aristocratic entrepreneurs.[3] The politicians who create organizations under political programs for social profit are political entrepreneurs.[4] Societies that create organizations for society profit are corporative entrepreneurs. This classification includes for-profit organizations, not-for-profit organizations, for-social-profit organizations, and for-society-profit organizations.

Single or simple definition will not suffice to describe perspectives, composition, and meaning of entrepreneurship. Therefore, several definitions will be helpful to comprehend the discipline. Since early, economists inquired into the nature of entrepreneurial behavior of capitalists. J.S. Mill isolated the risk-taker character of capitalists from their other capitalist characters and established entrepreneurship as the fourth factor of production.[5] Thus, entrepreneurship proliferates as a by-product of economics though it took its mileage with all industrial revolutions since the seventeenth century to emerge as an academic discipline as of today.

Adam Smith, in his seminal work *Wealth of Nations,* advocated the notion of entrepreneurship as human actions that lead to new waves in the division of labor.[6] Smith expected division of labor, through specialization, to play a significant role in augmenting national wealth. This notion perceived large-scale operations as favorable. Labor substituting machine tools and their proliferation across the industry were viewed as a means to deepen specialization which, in turn, helps market growth and national wealth creation. Smith believed that small-scale startups lack division of labor and do not produce a significant surplus, due to their smallness, even though they help create some individual wealth. Further, he made a distinction between productive and unproductive entrepreneurship; productive entrepreneurship creates wealth through division of labor whereas unproductive entrepreneurship (undertakings like litigation, security, robbery, piracy, and theft) rearranges wealth.

In general, business is equivalent to entrepreneurship, and businessman is equivalent to entrepreneur. This, at the very outset, prompts the need for differentiating between the two terms. The term "business" encompasses a vast spectrum of firms that engage in production, services, trade, and commerce. Every commercial entity, accordingly, is a business. However, it is also evident that some businesses grow while others stagnate or decline due to their innovation capabilities. The term "innovation" thus helps contrast between business and entrepreneurship. The businesses that are growing are innovative and thus are entrepreneurial.[7] So, the entrepreneurship is an inherent qualification of a perpetually growing business.[8] Entrepreneurship, thus, is an integral component that ensures the growth of a business. There cannot exist large businesses in absence of growth; without entrepreneurial input, every startup would end up with death. Venture that stagnates or declines due to lack of innovations after its creation does not qualify to be entrepreneurial.

The terms businessman and entrepreneur are customarily interchangeably used. Generally, owners of newly created businesses are referred to as entrepreneurs. However, successful innovators, throughout their careers as businessmen, also qualify for the title of entrepreneur. Lack of innovations would downgrade an entrepreneur to a mere businessman while bountiful innovations would upgrade a mere businessman to an entrepreneur. Therefore, business is different from entrepreneurship and so is the businessman from entrepreneur. Thus, it is clear that continuous innovations and hence growth can differentiate between entrepreneurship and business.[9]

Entrepreneurship is essentially a process that involves several uninterrupted functions. One who performs the functions belonging to entrepreneurship process can be identified as an entrepreneur. The knowledge of the functions that are performed by an entrepreneur helps describe entrepreneur and their inherent characters.[10] Below, we consider several definitions of entrepreneur and entrepreneurship furnished by various scholars. This exercise aims at identifying the functions performed by entrepreneur and the functions that belong to entrepreneurship. This comprehensive discussion of many definitions is helpful to grasp the essence of entrepreneurial functions.

Definitions and the Key Contributors

Richard Cantillon

Richard Cantillon (1680–1734), an Irish-French economist, described entrepreneur as the *"one who buys factors at certain price with a view to sell the output at uncertain price in the future facing the possibility of bankruptcy."*[11] This definition introduces a few important terms such as buying, selling, certain price, uncertain price, and bankruptcy. Cantillon conceives a production task without prior knowledge of the selling price of the goods produced. In the context of price uncertainty, as against contracted price, entrepreneur faces the possibility of bankruptcy.[12] According to this notion, entrepreneur deals with uncertain prices and thus risks bankruptcy of the business. And thus, it presumes risk as an inherent function of entrepreneur.[13]

Bernard Belidor

Bernard Forest de Belidor (1698–1761), a French engineer, defined entrepreneur as the *"one who performs tasks by bringing labor and materials at certain price and selling the resultant product at a contracted price."* This definition assumes that capital itself as entrepreneurship and it organizes other two factors of production: labor and materials. This notion highlights input–output relationship and the buying and selling price. In this scenario, entrepreneur engages in undertaking of contracted project obtained over bidding.[14] Under the contract, selling price is known to entrepreneur. But to make profit, entrepreneur carries out future operations and faces the challenge of keeping the cost of the project below the contracted (selling) price to earn a profit. This demands innovative actions to minimize costs at various cost centers across the project. Here, innovations in both production and managerial tasks help entrepreneur to gain efficiency and effectiveness that ensure profit. In this business context, profit can be realized only through bringing down the total cost of the project as the selling (handing over) price is contracted.

Adam Smith

Adam Smith (1723–1790), an English economist, defined entrepreneur as *"an individual, who undertakes the formation of an organization for commercial purposes by recognizing the potential demand for goods and services, and thereby acts as an economic agent and transforms demand into supply working as a manager, at the same time, intervening between the labor and capital."*[15] This definition highlights a few important terms such as formation of organization, demand, supply, economic agent, and manager. Interestingly, the formation of an organization is a major function of the entrepreneur according to Smith. The organization, once formed, operates as an economic agent based on the principle of efficiency to meet future demand by way of supply. This definition implies that the entrepreneur, functioning as a producer and a manager, capitalizes on the market opportunities to innovate products that can address market demand.

J.B. Say

Jean Baptist Say (1767–1832), a French economist, identified entrepreneur as *"an organizer of the business firms who unites all means of production factors and reconstitutes the value of the factors that are utilized and creates profit for himself. Therefore, entrepreneur need not possess factors of production but art of organizing and administration and knowledge of business."*[16] Accordingly, entrepreneur unites factors of production (land, labor, and capital) to create value. Profit is the economic rent yielded to entrepreneurship. In this notion, entrepreneur creates income from the factors of production they employ. Factors of production, owned by other parties, are organized by entrepreneurship. This definition also suggests that entrepreneurship involves functions such as organizing, administration, and sensing business. To Say, entrepreneur must possess "unerring market sense" to assess market needs and to fulfill them.

J. S. Mill

John Stuart Mill (1806–1873), in his book *The Principles of Political Economy (1848)*, mentioned that *"What a person expects to gain, who superintends the employment of his own capital, is always more, and generally much more, than this. The rate of profit greatly exceeds the rate of interest. The surplus is partly compensation for risk. By lending his capital, on unexceptionable security, he runs little or no risk. But if he embarks in business on his own account, he always exposes his capital to some, and in many cases to very great, danger of partial or total loss. For this danger he must be compensated, otherwise he will not incur it."*[17] By this means, Mill highlighted the entrepreneurial function of the capitalists and differentiated it from capital to identify entrepreneurship as the fourth factor of production. Until Mill's interpretation, entrepreneurship had been veiled in and inseparable from capital.

Every capitalist was not an entrepreneur to Mill. To him, not capitalists but entrepreneurs organize ventures. Unlike the conventional capitalists, entrepreneurs assume risks through venturing. For organizing ventures, they obtain capital from the capitalists giving guarantees. Conventional capitalists seek security for their capital and hence avoid risky portfolios. When guarantee is provided capitalists tend to lend and invest their monies. It is entrepreneur who risks investment and provides guarantees for the capital borrowed. Thus, one's will to associate or avoid risk demarcates the difference between entrepreneur from capitalist. Mill's notion elevated entrepreneurship as superior factor that has the capability of organizing other factors of production that would otherwise be idling.

Entrepreneurship is thus, much different from other factors of production: Land, labor, and capital. Entrepreneurship, as it desires, organizes these three factors with the aim of production of goods and services. They are used economically to minimize cost of production. Yet, entrepreneurship is never used minimally but maximally. Entrepreneurship does not add to cost of production and thus, is used maximally. Theoretically, entrepreneurship is not a resource like land, labor, and capital and so, it is not paid a salary. Therefore, cost of entrepreneurship is not included in cost of production. Harrington Emerson (1853–1931), differentiated the significance of entrepreneurship from other factors of production saying *"thinking (innovating) is more important than men, money, and materials in an organization."*[18] This approves the notion of J.S. Mill that entrepreneurship is a superior capacity which is rewarded not with salary but with profit. Accordingly, the cost cannot be allocated to entrepreneurship and so, it does not add to cost of production. This justifies maximization of entrepreneurship in contrast to minimization of other factors. Thus, entrepreneurship is not a mere factor, but a factor of factors.

Francis A. Walker

Francis Amasa Walker (1840–1897), an American economist, described entrepreneur as *"one who is endowed with more than average capacities in organizing and coordinating factors of production. Average capacity is rewarded with salary and superior capacity with profit."*[19] Accordingly, entrepreneur is a person with superior capacity who organizes and coordinates factors of production. And those who possess average capacity are non-entrepreneurs and hence employed as workers to assume lower responsibilities in a venture. This implies that the managers also possess average capacity and run routines, under guidance of an entrepreneur, for a salary. Entrepreneurs, in turn, earn profit as a rent for their superior capacities. On the contrary, entrepreneur is invisible in modern corporates. They are run by professional managers who earn amazingly high salaries or share profit. So, they ought to be persons with more than average capacities who play significant entrepreneurial role also in the organizations they lead. Accordingly, it is obvious that profit is connected to superior capacity while salary is connected to average capacity.

Carl Menger

Carl Menger (1840–1921), an Austrian economist, advocated that *"the entrepreneur acts as an economic agent who transforms resources into products and services. The entrepreneur transforms and gives added value."* Menger composed a useful diagram to depict value creation process as less useful resources are transformed into more useful goods.[20] Menger's model describes that the extent of resource transformation is determined by the opportunities for value creation. And the degree of value creation is determined by the profitability of value creation act. This notion identifies value creation for profit-making as entrepreneur's function. Entrepreneur, thus, transforms lower value products into higher value products.

Max Weber

Max Weber (1864–1920) was of the view that finance is key to entrepreneurship and that the Calvinists' parsimonious practices accrue funds required to finance entrepreneurial investments. Referring to the Puritans of the Church of England during the sixteenth and seventeenth centuries, Weber advocated that the Puritans composed a significant stake of entrepreneurs and thus, Puritan ethic also was prevalent among entrepreneurs.[21] Many English Puritans had engaged in entrepreneurship for the very reason that they were a religious minority and had been barred from accessing "other routes of social advance." Maria Brouwer (2000) mentions that other minorities like Jews and Christians also increasingly became merchants and moneylenders under the Ottoman Empire.[22] Entrepreneurship in these occupations was not regarded as much esteemed. Similarly, India's caste system had placed entrepreneurship as the occupation of the "Vaishya" caste; which was placed low on the social pyramid.[23]

Joseph A. Schumpeter

Joseph Alois Schumpeter (1883–1950), an Austrian-American economist, propagated the idea that *"entrepreneur is an innovator who carries out new combinations through innovations in product, technology, market, material, and form of organization."*[24] In Schumpeter's view, entrepreneur is an innovator, and their innovations are not confined to goods and services as commonly believed. In this view, entrepreneur engages in innovations and making new combinations relating to product, production, and market. In this case, an innovation can be a combination of several things; new materials, new technology, new production methods, new organization, and new market!

In Schumpeter's view, innovation is not a single act but an entire process of production and marketing that causes old inventories, ideas, technologies, skills, and equipment to become obsolete due to the process of continuous creations and destruction, commonly known as "creative destruction." Schumpeter said that both entrepreneurs and capitalists assume risk but operate in separate domains. Accordingly, venture owners who do not innovate are mere "capitalists" whereas those who innovate are "entrepreneurs." In this view, all entrepreneurs are capitalists, but all capitalists are not entrepreneurs. Schumpeter emphasizes that individuals who take risk in introducing new product, introducing new technology, adopting new production process, creating new markets, or creating new economic organization are entrepreneurs.[25]

Schumpeter identified the entrepreneur as one who creates ventures, innovates, challenges traditions, opposes old ways of doing things, and embraces new ways of doing things. Schumpeter believed that entrepreneur has to break with the environment that is hostile to radical behaviors. So, he advocated the notion that "entrepreneur breaks up the 'circular flow', steering the economy away from old paths and opening up possibilities hitherto unknown."[26] Schumpeter split between profit and bank interest and argued that profitability of marginal innovation equals the interest payment. Marginal entrepreneur's profit will only be sufficient to pay off the bank interest only as it is assumed that the venture is totally funded by the bank.

Any residual after interest payment reflects the soundness of innovation and entrepreneurial quality; the higher the residual the greater is the entrepreneurial quality. Thus, the profit after residual is a measure of the entrepreneurial quality. Entrepreneurs' goal to improve their personal and family wellbeing plus social position is reached if the profit will exceed the interest payment. Schumpeter differentiated between entrepreneur and manager highlighting differences of their roles. According to Schumpeter, innovation is not a vocation but the execution of strategic decisions.

Frank H. Knight

Frank Hyneman Knight (1885–1972), an American economist, observed in his book Risk, Uncertainty and Profit (1921) that *"entrepreneurs are specialized group of persons who bear risk and deal with uncertainty. Uncertainty is immeasurable and an uninsurable risk and a responsibility that cannot be salaried. In order to take risk, one has to be creative, innovative, confident, able and willing to extend guarantees."* This comprehensive definition highlights a few key skills that an entrepreneur should possess: creativity, innovativeness, risk-taking, provision of guarantees (to relevant parties), and holding responsibility.[27] Further, he emphasizes that tasks of entrepreneur cannot be salaried. Knight differentiates the entrepreneur from the salaried people in an organization and recognizes entrepreneur as a special person whose responsibility cannot be compensated with salary; so, they deserve to earn profit.[28]

Harrison Cole

Arthur Harrison Cole (1889–1974), an American economist, said *"entrepreneurship is the purposeful activity of an individual or a group of associated individuals, undertaken to initiate, maintain or aggrandize profit by production or distribution of economic goods and services."* This definition emphasizes that entrepreneurship can either be an individual or a group action.[29] The entrepreneurship function of large corporates is performed by groups; the boards of directors. Entrepreneurial action spreads across venture initiation, maintaining, and profit-making. Cole identifies the production of economic goods and services as the outcome of innovation. The nature of economic goods and services is that they can be commercialized seeking profit. According to Cole's notion, not only production and sales but distribution also is an economic activity that helps increase profit. Entrepreneurship, thus, is a series of economic activities that generates profit; the economic rent of the entrepreneurship.[30]

Everett E. Hagen

Everett Einar Hagen (1906–1993), an American economist, pointed out that the *"entrepreneur is an economic man who tries to maximize his profit by innovation."*[31] This simple but straightforward definition highlights innovation as the main task of the entrepreneur and the key function of profit maximization.[32] Again, this implies that innovation brings in profit and both innovation and profit are steadfastly connected. This notion suggests that venture is the mechanism that takes charge of innovation and profit maximization. This also has an implication that economic growth and wealth creation are connected to innovation and hence to entrepreneurship.[33]

John Galbraith

John Kenneth Galbraith (1908–2006), a Canadian-American economist, mentioned that *"Entrepreneur is one who accepts challenges and strives to achieve something."* Accordingly, accepting challenges is a unique skill of entrepreneur.[34] Many people ward off challenges in fear of risk and thus they belong to non-entrepreneurial class. Striving is an act as opposed to easygoing. Unlike easy goers, strivers achieve "something." To Galbraith, achieving goals such as wealth, social status, and goodwill is equivalent to achieving "something" which is a reward to the striver. Entrepreneur achieves wealth, social status, recognition, power, high consumption levels, ability to social works, and state of philanthropist.[35] Thus, the term "something" refers to many things that an entrepreneur earns.

Peter F. Drucker

Peter Ferdinand Drucker (1909–2005), an Austrian-American Management consultant, described entrepreneur as the *"one who always searches for change, responds to it and exploits it, through innovations as an opportunity."* The key words of this definition are change, response, opportunity, innovation, and exploiting.[36] The word change, in this context, refers to changes that take place in the macro business environment that comprises demography, industry, technology, environment, markets, attitudes, values, and lifestyles. Changes create opportunities for innovations. Entrepreneurs constantly search for opportunities emanating from changes and respond to them through innovations. Innovation is thus the means to exploit opportunities.

Drucker in his book Innovation and Entrepreneurship (1985) mentions that there can be ventures without entrepreneurs! It is an important question of how a venture can exist without an entrepreneur. Drucker gives the reason that one can operate a venture habitually (as a businessman) without founding it on entrepreneurial characters, i.e., without any novelty, creativity, or value creation. This notion is much helpful to differentiate entrepreneurship from non-entrepreneurship and to re-estimate the entrepreneur stock of a country. According to Drucker, there can be more ventures than entrepreneurs! Thus, it is a case in point to learn whether all smalltime vendors, shopkeepers, and "micro-entrepreneurs" are real entrepreneurs. He points out that McDonald's became entrepreneurial through revolutionized value creation for generic American food and redefining conventional restaurant operations to make a fast-food restaurant chain—a new type of venture.[37]

Drucker further argues that entrepreneurs are mostly non-capitalists, non-investors, non-business owners, and non-employers. Thus, they mostly borrow from banks and other financiers or finance businesses through equity capital. However, this generalization is more appropriate to new corporates, buyouts, acquisitions, and mergers. Drucker argues that most entrepreneurs are employed and thus, they are not employers either. It is true that corporate level entrepreneurs are employed as CEOs, directors, or managers in large organizations whereas smalltime entrepreneurs are all self-employed. Drucker, in this context, differentiated entrepreneur's personality traits from behaviors and expressed the notion *"entrepreneurship, then, is behavior rather than personality trait"* challenging also the conventional wisdom of entrepreneurship.[38]

David McClelland

David McClelland (1917–1998), an American psychologist, described the entrepreneur as *"a decision maker and one who does things new and better way and make decisions under uncertainty."* The most important notion of this definition is that the entrepreneur does things in new and better way.[39] Doing things new and better is required to better address needs and wants presented by markets. This, apparently, is innovation. The term "new" is connected to production process, technology, design, materials and to the goods and services with new capabilities.

The constant improvement and upgrading of goods and services aim at providing "better" satisfaction to the customers. Therefore, "doing new and better way" is essentially a function of entrepreneur. According to McClelland, entrepreneurs are achievement oriented so, they drive to excel, advance, and grow.[40] This notion challenges the "great man theory of entrepreneurship" and the "religious theories of entrepreneurship." He advocated that entrepreneurship is learned and that such learning can be encouraged fruitfully.[41]

Robert Ronstadt

Robert Ronstadt, an economist, defines entrepreneurship as *"the dynamic process of creating incremental wealth"* in his work of 1984. Ronstadt explains that wealth is created by individuals who assume major risks in the process of adding value to products. Entrepreneur infuses value into products by way of combining appropriate skills and resources. For creating wealth, products need not be entirely new or unique. Ronstadt referred to incremental wealth creation which can be perceived through incremental value creation, which again is the outcome of continuous value creation. The process of value creation thus, need not necessarily involve in production of something entirely new or unique. Other means such as delivery, after service, and warranties also can infuse value to products.[42]

He also advocates the notion *"entrepreneurship is the ability to create and build a vision from practically nothing; fundamentally it is a human, creative act. It is the application of energy to initiating and building an enterprise or organization, rather than just watching or analyzing."* Ronstadt further elaborates that *"entrepreneurship includes the ability to build an entrepreneurial or venture team to complement entrepreneur's skills and talents. It is the dexterity for sensing an opportunity where others see chaos, contradiction, and confusion. It is the possessing of the knowhow to find, marshal, and control resources."*

Intervention as Entrepreneurship

This illustration of definitions illuminates several perspectives of entrepreneur and entrepreneurship. Nonetheless, their inherent limitations call for a definition of eclectic nature. To satisfy this need, we define entrepreneur as the "*one who intervenes in addressing unsatisfied customer needs and wants by way of offering innovative solutions in pursuit of profit."* Accordingly, entrepreneur identifies common needs and wants, innovates and offers solutions to address them via market for earning a profit. Intervention is an external hand sought by people who are incapable of fulfilling their needs and wants by themselves. People's incapability to satisfy needs and wants by themselves creates opportunities for innovating solutions. Thus, unsatisfied needs and wants stimulate the intervener to propose solutions that can generate surplus for the producer and the consumer. The producer surplus is profit, and the consumer surplus is value. In this scenario, intervener assumes responsibility of entrepreneur.

Intervention, in this sense, involves in innovation and problem-solving. The word "entreprendre" means "to take between" and "intervene" means "to come between." So, the entrepreneur is one who comes between customer and their needs or wants. Entrepreneurs identify problems and intervene in solving them through innovating goods, services, processes, methods, technologies, materials, and markets. Every good or service produced and available for sale at the market is aimed at solving some kind of problem. The people who have problems find value in the right product and prepare to pay for it. If the solution is effective, the demand and profit will be high. Newer and better solutions fetch higher prices bringing greater profits.

Intervention is not confined to innovations aimed at private profit. Intervention is equally applicable to group and social profit contexts also. All entrepreneurs stive to make some kind of intervention in satisfying needs and wants of others and thus offer all forms of goods, services, processes, systems, methods, formula, designs, and technologies. And thus, it is interesting to note that behind every product, there is an intended intervention for an unresolved problem. The intervention concept discussed above is extensively elaborated to advance it as a theory in the Chapter five.

The Economic Impression

Entrepreneurship engulfs all human activities that are aimed at generating a surplus over the costs incurred. The purpose of generating a surplus is of economic nature and the surplus creation involves organizing of factors of production. Surplus is realized in the circumstance that the value of outcome exceeds the combined cost of inputs. In short, surplus is the excess over the value of input. Surplus is derived after deducting all costs from revenue and measured in monetary terms. Entrepreneurship is an economic activity that aims at generating surplus; generally known as profit. Profit, thus, is the economic rent for entrepreneurship. Private entrepreneurs earn private profit whereas public entrepreneurs earn public profit. And all entrepreneurs strive to generate national wealth.[43]

Entrepreneurial thinking has evolved since the time the man learned to generate surplus. The propagative nature of surplus influenced the proliferation of entrepreneurship. It helped increasingly and better serving human needs and wants. Entrepreneurship received a landmark recognition after J.S. Mill differentiated it from capital and expounded it as a factor of production. Since then, entrepreneurship has been crowned as the supreme factor, among the other factors of production, because of its merit in organizing production process which the other factors are not capable of. In the absence of entrepreneurship, other factors of production will lie redundant and no production process will be organized.

Entrepreneurship is directly connected to the level of economic development of countries. The higher the quality and the greater the supply of entrepreneurship in a country, the more advanced is the economy. Entrepreneurship quality refers to the effectiveness of entrepreneurial action whereas entrepreneurship supply refers to the stock of entrepreneurs operating in a country. In the USA, Germany, China, and the UK, the supply of entrepreneurs is less than that of Taiwan and Hong Kong in per capita terms but their effectiveness is high as they heavily engage in worldwide business operations. The global presence of American entrepreneur can be seen as almost every person in the world is using Google, WhatsApp, YouTube, Facebook, Android, Microsoft/Apple OS, McDonald's, and Pizza Hut and paying a royalty fee for them every moment. The number of Toyota cars on the streets and Sony TV sets at homes are indicators of global presence of the two Japanese companies. Names or brands of some large entrepreneurs are not known to many as they do not produce consumer goods or do otherwise produce components. As economically powerful as they are, the top 10 entrepreneurs of the world produce 5% of the World GDP (Table 1.1).[44]

In general, entrepreneurship forms national wealth and hence the level of economic development and living standard. Large corporates are entrepreneurial superpowers. The countries with large corporates thus, have become economic superpowers also. TheUSA, China, Japan, Germany, the UK, and France. have become economic superpowers

Table 1.1 World top 10 corporates

Rank	*Company*	*Country*	*Revenue (US$ Billion)*	*Cumulative revenue (US$ Billion)*
1	Walmart	USA	573	573
2	Amazon	USA	470	1043
3	China State Grid	China	461	1504
4	China National Petroleum	China	412	1916
5	CINOPEC Group	China	401	2317
6	Saudi Aramco	Saudi Arabia	400	2717
7	Apple	USA	366	3083
8	Volks Wagen	Germany	296	3379
9	China SCE	China	294	3673
10	CVS Health	USA	292	3965

Data Fortune 500 (2022)[45]

thanks to their entrepreneurial superpowers. In the Fortune 500, the largest corporates are sequentially listed against these countries. This proves that entrepreneurship and national income progressively correlate with each other. The Global Entrepreneurship Development Index data and per capita income of nations at current price in 2019 lineally correlates at $R^2 = 0.75$ as derived in Fig. 1.1. This indicates a strong relationship between the level of entrepreneurship and the economic advancement of nations.[46]

In Taiwan and Hong Kong, an incredibly large share of entrepreneurs in the population operates in their local or national markets without much impact on the global market. This suggests that effective entrepreneurs will help increase national wealth and foreign reserves while average entrepreneurs in a large number will help only unemployment problem and household earning, as Adam Smith stated. Entrepreneurship has created innumerable business organizations and private and public entrepreneurs. The number and the size of such organizations inflict various influences on life. The larger the number of organizations, the greater will be their influence. The countries with a large number of effective organizations enjoy high living standards whereas the countries with a large number of ineffective organizations have poor living standards. Organizational effectiveness is chiefly determined by management and management decisions are finally approved or disapproved

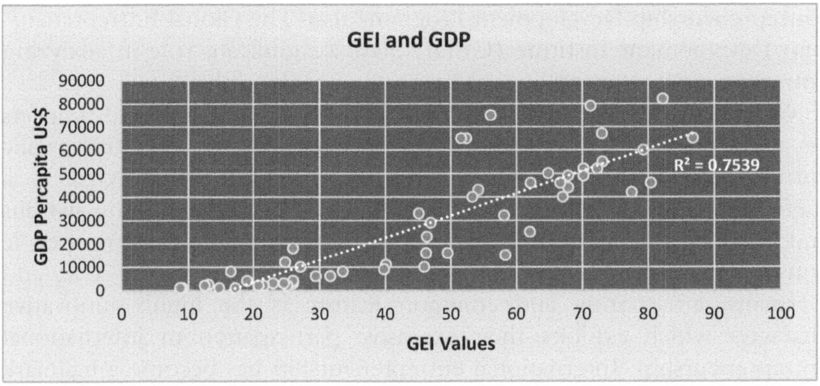

Fig. 1.1 GEI and GDP of selected countries (*Data* Global Entrepreneurship Index [2019], Statistics Times.com [2020])[47]

by entrepreneurs. Therefore, in all organizations, the topmost decision-maker is the entrepreneur and thus the organizational effectiveness is ultimately connected to entrepreneurship.

International flow of debts and donations is an indicator of success of entrepreneurship. Entrepreneurially rich countries are lenders and donators to entrepreneurially poor beneficiary countries. Technological advancement, effective management systems, and effective social systems of countries also are yielded to entrepreneurship. Goods and services, mode of production, logistics, distribution, marketing, and all other auxiliary services related to commerce are outcomes of entrepreneurship. Entrepreneurship is seen inevitably touching every aspect of social life and thus, dynamics and trajectories of social progress, as a whole, are guided by production of goods, services, technologies, systems, and thoughts which are yielded to entrepreneurship.

The Global Entrepreneurship Index (GEI) indicates the correlation between income disparity and entrepreneurial capacities of nations (Fig. 1.2). The volumes of production, consumption, trade, investment, debt, and reserves are thus determined by the level of entrepreneurship. Accordingly, economic progress of countries is now viewed as a function of entrepreneurship. This notion has led to implementation of worldwide

Entrepreneurship Development Programs also. The Global Entrepreneurship Development Institute (GEDI) plays a significant role in analyzing entrepreneurial strength of countries and in ranking them.

Global Entrepreneurship Index measures the nature and impacts of international entrepreneurship in relation to country-specific entrepreneurial skills, activities, and environment. Thus, GEI is a useful tool for comparing entrepreneurial competencies among nations and developing policies favorable for the improvement of country-specific entrepreneurship character. Of the USA, Japan, France, the UK, and Germany, an exciting and common feature is the highly innovative character which exhibits their extensive participation in international entrepreneurship. International entrepreneurship has become a hallmark of Global Value Chains and Global Supply Chains.[49]

The importance of study of international entrepreneurship was recognized by the United Nations and created the Center for Transnational Corporation (UN-CTC) as early as in the early 1990s. The World Investment Report (WIR) now published by the UNCTAD is an important outcome of the UN-CTC. The World Investment Report analyzes the nature, challenges, and trends of international entrepreneurship in terms of direct investment inflows and outflows, volume of international production and trade, new greenfield ventures, acquisitions and mergers,

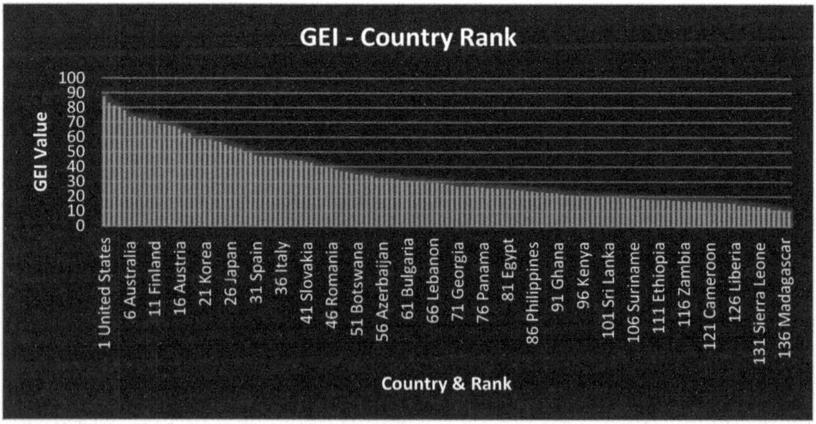

Fig. 1.2 GEI country rank (*Data* Global Entrepreneurship Development Index [2019])[48]

Table 1.2 Significance of international entrepreneurship

Item	*US$ Billion*
FDI Inflow	962
FDI Outflow	732
FDI Inward Stock	41,919
FDI Outward Stock	40,144
Earnings on Inward FDI	1837
Earnings on Outward FDI	1755
Greenfield Projects	604
Cross-border M&A	475
Sales of foreign affiliates	30,260
Value-added foreign affiliates	6463
Total assets of foreign affiliates	98,863
Royalties and License fee receipts	467
Employment by foreign affiliates (million persons) 80	

Data World Investment Report (2020)[50]

franchises, and royalties (Table 1.2). In addition to the WIR, the Global Entrepreneurship Monitor (GEM)[51] also is a useful source of extensive and comparative country analyses of international entrepreneurship.

Chapter Summary

The origin of the term entrepreneurship refers to the writings of J.B. Say whereas the French equivalent "entreprendre" appears in the seventeenth-century writings of Richard Cantillon. Entrepreneurship creates not only goods and services but also ventures. Entrepreneurship generates not only private profits but also social profits. Thus, entrepreneurship, in a broad sense, is an act of value creation (for individuals), venture creation (for entrepreneurs), and wealth creation (for nations). J.S. Mill detached the risk-taker role of the capitalist and redefined it as entrepreneurship; coining the fourth factor of production which was then admired by Francis A. Walker is a more than average skill that cannot be salaried and thus deserves profit. Adam Smith figured out productive entrepreneurs and unproductive entrepreneurs and advocated productive entrepreneurs create national wealth. Innovation fuels the growth engine of entrepreneurship.

Entrepreneurship has been defined by many scholars since the sixteenth century CE. The second section of the chapter illustrates the philosophies of Richard Cantillon, Bernard Belidor, Adam Smith, J.B. Say, J.S. Mill, Francis Walker, Carl Menger, Max Weber, Joseph Schumpeter, Frank Knight, Harrison Cole, Everett Hagen, John Gilbreth, Peter F. Drucker, David McClelland, Harington Emerson, and Robert Ronstadt on entrepreneur and entrepreneurship. After a lengthy review of their notions, the author concludes that the entrepreneur was born before the capitalist and thus, the entrepreneur is the parent of the capitalist; which relationship is absent in the Marxist notion. So, necessarily, one need not be a capitalist to become an entrepreneur. The author, also, advocates entrepreneurship as a process of intervention where entrepreneur intervenes in the unresolved needs and wants of the customer and proposes solutions to them via markets. The last section of the chapter deliberates on the economic perspective of entrepreneurship analyzing the relationship between entrepreneurial competencies of nations and their national incomes referring to the Global Entrepreneurship Index (GEI) and the Global Entrepreneurship Monitor (GEM). Then, the significance of international entrepreneurship is assessed referring to the World Investment Report (WIR) and the Fortune 500 magazine.

Review Questions

1. Describe the background that promoted entrepreneurship as a new field of study in the twentieth century.
2. "Entrepreneurship evolved from the French practice of 'entreprendre.'" Explain the meaning of "entreprendre" referring to the war logistics undertaking practices in France.
3. "The concept of entrepreneurship was derived splitting the concept of capital into two; so, entrepreneurship became the fourth factor of production revolutionizing fundamentals of economics." Explain.
4. Critically examine the statement "entrepreneurship is more than an average skill and thus it cannot be salaried but compensated with profit."
5. "Adam Smith identified two types of entrepreneurs: productive entrepreneurs and unproductive entrepreneurs." Differentiate between the two and explain why Smith despised unproductive entrepreneurs.

6. Select the most exciting contributions from among the main-stay definitions of entrepreneurship and discuss how they helped broaden the meaning of entrepreneurship.
7. Trace the shortcomings of the definitions of entrepreneurship and formulate your own definition to overcome them.
8. Discuss whether you agree with the propositions of the intervention hypothesis and its capability as an eclectic approach to entrepreneurship.
9. "Entrepreneur creates consumer surplus and producer surplus." Illustrate the connection between the two tracing the resulting value and profit also.
10. Differentiate between private profit and social profit and examine the circumstances that each is realized in entrepreneurship.
11. "Entrepreneurship organizes economic activities and thus it is referred to as the 'engine of growth and development'" also. Critically examine this statement.
12. Establish the connection between entrepreneurship and the formation of national wealth tracing evidence from recent Global Entrepreneurship Monitor (GEM).
13. "Global Entrepreneurship Index (GEI) establishes the connection between national entrepreneurial capacity and national income differentials." Analytically examine.
14. Pinpoint the areas that most of the countries are lagging behind but should strive to improve among the 14 fields proposed in the Global Entrepreneurship Development Report.
15. Estimate the dimension of international entrepreneurship and its significance in the world production and trade referring to the World Investment Report (WIR).

Additional Readings

1. The Economist, 2009. https://www.economist.com/news/2009/04/27/entrepreneurship
2. Fayol, H. 1949. *General and industrial management* (Constance Storrs, trans.) London: Sir Isaac Pitman & Sons Ltd. (Original work published 1916).

3. Thompson, F.M.L., 2002. Aristocrats as Entrepreneurs. In *Gentrification and the Enterprise Culture: Britain 1780-1980, Northampton shire*. Oxford University Press.
4. Mathew, M., and Joseph, T.S., 2011. A theory of political entrepreneurship. *Modern Economy, 2*(4), pp. 552–560.
5. Mill, J.S., 1848. *Principles of political economy with some of their applications to social philosophy*. London: Longmans, Green, and Co.
6. Smith, A., 1776. *An inquiry into the nature and causes of the wealth of nations*. London: W. Strahan and T. Cadell.
7. Philippe, A., 2014. What do we learn from Schumpeterian growth theory? In *Handbook of Economic Growth* (pp. 515–563). Philadelphia: Elsevier.
8. Sledzik, K., 2013. Schumpeter's view on innovation and entrepreneurship. *SSRN Electronic Journal*, pp. 89–95, https://doi.org/10.2139/ssrn.2257783.
9. Tobias, K., Andreas, K., and Christoph, S., 2009. Continuous innovation in entrepreneurial growth companies: Exploring the ambidextrous strategy. *Journal of Enterprising Culture, 17*(3), pp. 297–322.
10. Carton, R., Hofer, C., and Meeks, M., 1998. The entrepreneur and entrepreneurship: Operational definitions of their role in society. In *Singapore Annual International Council for Small Business Conference* (pp. 1–12).
11. Cantillon, R., 2015. *Essays on the nature of trade in general* (Antonion E. Murphy, trans.) Carmel, Illinois: Liberty Fund, Inc. (Original work published 1755).
12. Murphy, A., 1986. *Richard Cantillon: Entrepreneur and economist*. New York: Oxford University Press.
13. Thornton, M., 2020. Turning the word upside down: How Cantillon redefined the entrepreneur. *Quarterly Journal of Austrian Economics,* 23(3–4), pp. 265–280.
14. Robert, B., 1981. The Proto-history of Franchise Bidding. *Southern Economic Journal, 48*(2), pp. 464–474.
15. Smith, A., 1776. *An inquiry into the nature and causes of the wealth of nations*. London: W. Strahan and T. Cadell.
16. Say, J., 1855. *A treatise on political economy; or the production, distribution, and consumption of wealth,* (Clement C. Biddle,

trans.), Philadelphia: Lippincott, Grambo & Co. (Original work published 1803).

17. Mill, J.S., 1848. *Principles of political economy with some of their applications to social philosophy.* London: Longmans, Green, and Co.
18. Harrington E., 2016. *The twelve principles of efficiency.* London: Wentworth Press.
19. Walker, Francis A., 1888. *The wages question: A treatise on wages and the wages class.* London: Macmillan and Co.
20. Menger, C., 1950. *Principles of economics* (J. Dingwall and D.F. Hoselitz Glencoe, trans.) Illinois: Free Press. (Original work published 1871).
21. Weber, M., 1930. *The protestant ethic and the spirit of capitalism* (Talcott Parsons, trans.) New York: Charles Scribner's Sons. (Original work published 1905).
22. Brouwer, M.T., 2002. Weber, Schumpeter and Knight on entrepreneurship and economic development. *Journal of Evolutionary Economics, 12*, pp. 83–105.
23. Wilson, J., 1877. *Indian caste.* London: William Blackwood & Sons.
24. Schumpeter, J.A. 1934. *The theory of economic development* (translated by R. Opie). Cambridge, MA: Harvard University Press.
25. Schumpeter, J.A., 2017. *Essays on entrepreneurs, innovations, business cycles and the evolution of capitalism.* London: Routledge.
26. Brouwer, M. 2002. Weber, Schumpeter and Knight on entrepreneurship and economic development. *Journal of Evolutionary Economics, 12*, pp. 83–105.
27. Knight, F.H., 1942. Profit and entrepreneurial functions. *The Journal of Economic History, 2*(1), pp. 126–132.
28. Dold, M.F. and Rizzo, M.J., 2021. Frank Knight and the cognitive diversity of entrepreneurship. *Journal of Institutional Economics, 17*(6), pp. 925–942.
29. Cole, A.H., 1959. *Business enterprise in its social setting,* Cambridge, MA: Harvard University Press.
30. Cochran, T.C., 1975. Arthur Harrison Cole, 1889–1974. *Business History Review, 49*(1), pp. 1–5.
31. Hagen, E.E., 1960. The entrepreneur as rebel against traditional society. *Human Organization, 19*(4), pp. 185–187.

32. Hagen, E.E., 1980. *The economics of development.* Homewood Illinois: Richard D. Irwin.
33. Hagen, E.E., 1957. The process of economic development. *Economic Development and Cultural Change, 5*(3), pp. 193–215.
34. Galbraith, John K., 1967. *The new industrial state.* Boston: Houghton Mifflin.
35. Audretsch, D.B., 2015. Joseph Schumpeter and John Kenneth Galbraith: Two sides of the same coin? *Journal of Evolutionary Economics,* 25, pp. 197–214.
36. Drucker, P.F., 1985. *Innovation and entrepreneurship.* New York: Harper and Row.
37. Drucker, P.F. and Maciariello, J., 2014. *Innovation and Entrepreneurship*, New Jersey: Hoboken.
38. Drucker, P.F., 1985. Entrepreneurial strategies. *California Management Review*, 1985(02), 27–2.
39. McClelland, D.C., 1987. Characteristics of successful entrepreneurs. *The Journal of Creative Behavior, 21*(3), 219–233.
40. McClelland, D.C., 1965. Achievement and entrepreneurship: A longitudinal study. *Personality and Social Psychology, 1*(4), 389–392. https://doi.org/10.1037/h0021956
41. Audretsch, D.B., and Thurik, A.R., 2001. What's new about the new economy? Sources of growth in the managed and entrepreneurial economies. *Industrial and Corporate Change, 10*(1), pp. 267–315.
42. Ronstadt, R., 1984. *Entrepreneurship: Text, cases and notes.* Virginia: Lord Publishing.
43. Michael, A.H., et al., 2001. 'Strategic entrepreneurship: Entrepreneurial strategies for wealth creation. *Strategic Management Journal, 22*(6–7), pp. 479–491.
44. *Fortune 500 Companies, 2022.*
45. https://fortune.com/ranking/fortune500/
46. GEDI, *Global Entrepreneurship Development Report, 2020.*
47. https://statisticstimes.com/index.php
48. http://thegedi.org/global-entrepreneurship-and-development-index/
49. UNCTAD, *World Investment Report, 2020.*
50. https://unctad.org/publication/world-investment-report-2020

CHAPTER 2

Entrepreneurship Environment

Key Learning Points

- Entrepreneurial ecosystem.
- Entrepreneurial framework conditions.
- Formation of national entrepreneurship capacity.
- The 14 pillars of entrepreneurial ecosystem.
- Entrepreneurship environment.
- Controllable and uncontrollable spheres.
- Firm environment.
- Operational environment.
- Market environment.
- National business environment.
- International business environment.
- Micro and Macro entrepreneurship environment.
- Environmental stability and volatility.
- Risk and opportunities of volatile environment.
- Red Ocean and Blue Ocean Market environment.
- Need for entrepreneurial opportunity diagnosis.
- Internal and external environmental factors.
- The Entrepreneurial Opportunity Diagnostic Matrix.
- Entrepreneurial strategy formulation.
- Blue Ocean strategy.

© The Author(s), under exclusive license to Springer Nature Singapore Pte Ltd. 2024

M. Rajaratne, *Concepts, Processes and Practice of Entrepreneurship*, Palgrave Studies in Global Entrepreneurship,
https://doi.org/10.1007/978-981-97-6180-7_2

- Reengineering strategy.
- Niche market strategy.
- Retrenchment strategy.
- Managerial and entrepreneurial skills.
- Venture Classification Matrix.
- Four groups of ventures: LL, HL, LH, and HH.
- The inclusivity of entrepreneurial and managerial skills.

Introduction

Entrepreneurs face complex and volatile business environment. Medium and large scale entrepreneurs encounter more complex and challenging environment than micro and small entrepreneurs do. Among all entrepreneurs, multinational corporations face an extremely intricate, diverse, and challenging international environment that consists of multivariate social, political, economic, technological, and demographic factors.[1] Entrepreneurship environment consists of micro and macro environments; the micro environment is controllable to the entrepreneur while the macro environment is not. Entrepreneurs, therefore, are inescapably vulnerable to the macro environment.

Clever entrepreneurs, however, employ effective strategies to overcome challenges posed by the macro environment. Yet, in extreme cases, even large multinational corporations cannot overcome the challenges of the external environment. One-time photographic giant Kodak Inc.[2] failed to resist volatility of the external environment and faced bankruptcy. Volatility of the macro environment changes the circumstances under which entrepreneurial opportunities emanate and persist. Environmental volatility eliminates existing opportunities and generates new opportunities. Therefore, environmental volatility should not be always seen as depriving of opportunities as it triggers favorable conditions also. In all circumstances, and particularly in bad conditions, clever entrepreneurs recognize worthwhile venture opportunities.

Entrepreneurial Ecosystem

Entrepreneurial Ecosystem, an approach developed by the Global Entrepreneurship Development Institute (GEDI), describes entrepreneurial environment. Entrepreneurial ecosystem is comprised

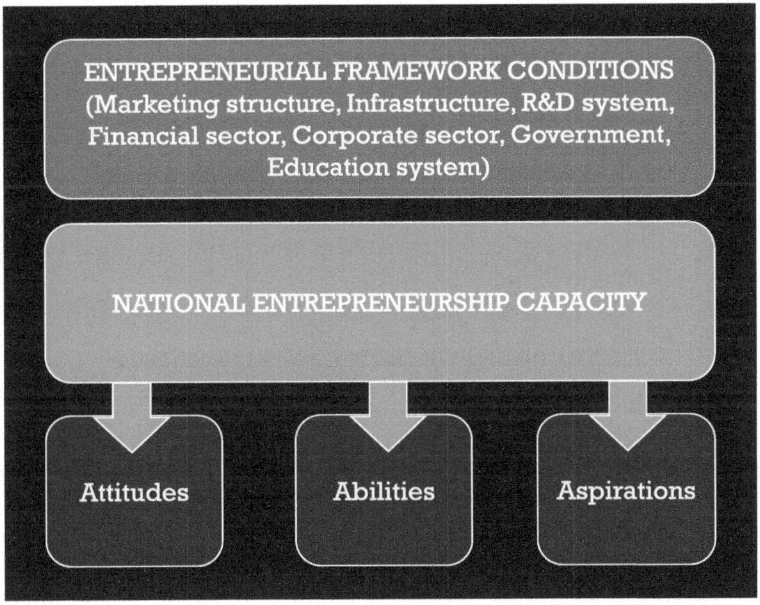

Fig. 2.1 Construct of the entrepreneurial ecosystem (Author portrayal based on GEDI Report, 2019[4])

of internal and external segments. Entrepreneurial outcomes are thus, subjected to external influences. The external segment, as indicated in Fig. 2.1, consists of seven elements: market structure, infrastructure, R&D system, financial system, corporate sector, government, and education system. These external elements influence internal elements identified as attitude, aspiration, and ability of the entrepreneur.[3] The entrepreneurial outcome thus, is configured by the external components of the ecosystem. According to this approach, entrepreneurial capacity of a country is determined by the dynamics of the external segment; which is also known as macro environment.

National Entrepreneurial Capacity

Entrepreneurial capacity of a nation is reflected by entrepreneurs' attitudes, abilities, and aspirations as a whole. Entrepreneur fitness then is believed to be constructed on 14 pillars. They determine the quantity of supply and quality of behavior of entrepreneurs. Therefore, GEDI recommends that the Entrepreneurial Ecosystem needs to be manipulated to enhance entrepreneurial capacity of a country.

The factors that affect entrepreneurial attitudes, abilities, and aspirations are extensively elaborated in *The* Global Entrepreneurship Development Report (2019: 15–18). Entrepreneurial attitudes in a population are constructed upon five pillars whereas entrepreneurship abilities are determined by four pillars and entrepreneurship aspirations are caused by five pillars as indicated in Table 2.1.

Entrepreneurship Environment

Entrepreneurship environment is more complex an affair than what was described above. This section, therefore, attempts to elaborate the composition of entrepreneurship environmental elements and their interactions (Fig. 2.2). Entrepreneurship environment basically comprises two spheres: controllable sphere and uncontrollable sphere. The controllable sphere comprises firm environment (internal environment) that is a composite of elements such as assets, liabilities, rights, skills, and internal stakeholders like owners, investors, and employees.[6]

The uncontrollable sphere is the external environment that lies beyond the firm environment and is comprised of four elements: operational, market, national, and international of which the impacts are uncontrollable and hence are challenges. Clever entrepreneurs adopt strategic innovations to overcome the challenges stemming from these uncontrollable elements. The uncontrollable environments need not be viewed as pessimistic always because they often produce circumstances that bring about unique business opportunities also. However, benefits from such opportunities will be yielded to strategic innovations only.[7] The uncontrollable sphere is a testing field for entrepreneurs as it demands critical entrepreneurial judgments and extraordinary innovations to overwhelm uncertainty and risk.

Firm Environment

The firm environment is the core environment that is controllable to the entrepreneur. Organizational form and formation, operations, expansion, internationalization, acquisition, merging, licensing, and going out of business are general decisions of a firm. The size and scale of a

Table 2.1 Elements of the entrepreneurial ecosystem

	Sub-index	*Pillars*	*Variables*
GLOBAL ENTREPRENEURSHIP INDEX	Attitudes	Opportunity perception	Opportunity recognition, economic freedom, property rights
		Start-up skills	Skill perception and education
		Risk acceptance	Risk perception and country risk
		Networking	Know entrepreneurs and agglomeration
		Cultural support	Career status and corruption
	Abilities	Opportunity startup	Opportunity motivation and governance
		Technology absorption	Technology level and technology absorption
		Human capital	Educational level and labor market
		Competition	Competitors and competitiveness
	Aspirations	Product innovation	New product and technology transfer
		Process innovation	New technology and Science
		High growth	Gazelle, finance, strategy, business sophistication
		Internationalization	Export and Economic complexity
		Risk capital	Informal investment and Depth of capital market

Author portrayal based on GEDI Report (2019)[5]

firm is determined by these decisions. In line with these decisions, recruitment, promotion, compensation, laying out, procurement, financial, and marketing decisions are taken by the entrepreneur. Entrepreneur is freer to make these decisions depending on the legal foundation of the firm. Firm environment of proprietorship is more controllable as the entrepreneur enjoys more liberties in the proprietary form of business.

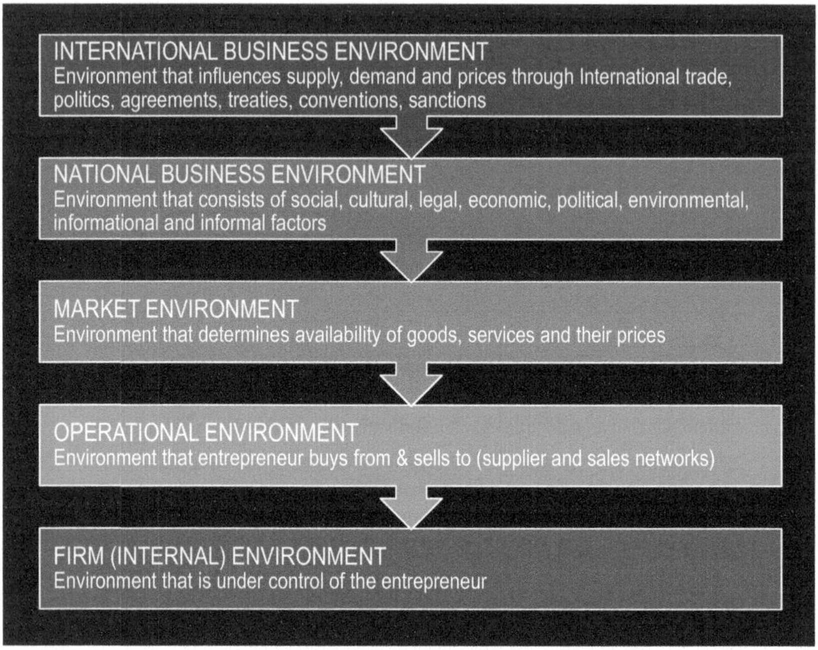

Fig. 2.2 Entrepreneurship environment (Author portrayal)

Proprietorship is not much regulated externally. However, in contrast, other firms like limited companies and large corporates are obliged to accord with complex regulations stipulated for such firms when making decisions in connection with above-mentioned circumstances. Yet, in general, every firm enjoys much freedom to decide internal affairs sans much external influences and thus, the internal environment is recognized as controllable.[8]

Operational Environment

Next to firm environment, the operational environment lies. It consists of seller networks, buyer networks, and professional agencies. Entrepreneur buys inputs from and sells outputs to this environment. The influence of this environment grows high as operations become complex. Since entrepreneur operates with certain parties in this environment, their behaviors, ethics, values, integrity, and accountability. are critical for the success or failure of the venture. In a circumstance where suppliers are steady and sales agencies are effective, entrepreneur can operate smoothly. In contrast, when suppliers and sales agents are frustrating, entrepreneur will find smooth operation is challenging. This suggests that a sound operational environment needs to be maintained for ensuring effective operations of a firm. Still, operations will be subjected to the challenges of market environment that lies beyond the operational environment.[9]

Market Environment

Market environment affects the operational environment either favorably or unfavorably. Components of the market environment include production, stock of inventories, prices, mode of delivery, competition among suppliers and producers, supply of factors of production, and auxiliary services. Market environment determines, at distance, the volume and scale of production and sales of individual entrepreneurs. When the market is competitive, the prices will be realistic and entrepreneurs will benefit from market efficiency. Price levels, surplus or scarcity of goods, supply of labor and wage rate, credits and interest rates, and land and its rent. are determined by market forces. Therefore, the market environment determines under what national market condition an entrepreneur will have to operate. Market environment is still influenced by national business environment.

National Environment

National business environment lies in the outermost sphere of the borders of a country. National business environment is national business climate that has overall bearing on the national entrepreneurship motion. Components of the national business environment include governance, legal system, monetary system, economic, political, environmental, cultural, and social policies, and international relations. Government can rule what and how to produce, quantity of production, who is to produce, who is not to produce, for whom to produce, what materials to be used, product and production standards, and price controls.[10] Price levels, interest rates, foreign exchange rates, environmental policies, bilateral and multilateral agreements, regional economic cooperation, physical and informational infrastructure, development programs, and the economic policy are sub-components of the national business environment.[11]

International Environment

International business environment is the most remote environment of all. The components of international business environment include international politics, sanctions and favors, trade and travel embargo, wars, rivalry, peace, international agreements, environmental protocols, conventions, safety standards of goods, exchange rate regimes, economic blocs, multinational corporations, international trade, commerce and finance, environmental concerns such as global warming, international health concerns such as pandemics, scientific and technological advancements. These factors determine the globalized business context which cannot be avoided or altered by individual entrepreneurs. International business environment influences price, quantity, standards, materials, technologies, and many other aspects of production, distribution, and sales of a firm.

It is now clear that the firm environment (internal environment) is in the core of the entrepreneurship environment surrounded and influenced by the components of external environment. In consequence, every business firm is closely or remotely and directly or indirectly influenced by the external environment. External environmental dynamics affect individual entrepreneurial operations negatively or positively. Therefore, the external environment should be perceived not only as an obstacle to entrepreneurship but as a source and means of venture opportunities also.

Environmental Dynamics

Entrepreneurship environment is inherently volatile because it is broadly comprised of volatile social, economic, political, and environmental factors. Therefore, entrepreneurs cannot expect stable environmental conditions for them to operate. This nature of entrepreneurship environment affects entrepreneurial actions either positively or negatively. In spite of this fact, some entrepreneurs always expect stable entrepreneurship environment believing that stable environment is by all means advantageous for business. However, against this common anticipation, some entrepreneurs choose to wrestle with volatile situations believing that they could discover exciting business opportunities under volatile environmental conditions.[12]

Stable environment is generally believed to produce business opportunities in abundance. It is obvious that entrepreneurial opportunities are more explicit and unambiguous in stable environment. Most entrepreneurs easily detect venture opportunities in stable environment because it is easier for them to plan, organize, forecast, and control and thus, business operations are convenient and less challenging. Sales and profits are also unquestionably stable in stable environments. Therefore, entrepreneurs generally prefer stable environment believing it is less risky and more profitable. The risk and challenge averting entrepreneurs prefer stable environment to unstable environment. However, because less risky environment is attractive to all entrepreneurs, the industry will become competitive and produce more rivals and less rewarding.[13]

In stable environment, market gets crowded as entrepreneurs increasingly enter the market. In this circumstance, market gets intensely competitive as many operators compete to grab a share of the existing market. This type of market is identified as "Red Ocean Market" (Kim, 2005)[14] which compels the producers to cut down cost and to push down prices in order to compete. Prices of the factors of production and inputs also rise due to competitive demand created by rivalry. Additional costs also will incur due to competitive advertising, product promotion, and product development which are aimed at market penetration. In the Red Ocean Market, all entrepreneurs finally face reduced profit margins and survival problems. Although stable environment seems less risky and more profitable, it is obviously risky due to escalated rivalry.[15]

In fear of uncertainty and high risk, many shrug off unstable environment. Yet, highly innovative entrepreneurs prefer unstable environment believing that it is more favorable for exciting innovations. In unstable environment, venture opportunities are more implicit and ambiguous and thus most entrepreneurs cannot readily spot venture opportunities. In order to exploit venture opportunities, this situation requires more inventive and innovative skills than in normal situation. When opportunities are implicit, market is less known to competitors and thus it is less crowded and less competitive. This type of market is called "Blue Ocean Market" (Kim, 2005).[16] In Blue Ocean Market, competition is low. Producers may tend to form collusion to manipulate market price and to make higher profits capitalizing on oligopolistic or monopolistic advantages. Also, bargaining power against factors of production and inputs is high among the entrepreneurs and thus they can keep the cost of factors of production low. The cost of advertising, promotion, and product development also can be maintained low as the competition is insignificant in Blue Ocean Market condition.

Entrepreneurial Opportunity Diagnosis

The preceding discussion reveals the fact that different environmental circumstances demand different entrepreneurial strategies.[17] Strategic entrepreneurial responses need to be designed taking the firm's internal environment also into consideration. Strategic outcomes of entrepreneurs can be derived from the relationships between internal and external environments of the firm.[18] Here, four different strategies are derived from a matrix in which responses of the firm meet different external environmental conditions. Entrepreneurial Opportunity Diagnostic Matrix (Fig. 2.3) guides entrepreneurs to recognize entrepreneurial strategies suitable for different circumstances they encounter.

Entrepreneurial Opportunity Diagnostic Matrix is constructed on two pillars: internal environment and external environment. Internal environment (firm environment) is comprised of factors such as management, capital, patents, inventive power, innovative capacity, product

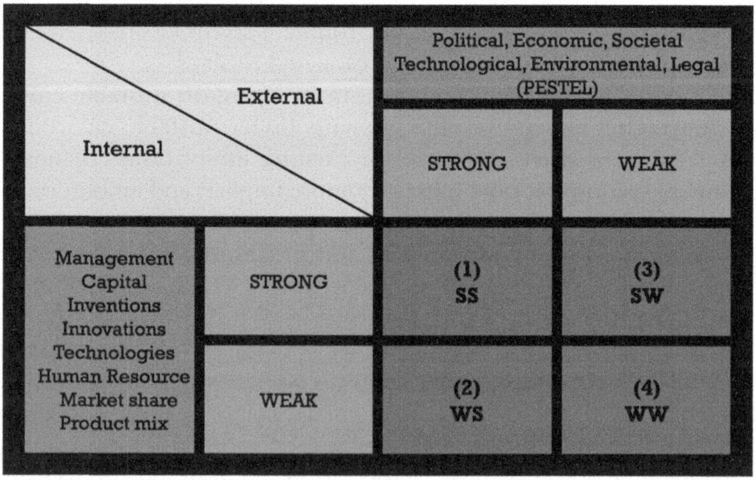

Fig. 2.3 Entrepreneurial opportunity diagnostic matrix (Author portrayal)

Situation	Characteristic	Strategy
SS	Internally Strong Externally Strong	BLUE OCEAN STRATEGY
WS	Internally Weak Externally Strong	RE-ENGINEERING STRATEGY
SW	Internally Strong Externally Weak	NICHE MARKET STRATEGY
WW	Internally Weak Externally Weak	RETRENCHMENT STRATEGY

Fig. 2.4 Strategic solutions (Author portrayal)

mix, technology, human skills, market share, and all other organizational capabilities. In contrast, external environment consists of political, economic, social, technological, environmental, and legal factors; which are commonly known as PESTEL factors.[19]

Environmental circumstances can either be strong or weak at different times and accordingly, four different situations are faced by entrepreneurs as indicated in Entrepreneurial Opportunity Diagnostic Matrix. Entrepreneurial strategies available for the entrepreneurs who encounter different situations are summarized in Fig. 2.4.

SS-Situation

This situation is characterized by strong internal capacity with optimistic external atmosphere. So, the SS situation is marked by abundant and explicit venture opportunities, crowded market, intense competition, and Red Ocean Market character. Entrepreneurial strategies required to overcome the market challenges of the SS situation are of three types. First, inventive and innovative strategies are required for production (for example, innovation of TVP curry flavors).[20] Second, strategic marketing programs are required to face market competition (for example, heavy advertising program to promote to eat Marmite[21] in addition to drinking habit). Third, strategies to leave Red Ocean Market and to reach Blue Ocean Market. These strategies will yield in growth, expansion, and sustainability of operations. As the firm's internal capability is strong in this situation, these strategies are financially quite feasible.

WS-Situation

This situation is characterized by weak internal capacity with optimistic external atmosphere. The main characteristics of this situation include opportunity rich circumstance, explicit opportunities, crowded market, intense competition (Red Ocean Market character), weak internal competitiveness, weak internal Research and Development position, weak marketing program, and lack of innovations. Facing competition and survival are challenges in this situation. Survival is considered as a game and the strategies are devised to win the game. Improving internal strength to switch to SS situation and the firm reengineering become major strategies.[22] In addition to these strategies, merging, alliance, licensing, and franchising are also available as alternative strategies.[23]

SW-Situation

This situation is characterized by strong internal capacity with pessimistic external atmosphere. The characteristics of SW situation include implicit opportunities, less competition, opportunities for innovation of low-cost products, opportunities in disguise (similar to "silver lining in the dark cloud"). The strategies relevant to this situation include cost effective production methods, use of new materials to cut down production cost, quality improvement to compensate high price, energy efficient production methods, and designing easy-to-operate simple and integrated products. Entering niche market (as Dilmah Tea[24] did), will be more useful than operating in the mass market in this situation. These strategies are quite feasible because the firm's internal capability is strong.

WW-Situation

This situation is characterized by weak internal capacity with pessimistic external atmosphere. The nature of the WW situation appears to be the worst among all situations indicated in the matrix. The WW situation is characterized by implicit opportunities, less competitors, shrinking mass markets, declining revenue and profit, increased overall costs, shrinking market opportunities, and demand. As internal capacity is weak, formulation of effective strategies to fight back will be remote. Therefore, retrenchment, reducing to simple product lines, cost minimization, merging with strategic partners, inviting another firm for acquisition, efforts to entering the SW situation will be suitable strategies for this situation.[25] The worst is that the firm may still find it difficult to introduce these strategies due to dire weakening financial and market positions. The failure in implementing the above alternative strategies shall compel the firm to go out of business and imminent closure. Kodak Inc. almost entered this "no come back zone" but managed to marginally escape.

Managerial and Entrepreneurial Skills

Entrepreneurs engage in innovation and operations roles and hence it is imperative for entrepreneurs to equip with two sets of skills.[26] Innovation role is entrepreneurial whereas operations role is managerial. Entrepreneurial role is basically non-managerial and managerial role is basically non-entrepreneurial. Yet, they are complementary at the top management level. In small and medium businesses, entrepreneurs engage in much managerial roles. On the contrary, the top management assumes entrepreneurial role of large corporates. Despite the manner they are exerted, both the roles jointly uphold venture success. Innovation skills involve venture creation and growth whereas operations skills involve venture management.[27]

When a firm is at its micro-level, entrepreneur equally plays both entrepreneurial and managerial roles. Yet, along with the growth of the firm, people are recruited to play managerial role. When the firm grows big, entrepreneur spends more of their time in entrepreneurial role leaving managerial role to others. Also, sometimes, entrepreneurs find their managerial skills are insufficient for much technical affairs and hire professional managers to perform them. This is the reason that entrepreneurs hire managers and assign their managerial responsibilities to professional managers. Yet, entrepreneurial responsibilities are evermore retained with the entrepreneurs. Though certain specialization between entrepreneurial and managerial skills is obvious in every circumstance, they are employed in conjugation because their collaborative and complementary function is essential for business success.[28]

Venture Classification Matrix

This ongoing discussion on entrepreneurial and managerial skills can be further explained with a matrix relationship as depicted in Fig. 2.5. Venture Classification Matrix provides a framework that is useful for perceiving different combinations of the two skills. Entrepreneurial skills include opportunity recognition, inventive, innovative, commercialization, organizing, intervention, and analytical skills. In contrast, Managerial skills comprise conceptual, human, technical, financial, planning, organizing, leading, and controlling skills.[29] These two skills can prevail at low or high level in a venture at a given time. Based on the degree of skill endowment, four different combinations can be identified as depicted in the Venture Classification Matrix. This helps classifying ventures into four different categories. Each category has a specific combination of managerial and entrepreneurial skills. The endowment of skills is determined as ventures give priority to each skill.

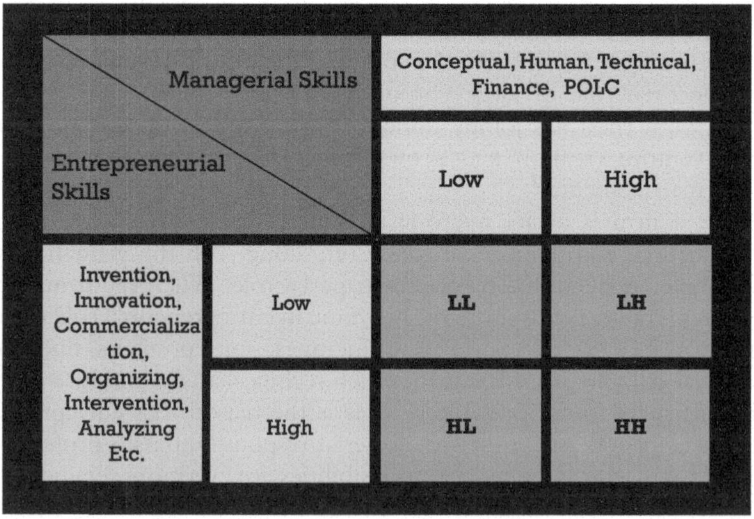

Fig. 2.5 Venture classification matrix (Author portrayal)

As both entrepreneurial and management skills are equally essential for venture success, Venture Classification Matrix helps entrepreneur to check whether the right combination of the two skills is employed in the venture. While proper combinations of skills contribute to venture prosperity, improper combinations retard venture growth. Thus, this matrix serves as a guide for entrepreneur to fine-tune skill combinations as demanded by venture objectives. Varied combinations of skills are required for ventures at their stages and according to the strategies implemented. Business strategies, in turn, are designed taking into consideration the opportunities and challenges induced by the wider business environment. Characteristics of each group of ventures are identified below.

The LL Group

- Low entrepreneurial skills
- Low managerial skills
- Lack of innovation
- Lack of product diversification
- Lack of business diversification
- Slow growth
- High operational costs
- Inefficiencies resulting from poor management
- Stability and sustainability problems
- Lack of industrial and market hegemony
- Struggling venture

The LH Group

- Low entrepreneurial skills
- High managerial skills
- Lack of innovation
- Lack of product diversification
- Normal growth
- Average overall efficiency
- Surviving on management competence
- Challenge of long-term survival sans innovation
- Management-driven venture

The HL Group

- High entrepreneurial skills
- Low managerial skills
- Innovations feasible
- Inefficiencies issues due to weak management
- Growth restricted to short and medium terms
- Difficulty in business diversification
- Moderate growth and moderate share prices
- Innovations stagnate due to weak management
- Insufficient funds for inventions and innovations
- Innovation-driven venture

HH Group

- High entrepreneurial skills
- High managerial skills
- Inventions and Innovations are feasible
- Fast growth due to innovation
- High earnings and share prices
- Product diversification is feasible
- Business diversification is feasible
- Enjoys favorable borrowing and investment conditions
- Operational hegemony in the business field
- Stability and sustainability accrued to management
- Innovation and management-driven venture

Skill swaps jeopardize venture objectives. Any compromise of entrepreneurial skills to managerial skills, or vice versa, thus, will bring negative or unsustainable results. In this setting, Venture Classification Matrix conceives the notion that skills in right combinations are pivotal for a venture to perform well; both entrepreneurially and managerially. Different business environments demand different combinations of skills and thus the entrepreneur needs to adopt suitable combinations of skills as demanded by different circumstances. Thus, Venture Classification Matrix is a useful tool for entrepreneurs to measure whether they adopt appropriate skill combinations in different situations.

In addition, it is noteworthy that most entrepreneurs set extremely high growth objectives in the short run or at the outset of the venture startup. Such growth objectives are merely unperceivable if the entrepreneur lacks exclusive innovation skills. Even if entrepreneur possesses inexhaustible management skills, growth objectives fall beyond reach due to lack of exclusive entrepreneurship skills. Growth objectives are mostly attuned to entrepreneurial skills while venture sustainability is attuned to managerial skills.[30] In the long run, to achieve business sustainability, exclusive managerial skills are required. Thus, growth and business sustainability targeting are pivotal in long-term strategic planning. Entrepreneurial and managerial skills are thus, mutually inclusive rather than exclusive.

Chapter Summary

Entrepreneurship environment consists of micro and macro environments. Micro environment is internal and controllable to the entrepreneur whereas the macro environment is external and uncontrollable. Environmental volatility eliminates some of the existing opportunities and generates new opportunities. Therefore, environmental volatility should not be always seen as depriving of opportunities as it triggers favorable conditions also. In volatile environment, an opportunity is similar to seeing silver lining in the dark cloud. Global Entrepreneurship Development Institute (GEDI) describes entrepreneurial environment as Entrepreneurial Ecosystem that consists of internal and external subsystems. The external subsystem consists of elements such as market structure, infrastructure, R&D, financial system, corporate sector, government, and education. These elements influence the internal subsystem that comprises entrepreneur's attitude, aspiration, and ability. Entrepreneurial outcome is configured by the dynamics of entrepreneurial environment.

This chapter also introduces a unique approach to entrepreneurship environment that advocates two spheres: controllable sphere and uncontrollable sphere. The controllable sphere comprises firm's internal environment that is a composite of elements such as assets, liabilities, intellectual property rights, skills, and the internal stakeholders like owners, investors, and employees. The uncontrollable sphere is comprised of four elements: operational, market, national, and international. Clever entrepreneurs adopt strategic innovations to overcome the challenges stemming from the Red Ocean Market and to sail to the Blue Ocean

Market. The uncontrollable environment, though challenging, is not pessimistic always because it produces circumstances that bring about unique business opportunities which demand entrepreneurial strategies. The Entrepreneurial Opportunity Diagnostic Matrix introduced here guides entrepreneurs in recognizing entrepreneurial strategies suitable for different circumstances.

Entrepreneurs engage in innovation and operations roles and hence it is imperative for them to equip with entrepreneurial and managerial skills. In small businesses, entrepreneurs assume much managerial roles whereas in large corporates, the top management assumes much entrepreneurial roles. Entrepreneurial skills involve venture creation and growth whereas managerial skills involve venture management. This relationship is described by the Venture Classification Matrix that conceives the notion that skills in right combinations are pivotal for venture performance. Growth objectives are mostly attuned to entrepreneurial skills whereas venture sustainability is attuned to managerial skills. For gaining business sustainability in all environments, entrepreneurial and managerial skills are seen mutually inclusive rather than exclusive.

Review Questions

1. Describe the composition of the Entrepreneurial Ecosystem stipulated by the Global Entrepreneurship Development Institute.
2. "National entrepreneurial capacity is determined by entrepreneurial attitudes, abilities, and aspirations according to the Global Entrepreneurship Development Institute." Critically explain.
3. Identify the components of entrepreneurship environment and discuss why the knowledge of each component is important for an entrepreneur.
4. "Some entrepreneurs prefer stable environment to unstable environment while some others prefer the inverse." Critically examine why.
5. Describe the controllable and uncontrollable spheres of the entrepreneurship environment and discuss the extent to which they impact on entrepreneur.
6. Explain how entrepreneur innovates their "firm environment" in response to the challenges posed by the elements of the external environment.

7. "The macro entrepreneurship environment is uncontrollable to the entrepreneur." Discuss this statement referring to Operational, Market, and National business environments.
8. Identify the components of the entrepreneurship environment. Explain how outer environmental components impact on each inner component.
9. Describe the propositions of Entrepreneurial Opportunity Diagnostic Matrix and critically evaluate the four different situations proposed by it.
10. "Entrepreneurial Opportunity Diagnostic Matrix is not only serves as a useful tool to diagnose environmental situations but also guides entrepreneurial strategy formulation for each situation." Elaborate.
11. Describe entrepreneurship situations that evoke the following strategies;

    Blue Ocean Market strategy
    Reengineering strategy
    Niche market strategy
    Retrenchment strategy.

12. Differentiate between Managerial skills and Entrepreneurial skills and discuss whether one skill is more important than the other.
13. Illustrate the construct and the propositions of the Venture Classification Matrix and discuss the strengths and weaknesses of ventures classified under each category.
14. Are entrepreneurial skills and managerial skills complementary? Provide arguments to establish your opinion.
15. Describe the characteristics of the venture class LL, HL, and LH and recommend a suitable remix of managerial and entrepreneurial skills for them to reach the class HH.

Additional Readings

1. Sundaram, A.K., and J.S. Black, 1996. *The international business environment: Text and cases.* New Delhi: Pentice Hall of India.
2. Peter, A.S., and Sarah, D.S., 2020. Rise and fall of Eastman Kodak: Looking through Kodachrome colored glasses. *American Journal of Humanities and Social Science Research,* 4(12), pp. 219–224.

3. Global Entrepreneurship Index, *Global Entrepreneurship Report, 2019.*
4. http://thegedi.org/global-entrepreneurship-and-development-index/
5. http://thegedi.org/global-entrepreneurship-and-development-index/
6. Omerzel Gomezelj, D., and Kušce, I., 2013. The influence of personal and environmental factors on entrepreneurs' performance. *Kybernetes, 42*(6), pp. 906–927.
7. Menguc, B., Auh, S., and Ozanne, L., 2010. The interactive effect of internal and external factors on a proactive environmental strategy and its influence on a firm's performance. *Journal of Business Ethics, 94*, pp. 279–298.
8. Kuratko, D.F., Hornsby, J.S., and Covin, J.G., 2014. Diagnosing a firm's internal environment for corporate entrepreneurship. *Business Horizons, 57*(1), pp. 37–47.
9. Bhat, S., and Khan, R., 2014. Entrepreneurship and institutional environment: Perspectives from the review of literature. *European Journal of Business and Management, 6*(1), pp. 84–91.
10. Dimitratos, P., Lioukas, S., and Carter, S., 2004. The relationship between entrepreneurship and international performance: The importance of domestic environment. *International Business Review, 13*(1), pp. 19–41.
11. Groşanu, A., Boţa-Avram, C., Răchişan, P.R., Vesselinov, R., and Tiron-Tudor, A., 2015. The influence of country-level governance on business environment and entrepreneurship: A global perspective. *Amfiteatru Economic Journal, 17*(38), pp. 60–75.
12. Luo, Y., Tan, J.J., and O'connor, N.G., 2001. Strategic response to a volatile environment: The case of cross-cultural cooperative ventures. *Asia Pacific Journal of Management*, 18, pp. 7–25.
13. Luo, Y., 2007. Are joint venture partners more opportunistic in a more volatile environment? *Strategic Management Journal, 28*(1), pp. 39–60.
14. Kim, C., 2005. Blue ocean strategy: From theory to practice. *California Management Review, 47*(3), pp. 105–121.
15. Kumar, S., 2023. Literature review red ocean strategy. *Global Journal of Management and Business Research*, 23(A9), pp. 71–75.

16. Kim, C., 2005. *Blue ocean strategy—How to create uncontested market space and make the competition irrelevant*. Boston: Harvard Business Review Press.
17. Godley, A.C., and Casson, M.C., 2015. Doctor, doctor: Entrepreneurial diagnosis and market making. *Journal of Institutional Economics, 11*(3), pp. 601–621.
18. Aloulou, W., 2002. Entrepreneurial orientation diagnosis in SMEs: Some conceptual and methodological dimensions. *Entrepreneurship Research in Europe: Specificities and Perspectives*, pp. 1–27.
19. Lee, E., Cho, Y., 2022. Effect of entrepreneurial ecosystem quality on entrepreneurship performance. *Journal of Korean Social Quality Management, 60*(3), pp. 306–332.
20. Textured Vegetable Protein (TVP). https://thedancingkitchen.food.blog/2019/12/01/sri-lankan-soya-meat-curry/
21. https://www.unilever.com.lk/brands/nutrition/marmite/
22. Kithinji, J., Rotich, G., and Kihara, A., 2021. Reengineering strategy and performance of large manufacturing firms in Kenya. *Journal of Business and Strategic Management, 6*(3), pp. 102–118.
23. Rohit, T., 1993. Business reengineering: A strategy driven approach. *Elsevier Long Range Planning, 26*(6), pp. 22–40.
24. https://shop.dilmahtea.com/
25. Mohammed, S.H., 2021. Merger & Acquisitions as important strategic vehicle in business. *Journal of Economics and Business*, 116(July August).
26. Lowden, J.S., 1988. Managerial skills for the entrepreneur. *Management Decision, 26*(4), pp. 35–39.
27. Tonidandel, S., Braddy, P.W., and Fleenor, J.W., 2012. Relative importance of managerial skills for predicting effectiveness. *Journal of Managerial Psychology, 27*(6), pp. 636–655.
28. Burgoyne, J., and Stuart, R., 1976. The nature, use and acquisition of managerial skills and other attributes. *Personnel Review*, 5(4), pp. 19–29.
29. Petrikova, D., and Sorokova, T., 2016. Managerial and entrepreneurial skills as determinants of business. *Polish Journal of Management Studies, 14*(1), pp. 184–194.
30. Burgoyne, J., and Stuart, R., 1976. The nature, use and acquisition of managerial skills and other attributes. *Personnel Review*, 5(4), pp. 19–29.

CHAPTER 3

Perspectives of Entrepreneur

Key Learning Points

- Scope of entrepreneur roles and functions.
- Cultural, ethical, legal, and economic responsibility.
- Designations of entrepreneur.
- Status of entrepreneurs: Business entrepreneur, Social entrepreneur, Charitable entrepreneur, Bureaucratic entrepreneur, Political entrepreneur.
- Traits of entrepreneur: Creative, Innovative, Self-motivated, Confident, Optimistic, Competent, Energetic, Flexible, Courageous, Aggressive, Patient, Dedicated, Visionary.
- Skills of entrepreneur.
- Role of entrepreneur: Innovation role, Managerial role, Administrative role.
- Responsibilities of entrepreneur.
- Importance of entrepreneur.
- Major types of entrepreneurs.
- Danhof classification.
- Facets of entrepreneur.
- Perceptions on entrepreneur.

© The Author(s), under exclusive license to Springer Nature Singapore Pte Ltd. 2024
M. Rajaratne, *Concepts, Processes and Practice of Entrepreneurship*, Palgrave Studies in Global Entrepreneurship,
https://doi.org/10.1007/978-981-97-6180-7_3

- Entrepreneur success factors: Curiosity, Experimentation, Adaptability, Decisiveness, Team building, Risk management, Determination, Strategic mindset, Focus, Growth management.
- Entrepreneurial challenges.

Introduction

Activities performed by entrepreneur spread across a vast scope. Entrepreneurial actions, in general, determine the perspectives of an entrepreneur. In this section, attempts are made to view entrepreneur in many perspectives. Entrepreneur plays multiple organizational roles, faces dynamic and volatile environments, and helps economic and social advancement of nations via value creation, generation of employment, tax payment, corporate social responsibility, and philanthropy.[1]

Scope of entrepreneur is not only confined to their business operations but proliferated into macro-social affairs also. Entrepreneurial actions, hence, consign responsibilities to entrepreneur in addition to those connected to their business. Entrepreneur is envisaged responsibilities such as social values, ethics, responsibilities, advancement of living, human rights, animal rights, consumer rights, labor rights, child rights, environmental conservation, resource conservation, good production practices, and operational standardization. This indicates that span of entrepreneur's operational scope has widened much beyond the internal stakeholders.[2]

Designations of Entrepreneur

Entrepreneur is identified with different titles in different occasions and at different organizational levels. Common titles used for identifying an entrepreneur include the following.[3]

- **Businessman:** Businessman is a common designation to identify an entrepreneur who engages in business for profit-making. In particular, smalltime operators, vendors, and middlemen are generally identified as businessmen while big businessmen are identified by their corporate designation plus the company name followed. E.g., CEO Microsoft Corp., Chairman Toyota Motor Corp.

- **Business leader:** The term business leader is used to refer to big businessmen who lead a conglomerate, group of companies, and business consortium. In this designation, leadership is highlighted rather than the entrepreneurial responsibility they shoulder. The term business leader is not used to describe an entrepreneur but to introduce an entrepreneur. Chairman or a president of a group of companies is recognized as a business leader. It is not uncommon for the term "business leaders' meetings." Corporates bigwigs attend such meetings.
- **Proprietor:** Sole owner of business is referred to as proprietor. Small enterprises are solely operated by proprietors. Along with the growth of ventures and transformation of their legal status, the designation undergoes changes; e.g., CEO, President, and Chairman. Legal status of ventures also undergoes changes to be dressed as (Pvt) Ltd., (Plc) Ltd., Inc., KK (Japan), and GmbH (Germany).
- **Chief Executive Officer:** Medium and large companies have created the Chief Executive Officer (CEO) post. The founder of a business, sometimes, serves as CEO. In case that the founder is elevated to the posts of President, Executive President, or Chairman, another person is appointed as CEO. They bear not only the responsibility of overall administration but also the entrepreneurial aspect of the firm. CEO is the most powerful and the highest paid post in the corporate sector and thus they are expected to perform entrepreneurial role in addition to administrative role.
- **President:** In large businesses, the post of President is created to obtain the service of the founder as a veteran. Usually, this requires ownership of sizeable volume of corporate shares also. Sometimes, the posts such as Senior President, Executive President, and Advisory President are created to keep the founder in as long as they are willing to serve.
- **Chairman:** The post of Chairman is seen in large companies as well as in government enterprises. The founder becomes the Chairman of private enterprises whereas the government appoints a Chairman for state sector corporations. This topmost post is sometimes delegated with executive/managerial authorities also drawing from the CEO.

Status of Entrepreneur

Entrepreneurs hold a few statuses in different settings of their operations and involvements as they belong to private, public, and social ventures. In any such setting, an entrepreneur plays inventive, innovative, and organizing roles to create value; monetary or otherwise. Entrepreneurs are identified by different statuses for involvement in different types of ventures.[4]

- **Business entrepreneur:** Business entrepreneur is motivated by private profit. Thus, they are identified as private entrepreneurs also. Business entrepreneur's participation can spread across micro, small, medium, or large businesses. Among all entrepreneurs, business entrepreneur is the most common type of entrepreneur.
- **Social entrepreneur:** Profit is shared among the business team that organizes social entrepreneurship.[5] Business objective of social entrepreneur is to enhance livelihood of his team by producing surplus income and sharing it among the team. By this means, social entrepreneur creates a social profit.[6] The beneficiaries of social entrepreneurship are usually economically backward, underprivileged, widows, socially, and discriminated. Hela Bojun[7] fast food chain introduced by the Department of Agriculture, Sri Lanka, is an example of social entrepreneurship.
- **Charitable entrepreneur:** Private entrepreneur who fully or partially sacrifices their profit to achieve charitable goals is a charitable entrepreneur.[8] Charitable entrepreneurs earn profit as does any other private entrepreneur, but spend the profit to achieve non-business objectives such as environment protection, child education, or animal welfare. In this instance, profit is business objective but the profit is used for non-business purposes. Here, among business objectives, welfare is prominent. Setting up of Embark chain of shops in Sri Lanka to fund caretaking of stray dogs is an example.
- **Bureaucratic entrepreneur:** Bureaucratic entrepreneurs are officers who bear higher positions in the public sector organizations. They are assigned responsibility to provide better social service.[9] Hence, the higher-level bureaucrats are expected to innovate their organizations and the services provided. So, they innovate their organizational structure, goods, or services they produce to impart social

profit. National School of Business Management (NSBM)[10] of Sri Lanka is an example.

- **Political entrepreneur:** Like bureaucrats, political entrepreneurs also engage in innovations aiming at increased social profit. Politicians with innovative ideas effectively contribute to the development of the country.[11] Establishment of Divisional Secretariats,[12] Board of Investment of Sri Lanka, Mahaweli Authority[13] are examples of the entrepreneurial endeavors of the politicians.

Traits of Entrepreneur

As entrepreneurs are "special" group of people with "more than average capacity" according to Walker as discussed earlier, it is comprehensible that entrepreneurs possess unique traits.[14] And entrepreneurs are self-invented personalities whose thinking, characteristics, and behaviors are different.[15] The study of traits of entrepreneur has become popular for two reasons. Firstly, the debate on the topic "whether entrepreneur is born or made" has aroused interest of researcher in investigating entrepreneurial traits. Secondly, the social discourse of entrepreneurship has urged scholars to distinguish entrepreneurs from other trades.[16] Also, entrepreneur trait is an important denominator to recognize trainees for entrepreneurship development programs. The major traits of entrepreneur are presented below.

- **Creative**—The ability to invent new knowledge useful for innovation of new and better goods and services.
- **Innovative**—The drive and capacity to bring about new and better goods and services.
- **Self-motivated**—The intrinsic motivation that comes from within rather than from outside and the resilience to maintain it without getting demotivated.
- **Confident**—The confidence of the business concept and plan, own and subordinates' skills, operations, and business success.
- **Optimistic**—The ability to foresee the future positively against pessimism that retards future endeavors.
- **Competent**—The competency in innovation and multitasking in performing various organizational tasks and functions.

- **Energetic**—The undiminishing stamina that is needed for relentless engagement in business operations.
- **Flexible**—The quality of adjustability to circumstances when and where they occur in the internal and external business environment.
- **Courageous**—The ability to face unexpected and unpredicted situations, challenges, and to overcome adversities.
- **Aggressive**—The character of not being exhausted and subjugated by challenges and tediousness of work.
- **Patient**—The ability to view and handle all situations calmly regardless that they are favorable or unfavorable.
- **Dedicated**—The quality of being attached wholeheartedly to decisions, tasks, and functions until success is accomplished.
- **Visionary**—The thinking power of perceiving venture destiny, potentials of innovations, and markets.

Skills of Entrepreneur

Entrepreneur's responsibility is to achieve specific goals and to maneuver the venture to a planned destination. The comprehensiveness and complexity of the tasks involved in these affairs demand a broad range of skills. They fall into two categories: entrepreneurial skills and managerial skills. Venture success is resulted from both these skills. Entrepreneurial skills are required to accomplish a venture whereas managerial skills are required to manage it.[17] Unlike in the past, now attention is paid to inculcate entrepreneurial skills for developing entrepreneurial capacity of nations. Therefore, the educational aspect of entrepreneurial skills has become increasingly important.[18] Both these categories comprise a large set of skills as listed below.

Entrepreneurial Skills

- Conceptual skill—To evoke ideas relating to creativity and business vision.
- Investigative skill—To explore business opportunities, markets, distribution, and technologies.
- Analytical skill—To assess business potentials, to measure them, and to make decisions.
- Technical skill—To determine jobs, tasks, and their orders.

- Inventive skill—To create new knowledge required for production of goods and services.
- Innovative skill—To produce useful goods, services, means, methods, and materials.
- Organizing skill—To organize tasks, resources, and overall operations.
- Criticism skill—To assess own drawbacks and to bear critiques from others for improvement of products.

Managerial Skills

- Delegating skill—To assign jobs, tasks, and responsibilities to subordinates.
- Coordinating skill—To connect different operations to bring about one whole system.
- Decision-making skill—To collect information, analyze them, and select right option from wrong option.
- Human skill—To deal with internal and external stakeholders.
- Communication skill—To compile messages transmit, persuade, receive feedback or right response from the receiving end.
- Commercial skill—To adopt marketing strategies to commercialize innovations.
- Leadership skill—To enhance motivation, industrial peace, sustain business, maneuver venture to reach envisioned destination.
- Finance skill—To estimate, forecast, trace, acquire, make finance available for operations, and control.

Role of Entrepreneur

Entrepreneur functions as an innovator, manager, and administrator. The innovation role includes not only innovation of goods and services but creation of venture also.[19] Once created, the venture engages in production and selling that demand managerial roles to guarantee operational efficiencies.[20] Then comes the administrative role that is required to ensure overall effective maintenance and sustenance of the venture. Venture creation, management, and administration delegate an entrepreneur a vast responsibility which, in turn, demands wide-ranging roles to play aiming at building a successful venture.[21] Entrepreneur, thus, instinctively assume innumerable sub-roles also therein.

Innovation Role

Innovation role relates not only to bringing about products and commercializing them but creation of business organizations also.[22] Accordingly, innovation role comprises the following sub-roles also.

- Searching for venture opportunities
- Organizing and combining resources
- Assuming uncertainty and risk
- Inventing, innovating, and intervening
- Commercializing to deliver innovations
- Reconstituting factor incomes
- Bringing about value creation
- Creating a venture

Managerial Role

Managerial role involves efficiently handling of organizational operations. Management is an inevitable role that encompasses all venture activities from the inception of a venture. Management role differs from small to larger ventures. In small ventures, usually, entrepreneur solely plays almost all managerial roles. But in large ventures, entrepreneur obtains the service of professional managers for distinctive business functions. In small ventures, business functions are not specialized and thus entrepreneur performs them all. Managerial roles connect to production function, personnel function, finance function, marketing function, and security function that every commercial entity is constituted upon.[23]

Administrative Role

Administration is an intricate job at large firms; and is more important as Fayol mentioned. Entrepreneur cannot effectively play all administrative roles in large and complex firms due to incapacity and thus resort to specialize organizational functions to guarantee effective operations.[24] Accordingly, managers are appointed and authority is delegated to them for carrying out organizational functions. Administrative role is a right, if not the prime responsibility, of entrepreneurs and so it is normally retained in their hands. When entrepreneur finds holding of administrative responsibility retards performance, they appoint top management and delegate the topmost authority also at a point.[25] Administrative role includes several duties:

- Planning; setting the vision, mission, goals, and objectives
- Organization of operations and coordinating
- Leading the venture as a whole according to the business plan
- Controlling the operations according to the preset plans, objectives, and standards
- Assuming the responsibility for venture success and failure
- Holding accountable to the stakeholders.

Responsibility of Entrepreneur

Ventures are created to produce goods and services by way of resource transformation and commercialize them. In this process, inputs are obtained from the society, and goods and services are produced for the use of the society. For this reason, social life is closely connected to organizations. Due to this pivotal connection between organizations and the society, entrepreneurs as heads of organizations are responsible for maneuvering organizations for the uplift of the society.[26] Main responsibilities of entrepreneurs are identified below.

- Remunerating own opportunity cost. Every entrepreneur has their opportunity cost of time. Therefore, entrepreneur should make a reasonable profit to remunerate the earnings they sacrificed for becoming an entrepreneur.
- Creating incomes for the factor suppliers. Entrepreneur should generate sufficient income from the business to pay off the rents and fees for the factors of production he used in the business operations.
- Correct use of resources. Incorrect use of resources causes private and social costs. Therefore, waste reduction, worker safety, foreign exchange saving, and resource saving. are major concerns of entrepreneur's responsibility.

- Minimizing environmental damage. Every product causes damage to the natural environment along the supply chain. Therefore, environmentally friendly policies and ethical practices should be adopted across the supply chain.
- Caring socio-cultural values. Socio-cultures are diverse and thus, multi-cultural, multi-religious, and multi-ethnic concerns are common in every society. Entrepreneurs are supposed to tolerate cultural diversities and prevent from enmities against any socio-cultural section.
- Abiding by laws and regulations. Organizations ought not to breach laws to gain undue benefits. For maintaining clean supply chain, entrepreneurs must avoid irresponsible conducts.
- Enhancing wellbeing of stakeholders. Both internal and external stakeholders expect monetary or non-monetary gains and thus, gratification of reasonable expectations of the stakeholders is the responsibility of the entrepreneur.
- Caring social responsibility. Corporates generally hold enormous wealth and economic power. This entails responsibility to soothe and caretake the parties affected by the venture, when and where the necessity arises.
- Careful handling of operations. Entrepreneurs are not supposed to handle business operations hazardously as such practices can damage workers and neighbors. The accident of Union Carbide plant in India is an example of careless handling of operations that killed several thousands of people.
- Ethical practices and fair policies. Entrepreneurs are a powerful segment of the society. Their behavior and attitudes matter the stakeholders and the society, in general. Entrepreneur is held responsible as unethical business practices, and unfair dealings cause social unrest and thus, they should minimize infliction on the society.
- Preventing from anti-social actions. Corporates hold enormous wealth and they are more powerful than small countries in terms of GDP. Similarly, a few corporates dominate the GDP of the country where they operate. Therefore, entrepreneur should act responsibly not to fund and nurture anti-social, terrorist, and extremist elements.

Importance of Entrepreneur

Importance of entrepreneur is determined by several factors. As ventures are social entities, they are useful to many aspects of social life.[27] Entrepreneurs are steersmen of ventures who perform many important tasks to achieve venture and social objectives as described below.

- Entrepreneur produces, distributes, and sells useful goods and services to the society, which means, relieving social stress.
- Entrepreneur creates income for factors of production that are owned by the public. Factor owners earn incomes only if entrepreneurs demanded them.
- Entrepreneur creates surplus that helps improve national wealth; which is identified as national income. Higher surpluses have caused higher national incomes.
- Entrepreneur brings about innovations useful for social progress. Modern metropolitan life indicates social progress from the life of stone age.
- Entrepreneur is pivotal to industrial development. Entrepreneur contributes to economic and industrial development through technological innovations and industry organization.
- Entrepreneur is an important taxpayer. Entrepreneur pays corporate tax and income tax. Entrepreneur breeds new taxpayers also through supply chains and employment.
- Entrepreneur is an important saver and an investor in the economy. Entrepreneur retains earnings and invests them in Treasury Bills, Treasury Bonds, Development Bonds, and Corporate Shares.
- Entrepreneur is a major donor. Entrepreneur donates money and materials to his alma mater, hospitals, education institutions, economically backward people, and to the countries in trouble.

Types of Entrepreneurs

Entrepreneur types have evolved during the past few centuries at a rapid rate during the past few decades due to growing business models. In consequence, many different types of entrepreneurs are present today. Major criteria to classify entrepreneurs include business models, mode of operations, ownership, scale, and legal foundation as indicated in Fig. 3.1. Common types of entrepreneurs are described below.

Based on Ownership
Private Entrepreneur (Proprietorship, Partnership, Private Limited Company)
Public Entrepreneur (Public Limited Companies)
Joint Entrepreneur (Joint Venture, Public–Private Partnership)
State Entrepreneur (Corporations, Authorities, Boards)
Foreign Entrepreneur (Multinational Corporations)
Cooperative Entrepreneur (Cooperative societies)

Based on Size
Micro Entrepreneurs
Small Entrepreneurs
Mid-size Entrepreneurs
Corporate Entrepreneurs

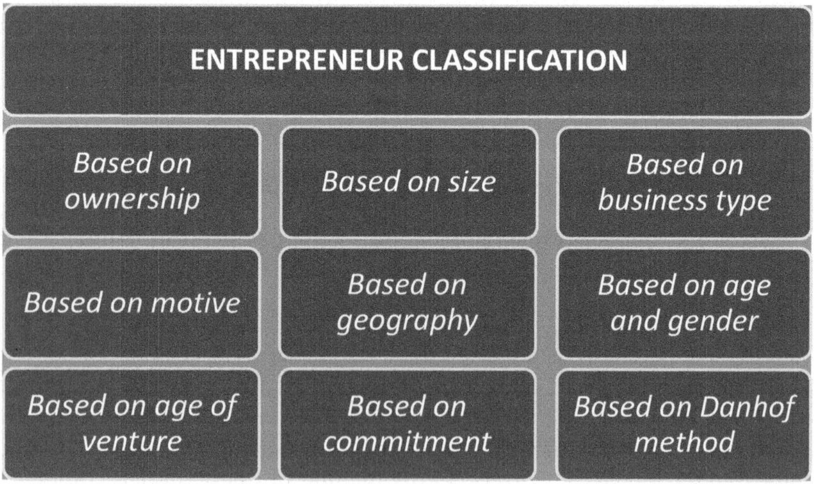

Fig. 3.1 Entrepreneur classification (Author Portrayal)

Based on Business Type
Trading Entrepreneur
Manufacturing Entrepreneur
Service Entrepreneur
Agricultural Entrepreneur
IT Entrepreneur
Construction Entrepreneur

Based on Motive
Inventive Entrepreneur (Sony, Apple)
Imitative Entrepreneur (Biscuits, soap)
Development Entrepreneur (Bullet train)
Induced Entrepreneur (Sanyo, Bata International)

Based on Spatial Presence
Local Entrepreneurs
National Entrepreneurs
International Entrepreneurs
Global Entrepreneurs
Transnational Entrepreneur

Based on Age and Gender
Young Entrepreneurs
School (children) Entrepreneurs
Women Entrepreneurs

Based on Age of Venture
Start-up Entrepreneurs
New Entrepreneurs
Old Entrepreneurs

Based on Commitment
Full-time Entrepreneurs
Hybrid Entrepreneurs
Self-employed Entrepreneurs
Seasonal Entrepreneurs

Based on Danhof's Classification
Innovative Entrepreneurs
Imitative Entrepreneurs
Fabian Entrepreneurs
Drone Entrepreneurs

Entrepreneur in Different Faces

Venture is comprised of three major communities: entrepreneur/s, managers, and workers. Each community has a unique role to play and any lapse would result in ineffective venture. Among them, entrepreneur creates organizations and lays out organizational system that exists even in their absence. Managers develop and implement effective management subsystems to run a venture. Management subsystems are founded on processes, procedures, rules, and regulations in a way to facilitate organizational functions. Workers perform specific tasks according to standards and parameters set by the main system and subsystems.

Although entrepreneurs have unique identity, the different roles they play in a venture instill in them some other appearances also. Entrepreneurs sometimes perform multiple organizational roles. Multitasking of entrepreneur is often observed in small ventures where entrepreneur performs entrepreneurial, managerial, and technical tasks at a time (Fig. 3.2). It is obvious, thus, multitasking of an entrepreneur involves non-entrepreneurial tasks also. In most cases, the scope of the duty of entrepreneur is wide and encompasses much managerial tasks also at the early stages of a venture even in medium and large-scale ventures. Corporates, however, adopt sharp differentiation between the entrepreneurial and managerial roles and thus the tasks perform by managers are heavily differentiated from those performed by entrepreneurs unlike in smaller firms.

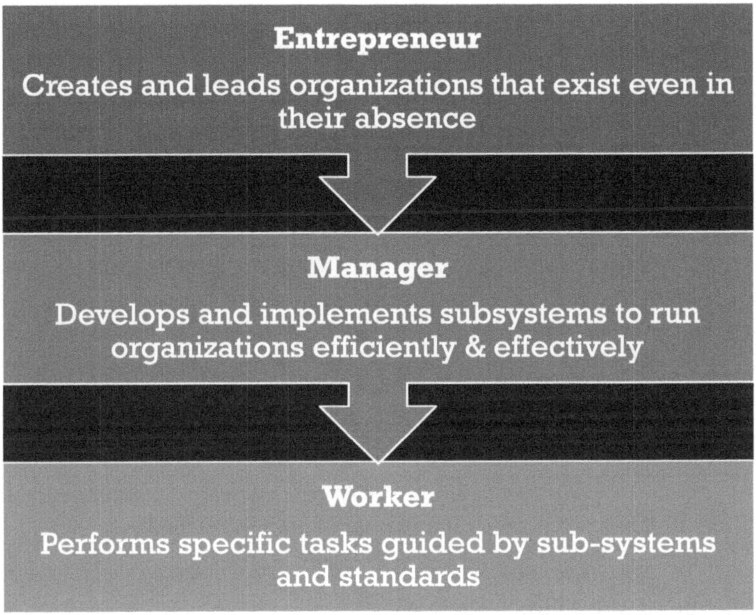

Fig. 3.2 Entrepreneur, manager, and worker (Author Portrayal)

Although a sharp distinction between entrepreneurial and managerial roles prevails in large corporates, entrepreneurial figure is mostly ambiguous as large corporates are governed by professional managers who perform entrepreneurial role in the capacity of Chief Executive Officer (CEO). Figure 3.3 summarizes the roles of entrepreneur and manager, in general.

Scope of the Entrepreneur's Duty
Creation of organizations
Generation of employment
Assigning tasks to subordinates
Exercise of own authority
Owning firms
Innovation
Promoting subordinates
Making profit or loss
Facing uncertainty

Fig. 3.3 Role of entrepreneur and manager (Author Portrayal)

Scope of the Manager's Duty
Running organizations
Performing duties
Carrying out tasks
Exercising delegated authority
Serving as an employee
Earning a salary
Attaching to a workplace
Maintaining managerial functions
Getting promoted
Getting fired

Managerial Entrepreneur

An entrepreneur who exhibits managerial role is a managerial entrepreneur.[28] Konosuke Matsushita, Chairman of Panasonic Corporation, once cut his own one-day salary in compensation for employing an ineffective transport manager. Subsequentially, the transport manager's one-day salary was cut because a driver he had employed failed to deliver his service punctually. Finally, the driver's one-day salary also was cut for his failure to effectively. This instance exhibits Matsushita's role as a manager rather than that of an entrepreneur.

Technical Entrepreneur

In some instances, entrepreneur is seen spending time as a technical worker such as cashier, salesman, or technician. Entrepreneurs who perform operational tasks are identified as technical entrepreneurs.[29] Technical tasks consume valuable time of entrepreneur which could otherwise be spent for inventive and innovative tasks. Entrepreneurial tasks are compensated with profit whereas technical tasks are paid with salaries. Technical tasks can be performed by people with "average capacity." Entrepreneur must engage in entrepreneurial tasks because their time is more precious than that of a technical worker.[30]

Entrepreneurial Manager

Some managers play the role of entrepreneur. So, they are entrepreneurial managers. Some managers develop organizations through their innovative inputs and thus they are rewarded with corporate shares; an opportunity for sharing profit. Some CEOs of large organizations are paid extremely high salaries and in return, they are expected to play entrepreneurial role in the organization. So, they are entrepreneurial managers.[31]

Corporate Entrepreneur

Corporate entrepreneur is alternatively identified as intrapreneur also. Corporate entrepreneur emerges from large corporates when outstanding and innovative ideas of employees are recognized to be supported to realize new innovations outside the main and general business interests.[32] If the new ideas are promising, the company might take interest in supporting the employee to operate as an intrapreneur. Company provides chosen employees with facilities for research and development and sponsors with resources, and technology. The employee, despite still being an employee, operates an independent business unit under the purview of the company.[33] A successful intrapreneur can operate as a sub-contractor to the mother company, amalgamate operations with the mother company, or leave the company to start his own enterprise. Whirlpool promotes intrapreneurs outside the company by recognizing innovations that align with the proposals of the company.[34] This topic will be lengthily described in a later chapter of this book.

Social Entrepreneur

Social entrepreneur aims at benefit of the people who join in pursuing social course that helps the community at large. Social entrepreneur creates a venture for and with a selected group of people to obtain their participation. Social entrepreneur capitalizes on abilities, skills, connections, and resources of the participating members within the group. Social entrepreneur aims at improving group education, health, economic, and social wellbeing. Further, social entrepreneurs adopt wider purposes such as poverty alleviation of less-privileged sections of the society, environmental conservation, citizenship empowerment, and women empowerment.[35] The less privileged includes those who are discriminated against color, caste, ethnicity, and gender, and the widows, war-affected, displaced, and handicapped. Social entrepreneur operates with the purpose of earning profit but sharing it among the group or investing in a social course.[36] Producer cooperatives are primarily a form of social entrepreneurship. Hela Bojun[37] (Sri Lankan social enterprise franchise) restaurant chain of the Department of Agriculture, Sri Lanka is an example of social entrepreneurship.

Hybrid Entrepreneur

Hybrid entrepreneur is one who organizes a venture while working as a full-time employee for another organization.[38] This type of venture is operated by entrepreneur's family members or subordinates (employees) as the owner is working full-time elsewhere. Hybrid entrepreneurs are mostly invisible but they play the entrepreneurial role behind the screen. However, the owner engages in business primarily during evenings, weekends, or online.[39] Some hybrid entrepreneurs are well organized as any other regular business by way of creating strong organizational structure. Hybrid entrepreneurs are common in online businesses at present. Some hybrid entrepreneurs operate as family businesses where family members take care of the business while the entrepreneur is engaged in another career.[40]

Perceptions on Entrepreneur

There are frequently asked questions (FAQs) about entrepreneur. While definitions of entrepreneurship help answer many of these FAQs, here it is attempted to provide a brief discussion on several such questions.

Q: Entrepreneurs are doers, not thinkers?
A: *Entrepreneurs think first and do then as conceptualization of business lays foundation for operations.*
Q: Entrepreneurs are born, not made?
A: *Some entrepreneurs are born with certain skills but entrepreneurial skills are imparted nowadays by entrepreneurship development programs also.*
Q: Entrepreneurs are always inventors?
A: *Entrepreneurs are not necessarily inventors. Entrepreneurs can use, buy, license, or franchise inventions of others.*
Q: All what entrepreneur needs to possess is money?
A: *Entrepreneurs can obtain money from other sources if they possess effective entrepreneurship skills and entrepreneurial plans. So, possession of money is secondary to entrepreneurship skills.*
Q: Entrepreneur needs luck?
A: *Luck is a random opportunity brought about by synchronization of internal and external circumstances. Clever entrepreneurs capitalize on luck or opportunities that come on their way.*
Q: Entrepreneur more frequently fails than succeeds?
A: *If and when entrepreneurial skills are insufficient or inappropriate to exploit specific opportunity, failure is inevitable. Appropriate skills will help success.*
Q: Entrepreneurs are gamblers?
A: *Entrepreneurs are not gamblers but they appear so because they inherently face uncertainty and risk like gamblers.*
Q: Entrepreneurs are profit makers?
A: *Entrepreneurs can make profit only through innovation of useful products that can successfully address customer needs and wants.*
Q: Entrepreneurs become rich as they exploit?
A: *Entrepreneurs exploit opportunities but they can become rich through successful value creation only.*
Q: Government entrepreneurship can replace private entrepreneurship?
A: *Government entrepreneurship cannot replace private entrepreneurship as both are complementary. Private and government entrepreneurs can jointly operate through Private–Public Partnerships (PPP) for favorable outcomes.*
Q: Social entrepreneurs are more important?

A: *Social entrepreneurs engage in selected fields of operations with specific objectives. Thus, they cannot be more important because they do not satisfy overall social needs and wants.*

Q: *Must women entrepreneurs play an important role in entrepreneurship?*

A: *Entrepreneurial behavior of men and women are similar. Women entrepreneurship is important as a means of women empowerment.*

Entrepreneur Success Factors

Entrepreneurial success is determined by a number of factors regardless of the size of venture. The vigor of the success factors from the business startup will be helpful to create a successful large corporate later in the entrepreneurial journey.[41] The entrepreneurial success factors are summarized in Fig. 3.4.

Sense of Continuous Curiosity
Curiosity is connected to the discovery of business opportunities and essential for invention. Continuity of curiosity helps venture growth in the long run through continuous innovation.

Will for Experimentation
Once opportunities are detected, experiments need to be performed to verify possibilities for invention and innovations. Without experimentation, neither inventions nor innovations are possible. Experimentation provides the entrepreneur with knowledge helpful to validate business ideas and their potentials.

Adaptability to Business Environment
Business environment constantly changes and those changes bring forth new challenges and opportunities. Thus, adaptability, instead of resistance, bestows new business avenues. Adaptive and agile entrepreneurs quickly respond to changes and exploit them as Peter F. Drucker mentioned. The unexpected moves in the business environment bring fortune to adaptive entrepreneurs.

Decisiveness over Indecisiveness
Making difficult decisions quickly and accurately is a key success factor. Business organization is a sea of decisions and thus the ability of decision-making is crucial not only for business policies and strategies but also for day-to-day operations. Confidence in decision-making is backed by entrepreneurial intuition also.

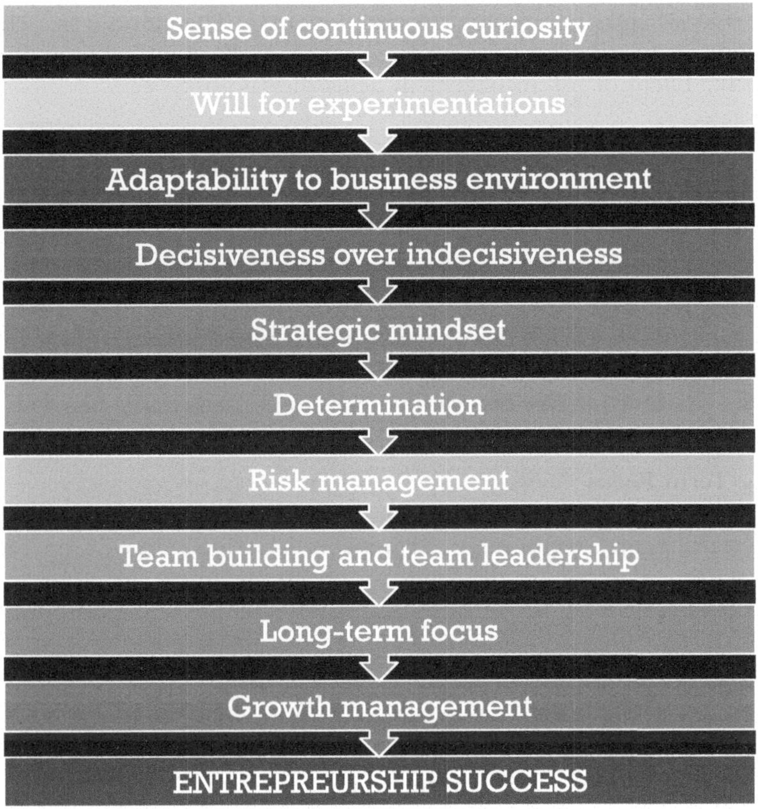

Fig. 3.4 Entrepreneur success factors (Author Portrayal)

Team Building and Team Leadership
Effective and well-managed teams are essential for successful business operations. Business building is a direct and positive outcome of team building. For a fast-growing business, founder's skills are insufficient. This problem is overcome by building the organization into an effective team.

Risk Management
Risk is an inherent character of entrepreneurship and thus the risk management is pivotal to entrepreneurial success. High profits associate

high risks whereas low profits associate low risks. Therefore, it is a challenging task for the entrepreneur to select the right point between profit and risk. Talent of risk management helps alleviate risk.

Determination

Determination is the key to business startup, organization, and expansion. Risk, uncertainty, failure, disputes, and challenges are common in business. Facing them with determination only can create a successful business.

Strategic Mindset

Internal and external environments often pose business challenges. Medium and long-term strategies are needed to successfully face the challenges. Key function like innovation needs to be strategically handled for business success.

Long-Term Focus

Long-term business survival, growth, and success are more challenging than starting up a venture. Entrepreneurs who focus heavily on business startups but not on the long-run operations often fail. Long-term focus is essential for long-term success, substantial growth, and business sustainability.

Growth Management

Long-term business survival and short-term business dynamics depend on the capability of growth management. Growth should be planned and achieved during short, medium, and long run. In all periods, the planned growth needs to be maintained. Both lower growth as well as higher growth can be harmful as happened to Osborne Computers of USA. Growth management techniques are applied to plan and achieve venture growth.

Entrepreneurial Challenges

Entrepreneurship is a challenging process. Many do not wish to face this challenge and thus, do not prefer to become entrepreneurs. The paucity of entrepreneurs in a society is a mark of shrugging off challenges. Entrepreneurship starts with identifying the unresolved needs and wants of people. Though explicit needs and wants do not pose much challenge, identifying implicit needs and wants is really challenging a task. Isolation of an exact business opportunity out of a large number of needs and wants that prevail at any given time is equally challenging. Invention is a key task of entrepreneurship that aims at satisfying unsatisfied needs and wants. Invention is a much challenging task because it requires investment, time, effort, expertise, and equipment for realizing an idea to solve needs and wants problems. And it is a more challenging task to finalize an invention before the opportunities expire.[42]

The greatest challenge among all that an entrepreneur encounters is converting inventions into innovations. Innovations are goods and services proposed to newly or better address unresolved needs and wants-related problems. Conversion of inventions into innovation is most challenging because it requires a production process which requires organization of investment, working capital, machineries, plants, and personnel. Also, the production process and the resulting products should comply with environmental and industrial standards. Obtaining licenses, permits, approvals, and standards is also challenging tasks. It is also a challenging task for the entrepreneur in guaranteeing that the innovations newly or better address problems and are practicable as well as reliable. Failing in facing this challenge is failing in addressing needs and wants; in other words, failing in entrepreneurial mission.

Entrepreneur operates with internal and external stakeholders and it is their responsibility to satisfy them all. This is a much challenging task as different stakeholders have different expectations and there can arise conflicts with expectations of one set of stakeholders when the expectations of others are satisfied. For instance, when customer satisfaction is enhanced through supplying high-quality products at a lower price by compromising profit, the investors will be unsatisfied as return on investment (ROI) lowers. The larger the stakeholder base and expectations the greater will be the challenge an entrepreneur encounters.[43]

Entrepreneurship embarks on venture creation. From the start-up stage, the entrepreneur encounters many challenges at different stages of the venture. Market positioning, increasing market share, gaining market and R&D hegemony, dealing with external challenges, adjusting to internal challenges such as shifting from one legal form to another legal form of organization (proprietorship to limited company) as the venture grows, transforming owner-management to professional management, managing venture growth, adapting to rapid technological changes, adjusting to social and changes, managing internationalization of the firm, dealing with corporate social responsibility and adopting corporate ethics, and crisis situations[44] are the areas from where most entrepreneurial challenges emanate.

Chapter Summary

Scope of entrepreneur is not confined only to business operations but it proliferates into socioeconomic affairs also. Entrepreneur is envisaged responsibilities such as social values, ethics, responsibilities, advancement of living, human rights, consumer rights, labor rights, child rights, animal rights, environmental conservation, resource conservation, good production practices, and operational standardization in addition to those of internal stakeholders. Responsibility of entrepreneur includes remunerating own opportunity cost, constituting incomes for the factors contracted, correct use of natural and manmade resources, minimizing environmental damage, caring socio-cultural values, abiding by laws and regulations, enhancing wellbeing of stakeholders, social responsibility, safety operations, ethical practices, fair policies, and preventing from anti-social actions.

Entrepreneur is designated as a businessman, proprietor, business leader, Chief Executive Officer, President, or Chairman depending on the business setup and scale. Also, entrepreneur is classified as business entrepreneur, social entrepreneur, charitable entrepreneur, bureaucratic entrepreneur, and political entrepreneur and is identified as creative, innovative, self-motivated, confident, optimistic, competent, energetic, flexible, courageous, aggressive, patient, dedicated, and visionary. Entrepreneur possesses conceptual, investigative, analytical, technical, inventive, innovative, organizing, criticism, and managerial skills and plays innovation, managerial, and administrative roles. Entrepreneur is important as a producer, distributor, and seller of useful products to address social needs and wants and to relieve social stress. Entrepreneur is also a creator of factor income, surplus, and national wealth. They are an agent of social progress through innovations, industrial development, and economic development. Entrepreneur is an important taxpayer, employer, sub-contractor, saver, major donor, and an investor in government portfolios and share market.

Entrepreneurs are categorized into a few types based on venture ownership, size, type, motive, geography, age, gender, age of venture, and the classification of Clarence Danhof. Entrepreneurs are also categorized as technical entrepreneurs, managerial entrepreneurs, corporate entrepreneurs, social entrepreneurs, women entrepreneurs, family entrepreneurs, and hybrid entrepreneurs. Entrepreneur success depends on several factors: sense of constant curiosity, will for invention and innovation, adaptability to business environment, determination, team building, team leadership, risk management, long-term focus, strategic mindset, and growth management.

Review Questions

1. Explain whether the entrepreneur's roles and functions stretch beyond the internal affairs of a venture.
2. What are the cultural, ethical, legal, and environmental responsibilities of the entrepreneur? Explain why entrepreneur is required to honor these responsibilities.
3. "Entrepreneur is a generic title used for a person involved in business activities." Describe the other such terms that are alternatively used for entrepreneur.
4. a. Is businessman different from entrepreneur?
   b. Is business different from entrepreneurship?
5. Describe the uniqueness of each of the following terms;

   Business entrepreneur
   Social entrepreneur
   Charitable entrepreneur
   Bureaucratic entrepreneur
   Political entrepreneur.

6. Can anyone be an entrepreneur without owing to the personal traits such as being Creative, Innovative, Self-motivated, Confident, Optimistic, Competent, Energetic, Flexible, Courageous, Aggressive, Patient, Dedicated, and Visionary? Explain why.
7. "Entrepreneur possesses both entrepreneurial and managerial skills. Compromise of each will result in adverse effects on the venture." Discuss.
8. Explain why entrepreneur is required to play the following roles simultaneously in entrepreneurial career;

Innovation role,
Managerial role, and
Administrative role.

9. "Entrepreneur can be successful only if they care for their responsibilities." Identify the major responsibilities of entrepreneur and elaborate how entrepreneur should commit to the responsibilities.
10. Explain why entrepreneur is important to the society. Describe the state of a society in absence of entrepreneurs.
11. Identify the different types of entrepreneurs based on the classifications of ownership, size, venture type, motive, geography, gender, and age of venture.
12. Explain why entrepreneurs are identified as Managerial entrepreneur, Technical entrepreneur, and Entrepreneurial manager.
13. Answer the frequently asked questions about entrepreneur that reflect different perceptions of entrepreneur.
14. Describe the entrepreneurial success factors critically examining the relevance of personal attributes and personal abilities also.
15. "Challenges for entrepreneurship retard supply of entrepreneurs." Examine the validity of this statement referring to how challenges thwart entrepreneurship.

Additional Readings

1. Bird, B., Schjoedt, L., 2017. Entrepreneurial behavior: Its nature, scope, recent research, and agenda for future research. In Brännback, M., Carsrud, A. (eds) *Revisiting the entrepreneurial mind. International studies in entrepreneurship*, vol 35. Cham: Springer.
2. Cornwall, J.R., 1998. The entrepreneur as a building block for community. *Journal of Development of Entrepreneurship, 3*(2), pp. 141–148.
3. James, W. Carland, F., et al., 1984. Differentiating entrepreneurs from small business owners: A conceptualization. *Academy of Management Review*, 9(2), https://doi.org/10.5465/amr.1984.4277721
4. Bogdan, N., Agnieszka, S., Marcin, O., 2011. Businessmen, managers, leaders: Why is it hard to be an entrepreneur? *Prace*

Naukowe Uniwersytetu Ekonomicznego we Wrocławiu, No. 224, pp. 98–111.
5. Ana, M.P., Murdith, M., 2006. Social entrepreneurship: Critical review of the concept. *Journal of World Business, 41*(1), pp. 56–65.
6. Thompson, J.L., 2002. The world of the social entrepreneur. *International Journal of Public Sector Management, 15*(5), pp. 412–431. https://doi.org/10.1108/09513550210435746
7. https://www.localguidesconnect.com/t5/General-Discussion/Hela-Bojun-Hala-Sri-Lankan-local-food-Outlet/td-p/1348709
8. Eleanor, S., Jillian, G., et al., 2011. Exploring contemporary entrepreneurial philanthropy. *International Small Business Journal, 31*(5). https://doi.org/10.1177/0266242611429164
9. Bien, B. Mitchel, Y.A., 2002. Bureaucratic entrepreneurship and institutional change: A sense-making approach. *Journal of Public Administration Research Theory, 12*(4), pp. 525–552.
10. https://www.nsbm.ac.lk/story-of-nsbm/
11. Mark, S., and Paul, T., 1992. Toward a theory of political entrepreneur: Evidence from local government. *American Political Science Review,* 86(3), pp. 737–747. https://doi.org/10.2307/1964135
12. https://en.wikipedia.org/wiki/Divisional_secretariats_of_Sri_Lanka.
13. https://mahaweli.gov.lk/
14. Sari, P.K., William, R.K., and Tina Xu, 2018. Personality traits of entrepreneurs: A review of recent literature. *Foundations and Trends in Entrepreneurship, 14*(3), pp. 279–356.
15. Florentine, U.S., and Dominik, K.K., 2022. Personality trait difference across types of entrepreneurs: A systematic literature review. *Review of Managerial Science, 16*, pp. 713–749.
16. Walter, S.G., Heinrichs, S., 2015. Who becomes an entrepreneur? A 30-years-review of individual-level research. *Journal of Small Business and Enterprise Development*, *2*(22), pp. 225–248.
17. Stuetzer, M., Obschonka, M., et al., 2013. Where do entrepreneurial skills come from? *Applied Economics Letters, 20*(12), pp. 1183–1186.
18. Leon, R.D., 2017. Developing entrepreneurial skills. An educational and intercultural perspective. *Journal of Entrepreneurship, Management and Innovation, 13*(4), pp. 97–121.

19. Erken, H., Donselaar, P., and Thurik, R., 2018. Total factor productivity and the role of entrepreneurship. *The Journal of Technology Transfer, 43*(6), pp. 1493–1521.
20. Li, C., Murad, M., et al., 2020. Entrepreneurial passion to entrepreneurial behavior: Role of entrepreneurial alertness, entrepreneurial self-efficacy and proactive personality. *Frontiers in Psychology, 11*, p. 516989.
21. Sajilan, S., Hadi, N.U. and Tehseen, S., 2015. 'Impact of entrepreneur's demographic characteristics and personal characteristics on firm's performance under the mediating role of entrepreneur orientation', *Review of Integrative Business and Economics Research, 4*(2), p. 36.
22. Sledzik, K., 2013. 'Schumpeter's view on innovation and entrepreneurship. *SSRN Electronic Journal*, 89–95. https://doi.org/10.2139/ssrn.2257783
23. Lowden, J.S., 1988. Managerial skills for the entrepreneur. *Management Decision, 26*(4), pp. 35–39.
24. Stanislav, D.D., William, P.B., 2005. Organizational roles and transition to entrepreneurship. *Academy of Management Journal, 8*(3), https://doi.org/10.5465/amj.2005.17407910
25. Monzani, L., Mateu, G., et al., 2021. Reducing the cost of being the boss: Authentic leadership suppresses the effect of role stereotype conflict on antisocial behaviors in leaders and entrepreneurs. *Frontiers in Psychology,* 12. https://doi.org/10.3389/fpsyg.2021.760258
26. Vallaster, C., Kraus, S., et al., 2019. Responsible entrepreneurship: Outlining the contingencies. *International Journal of Entrepreneurial Behavior & Research, 25*(3), pp. 538–553.
27. Osorio, A.E., Settles, A., 2022. Entrepreneur is so much more than just money making: Reclaiming the space of entrepreneurship in society. Ozkazanc-Pan, B., Osorio, A.E., Dutta, D.K., Gupta, V.K., Javadian, G., Guo, G.C. (eds), *Modern classics in entrepreneurship studies.* Cham: Palgrave Macmillan. https://doi.org/10.1007/978-3-030-61029-6_8
28. Moon, M.J., 1999. The pursuit of managerial entrepreneurship: Does organization matter? *Public Administration Review,* pp. 31–43.

29. Jones-Evans, D., 1996. Technical entrepreneurship, strategy and experience. *International Small Business Journal, 14*(3), pp. 15–39.
30. Cooper, A.C., 1973. Technical entrepreneurship: What do we know? *R&D Management, 3*(2), pp. 59–64.
31. John, A.P., Tracy, R.K., and D. Keith Robbins, 1997. 'Effects of managers' entrepreneurial behavior on subordinates', *Journal of Business Venturing, 12*(2), pp. 147–160.
32. Kuratko, D.F., Hornsby, J.S., and Covin, J.G., 2014. Diagnosing a firm's internal environment for corporate entrepreneurship. *Business Horizons, 57*(1), pp. 37–47.
33. Burgers, H., and Vareska, V.V., 2016. Who is the corporate entrepreneur? Insights from opportunity discovery and creation theory. *Handbook of Research on Corporate Entrepreneurship* (pp. 64–86). London: Edward Elgar.
34. Thornberry, N.E., 2003. Corporate entrepreneurship: Teaching managers to be entrepreneurs. *Journal of Management Development, 22*(4), pp. 329–344.
35. Constant, B., 2017. *Social Entrepreneurship—Managing the creation of social value.* New York: Routledge.
36. IGI Global, 2019. *Social entrepreneurship—Concepts, methods, tools, and applications.* Pennsylvania: IGI Global.
37. https://web.facebook.com/UNDPSriLanka/posts/hela-bojun-hala-food-stalls-promoting-true-sri-lankan-taste-of-nutritious-local-/1274427542591765/?_rdc=1&_rdr
38. Kriskaya, L., Kolvereid, L., and E.J. Isaksen, 2017. Hybrid entrepreneurs: Characteristics and achievements. *Entreprendre & Innover, 34*(3), p. 7.
39. Demir, C., et al., 2022. Hybrid entrepreneurship: A systematic literature review. *Journal of Small Business and Entrepreneurship, 34*(1).
40. Thorgren, S., Nordström, C., and Wincent, J., 2014. Hybrid entrepreneurship: The importance of passion. *Baltic Journal of Management, 9*(3), pp. 314–329.
41. Raduan, C.R., Naresh, K., and Lim Li Yen, 2006. The dynamics of entrepreneurs' success factors in influencing venture growth. *Journal of Asia Entrepreneurship and Sustainability, 11*(2).
42. Robinson, D.A., 2004. Entrepreneurial challenges in South Africa. *Journal of African Business, 5*(2), pp. 173–185.

43. Dennis, P.S., Jeffrey, G.C., 1998. Time, growth, complexity, and transitions: Entrepreneurial challenges for the future, *Entrepreneurship Theory and Practice, 22*(2). https://doi.org/10.1177/104225879802200205
44. Gagan, D.S., Sascha, K., et al., 2024. Entrepreneurial challenges of COVID-19: Re-thinking entrepreneurship after the crisis. *Journal of Small Business Management, 62*(2), pp. 824–846.

PART II

History and Theory of Entrepeneurship

CHAPTER 4

Evolution of Entrepreneurship

Key Learning Points

- The early history.
- Sense of synergy and teamwork.
- Origin of entrepreneurial thought.
- Reasons for entrepreneurship.
- Surplus production and barter system.
- Historical perspectives of entrepreneurship.
- New Guinea in 17,000 BCE.
- Farm production in 10,000 BCE.
- Emergence of entrepreneurial class.
- Emergence of trade and cities.
- Cross-border trading.
- The medieval history.
- Colonization, trade, and production.
- Entreprendre and Undertaking.
- Pre-industrial revolution production systems.
- Industrial revolution and factory system.
- The modern history.
- World Wars, world peace, open market regimes, and entrepreneurship.
- From mercantilism to free float exchange rate regimes.

© The Author(s), under exclusive license to Springer Nature Singapore Pte Ltd. 2024

M. Rajaratne, *Concepts, Processes and Practice of Entrepreneurship*, Palgrave Studies in Global Entrepreneurship,
https://doi.org/10.1007/978-981-97-6180-7_4

- Economic policy changes toward open market.
- Institutional support for international trade.
- Renaissance of technology and management.
- Modern social discourses.
- Consumerism, mass production, and mass marketing.
- Internationalization of business operations.
- Entrepreneurship development drive.

Introduction

The history of entrepreneurship dates back to the origin of commencement of human activities for living. Hunting was the primary activity of the humans in the pre-historic times. Primarily, hunting is aimed at hunting of food. As families grew, more food was needed and more effective hunting was indispensable to secure a sufficient amount of food. The sense of synergy occurred to the ancient man by experience and they learned to use simple tools and techniques which, in consequence, eased hunting and the volume of food huntable. This was the initial form of production of surplus food. The surplus, in turn, generated some kind of wealth in the caves. This, even without barter, is the first sign of entrepreneurship as wealth creation is in place yielded to accumulation of surplus; which can be named as "hunterpreneurship."

Since ancient times, the human kind rapidly learned the making of tools, methods, and techniques which helped producing surplus throughout the history. The primary entrepreneurial thoughts then advanced to production and barter, manufacturing, commerce and trade, and service and information technology consecutively transforming human life. As of today, technological marvels have created "technopreneurs" who are detailing the human life to an unforeseen shape. The evolution of entrepreneurs occurred as renaissances progressed. So, the hunterpreneur transformed into technopreneur as of today passing many milestones such as farmerpreneur, barterpreneur, hyper-producer-preneur, servicepreneur, etc., as summarized in Fig. 4.2.

The Early History

Sense of Synergy and Teamwork

Individual hardly ever possesses all hunting skills at high level and cannot perform a hunting task as effectively as a team does. Thus, the ancient people went on hunting in teams of different sizes and different skill combinations. Teams were formed as team efforts were more productive than individual efforts. Thus, teams were formed to pool skills of individuals for better hunting. Even in its ancient form, hunting involved a few activities such as tracing, chasing, killing, slaughtering, and carrying the meat back home. Each activity required different skills and when forming a team, the leader sought after individuals with right skills for each task. Leader's responsibility was to form a team with right skills to ensure effective hunting. With the sense of synergy (greater output), ancient men put collective efforts to perform tasks. In consequence, based on the notion of synergy, teams were formed to carry out jobs and tasks. Teams produced a surplus which was then bartered with surpluses of other goods produced by different teams. This not only led to proliferation of the barter system but also the fundamentals of economics.[1]

In ancient times, people were struggling to satisfy their basic needs with scarce goods. Scarcity had been aggravated by individual's incapacity to produce what they needed. In this backdrop, people recognized the sense of synergy that helps generate surplus of goods. Surplus was useful to satisfy the needs of those who lack the capacity to produce. Capitalizing on synergy, teams were formed to engage in effective hunting. Innovations such as tools and methods were consumed by teams to improve their production and surplus. Those who managed to produce an excess began to exchange their surpluses with those of the others.[2] The men who had sufficient amount of food sought for more goods exhibiting new needs and then wants. This gradually gave rise to value creation and commercialization as depicted in Fig. 4.1.

New Guinea in 17,000 BCE

In New Guinea, around 17,000 BCE, locals exchanged volcanic slates as hunting tools with goods like skins and meats (Ryan Alli, 2018). Near the volcanic site, volcanic slates were abundant while animals and vegetations were scarce. Yet, goods such as meats, skins, and yams were abundant in the habitats in the thick forests where volcanic activities were absent.

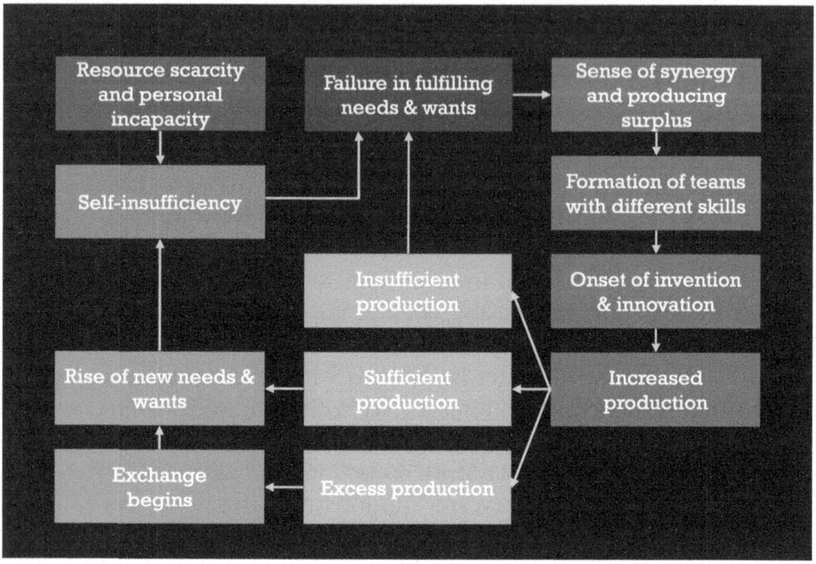

Fig. 4.1 Origin of entrepreneurial thought (Author portrayal)

This disparity encouraged the locals living near the volcanic site to collect volcanic slates, to carry them to a different locality, and to exchange them with other essentials produced in excess by those inhabitants. Both parties were satisfied as their exchanges created value for them. The motive of this basic transaction, though primitive, has been a form of value creation; which has evolved in numerous directions as of today.[3]

The modus operandum changed from hunting to cattle ranching which engaged in value creation through breeding cattle that can bring higher livestock output. Cattle ranchers developed a set of skills to generate higher output which aimed at producing a surplus after meeting the producer consumption. Maha Gopalak Sutra, in the Buddhist tradition, recommends 11 skills that help cattle ranchers to optimize sustainability of the cattle and to maximize the output. The practices adopted to generate increased surplus then helped increase exchange with other essentials.

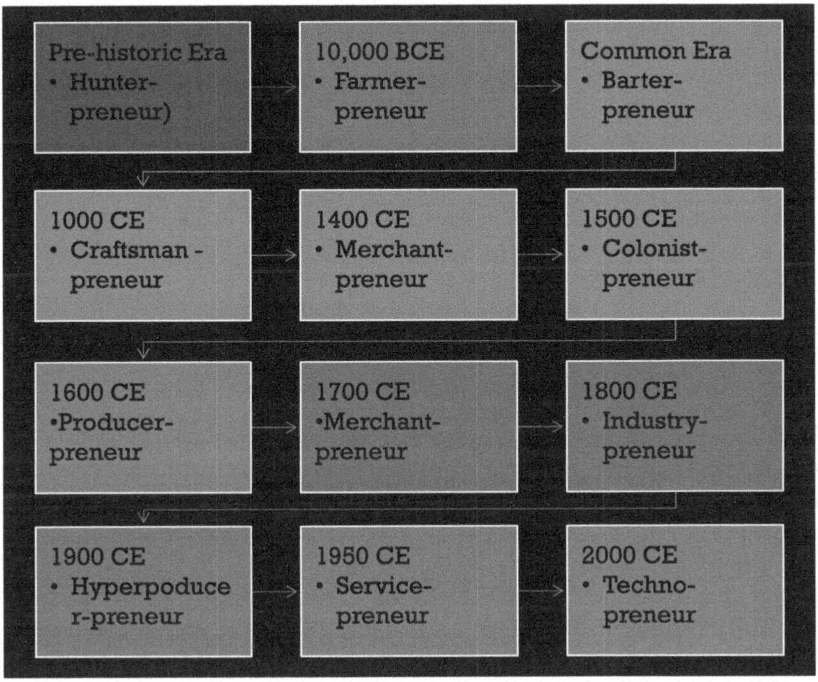

Fig. 4.2 Evolution of Entrepreneur (Author portrayal)

Agricultural Era

The agricultural era which is believed to have dawned 12,000 years ago led to stationary human living. Stationary living encountered with fixed supply of land and limited amounts of resources connected to it. This should be seen as the dawn of a new paradigm that was characterized by resource scarcity in contrast to needs and wants. Scarcity of supply of resources compelled the farmers to maximize their outputs from the limited resources at hand. This aroused the concerns of productivity among the farmer community. Productivity concern then promoted specialization in which a farmer could produce more of a certain crop. However, as farmers required non-farm products also for making their livelihood, another class of people found opportunities in producing goods that the farmers could not produce.[4]

This, in consequence, created two classes of people in the society: farmer and non-farmer class. The non-farmer class engaged in pottery, iron works, fabric making, and several other trades. They produced with the aim of exchanging their output with farm produce. Specialization systematically and rapidly spread in the society giving rise to numerous social classes also which was later identified as the class system and social stratification or even caste system. Every producer tried to increase varieties and quantities of output by employing creative ideas in production. Increased output and the surplus thereupon instilled a comprehensive barter system; the early form of systematic trade.[5]

Emergence of Trade and Cities

Trading infused dependency on goods produced by other parties. Trade dependency became the norm in contrast to self-sufficiency which prevailed for a long time. As trading became intensive, money was invented as a medium of exchange.[6] Money made trading easier and more prevalent activity. Trade formed trading centers and markets which then gradually developed into towns and cities.[7] City life is an outcome of manufacturing, trading, and auxiliary services concentrated in cities. People began to settle in cities to make a living by producing goods and services that fetch higher prices. It is believed that the city life emerged as early as 4,000 BCE; the Sumerian city of Uruk has been home to some 50,000 people by that time.[8]

Inter-Territorial Trade

Trading with neighboring territories transformed into inter-territorial trade along with producers across territories where producing surplus for trading to earn a profit. This is the initial state of international trade in contrast to domestic trade that prevailed until the inter-territorial trades emerged. Traders found that certain goods produced in excess in one country were rare in another country.[9] Thus, the traders were knowledgeable of the goods that generated higher profits in cross-border trade. Initially, salt from Africa was traded across the Roman Empire. And Chinese goods were inter-territorially traded over the Silk Roads that connected East Asia with the Middle East and Eastern Europe.[10] Products such as coffee, lemons, and oranges from Arabia were traded across

Europe. Possibilities of gains from surplus production and sales eventually led to surge in world production and sales.[11]

The Medieval History

The political economy of cross-border trade, by the medieval period, supported collection of wealth as much as possible in the form of gold and silver. This mercantilist norm heralded a new era of trade in the medieval period. Money and banking systems, even in primitive form, also were in place in Europe.[12] Money lubricated the wheels of commerce. Collection and production of commodities in large quantities for domestic and international trade became increasingly a predominant economic activity in Europe. Gains from trade encouraged traders to explore new destinations to engage in trade which later impelled colonialism.[13]

Colonization and Trade

Colonization became the spell of political economy of trade and production. Gains were incomparably high against free trade under colonial trading system. The Portuguese, Spanish, Dutch, French, and English, with support of their naval and gun power, rushed to colonize the world.[14] Colonization, in its first phase, was limited to the collection of commodities via Trading Companies (E.g., Dutch East India Trading Company and British East India Trading Company) but later, however, they initiated ventures also in their respective colonies.[15] Coffee, tea, rubber, cocoa, and sugar cane plantations are examples of early colonial ventures. Subsequently, colonial ventures spread in different industries and across continents in conjunction with European technologies, entrepreneurship, management, and economics.[16]

Entreprendre and Undertaking

France, being a country that encountered frequent wars in the history, opted to contract construction and logistics projects to the private sector because the military was overburdened with wars.[17] Private enterprises of this type were called "entreprendre" *(˜a.tʁə.pʁ˜adʁ)* in French.[18] Entreprendre was a common venture type in war logistics in the sixteenth century. The term "entreprendre" has been in use since then to differentiate the undertaking of civil contracts from other ventures.[19]

The term entreprendre was transliterated into English as entrepreneur (and entrepreneurship) in the early 1800s to mean "undertaker" (and undertaking).[20] However, before long, the scope of the term entrepreneurship widened to harbor every business enterprise into it. In particular, in the seventeenth century, the first Industrial Revolution transformed enterprises through machines and then through management.[21] Machines introduced sweeping changes to mode of production whereas management transformed production system. Production system evolved from the Domestic System to Putting-out System, and finally to the Factory System. Among them, the Factory System is a classic outcome of the Industrial Revolution where mode of production and production system are seen exceptionally progressed.[22]

Pre-industrial Revolution Production Systems

In the Domestic System, cotton fabric was produced domestically on micro scale with hand-operated primitive tools. The output was sold at the fair (weekly market) by the producers themselves. Fabric weavers purchased cotton from the cotton vendors at the same fair.[23] Domestic System was operated by small producer-entrepreneurs. Meanwhile, some intermediate persons found the Domestic System to be primitive and unproductive.[24] So, they recognized novel opportunities in the process of production and sales. They supplied machines and cotton to the domestic producers and collected the output paying for the labor; daily wages were replaced by this means because the domestic operators produced fabric as contractors. The middlemen collected the contracted output and sold them at the fair; this intermediary affair was called the Putting-out System. This gave rise to entrepreneurs of small scale who did not produce but did sell; the seller-entrepreneurs.[25]

Industrial Revolution and Factory System

Finally, the Factory System emerged as a solution to the drawback of the Putting-out System. Entrepreneurs of the Putting-out System wanted tighter control and close monitoring over the machines, tools, and materials supplied to domestic operators, the volume of production yielded to the supplies, and the quality of the output.[26] These controls were necessitated by misappropriation and malpractices experienced by the entrepreneur as the production occurred out of his sight. Innovative ideas of the entrepreneurs to overcome those embezzlements later gave birth to Factory System in which entrepreneur organizes production at a single place called factory where machineries are fixed, inventories are available, and people come for work.[27]

Entrepreneurs, by this means, were able to control theft, waste, and wear and tear of machine tools. As the operations grew large, entrepreneur individually was not able to look after every function of the factory. Therefore, entrepreneur appointed personnel to look after the factory affairs. They were supposed to look after every aspect of operations to control cost, finance, workers, inventory, and product quality. The people who were delegated the authority of control of each aspect of operations were accordingly designated as production controller, quality controller, inventory controller, finance controller, and personnel controller. Later, in the modern business context, the controllers were retitled as managers for the influence of the management pioneers of the twentieth century. The Factory System created large establishments where entrepreneur, controller (manager), and working class became distinctive.[28]

It is interesting to note that entrepreneur behavior has accorded to Say's Law of Markets that appeared in *Treatise on Political Economy* (J.B. Say: 1803). Say's Law advocates that "*A product is no sooner created, than it, from that instant, affords a market for other products to the full extent of its own value.*" He further elaborated, "*as each of us can only purchase the productions of others with his own productions – as the value we can buy is equal to the value we can produce, the more men can produce, the more they will purchase.*" Entrepreneurs collectively and in large scales have been producing goods and services that have created demand by themselves for each other's goods. This later prompted the notion of "Supply-side Economics" also that propagated entrepreneurship capitalizing on the possibility for innovations.[29] Adam Smith's proposition that large entrepreneurs are more productive as they engage in division of labor has also been equally approved by the large-scale entrepreneurs that emerged during the past several decades.[30]

The entrepreneurial thinking seems to have been evolving since the pre-historic period as people began to sense the marvel of synergy. This gradually led to production surplus and trade which then was formally organized and developed as ventures. The evolution of ventures yielded in evolution of entrepreneurs also from "hunterpreneur" in the pre-historic era to "technopreneur" in the twenty-first century as depicted in Fig. 4.2.

The Modern History

The dawn of modern history of entrepreneurship is connected to the Factory System. Efficiency and effectiveness of operations became the mantra of ventures. Manufacturing, mining, agriculture, plantations, and any other industry were assessed by their competence of efficiency and effectiveness. Emergence of management, that advocated organizational efficiency and effectiveness since the early twentieth century ladened entrepreneur with the responsibility of both leading and establishing comprehensive management systems in organizations. Entrepreneurs were encouraged by management as professional managers can share business challenges together with entrepreneurs. Thus, much of venture creation and success during the past century can be credited to management besides inventions and innovations.[31]

World Wars and Aftermath

The world wars and the cold war largely contributed to inventions, innovations, supply chains, and logistics paving the way for advancement of entrepreneurship.[32] Technological and marketing advancements facilitated mass production and mass marketing. The doors of international markets were gradually opened as free market system was established globally with the support of the World Bank, IMF, GATT, WTO, and UNCTAD.[33] Liberal trade policy, direct investment policy, exchange rate policy, financial system, and regional economic integrations such as free trade areas (FTA) and common markets such as European Union (EU) formulated an entrepreneur-friendly atmosphere globally.[34]

Technology Miracles

Technology miracles such as invention of integrated circuit (IC), transistor, Wi-Fi, memory chips, data processors, display technologies, 3-D printing, artificial intelligence, and remote sensing devices revolutionized the manufacturing industry and created immense opportunities for entrepreneurship. Further, food processing technologies, agrochemical, material making, assembly lines, and automation not only created opportunities in production but they led to cost competitive production systems also creating market opportunities for prospective entrepreneurs. Competitive advantage of nations encouraged gains from global value chains, interdependency, and internationalization of the firm. Industry 4.0 looming in the twenty-first century directs entrepreneurs to a wide spectrum of opportunities in digital, remote sensing, and artificial intelligence.[35]

Modern Social Discourses

New concepts such as environmentalism, feminism, personal wealth, education, health, traveling, personality, and distance operations were heavily propagated presently. These concerns have affected the entrepreneurial environment that existed so far. Environmental concerns required production of environmentally friendly goods.[36] Feminism led to women empowerment via women entrepreneurship.[37] Personal wealth concern promoted the notion of becoming rich and one's own boss rather than working as an employee and living a modest life. Increased demand for education, health, traveling, and distance operations modes created enormous opportunities for new ventures. Also, global production and operational standards such as ISO promoted better operations practices that bring about newer opportunities.[38] Also, much of recent developments have created abundant entrepreneurship opportunities in the service sector.[39]

Mass Production and Mass Marketing

Entrepreneurship is a relatively young academic discipline which is not theoretically deep rooted. Yet the concept of entrepreneurship dates back to the origin of team building by the ancient man. Entrepreneurship evolved gradually in the form of livelihood activities, in the first place, and then in the form of business. Technological marvels steamed the engine of entrepreneurship in the modern history and the development of commerce, management, economic freedom, and social progress also accelerated venture creation. Mass marketing, mass production, consumerism, personal wealth, and economic development encouraged large firms. Some large firms produce for the whole world. Large firms adopt sub-contracting, global value chain, and logistics that invite thousands of small entrepreneurs to take part in.[40]

In large firms, entrepreneur became less visible while managers became more visible. In today's big businesses, managers play some of the roles that the entrepreneur played earlier. Thus, the former has become entrepreneurial managers. Entrepreneurs are much visible in micro, small, and medium size ventures whereas professional managers and director boards, in place of entrepreneurs, are visible in corporates. Government entrepreneurship is also prominent in some countries in both for or not-for-profit concerns. This indicates that entrepreneurship has evolved in new directions also to address, differently or better, needs and wants of the society. Not only in the capitalist world but in the socialist world also, entrepreneurship is equally important as it plays the catalytic role of economic and social development. Entrepreneurship is an indispensable means of intervention to address human needs and wants which are on the rise.[41]

Internationalization of Business

Entrepreneurship started to take new forms, particularly since the end of the WWII. The USA became the world superpower and technology and management leader. The new world order underpinned by political power balance is seen in the backdrop of international trade. Mass production and mass sales became the spell of the world production and trade. World market was transformed into a global market and product standardization became common. Licensing and franchising became a significant mode of local and international business.[42]

International fund flows by means of foreign direct investment (FDI), multinational corporations, and the open market economic policies that were widely embraced by nations significantly contributed to change the entrepreneurship landscape of the world.[43] Further, social and psychological changes that occurred after the WWII encouraged entrepreneurial sentiment among many. Development of technology and management systems facilitated entrepreneurs to operate and control ventures from distance giving rise to international enterprising.

Entrepreneurship embraced wide recognition as an engine of growth which, in turn, stimulated entrepreneurship development programs in every nation as a means to economic growth and alleviation of unemployment, income inequality, and poverty.[44] Vocational skill development for the youth, repeal of employment laws to permit public sector workers to own and operate ventures, and widespread capitalist value system that bestows social recognition to entrepreneurs and their achievements helped boost entrepreneurial drive of individuals and nations in the new world during the past decades.[45]

Impact of COVID-19

COVID-19 erupted as an epidemic in 2019 in Wuhan Province, China and transformed itself into a global pandemic that caused catastrophic impact on the world economy and the life as a whole well until 2022. Some countries immensely suffered while others mildly suffered. Despite the diverse health impact of countries, entrepreneurial activities became standstill as social mobility was restricted and isolation was imposed for a long period. Travel restrictions, transportation restrictions, and lockdowns were common during the period. At the initial phase of the pandemic, these restrictions heavily retarded global and local value chains and supply chains. Entrepreneurial operations thus, were depressed pausing procurement and operations. In the entrepreneurship spectrum, upstream suppliers, manufacturers, distributors, and traders suffered and the factor suppliers including employees began to lose their income which then stressed the consumer market.[46] The seriousness of the impact of the pandemic on industry is indicated in Tables 4.1 and 4.2.

Thus, in a means-end chain like effect, production and auxiliary services shrunk disturbing almost all usual entrepreneurial activities around the world. Lockdowns and social distancing adversely affected every business from bakeries to airlines. However, the hardest hit areas included the SME sector and the "non-essential" services. Leisure, entertainment, tourism, traveling, etc., were banned and restricted and thus, many entrepreneurs had no immunity to operate their businesses; so, closing down was imminent. The pandemic drastically changed the international entrepreneurship landscape also heavily restricting the volume of international operations of ventures as indicated in Table 4.3.

Table 4.1 Impact of COVID-19 on entrepreneurial landscape

Item	*Percentage*
Reduction in consumer demand	88
Supply chain disruptions	34
Delays of state entrepreneurships	26
Distribution channel disruptions	25
Reduced investor demand	21

Data Youth Co-Lab Survey (March 2020)[47]

Table 4.2 Impact of COVID-19 on industry landscape

Average earnings revisions as of May, 2019	*Percentage*
Total	–36
Primary	–65
Mining, quarrying, and petroleum	–70
Agriculture, forestry, and fishing	–01
Manufacturing	–34
Motor vehicles and other transport equipment	–50
Textiles, clothing, and leather	–50
Basic materials	–49
Machinery and equipment	–47
Other manufacturing	–39
Computer, electronic, optical	–28
Products and electrical equipment	–20
Food, beverages, and tobacco	–15
Pharmaceuticals, medicinal chemicals products	–14
Services	–35
Accommodation and food service activities	–94
Transportation and storage	–63
Other services	–44
Business activities	–32
Information and communication	–31
Trade	–28
Financial and insurance activities	–23
Construction	–21
Electricity, gas, water, and waste management	–16

Data World Investment Report, UNCTAD (2020)[48]

On the contrary, some entrepreneurs strived and were successful in discovering the "silver lining" in the dark cloud. They invented technologies, methods, products, as well as business models. Entrepreneurs in information technology field innovated software for remote and distance operations which were useful for the service entrepreneurs.[50] The software devices for working from home, food delivery, online medical consultation, online teaching, and drone delivery are some of the innovations of the IT sector. Some other entrepreneurs responded by innovating new business models such as Uber Eats, Online classrooms, Online campuses, and Realtime doctor consultations. Further, an array

Table 4.3 Impact of COVID-19 on international entrepreneurship landscape

Item	*Percentage*
Reduction in FDI Inflows:	
World	–35
Developed countries	–58
Developing countries	–66
Growth rate of Greenfield investment:	
Developed countries	–42
Developing countries	–19
Growth rate of Cross-border M&A:	
Developed countries	–10
Developing countries	–24
Global FDI inflow components:	
Equity	–55
Reinvested earnings	–07

Data World Investment Report, UNCTAD (2021)[49]

of goods like face masks, sanitizers, cleansing-related devices, and immunity boosting drugs. Large entrepreneurs such as SmithKline and Pfizer invented immunity vaccines. New micro and small entrepreneurs emerged regionally to serve regional markets.[51]

Overall, COVID-19 evoked entrepreneurial thinking and contributed to an array of new opportunities for invention and innovations that helped address the needs and wants that emerged from this special circumstance. Governments too reoriented their policies toward supporting entrepreneurs, promoting research, and protecting entrepreneurs. All private, corporate, and public innovations to overcome challenges posed by COVID-19 are seen as its positive side. Erasmus+, in a study conducted in 2021, under the title "*Impact of COVID-19 on entrepreneurship*" concludes, like many other entrepreneurship scholars, that the inventions and innovations carried out during the pandemic period would be helpful for enterprising in the post-COVID-19 period also. It is obvious that COVID-19 has redrawn the contour of contemporary entrepreneurship.[52]

Chapter Summary

Entrepreneurship emerged and evolved as a practice for millennia and only in the past few centuries it caught attention of scholars. The history of entrepreneurship is traced to early, medieval, and modern history. The early practice of entrepreneurship dates back to the stone age. Insufficiency of food and incapacity to produce sufficient amount of food triggered the sense of synergy. This helped the production of foods in constant surplus and barter them with the neighborhood. Early entrepreneurial activities were traced to New Guinea, in 17,000 BCE, where the locals living near the volcanic sites collected volcanic slates useful as hunting tools and bartered them with goods like skins and meats produced by the inhabitants in the thick forests where animals were abundant.

The disparity in availability of goods or ability to production of complementary goods made a platform to barter them. This is the earliest mode of value creation from which both parties who engaged in the barter enjoyed a surplus. The agricultural era, which dawned 12,000 years ago, led to stationary human living. Fixed supply of land, resources, and scarcity of food were the characteristics of the society in that era. This raised the need for increasing productivity that led to specialization, surplus, and exchange of farm products with non-farm products. Accordingly, entrepreneurial sense emerged in both farmer and non-farmer classes. Class system and caste system also came to being as a result. Trade emerged as money was introduced to facilitate exchange. Trading centers, markets, and cities like Uruk, home to 50,000 people, were formed as early as 4,000 BCE. Entrepreneurs found opportunities in intra-territorial trade first and then in inter-territorial and international trade. Salt from Africa to the Roman Empire, silk and rice from China on the Silk Roads to the Middle East, and coffee and orange from Arabia to Europe are examples of early trade.

In the Medieval period, mercantilism that commanded international trade, money and banking systems, Trading Companies, and colonization were significant forces behind the development of entrepreneurship. Coffee, tea, rubber, cocoa, and sugar cane plantations and investment of their earning in other ventures made a big impact on cross-border entrepreneurship development. French government's initiatives to invite private undertakers as "entreprendre" dawned a new era in entrepreneurship. In the modern history, the Industrial Revolution revolutionized the entrepreneurial sphere and transformed enterprises from Domestic System to Putting-out System to Factory System. Entrepreneurship thrived during World Wars and the Cold War due to the advancement of inventions, innovations, supply chains, logistics, and then mass production and mass marketing. Open economy, free market system, World Bank, IMF, GATT, WTO, and UNCTAD extend institutional support for liberalization of trade, exchange rate, direct investment, and financial policies.

Regional integration, free trade areas, and common markets formulated an entrepreneur-friendly atmosphere globally. Technology miracles revolutionized operations and management of industries and created wide-ranging entrepreneurial opportunities worldwide. Environmentalism, feminism, education, health, traveling, personality, subcontracting, global value chain, logistics, industry standardization, and entrepreneurship development programs (EDP) have revolutionized the entrepreneurship landscape. Today, entrepreneurship has embraced wide recognition as an engine of growth in both capitalist and socialist regimes. Multinational corporations and FDI friendly policies worldwide have let the cross-border flow of capital, management, technology, resources, and even human resources paving the way for internationalization of entrepreneurship.

COVID-19 occurred in Wuhan, China and spread rapidly across the world and every nation fell victim to it. The pandemic was highly contagious and thus special cures and preventive measures were immediate needs. Mobility of people was contained and measures like lockdowns, isolation, and 14-day quarantine were imposed by governments. They caused the whole entrepreneurial world to standstill. However, diagnoses, cures, immunization, prevention, food supply, and maintenance of essential services were inescapable and thus, innovations were evoked by many. New products like special facemasks, sanitizers, new drugs and vaccines, and health apparatuses rapidly innovated. Logistics systems, working from home methods, drone services, online education, etc., were innovated synthesizing information technology as entrepreneurs were inspired to find solutions. COVID-19, thus, not only created opportunities to innovate goods and services for the short-term needs but also changed the trek of entrepreneurship.

Review Questions

1. "The history of entrepreneurship dates back to the stone age." Make an enquiry into the early age of entrepreneurship.
2. Examine how synergy encouraged teamwork, teamwork improved productivity, and productivity helped create surplus at the early age.
3. Explain how surplus production fostered the barter system during the agrarian era.
4. What is the entrepreneurial class? Explain how the entrepreneurial class emerged along with the rise of trade and cities in the medieval age.
5. "Colonialization inspired cross-border production and trade and hence international entrepreneurship, under the colonial system." Discuss providing historical evidence.
6. Describe how the concept of "entreprendre" led to the undertaking of projects in the sixteenth century and its contemporary prevalence also.
7. "Industrial Revolution transformed the Domestic System into Factory System." Explain how entrepreneurship evolved during the seventeenth and eighteenth centuries in Europe.
8. Identify the major forces and their impacts that strengthened the entrepreneurship in the twentieth century.
9. Evaluate the impact of free float exchange rate policy, open market policy, entrepreneurship liberalization and development policy, Free Trade Zone policy, and free trade policy on entrepreneurship development in the twentieth century.
10. Describe the role of international organizations that help entrepreneurship in terms of intellectual property protection, trade regulation, trade financing, and entrepreneurship development at present.
11. Evaluate the role of management and technological development in revolutionizing entrepreneurship to the present state.
12. Explain how entrepreneurship has been evolving through consumerism, mass production, mass marketing, free trade, Foreign Direct Investment, Global Value Creation, and Global Supply Chain.

13. "COVID-19 was non-man-made-marvel that revolutionized entrepreneurship." Critically examine how COVID-19 conceived new entrepreneurship thoughts and reinvented the wheels of contemporary entrepreneurship.

Additional Readings

1. Ryan, A., 2018. The history of entrepreneurship from ancient trade to the industrial age. https://startupguide.com/history-of-entrepreneurship-from-ancient-trade-to-the-industrial-age
2. Bögenhold, D., 2019. Changing ideas and contours of entrepreneurship in the history of thought: On the fluidity and indefiniteness of a term. *International Review of Entrepreneurship, 17*(2).
3. Ben, R.F., 2019. *Big-men and business: Entrepreneurship and economic growth in New Guinea Highlands.* Honolulu: Hawaii University Press.
4. Hynes, N., 2019. Something new under the sun? A case study of modern Italian barter systems. *Journal of Applied Business and Economics, 21*(2), p. 27.
5. Nyoko, A., Fanggidae, R., and Ose, M., 2022. The study of the barter trading system at Wulandoni barter market. *Proceedings of the 1st International Conference on Social, Science, and Technology,* Tangerang, Indonesia.
6. David, S.L., Joel, M., and William Baumol, 2010. *The invention of enterprise: Entrepreneurship from ancient Mesopotamia to modern times.* Princeton: Princeton University Press.
7. Laneri, N., 2014. The lifestyle of ancient entrepreneurs: Trade and urbanization in the ancient near east during the early 2nd Millennium BC. *Papers in Honor of Maurizio Tosi for his 70th birthday* (pp. 401–409). Oxford: Archaeopress.
8. Jeff, H., 2014. The invention of enterprise: Entrepreneurship from ancient Mesopotamia to modern times. *The European Legacy, 19*(4), pp. 509–510.
9. Bitros, G.C., and Karayiannis, A.D., 2008. Values and institutions as determinants of entrepreneurship in ancient Athens. *Journal of Institutional Economics, 4*(2), pp. 205–230.

10. Kudabay, A.A., Mukanova, G.K., and Yanchuk, V.A., 2021. The silk road and business communications in the ancient east. *Istorie/History*, *703*, p. 7.
11. Chan, W.K., 2010. Chinese entrepreneurship since its late imperial period. *The Invention of Enterprise: Entrepreneurship from Ancient Mesopotamia to Modern Times*, *10*, p. 469.
12. Casson, M., and Catherine Casson, 2014. The history of entrepreneurship: Medieval origin of a modern phenomenon. *56*(8), pp. 1223–1242.
13. Robert, F.H., and Albert N.L., 2009. *A history of entrepreneurship*. London: Routledge.
14. Dietz, S., 2020. *Entrepreneurship in the age of empire: Colonialism, collaboration and exploitation*. Routledge.
15. Bosma, U., 2014. The economic historiography of the Dutch colonial empire. *TSEG-The Low Countries Journal of Social and Economic History*, *11*(2), pp. 153–174.
16. Arkin, M., 1981. Entrepreneurship and the English East India Company—A review article. *Business History*, *23*(1), pp. 91–95.
17. Bamford, P.W., 1957. Entrepreneurship in Seventeenth and Eighteenth Century France: Some general conditions and a case study. *Explorations in Economic History*, *9*(4).
18. Hoselitz, B.F., 1955. Entrepreneurship and capital formation in France and Britain since 1700. In *Capital formation and economic growth* (pp. 291–337). Princeton University Press.
19. Hoselitz, B.F., 1951. The early history of entrepreneurial theory. *Explorations in entrepreneurial history*, *3*(4).
20. Munro, J.H.A., 2006. Entrepreneurship in Early-Modern Europe (1450–1750): An exploration of some unfashionable themes in economic history. *Tecipa*, 257. University of Toronto.
21. Murray, J.M., 2010. Entrepreneurs and entrepreneurship in medieval Europe. *The invention of enterprise: Entrepreneurship from Ancient Mesopotamia to Modern Times*, *10*, p. 88.
22. Redlich, F., 1955. Entrepreneurship in the initial stages of industrialization (With Special Reference to Germany). *Weltwirtschaftliches Archiv*, pp. 59–106.
23. Shepherd, A., and Toms, S., 2019. Entrepreneurship, strategy, and business philanthropy: Cotton textiles in the British industrial revolution. *Business History Review*, *93*(3), pp. 503–527.

24. Itoh, M., and Tanimoto, M., 1998. Rural entrepreneurs in the cotton-weaving industry of Japan. *Toward the rural-based development of commerce and industry: Selected experiences from East Asia*, pp. 47–68.
25. Itoh, M., and Tanimoto, M., 1998. Rural entrepreneurs in the cotton-weaving industry of Japan. *Toward the rural-based development of commerce and industry: Selected experiences from East Asia* (pp. 47–68).
26. Attar, M.A., 2015. Entrepreneurship, knowledge, and the industrial revolution. *Economics*, *9*(1), p. 20150003.
27. Wilson, C., 1957. The entrepreneur in the industrial revolution in Britain. *History*, *42*(145), pp. 101–117.
28. Geraghty, T.M., 2007. The factory system in the British industrial revolution: A complementarity thesis. *European Economic Review*, *51*(6), pp. 1329–1350.
29. Knight, F., and Schumpeter, J., 2015. Supply-side theories of entrepreneurship. *Public Sector Entrepreneurship: US Technology and Innovation Policy*, p. 28.
30. Newbert, S.L., 2003. Realizing the spirit and impact of Adam Smith's capitalism through entrepreneurship. *Journal of Business Ethics*, *46*, pp. 251–258.
31. Sathe, V., 1989. Fostering entrepreneurship in the large, diversified firm. *Organizational Dynamics*, *18*(1), pp. 20–32.
32. Godley, A., 2010. Culture, opportunity and entrepreneurship in economic history: The case of Britain in the twentieth century. In *Historical foundations of entrepreneurship research*. Edward Elgar Publishing.
33. Coulibaly, S.K., Erbao, C., and Mekongcho, T.M., 2018. Economic globalization, entrepreneurship, and development. *Technological Forecasting and Social Change*, 127, pp. 271–280.
34. Szerb, L.A., Acs, Z., and Autio, E., 2013. Entrepreneurship and policy: The national system of entrepreneurship in the European Union and in its member countries. *Entrepreneurship Research Journal*, 3(1), pp. 9–34.
35. Balachandran, V., and Sakthivelan, M.S., 2013. Impact of information technology on entrepreneurship (e-entrepreneurship). *Journal of Business Management & Social Sciences Research*, *2*(2), pp. 51–56.

36. Jamison, A., 2001. Environmentalism in an entrepreneurial age: Reflections on the greening of industry network. *Journal of Environmental Policy & Planning*, *3*(1), pp. 1–13.
37. Jamison, A., 2001. Environmentalism in an entrepreneurial age: Reflections on the greening of industry network. *Journal of Environmental Policy & Planning*, *3*(1), pp. 1–13.
38. Eugene, T.K., 2020. International standards: Catalyst or barrier for innovative entrepreneurship in Singapore? https://ink.library.smu.edu.sg/sol_research/3823
39. Dobón, S.R., and Soriano, D.R., 2008. Exploring alternative approaches in service industries: The role of entrepreneurship. *The Service Industries Journal*, *28*(7), pp. 877–882.
40. Wang, J., and Tan, Y., 2020. Social factory as prosaic state space: Redefining labour in China's mass innovation/mass entrepreneurship campaign. *Environment and Planning A: Economy and Space*, *52*(3), pp. 510–531.
41. Ghani, E., Kerr, W., and O'Connell, S., 2011. Promoting entrepreneurship, growth, and job creation. *Reshaping tomorrow*, pp. 168–201.
42. Wright, R.W., and Dana, L.P., 2003. Changing paradigms of international entrepreneurship strategy. *Journal of International Entrepreneurship*, *1*, pp. 135–152.
43. Hong, S., Reed, W.R., et al., 2021. Does FDI promote entrepreneurial activities? A meta-analysis. *World Development*, *142*, p. 105436.
44. Kressel, H., and Lento, T.V., 2012. *Entrepreneurship in the global economy: Engine for economic growth*. Cambridge University Press.
45. Zvavahera, P., Chigora, F., and Tandi, R., 2018. Entrepreneurship: An engine for economic growth. *International Journal of Academic Research in Business and Social Sciences*, *8*(11), pp. 55–66.
46. Amankwah-Amoah, J., Khan, Z., and Wood, G., 2021. COVID-19 and business failures: The paradoxes of experience, scale, and scope for theory and practice. *European Management Journal*, *39*(2), pp. 179–184.
47. https://www.google.com/search?q=Youth-Co+Lab+services+link&client=firefox-b-d&sca_esv=e8f1cfb632bd06ad&sca_upv=1&source=lnms&sa=X&ved=2ahUKEwidr_fu3fWFAxXKR2wGHRaHCVcQ0pQJegQIAhAC&biw=823&bih=648&dpr=1.36

48. https://unctad.org/topic/investment/world-investment-report
49. https://unctad.org/topic/investment/world-investment-report
50. Maritz, A., Perenyi, A., De Waal, G., and Buck, C., 2020. Entrepreneurship as the unsung hero during the current COVID-19 economic crisis: Australian perspectives. *Sustainability*, *12*(11), p. 4612.
51. Seetharaman, P., 2020. Business models shifts: Impact of Covid-19. *International Journal of Information Management*, 54, p. 102173.
52. Giones, F., Brem, A., et al., 2020. Revising entrepreneurial action in response to exogenous shocks: Considering the COVID-19 pandemic. *Journal of Business Venturing Insights*, *14*.

CHAPTER 5

Theory of Entrepreneurship

Key Learning Points

- Introduction.
- Influence of economics and management renaissance.
- Economic theory of entrepreneurship.
- Sociological theory of entrepreneurship.
- Psychological theory of entrepreneurship.
- Displacement theory of entrepreneurship.
- Inducement theory of entrepreneurship.
- External factor theory of entrepreneurship.
- The environmental school of thought.
- The finance school of thought.
- The displacement school of thought.
- The entrepreneurial trait school of thought.
- The venture opportunity school of thought.
- The strategy formulation school of thought.
- Mountain gap strategy.
- Great chef strategy.
- Unique product strategy.
- Unique resource strategy.
- Need for a new theory.
- The Intervention Hypothesis.

© The Author(s), under exclusive license to Springer Nature Singapore Pte Ltd. 2024
M. Rajaratne, *Concepts, Processes and Practice of Entrepreneurship*, Palgrave Studies in Global Entrepreneurship,
https://doi.org/10.1007/978-981-97-6180-7_5

- Phases of intervention; The 10-i steps: identification, isolation, imagination, invention, innovation, infiltration, intervention success, intervention continuation, intervention failure, intervention re-started.
- Intervention Hypothesis and Entrepreneurship Development Programs (EDPs).

Introduction

It is generally accepted that views on entrepreneurship have been around in Europe during renaissance in the fifteenth century. However, it should not be forgotten that topics of entrepreneurship have been present in Sumerian, Egyptian, Chinese, and Indian cultures and in their religious teachings.[1] Concepts of entrepreneurship have gradually developed during the past several centuries. Entrepreneurship concepts initially grew under the purview of economics during the past few centuries. Yet, the first Industrial Revolution in the seventeenth century and renaissance of management through the nineteenth century significantly enriched the theory of entrepreneurship.[2] Among those who significantly contributed to the development of entrepreneurship theory economists, management specialists, sociologists, and psychologists are at the forefront. The theory base of entrepreneurship comprises mono theories as well as schools of thoughts.[3] As a backdrop to the theory of entrepreneurship, Fig. 5.1 elaborates the determinants of entrepreneurial action.

Major Theories

Economic Theory

The economic theory of entrepreneurship propagates the notion that economic variables generate entrepreneurial opportunities and hence entrepreneurs. Accordingly, the state of the economy, i.e., progress or regress, is crucial in conceiving venture opportunities in a country with which entrepreneurs emerge as they exploit them through innovations.[5] The economic theory of entrepreneurship proclaims that the venture opportunities generated through economic dynamics and the intensity of their exploitation by entrepreneurs instigate entrepreneurship which hence determines the supply of goods and services in the economy.[6]

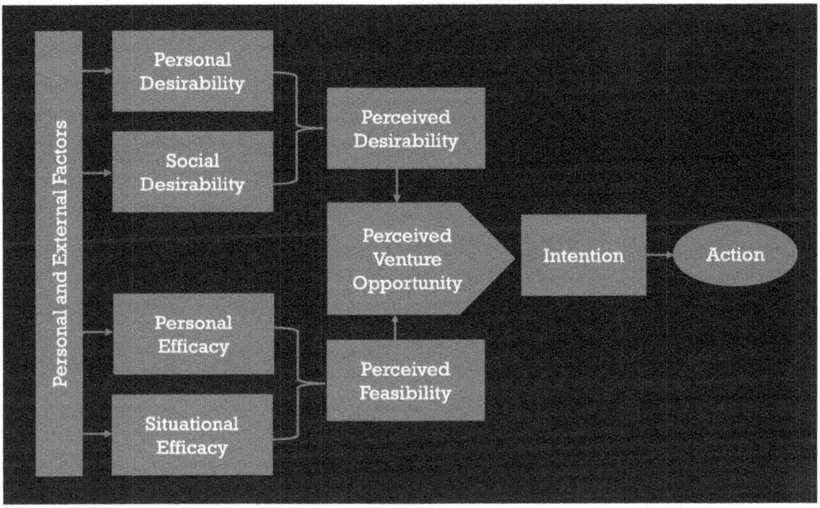

Fig. 5.1 A theory of entrepreneurial action (Author portrayal based on Krueger (2003))[4]

Both national and global economic policies affect the general business environment that is being faced by an entrepreneur. Open and free market economic policy leads to expansion of trade and production opportunities while closed market policy leads to their contraction. Free market policies promote free trade, free investment, free ports, and tax-free regimes.[7] Hong Kong, Singapore, and Dubai are a few examples of this kind that experienced thriving entrepreneurial activities during the past half a century. Thus, free market policies are opportune for entrepreneurs to engage in investment, production, trade, and other commercial functions nationally and internationally.[8]

Governments adopt export promotion or import substitution policies to achieve certain industrial development goals. Export promotion comes in a package of policy action that normally includes floated foreign exchange rates, lifted tariff barriers, unrestricted foreign exchange facilities, export promotion programs, export-oriented foreign investments, and preferential credits and interest rates for exporters.[9] On the contrary, import substitution policy restricts imports via tariff barriers, quantity restrictions, import bans, and discriminatory exchange rates. Import restrictions result in shortage of commodities which contrariwise infuses opportunities for producing domestically.[10]

Capital is regarded as a major impetus for entrepreneurship. Domestic capital formation is chiefly dependent on domestic savings. Foreign capital is also obtained in the form of loan, direct investment, and equity capital for business projects. Investment promotion policy and capital markets play a significant role in enhancing availability of finance for business.[11] The interest rate policy plays a vital role in promoting savings and capital formation, thereby. The economic theory advocates that low interest rates and finance with minimum collaterals stimulate entrepreneurs to invest in exploiting new venture opportunities. Thus, increased accessibility to capital, low interest rates, and minimum collaterals are stimuli to breeding entrepreneur according to the economic theory.[12]

Invariably, industrial policy has a connection to industrial opportunities. Industrial policy can have one or combination of strategies such as infant industry protection, private sector leadership, state entrepreneurship, public–private partnership, revitalization of local and traditional industry, industrial development programs, and small and medium enterprise (SME) development. In support of some of these policies, physical infrastructure like industry incubators, workshops, marketplace, and trade stalls are also provided by governments. Price policy, interest rate policy, exchange rate policy, and wage rate policy determine the cost of production and market price. Cost, in turn, determines industrial competitiveness. Controlled markets cause lower competitiveness and contract entrepreneurial activities whereas laissez-faire markets stimulate entrepreneurial activities and venture creation.[13]

Modern amenities, transport and distribution infrastructure, information technology, utility goods such as electricity, water, gas, and internet connection are useful for inception of new ventures and expansion of the existing ventures. Access to information about materials, technologies, machineries, markets, and competition that comprise valuable inputs in the production process is also vital for venture inception. Wage rate, interest rate, exchange rate, inflation, concessions for production, incentives for exports, and government sponsorship for crucial sectors such as energy, health, and education are favorable for new and existing ventures. All these outcomes are directly or indirectly connected to economic policy sphere. Thus, in general, economic factors help explain how entrepreneurship is locally and globally stimulated under different economic circumstances.[14]

Sociological Theory

Sociological theory explains that venture opportunities and exploitation of them are determined by social structure, values, ethics, beliefs, rituals, and taboos. Social dynamics determine market dynamics and entrepreneurs' response in exploiting them as opportunities. Sociological theory thus, assumes every innovation is consequent to social change. Sociological theory considers several elements of social behavior that give rise to entrepreneurship. They include social values, social acceptance of business, and social status of entrepreneur. Social values are comprised of sub-elements such as beliefs, customs, and taboos and their changes caused by political, environmental, technological, and economic factors. Accordingly, these social factors determine the supply of entrepreneurs in every society.[15]

Social beliefs, customs, and taboos determine what to and what not to consume, when to and when not to consume, and what volume to consume. Beliefs, customs, and taboos set guidelines for production and consumption. So, they influence the choice of materials, ingredients, process of production, designs and styles, colors, and patterns of goods. Also, they affect volumes, patterns, and frequencies of consumption. For example, Hindus are guided not to consume beef while Muslims are guided not to consume pork. Vegans refrain from consuming all animal products. They refrain from buying even leather products. On the other hand, Buddhists and Jains are taught to refrain from consuming meat as meat eating is against compassion and humanity.[16]

Some beliefs alleviate opportunities for production of certain goods but they contrarily create opportunities for production of alternative goods. Soybean-based textured vegetable protein (TVP), commonly known as soya meat, is an alternative product for beef, pork, chicken, and fish aimed at vegetarian market. The Islamic rules such as non-exposure of hair, face, and toes have generated opportunities for production of additional garments and ornaments to cover them. Religious rituals conducted by shrines, temples, and churches consume a large number of goods specific to those rituals. As an example, pooja (offerings) require many goods to be offered to gods and those pooja goods are sold at shops near religious places. Religious aspect of life creates demand for those goods, and in consequence, they create entrepreneurial opportunities for innovation. In contrast, the liberal thoughts advocated by the Westerners have created opportunities in production of modern fashionable goods.[17]

Social attitudes influenced by economic development and high personal income have revolutionized consumption and created modern consumerist society in which consumption of products in great volumes and in vast diversities are characteristics. This new trend of social behavior has created innumerable opportunities in mass production. Like goods, services are also heavily demanded at present to satisfy the wants for convenience, comfort, beauty, entertainment, amusement, and leisure. In consequence, service products consume much of the personal income. As a result, enormous entrepreneurial opportunities are created in the areas of travels, tours, games, sports, fitness, health, music, and movies. Performance of services requires certain goods also as inputs. For performance of the services such as travels and tours, sports, movies, musical shows, fitness and training goods such as transport equipment, sports gear, fitness goods, and healthy foods are demanded. Social progress thus, has become a source of innumerable entrepreneurial opportunities.[18]

Social acceptance and social status of entrepreneurs play an important role in supply of entrepreneurs in a country. Some societies highly value business and businessmen whereas some others do not. Societies like China, Hong Kong, and Japan are in abundance of entrepreneurs because social recognition for entrepreneurship is astonishing in them. High concentration of entrepreneurs in a society creates an environment conducive for competitively perceiving entrepreneurship opportunities. In competitive atmosphere, entrepreneurs operate shrewdly to recognize subtle and trivial opportunities also as explicit opportunities are already almost exploited. Goods and services that can satisfy inconspicuous needs or wants are indicators of smart innovations aimed at niche markets. Thus, the higher the supply of entrepreneurs in a society the wider the innovations of that society. China produces goods in an unimaginably great diversity and proves this argument.[19]

In the societies where entrepreneurs have high social status, supply of entrepreneurs is also high. Thus, in the societies where enterprises and entrepreneurs are heavily recognized, people get stimulated to engage in entrepreneurship. Capitalist countries have amazingly benefited from this social phenomenon in contrast to socialist countries. In socialist countries, government entrepreneurship is predominant and private entrepreneurship is restricted. Sociological theory thus, propagates the notion that social phenomena are pivotal to the generation of entrepreneurial opportunities that in consequence create entrepreneurs.

Accordingly, social forces are believed to be the key input for the advancement of entrepreneurship.[20]

Psychological Theory

The psychological theory of entrepreneurship has been formulated considering needs, attitudes, and perceptions that influence decisions of individuals to become entrepreneurs. Accordingly, the choice to become an entrepreneur or not is a personal decision fashioned by psychological reasons. There may be favorable economic factors, sociological background, entrepreneurial traits, and intuition, inducement, and cooperation and support that encourage a person to become an entrepreneur. Yet, it is still a question why many do not think and behave entrepreneurially. Answers to this question are investigated by the psychological theory.[21]

The need for achievement is a major factor that explains psychological behavior of persons. Human needs are constructed in a hierarchical form and people endeavor to fulfill their needs systematically on the hierarchy (Maslow, 1943).[22] Making a living, accumulating wealth, and achieving power and positions are some of the major needs of people.[23] Entrepreneurship is a lucrative avenue for those who look for avenues to fulfill these needs. However, those who lead a modest life are not fascinated by many needs and shy away from entrepreneurship. Intensity and level of need and their fulfillment widely differ among people. The differences in attitudes on needs determine the degree of entrepreneur supply in a society. In a nation where there are many who wish to be rich and economically powerful, its entrepreneurial attitude is strong and prevalent. In circumstances of extensive psychological needs of the general public, entrepreneurial response to satisfy them is also extensive. Thus, needs inspire psychological motive for entrepreneurship.[24]

Attitudes promote a person's will for entrepreneurship. Choice of employment or doing business, becoming a subordinate or a leader, bearing or avoiding risk, accepting or avoiding challenges, living with freedom, or being occupied are reflections of attitudes. Entrepreneur is a person who basically bears risk, accepts challenges, forgoes freedom, leads teams, and bears responsibilities. Those who have positive attitudes and wish to inculcate such wills destine to become entrepreneurs whereas those who bear negative attitudes will refrain from becoming entrepreneurs. This explains why the supply of entrepreneurs is chiefly determined by personal attitudes toward entrepreneurship.[25]

Perceptions are also important in making of an entrepreneur. Some perceive chances for fulfilling needs and wants of people by way of innovating goods and services deliverable through the market to address unsatisfied needs and wants and improve convenience and comfort.[26] In addition to production of goods, customer care, hospitality, problem-solving, and professional services are useful passions for entrepreneurs. High egoistic concerns and self-esteem, on the contrary, deter entrepreneurial spirit of a person. Passion for profit-making and bourgeoning encourage longing for entrepreneurship. Social entrepreneurship is perceived as the passion for uplifting backward and disadvantaged segments of the society. Thus, psychological theory of entrepreneurship propagates that the psychological state of a person makes an entrepreneur.[27]

Displacement Theory

Displacement theory advocates the notion that entrepreneurship is a typical response to the displacement of a person. Displacement can occur due to loss of several things: job, prestige, respect, family affiliation, clan affiliation, inherited wealth, habitat, and decent living. Displacements are categorized as economic, political, socio-cultural, and geoclimatic. Displacement, in broad sense, is loss of present status quo of a person in terms of employment, wealth, relationship, affiliation, ego, habitat, and respect. Those who are displaced are compelled to regain their past status quo. According to displacement theory, this challenge breeds entrepreneurs.[28]

Loss of employment ultimately leaves persons without income. Even skillful person may not find another employment after loss of their job. Loss of job is economic displacement and to overcome it a person may tend to capitalize on their skills, experiences, learnings, connections, and instincts in a productive manner. All these aptitudes can mostly take refuge in doing business as an alternative profession. Wars, conflicts, and migration displace people from their habitat and locate them in unfamiliar places. This eventually leaves people without occupational income. Loss of wealth urges people to seek alternative means of making a living.[29]

Most migrants end up with casual jobs and lower living standards. Commonly the risky, untidy, dangerous, and extreme jobs will become their occupations. Though they may engage in such occupation for some time, they later try out alternatives to reinstate their living standards by doing business.[30] The intensity of entrepreneurial drive of migrants is determined by their learning of the new culture, connections, and language. Loss of income, respect, and ego due to retirement also encourages retired persons to give a fresh start to their lives through new endeavors. In all such circumstances, entrepreneurship is seen as the most common and frequent alternative engagement of displaced persons.[31]

Displacement theory of entrepreneurship argues that displacement builds courage in those who are displaced to look for opportunities in business. Businesses of the Chinese and Indian migrants across the world are often quoted as examples of entrepreneurial moves of migrants.[32] Authentic restaurants, culinary ingredient shops, clothing, and ritualistic goods are common enterprises of Chinese and Indian migrants. "China Town" in every corner of the world is a symbol of Chinese migrant entrepreneurship.[33] Small enterprises initiated by retired persons or job losers are also examples of entrepreneurship upon termination of their monthly salary.

COVID-19 pandemic caused millions to lose their jobs around the world. Many of them overcame their lives by starting entrepreneurship from scratch.[34] Home delivery, garage sale, jumble sale, and car-boot sale mushroomed during the pandemic period proving that displacement pushes people to entrepreneurship. The displaced capitalized on their savings, connections, networks, experience, and knowledge that they had gained from previous employments. Another reason for the displaced persons to engage in entrepreneurship is to catch up with high-income levels instead of making income for simple living. Though every displacement does not account for entrepreneurship, there seems obvious rise of entrepreneurs among the displaced.[35]

Inducement Theory

Entrepreneurship has been appropriated to inducement of another party also. Accordingly, entrepreneurship is induced by family, politics, society, corporate, and environment. Inducement theory implicates that entrepreneurship is rather extrinsic than intrinsic, assuming that external factors play a significant role in creating an entrepreneur. This is quite a matter that deserves attention. The inducement perception has arisen in contrast to the widely received view that entrepreneurship is an intrinsic phenomenon. Therefore, inducement theory challenges the conventional wisdom that propagates the notion that entrepreneurship is an intrinsic phenomenon.[36]

Family inducement is the most common form that includes physical assets, financial support, knowhow, or formula as inducements provided by the family to its intimate members to initiate ventures.[37] Sanyo Corporation of Japan is a classic example of family inducement. Sanyo was founded by Ino-Ue with the support of his brother-in-law Konosuke Matsushita—the founder of Panasonic Corporation. When Matsushita moved to a new factory premises, the old factory together with some machineries, workers, and the rights to produce several products that were produced under the National brand were given away to Ino-Ue to initiate his own business. The outcome was Sanyo Corporation. Family-induced entrepreneurship is different from family business because family business is a continuation of business legacy by family members whereas family-induced business is a newly established venture.[38]

Caste inducement is another aspect of the inducement theory. Caste molded social system over the past millennia. In the tradition, production, art and craft, and several other professions are related to caste. Caste system thus, is a system of traditional knowledge and profession. Production system was not necessarily designed as a commercial endeavor in the feudal era. Yet, entrepreneurial era as of today, caste-based traditional knowledge systems are useful means of value creation. Caste-specific knowhow has been passed down to generations in the descend and they possess the knowledge system traditionally as if a copyright or patent. So, the later generations can use that knowledge system to start up business. Accordingly, caste has been an inducement for the later generations to initiate ventures on unique traditional knowledge systems. Family businesses in brewery, butchery, jewelry, handcrafts, and certain entertainment have evolved from caste inducements.[39]

Ethnic groups possess exclusive knowledge and practices of doing things learned from their ethnocultural background and training. Passing on ethnic businesses to descendants is regarded as a family responsibility which later generations carry on within the same ethnic group. The professions that are ethnically inherited confine to certain ethnic groups and are identified as ethnologically induced. Authentic Chinese, Indian, and Japanese restaurants, Japanese paper umbrellas and potteries, Iranian rugs, and Indian sarees are examples of ethnologically induced enterprises. Clan relationship also plays an important role in inducement. Old boys of leading schools, who are presently entrepreneurs, provide their juniors with information, networking, connections, and sub-contracts as initial inducements for business startups.[40]

Culture of China, Hong Kong, and Japan provides impetus for starting business. Culture of Sri Lanka, Nepal, and Bhutan generally regard doing business is less esteemed occupation. This has resulted in poor supply and quality of entrepreneurship in the latter. So, it is obvious that entrepreneurship thrives where social inducements are abundant. In addition to general inducements, there can persist specific inducements also. The societies that cherish natural environment provide inducements for environmentally friendly businesses by way of financial and tax concessions. Some banks and financial institutions also induce environmentally friendly businesses through concessionary finance. As a result, environmentally friendly enterprises have emerged in large numbers in the recent past around the world, in particular, in the Scandinavian region. Hybrid, paperless, wireless, and fuel-efficient devices and operations are some examples of environmentally friendly enterprises. The platform for Carbon Rights is an international inducement to production with low carbon emission.[41]

Governments and non-government organizations also provide inducements for selected groups to initiate entrepreneurship. Inducement extended to social entrepreneurship and women entrepreneurship by government and non-government organizations is a case in point.[42] Entrepreneurship Development Programs (EDPs) of government and other organizations provide inducements for entrepreneurship by way of imparting business knowledge, knowhow, training, links, networks, finances, technologies, incubators, and markets. Micro-credit and thrift societies, religious movements for poverty alleviation, government agencies, banks, and international agencies such as JAICA, KOICA and USAID are major inducement providers for entrepreneurship. The inducement theory thus advocates that where there are inducements, there are opportunities for venture creation.[43]

External Factor Theory

According to external factor theory, entrepreneurial opportunities arise from external factors. External factors include government, non-government organizations, corporates, entrepreneurship development programs, urbanization, availability of market information, opportunity for sub-contracting, infrastructure development, and availability of venture capital. It is believed that dynamics of these factors create entrepreneurial opportunities. According to this theory, those who look for entrepreneurial opportunities should look into the dynamics of external factors.[44]

Government, by all means, is a powerful external agent that influences entrepreneurship via new projects, business promotion programs, free market policy, industrial development, regional development, regional cooperation agreements, import controls, export promotion, poverty alleviation programs, scientific research, and enhancing public demand. All these actions create opportunities for entrepreneurship. NGOs also play an alternative role in promoting entrepreneurship among socioeconomically backward and disadvantaged sections of the population.[45] Large corporates create venture opportunities via sub-contracting, supply chains, and intrapreneurship.

Large infrastructure projects such as airport, harbor, highway, petroleum processing, iron and steel, auto-making, and power generation create extensive opportunities for supportive ventures. Projects of this nature are powerful enough to develop entirely new townships which, in turn, create extensive opportunities for many other ventures also. Toyota City of Nagoya and Silicon Valley of California are classic examples of the cities that have generated tens of thousands of new venture opportunities. Urbanization and town creation, similar to the aforementioned situation, stimulate innumerable entrepreneurial opportunities. The highway restaurant history describes how casual rest areas under forest cover, discovered by commuters, later turned into restaurants and then into restaurant chains witnessing to the relationship between highway construction and venture opportunities.[46]

Environmental School

Environmental school of thought advocates external environment as the key to entrepreneurship. According to this school, the external environment is volatile and thus, it causes unpredictable occurrences giving rise to needs and wants which require entrepreneurial intervention to address them. The COVID-19 pandemic is an example which created demand for an array of new goods and services such as hand sanitizer, face mask, vaccine, and home delivery apps. The Oil-Shock in the 1970s paved the way for Japanese automakers to export fuel-efficient small cars to the USA and Europe. This move was followed by all automakers engaging in innovating fuel-efficient cars in the later decades. World War I and II urged the production of new equipment, machinery, technologies, and commodities for the use of the military. After the wars ended, most of those goods were altered to be sold in the consumer market. Advanced equipment and technologies used in the Apollo-11 lunar mission by NASA have been transformed into photographic, telecommunication, computing, wireless, and remote sensing products at present. The movement for protection and conservation of natural environment has created venture opportunities in environmentally friendly productions such as electric and hybrid cars, paperless technologies, and many other products certified under ISO 14001.

Finance School

Finance school elaborates that capital as the key to entrepreneurship. Accordingly, given that every other factor is favorable, entrepreneurship can only be realized through finance. This notion advocates the view that financial input as the first-order factor. Equity capital, debt capital, venture capital, financial support, micro finance, lottery wins, and wealth inheritance are identified as sources of finance. Thus, regardless of the size of operations, finance is equally important to every enterprise. This school of thought advocates that finance is the determinant factor of entrepreneurship and thus without adequate finance, ventures cannot be initiated. This belief is widespread and tends to prompt every potential entrepreneur to believe that capital or finance as the first and foremost factor of entrepreneurship. The mushrooming financial institutions that provide finance to address financial requirements of ventures at present are a proof of this notion.

Displacement School

Displacement school of entrepreneurship advocates that political, economic, and cultural displacements as reasons for initiation of ventures. Accordingly, those who are displaced encounter adverse situations and choose entrepreneurship to overcome them. While not all the displaced persons engage in entrepreneurship, a considerable number initiates ventures and some of them are rated as highly successful. Displaced persons generally rely on nothing but courage and dedication targeting success and sustainability. Also, the displaced can start humbly in unfamiliar locations as their ego matters not. The displaced normally initiate ventures that require the least amount of capital, skills, and experience and thus they are usually easy to start small or micro scale. Biographies of once displaced but distinguished entrepreneurs reveal that their start as entrepreneurs has been incredibly humble.

Entrepreneurial Trait School

The entrepreneurial trait school propagates the notion that only unique talents and traits can start ventures. The advocates of this school believe that entrepreneurs are born; one can become an entrepreneur with born talents and traits. Leadership, organizing skill, endurance, intuition, and courage are believed to be inherited from birth according to the trait school. However, the trait school now extended its scope to include the belief that entrepreneurs can also be made. Making of an entrepreneur requires inculcating certain entrepreneurial qualities, skills, and characteristics in persons through training, education, exposure, and development. Entrepreneurship Development Programs (EDPs) are catalytic in inculcating entrepreneurial traits in persons. Development of entrepreneurial traits is the key input for the accomplishment of entrepreneurship.

Venture Opportunity School

Venture opportunity school elaborates opportunity as a precursor to entrepreneurship and without opportunities, entrepreneurship cannot come into effect. Opportunities are created by occurrences in the local and global environments. Accordingly, political, economic, social, demographical, psychological, technological, and environmental changes create opportunities. All opportunities represent needs and wants of people. New needs and wants are created in the first instance and then they are altered by circumstances. Demands for goods and services can be related to the demographic factors such as birth, death, age structure, schooling, marriage, income, education, health, religion, and ethnicity. The changes taking place in relation to these factors create demand for goods and services. Entrepreneurs strive to address demands through innovation of useful goods and services.

Identification of opportunities can be further explained through Window and Corridor principles.[47] The window principle describes that an opportunity is not open always but it opens and closes as if a window does. Thus, an opportunity lasts for a short period of time and if not recognized and catered to, it disappears. It is also conceivable that one opportunity is wiped out by another opportunity that rises later. Therefore, the entrepreneur must swiftly exploit opportunities as they last. Too early and too late attempts to exploit opportunities are not useful entrepreneurial actions. If the windows are not open, the entrepreneurial action will be futile as opportunities are not set. In case that entrepreneurial action is too late, the windows of opportunities will no longer prevail.

Introduction of digital watch in the early 1960s by the US watchmaker Hamilton Watch Company is believed to be too early an entrance to the market. Apart from the technical flaws and its high price, the watch was unsuccessful before long as the market for a digital watch was not ready as technophiles were scant in the society. But, the Japanese corporations such as Casio, Citizen, and Seiko launched digital watches during the reverberation of the Apollo-11 lunar expedition with which the windows opened for digital goods. Then, the US watchmakers attempted to make a comeback but that also was unsuccessful as the window was closed and the market was crowded.

The corridor principle describes an array of opportunities that occur to an existing entrepreneur. Corridor resembles a set of windows that open and close along the business corridor an entrepreneur walks. Each window resembles a venture opportunity and when a window is seen open, entrepreneur can consider innovations to exploit the opportunity. The notion of corridor thus is an array of opportunities available for an entrepreneur who is already in business. Socioeconomic and technological changes create opportunities as time evolves. Entrepreneurs who can recognize such changes and opportunities can swiftly exploit them effectively.

The dramatic socio-cultural and economic changes that took place since 1980s in Sri Lanka created demand for instant foods. A vast spectrum of instant food items found their way to the market. The response of Nikado Private Ltd.[48] to the market changes is a classic example of recognition of opportunities along the corridor and responding to them through innovations of goods such as instant noodles, instant hopper mix, string hopper mix, instant dosai mix, and instant wadai mix. Nikado was the market leader of Papadam, the only instant food in Sri Lanka for many decades, and thus it was convenient for the company to grasp opportunities and introduce new items also as instant food.

Strategy Formulation School

The strategy formulation school describes entrepreneurship as a strategic response to opportunities. Accordingly, each business is based on a specific strategy. In other words, entrepreneurship is yielded to strategies and every venture represents a specific strategy. The strategy formulation school consists of four strategies as described below.[49]

Mountain gap strategy—Mountain gap is the space between two mountains. In entrepreneurship, the needs and wants that remain unaddressed between two large markets are identified as a mountain gap. Between two large markets, a third market exists. Strategic entrepreneurs identify this market space and innovate goods and services for it. This strategy creates a new market. Examples of mountain gap strategy include innovation of the three-wheeler; a transport equipment that comes in between motorcycle and automobile. Similarly, the meat flavored soya meat (TVP) is strategically produced as an alternative food in between nonvegetarian and vegetarian markets.

Great chef strategy—Entrepreneurship strategy is sometimes based on a unique person. This notion is constructed based on the idea that chef is always pivotal to the success of a restaurant. Kentucky Fried Chicken (KFC) poses its founder David Sanders as its great chef exhibiting his posters and figures on the restaurant premises. Konosuke Matsushita and Steve Jobs have been the great chefs of Panasonic Corporation and Apple Corporation, respectively.

Unique product strategy—Some goods and services are produced according to a strategy. Authentic products are examples of this strategy. For instance, serving food items like sushi, sashimi, teriyaki, and tempura is a unique strategy for maintaining authenticity of a Japanese restaurant. Further, Japanese Geisha is a service unique to Japanese culture which cannot be duplicated by other cultures and thus the Japanese find it as a strategy to start a traditional hospitality business.

Unique resource strategy—Some enterprises are based on a unique resource or a location. For instance, access to mineral-rich unique water sources is a strategic position for initiating mineral water bottling. Some hotels are located as beach hotels or nature resorts where beach or nature is the unique and strategic resource. The ownership or access to unique resources is essential for this business strategy to get underway. Below-mentioned products are specialized in certain regions due to their availability in those regions only. In a few Indonesian districts, based on the coffee beans defecated by civet cats (Toddy cat), a rare resource, the most expensive Civet Coffee (Kopi luwak) is produced. Unique Indlovu Gin is produced in South Africa based on elephant dung. Tatami, unique flooring product, is made in Japan based on rice paddy straws. The palm species Caryota urens is a unique resource for making syrup and jaggery in Sri Lanka.

The Need for a New Theory

The orthodox theory describes the factors such as economic, sociological, psychological, financial, displacement, strategy, personal trait, and opportunity, individually or collectively, cause entrepreneurship. And it advocates entrepreneurship as a process that passes through four steps: opportunity identification, invention, innovation, and commercialization which are entrepreneurial activities only. An important question left unanswered by the orthodox theory is what the "absolute role" of entrepreneurship is.

Among many roles that an entrepreneur plays, the most fundamental and central role that cannot be detached from entrepreneur is "intervention." Every entrepreneur makes interventions to satisfy needs and wants of people by way of offering marketable solutions to their needs and wants-related problems. Intervention is an inclusive effort that perceivably lays foundation for entrepreneurship itself and integrates all entrepreneurial roles and activities in a scheme. Thus, venture formation, venture performance, and venture sustainability are inseparably connected to intervention. The very meaning of intervention is the entrepreneur "coming in between" the customers and their unresolved problems.

Orthodox theory has ignored the entrepreneur's role of intervention despite the fact that the whole entrepreneurship process is designed to intervene in satisfying customer needs and wants. It is commonplace that doctors intervene in patients who struggle to survive and thus, the term intervention is frequently used in the medical profession. Entrepreneur, in contrast, intervenes when people struggle to satisfy their needs and wants. In this context, entrepreneur plays the all-inclusive role of an intervener. Entrepreneur's intervention is unlimited because human needs and wants are also unlimited. Innumerable goods and services, their quality, and upgrades are evidence of countless interventions.

Unlimited needs and wants arise from psychological and physiological factors and as a result of wants tempt promotional activities of entrepreneurs. People seek external means to address needs and wants when they cannot address needs and wants by themself. Living with unsatisfied needs and wants is living with problems, stress, and frustration. Human being chooses not to live with problems and attempts various means to solve as they arise. Some individuals find self-help and jungle fixes for problems, but the masses still need an external intervention to solve their problems. This compels people to seek someone's intervention.

The Intervention Hypothesis

An important question is why entrepreneurs get inspired to intervene in problems of others. Entrepreneurs seek both intrinsic and extrinsic rewards in return of intervention. Extrinsic rewards such as profit, personal wealth, social recognition, prestige, and good life and the intrinsic rewards like happiness, satisfaction, and self-actualization are yielded to intervention in common problems. The desire for extrinsic and intrinsic rewards is connected to psychological motives of entrepreneurs.

Profit is the major force that motivates entrepreneur to execute intervention. The congenital relationship between intervention and profit maintains momentum of intervention action. This sets the premises for entrepreneurship to earn profit as its economic rent. This fosters the general thesis that the ability to intervention brings about entrepreneurship. The theories elaborated previously describe the circumstances and motivational factors such as finance, displacement, opportunities, economic soundness, sociological background, and psychological factors under which entrepreneurship arises. But they lack formidable reasoning as to why and how entrepreneurship emerges and works. This background urges a new approach that can abridge the theoretical gap and, in response, the Intervention Hypothesis was formulated (Fig. 5.2).

According to the Intervention Hypothesis, entrepreneurship process consists of 10 phases; six core phases plus four extended phases, where entrepreneur must exhibit their uncompromising abilities throughout.

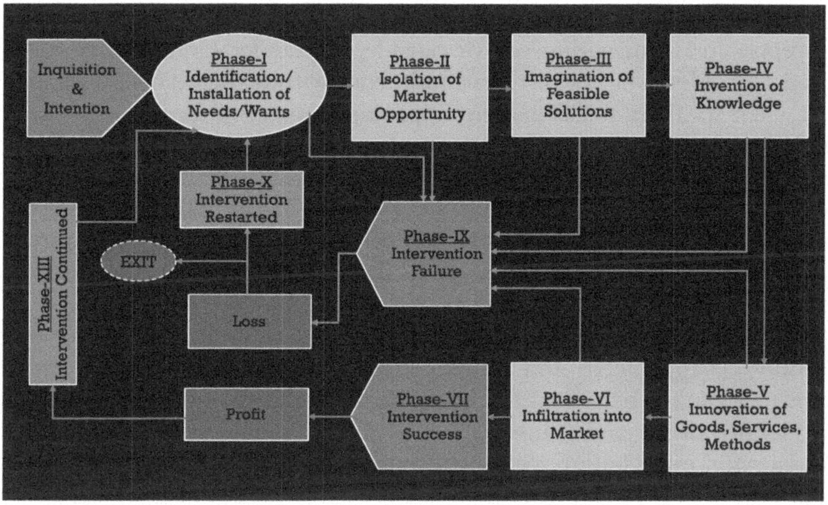

Fig. 5.2 The intervention hypothesis (Author portrayal)

Intervention hypothesis advocates that intervention process casts entrepreneurship. Intervention hypothesis advocates an aggregate and eclectic approach that helps address fundamental weaknesses of the mainstream theory of entrepreneurship. This hypothesis disputes the present entrepreneurship theories as they are constructed upon circumstances such as economic and social conditions, displacements, finance, inducements, and external factors. Intervention hypothesis advocates entrepreneurship as a response to needs and wants related to common problems aiming at offering marketable solutions to address them. Intervention hypothesis is constructed on 10 phases (i-10) and their interconnection is described in the next section. Intervention is a dynamic process that continues until needs and wants are effectively addressed.

Phases of Intervention

1. Identification

Intervention process starts with identification of problems that cannot be resolved by the individuals themselves who face them. Curiosity is a prerequisite for detecting problems. A problem could occur to entrepreneur from within self or outside. Alexander Graham Bell identified a problem that occurred to him from within. Bell did not want to yell when speaking to his hearing-impaired mother and thus, investigated the ways to amplify sound to improve her hearing. Konosuke Matsushita of Panasonic Corporation identified a problem that occurred to him from outside. Matsushita heard as two siblings in the neighborhood disputed on inability to simultaneously use two electrical devices on a single power cord. Matsushita devised the ways to distribute electricity between two electrical devices.

In the process of identification of needs and wants, entrepreneurs firstly identify existing needs and wants of people emanating from the problems that cannot be solved by themselves. This is the most common way to identify needs and wants. These problems themselves create opportunities for intervention. Secondly, entrepreneurs tend to create needs and wants in people through marketing strategies. This is possible in the areas such as food supplements, fitness goods, beauty products, ornamental goods, and environmentally friendly products where psychological influence on the buying decision is high. Thirdly, in certain circumstances, entrepreneurs alter and modify the present needs and wants of the people and install needs and wants on people. The chewing need that has continued throughout the human history has now been modified to chewing gums. Shape-up Teas and Fitness Gyms are innovations mostly after installed needs and wants. Fourthly, entrepreneurs initially identify materials (instead of needs and wants), and intuitively convert them into goods contemplating needs and wants. Classic examples include elephant poo paper of Sri Lanka, elephant dung gin of South Africa, and civet coffee (Kopi luwak) of Indonesia which were initially ridiculed rather than were sought. Fifthly, entrepreneurs identify not only individuals' needs and wants but public needs and wants also. Alternatives for fossil fuel and Ozone friendly gases are the needs of governments. This need is identified and catered to through innovating solar power equipment, electric vehicles, and new types of gases.

2. Isolation

Unfulfilled needs and wants cause dissatisfaction, frustration, threat, and vulnerability among people. Thus, the unfulfilled needs and wants are a source of opportunities that demand external intervention. For making an intervention, isolation of opportunities is a prerequisite for identifying exact needs and wants. Customer sensitivity, physiology, and psychology of needs and wants, and drawbacks of existing products can differentiate and isolate opportunities that stem from needs and wants-related problems. Isolation of an opportunity helps entrepreneur to identify the opportunity precisely and so they can devise exact intervention via market. Isolation of opportunities is the critical factor that enables entrepreneur to practically engage in intervention.

3. Imagination

Imagination of feasible solutions to address needs and wants of prospective customers is an essential step after identification of problems. Entrepreneur first imagines only hypothetical solutions that might solve problems. Useful imaginations are feasible for entrepreneurs whose intuition, experience, exposure, abilities, knowledge, and technological geniuses are extensive. Solutions beyond innovative capacity cannot solve problems as such products cannot be produced. Therefore, imaginations should be within the entrepreneur's capacity. Imagination is a hint of a product idea that precedes invention and innovation.

4. Invention

Knowledge of a new product is evoked from invention. Invention is primarily derived from imagination which provides only a general idea or picture of a product that is not refined enough to impart useful knowledge required for innovation. Invention is a process that involves steps such as idea germination, incubation, experimentation, realization, and verification. Invention sometimes is a rigorous process that consumes lots of time, resources, and efforts. Entrepreneurs themselves can accomplish inventions or otherwise they can acquire already invented ideas from outside by way of purchasing, licensing, or franchising. Research, fundamental research, and experiments are sources of invention.

5. Innovation

Innovation is the means of converting ideas generated from invention into products; goods and services that can practically address needs and wants. Innovations thus are useable products like goods, services, means, and methods derived from inventions. Innovations are the means to intervention and without them, intervention is impossible. In line with this argument, every commercialized product is a proposed solution to a common problem. So, it is comprehensible that attempted resolution is there behind every product. Simple products are solutions to simple problems while complex products are solutions to complex problems; paper clip is a simple product whereas a powerplant is a complex product. For innovation, a few approaches such as invention, extension, duplication, synthesis, and product development are adopted.

6. Infiltrating Markets

Commercialization is the channel that takes innovations to those who look for them. Infiltration into markets is the means to take innovations to prospective customers. This process is generally known as commercialization also. Marketing strategies such as product, price, place, and promotion (4Ps) are employed to gain successful infiltration into markets. Market infiltration is an incessant process subsequent to the innovation process. With infiltration into market, the core intervention steps are completed.

7. Intervention Success

Intervention success is the outcome of success of phases 1 through 6. Failure of any single phase inhibits intervention. Drawbacks relating to these phases arise from misjudgment in problem investigation and misreading of needs and wants. Misjudgments lead to production and sales of goods and services incapable of solving problems. Intervention success depends on the capability of addressing physiological and psychological needs solving consumer problems. Thus, profit is accrued only to successful intervention. Profitability then leads to the improvement of other business ratings such as share price, market share, brand loyalty, and brand value. Intervention is subject to competitiveness as there can be competition to intervention.

8. Intervention Continued

The rate of success in the first cycle of intervention inspires entrepreneur to continue intervention process. Intervention process is continued as long as the key indicators of success such as market share, profitability ratios, and share prices remain within expected range. The first cycle of intervention process is completed with this phase. However, with or without reinventing the wheel, intervention process can enter further rounds.

9. Intervention Failure

Failure in intervention is borne to failure in the phases from 1 to 6. Failure of intervention results in losses. Here, entrepreneur has two options. If the future of intervention seems gloomy and no sign of success, entrepreneur can decide to exit from the intervention process. Otherwise, they can opt for reinventing the wheel to recharge intervention process from phase 1.

10. Intervention Re-started

At restart, intervention process reverts to the investigation phase for re-reading the problem accurately. Restarting intervention refreshes the intervention cycle in which all the phases from phase 1 to 6 are repeated and fixed for errors. In this fresh cycle, entrepreneur must strive to enter phase 7 of the process. Repeated failures in entering phase 7 will compel the entrepreneur to discontinue the intervention process.

Importance of the Intervention Hypothesis

This hypothesis advocates intervention, in solving problems emanate from needs and wants, as the mission of entrepreneurship. Intervention consists of 10 phases; out of which 6 are core and the rest are subordinate. Effective intervention generates profit that fuels the intervention process. Intervention will continue as long as it is profitable. Losses incurred suggest entrepreneur to reengineer the intervention process or otherwise to exit from it.

This hypothesis identifies a systematic relationship of numerous phases involved in intervention. It constructs a rational existence and relationship of each phase of the system. Thus, it embraces generality and applicability also. These key features elevate this hypothesis to eclectic state as it wholly deals with the entrepreneurship process. In essence, this hypothesis advocates that every entrepreneurial urge ascends from curiosity to solve a problem which is followed by 10 complementary and sequential actions that construct the process of entrepreneurship.

This hypothesis advocates the notion that entrepreneurship emerges from needs and wants-related problems. So, "no problem no entrepreneurship." The problems referred to here, in turn, are entrepreneurial opportunities. The intervention hypothesis, therefore, is a problem-based approach to entrepreneurship unlike the resource-based approach adopted by Entrepreneurship Development Programs (EDPs). EDPs customarily consider capital, labor, materials, and technology as impetus for entrepreneurship. The intervention hypothesis, in contrast, reckons unresolved needs and wants as venture opportunities. Resources are limited but needs and wants are unlimited. Entrepreneurship development thus, must focus on needs and wants treating resources as subordinate to needs and wants. This elevates the applicability of the intervention hypothesis as a useful tool for entrepreneurship development in place of the resource-based approach to EDPs that have limited scope.

Chapter Summary

The concept of entrepreneurship emerged and grew under the purview of economics during the past few centuries. Industrial Revolution and management renaissance significantly contributed to the theory of entrepreneurship. Presently, several theories are deliberated in entrepreneurship textbooks: economic theory, sociological theory, psychological theory, displacement theory, inducement theory, external factor theory, and entrepreneurship school of thought. Under entrepreneurship school of thought, environmental school, finance school, displacement school, entrepreneurial trait school, venture opportunity school, and strategy formulation school are included.

Economic theory of entrepreneurship considers economic development policies, macroeconomic management policies, global economy, economic dynamics, modern amenities, infrastructure, and information technology to generate entrepreneurial opportunities and hence entrepreneurs. Sociological theory assumes every innovation is consequent to social change and thus, venture opportunities are determined by social structure, values, ethics, and beliefs. Psychological theory considers that human needs, wants, attitudes, and perceptions induce entrepreneurial thinking. Displacement theory advocates entrepreneurship as a typical response to economic, political, socio-cultural, and geoclimatic displacements which cause loss of job, prestige, respect, family affiliation, clan affiliation, inherited wealth, habitat, and decent living. Inducement theory explains entrepreneurship as an incentivized outcome of another party like family, society, corporates, and environment. External factor theory argues venture opportunities arise from external factors such as government policy, support from organizations and corporates, entrepreneurship training, sub-contracting opportunity, infrastructure development and urbanization, availability of information, and venture capital.

Entrepreneurship school of thought comprises environmental school, finance school, displacement school, entrepreneurial trait school, venture opportunity school, and strategy formulation school. Environmental school advocates external environment as the key to entrepreneurship.

Finance school highlights capital as the key and entrepreneurship can only be realized through finance. Displacement school argues that displaced persons choose entrepreneurship to overcome adverse situations they encounter. Entrepreneurial trait school proposes unique talents to help start of ventures. This school propagates the notion that entrepreneurs are born with talents and traits. Venture opportunity school elaborates opportunity as a precursor to entrepreneurship. Opportunities are caused by occurrences in the local and global political environments. Strategy formulation school describes entrepreneurship as a strategic response to opportunities. It elaborates businesses are based on strategies such as Mountain gap, Great chef, Unique product, and Unique resource.

The orthodox theory of entrepreneurship is a composite of individual theories such as economic, sociological, psychological, financial, displacement, and personal traits. All these theories lack the most fundamental and central role of entrepreneurship, i.e., intervention. Every entrepreneur makes interventions to satisfy needs and wants-related problems of people by way of offering marketable solutions. The inspiration to intervene in problems of others arises from intrinsic and extrinsic rewards in return. Extrinsic rewards include profit, personal wealth, social recognition, prestige, and good life whereas intrinsic rewards include happiness, satisfaction, and self-actualization. The intervention hypothesis proposed herein is an alternative to the orthodox theory. This aggregate approach aims at addressing the fundamental drawbacks of the mainstream theory of entrepreneurship.

Intervention hypothesis is constructed on 10, referred to as i-10, complementary and sequential stages phases considering intervention as a dynamic process that continues until the problems of human needs and wants are effectively addressed. The needs and wants are connected to individuals and/or organizations. The 10 pillars on which the intervention hypothesis is constructed include the following: identification of needs/wants, isolation of opportunity, imagination of solution, invention of knowledge, innovation of solution, infiltration into market, intervention success, and intervention continuation, or intervention failure and intervention restart. Effective intervention generates profit that fuels continuity of the intervention process. Any losses incurred suggest entrepreneur to reengineer the intervention process or otherwise to exit from it. The intervention hypothesis not only answers why of entrepreneurship but how of entrepreneurship also. Entrepreneur curiosity is the keystone of the urge for intervention. One who has the urge engages in intervention.

This hypothesis iterates the notion that entrepreneurship emerges from needs and wants-related problems; so, no problem no entrepreneurship. The intervention hypothesis reckons unresolved needs and wants as venture opportunities. Thus, this hypothesis is a problem-based approach to entrepreneurship unlike the resource-based approach adopted by Entrepreneurship Development Programs (EDPs). EDPs customarily consider capital, labor, materials, and technology as impetus for entrepreneurship. This hypothesis, thus, recommends entrepreneur must focus on needs and wants-related problems and treat resources as subordinate. The intervention hypothesis deviates from all other theories but coexists with the psychological theory because entrepreneurial intervention is concomitant to psychological phenomenon.

Review Questions

1. Describe the lineage of economic and management thoughts traceable in entrepreneurship theory.
2. (a) What are the chief arguments of the economic theory of entrepreneurship?

   (b) Discuss how the economic circumstances contribute to rise of entrepreneurship opportunities.
3. Describe the sociological theory of entrepreneurship and explain how the sociological factors determine entrepreneurship.
4. "The most predominant among all is the human psychology in inspiring motives for entrepreneurship." Discuss.
5. Describe the major types of displacements and argue how powerful are displacements to create entrepreneurs. Provide suitable examples to support your arguments.
6. "Some become entrepreneurs solely due to inducement." Identify the major types of inducements and discuss this statement giving examples.
7. What are the external factors that cause entrepreneurship? Explain how they influence entrepreneurship.
8. "The environmental school of thought propagates the notion that external environmental factors induce entrepreneurship." Discuss giving examples.

9. Critically examine whether entrepreneurship can be appropriated to finance as the finance school suggests.
10. Argue whether entrepreneurial traits are inherited or can be imparted by Entrepreneurship Development Programs.
11. "Opportunities generated in the environment due to various reasons are pivotal for entrepreneurship." Elaborate this statement by giving suitable examples.
12. What are the major propositions of the strategy formulation school?
13. Explain how do the following strategies create entrepreneurship opportunities;

    Mountain gap strategy
    Great chef strategy
    Unique product strategy
    Unique resource strategy.

14. Discuss limitations of the orthodox theories of entrepreneurship and assess the significance of the Intervention Hypothesis as an alternative theory, also, highlighting its foundation, construct, and merits.

Additional Readings

1. Cassis, Y., and Minoglou, I.P., 2005. Entrepreneurship in theory and history: State of the art and new perspectives. *Entrepreneurship in theory and history*, pp. 3–21.
2. Brown, C., and Thornton, M., 2013. How entrepreneurship theory created economics. *Quarterly Journal of Austrian Economics*, *16*(4).
3. Kuratko, D.F., 2011. Entrepreneurship theory, process, and practice in the twenty-first century. *International Journal of Entrepreneurship and Small Business*, *13*(1), pp. 8–17.
4. Krueger Jr, N.F., 2003. The cognitive psychology of entrepreneurship. In *Handbook of entrepreneurship research: An interdisciplinary survey and introduction* (pp. 105–140). Boston, MA: Springer US.
5. Schumpeter, J.A., 1965. Economic theory and entrepreneurial history. In *Explorations in enterprise* (pp. 45–64). Harvard University Press.

6. Baumol, W.J., 1968. Entrepreneurship in economic theory. *The American economic review*, *58*(2), pp. 64–71.
7. Steiner, P., 1998. Jean-Baptiste Say: The entrepreneur, the free trade doctrine and the theory of income distribution. *G. Faccarello (ed.)*, pp. 196–228.
8. Smith, G.H., 1979. Justice entrepreneurship in a free market. *Journal of Libertarian Studies*, *3*(4), pp. 405–426.
9. Obaji, N.O., and Olugu, M.U., 2014. The role of government policy in entrepreneurship development. *Science Journal of Business and Management*, *2*(4), pp. 109–115.
10. Smallbone, D., 2020. Entrepreneurship policy: Issues and challenges. In *Understanding the development of small business policy*, pp. 6–23.
11. Hong, S., Reed, W.R., Tian, B., Wu, T., and Chen, G., 2021. Does FDI promote entrepreneurial activities? A meta-analysis. *World Development*, *142*, p. 105436.
12. Brophy, D.J., and Shulman, J.M., 1992. A finance perspective on entrepreneurship research. *Entrepreneurship Theory and Practice*, *16*(3), pp. 61–72.
13. Aghion, P., 2011. Industrial policy, entrepreneurship and growth. *Handbook of research on innovation and entrepreneurship*, pp. 45–54.
14. Audretsch, D.B., Heger, D., and Veith, T., 2015. Infrastructure and entrepreneurship. *Small Business Economics*, *44*, pp. 219–230.
15. Thornton, P.H., 1999. The sociology of entrepreneurship. *Annual review of sociology*, *25*(1), pp. 19–46.
16. Jakob, E.A., Isidor, R., Steinmetz, H., Wehner, M.C., and Kabst, R., 2019. The other side of the same coin–How communal beliefs about entrepreneurship influence attitudes toward entrepreneurship. *Journal of Vocational Behavior*, *112*, pp. 431–445.
17. Dana, L.P. ed., 2010. *Entrepreneurship and religion*. Edward Elgar Publishing.
18. Greenfield, S.M., and Strickon, A., 1981. A new paradigm for the study of entrepreneurship and social change. *Economic Development and Cultural Change*, *29*(3), pp. 467–499.
19. Gehman, J., and Soublière, J.F., 2017. Cultural entrepreneurship: from making culture to cultural making. *Innovation*, *19*(1), pp. 61–73.

20. Sobel, R.S., Dutta, N., and Roy, S., 2010. Does cultural diversity increase the rate of entrepreneurship? *The Review of Austrian Economics*, *23*, pp. 269–286.
21. Frese, M., and Gielnik, M.M., 2023. The psychology of entrepreneurship: action and process. *Annual Review of Organizational Psychology and Organizational Behavior*, *10*, pp. 137–164.
22. Maslow, A. H. (1943). A theory of human motivation. *Psychological Review*, *50*(4), 370–396. https://doi.org/10.1037/h0054346
23. Deshmukh, T., and Sucheta, P., Relevance of Maslow's hierarchy of needs to entrepreneurs. *Pramana Research Journal*, *9*.
24. Gorgievski, M.J., and Stephan, U., 2016. Advancing the psychology of entrepreneurship: A review of the psychological literature and an introduction. *Applied Psychology*, *65*(3), pp. 437–468.
25. Botsaris, C., and Vamvaka, V., 2016. Attitude toward entrepreneurship: Structure, prediction from behavioral beliefs, and relation to entrepreneurial intention. *Journal of the Knowledge Economy*, *7*, pp. 433–460.
26. Wärneryd, K.E., 1988. The psychology of innovative entrepreneurship. In *Handbook of economic psychology* (pp. 404–447). Dordrecht: Springer Netherlands.
27. Fodor, O.C., and Pintea, S., 2017. The "emotional side" of entrepreneurship: A meta-analysis of the relation between positive and negative affect and entrepreneurial performance. *Frontiers in Psychology*, *8*, p. 246712.
28. Nyström, K., 2020. Entrepreneurship after displacement. *Small Business Economics*, *54*(2), pp. 475–494.
29. Kwong, C.C., Cheung, C.W., Manzoor, H., and Rashid, M.U., 2019. Entrepreneurship through Bricolage: A study of displaced entrepreneurs at times of war and conflict. *Entrepreneurship & Regional Development*, *31*(5–6), pp. 435–455.
30. Fatoki, O., and Patswawairi, T., 2012. The motivations and obstacles to immigrant entrepreneurship in South Africa. *Journal of Social Sciences*, *32*(2), pp. 133–142.
31. Ram, M., Jones, T., and Villares-Varela, M., 2017. Migrant entrepreneurship: Reflections on research and practice. *International Small Business Journal*, *35*(1), pp. 3–18.

32. Dheer, R.J., 2018. Entrepreneurship by immigrants: A review of existing literature and directions for future research. *International Entrepreneurship and Management Journal*, *14*, pp. 555–614.
33. Zhou, M., and Liu, H., 2014. Transnational entrepreneurship and immigrant integration: New Chinese immigrants in Singapore and the United States. In *Immigration and work* (pp. 169–201). Emerald Group Publishing Limited.
34. Liñán, F., and Jaén, I., 2022. The Covid-19 pandemic and entrepreneurship: Some reflections. *International Journal of Emerging Markets*, *17*(5), pp. 1165–1174.
35. Usman, M.A., and Sun, X., 2022. Global pandemic and entrepreneurial intention: How adversity leads to entrepreneurship. *Sage Open*, *12*(3), p. 21582440221123421.
36. Tíryakí, A., 2005. Theories of entrepreneurship: A critical overview. *Dumlupınar Üniversitesi Sosyal Bilimler Dergisi* (13).
37. Powell, G.N., and Eddleston, K.A., 2017. Family involvement in the firm, family-to-business support, and entrepreneurial outcomes: An exploration. *Journal of Small Business Management*, *55*(4), pp. 614–631.
38. Edelman, L.F., Manolova, T., Shirokova, G., and Tsukanova, T., 2016. The impact of family support on young entrepreneurs' start-up activities. *Journal of business venturing*, *31*(4), pp. 428–448.
39. Iyer, L., Khanna, T., and Varshney, A., 2013. Caste and entrepreneurship in India. *Economic and Political Weekly*, pp. 52–60.
40. Volery, T., 2007. Ethnic entrepreneurship: A theoretical framework. In *Handbook of research on ethnic minority entrepreneurship*, *1*, pp. 30–41.
41. Volery, T., 2007. Ethnic entrepreneurship: A theoretical framework. In *Handbook of research on ethnic minority entrepreneurship*, *1*, pp. 30–41.
42. Raj, P.B., 2018. Women entrepreneurship and government support in present scenario in the context of India. *IOSR Journal of Business and Management*, *20*(2), pp. 25–31.
43. Singh, S.K., and Ram, P., 2017. Entrepreneurship development in India: Opportunities and challenges. *Splint International Journal of Professionals*, *4*(3), pp. 75–81.
44. Ahmed, I., Nawaz, M.M., and Ramzan, M., 2012. Do external factors influence students' entrepreneurial inclination?

An evidence-based approach. *Edited by Thierry Burger-Helmchen*, p. 51.

45. Auplat, C., 2006. Do NGOs influence entrepreneurship? Insights from the developments of biotechnologies and nanotechnologies. *Society and Business Review*, *1*(3), pp. 266–279.
46. Woolley, J.L., 2014. The creation and configuration of infrastructure for entrepreneurship in emerging domains of activity. *Entrepreneurship Theory and practice*, *38*(4), pp. 721–747.
47. Holt, D.H., 216. *Entrepreneurship: New venture creation* (1st ed.). New Delhi: Pearson India.
48. https://nikado.lk/
49. Kuratko, D., and Richard, M. H., 2004. *Entrepreneurship—Theory, process and practice* (12th ed.). Mason, Ohio: Thomson–Southwestern.

PART III

Entrepreneurship Process

CHAPTER 6

Opportunity Recognition Process

Key Learning Points

- Introduction.
- Market gaps and venture opportunities.
- Explicit and implicit opportunities.
- The Red Ocean and Blue Ocean Markets.
- Window and Corridor principles.
- Sources of venture opportunities.
- Physiological and psychological needs.
- Economic Factors.
- Industrial Factors.
- Socio-cultural Factors.
- Demographic Factors.
- Legal Factors.
- Infrastructural Factors.
- Sense of opportunity recognition.
- Opportunity recognition methods.
- Sensitivity observation and survey method.
- Product drawback analysis method.
- Invention search method.
- Mind mapping method.
- Brainstorming method.

© The Author(s), under exclusive license to Springer Nature Singapore Pte Ltd. 2024

M. Rajaratne, *Concepts, Processes and Practice of Entrepreneurship*, Palgrave Studies in Global Entrepreneurship,
https://doi.org/10.1007/978-981-97-6180-7_6

- Intuition method.
- Resource conversion method.
- Habit adoption method.
- Ritual adoption method.

Introduction

Entrepreneurship is neither a single activity nor a set of isolated activities. Instead, entrepreneurship involves several functions in a designated order and a large number of interconnected activities to them. Entrepreneurship is not equivalent to venture creation but, a venture is definite outcome of the entrepreneurship. Venture is not feasible without entrepreneurship and that entrepreneurship is not feasible without venture. Peter F. Drucker (1985)[1] pointed out *"All new businesses have many factors common. But to be entrepreneurial, enterprise should create something new, different, and better that transmute values."* Accordingly, entrepreneurship is not mere opening of a venture but an intricate process that eventually creates ventures.[2] Seemingly, entrepreneurship is a comprehensive process that customarily comprises the following sub-processes *(this section does not follow the 10 phases proposed in the intervention hypothesis above as if the case of a doctoral thesis).*

1. Opportunity Recognition Process
2. Invention Process
3. Innovation Process
4. Business Planning Process
5. Business Modeling and Creation Process
6. Growth Management Process

Entrepreneurship process starts with opportunity recognition. Venture is created to exploit opportunities and thus venture is an outcome of the entrepreneurship process that engulfs major functions such as invention, innovation, and commercialization, among other functions. Opportunities prompt invention; exploration of solutions to problems and thereby creating knowledge.[3] Knowledge creation may or may not have a commercial intention although invention is an intellectual property that can be sold, licensed, or used for commercial purposes. Invention is then applied to innovation, i.e., to produce goods and services to address needs and wants. In this context, opportunity serves as an indicator of market gap, invention serves as the knowledge required for innovation, and innovation serves as the means to fill the market gap.[4]

Innovations are either pulled by markets or pushed to markets depending on the intensity of demand. In strong demand scenario, innovations are pulled by markets. Need satisfying goods, speculative or dream goods, hi-tech goods, designer and branded goods, and scarce goods tend to be pulled by the market. Personal mobile audio set was a dream of American youth in the late 1970s. Sony Walkman was the solution and it was pulled in millions of units by the Americans. Facebook, YouTube, Windows OS, and Android OS are also examples of the goods that are pulled by market. Profound market opportunities pull innovations. Innovations of this nature can gain monopolistic advantages initially and then maintain market hegemony at a later phase.[5]

In contrast, certain innovations need to be pushed to the market via marketing strategies. Non-essential goods, abundant goods, common goods, sub-standard goods, and sometimes average innovations are required to be pushed to the market. In competitive markets where many varieties, brands, and a wide range of prices are offered, price leadership and monopolistic advantages are minimal or absent, profit margin is thin, market share is small or stagnating, and marketing strategies are employed to push the products to markets. Products based on common opportunities require extensive marketing effort to push them to the market.[6]

Explicit and Implicit Opportunities

Market gaps are indicators of market opportunities and market opportunities, in turn, are either explicit or implicit. While most entrepreneurs can recognize explicit opportunities, only clever entrepreneurs can recognize implicit opportunities. Explicit opportunities draw attention of many entrepreneurs while implicit opportunities draw attention of a few. Thus, the character of opportunity determines the degree of entrepreneur crowding. Explicit opportunities create high entrepreneur crowding which causing "Red Ocean Markets." In contrast, implicit opportunities create low entrepreneur crowding causing "Blue Ocean Markets." Monopolistic advantages prevail under Blue Ocean Market condition while only nominal returns are feasible under Red Ocean Market condition.[7]

Explicit opportunities propose obvious chances to produce goods or services. When automobiles are abundant, opportunities are naturally created for repair work and auto service. Entrepreneurs can readily recognize the need for such services and make decisions accordingly to commence ventures in those fields. When opportunities are explicit, major needs and wants are easily addressed. Yet, subtle opportunities are left behind. Only clever entrepreneurs can recognize subtle needs and wants. Refined goods and services produced in Japan and China, for example, are a case in point in contrast to the products of low-income economies like India. China, with its advanced entrepreneurial culture, leads the world market supplying hundreds of thousands of goods to fulfill subtle needs and wants. Thousands of car accessories and household accessories are a classic case in point. As unique as those innovations, prospective customers cannot even imagine how entrepreneur has recognized their needs.[8]

Window and Corridor Principles

Venture opportunities are detected either through "Windows" or "Corridors." Window principle describes that a chance to detect an opportunity is similar to that something is seen through a window when it is open. But until window is open and after it is closed, it is impossible to see through it. Venture opportunity can appear and disappear at any time and usually an opportunity does not last for an extended period of time.[9]

Opportunity should, thus, be detected before it expires or is wiped out due to rise of new circumstances. Entrepreneur's response to an opportunity too early or too late will not be helpful to build a successful venture. Digital wristwatch production is a case in point. American watchmaker Hamilton was to first produce digital watch in 1957. But it is destined to have low sales volumes due to low consumer reception for digital watches. American digital watchmaker failed as it was too early for it to innovate digital wristwatches as consumers were still fond of analog wristwatches.

However, the success of Apollo-11 lunar voyage in 1969 was capable of transforming the human mind in the direction to trust and embrace digital devices. And digital gadgets even became a sign of style of living. So, the window for digital watchmaking was truly open only since the early 1970s. It was at this time that the Japanese watchmakers such as Casio and Citizen entered the market. Japanese digital watchmakers were neither too late nor too early to respond to the opportunity. The

American watchmakers, who failed being too early, re-entered the digital watchmaking in 1970s. By that time, the market was flooded with the Japanese brands such as Casio and Citizen and the American watchmakers failed again as their re-entry was too late.

Corridor principle describes the phenomenon of occurring opportunities to entrepreneurs those who are currently engaged in business. It is assumed that there are many windows along a corridor. When walking through a corridor passing numerous windows, opportunities could be seen through the windows that are open. The entrepreneurs who detect opportunities can swiftly respond to them by innovating suitable products before the windows get closed. By this way, corridor principle describes that the present entrepreneurs can diversify their product lines by innovating new products and can benefit from economies of scope. Product diversification of large corporates such as Sony, Panasonic, Samsung, LG, and many others for several decades has been clear evidence of corporate responses to opportunities detected along corridor.

Papadam (papad) was the only instant food in Sri Lanka until the mid-1980s and Nikado Company Ltd.[10] was the prominent papadam maker and distributor island-wide. After 1977, with implementation of the open market economic policies, Sri Lanka experienced rapid socioeconomic change. Export Processing Zones, foreign employment policy, financial sector liberalization, entrepreneurship liberalization, and social mobility caused extensive social change during the past few decades resulting in new job opportunities, incomes, modern lifestyles, and attitudinal change.[11] This new socioeconomic environment urged the demand for a large number of different food items. Nikado Ltd. spotted these new opportunities and harnessed them innovating a large number of instant food items under Nikado brand. They included instant noodles, instant hopper (Sri Lankan food) mix, instant string hopper (Sri Lankan food) mix, instant dosai (South Indian food) mix, instant wadai (South Indian food) mix, instant soya meats, and a few more.

Sources of Opportunities

Opportunities are represented by needs and wants which arise from the changes that take place in the wider environment comprised of an array of economic, social, industrial, technological, environmental, legal, demographic, and infrastructural factors (Fig. 6.1). Awareness of the changes taking place in them helps entrepreneur to recognize opportunities as they

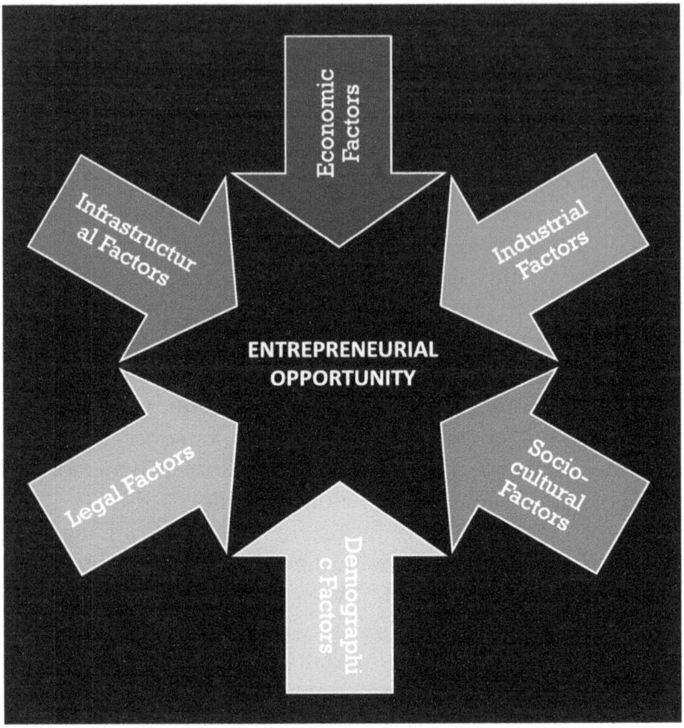

Fig. 6.1 Sources of entrepreneurial opportunities (Author portrayal)

arise in the wider environment. These factors individually or collectively set motion to environmental dynamics discussed below.[12]

Economic Factors

Changes in economic environment are caused by macroeconomic and economic policy dynamics. Economic growth rate, interest rate, foreign exchange rate, tax rate, inflation rate, money supply, fiscal policy, development policy, monetary policy, trade policy, industrial policy, and market policy are key economic variables.[13] The changes taking place in these variables can either stimulate or impede venture opportunities. So, they affect entrepreneurs positively or negatively. In presence of open market policy, market protection and infant industry protection are less strict and thus imports flood into local markets creating fierce competition. This policy, for instance, can eliminate opportunities for domestic production and sale but it can instead create new opportunities in distribution, logistics, and trade.[14]

In case of a new investment policy that promotes foreign investors in local industries, local producers could be pushed out of their industries. On the contrary, new opportunities in sub-contracting, support industry, and logistics will be created under new circumstances.[15] When the exchange rate policy regime changes from fixed exchange rate to floating exchange rate, and for which reason the local currency depreciates, local entrepreneurs find more opportunities in production for export markets. Yet, appreciated local currency, on the other hand, creates opportunities in import business.[16]

High tax rates, interest rates, wage rates, and inflation translate into higher cost of production and higher prices which will discourage entrepreneurs while lower rates of which, on the contrary, will encourage entrepreneurs.[17] At times, economic variables are sound, economic expansion is experienced. Economic expansion is consequent to expansion in production and consumption; which is known as increase in supply and demand. In economic contraction, decreasing demand diminishes opportunities for production. However, economic contraction is not always pessimistic as new economic circumstances can stimulate new opportunities. The economic contraction during the Oil-Shock in the early 1970s created opportunities to produce fuel-efficient vehicles. Japanese automakers capitalized on this new opportunity, with their fuel-efficient autos, to penetrate into the US and European automobile market.[18]

Industrial Factors

Production technology, production methods, materials, value chain, logistics, and management are the major causes of industrial changes. A single change in a factor like technology can create or eliminate opportunities in many fields of production. Invention of the Transistor, Integrated Circuit (IC), Processors, Memory chips, Application software, Diode panel, Lithium battery, RAM, and ROM caused sweeping changes in the electronic and telecommunication industries. Those inventions led to innovations in the fields of computers, smartphones, televisions, household electricals, and transportation equipment. New technology similarly wiped out hundreds of analog products from the market eliminating the opportunities that lasted for decades.[19]

Production of innumerous new goods has thus, been an outcome of new technologies. Invention of Lithium-Ion battery technology, for example, created opportunities for production of mobile electronic devices. Powerful, lightweight, and small batteries helped production of the mobile phone which otherwise could have been impossible. Minimization technology, cordless technology, Wi-Fi technology, and software helped production of all-in-one versatile tool called smartphone. Invention of electronic, telecommunication, robot, and artificial intelligence technologies has created innumerous opportunities in the manufacturing and service sectors. All industrial products being used since the past several decades should be seen as outcomes of industrial changes.

Changes that take place in relation to materials also create immense business opportunities. Packaging materials changed from wood, glass, metals, plastics, and to paper as of today. This change created opportunities in production of all these materials in the first place and then in numerous disposable goods such as cartons, ballpoint pens, soft drink bottles, lunch trays, and disposable shaving razors. Invention of new materials has created innumerous opportunities in production of building materials during the past few decades. Invention of new materials has partly been a response to minimize natural materials. Synthetic materials produced in abundance and thus their unit cost as well as unit price was minimal. Opportunity for production of lightweight, low cost, durable, and refined goods became prevalent with new materials.[20]

Production methods and management-induced changes also create venture opportunities. Initiatives of Ford Corporation to assemble vehicles on a conveyor belt introduced an entirely new production system popularly known as assembly line; an eye opener of cost-efficient production system. This new production system was embraced by almost every mass manufacturing. The Just-In-Time (JIT) production method introduced by Toyota Motor Corporation of Japan quickly spread to manufacturing firms and then to service ventures.[21] These production systems generated sub-contracting opportunities for entrepreneurs to participate in. Modern telecommunication methods also have opened opportunities in e-commerce businesses for large players like AliExpress and Amazon Inc. and millions of individuals.

Socio-Cultural Factors

Social values, beliefs, perceptions, ethics, and responsibilities guide social behavior. These elements are not static but take their shape due to education, political thoughts, international exposure, urbanization, and wars. The changes take place with respect to these elements can result in negative or positive impacts to entrepreneurs.[22] Yet, they realize useful opportunities in both situations. Cultural exposure during the past few centuries has caused significant changes in consumer values and consumption patterns. Clothing, food, beverages, housing, household furniture, electrical goods, work, health, and fitness are dramatically becoming uniform across cultures. So, the cultural distinctiveness is drastically tapering. Cultural distinctiveness creates opportunities for production of specific goods like chopsticks in the East but with adoption of the Western lifestyles, opportunities for production of spoon and fork also have soared. Additionally, opportunities for production of uniform and global products like iPhones and Denim also are common as a result.

Travels and tours have become an essential part of life in modern societies against the relative immobility that prevailed in the past. People's mobility generates immense opportunities in transportation, hospitality industry, and related other services.[23] Value systems in relation to education, decent life, and housing also have created immense opportunities in the service sector. Nightlife, nightclubs, eating out, motor racing, amusement parks, leisure, and sports are marks of changing lifestyle and they also create new venture opportunities.[24] Needs and wants emanating from lifestyles demand goods and services. Beauty, health, and fitness are concerns of modern life. As a result, opportunities are created in the areas of fitness and beauty products, fragrances, vitamins, food supplementary, and health insurance.[25]

Beliefs in virtue, sin, gods, demons, and performance of rituals also create venture opportunities.[26] Shops operating near temples and shrines, and the goods they sell are examples of the opportunities for production and sale created by social beliefs and behaviors. Democracy, rights to education, rights to health, social security, and care for elderly are social values at present.[27] These areas of social concerns demand goods and services giving rise to venture opportunities. Some of these concerns are related to improvement and maintenance of living standards and are the sources of demand for newer goods and services. It is, therefore, obvious that every social change is a source of venture opportunities.

Demographic Factors

Demography is a subject of population analytics. It includes population characteristics such as birth rate, death rate, population growth rate, population size, age structure, education, health, income, and civil status. Changes in these characteristics determine different needs and wants of the population and hence consumer demand. Birth, life, and death, and emotions such as attachment, lust, maliciousness, insecurity, and delusion are connected to the conduct of life that are the sources of needs and wants. It is this physiological and psychological state of the human that compel entrepreneurs to incessantly engage in innovations. Entrepreneurs who are sensible in human life cycle and psychology of emotions recognize commercially viable opportunities and devise means to address them commercially through innovation of goods and services.[28]

Age is a major determinant of composition of demand of goods and services. Bottom-heavy population structure has a large child population and thus, opportunities rise to address children's needs and wants; Children's medicine, toys, educational goods, schooling goods, child healthcare facilities, kindergarten, educational services, children's parks, games, and sports goods are examples. In a country where top-heavy population structure is present, the composition of elderly is significant and thus, there will be more opportunities to produce medicine for adults, healthcare services, care taker services, homes for elderly, walking-aid, hearing-aid, etc.

Number of annual marriages is a source of demand for hotel facilities, catering, flower arrangements, homes, furniture, household goods, and electronics. More marriages lead to more pregnancies which, in turn, create opportunities for maternity healthcare, maternity goods, infant healthcare, and infant goods. Further, more births generate more demands for maternity and infant care in contrast to more deaths generate more demand for funeral parlors and funeral goods. Educational aspect of the population creates opportunities for supply of education facilities, hostels, laboratories, research equipment, computers, and software.

Population is classified into low-income, middle-income, and high-income classes. The bigger the low-income class the smaller will be the volume of sales resulting in less opportunities for production. Further, the demand for want satisfying fashion and luxury goods will be limited. Yet, when the income grows and the middle class expands, demand is created for housing, household equipment, electronics, automobiles, restaurant, education, sports, gymnasium, fashion, and fancy goods. With a significantly large high-income class, opportunities arise for tours and travels, branded goods, high end hotels and restaurants, authentic cuisine, luxury housing, and living. This indicates different income classes promote operations of different types of businesses sponsoring different venture opportunities.[29]

Legal Factors

Changes in the legal sphere occur due to introduction of new laws, abolishing of old laws, tightening or relaxation of laws by the law making and law enforcement authorities. Changes in the legal sphere are inflicted by political changes also. Democracies respect personal liberties and ensure freer human behavior. Non-democracies, on the other hand, have less concern for human rights. Political belief reflects on the economic policy also. Import bans, distribution and marketing restrictions, consumption quota, import quota, foreign exchange quota, and many other similar restrictions are common in closed economies. They adversely affect quantity of production and consumption.[30]

Prohibition of beauty parlors, photography, and education for women by Taliban government in Afghanistan has eliminated venture opportunities in those areas. East and West Germany made a reunion, after demolishing the Berlin Wall, and made one Germany in 1991. This political change introduced sweeping changes to the legal system of East Germany and as a result, opportunities in trade and investment prospered immensely. Laws affect exports, imports, foreign investment, and foreign exchange conversions also. There can be temporary or permanent tightening or otherwise relaxation of these laws. At times these laws are relaxed, entrepreneurs find fresh opportunities for business whereas at times laws are stricter business opportunities are hindered. Some other times, entrepreneurs will have to go out of business when certain goods import bans are imposed.

The Soviet style political regime between 1970 and 1977 in Sri Lanka brought the Business Undertakings Acquisitions Act of 1971 and largely restricted private entrepreneurship.[31] The Land Reform Act of 1972 and 1975 abolished foreign ownership and restricted the extent of local ownership of plantations and other agricultural affairs. Nationalization of private enterprises and establishment of state enterprises were key features of that economic model. The state penetrated into all business areas such as production, distribution, marketing, import, export, banking, and insurance. In contrast, with the introduction of the open and free market economic policies in 1977, the above Acts were abolished and new legislations were brought to empower the private entrepreneurs. Trade liberalization, financial sector liberalization, and entrepreneurship liberalization were the key features of the policy regime after 1977. This new environment increasingly conducive for private entrepreneurs and in consequence, hundreds of thousands of business startups emerged in a short period of time.

Excessive use of *R22 Chlorofluorocarbon* gas was found to be the cause of the Ozone layer depletion. This scientific revelation then appealed abandonment of the gas. Alongside, the businesses based on R22 gas began to decline. Yet, new opportunities arose with the replacement gas, *R134A Tetrafluoroethene*. Again, as *R134A gas was found to be greenhouse portent, the R438A Freon and R600A Iso Butane were permitted as refrigerator gases. This opened up new opportunities in new gas businesses.* Automobile and factory *missions* became a concern of air pollution and hence emission test systems were obligated by environment laws and policies to reduce emissions. This initially restricted business opportunities but later led to production of environmentally friendly vehicles, machineries, production systems, and factories. Production of hybrid and electric cars are examples.

The COVID-19 outbreak occurred as a natural course that ruthlessly destroyed business opportunities due to lockdowns, social distancing, and travel restrictions. The pandemic, at its onset, rapidly eradicated ventures and venture opportunities. Yet, demand for new products rose gradually opening up new business opportunities in production of face masks, sanitizers, vaccines, and immunity booster goods. As the world prepared to face this health challenge, opportunities in production of new goods and services emerged. Opportunities emerged not only for production of new health goods, but for systems like remote operations, working from home, online education, and online delivery also. In short, the initially disadvantaged COVID-19 pandemic later created innumerous opportunities for new business paradigm.[32]

Infrastructural Factors

Supply of utility services such as electricity, gas, water and the infrastructure such as airports, seaports, and road networks to remote areas creates new venture opportunities in those areas. Without certain utility services some production and services are not feasible. Supply of electricity, water, and gas in rural areas has fashioned hundreds of thousands of micro and small entrepreneurs during the past few decades. Electricity and gas supply not only created opportunities in rural sector production of goods but also in operation of rural eateries, juice bars, ice cream parlors, beauty parlors, and many other ventures which would not have been feasible without such utility services. Power supply to remote areas has promoted business opportunities in resort hotels, mining, excavation, milling, and processing. In general, rural sector entrepreneurship development has much to do with increased access to utility services.[33]

With infrastructure development, numerous opportunities arise in trade and manufacturing. Ports, airports, and urban and rural development projects are examples of infrastructure development. While new road networks create opportunities in transportation and trading, alternative roads may erode existing opportunities as road traffic will be altered. In Sri Lanka, Colombo Port City, as a new infrastructure development project, will create thousands of new entrepreneurial opportunities. The four-decade-old Gam-Udava regional development project has created many small towns and innumerable business opportunities in them. It is obvious that these new towns now serve as entrepreneurship opportunity hubs.

Gam-Udava[34] project set up a few factories, in a selected area, that employed a few thousand workers. These factories together with a few newly established government offices injected new incomes into the area through salaries. This created a demand for goods and services in the new township. Small trading entrepreneurs set up ventures to capitalize on these opportunities. Large and growing number of ventures in those townships after three decades witness to creation of ventures through that project. An American highway pierced a private land and the landlord noticed that the travelers used his land to stopover, refresh, and relax, and the land becoming untidy and unhygienic. He was annoyed at the beginning, but then he volunteered to facilitate the travelers with restrooms, benches, tables, and dustbins. Later, the owner found it an opportunity to open a restaurant there. This is believed to be the US highway restaurant history.

Sensing Venture Opportunities

To explore useful venture opportunities, more than an average sense is essential. With average sense, only average opportunities can be recognized. It is common for those who recognize average opportunities become average entrepreneurs. In contrast, those who are with more than average sense can recognize opportunities that help start exclusive ventures. Examples of modern exclusive ventures include Android, AliExpress, and Uber. The sense of entrepreneurship described here does not advocate the notion that the entrepreneur should possess a thorough sense of everything. But among the most essential is the entrepreneurial sense which is gained intuitively or by training and experience. Venture opportunity exploration requires a synthesis of many senses as described below.[35]

Sense of the technology and technological development
Sense of materials, machineries, formula
Sense of production knowhow
Sense of customer needs and buying behavior
Sense of distribution channels and networks
Sense of the competitors and competition
Sense of product promotion
Sense of human skills needed
Sense of socioeconomic and political trends
Sense of demographic trends
Sense of world economic trends
Sense of environmental changes and challenges

Opportunity Recognition Methods

As emphasized previously also, venture opportunities comprise of unsatisfied needs and wants that have commercial potentials. Opportunities arise infinitely in every circumstance but entrepreneurs recognize only suitable and viable ones out of them for venture creation.[36] Therefore, methodical and systematic search of opportunities is essential for recognizing appropriate opportunities. Recognition of opportunities is thus, the foremost action of the entrepreneurship process. This requires special traits and efforts. Clever entrepreneurs recognize venture opportunities through intuition whereas average entrepreneurs recognize them through exploration; by way of techniques such as research, surveys, or experiments.[37] The need and simplicity or complexity of these techniques depend on the need or want aimed to be addressed. Further, entrepreneurs adopt two approaches to identify venture opportunities: (1) selective approach and (2) open approach. Selective approach, first chooses a business field and then identifies a suitable opportunity. In contrast, the open approach searches for an opportunity from among many fields, picks a suitable one, and then initiates venture in that field. The opportunity recognition methods identified in this section accord with both these approaches.

Sensitivity Observation and Survey Method

Market surveys are conducted to make observations into present and prospective consumer behavior. Observations identify the extent to which products satisfy customer needs and wants, what features are lacking in the products presently available, what products are scarce, and what products would have potential demand. Observations look into the customer sensitivity to different aspects of a product. Observations are carried out with human eyes, electronic devices, and through survey methods. Observations are made informally or formally and publicly or secretly. Observations are directed to recognize customer response to existing products as well as to proposed products.

Observations are made to initially see if customers are satisfied with the products available in the market. Then, at the consumption stage, the real level of satisfaction is observed and measured. Finally, customer sensitivity is observed in relation to price, performance, design, technology, prestige, and convenience of use of the products. This information helps entrepreneur to identify opportunities and to respond to them through innovations that include new products, quality and design improvements, or alterations to existing products; innovative pricing, presentation, packing, and distribution. Large corporates conduct both market surveys and marketing research to recognize opportunities conceived in markets in relation to varied sensitivities (Fig. 6.2).

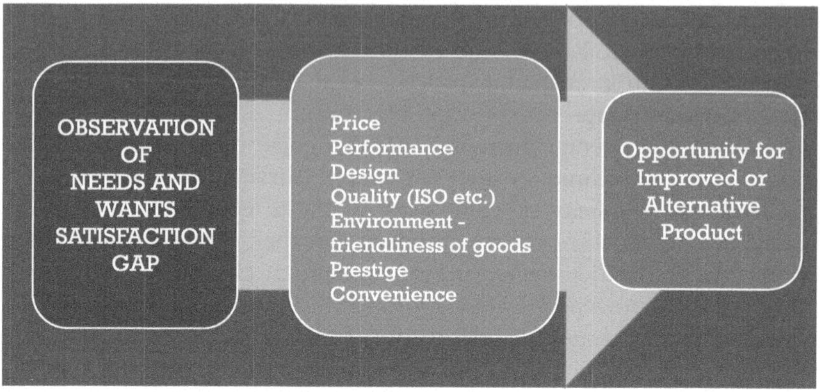

Fig. 6.2 Sensitivity observation method (Author portrayal)

Drawback Analysis Method

Analysis of technical drawbacks of existing products is a means to recognize opportunities for product enhancement. Existing products sometimes are not coherent with customer needs for quality, functionality, durability, and reliability. Further, products are pulled by customers, for their unique features, when they are first introduced but later, customers may realize drawbacks of the products and find less value in them. With the perceived low value, product will not sell as it did earlier. This state indicates the need for further development of the existing products. General, scientific, and technical analyses help recognize product flaws. Significant drop in the value of a product provides ample opportunities for their improvement, alteration, and development. Product drawback analyses are carried out by means of reverse engineering, disintegration, and dissection of goods to detect functional errors related to engineering, production, function, material, and design. The need for error-free and better products results in new entrepreneurial opportunities (Fig. 6.3).

Invention Search Method

For intervening in solving needs and wants-related problems, the ideas and knowledge required for production of goods and services, i.e., invention, must be searched for. Governments, laboratories, corporates, and individuals sometimes publish their inventions for the public use for free

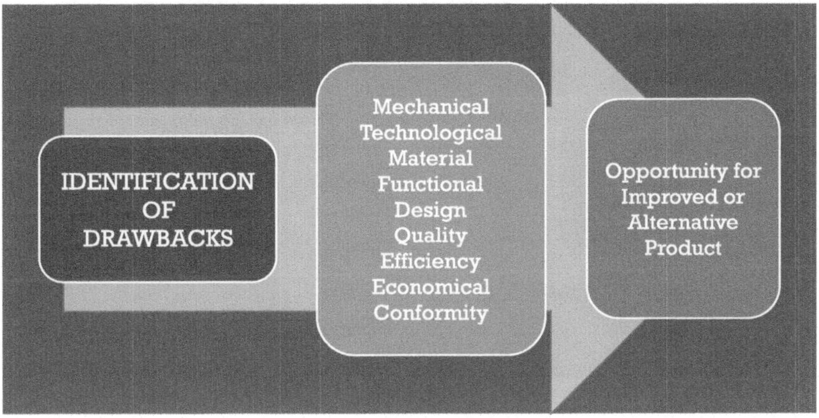

Fig. 6.3 Drawback analysis method (Author portrayal)

of charge. Inventions of private organizations and individuals usually patent their inventions and thus, cannot be obtained free of charge. Thus, they can only be used if purchased or licensed or franchised. Entrepreneurs themselves also engage in experimenting and fundamental research in search of invention. Inventions can be identified in areas such as materials, production methods, formulas, designs, new uses of existing products, simplification of goods, process of production, and new technologies (Fig. 6.4). Inventions lead either to entirely new product like Ajinomoto or improved product like smartphone.

Mind Mapping Method

Mapping of one's own mind is a helpful technique to ascertain an area of business and the opportunities connected to it in contrast to many other business areas and opportunities. Earth shaking and high-risk products are feasible to some entrepreneurs while average and low-risk products are feasible for some others. When selecting to innovate a product, technical, financial, and professional feasibilities of entrepreneur also matter. Mind mapping technique, as depicted in Fig. 6.5, facilitates entrepreneurs to recognize feasible area and feasible product within a large range of possibilities for innovation. In particular, mind mapping technique guides

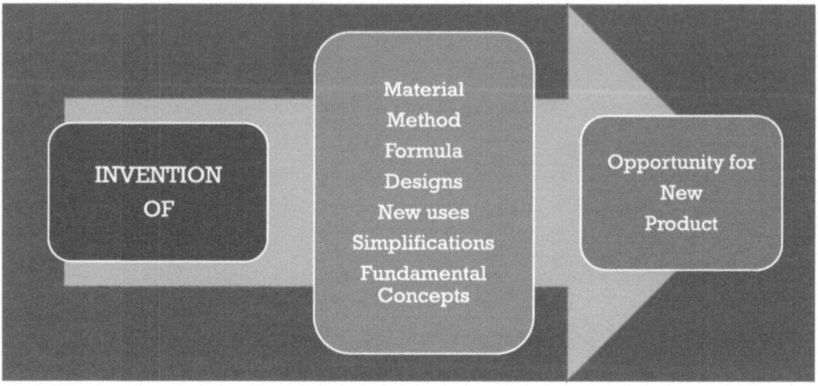

Fig. 6.4 Invention search method (Author portrayal)

entrepreneur in selecting a product area and idea appropriate to him from a general scenario of opportunities.

Mind mapping technique guides entrepreneur to a specific choice of a product from a general option of products. In mind mapping technique, firstly, a field of business is selected from production or service.

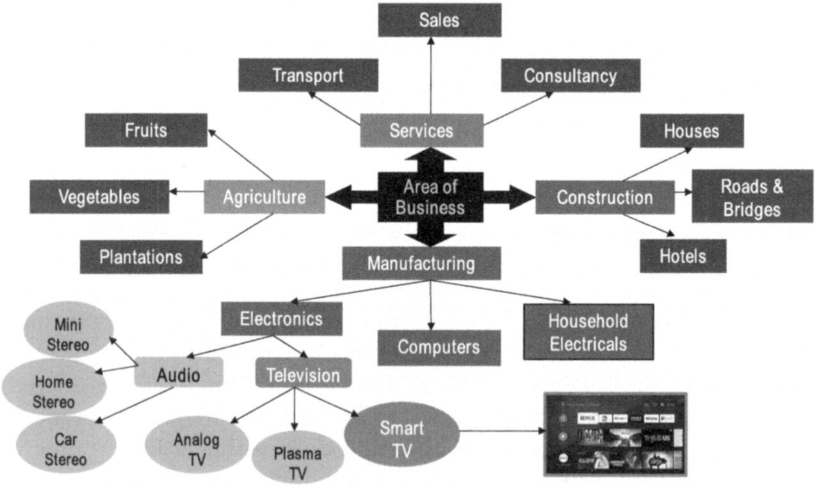

Fig. 6.5 Mind mapping technique (Author portrayal)

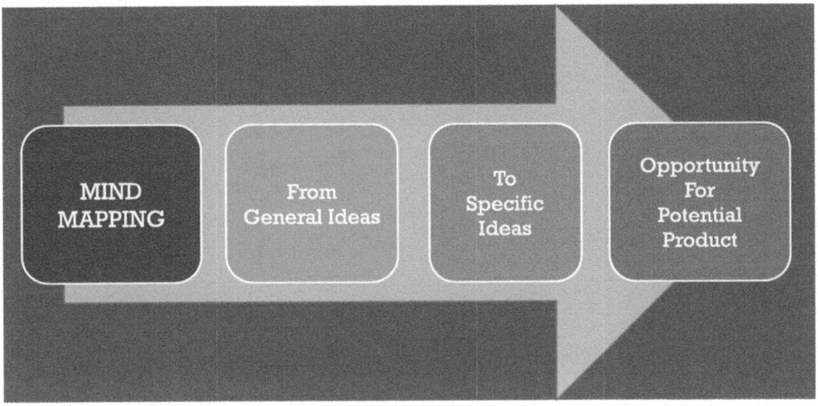

Fig. 6.6 Mind mapping method (Author portrayal)

Then specific industry is selected. For instance, having selected the finance industry, a sub category needs to be isolated from it. Sub categories of the finance industry are banking, pawning, leasing, microfinance, and investment. In case of electronics industry, sub categories will include manufacturing of audio, video, computer, and mobile phone. In this detailing-out process, finally, a single product is identified from the sub category or micro-category according to the preference and capabilities of the entrepreneur. The mind mapping method is an assistant for an entrepreneur to figure out and pick up the specific opportunity from general and broad spectrum of opportunities as indicated in Fig. 6.6.

Brainstorming Method

Brainstorming stimulates mind to ascertain opportunities out of the blue. Brainstorming is a team activity and the team should be aware of the firm's vision, mission, assets, liabilities, strengths, weaknesses, and individual member capabilities. This technique helps the team to come up with brand new ideas subject to the firm's capacity. Brainstorming is usually performed by small teams but both in startups as well as in corporates. At the inception of Sony, it was habitual for the members engage in brainstorming to figure out an exact product development opportunity. They came up with the suggestions to make "Bean Bun" (mame pan, in Japanese), Rice cookers, electric mats (kotatsu, in Japanese), radio

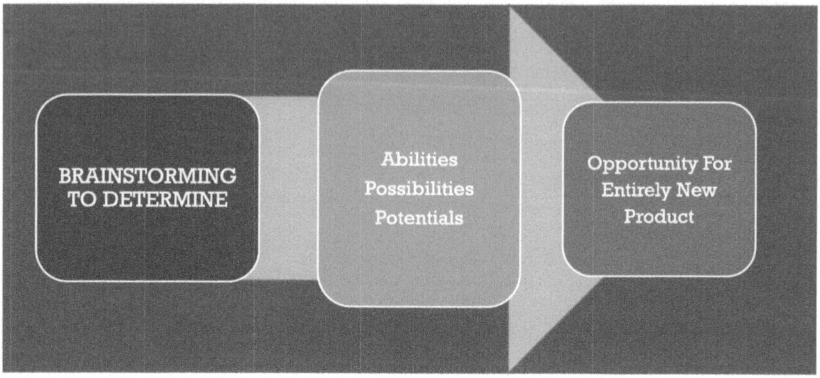

Fig. 6.7 Brainstorming method (Author portrayal)

parts, etc. However, Ibuka, the senior and the pioneer ridiculed all that saying "something else" was there in his mind.[38] Though the team was disappointed at the beginning, they gradually realized what Ibuka had in his mind and recognized potentials of making audio and video apparatus. Sharp Corporation of Japan, in an interview revealed that it assigns a few teams to develop a single product and the teams engage in brainstorming to identify the product and its features from scratch.

Participants of brainstorming exercise collectively come up with innovative ideas considering the feasibility, challenges, risk, marketability, and profitability of an idea and its overall suitability to the firm's vision and mission. Brainstorming matches potential opportunities with feasibilities and helps bring about an entirely new product or service. Brainstorming, thus, helps recognizing abilities, possibilities, and potentials in recognizing and capitalizing on an opportunity (Fig. 6.7).

Intuition Method

Intuition triggers ideas that other techniques cannot. Intuition is not a method or a technique, but a power of the brain that recognizes new combination of resources, technologies, and markets. to create something new or better. The people who are blessed with intuition can recognize opportunities that no other person can even imagine. Therefore, intuition-led opportunity recognition can bring about novel products and services (Fig. 6.8). The outcomes should not necessarily be earthshaking

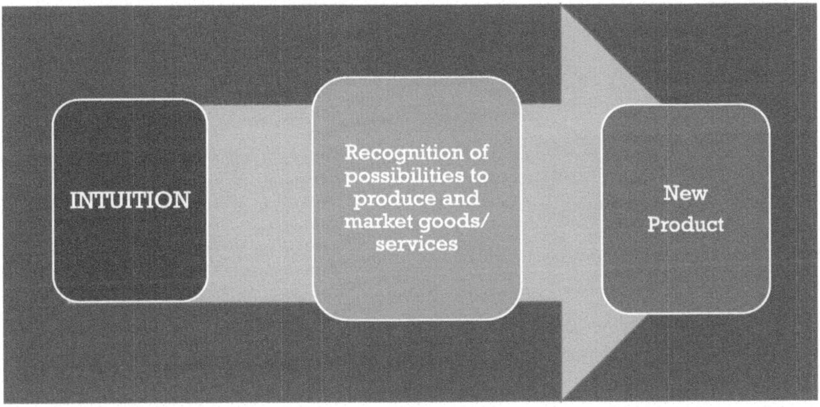

Fig. 6.8 Intuition method (Author portrayal)

products that are based on unimaginable technology. Intuition-led products can range from a simple product like elephant poo paper, elephant whisky, and 3M's sticky notes to Tesla's farfetched space docking station. Although intuition is identified as a method, the knowledge behind intuition cannot be transferred to others.

Resource Conversion Method

Conversion of materials and spaces can bring about innovations (Fig. 6.9). Entrepreneurs usually attempt to convert materials they are familiar with and have easy access to. Entrepreneurship Development Programs, therefore, suggest that opportunities are usually connected to the availability of resources in close proximities. Resources are comprised of materials and spaces. Availability of elephant dung in the close proximity of Elephant Orphanage flares up opportunities for conversion of it into poo papers; which then used to produce greeting cards. Similarly, building spaces that do not possess license to operate pubs are converted into "bring-your-bottle" restaurants where customers, at a corkage, can enjoy alcoholic beverages.

Spaces at mountains, rivers, beaches, and plateaus are resources worthy of converting into hotels and amusement parks; which is a common practice of resource conversion. Stationery shops near schools, offering articles near churches and temples, and thirst-quenching goods near playgrounds

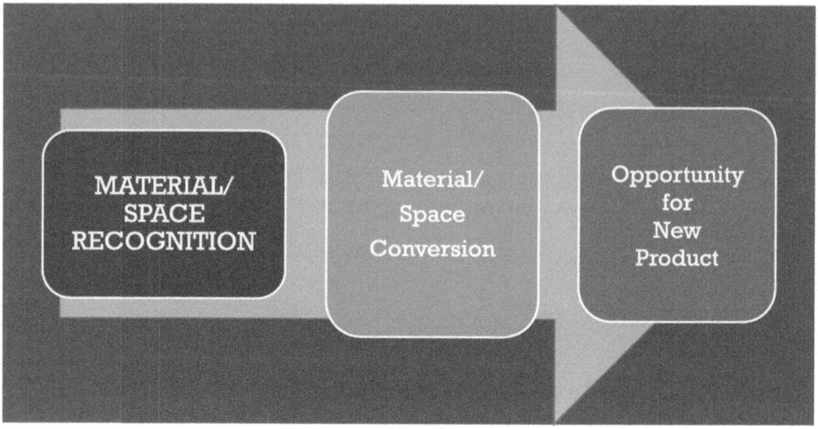

Fig. 6.9 Resource conversion method (Author portrayal)

are examples of conversion of spaces into ventures. Feasibility of conversion of resources is commonly recognized as opportunities for innovation. A large number of ventures are created to harness wastes and to innovate useful products.

Harnessing waterfalls to produce hydropower and recycling paper, plastic, rubber, fabric, garments, factory disposals, human and animal wastes, and biomass are instances of resource conversion. Both manmade wastes and natural wastes are thus recognized as resources for conversion. Under the Japanese "mottai-nai" assumption, resource conversion opportunities are recognized in relation to natural or near-waste resources. Japanese Rotenburo and Nothenburo (open-air hot spring bathing facility) are a classic example of conversion of hot springs (Onsen) into lucrative business.

Habit Modification Method

Habits are long-standing practices. Individuals and communities are adapted to habits for generations. Habit of masses is an important mark for an entrepreneur to derive opportunities for innovation of goods and services (Fig. 6.10). Some habits continue amidst social and health concerns over them. Chewing (something) has been an age-old habit of people in every region of the world. People learned to chew various kinds

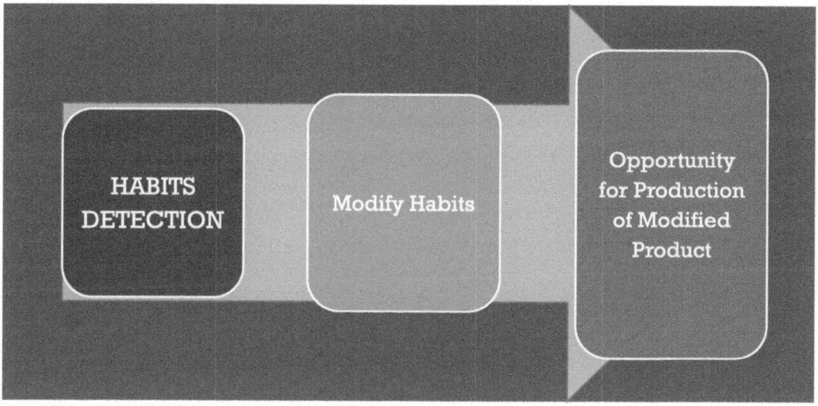

Fig. 6.10 Habit modification method (Author portrayal)

of leaves such as tobacco, betel leaf, coca leaf, or Guayusa leaf as a means to relieve from stress.

The habit of chewing was seen by entrepreneurs as an opportunity to produce candies and gummies for chewing. Gummies have grown into a US$ 19 billion market in addition to US$ 66 billion candy market. World candy and gummy markets are growing at the phase of 10% annually. The chewing habit has now spread to children also from adults. Further, unlike leaf chewing, the habit of gummy chewing is allowed at the workplace, schools, and universities for almost all ages. Canada and a few States in the USA have permitted cannabis-based gummies for adults. This reveals that the old-fashioned chewing habit has now been converted into the modern way of chewing.

Ritual Adoption Method

People belong to varied cultures and every culture is enriched with long-standing rituals. While rituals emanate from historically established social beliefs, religious practices play a predominant role in it. At temples, shrines, churches, mosques, or any other religious place, rituals like prayers, sacrifices, offerings, and pooja are commonly performed. Every ritual requires certain products for offerings or sacrifices. Also, in many cultures, ornaments and costumes represent social ritualistic behaviors. Dresses and ornaments are worn to distinguish cultural attachments and

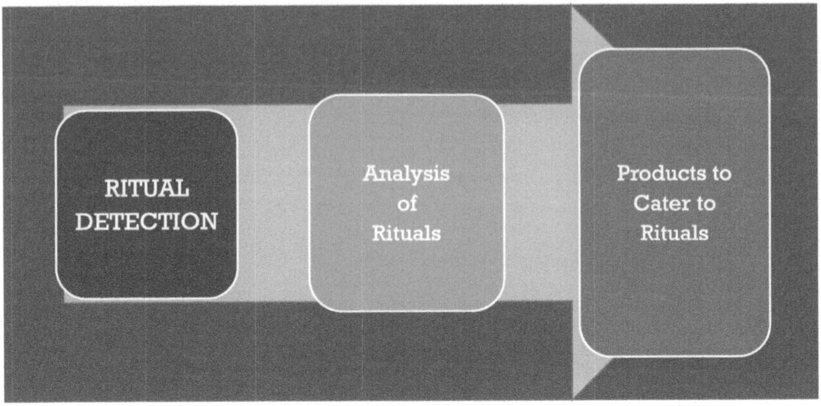

Fig. 6.11 Ritual adoption method (Author portrayal)

beliefs. The goods that are required for social or religious rituals are demanded in large quantities in every society creating opportunities for production of the same (Fig. 6.11).

For instance, in Indian culture, in particular, from birth to death and after death of a person, a large number of rituals are performed and each such ritual requires specific products and costumes. Further, a large number of gods are being believed by people and thus, there are peculiar rituals to satisfy each god for receiving their blessing. Commonly, ritualistic goods are being sold in front of temples, churches, shrines, and mosques. Further, specialized shops sell ritualistic products in every culture. Practice of rituals and ritualistic festivals helps determining immense opportunities for production of specific goods.

Chapter Summary

Venture is not feasible without entrepreneurship and that entrepreneurship is not feasible without venture. Thus, entrepreneurship is not mere opening of a venture but an intricate process comprised of the following major sub-processes: opportunity recognition, invention, innovation, business planning, business modeling, venture creation, and growth management. They all are interconnected in a designated order leading to the final outcome of a sustainable venture. Among which recognition of opportunities is thus, the foremost action of the entrepreneurship process.

Opportunities are sometimes called market gaps. Also, opportunities are identified as market opportunities, venture opportunities, or business opportunities; which terms are interchangeably used in textbooks. However, according to intervention hypothesis, opportunities are unfulfilled needs and wants of individuals or organizations. Opportunities are either explicit or implicit. While it is easy to recognize explicit opportunities, special entrepreneurial talents are required to recognize implicit opportunities. Explicit opportunities create highly competitive Red Ocean Markets whereas implicit opportunities create competition free Blue Ocean Markets. The entrepreneurs who operate in the Blue Ocean Markets enjoy market hegemony and monopolistic advantages. The "Window" and "Corridor" principles describe the nature of venture opportunities, and how and when they arise and vanish. Opportunities are represented by needs and wants that arise from physiological or psychological factors primarily. And they are mostly influenced by the dynamics of economic, social, industrial, technological, environmental, legal, demographic, and infrastructural factors in the wider environment.

More than an average sense of entrepreneurship will explore exclusive opportunities whereas an average sense will identify average opportunities. Thus, exclusive or average ventures are reflections of the opportunity recognition skills of an entrepreneur. The opportunity recognition ability can be appropriated to entrepreneurial training, experience, or intuition. Opportunity recognition is an explorative endeavor that requires a synthesis of senses and methods. This chapter lengthily deliberates several methods entrepreneurs employ to recognize venture opportunities. They include observation or survey method, product drawback analysis method, invention search method, mind mapping method, brainstorming method, intuition method, resource conversion method, habit adoption method, and ritual adoption method.

Review Questions

1. Explain whether entrepreneurship is an action or a process and elaborate the sub-processes of entrepreneurship.
2. Which definition do you prefer to accept from the following in describing venture opportunities; "market gaps" or "unfulfilled needs and wants?" Explain why.
3. Differentiate between explicit and implicit opportunities and describe the circumstances they occur.

4. Explain how explicit opportunities lead to Red Ocean Market and implicit opportunities lead to Blue Ocean Market.
5. "Window and Corridor principles powerfully explain the rise and fall of entrepreneurial opportunities and recommend the right time for entrepreneur to respond to them." Elaborate this statement.
6. Describe the sources of venture opportunities and the prospective startups that might find them useful to exploit.
7. Explain what types of senses that can be useful for an entrepreneur to cleverly recognize venture opportunities.
8. "Sensitivity observation method can reveal a host of opportunities stemming from unfulfilled needs and wants." Discuss.
9. What is the product drawback analysis method? Explain how this method is useful for imitative entrepreneurs.
10. Explain how external sources of inventions can be useful for an entrepreneur to recognize venture opportunities.
11. Describe how the Mind Mapping exercise can help isolating a specific opportunity in a specific industry among many.
12. "Brainstorming is a popular method adopted for ascertaining venture opportunities." Explain whether startups also can benefit from brainstorming as the corporates do.
13. Is intuition a method or a trait? Explain how intuition functions in ascertaining opportunities.
14. Describe the merits of resource conversion method and explain why resource-based entrepreneurship is promoted by Entrepreneurship Development Programs.
15. "Human habits create tremendous opportunities for entrepreneurship." Explain this statement referring to an industry that has adopted human habits as its business opportunity.
16. "Rituals are signs of venture potentials." Relate rituals to venture opportunities and recognize their vastness for innovation of goods.

Additional Readings

1. Drucker, P.F., 1985. *Innovation and entrepreneurship*. New York: Harper and Row.
2. Moroz, P.W., and Hindle, K., 2012. Entrepreneurship as a process: Toward harmonizing multiple perspectives. *Entrepreneurship theory and Practice*, *36*(4), pp. 781–818.

3. Olson, P.D., 1985. Entrepreneurship: Process and abilities. *American Journal of Small Business*, *10*(1), pp. 25–31.
4. Carayannis, E.G. ed., 2020. *Encyclopedia of creativity, invention, innovation and entrepreneurship*. Cham: Springer International Publishing.
5. Brem, A., and Voigt, K.I., 2009. Integration of market pull and technology push in the corporate front end and innovation management—Insights from the German software industry. *Technovation*, *29*(5), pp. 351–367.
6. Brem, A., and Voigt, K.I., 2009. Integration of market pull and technology push in the corporate front end and innovation management—Insights from the German software industry. *Technovation*, *29*(5), pp. 351–367.
7. Dimov, D., 2021. From "Opportunity" to opportunity: The design space for entrepreneurial action. *Journal of Business Venturing Design*, *1*(1–2), p. 100002.
8. Smith, B.R., Matthews, C.H., and Schenkel, M.T., 2009. Differences in entrepreneurial opportunities: The role of tacitness and codification in opportunity identification. *Journal of small business management*, *47*(1), pp. 38–57.
9. Holcombe, R.G., 2003. The origins of entrepreneurial opportunities. *The Review of Austrian Economics*, *16*, pp. 25–43.
10. https://nikado.lk/
11. Pallegedara, A., 2019. Food consumption choice and demand by the Sri Lankan households: Trends, drivers and policy implications. *Journal of Agribusiness in Developing and Emerging Economies*, *9*(5), pp. 520–535.
12. Fuduric, N., 2008. The sources of entrepreneurial opportunities: Individuals & the environment. *Doctoral Research Paper*. Department of Planning and Development, Aalborg University.
13. Carlos Díaz-Casero, J., Ángel Manuel Díaz-Aunión, D., Cruz Sánchez-Escobedo, M., Coduras, A., and Hernández-Mogollón, R., 2012. Economic freedom and entrepreneurial activity. *Management Decision*, *50*(9), pp. 1686–1711.
14. Vidal-Suñé, A., and López-Panisello, M.B., 2013. Institutional and economic determinants of the perception of opportunities and entrepreneurial intention. *Investigaciones Regionales-Journal of Regional Research*, *26*, pp. 75–96.

15. De Marchi, V., Giuliani, E., and Rabellotti, R., 2018. Do global value chains offer developing countries learning and innovation opportunities? *The European Journal of Development Research*, *30*, pp. 389–407.
16. Rafindadi, A.A., and Yusof, Z., 2014. Are the periods of currency collapse an impediment to entrepreneurship and entrepreneurial haven? Evidence from regional comparison. *International Journal of Economics and Financial Issues*, *4*(4), pp. 886–908.
17. Wood, M.S., Bylund, P., and Bradley, S., 2016. The influence of tax and regulatory policies on entrepreneurs' opportunity evaluation decisions. *Management Decision*, *54*(5), pp. 1160–1182.
18. Aceytuno, M.T., Sánchez-López, C., and de Paz-Báñez, M.A., 2020. Rising inequality and entrepreneurship during economic downturn: An analysis of opportunity and necessity entrepreneurship in Spain. *Sustainability*, *12*(11), p. 4540.
19. Zahra, S.A., 2008. The virtuous cycle of discovery and creation of entrepreneurial opportunities. *Strategic Entrepreneurship Journal*, *2*(3), pp. 243–257.
20. Roscoe, P., Discua Cruz, A., and Howorth, C., 2013. How does an old firm learn new tricks? A material account of entrepreneurial opportunity. *Business History*, *55*(1), pp. 53–72.
21. Winston Jr, R., and Heiko, L., 1990. Just-in-time and small business evolution. *Entrepreneurship Theory and Practice*, *14*(4), pp. 51–64.
22. Thornton, P.H., Ribeiro-Soriano, D., and Urbano, D., 2011. Socio-cultural factors and entrepreneurial activity: An overview. *International Small Business Journal*, *29*(2), pp. 105–118.
23. Solvoll, S., Alsos, G.A., and Bulanova, O., 2015. Tourism entrepreneurship–review and future directions. *Scandinavian Journal of Hospitality and Tourism*, *15*(sup1), pp. 120–137.
24. Chin, O., and Harun, M.Z.M.B., 2015. Night market: A platform for creating new entrepreneurs. *Humanities and Social Sciences*, *3*(1), pp. 32–36.
25. Berry, S., 2023. The work of building beauty? An analysis of work-related motivations for women entrepreneurs in the beauty industry.
26. Dana, L.P., 2021. Religion as an explanatory variable for entrepreneurship. In *World encyclopedia of entrepreneurship* (pp. 535–552). Edward Elgar Publishing.

27. Dahrendorf, R., 1996. Economic opportunity, civil society and political liberty. *Development and Change*, *27*(2), pp. 229–249.
28. Kohlbacher, F., Herstatt, C., and Levsen, N., 2015. Golden opportunities for silver innovation: How demographic changes give rise to entrepreneurial opportunities to meet the needs of older people. *Technovation*, *39*, pp. 73–82.
29. Galindo Martin, M.A., Méndez Picazo, M.T., and Alfaro Navarro, J.L., 2010. Entrepreneurship, income distribution and economic growth. *International Entrepreneurship and Management Journal*, *6*, pp. 131–141.
30. Jacquemin, A., and Janssen, F., 2017. Entrepreneurs using regulation as a source of opportunity: A study combining quantitative and qualitative approaches. In *Exploring the entrepreneurial society* (pp. 35–45). Edward Elgar Publishing.
31. http://www.commonlii.org/lk/legis/num_act/bua35o197 1424/
32. Krishnan, C.S.N., Ganesh, L.S., and Rajendran, C., 2022. Entrepreneurial Interventions for crisis management: Lessons from the Covid-19 Pandemic's impact on entrepreneurial ventures. *International Journal of Disaster Risk Reduction*, *72*, p. 102830.
33. Tseng, C.C., 2012. Linking entrepreneurial infrastructures and new business development: Entrepreneurship development in Taiwan. *The Journal of Entrepreneurship*, *21*(1), pp. 117–132.
34. https://www.news.lk/news/business/item/12748-govt-to-rel aunch-gam-udawa-program
35. Hill, R.C., and Levenhagen, M., 1995. Metaphors and mental models: Sensemaking and sensegiving in innovative and entrepreneurial activities. *Journal of Management*, *21*(6), pp. 1057–1074.
36. Ardichvili, A., and Cardozo, R.N., 2000. A model of the entrepreneurial opportunity recognition process. *Journal of enterprising culture*, *8*(02), pp. 103–119.
37. Hajizadeh, A., and Zali, M., 2016. Prior knowledge, cognitive characteristics and opportunity recognition. *International Journal of Entrepreneurial Behavior & Research*, *22*(1), pp. 63–83.
38. Morita, A., Reingold, E.M., and Shimomura, M., 1992. *Made in Japan: Akio Morita a Sony*. Pragma.

CHAPTER 7

Invention and Innovation Process

Key Learning Points

- Meaning and scope of invention.
- Invention and intellectual property rights.
- Invention as an input of innovation.
- Invention as a process.
- Invention and knowledge creation.
- Knowledge creation in numbers.
- Innovation process.
- Analytical planning.
- Organizing resources.
- Implementation.
- Commercial application.
- Facets of innovation.
- Mission of innovation.
- Means of innovation.
- Sources of innovation.
- Steps of innovation.
- Types of innovations.
- Nature of innovation.
- Orientations of innovation.
- Imagination.

© The Author(s), under exclusive license to Springer Nature Singapore Pte Ltd. 2024

M. Rajaratne, *Concepts, Processes and Practice of Entrepreneurship*, Palgrave Studies in Global Entrepreneurship,
https://doi.org/10.1007/978-981-97-6180-7_7

- Problem-solving.
- Exploitation.
- Skill based.
- Material based.
- Preference based.
- Fashion orientation.
- Beauty orientation.
- Health orientation.
- Art and design orientation.
- Profession orientation.
- Value creation and innovation chain.
- Innovation path and power.

Introduction

Invention and innovation are key functions of entrepreneurship process. Invention is the foundation of innovation as invention creates the knowledge required for innovation. Therefore, invention involves in creation of knowledge whereas innovation involves in creation of goods and services which includes means, methods, systems, formulas, and designs also. Invention and innovation are complementary to each other. Invention is not useful either to the customer or to the entrepreneur as long as something useful is not produced. Invention is thus, only useful if goods or services are innovated based on it. Invention will be useful to the inventor if it is adopted for innovation or otherwise licensed or sold. Invention is described as a process that involves a few steps.

Similarly, innovation is also identified as a process. Invention process feeds into the innovation process and thus, they are interconnected. However, though mutually inclusive, there is no theory that invention and innovation are performed by the same person or firm. In fact, invention can be conducted separately even by an unknown party. Innovator sometimes performs searches to find out inventions from outside. If the right invention is available for sale or licensing, the innovator can purchase it outright or license it at royalty fee. If the invention is lawfully registered, the inventor can claim rights for the invention as an intellectual property. Innovator also can claim rights for product design, shape, look, trade name, brand name, persona, etc., if they are not claimable to the inventor.

Invention Process

Invention process, which is also referred to as creative process in some textbooks, is an indispensable function that creates knowledge required for innovation which, in turn, is the function that brings about new and better things into existence.[1] Invention produces creative knowledge useful for production of goods and services; so, invention feeds into innovation as indicated in Fig. 7.1.[2] The knowledge referred to herein is broad and thus it encompasses not only production knowhow but also technology, techniques, materials, designs, and product presentation. Unique knowledge created by invention is an intellectual property that can be legally protected as a right of the inventor by means of patents, copyrights, design rights, and trademarks.[3] Once ownership of invention is legally claimed by an inventor, the invention becomes their asset which grants the rights to sell, license, or franchise. Although invention is an indispensable input for innovation, it is not inevitable that an entrepreneur possesses it. Entrepreneur can acquire inventions from outside in case that they cannot invent by himself.

Entrepreneur has the options of buying, licensing, or franchising inventions of another party by paying for it. In case of licensing or franchising,

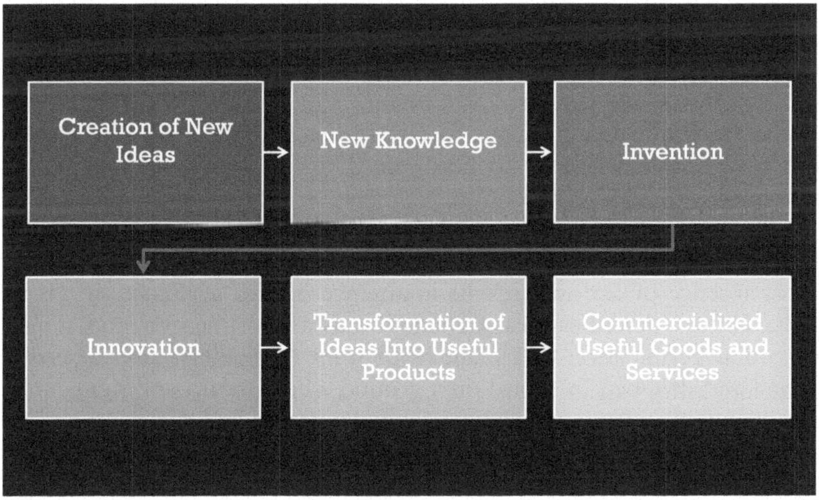

Fig. 7.1 Invention as an input (Author Portrayal)

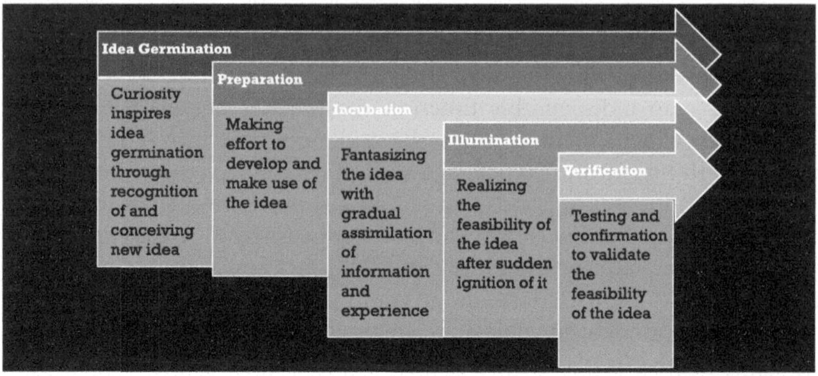

Fig. 7.2 Invention process (Author Portrayal)

the fee involved is referred to as royalty. Inventions can be acquired free of charge at times when the inventor has not obtained legal rights for the invention. Also, inventions of governments and charity organizations are generally available free of charge. Invention is a process that evolves the following steps: Idea germination, Preparation, Incubation, Illumination, and Verification[4] as indicated in Fig. 7.2.

Idea Germination

Idea germination is the first and foremost step of the invention process. Idea germination is equivalent to conceiving of unique idea as a solution to a problem related to needs or wants of people. Curiosity is a prerequisite to idea germination. Curiosity is aroused in a person due to enthusiasm for an incident, happening, problem, or need or want. For those who are not curious, happenings around them will go unnoticed. Thus, absence of curiosity results in absence of idea germination. David Holt (2000)[5] describes idea germination as a rare phenomenon similar to natural germination of a plant, with scant probability, after a seed is carried and dropped by a bird on a ground where fertile soil, right moisture, and temperature are present for germinating and surviving against insects, animals, and human, or hostile weather conditions like landslides, volcanos, and bushfire.

In his childhood, Alexander Graham Bell was curious about why his mother was hearing impaired, how she hears only when spoken to her loudly, and how to amplify his voice so that he could communicate well with his mother. Young Bell wanted to overcome the problem that he had to speak loudly. Konosuke Matsushita (founder of Panasonic Corp.), at his young age, heard a quarrel between two siblings from a neighborhood residence in an evening. Brother wanted to read for the examination while the sister wanted to iron press her uniform for schooling on the following day. According to the way that electricity had been supplied to the house, either the lamp or the electric iron could be operated at a time. Japanese houses for the working class, in the turn of the twentieth century, usually had one room, a sitting area, and a kitchen with simple electrical wiring chiefly for lighting purpose. The dispute erupted because neither brother nor sister prepared to compromise. This incident germinated the idea in Matsushita's mind to solve the problem. He then developed a dual holder[6] that can house a light bulb and a connector at the same time. This device helped distributing electricity between two electrical devices.

Preparation

Once an idea is germinated, inventor engages in exploring the idea from every possible perspective. This requires wider knowledge which is gained from publications, association of people, discussion of the idea with others, attending seminars and workshops, and experimentation. The knowledge will help the inventor to further develop the idea with a focus. This takes varied time periods depending on the complexity of the idea and the dedication of the inventor. Some keep gathering information, experimenting, and fine-tuning the idea for a long period of time and end up without realizing the feasibility of the idea while some others within an incredibly short period of time reach the next stage of the invention process.

Preparation requires dedication, enthusiasm, patience, and endurance. Graham Bell (with Thomas Watson, who later founded IBM Corporation) entered the preparation stage and initiated learning the principles of basic physics and started experiments. Matsushita took time in learning how electricity works and figuring out a method to divide and distribute electricity. At times the inventor is not driven by the passion of entirely new invention, they would engage in working on the knowledge derived from existing inventions. For example, the writing tool in the form of a quill is an invention in the past. Yet, the nib pen and the fountain pen are subsequently invented based on the knowledge of the first invention. Ballpoint pen is a new invention, whereas the ballpoint pen with multi-color heads, different head thicknesses, and push button to replace the clip are developed based on the knowledge of the first invention.

Incubation

Preparation stage is followed by the incubation stage. In case that the idea is not enlightened during the preparation period, the idea inadvertently enters an incubation period. There is no specific time period for incubation. For different ideas, it takes different lengths of time. It will be days, weeks, months, years, or decades. In the incubation period, some ideas may die or otherwise be wiped out by another idea. In some cases, the inventor may die during the incubation period without disclosure of any progress of the idea. In some cases, ideas bypass the incubation stage and progress to the illumination stage rapidly.

Creative ideas progress passively in the incubation phase while the inventor is actively engaged in their routine activities. Incubation period is also known as a period of fantasizing or dreaming of an idea where it nurtured slowly. Passive engagement in information gathering, analyses, experiments, and knowledge hunting through participating in workshops, forums, and seminars are seen during the incubation period. Assimilation of information, development of knowledge, learning from experiments are major achievements perceived during this stage. Incubation is metaphorically described similar to that of a hen that incubates her eggs while living the daily life.

Illumination

Illumination is the most anticipated and anxious stage of the invention process though it is not the final stage of the process. Some inventors realize the idea in the early stages whereas many realize the creative idea accidentally in connection to some other occurrences during the incubation period. Illumination is rather abrupt than a gradual phenomenon on many occasions. In whichever the case, at the illumination stage, the idea is ignited for its feasibility. Alexander Graham Bell accidentally experienced that sound transmits through a steel rod. There, he ignited the idea that it was feasible to carry sounds from one location to another. This gave birth to the telephone many years later. Konosuke Matsushita realized the method of splitting a single electrical path into two. So, he developed the double holder and an electrical adapter that connects to one mouth of the double holder. Thomas Edison realized voice recording and replaying recorded voices on the cylindrical phonograph which led to all sorts of recording marvels thereafter.

Verification

Verification is the final stage of the invention process. After realizing the feasibility of an idea, it is essential to verify and confirm its feasibility by repeating the method until the idea is repeatedly proven feasible. This stage is described as testing and validation also. Once the idea is validated, the inventor engages in record-keeping of the procedures followed. However, it should also be remembered that some inventions are not readily useful. The world's tiniest piano, invented to the size of an inch several years back, is not useful as it does not solve any problem. Yet, the knowledge behind this invention is indirectly useful to future innovators who look for the ways to reduce size of goods and components. The tiny devices such as cameras, video cameras, radios, recorders, scanners, clocks, speakers, and microphones assembled inside a smartphone are examples of miniscule inventions.

Invention and Knowledge Creation

All the labor involved in the invention so far turns into new knowledge which is identified as an invention. In summary, entrepreneur can either invent or buy, license, franchise, or obtain inventions from the public domain. Inventions can be identified in the fields of goods, services, markets, materials, and methods. Inventions lead to production of new or better goods, services, inputs, and new or better ways of serving market, new or better methods of production, delivery, logistics, storage, advertising, and customer care. Therefore, all the innovations in the form of goods, services, materials, and methods represent the knowledge created through the invention (creative) process.[7]

Entrepreneur has the options of buying, licensing, or franchising inventions of another party by paying for it. In case of licensing or franchising, the fee involved is referred to as royalty. Inventions can be acquired free of charge at times that the inventor has not obtained legal rights for the invention. Also, inventions of governments and charity organizations are

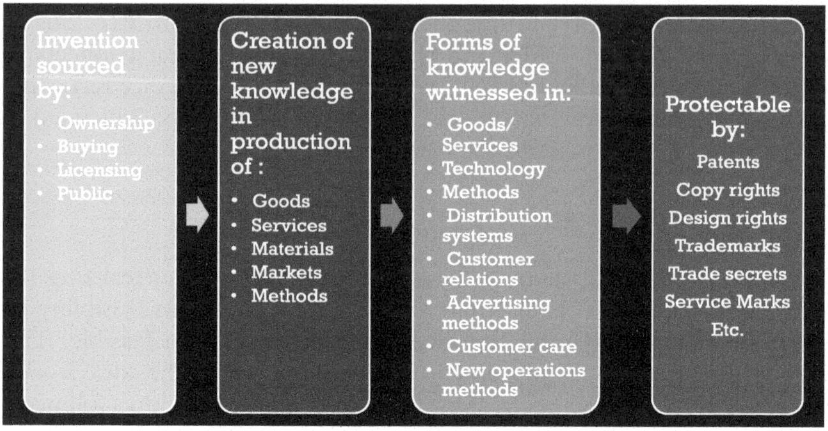

Fig. 7.3 Invention and knowledge creation (Author Portrayal)

generally available free of charge. According to Fig. 7.3, invention has a few sources, it creates new knowledge in several areas, and the original knowledge is an intellectual property that can be protected through registration of it to obtain rights in order to block infringements.

Ownership of Creativity

Governments, multinational companies, and many small and medium size companies annually spend considerable amount of money on invention which is known as Gross-domestic Expenditure on Research and Development (GERD). It is estimated that world GERD in 2020 was US$ 2.4 trillion (Refer to estimated World GDP of US$ 85 trillion). World Intellectual Property Indicators (WIPI) reports that 3.46 million patent applications, 15.5 million trademark applications, and 1.48 million industrial design applications have been placed at the Intellectual Property Offices across the world in 2022; out of which China alone filed 1.58 million patent applications. China was followed by the USA, Japan, South Korea, and Germany and they, respectively, filed 0.51 million, 0.40 million, 0.27 million, and 0.16 million patent applications. Table 7.1 indicates the magnitude of patent ownership by leading inventors.

Tables 7.2 and 7.3 summarize the figures of the Annual Report of Global Research and Development, 2021 to grasp an idea of the world

Table 7.1 World's top 20 inventors

IPO Rank	*Company*	*Country*	*Number of patents (2022)*
1	Samsung Electronics Co.	Korea R.O.	8,513
2	IBM Co.	USA	4,743
3	LG Co.	Korea R.O.	4,580
4	Toyota Motor Co.	Japan	3,056
5	Canon Co.	Japan	3,046
6	Taiwan Semiconductor Co.	Taiwan	3.038
7	Huawei Technologies Co.	China	3,023
8	BOE Technology Group	China	2,725
9	Raytheon Technologies	USA	2,684
10	Qualcomm Co.	USA	2,656
11	Sony Co.	Japan	2,638
12	Intel Co.	USA	2,501
13	Dell Technologies	USA	2,445
14	Apple Inc.	USA	2,313
15	Alphabet Inc.	USA	2,077
16	Amazon.com Inc.	USA	2,051
17	Micron Technologies Inc.	USA	1,921
18	Microsoft Co.	USA	1,888
19	Hyundai Motor Co.	Korea R.O.	1,786
20	Hitachi Ltd.	Japan	1,557

Data: Intellectual Property Organization (2022)[8]

gross R&D expenditure by corporates, countries, and regions. Out of the US$ 2.5 trillion spent in 2021 by the world, the top ten spenders contribute to almost US$ 2 trillion and out of which the USA and China alone spend UD$ 1 trillion. The new trends in R&D expenditure mark that China, India, and Asia are catching up with the West in terms of R&D expenditure as well as in intellectual property ownership, which is a mark of entrepreneurial capacity of new nations.

Innovation Process

Innovation is the most magnificent function of an entrepreneur. Innovation is the process that transforms creative ideas or concepts, generated by invention, into useful goods and services by way of organizing and creating value for resources.[10] In contrast to invention, every innovation has three distinctive features: personality, functionality, and utility. Innovation targets and exploits opportunities that arise from changes taking

Table 7.2 Top 10 spenders in R&D

Rank	*Company*	*Country*	*US$ billion*
1	Amazon.com Inc.	USA	40.43
2	Alphabet Inc.	USA	27.3
3	Huawei Technologies Co.	China	20.0
4	Microsoft Co.	USA	19.3
5	Apple Inc.	USA	18.7
6	Samsung Electronics Co.	Korea R.O.	17.8
7	Intel Co.	USA	13.2
8	Alibaba.com Inc.	China	7.4
9	IBM Co.	USA	6.3
10	Oracle Co.	USA	6.0

Data: R&D World (2021)[9]

Table 7.3 Global R&D expenditures

Region/Country	*R&D Expenditure (US$ Billion)*	*R&D Global Share (%)*
USA	609.7	25.0
China	563.7	23.2
Japan	191.0	7.8
Germany	130.0	5.3
India	96.5	4.0
Korea R.O	92.2	3.8
Top Ten Countries	**1909.8**	**78.5**
North America	658.4	27.0
South America	52.6	2.2
Europe	499.7	20.5
Africa	21.2	0.9
Middle East	57.9	2.4
Russia CIS	65.8	2.7
Asia	1,078.8	44.3
All Countries	**2,434.3**	**100.0**

Data: R&D World (2021)

place in the social, natural, and psychological spheres for making interventions. As depicted in Fig. 7.4, innovation is a process that progresses through four stages: analytical planning, organizing resources, implementation, and commercialization. Innovation leads to creation of ventures

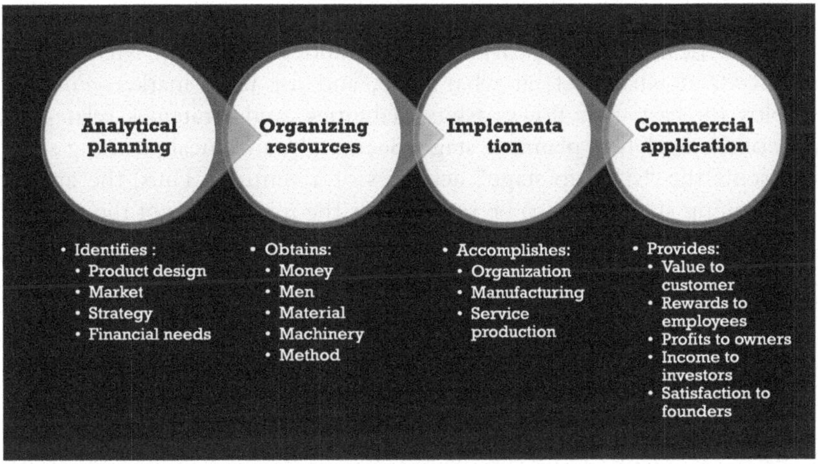

Fig. 7.4 Innovation process (Author Portrayal)

for making profit. Continuity of innovations is indispensable for growth and sustainability of a venture.[11]

Lack of innovations and delays of innovations compared to other major competitors led the multibillion-dollar US company Kodak to bankruptcy in the past decade encountering many business catastrophes like share price collapse from US$ 106 to US$ 0.17 and being kicked out from the New York Stock Exchange.[12] Therefore, innovation is a task that appears on the to-do-list always in order to avert falling behind in innovation. The CEO of Intel Corporation, the industry leader of computer processors, once stated in an interview with Japanese NHK[13] television channel that the company's technology leadership depends on steadiness of invention and innovation and even a trivial drawback could destroy its industry leadership overnight, and get defeated to a closest rival like Samsung of South Korea.

Analytical Planning

Innovation process comprises four activities: analytical planning, resource organizing, operations implementation, and commercial application. At the analytical planning stage, product analysis, market analysis, financial analysis, and strategic planning are identified as essential tasks. These analyses are helpful to recognize innovations that can reduce business risk. Analytical planning provides a prior understanding of what will be produced, at what cost, at what price, and for what market. Further, it helps forecast cash flows, assets, liabilities, and strategies related to tasks of the analytical planning stage. Seemingly, analytical planning stage represents the "start-up stage" activities of a venture. Thus, the analytical planning stage can also be regarded as the initial stage of the venture creation process.

Organizing Resources

The second stage of the innovation process involves in organizing resources. After the planning stage, production can be carried out and every production is an outcome of combinations of resources. Therefore, the resources identified need to be organized according to the operational plans already finalized. Resources basically include money, men, materials, machineries, and methods. In addition, space, plant, warehouse, and buildings for office and residence are also required. At this stage, resource identification and procurement are required to be carried out. Some of the assets and resources can be positioned at different locations according to how the production process is designed. In international entrepreneurship, location of production is chiefly determined by the Global Value Chains, Global Supply Chains, and the Smiling Curve. Unlike how Ford Corporation did in the past, for example, all operations need not be centralized at a single location at present because organizing is made easy by widespread technology, transportation, and communication.

Implementation

The third stage of the innovation process is implementation of production facility. For initiating production, founding of an organization (venture) is a prerequisite. There are many organizational types for an entrepreneur to choose from. They are proprietorship, partnership, private limited company, public limited company, and cooperatives. Proprietorships and partnerships may or may not be registered while it is mandatory for all other forms of organizations to acquire proper registration. In general, all business organizations, regardless of their legal construct, are required to obtain permissions and licenses from the local authorities, environmental agencies, and other relevant bodies for operations. Mining, material processing, manufacturing, performing medical, accounting, and legal services, selling pharmaceuticals, etc., for example, require specific permissions and licenses.

Commercial Application

The final stage of innovation process involves commercial application of the goods and services produced. Commercial application can be explained as basic selling or marketing process to achieve commercial objectives of the venture. Innovations must be capable of reconstituting the rent of all the factors of production used and satisfying all the stakeholders. In commercialization, innovations should bring about value to customers, profit to entrepreneur, income to investors, rewards to employees, satisfaction to founders, compensation to sacrifices, tax to the government, and sustainability to the firm. Accomplishment of these objectives depends on the success of commercialization of the products.

Some large businesses like multinational corporations create separate organizations for handling sales. Toyota Tsusho Corporation, for example, handles sales and develops business for the Toyota Motor Corporation. The "Smiling Curve" depicts how different stages of operations are distributed across countries. Accordingly, high innovation activities are organized by the headquarters of companies and commercialization is integrated into the headquarters generally via affiliated companies. Operations and productions are mostly sub-contracted to overseas operators or organized abroad by the company itself.

Invention, Innovation, and Venture

Figure 7.5 indicates the relationship among three functions described in the previous sections. The foremost aim of entrepreneurship is to create a venture. Venture creation requires invention that helps create knowledge required for innovation; the major function of entrepreneurship. The entrepreneurial character arises from innovation as it engages in value creation identified as consumer surplus and producer surplus without which consumers and producers, respectively, prevent from purchasing and production. The operational aspect of entrepreneurship thus, is yielded to innovations which cannot be run without forming organizations. Management comes to matter at the stage of creation of organizations.

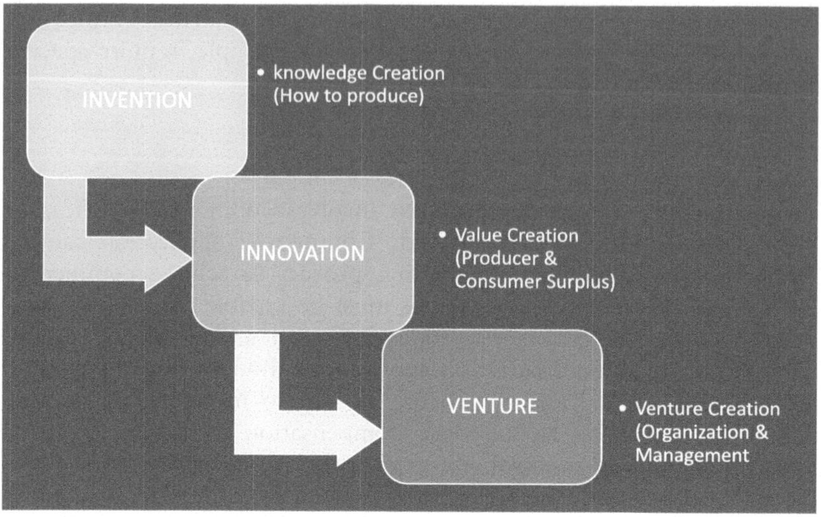

Fig. 7.5 Invention, innovation and venture (Author Portrayal)

Facets of Innovation

Mission of Innovation

Every innovation has its own mission to solve specific needs or wants. Needs are physiological and are referred to as real needs. Basic requirements such as food, water, clothes, and shelter that are essential to live a basic life are identified as needs. With the progress of living standards and living styles some wants have presently turned into needs. The goods such as vehicles, refrigerators, and mobile phones were once regarded as luxuries or wants. But now they have become needs as without them today's living is difficult. Although entrepreneurship involves addressing needs, it does not prefer a minimalist life essentially because such life only barely creates opportunities for innovations. Consumerism, on the contrary, associates a vast spectrum of needs and wants that creates innumerous opportunities for innovation.

While needs are physiological, wants are psychological and thus the latter are described as emotional needs also. In fact, wants are a set of preferences of individual persons. Thus, wants are connected to tastes, preferences, and choices of individuals. The scope of wants can spread from cheap products to luxuries and thus wants are unlimited whereas needs are limited. For example, if the need is food, the wants connected to it will be rice, meat, fish, and bread. Again, the want for fish can have further preferences such as salmon, tuna, cuttlefish, prawns, and lobsters. If the preference is for salmon, then choices such as salted salmon, smoked salmon, or raw salmon (sashimi) are considered as refined choices. In case the need is a drink, the wants related to it can have preferences such as water, tea, coffee, milk, juice, and carbonated drinks. If coffee is chosen as the want, it further extends to Georgia coffee or Java coffee. Then this is further refined as choice for black coffee, milk coffee, brewed coffee, and instant coffee. Then again, it takes further preferences such as Americano, Cappuccino, Espresso, and Mocha.

Want satisfying goods and services are produced to satisfy personal tastes, likes, and choices. And thus, the wants satisfying products tend to be innumerous as wants are infinite. Wants represent social class, living standards, personal status, professional status, personal style, and personal taste. In response to wants, entrepreneurs produce innumerous goods and services. Therefore, wants are the driving force of innovation in contrast to needs. Needs are common and wants are distinctive. As an example, in a cross section of types of wristwatches, the price range spans from one US dollar to US$ 31.19 million (Patek Philippe watch, Code 6300A-010).[14] All these watches are primarily made to indicate time. However, wearing an expensive wristwatch is a want satisfying act. A few branded products that are produced to satisfy psychological needs include Rolls-Royce cars, Gucci products, Rolex watches, Montblanc pens, and Patek Philippe watches. The want satisfying services include space trip by Tesla Co. and vacation on luxury cruise, seven-star hotel like Palm Jumeirah Hotel of Dubai.

Means of Innovation

Innovations can be brought about by several means, namely; invention, extension, duplication, and synthesis. Knowledge created by invention is converted into innovations like new products, methods, and processes. Telephone, light bulb, compact disc, plastics, conveyor belt assembly system, intercontinental parcel delivery service, computer and software, ship, and airplane are examples of innovations. Innovations, not necessarily, are state-of-the-art technology like remote sensing and artificial intelligence but also are simple products such as screw driver and screw nail. Every product, regardless of the state of technology, therefore, is an outcome of invention.

Extension is a means to develop new uses of existing goods, services, and processes. Home delivery of foods, Uber taxi service, and mobile banking are examples of extension of existing services. While traditional restaurant, taxi, and banking services continue to exist, they are extended by these means. For the conventional telephone, emailing, messaging, videoing, photographing, sound recording, scanning, storing, retrieving, navigating, and voice recognition capabilities are introduced as extensions to make the smartphone. Through development of and alteration to the existing products, extension can be exerted to a wide spectrum of goods and services. Introduction of multicolor leads to a ballpoint pen is an extension of the common ballpoint pen and the introduction of veggie-burger to the menus of the McDonald's fast-food restaurants are examples of a product extension. After an entrepreneur introduces commercially viable new product, other entrepreneurs who recognize its market potentials introduce extensions to it by adding new features and functions to differentiate their versions from the original product.

Duplication is another means of innovation. Creative replication is the method of duplication. The small burger restaurant, operated by Richard McDonald and Maurice McDonald in California, was reconstructed as McDonald's Corporation; a worldwide fast-food restaurant chain by Raymond Kroc by way of extension through franchising. The popularity and profitability of McDonald's triggered worldwide duplication of burger restaurants with similar looks. Duplication is very common among smalltime enterprises and in light-engineering manufacturing very much due to commonness of the technology and production processes. Fashionable goods, garments, and low-tech electronics are mostly duplicated among all products. Although intellectual property rights are implied to prevent duplication, advanced copies of the original goods like San-Zai products of China are not uncommon in the markets. Yet, Red Bull provides an example for legally duplicated products. Krating Daeng,[15] the energy drink produced by Chaleo Yoovidya of Thailand, was duplicated with some extensions also to innovate Red Bull by Dietrich Mateschitz of Austria to form a joint company.

Synthesis is another means of innovation. In synthesis, existing concepts are synthesized into new formulations. Here, conventional operations are combined with new systems and technologies, and newer products are made to overcome the issues persisting with the conventional products. Services sector is mostly prone to synthesized innovations. Online education, for example, is a combination of conventional teaching and the Zoom technology which together innovate better distance learning service. The conventional call-up taxi service was synthesized with telecommunication and GIS technology by Travis Kalanick and Uber Taxi Service was born. This was further synthesized with restaurants to innovate Uber Eats online delivery service. Synthesized services such as online medical services, TripAdvisor, and Booking.com are also examples of innovations under synthesis method.

Sources of Innovation

Innovations are realized through a few sources or roots: research, development, accidental discoveries, and incongruities. Among them, research is a prominent source of innovation. Research creates new knowledge useful for innovation. Fundamental research creates entirely new knowledge that never existed. Knowledge created through research spreads across various fields of production and thus is capable of generating a vast array of products. Integrated Circuit (IC), Transistor, RAM, ROM, OS, Application software, Remote sensing, and Artificial Intelligence have revolutionized the electronic industry during the past several decades since 1950s. Radio, Cassette recorder, Television, Telephone, Video player, Camera, Computer, Car electronics, Aviation, and Space electronics are examples of the goods that have emerged from the findings of fundamental research.

Another source of innovation is product development. This refers to improvements to products that are currently available in the market. Product development is achieved through improving utility, durability, reliability, quality, design, and technicality. Product development essentially engages in making better and improved products against what is existing. Following examples highlight the transformation of some products into better products; ink pen to ballpoint pen, incandescent bulbs to LED bulbs, conventional phones to smartphones, conventional cameras to digital cameras, and conventional foods to instant foods. It is obvious that research leads to new products while development leads to better products. Better products are made associating various findings of product development research and experiments.

Accidental discovery is also a source of innovation. In the process of research, an entirely different and unexpected finding can occur to the researcher. Similarly, if the research outcome goes wrong, the mistaken outcome sometimes appears to be a useful innovation. Discovery of Penicillin is a classic example of a discovery by mistake. Alexander Fleming, who had been experimenting on growth of bacteria, accidentally found a green substance killing some of his bacteria. Fleming, who was puzzled by the bacteria killing substance, redirected his research to explore the capability of the enemy of his bacteria. He isolated *Penicillium notatum* from the green substance, grew more of it, and experimented to see how many other bacteria it could kill. He found *Penicillium notatum* could kill many types of bacteria. Based on the knowledge of his accidental discovery, he innovated Penicillin, the drug many other researchers were experimenting to discover. Post-It notes, Corn flakes, Potato chips, Microwave oven, and Clay putty also are examples of innovations from accidental discoveries.

Incongruity became a source of innovation as challenging circumstances urge turning impossibilities into possibilities. Delivery of parcels and mails overnight became a need in the USA. Being a country with 4,500 kilometers from east to west, 2,500 kilometers from north to south, and 9.8 million square kilometers of land extent, fulfillment of this need was awfully challenging and beyond imagination. However, Frederick Smith who founded FedEx overcame this challenge through the innovation of mail and parcel delivery methods. Another case of incongruity is making a radio to fit into a shirt pocket in 1950s. That time, average size of a radio was a few cubic feet. Sony Corporation overcame this challenge by innovating the model TR-610, a small radio that fits into a shirt pocket. In 1979, Sony produced the pocketable cassette player, Walkman model TPS-L2.[16]

Document sharing, real-time communication, and linking via computers were unfeasible without an appropriate telecommunication device. The need for the interconnection among the researchers of Conseil Européen pour la Recherche Nucléaire (CERN) and then the scientists across the world was fulfilled after innovation of the World Wide Web (WWW) by Tim Berners-Lee in 1989. Innovation of the Modulator-Demodulator (Modem) by Bell Telephone company since many decades and innovation of the powerful search engine "Google" by Larry Page in 1998 revolutionized the data and information communication. These innovations together turned unfeasible into feasible, undoable into doable, unreachable into reachable, and telecommunication incongruities into congruities.

Steps of Innovation

Innovation involves several steps as described below.

- Recognition of real and potential needs and wants as opportunities.
- Search for sources and means of innovation.
- Organizing resources and facilities required for innovation.
- Production of goods and services to satisfy customer needs and wants.
- Continuous innovations to address changing needs and wants.
- Introducing improvements to products to make them new or better.

Types of Innovations

Innovation brings about goods, services, methods, and formulas that are supposed to be new or better products. All innovations can be classified into several products as follows. Accordingly, innovations must have two features; novelty and improvement/upgrading.

- New or better products
- New or better services
- New or better techniques for productions
- New or better ways of delivering services
- New or better practice of operations
- New or better ways of informing customers
- New or better ways of organizing business.

Forms of Innovations

Innovations can be categorized as follows based on their nature.

- **Destructive innovations**

  This has reference to Schumpeterian school of creative destruction. Some innovations wipe out existing ones and install versatile new products.[17] Following examples explain a few destructive innovations; typewriter was wiped out by the personal computer (PC), still and motion photo film was eliminated by the digital photographic devices, CRT monitors were replaced by LCD and LED monitors, quinine (an antimalarial drug) was retired by chloroquine.

- **Disruptive innovations**

  The innovations that challenge stereotype practices and break traditions, protocols, ethics, and established practices to create markets are identified as disruptive innovations.[18] Alexa Clay and Kyra Maya Phillips (2016) promulgated the notion that disruptive innovations are brought about through five routes: Hustle, Copy, Hack, Provoke, and Pivot.[19] Fashion shows, nightclubs, lunar voyage, Camel milk club of USA, and pirated goods such as software and generic drugs are examples of disruptive innovations.

- **Breakthrough innovations**

  Some innovations, in the form of entirely new products, introduce breakthroughs in human living and the society transforming conduct of the life. Electricity, gas, internet, digital technology, remote control and wireless technology, space and aviation technology, medical equipment, drugs, and treatment methods are those innovations that have made breakthroughs in many aspects of the human life.

- **Radical innovation**

  Some innovations challenge conventional goods or traditional practices but do not eradicate them. Fixing a small motor on the conventional foot bicycle led to innovation of the motor bicycle but the conventional bicycle was not eradicated by the motor bicycle. The conventional fossil fuel engine was replaced by an electric motor in automobiles while conventional autos do remain in the market.

- **Incremental innovation**

  Some innovations can continuously add value to a stable product through a long period of time. Additions such as air conditioner, power shutters, power mirrors, navigation system, audio system, ABS, and hill-assist do not change the mechanism of a motor car but are incremental to it. Smartphone also is an example for a product of incremental innovation that contains a large number of devices built into it.

- **Sustained innovation**

  Minor innovations introduced to basic food items, and garments are examples of sustained innovations. Sustained innovations are basically needed for sustaining market share. Malted milk and ice cream in different flavors, biscuits in stylish packs, and garments with different colors and designs are examples. Restaurants, bars, and salons also introduce minor innovations to their products aiming at sustaining market share.

Orientations of Innovation

Innovations can be traced to various orientations according to the purpose of innovation.

- **Imagination-based orientation**
  Products innovated based on entrepreneur's imaginations belong to this category. Pocket radio was innovated because SONY Corporation wanted to produce a small size radio to amaze radio makers and customers.
- **Problem-solving orientation**
  Some innovations aim at solving specific problems. Walkman was innovated to make music available at anyplace, anytime, and for anyone maintaining listener's privacy.
- **Exploitation orientation**
  Products are innovated to make a quick profit through exploiting market opportunities. Inferior and imitation goods with meager commitment to quality, reliability, and customer loyalty belong to this category.
- **Skill-based orientation**
  Some products are innovated purely based on skills of the innovator. Beauty salon and bakeries are operated based on specific skills and experience of the entrepreneur.
- **Material-based orientation**
  Availability and familiarity of a material urge innovation of goods from that material. Innovations of poo paper from elephant dung is an example.
- **Preference-based orientation**
  Products are innovated in the field preferred by the entrepreneur. Herbal products, authentic food, and nature goods are examples of this category.
- **Fashion orientation**

Some entrepreneurs are fond of fashionable goods and beauty products such as jewelry, garments, and shoes and thus their innovations are fashion oriented.

- **Beauty orientation**

  Beauticians innovate beauty enhancement products such as cream, lotion, hair dyes, and lipsticks and operate beauty parlors.
- **Health orientation**

  Innovation of health and medical products is a result of health orientation of the entrepreneur. Ayurvedic medicines are a common example of the entrepreneur's health orientation.
- **Art and design orientation**

  Some innovations are connected only to artistic and design skills of entrepreneur. Flower vase, simple ornamental goods, and greeting cards are outcomes of arts and design orientation.
- **Profession orientation**

  Profession and technical skills of persons mostly have connection with their innovations. After retirement and economic displacement, many engage in innovations in the fields they have gained skills and use the relationship networks they have access to.

Innovation as a Chain

Carl Menger (1871) advocated the notion to describe innovation as a chain like resource transformation process.[20] According to him, entrepreneur is the agent who undertakes resource transformation. Menger pointed out resource transformation takes place as value is added to resources of less value with an intension to produce most wanted goods compared to least wanted goods considering the demand for the most wanted goods. In the value addition chain, resources are converted from the state of "no use" to the state of "some use" or from the state of "less use to the state of more use." Accordingly, resource transformation is seen as a chain and a continuous process aimed at addressing human needs and wants and thereby earning profit.[21] The incentive for value addition is profit and profit, in turn, determines the extent to which a resource is transformed (Fig. 7.6).

The innovation chain advocated by Menger has its own logical sequences. First, entrepreneur identifies human needs and matches

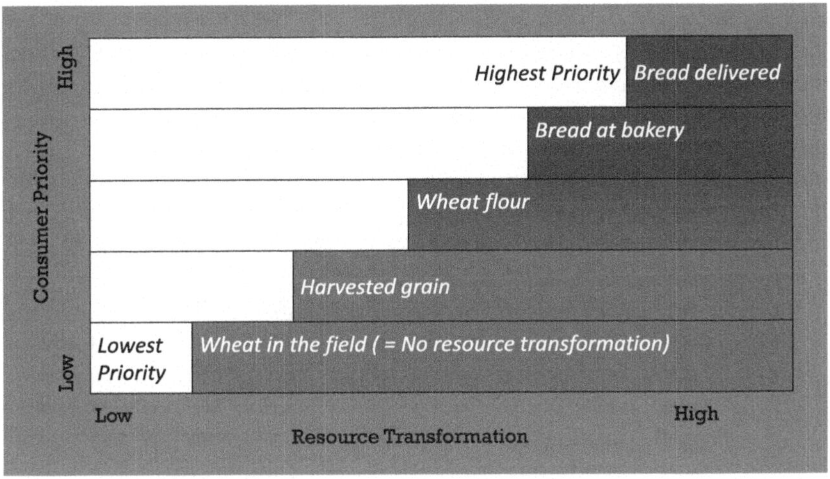

Fig. 7.6 Value addition and consumer priority ladder (*Source* Author portrayal based on Menger [1871])

resources with them. Then he specifies the resources that need to be transformed and the extent to which they need to be transformed. Second, the resources are transformed to exploit market opportunities. Third, consequent to resource transformation, useful goods and services are produced. Fourth, these goods and services are aimed at newly, differently, or better satisfying customers. Goods with this capacity qualify themselves as marketable innovations. Fifth, the convertibility of the resource and the profitability of resultant innovations determine the length of the innovation path—the value chain.

Menger's material transformation and value-added model describes that the wheat grain in the field is of least value to the customer because it cannot be readily consumed. Therefore, consumers give least priority to the grain in the field and do not demand it. But the middlemen demand the grains and collect, transport, and make them available at the market in bulk. Now the grain fetches some value because it is of some use to consumers. Thus, consumers' priority is now improved by one step. When the grain passes through further value addition to turn itself into wheat flour, the product is of high value and thus higher priority is given by consumers. The product is now easier to buy, consume, and transform into many other readily consumable goods such as bread, pastries, buns, biscuits, and cakes. Finally, at the point that the baked products are delivered to consumer's doorstep, consumers are willing to pay the highest price as the products are of the highest priority. Through this example, Menger vividly described, in a chain like metaphor, how a resource undergoes different stages of transformation, value addition, and consumer priority. Value addition to resources is perceived through conversion, changing, improvement, combination, and separation of materials.

- Conversion is a major action of innovation. Extraction of spirits from herbs, deriving polyurethane from petroleum residues, and making paper out of lumber are common examples for conversion. Conversion is most common in production process. Conversion process, depending on the conversion job, takes simple to complex forms. Conversion of timber into wooden furniture is a simple form while conversion of crude oil into lubricant is a complex form.
- Changing includes the actions that alter the original shape, chemistry of resource, place of availability, and available amounts of a good or a resource. All these actions add value to a product. Trade is the most common practice among exerting change. Place of availability is changed via transportation of goods to locations where customers want to buy them. Changing the texture of iron ores through melting to make pig iron and steel, changing raw vegetables and grains through cooking to make food, changing the form of plastic to produce various goods and materials, changing to produce new goods via changing appearance, shape, size, weight, taste, and fragrance of existing goods, changing for introducing new uses such as alcohol into hand sanitizer, changing plant properties to produce genetically altered varieties, changing the form and extract substances and spirits, changing the sale quantity from wholesale to retail, changing temperature from warm to cold or vice versa; hot coffee to iced coffee or iced coffee to hot coffee, are examples for the action of change.
- Examples for action of improvement include improving the quality of rough furniture by polishing them, improving the water quality by treating, improving beauty through treatment, improving fitness through gym, improving knowledge through education, and improving health through medical services. Improvement is a common action in relation to most of the goods that not only include consumables but technologies, processes, and services also.

- Combination is a practice adopted in most production processes. Almost all industries like education, hospitality, and manufacturing, combination practice is very common. Manufacturing of computers, vehicles, airplanes, ships, cement, ceramic, garments, and foods such as cakes, biscuit, and buns are combinations of different components or ingredients. In modern manufacturing culture, value chains and assembly lines are constructed to exert combination action to finish a product. Beautification service such as giving a facial treatment is an outcome of combination of many beauty goods. Therefore, both goods and services require combination of components, ingredients, and parts to finish a product.
- The action of separation is seen in oil refineries to remove additives from crude oil at different levels to produce different fuel types for vehicles, ships, and airplanes. Separation of life of an animal to obtain meat, separation of a salvage vehicle into auto parts for re-use, separation of additives from metals and minerals, and separation of substances from plants are some examples. Separation is carried out through sifting, winnowing, silting, and melting also. After separation, crudeness is removed and usability is improved. All these value addition actions or a few can be seen in every product we consume.

Innovation Path

Figures 7.7 and 7.8 depict innovation path constructed based on the Menger's proposition. This graph plots value addition (and the consumer priority) on axis X and the profit level on axis Y. The resulting innovation path indicates positive relationship between value addition and profit. The sub-line rising from the normal innovation path depicts super innovation that indicates higher innovation and higher profit. Normal innovation path is connected to the value addition process that starts from the point where the live chicken is for sale and to the point where barbequed chicken is served. This graph indicates the possibilities for an entrepreneur to deviate from normal chicken processing to other innovations as KFC does. Varied chicken dishes unique to KFC are of higher value addition and they create higher profit. These alternatives suggest that transformation of materials can vary and produce super innovations on the capability of entrepreneur to generate higher value to the customer which, in turn, generates producer surplus that creates higher gains to the producer.

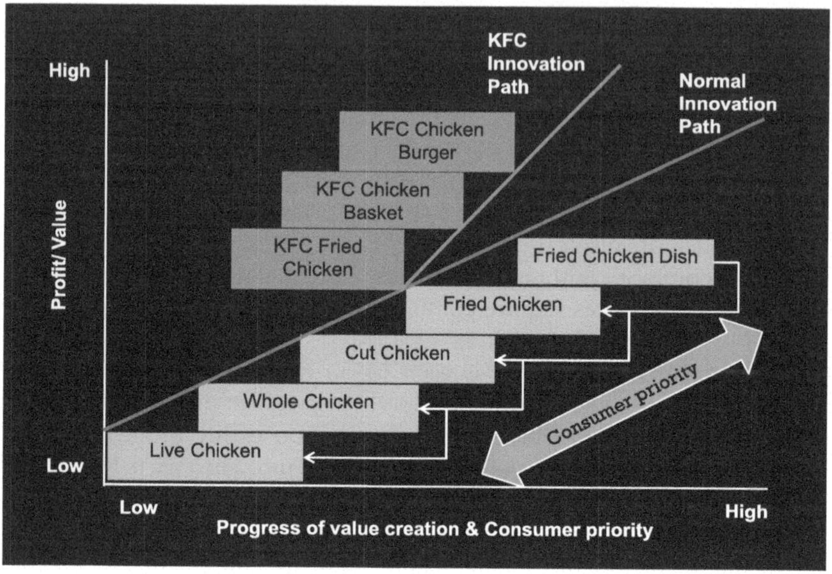

Fig. 7.7 Innovation path (Author Portrayal)

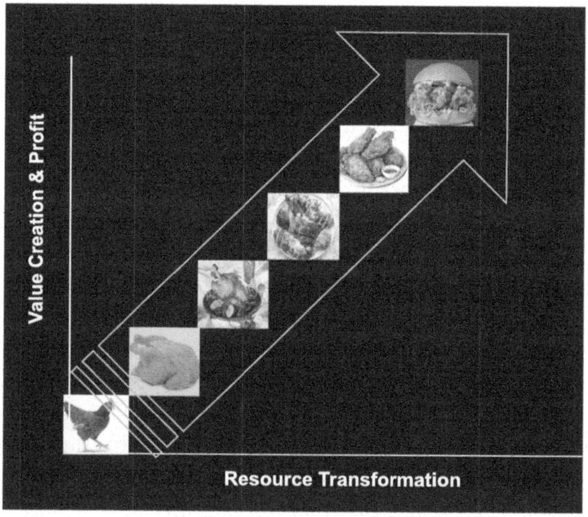

Fig. 7.8 Innovation path—example (Author Portrayal)

Innovation Power

While different degrees of innovations associate different levels of value creation and profits, characteristics of resources also have bearings on the value creation process. Some resources have immense possibilities to innovation whereas some others do not. In Fig. 7.9, three different situations of value creations are considered. They are super innovation, normal innovation, and limited innovation according to the inherent characteristics of resources. These concepts are described taking three different types of resources into consideration: wheat flour, rice flour, and millet flour.

First, let us assume that the super innovation path is connected to wheat flour and cake made of it as the highest value-added product. Among all wheat-based products, cake can generate the highest profit. The entrepreneurs who are in cake business thus, usually post higher earnings (point C). Second, rice flour is assumed as connected to the average innovation path. Rice flour is less versatile and thus, it is assumed that the best possible value addition to it is oilcake. Compared to cake, oilcake is less prioritized in consumption and thus it generates less profit at point B.

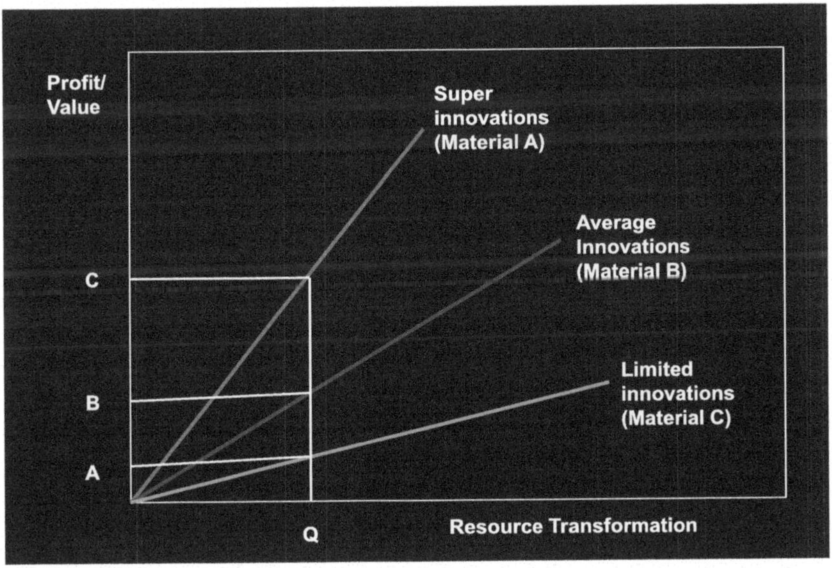

Fig. 7.9 Innovation power (Author Portrayal)

Third, let us assume millet flour as the resource connected to the limited innovation path. The highest value-added product of millet flour would be the "leaf waffle" which is least prioritized by consumers among these three products. Thus, millet flour has the least possibility to bring about innovations and value addition as indicated at point A.

When value addition possibility of all the three types of flour is set at Q, it is obvious that each resource generates differential profits at A, B, and C, respectively. This concludes that resources have differential possibilities to value addition. The higher the possibility of value addition, the greater the possibility of earnings. The earning differentials between millet waffle maker and the cake maker is the case in point. Obviously, the entrepreneur who makes cakes would create more personal wealth than that of the millet waffle maker. This discussion assumes that the resource transformation technology, consumer behavior, and invention and innovation capabilities of entrepreneurs are fixed.

Innovation path, in practice, can pass through three stages: growth, saturation, and decline. When innovation cannot hold onto its growth momentum, it saturates and then declines. Innovative momentum is determined by three factors: entrepreneurial capability, managerial capability, and external environment. The weakening innovative power results in weak value addition and lower profit. Highest profit level is reached when innovation is at its top and profitability starts to diminish thereafter. Thus, it is irrational for an entrepreneur to cling onto the same products seeking higher profit. As an option, entrepreneur can re-innovate the product to add more value. Declining stage suggests the entrepreneur to re-make the product, reengineer production, or retrench.

Innovative power rests on either scientific or traditional knowledge. When either of these knowledges is lacking, innovations tend to lag. If, again, the above examples of different resources are considered here, the innovations based on them are seen largely different across nations. For instance, Japan possesses both scientific and traditional knowledge to add high value to rice. Out of rice, Japanese make variety of extremely high value-added Mochi (rice-cake) whereas Sri Lankans make low value-added rice cakes. Also, Japanese possess both scientific and traditional knowledge to produce rice biscuit, rice porridge, Nigiri, pre-cooked rice, pre-cooked rice and curry, rice bread, Sushi, and rice wine (Sake). Japanese entrepreneurs possess fine knowhow to produce an opulent flooring material, Tatami, out of paddy straws. But Sri Lanka, as a rice grower, does not possess any of these knowledges to innovate high value-added goods out of rice. Americans produce refined goods such as cornflakes, corn soup, and corn plastic out of corn. Sri Lanka, too, grows corn but has no knowledge in innovating higher value-added goods out of corn. Therefore, it is an important fact that materials themselves as well as the knowledge base of a nation determine innovative power differentials.

Chapter Summary

Invention process, also known as the creative process, creates knowledge required for innovation. The knowledge referred to herein relates not only to invention of prototype, but also designs, formula, and product presentation. The knowledge created by invention is an intellectual property that can be legally protected as a right of the inventor by means of patents, copyrights, design rights, trademarks, and trade secrets. When legally owned, the invention becomes an asset of the inventor. So, the invention can be sold, licensed, or franchised. Though invention is indispensable for innovation, it is not inevitable for an entrepreneur to invent or possess it because inventions can be acquired, licensed, or bought from their owners. Invention is licensed or franchised at a fee called royalty. Yet, unregistered inventions and those of governments and charity organizations are available free of charge.

Invention process takes the following steps: idea germination, preparation, incubation, illumination, and verification. Backed by curiosity, idea germination is equivalent to conceiving of an idea as a solution to a need or want-related problem. Gathering additional knowledge, and experimentation are directed to explore the idea from every perspective at the preparation stage. If a breakthrough is not experienced during the preparation period, the idea inadvertently enters an incubation period where it nurtures slowly and progresses passively. Illumination is mostly an abrupt and accidental ignition of the idea that ends the incubation period. Illumination is realization of the idea for its feasibility. The idea is then repeatedly tested, verified, validated, and confirmed for its feasibility by using the methods or process followed.

Entrepreneur can invent, buy, license, franchise invention or obtain it free of charge from the public domain. Invention provides knowledge to produce new or better goods, services, materials, production methods, mode of serving market, delivery, logistics, storage, advertising, and customer care. In 2020, Gross Expenditures for Research and Development (GERD) has been US$ 2.4 trillion (Refer to World GDP of US$

85 trillion) of which the share of top 10 countries including the USA, China, Japan, and Germany is almost US$ 2 trillion in which the USA and China alone shared almost 50% of it. World Intellectual Property Indicators 2022 (WIPI) reports 3.46 million applications have been filed across the globe. The highest number of patents are claimed by, respectively, Samsung, IBM, LG, Toyota, and Canon in 2022 and their total number is 27,500 patents.

Innovation transforms creative ideas generated by invention process into useful goods, services, processes, and methods. Innovation process progresses through four stages: analytical planning, organizing resources, implementation, and commercialization. Innovations target opportunities that arise from changes taking place in the socioeconomic, natural, and psychological spheres and produce new or better and useful marketable products seeking profit. Innovations initiate with identifying real and potential needs and wants and continue to innovate products that can better address changing needs and wants.

The mission of innovation is to intervene in solving needs and wants-related problems of people and thus, innovations such as products, methods, and processes must have three distinctive features: personality (features), functionality, and utility. Innovations are realized through a few sources: research, development, accidental discoveries, and incongruities. Innovations are brought about by several means such as invention, extension, duplication, or synthesis. Also, innovations appear in a few types: goods, services, methods, means, and formulas. The character of innovations is described as destructive, disruptive, breakthrough, radical innovation, incremental, or sustained innovations. Innovations are orientated on imagination, skill, material, preference, problem-solving desire, exploiting purpose, art and design, fashions, beauty, and health.

Carl Menger advocated innovation as a process of resource transformation. Accordingly, entrepreneur undertakes to add value to resources with the purpose of making them the most sought for goods in contrast to the least wanted state in the form of a resource. In this process, resources are converted from the state of "no use" to the state of "some use" or from the state of "less use to the state of more use." Innovation Path introduced in this chapter identifies three paths of innovations: average, limited (below average), and above average (super). Every innovation path passes through three stages of its life: growth, saturation, and decline. When innovation cannot hold onto its value creation momentum, it saturates and then declines. This is determined by three factors: innovation capability, managerial capability, and external factors.

Review Questions

1. What is invention and why is it important in entrepreneurship?
2. "Invention turns out to be an intellectual property of a person or an organization." Elaborate.
3. Explain the invention process through the following steps;
    a. Idea germination
    b. Preparation
    c. Incubation
    d. Illumination
    e. Verification.
4. Describe the relationship between interdependence of the invention process and the innovation process.
5. Conduct a mini web survey to find R&D expenditures and intellectual property rights of nations in the recent years.
6. Explain the importance of and the need for research and development effort for entrepreneurs.
7. Describe the innovation process referring to the following steps;
    a. Analytical planning
    b. Organizing resources
    c. Implementation
    d. Commercial application.
8. Describe the vision and mission of innovation and by which means innovations are accomplished.
9. Provide an account on the sources of innovations. Describe each with a specific example.
10. "Innovation is not confined to goods." Expand this statement introducing other types of innovations also into your list.
11. Describe the features of the following forms of innovations;
    a. Destructive innovation
    b. Disruptive innovation
    c. Breakthrough innovation

d. Radical innovation
e. Incremental innovation
f. Sustained innovation.

12. What are the orientations of innovations? Enquire into the reasons behind different orientations.
13. Depict the relationship among resource conversion, innovation, demand priority, value creation, and profit and derive an innovation path specific to your example.
14. Explain, with examples, the possibilities of adding extraordinary value in the resource transformation process deviating from the normal innovation path.

Additional Readings

1. Arthur, W.B., 2007. The structure of invention. *Research Policy*, *36*(2), pp. 274–287.
2. Schoen, J., Mason, T.W., Kline, W.A. and Bunch, R.M., 2005. The innovation cycle: A new model and case study for the invention to innovation process. *Engineering Management Journal*, *17*(3), pp. 3–10.
3. Kanagavel, P., 2003. Intellectual property rights: A comprehensive overview. *Journal of the Patent and Trademark Office Society*, *85*, p. 663.
4. Carayannis, E.G. ed., 2020. *Encyclopedia of creativity, invention, innovation and entrepreneurship*. Cham: Springer International Publishing.
5. Holt, D.H., 2000. *Entrepreneurship: New venture creation*. New Delhi: Prentice-Hall of India.
6. https://panasonic.net/electricworks/about/history.html.
7. Bergman Jr, B.J., and McMullen, J.S., 2020. Entrepreneurs in the making: Six decisions for fostering entrepreneurship through maker spaces. *Business Horizons*, *63*(6), pp. 811–824.
8. https://www.wipo.int/publications/en/series/index.jsp?id=37.
9. https://forecast.rdworldonline.com/.
10. Barnard, B., and Herbst, D., 2018. Entrepreneurship, innovation and creativity: The creative process of entrepreneurs and innovators. *Available at SSRN 3195912*.

11. Carayannis, E.G., Samara, E.T., and Bakouros, Y.L., 2015. Innovation and entrepreneurship. *Theory, Policy and Practice*, p. 218.
12. Gershon, R.A., 2013. Innovation failure: A case study analysis of Eastman Kodak and Blockbuster Inc. In *Media management and economics research in a transmedia environment* (pp. 62–84). Routledge.
13. https://www3.nhk.or.jp/nhkworld/.
14. https://www.patek.com/en/home.
15. https://www.kratingdaeng.co.id/.
16. https://www.walkman-archive.com/gadgets/walkman_sony_01_tps-l2_eng_v3.htm.
17. Garcia-Macia, D., Hsieh, C.T., and Klenow, P.J., 2019. How destructive is innovation? *Econometrica*, *87*(5), pp. 1507–1541.
18. Christensen, C., Raynor, M.E., and McDonald, R., 2013. *Disruptive innovation*. Brighton, MA, USA: Harvard Business Review.
19. Clay, A., and Phillips, K.M., 2016. *The Misfit Economy: Lessons in creativity from pirates, hackers, gangsters and other informal entrepreneurs*. Simon and Schuster.
20. Menger, C., 1950. *Principles of economics* (J. Dingwall and D.F. Hoselitz Glencoe, trans.) Illinois: Free Press. (Original work published 1871).
21. Kirzner, I.M., 1978. The entrepreneurial role in Menger's system. *Atlantic Economic Journal*, 6(3), pp. 31–45.

CHAPTER 8

Intellectual Property Rights Registration

Key Learning Points

- Introduction.
- Determinants of intellectual property.
- Sources of intellectual property.
- Intellectual property and entrepreneurial strength.
- Types of intellectual properties.
- Inventions and intellectual properties.
- Intellectual property protection against counterfeiting.
- Registering rights of intellectual property.
- Intellectual property rights laws.
- World Intellectual Property Organization (WIPO).
- National and local Intellectual Property Organizations.
- UNESCO and WTO in intellectual property protection.
- Types of intellectual property rights.
- Copyrights.
- Patent Rights.
- Trademark.
- Design Right.
- Trade Secrets.
- Image Right.
- Procedures for intellectual property right registration.

© The Author(s), under exclusive license to Springer Nature Singapore Pte Ltd. 2024

M. Rajaratne, *Concepts, Processes and Practice of Entrepreneurship*, Palgrave Studies in Global Entrepreneurship,
https://doi.org/10.1007/978-981-97-6180-7_8

Introduction

The most precious, important, and useful property of a venture is its inventions and innovations; unique knowledge and the goods or services produced and commercialized. Venture success relies chiefly on production and sales of useful goods or services to customers. Lack of useful goods or services is a mark of lack of inventions and innovations. Successful inventions and innovations are an indicator of profitability also. Therefore, always, there is a threat of counterfeiting successful goods and services to siphon profit from lucrative markets.[1] Once counterfeited products enter the market, the market share of the original innovator tends to lose. This situation is counterproductive to the venture as it already has spent significant amount of money on research and development, machineries, facilities, plants, and personnel training and finds it will be difficult to recover the initial investment or attain reasonable return on investment.[2] Counterfeit can also retard entrepreneurial spirit. This unpleasant, challenging, and formidable experience urges authentic entrepreneurs to develop anti-counterfeit measures. Anti-counterfeit measures are exerted through intellectual property (IP) rights. Intellectual property rights can protect inventions as counterfeiter knows counterfeiting of registered intellectual property is an infringement of intellectual property law. In case of counterfeiting, the intellectual property right holder can file lawsuits to claim damages from the infringing party.[3]

Inventions and Intellectual Properties

Intellectual property rights aim at providing legal protection against counterfeiting research findings, formula, trade secrets, product designs, and any other original ideas. The goods that cannot easily be counterfeited help the venture to operate without challenges. But most ventures that do not possess strong brand names often face counterfeit challenge.[4] Therefore, it is imperative for the entrepreneur to be proactive to protect their findings, goods, and services. World Intellectual Property Organization (WIPO) established in Geneva is the international office where an entrepreneur can register his intellectual property internationally.[5] Entrepreneurs also can register their intellectual property at local office of a federal state or a country.

National Intellectual Property Organization (NIPO)[6] of Sri Lanka, United States Patent and Trademark Office (USPTO),[7] Japan Patent Office (JPO) are examples for country office of intellectual property registration. Original knowledge and works are recognized as intellectual property by the United Nations,[8] GATT, World Trade Organization,[9] and governments also. So, the counterfeiters, if caught, will have to face litigation at local or international courts depending on the relevance of jurisdiction of the counterfeit case. Intellectual properties can thus be protected through legal enactments such as copy rights, patents, trademarks, design rights, trade secrets, and image rights.[10]

Types of Intellectual Properties

Intellectual property becomes a right only if it is duly registered by the original inventor or innovator at an Intellectual Property Rights office. This helps entrepreneur to legally claim rights for the creative works and to protect creative ideas against infringement. Major works are registered as intellectual properties under persisting laws whereas less important works are not protected. When registering intellectual properties, owner can target protecting the following creativities.[11]

- Literary and artistic works
- Plays, films, and musical works
- Computer programs and databases
- Drawings, paintings, photographs, and sculptures
- Architectural designs
- Performances such as sound recordings and broadcasts
- Inventions such as unique knowledge and technologies
- Industrial plans, designs of goods, machineries, shops
- Trademarks, service marks, commercial names
- Images and designations
- Layout designs of integrated circuits
- Plant and crop varieties
- Geographical indications
- Undisclosed information including trade secrets
- Secret formula.

Intellectual Property Protection

In addition to intellectual property protection, an entrepreneur can seek protection against unfair competition also under the international legal frameworks such as Anti-dumping, Antitrust, Anti-monopoly, and Fair-trade laws. These laws entrust entrepreneur with legal rights to thwart trade-related damage. As intellectual property is an individual or corporate right, the owner can use or otherwise sell or license it at a fee.

Intellectual Property Rights have been recognized by several international conventions considering the importance of technology advancement, business development, economic growth, human creativity, employment generation, and social progress resulting from intellectual properties. Geneva based World Intellectual Property Organization (WIPO) of the United Nation Organization is the main global agency that protects and promotes intellectual property rights. It administers 26 international conventions on intellectual property and has 191 member states.[12]

In addition, UNESCO monitors the Universal Copyright Convention. The World Trade Organization monitors the Trade-Related Intellectual Property Rights Agreement (TRIPRA) whereas the International Union for the Protection of New Varieties of Plants monitors the International Convention for the Protection of New Varieties of Plants.[13] Further, copyright and patent right offices are established by individual countries from which entrepreneurs can obtain rights to protect their creativities. Entrepreneur can protect their products simultaneously through claiming more than one right. For example, Coke is simultaneously protected by trade secret, trademark, design right, and patent.[14]

Intellectual Property Registration

Designated process is laid down for registration of intellectual property of a person or an organization. The person or organization that contemplate to register intellectual property is required to approach the Intellectual Property Office of the relevant country and submit an application to obtain registration for the rights being claimed. If the rights are claimed internationally, registration must be obtained from WIPO. A country office of intellectual property rights can register rights confining to its jurisdiction areas. However, intellectual property can be registered in multiple countries also if required. To seek protection in a large number of countries, an entrepreneur chooses to register intellectual properties in multiple locations; countries or states as applicable.[15]

In the USA, each state has its own Intellectual Property Office and thus registration is required in each state as IP registration in one state is not valid in another state. Steps involved in intellectual property registration can slightly vary across countries and states because they adopt different legal systems. While Fig. 8.1 depicts a simple flow process of Intellectual Property registration, the steps given below present a general procedure of IP registration.[16]

1. Obtain a trademark application from the Intellectual Property (IP) office.
2. Submission of the duly filled Trademark Application to the IP office.

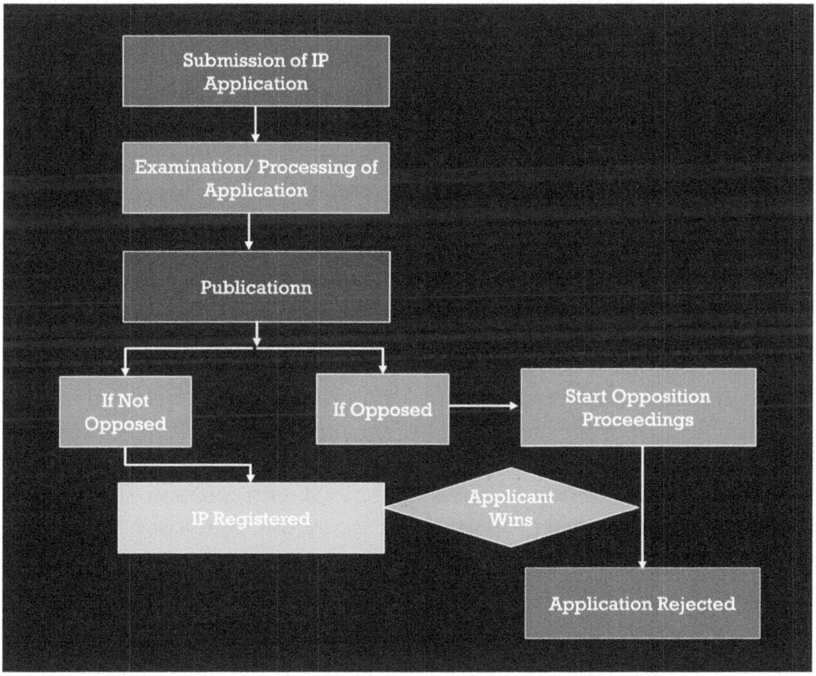

Fig. 8.1 Intellectual property registration procedure (Author Portrayal)

1. A number will be allocated to the application and acknowledgment will be given by the IP office.
2. Opening a file for the application at the IP office.
3. Examination of the claim to see whether the applicant's claim is acceptable under the IP law.
4. Payment of the fee for publication of the Mark if the claim is accepted.
5. Mark is published in the Government Gazette.
6. Period of three months will be given to any party to lodge objections to the Mark published.
7. If there are no objections within three months, the applicant will be asked to pay the registration fee.
8. Upon payment of the fee, Mark will be registered.
9. Certificate of a Registration of Mark will be issued by the IP office to the claimer.
10. Maintaining the registered Trademark (Change of name, and or address, alterations of the Mark, and renewal).

Intellectual Property Rights

Entrepreneur must be aware of his rights at the early stage of invention and innovation as both these creativities can be protected through property rights laws. At both invention and innovation stages, creativities are originated with or without the knowledge of entrepreneur. Yet, those creativities qualify for registration as originalities which then become rights. Entrepreneur's failure to recognize own originalities will cause loss of the grip of protection. Once the originalities are exposed in the commercialization process without or prior to obtaining legal rights, useful intellectual properties will transfer to the hands of competitors who are free to use them as infringement laws do not apply. Therefore, from the early stage and during business operations, entrepreneur should keep track on their intellectual properties and secure due protection under suitable method or methods. For example, Coca-Cola protects the bottle of Coke through patent right, copyright, trademark, trade secret, and design right obtained for several of its features. Entrepreneur can choose protection methods from the following as applicable.[17]

Copyrights

Copyright provides legal protection for original ideas and their expressions. Copyright protection is automatically exerted even without proper registration. Unlike patents and trademarks, the author of the work need not assert the rights of ownership of his work with special effort; so, copyright registration is not mandatory. In many instances, copyright notice is indicated by the one who claims copyright with © and the statement "All Rights Reserved." However, copyright registration is useful in case of a litigation against copyright infringement. Whether registered or not, copyrights last for the life of the author plus 70 more years. Copyrights can be claimed for original works such as arts, literature, music, movies, sound recording, broadcasts, computer programs, and databases written or presented in a tangible or visible form.[18]

The owner of a copyrighted work has the right to reproduce their work. Production of derivative work like movie or a drama based on a book and the works of repetitive nature such as movie, drama, and song infringe copyright laws unless the author's permission is obtained and royalty is paid. Products that carry many features worthy to be copyrighted can be discretely protected by the copyright laws. For instance, images and word-arts appear on a product or its packaging, labels and product names, product itself like a book, and distinctive webpages can be protected by copyright laws.[19]

Literary and artistic works associated with products are also protectable under copyright law. Compared to other protection methods, copyright registration is inexpensive method. Copyright owner often finds the attorney fees are greater than the damage caused by copyright infringements. So, the copyright law allows the owner to demand attorney fees from the infringers. The provisions for demanding attorney fees from an infringer carry significant influence on the infringer to refrain from infringement or to early settlement of a case. This advantage prevails, for the owner, only if the copyright is registered. Otherwise, the copyright owner, the suing party, is obliged to bear the attorney fees or else, a separate lawsuit is required for him to claim that expense.

Copyright laws protect only the original works that are fixed to a tangible medium of expression. This means that the literary or creative works that seek copyright must be in written, printed, electronic, or any other tangible form. Examples of copyrightable works include movies, videos, photos, books, diaries, articles, and software. Copyright does not protect scientific formula, recipe, engineering designs, knowhow, ideas, and information which can be protected under patent rights. While a software program is a patentable item, its creative features can be protected by copyrights. Copyright is automatically secured to the author or creator at the time a product of creative expression is made in a tangible form. The works of the above characteristics created on or after January 1, 1978 are eligible for copyright protection for the author's life plus 70 years. The enforcement of copyright law may be limited to local or national jurisdictions. Copyright can be enforced internationally if the countries concerned have entered into international copyright conventions.[20]

Patent Rights

Patent is a right granted for any original and inventive device, substance, method, or process. Patent blocks others using, producing, or selling the patented items without a permission of the patent owner. Patents are registered to individuals, groups, or an organization or both as inventors. Patent owner has rights to permit or license the patent for others to use in production. Patent owner also has the option to sell their patent rights to another party. Patents are sometimes registered in foreign countries also for the purpose of making the international competitors aware of the patent owner. This will help others to contact the registered owner of the patent in case of purchasing or licensing the patent. Once registered, a patent protects the rights of the owner for a period of 20 years.[21]

Patents are of two types: Utility patents and Design patents. Utility patent protects a useful machine, process, manufacture, and composition of a matter. Design patent protects the ornamentation features of a product such as appearance, look, and shape. Entrepreneur must identify the most suitable type of patent among the two or consider both the types to simultaneously protect his right of original works. When an entrepreneur believes the utility (function) of an invention is of prime importance, utility patent would be a more suitable protection for that invention. But if aesthetic features of the invention are considered as more important, design patent would be the right option of protection. When entrepreneur finds both utility and design are significant aspects of the invention, patent rights must be obtained to protect both the aspects.

In case of meager funds, entrepreneur is compelled to select one type of patent that better suits to protect the invention. In this instance, entrepreneur should select the strongest aspect of the invention to be patented. Design patents are useful for barring sale of counterfeits. In international trade, goods identical to the original goods can be blocked at the Customs when imported. Once counterfeit goods are imported, the producers, importers, distributors, sellers, and users can be sued for infringement of the patent. The authority in relation to exerting patent rights laws, however, is agreed upon by the relevant trading partners.

By obtaining design patent, entrepreneur can block others from selling products that look like the original products. Several design patents can be obtained to protect different aspects of a single product in case the product is versatile in its designs. For example, Apple iPhone is protected for the housing design, logo design, container and packing design, and appearance of the icons on the phone screen. While the term for a utility patent is generally 20 years, design patent covers 15 years from the grant date of the patent.[22]

Trademarks

Trademark is a right that is granted over a word, phrase, letter, number, sound, smell, shape, logo, picture, or packaging that a firm uses to represent its products or services. Trademark distinguishes goods or services from other competitive products. Trademarks can be commonly identified as names, phrases, sounds, or symbols used in association with goods or services. For example, Cable News Network (CNN) is protected with the following trademarks; name—"CNN," word-art—cursive artwork with white line depicting CNN between two red lines, and unique music intro. All major manufacturers, Traders, IT companies, Family restaurants, showcase their trademark identity. Trademark often connects a brand to represent the quality of goods and services for building reputation. Trademark protection initially lasts for 10 years after registration but can be renewed thereafter for periods that the entrepreneur wishes.[23]

Trademark is essential to build business reputation. Therefore, entrepreneur should initially register trademark to block potentials for another person using the trademark. Unregistered trademarks are sometimes used by other persons and when such action is discovered, the original user will have to adopt alternative trademark. Ironically, the entrepreneur who originally used the trademark without registering it might later face trademark infringement case for using their own trademark which others have registered as of theirs. Name of a product and name of the maker (company) or the symbolic representation of the company are considered as trademarks. Under trademark law, a trademark is anything by which customers recognize a product or the source (maker) of a product. Therefore, trademark is typically the words, names, or symbols associated with the product or service. Trademarks made up of words are considered as wordmarks; SONY is an example. The word-art name "MITSUBISHI" is an example for wordmark while its three-diamond symbol is a trademark. Trademark protects the company name as well as the products that are introduced under the company name or logo.[24]

Trademarks are imbued with sound, color, design, shape, fragrance, slogan, flavor, or any other thing of a product that can remind customers of the original product or its producer. If a product reminds the customer of another product or a maker that they have consumed or seen in the past, the latter is a counterfeit. The most common types of trademarks are wordmarks, logos, and slogans attached to a product. If the product configuration and packaging can recall the maker of the goods, such configuration can be protected and registered as a trademark. A trademark can merely be used without registration at the start-up stage, but it is important to be registered as the venture grows. The feel, taste, design, features, appearance, logo, symbol, fragrance, color, and slogan of a product and the goodwill, loyalty, history, and trustworthiness of the firm are the hallmarks of trademark.

Before using or registering a trademark, a search for trademarks should be conducted to find out whether the same is being used by someone or already registered. If the proposed trademark is not registered or not being used by another party, trademark application process can be initiated. In fact, registration of a trademark is optional because a trademark is simply accrued to the user of it if it has been a unique mark in commerce for a significantly long period of time. When selling a product or performing a service under a brand name, without registration, trademark rights can be asserted under the common law in a smaller geographical region where the brand name is used. In this instance, it is not obligatory for the entrepreneur to register the trademark at the Trademark Office. In case of a litigation, the attachment to and association with the trademark has to be proven with historical evidence by the original user of it. Trademark registration allows entrepreneur to secure trademark rights beyond a small locality. Trademark can also be registered in wider jurisdiction areas covering a state, country, region, or the world. Wider coverage of trademark protection is sought by national and international scale businesses.[25]

Design Rights

Design is the appearance of a product that gives it a unique expression. It could be a logo, brand name, trademark, packaging, shape, artwork, or word-art. Registered design is an exclusive right that the owner can commercially use, license, or sell. Design registration gives legal rights for the entrepreneur to appeal against unauthorized use and counterfeiting of his design. In essence, design right helps protect the way a product looks. In case that the design has a technical function of the product or the design naturally relates to utility of the product, design right may not be a suitable method of protection. But patent can be more suitable for protection of products with aforementioned design. A design must be new, unique, and registered in overseas jurisdiction in order for claiming right. A design is not registrable if the design is indecent, culturally offensive, dictated by the very technical function of the product, or does not possess uniqueness.[26]

There are legal provisions for the protection of unregistered designs also. The protection granted to the owner of an unregistered design is different to that of a registered design. Therefore, the entrepreneur should properly weigh the merits and demerits of design registration and consult legal advisors before making decision to or not to register the design. Design rights can protect the whole or a part of a product. The appearance of a product, lines and contours, colors, shape, texture, materials, or ornamentation of the product can be separately registered. For instance, while a motor car itself is a design, its parts such as headlamps, tail lamps, doors, seats, and meter board also have designs that can be protected separately by design rights.

Legal rights prevail for designs in three different forms: unregistered design rights, registered design rights, and artistic copyright (the copyright law was described in the earlier section). Unregistered design rights and copyright arise automatically and thus the owner is provided with exclusive rights against the designs being copied. However, because there are limitations on unregistered design rights, it is always better for the entrepreneur to register designs where possible in order to maintain design-based competitiveness and to prevent others from copying the same design. Design registration is a formal step to claim design rights.

Once the design is registered, the owner is granted rights to license or sell it. If the owner wishes to stop production of goods belonging to a certain design or a model, they still can license or sell the design during the valid period of the design rights.

After registration, design rights last for 5 years initially. But the rights can be renewed for up to 25 years stepwise thereupon. For unregistered designs, rights arise automatically and last for a period of 10 years counted from the end of the year of first commercialization of a product connected to a certain design. This period will be limited to 15 years from the end of the year when the product was first designed but no products were sold since then for a period of 5 years. Unregistered design rights are restricted to shape and configuration of a product. There is a version of unregistered design rights in Europe referred to as "unregistered community design right." The term for the community unregistered design right will live up to 3 years after creation.[27]

Product design helps with branding and creating image of a business. Thus, design serves as an intangible asset which has monetary value. The design rights holder can, therefore, license the design to another party under commercially agreed terms. Like trademarks, design rights can be registered in one country, group of countries such as European Union, and worldwide. Following factors are considered when granting design rights.

1. Product novelty (design must be new, and not the same as any design which is already publicly available).
2. Individual character (design must have individual character, the overall impression of the design that is different from the appearance of already known designs).
3. Appearance of the product (which must not be wholly determined by its technical function).

Trade Secrets

Trade secrets can be a formula, pattern, device, or compilation of data that grant an advantage over competitors. To protect a secret, a business must prove that the secret adds value to the company. Restricting trade secrets to a handful of senior executives is common practice of companies. Trade secret is a valuable information possessed and protected by a firm. The owner of the secret has to prove that "reasonable" measures are taken to maintain secrecy. Secrets include information such as business plans, customer lists, research findings, and ideas related to research and development. Trade secrets are neither submitted for approval nor accepted by government agency for examination, approval, or registration. Thus, to establish something as a trade secret, it is required that the information regarding the secret should be concealed but accessible to those who have an obligation to know it.[28]

In an event of disclosure of secret, it should be done only under a non-disclosure agreement. When steps are taken to keep useful information a secret, that information itself becomes a trade secret. In case that someone misappropriates trade secret, the owner should prove it in a court of law that that information qualifies to be a trade secret. In case of secret misappropriation, the owner of the trade secret has to prove that the misappropriation has caused significant damage. Also, it is required to prove the appropriate steps were taken to maintain the secrecy. Trade secret protection lasts until the information is no longer valuable to its holder, no more a secret, or the owner no longer takes reasonable steps to maintain its secrecy.

Trade secret law protects secret information from misappropriation. Trade secret misappropriation is defined as wrongful and dishonest act of acquiring secret information belongs to another party. In industry, it is not uncommon to observe organized act of industrial spy. Industrial spy spreads across spying of trade secrets, designs, software, and formula. Therefore, the owner of the trade secret can sue those who steal and misappropriate trade secret information. However, if the owner voluntarily reveals trade secret information without limitation, they cannot sue anyone against misappropriation because misappropriation cannot be logically established. It is possible for information to lose its status as a trade secret. This occurs due to lack of reasonable effort to protect the information and the information is actually no longer a secret.

Most inventions start with trade secrets but the secrecy dilutes as goods and services are produced and commercialized based on that secret information. Entrepreneur should take strict measures to prevent leak of information from the laboratory at the experimental stage of inventions. Trade secret is important to be protected in the short term because it is extremely difficult to protect trade secrets in the long term. Reverse engineering of information does not account to a dishonest act. Acquisition of information through reverse engineering thus cannot be treated as misappropriation or wrongful appropriation. Thus, trade secret protection is not very useful and practical for mechanical and software products because reverse engineering can be performed through catalogs and interface available to the public. Therefore, entrepreneurs can benefit from trade secret protection as long as the ideas and inventions can be held secret.[29]

Image Rights

Image right is the expression of a personality in the public domain. Image rights legislations enable a dignitary to register their personality. In the law, a personage (dignitary) is described as a natural person, a legal person, a joint personality (two or more natural or legal persons) who are intrinsically linked and who together have a joint personality, a group (two or more natural or legal persons) who are publicly perceived to be linked in a common purpose and who together form a collective group or team, a fictional character of a human or non-human. The real name of the personage need not be the name of the registered name; for example, Mr. Bean is the personality name of Rowan Atkinson. The music groups Abba and Beatles, Spider-man, Ultraman, Totoro are other examples for different personalities.[30]

Personality holder can commercially exploit the personal attributes such as voice, signature, appearance, silhouette, feature, face, expressions (verbal or facial), gestures, mannerisms, any other distinctive characteristics or personal attribute of a personage, any photograph, illustration, image, picture, moving image, electronic or other representations of the personage. Although there is no specific law in the UK dealing with image rights for individuals, there are various laws which can be applied to protect a personality of significant reputation and the goodwill connected to the image of an individual.[31]

Unauthorized use of an image for marketing can mislead the public into believing that a product has been endorsed by the image holder. This is a case in point that the individual's image is damaged. If image of an individual is used to promote a product without permission, then it will be treated as a damage to the reputation and thus it sanctions the affected personality to file defamation case against the party that used their image. The advertising codes require advertisers to secure consent of celebrities and others to embed their images in advertisements; failure in which is treated as misappropriation of images.

Under Consumer Protection and Unfair Trading Regulations, no business entity can falsely claim that a product has been endorsed or approved by celebrities. Without their expressed permission, images of celebrities cannot be used to promote products. Permission obtained from the photographer may not be sufficient to use an image though they have the rights of the photograph. Permission should be obtained from the relevant celebrity him/herself. Using dead celebrities or using their holograms to promote products are generally unlawful. Although the US laws protect rights of the dead celebrities, there is no such legal protection in the UK. However, as a matter of courtesy, it is required to obtain permission from the relevant parties of the dead celebrity. Artificial Intelligence (AI) is capable of reproducing still and video images of dead or live personalities with their voices also and thus the works of AI in this connection come under purview of the law of Image Rights.[32]

Chapter Summary

Inventions and innovations are the most precious assets of a venture and called intellectual property. Intellectual property represents unique knowledge behind the goods and services produced and commercialized. Intellectual property also is an indicator of entrepreneurial health of a venture. These intellectual properties are vulnerable to counterfeiting by competitors and imitators for siphoning profit from lucrative markets. Counterfeiting can retard entrepreneurial spirit of entrepreneur due to loss of grip of intellectual properties, unfair competition, and involvement in elongating court cases against the counterfeiters. In order to spoil the treat of counterfeiting and to protect the original ideas, a legal and institutional mechanism has been developed to register the rights of intellectual property of the original inventor.

Intellectual property rights laws aim at providing legal protection against counterfeiting the original ideas viz. research findings, formula, trade secrets, product designs, and any other original ideas. World Intellectual Property Organization (WIPO) and country-specific intellectual property offices are established to acknowledge intellectual property rights. Inventors and entrepreneurs can register their intellectual property internationally at the Geneva-based World Intellectual Property Organization of the United Nation Organization. WIPO protects and promotes intellectual property rights, administers 26 international conventions on intellectual property, and has 191 member states. Entrepreneurs or inventors can register their intellectual property at local office of a federal state or a country also and claim the rights. National Intellectual Property Organization (NIPO) of Sri Lanka, United States Patent and Trademark Office (USPTO), Japan Patent Office (JPO) are examples for country offices of intellectual property registration. In addition, UNESCO and WTO also have their own jurisdiction areas of intellectual property protection.

Rights for intellectual property can only be claimed if the original inventor or innovator duly registers the original idea at an Intellectual Property Office. This helps the owners of original ideas to legally claim rights for their creative works and to protect them against infringement. The Intellectual Property Office has developed several methods of intellectual property protection from which entrepreneurs or inventors can choose as appropriate. These methods include Copyright, Patent right, Trademark, Design right, Trade secrets, and Image right. Intellectual Property Office adopts a designated procedure in accepting and registering property rights after an application is filed for registration. Intellectual property can be registered in a single country, multiple countries, or internationally at the choice of the applicant.

Review Questions

1. Distinguish intellectual property from intellectual property right.
2. What are the determinants of intellectual property rights?
3. Describe the relationship among the following;

    a. Invention
    b. Innovation
    c. Intellectual property.

4. "Intellectual properties are vulnerable to counterfeiting." Explain what is counterfeiting and why intellectual property needs to be protected against counterfeiting.
5. What is the World Intellectual Property Organization (WIPO) and its role in protecting intellectual property rights?
6. Describe, providing examples, national and local intellectual property organizations and their jurisdictions in protecting intellectual properties.

7. Examine the authority vested in the UNESCO and WTO as alternative intellectual property protection institutions.
8. Elaborate the procedures for and subsequent steps of registration of intellectual properties with the World Intellectual Property Organization.
9. Describe the circumstances where intellectual property rights arise and how such rights can stand against infringement of intellectual property.
10. Explain the circumstances where Copyrights emerge and the methods of their protection.
11. Describe the characteristics of Patent Rights and the procedure of patenting an invention.
12. Distinguish Trademarks from patent rights providing examples for the circumstances where they conflict and stand out.
13. "Design rights sometimes can conflict with patents, copyrights, and trademarks." Describe how design rights can be established in reconciliation.
14. "Trade Secret is a registered right of the owner of undisclosed information." Discuss the special features of Trade secrets and the possibility for protection.
15. Describe how an image is raised to fetch market value and then to protect it through Image Rights.

Additional Readings

1. Giannakas, K., 2002. Infringement of intellectual property rights: Causes and consequences. *American Journal of Agricultural Economics*, *84*(2), pp. 482–494.
2. Demeré, B.W., Sedatole, K.L., and Wilson, J.M., 2022. Counterfeiting and anti-counterfeiting costs: An application of cost of quality concepts. In *Brand protection and the global risk of product counterfeits* (pp. 141–158). Edward Elgar Publishing.
3. Romer, P., 2002. When should we use intellectual property rights? *American Economic Review*, *92*(2), pp. 213–216.
4. Sharma, D.K., 2014. Intellectual property and the need to protect it. *Indian Journal of Scientific Research*, *9*(1), pp. 84–87.
5. Birkbeck, C.D., 2016. *The world intellectual property organization (WIPO): A reference guide*. Edward Elgar Publishing.

6. Amaradasa, R.M.W., De Silva, M.A.T., and Pathirage, R.P., 2002. *Patents in a small developing economy: A case study of Sri Lanka.*
7. Kim, J., and Lee, S., 2015. Patent databases for innovation studies: A comparative analysis of USPTO, EPO, JPO and KIPO. *Technological Forecasting and Social Change*, *92*, pp. 332–345.
8. Kim, J. and Lee, S., 2015. Patent databases for innovation studies: A comparative analysis of USPTO, EPO, JPO and KIPO. *Technological Forecasting and Social Change*, *92*, pp. 332–345.
9. Byrne, J.G., 1995. Changes on the frontier of intellectual property law: An overview of the changes required by GATT. *The Duquesne Law Review*, *34*, p. 121.
10. Pandey, N., and Dharni, K., 2014. *Intellectual property rights*. PHI Learning Pvt. Ltd.
11. Hettinger, E.C., 1989. Justifying intellectual property. *Philosophy & Public Affairs*, pp. 31–52.
12. Jorgenson, L., and Fink, C., 2023. WIPO's contributions to international cooperation on intellectual property. *Journal of International Economic Law, 26*(1), pp. 30–34.
13. Thippeswamy, S., 2017. Plant variety protection: A historical perspective. *International Journal of Development Research*, *7*(11), pp. 16839–16843.
14. Gaikwad, A., and Dhokare, C.S., 2020. A study of intellectual property rights and its significance for business. *Journal of Information and Computational Science, 10*(2), pp. 552–561.
15. Curci, F.X., 2002. Protecting your intellectual property rights overseas. *Transnational Law*, *15*, p. 15.
16. Febriany, T.A., Kurniawan, H.Y., and Setiyawan, D., 2022. The implementation of intellectual property registration for startups in the industrial revolution era 4.0 in Pontianak. *Indonesia Law Reform Journal*, *2*(3), pp. 382–388.
17. Carroll, M.W., 2009. One size does not fit all: A framework for tailoring intellectual property rights. *Ohio State Law Journal*, *70*, p. 1361.
18. Goldstein, P., Lillick, S.W., and Lillick, I.S., 1989. *Copyright: Principles, law, and practice* (Vol. 1). Boston, MA: Little, Brown.
19. Joyce, C., Ochoa, T.T., Carroll, M.W., Leaffer, M.A., and Jaszi, P., 2016. *Copyright law* (Vol. 85). Durham, NC: Carolina Academic Press.

20. Brownlee, L.M., 1995. Recent changes in the duration of copyright in the United States and European Union: Procedure and policy. *Fordham Intellectual Property, Media and Entertainment Law Journal*, *6*, p. 579.
21. Andersen, B., 2004. If 'intellectual property rights' is the answer, what is the question? Revisiting the patent controversies. *Economics of Innovation and New Technology*, *13*(5), pp. 417–442.
22. Love, B.J., 2019. *Patent duration* (pp. 310–325). Edward Elgar Publishing.
23. Peguera, M., 2014. Trademark functions and trademark rights. *Available at SSRN 3693270*.
24. Geamanu, R.G., 2018. The right to image, to name, to registered office, to logo, to trademark of the legal entity (company) and the means of protecting them according to the new civil code. *Romanian Review of Private Law*, p. 102.
25. Zlatovic, D., 2011. Recognition, duration and effects of a trademark according to the new trademark law in Bosnia and Herzegovina. *Zbornik Pravnog fakulteta Sveučilišta u Rijeci*, *32*, p. 927.
26. Monseau, S., 2011. European design rights: A model for the protection of all designers from piracy. *American Business Law Journal*, *48*, p. 27.
27. Marshall, J., 2022. Rights beyond the registration: From black and white to grey. *Journal of Intellectual Property Law and Practice*, *17*(2), pp. 193–198.
28. Hannah, D.R., 2006. Keeping trade secrets secret. *MIT Sloan Management Review*, *47*(3), p. 17.
29. Yeh, B.T., 2014. *Protection of trade secrets: Overview of current law and legislation* (Vol. 5). Congressional Research Service.
30. Logeais, E., and Schroeder, J.B., 1997. The French right of image: An ambiguous concept protecting the human persona. *The Loyola of Los Angeles Entertainment Law Review*, *18*, p. 511.
31. Thompson III, R.T., 2009. Image as personal property: How privacy law has influenced the right of publicity. *The UCLA Entertainment Law Review*, *16*, p. 155.
32. Reiter, E.H., 2001. Personality and patrimony: Comparative perspectives on the right to one's image. *Tulane Law Review*, *76*, p. 673.

CHAPTER 9

Feasibility Planning Process

Key Learning Points

- Introduction.
- Feasibility planning and business planning.
- Need for feasibility planning.
- Costs and benefits of feasibility planning.
- Audience of a feasibility plan.
- Feasibility planning premises.
- Business environment analysis.
- PESTEL analysis.
- Five Force framework.
- SWOT Analysis.
- Product-Market analysis.
- Portfolio analysis.
- Stage of the industry.
- Developing a feasibility plan.
- General considerations of feasibilities.
- Purpose of a feasibility plan.
- Feasibility plan in the eyes of executives.
- Major elements of a feasibility plan.
- Overall soundness of a feasibility plan.
- Elements of a feasibility plan.

© The Author(s), under exclusive license to Springer Nature Singapore Pte Ltd. 2024

M. Rajaratne, *Concepts, Processes and Practice of Entrepreneurship*, Palgrave Studies in Global Entrepreneurship,
https://doi.org/10.1007/978-981-97-6180-7_9

- Executive Summary.
- Business concept description.
- Product and service plan.
- Marketing plan.
- Operations plan.
- Human resource plan.
- Financial plan.
- Administrative plan.

Introduction

Feasibility planning is a key step of the venture creation process. Although, sometimes, it is obvious that ventures are created without formal feasibility analyses, it should be noted that every entrepreneur makes reasonable feasibility judgment prior to creation of venture. With realization of innovation and commercial feasibility of products, entrepreneur inspires to initiate a venture. This implies that feasibility planning is a venture pre-start-up stage activity.[1] Although some entrepreneurs tend to enter the start-up stage of a venture without much preparations in the pre-start-up stage, it is worthwhile spending some time to study and analyze feasibility of the intended venture. Therefore, as a pre-start-up activity, feasibility planning is considered a key step of the venture creation process.[2]

Feasibility planning, also known as business planning, produces feasibility plans or business plans. Feasibility plans are not only essential for new ventures but also for existing ventures at times they consider starting new business units, amalgamation, merger, acquisition, and new projects. Feasibility plans are essential for guiding business operations and guaranteeing their success. Smalltime entrepreneurs usually escape formal feasibility planning steps in order to save cost and time. This is partly due to poor knowledge of advantage of business planning. Quite often, most entrepreneurs estimate business feasibility in instinct. It is interesting to note that some entrepreneurs do not prepare feasibility plans but start ventures while some others prepare plans but do not start ventures. Those who do not seem to develop business plans in fact have business plans in their minds. And some entrepreneurs develop business plans but create ventures belatedly.[3]

Audience of a Feasibility Plan

Feasibility plans are indispensable for large businesses due to several reasons. Unlike proprietorship, large ventures are not created by individuals. Large ventures are created by a group of persons who are investors, venture capitalists, managers, lenders, lessors, governments, and foreign partners. Therefore, the feasibility plan is used as a device of formal communication also among the involving parties. In this sense, a feasibility plan is useful as a communicating and convincing device. Feasibility plan describes the type of business, why, when, with whom, and how the business is planned and operated. Business plans are presented to relevant parties to communicate and convince business concept and operational perspectives. A business plan is generally presented to the following parties.[4]

- Bankers: For borrowing and operating as guarantors for transactions.
- Financiers: For obtaining venture capital, leasing, and financing.
- Partners: For obtaining equity capital, operation licenses, management, etc.
- Investors: For obtaining investment in equity capital.
- Insurers: For obtaining insurance policies for company properties, transactions, and third-party damages.
- Government authorities: For obtaining business registration, licenses, clearance, concessions, and entitlements.
- Trade unions: For convincing the commitment to labor laws and welfare pertaining to the industry.
- Pressure groups: For assuring responsible operations, standardized and ethical practices.

Planning Premises

Identifying planning premises is an important task in the feasibility planning process. Venture differences evoke analyses of different elements in the planning premises. These elements include general business environment, feasible fields of business, feasible forms of business, and industry competitiveness and risk. They are discussed in detail in the following sections.[5]

Business Environment Analysis

General business environment is comprised of the operational, market, national, and international business environments as depicted in Fig. 9.1. Business environment is comprised of social, economic, political, and environmental components, which are characteristically unstable and volatile and thus, they cause unstable external environment for entrepreneurship. The nature of business environment can affect entrepreneurs either positively or negatively. Some entrepreneurs expect a stable environment at all times while some other entrepreneurs prefer wrestling with volatile situations to discover new business opportunities.[6]

Stable environment is believed to create steady business opportunities. In stable environment, opportunities are explicit and unambiguous and thus, it is quite easier for entrepreneurs to recognize venture opportunities. Also, stable environment makes it easier for the entrepreneurs to plan

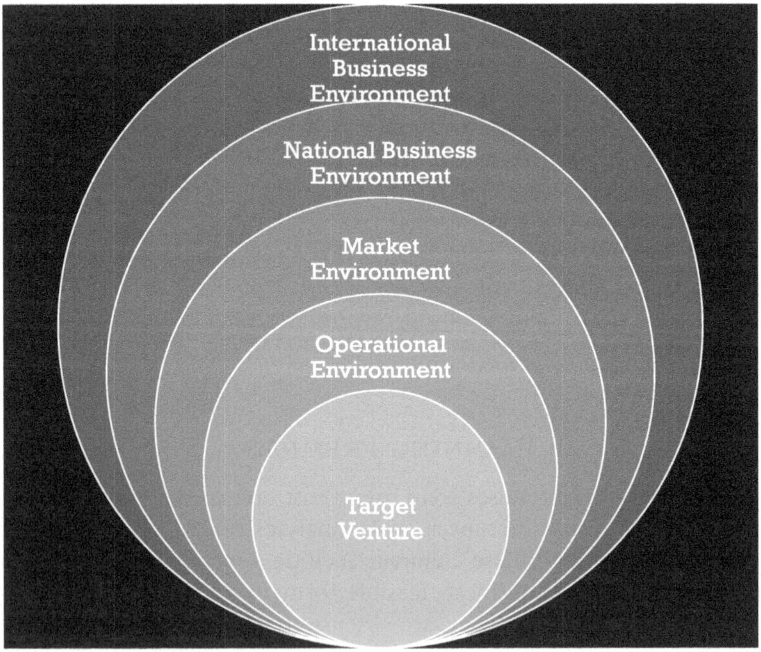

Fig. 9.1 Business environment (Author Portrayal)

and forecast business. In this premise, operations become convenient, less challenging, predictable, and feasible. Entrepreneurs generally believe that this kind of environment is less risky and hence entrepreneur-friendly. For these reasons, some entrepreneurs prefer stable environment to unstable environment.

However, stable environment causes the market to be crowded as many entrepreneurs enter predicting that the market is highly lucrative. This situation is identified as "Red Ocean" market condition.[7] In the Red Ocean, many competitors operate and hence the market is intensely competitive. This leads to push down the consumer prices due to competition and to push up the producer prices due to increase in factor costs. These two forces squeeze the profit margin. Additional costs are also incurred in competitive environment due to urge for advertising, promotion, and product development to maintain the market share. Finally, profit tends to decrease due to increase in cost of production and cost of sale and decrease in market prices.[8]

High cost, low profit imbued, and high market risk in the crowded market discourage operating in the competitive market. This is a good reason for entrepreneurs to withdraw from the mainstream market and to search for alternative markets where competition is less. Entrepreneurial opportunities are less explicit in alternative markets and thus, only a few entrepreneurs who are clever enough to recognize opportunities and confident enough to operate enter this market. Alternative markets are unestablished markets that will be less crowded and less competitive. However, these markets require more inventive and innovative skills to exploit opportunities in them compared to normal markets. This market condition, characterized by abundance of opportunities and absence of competition, is identified as "Blue Ocean" Market. Blue Ocean Market is either monopolistic or oligopolistic and thus, high profit margins are feasible. This is due to the phenomenon of low competition in factor market as well as in the product market.[9]

PESTEL Analysis

The PESTEL (Political, Economic, Social, Technological, Environmental, Legal) analysis is helpful for analyzing business environment in which the entrepreneur is planning to set up their prospective venture. F.J. Aguilar (1967)[10] introduced PEST (political, economic, social, and technological) analysis as an analytical tool for macro business environment.[11] Since

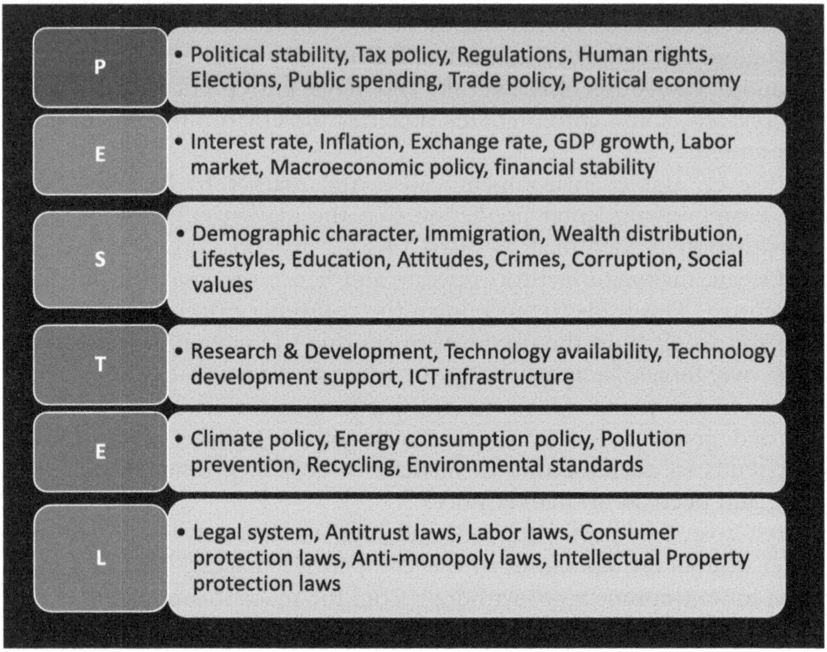

Fig. 9.2 The PESTEL framework (Author Portrayal)

its debut, this tool was developed by adding components to it by many scholars. By now, the variant PESTEL has become the most popular among them. Each PESTEL component comprises several variables that help analyze the macro business environment as indicated in Fig. 9.2.

Five Force Framework

Reasonable analysis of the rivalry factor is essential for an entrepreneur to understand the gravity of market competition. Business rivalry occurs in a market where several market leaders operate. In oligopolistic competition, intense rivalry is unavoidable. The Five Force Model of Michael Porter (1985)[12] is a generally accepted tool for analyzing business rivalry. This model helps the entrepreneur to estimate the elements that construct competitive environment and the degree of competition in the market. The Five Force Model advocates that business rivalry is instigated via four external forces: (1) threat of new entrants, (2) threat of substitutes, (3) bargaining power of suppliers, and (4) bargaining power of buyers. Internal strength is the fifth force that the firm employs to ward off external forces of rivalry. Entrepreneur is compelled to unleash strategies to counter the rivalry emanating from the external forces. This model is useful for the entrepreneur to learn competitiveness aspect of business environment and plan innovations and venture strategies.[13]

SWOT Analysis

It is believed that the SWOT analysis was proposed by Albert Humphrey of Stanford Research Institute, USA, with the aim of estimating strategic fitness of a firm (while some accredit it to Edmund P. Learned, C. Roland Christensen, Kenneth R. Andrews, and William D. Guth for carrying the concept in *Business Policy: Text and Cases* in 1965). The SWOT analysis recommends consideration of internal and external factors that are useful to forming business strategies. Internal factors are identified as internal strengths and internal weaknesses; and external factors are categorized as external threats and external opportunities. Although the SWOT analysis aims at helping strategic decision-making process of existing firms, it can also be a useful tool for pre-startups. The SWOT analysis helps prospective entrepreneurs to weigh opportunities amidst threats and to match them with entrepreneur's strengths and weaknesses when considering starting up of new venture. The SWOT analysis is a useful guideline for preparation of feasibility plan.[14]

Product-Market Analysis

Igor Ansoff (1957)[15] introduced the Product-Market Matrix which was later coined as Ansoff Matrix. This tool helps strategic decisions to increase sales revenues. Ansoff Matrix considers two market factors: product and market. Then the products are further divided into two as new products and present (existing) products. Market is also divided into two as new and present (existing) markets. Based on the arrangement of these four scenarios, Ansoff introduces four strategies: Market penetration, Market development, Product development, and Product-Market diversification. This matrix is useful as a tool for analyzing general business feasibility as it provides guidelines for the entrepreneur to develop appropriate strategies for a prospective venture. The Product-Market Matrix is helpful for entrepreneurs when developing the business/feasibility plan.[16]

Portfolio Analysis

Analysis of relevant product portfolios of competitors is equally important for an entrepreneur to develop a sound business plan. Bruce Henderson introduced his Growth-Share Matrix as a strategic planning tool to Boston Safe Deposit and Trust Company, which became independent as Boston Consulting Group (BCG) in 1970s. This matrix later became popular as the BCG Matrix. The BCG matrix is constructed on two pillars: market share and market growth. In relation to market share and market growth, cash generation and cash absorption of business sections or products are estimated. Then, based on the revenues and costs and inward and outward cash flows, strategies are recommended for business section or product line. Accordingly, the BCG matrix identifies four possible outcomes: Cash-cow, Star, Dog, and Problem-child.[17]

This analysis is helpful for prospective entrepreneurs for analyzing feasibilities of a proposed venture or product, prior to making the entry decision, in contrast to the present portfolios of the competitors in the industry. This matrix is useful for start-up entrepreneurs as it provides analysis of market and financial status of business segments or products that are relevant to the products that the prospective entrepreneur is considering to launch via the start-up venture. With the use of BCG matrix, entrepreneur can assess current market and industry scenarios and estimate advantages and disadvantages of each before launching a business.

Stage of the Industry

Prior to creating a venture, it is useful for an entrepreneur to be familiar with the stage of the industry which his venture belongs to. Industry life cycle provides useful insights for entrepreneur to understand the stages of life an industry. After introduction of a product, it passes through the stages of growth, maturity, and decline. These stages can be viewed in industry also in relation to industrial sales and profit. At the introduction and growth stages, an industry experiences increased competition from substitutes. Thus, an industry that hovers at these two stages is challenging for an entrepreneur as competition is intense.[18]

On the contrary, at the stages, competitors engage in heavy advertising and promotional activities that help the market to expand; new entrants can benefit from the market expansion and easily position in the market with substitutes. The maturing and declining stages of an industry suggest that sales and profits tend to decline in that industry. Therefore, entering into an industry at the maturing and declining stages are risky as the market is contracting. To remain in the market at this phase, strategies such as product diversification, market segmentation, and niche market are essential. When preparing a feasibility plan, analysis of the stage of the industry is beneficial as it helps entrepreneur to determine the right time to enter the market with right strategies suitable for each stage of the industry life cycle. Different stages in the industry pause different business conditions that may or may not be beneficial for startups. Therefore, entrepreneurs must be aware of the stage of the product life cycle and contemplate costs and benefits when entering the market.

Developing a Feasibility Plan

General Considerations

Feasibility plan is developed either by entrepreneur or by a professional designated for the task. Three approaches are seen in preparation of feasibility plans. First, entrepreneur prepares the plan when they possess sound educational background and knowledge of business planning. Still, entrepreneur may consult knowledgeable persons if they lack required competency. Second, for large ventures, entrepreneur appoints a team to prepare feasibility plan consulting professionals. Third, in creating corporates that are complex and of high risk, feasibility plan development is entirely contracted to professional firms.[19]

Length of a feasibility plan depends on the scope and scale of the proposed venture. However, it is generally agreed that the length of a feasibility plan should confine to 40–50 pages. But additionally, several pages can be appended as annexures according to requirements. Cash flow forecasts, estimates of final accounts, sales forecasts, administrative structure, licenses, and patents are usually appended as annexures. Information provided in the feasibility plan should be specific, realistic, short, straightforward, and focused. Yet, it is essential to indicate contingencies also toward goals and alternative strategies in case of business environment changes.[20]

Prospective readers of a feasibility plan include higher ranking public and private sector officers, executives, investors, lenders, bankers, and financiers who are usually busy and shrug off reading lengthy reports. Thus, the content of the feasibility plan should directly answer probable questions rather than inviting the readers to raise questions out of the content. Feasibility plan should be written to present a precise business proposal to relevant external parties in a way to convince them quickly and comfortably. Primarily, it is the convincing ability of a feasibility plan that helps securing patronage from the external parties. Additionally, feasibility plan is helpful for guiding entrepreneur and their team in conducting the business once initiated.

Executives look at three main characteristics of a feasibility plan: (1) creativity worthiness, (2) market worthiness, and (3) financial viability. In the corporate sector, "Five-minute Reading" is a norm in reading a business proposal. Executives initially spend five minutes to grasp essential points in the proposal. Therefore, when preparing a feasibility plan, the planners should emphasize on the key content only. In addition to content of the plan, attention should be paid to appearance, length, title, summary, and the page of contents also to ensure the plan is attractive and readable. Executives initially rush to look at the five points mentioned below (FUQCO).[21]

1. Financial structure and soundness of the balance sheet
2. Unique feature of the venture
3. Quality of the entrepreneur
4. Characteristics of the venture
5. Overall soundness of the proposal.

Business plan should essentially express the feasibility of several functional areas of the proposed business. Any unfeasibility seen in them will prove the venture to be undoable. Therefore, the planners must be able to certainly determine and confidently express feasibility of the following functional areas of the proposed business. Score card method is useful for determining general business feasibilities, as a background pilot survey of the following areas, prior to preparation of true feasibility plan.[22]

1. Technological feasibility
2. Environmental feasibility
3. Management feasibility.
4. Production feasibility
5. Technical feasibility
6. Social feasibility
7. Legal feasibility
8. Organizing feasibility
9. Resource procurement feasibility
10. Marketing feasibility
11. Financial feasibility.

Elements of a Feasibility Plan

There is no rule or theory that specifies the number of elements itemized in a feasibility plan. Yet, it is generally agreed by every planner that a feasibility plan should consider a limited number of elements. Under each element, relevant information is detailed out. There are several principles that guide the volume and quality of the details provided. Accordingly, the information should be appropriate and short, properly organized, orientated to future, unexaggerated, identifying critical risks, focused on specific opportunity, identifying target market, and capturing reader's interest. As far as the number of elements is concerned, some scholars propose 10 while others confine to 6 elements as appropriate for a business plan. The order of the elements arranged in a business plan is not fixed.[23] Here, eight elements are identified as appropriate for a feasibility plan. A feasibility plan contains the following essential elements (Fig. 9.3).

1. Executive summary
2. Business concept
3. Products or services
4. Marketing plan
5. Operations plan
6. Personnel plan
7. Financial plan
8. Administrative plan

ELEMENT	• DETAILS
Executive Summary	• Venture defined, product/services identified, market characteristics identified, financial structure and administrative structures are identified, founders, managers etc. are introduced, Name & address given.
Business Concept	• Purpose of the venture, Legal form, Vision, Mission, Strategies, Objectives of the founders; Validity, strength, and competency of the concept.
Product & Service Plan	• Function and nature of the products/ services; owners' interest in product; attribute and technical profile of the team; Product/service protection; Licensing/ franchising.
Marketing Plan	• Customer scenario, market & market segments, industry structure, sales forecast, competition, market strategy: pricing, promotion, distribution, product strategy: warranties, guarantees, after service, technical support.
Operations (Production) Plan	• Operational processes, Plants, facilities, location, inventory and materials, resource procurement, machineries, technology, security, insurance, and safety.
Human Resource Plan	• Profile of founders, key personnel, investors, management team and the role etc. Secretaries, Auditors, Consultants.
Financial Plan	• Financial forecasts, cash flow estimates, assets and liabilities, break-even projections, source of venture capital etc. financial statements.
Administration Plan	• Administrative and organizational structure, Policies, Procedures & Rules, Ethics, CSR.

Fig. 9.3 Structure of feasibility plan (Author Portrayal)

Executive Summary

Executive summary contains the key information of all elements of the feasibility plan in concise. Therefore, although the executive summary appears as the first section of a feasibility plan, it is written after all other sections are completed. The purpose of the executive summary is to briefly present the business proposal to the prospective bankers, lessors, investors, venture capitalists, partners, and other major stakeholders.[24] The length of the executive summary should be limited to two to three pages. Also, the executive summary should be concise, compact, specific, steady, readable, convincing, and stimulating. Executives normally spend only a few minutes in reading the summary and thus, a few minutes are critical for the decision to accept or reject the business plan. Content of the executive summary is described below.[25]

- **Business name and location**—Name of the business proposed, whether the name is registered, what is the trademark, where the head office and factories or service points are located.
- **Business concept or the idea**—What the business is about, why it is important and necessary, what industry the venture belongs to, and how unique the business concept is.
- **Business purpose, vision, and mission**—What problem to be intervened via market, how, when, and where to intervene, and what long-term purpose to be achieved through what means.
- **Business objectives**—What to be achieved by the business for its stakeholders in short, medium, and long term and what business milestones to be reached and passed consecutively.
- **Organizational type**—What organizational form is considered (proprietorship, partnership, limited liability company, etc.) and its suitability to achieve business objectives.
- **Products and production process**—What type of goods or services are produced when, under what production process, what quality standards, and what procurement plans and practices.
- **Market and marketing plans**—What market is targeted and what marketing plans to be implemented. How and where to sell under what marketing strategy. Expected market share, growth, and sales sustainability.
- **Financial structure and financial plans**—From what sources of finance what amounts are procured, expenditure plans, financial

dynamics and health, financial forecasts, estimates, breakevens, financial statements.

- **Administrative structure**—How the operations are organized (as departments, divisions, branches, etc.), what authorities and responsibilities are delegated, and what regulations, procedures, and rules are adopted.
- **Founders and managers**—Who the founders and key managers are and what their backgrounds, experiences, skills, and track records are, and what roles they are assigned.
- **Social responsibility and ethics**—What social cost and benefits are caused, and the mechanism to care social responsibility, ethics, and environmental concerns.
- **Compliances**—What local or international industrial standards and legal compliances are required and how they are met.

Business Concept Description

Description of the business concept provides key information of the business. In addition to the business concept itself, information such as name, address, and legal status of the business, vision, mission, strategies, and objectives are also identified in this section. For every new venture, there needs a valid business concept which is essentially the soul of the venture. Business concept is described in several steps to persuade persons and firms whose partaking is expected. Those steps are briefly described below.[26]

- **Business concept**—What the business is about, what makes the business important and necessary, what the purpose of the business is, and in what industry it is to operate. What problem, when, and where to be intervened, what consumer needs and wants are to be addressed and how, and what satisfactions are aimed to be guaranteed to customers.
- **Validity and uniqueness of the business concept**—Why the business concept is unique, why it is worthy and suitable to start a business, whether the concept is periodically or perpetually valid.
- **Vision and Mission**—What is the end goal of the business, how long it will take to reach the goal, and what strategic path is required.

What strengths are there to face and win challenges, what constraints are identified, and how the business objectives are met.

- **Business objectives**—Specific, measurable, achievable, realistic, and time-bound (SMART) objectives in the functions of production required to achieve sales, cost, profit, market share, and growth objectives.
- **Business scale**—What size or the operational scale is at the startup and expansion milestones. Scale of production, inventory, sales, human resource, and level of technology are identified.
- **Short-term business survival**—Tactics of short-term survival, positioning the business in the market, connections and networks, technical and marketing capability for short-term survival, trademark, and brand name strategies.
- **Break-Even Point and profitability**—Break-even forecast, output and revenue at the break-even point (BEP), time spent to reach break-even point, financial losses up to BEP, and profit volumes thereafter.
- **Business in the long run**—The direction of the business after startup, expansion milestones, diversification plans, competitiveness, and market share strategies.
- **Compliances**—Legal compliances, environmental compliances, international compliances, quality compliances, and permissions for inception and operations, social and environment impact assessment certification, and the contracts entered into.
- **Social responsibility**—Social cost of the business, pressure group influences, ethical concerns, ways to carry out social responsibility.

Product and Service Plan

This section should provide detailed information on the intended products of the venture. Products are the outcomes of entrepreneurial endeavor and they include either goods or services or both.[27] Feasibility of production, capability of products to guarantee customer satisfaction, and other relevant details are included in this section.[28]

- **Nature of the products**—Whether the products are consumables, intermediate goods, or investment goods. Whether the product is for every and any customer or only a group of customers selected based on demographic characteristics. Whether the product is essential or luxury. Whether the life cycle is long or short. Whether the product can easily be imitated.

- **Function of the products**—How the good or the service works on the customer to satisfy needs or wants. Whether the products provide additional features compared to those of competitors. Whether the products can perform the anticipated functions trouble free.
- **Raw materials and inventory**—Identification of type of raw materials, sources of supply, supply chains, sustainability of supply, quality, quantity, and future price of raw materials.
- **Production technology**—Type and level of technology adopted, suitability and adaptability of the technology, cost of technology, Research and Development capabilities, laboratories, and facilities.
- **Production processes and scale**—Manual or machine-based production, process of production, scale of production, assembling, sub-contracting, relevance of value chains, and production control methods such as JIT and TQM.
- **Contingent plans**—Alternative sources of supplies of components and materials in case of breakdown of usual supply chain. Alternative measures for machine breakdowns. Alternative measures to face labor strikes and natural disasters.
- **Intellectual property rights**—Whether protection of intellectual properties of the venture is essential, measures of product and service protection such as copyrights and patent rights.

Marketing Plan

Marketing plan describes marketing aspect of the venture. Marketing is pivotal to business as the venture success mostly depends on successful marketing program. Therefore, well-defined marketing plan is essential for convincing business partners. Market and marketing research is conducted to derive information required to develop marketing plan. Following details are generally presented in a marketing plan.[29]

- **Industry composition**—Market structure such as monopoly, oligopoly, or perfect market and determination of price.
- **Expected competition**—Rivals, rivalry, and means of rivalry such as price, quality, technology, and distribution.

- **Customer scenario**—Types of customers, size of the market, expected market niche, demographic characteristics of the customers such as income, education, age, and gender.
- **Marketing strategy**—How the product, price, place, and promotion (4Ps) strategies are designed to launch a successful marketing program.
- **Sales forecast**—Daily, weekly, monthly, or yearly sales forecasts of each product at each market based on the nature of goods and services presented. Forecasts are usually expressed in terms of value rather than volumes.
- **Customer care programs**—Provision of warranties, guarantees, maintenance and service, and technical support and how they are offered and operationalized.
- **Brand identity**—Establishing brand and brand image, trademark, service mark, physical appearance of the business firm, uniforms of the workers, communication materials, and templates.
- **Trade networks**—Whether own distribution and sales networks are developed or trading and distribution are contracted to designated trading firms.

Operations (Production) Plan

Operations plan describes the dimensions of the production process. Production plays the most crucial role in innovation. The key responsibility of the production process is to bring about right innovations. Failure in production adversely affects other business functions and the whole venture. Therefore, the interested parties enthusiastically look into the operational plan of the proposed business. Thus, the entrepreneur should present the operations plan with a focus on the following essential aspects.[30]

- **Operational scale**—Scale of operations: small, medium, or large. Justification for the chosen economical size of operations and the scale in terms of market, finance, technology, supply of materials, and labor.
- **Operations process**—Transformation process of materials, key activities in different phases of production, time span, flow of the

production process, operational techniques such as assembly lines, lean manufacturing, Just-In-Time (JIS), and Six Sigma.

- **Organization of operations**—Production coordination, production integration, operational structure such as departmentation, production units, spatial divisions of production facilities, sub-contracting, and value chain networks.
- **Location and facilities**—Geographic location of plants or service points, facilities such as buildings, and space with accessibility to them. Utilities such as source of energy (power), water and gas, and waste disposal. Logistics related to supply of resources and shipment of finished products, and transportation routes such as land, sea, and air.
- **Production technology**—Level of technology used (high-tech, medium-tech, or low-tech), real-time technology, distance operations technology, machinery and equipment employed, computer-aided design (CAD), and computer-aided manufacturing (CAM).
- **Production team**—Profile of the production team, team attributes: technical skills, innovative skills, experience, expertise, qualifications.
- **Safety, security, and insurance**—Personnel safety from machine and industrial hazards, safety of machineries, equipment, and assets. Health and property insurance. Safety measures of proximate bio environment.
- **License and permissions**—Production licenses and permissions acquired from authorities. Agreements on use of patent and copyrights, clearance from departments such as environment, export and import, and defense. Agreements for operations through franchise or other royalty arrangements.

Human Resource Plan

Human resource plan describes the aspects of the human factor affiliated with the proposed venture. Business plan is operationalized by and through human resource. Human resource structure stretches from the founders to the lowest ranking subordinates. The key concerns of a human resource plan are described below.[31]

- **Profile of founders**—Entrepreneurial strength of the founders: experience, success stories, track records, past and present involvement with other organizations, corporate links, professional and social affiliations.
- **Key personnel**—Profile of key persons such as Chairman, CEO, managers, consultants, accountants, auditors, partners, and partner organizations. Managerial experience, success stories, track records, past and present involvement with other organizations, corporate links, and professional and social affiliations. Role and responsibility of the top management. Special ownerships such as licenses, patents, and copyrights of the key persons.
- **Investor profile**—Business profile of the parties already agreed to consider investments: banks, corporates, venture capitalists, lessors, and lenders. Agreements and conditions of such agreements, if any.
- **Recruitment and remuneration**—Policies and procedures of recruitment, remuneration, training, promotion, demotion, firing. Commitment to labor regulations.
- **Motivational measures**—Personnel motivation methods, compensation, healthcare, bonus and other benefits, labor turnover, conflict resolution, and grievances handling.

Financial Plan[32]

The numeric summary of all operations of the venture is presented in the financial plan. In this section, financial estimates related to all operations are produced based on realistic calculations and forecasts. These estimates include fund requirements, source and use of funds, revenues and expenditures, profitability, assets and liabilities, balance sheet, and other financial statements of the venture. Content of a financial plan is briefly presented below.

- **Capital requirement**—Initial capital, additional funds, working capital requirement for the start-up stage, and fund requirements for the growth stages.
- **Source and use of funds**—The source of funds, amounts, and the methods of fund procurement, reliability of the sources, costs, and conditions applicable to the selected source. The end use of funds and the amounts obtainable.

- **Cash flow budgeting**—Monthly, quarterly, and annual sales revenues forecasts, other incomes and itemized costs to be incurred for one-year period. Extended cash flow budgeting for another two-year period.
- **Financial statements**—Accounting documentations such as Cash flow statement, Income Statement, Profit and Loss Account, Break-Even projections, Financial Ratio estimates, and projected Balance Sheet. Asset and liability schedules and structure, debtors, creditors, liquidity, and tax liabilities.

Administration Plan

Administrative plan describes how the venture is managed. Organizational structure of the venture, delegation of authority, reporting system and responsibility, accountability, rules, and regulations are the key elements of the administrative plan. Management, administration, guidelines, policies, procedures, standards, and rules comprise an enormous part of the administrative plan. They are described below.[33]

- **Organizational structure**—Tall or flat organizational hierarchy, positions at each administrative level and organizational hierarchy, number of subordinates under each managerial position.
- **Administrative procedures**—Predetermined policies, procedures, rules, and regulations that guide and govern the venture, conflict management procedures.
- **General management**—Managerial positions, delegation of authority and responsibility, reporting system, positional powers, positional responsibilities and positional accountabilities, decision power, etc.
- **Ethics and Social Responsibility**—The ethical practices and social justice (which are not directed by laws), means of caring Social Responsibility, depth and width of Social Responsibility action.

Chapter Summary

Feasibility planning looks into feasibility of a business and thus, is called business planning also. Feasibility planning produces feasibility plans or business plans and is a key step in the venture creation process. Feasibility planning is pre-start-up stage activity of a venture. Some entrepreneurs create ventures without a formal feasibility; but they make reasonable feasibility judgments prior to venture creation. Feasibility plans are essential for both new ventures and also for the existing ventures when they plan to engage in new business units, amalgamation, merger, acquisition, and new projects. Feasibility plans guide business initiation and operations. However, smalltime entrepreneurs usually avoid formal feasibility planning as it costs money and consumes time which are precious at the pre-start-up stage. Business plan looks into a large number of general feasibilities as well as feasibilities of business functions.

Business plan should not contain too many elements in it. It is almost generally agreed upon that a business plan is written under the following sub-headings: Executive summary, Business concept, Product or service, Marketing plan, Operations plan, Personnel plan, Financial plan, and Administrative plan. Business plan should avoid details but should not be too short. Also, there is no generally accepted length of a business plan either. Business plan is prepared to communicate and convince a potential lucrative business to several parties such as bankers, investors, lessors, government officials, and managers. Business plan addresses why, when, with whom, and how the business is operated. Business plan comes out from planning premises that is comprised of general business environment, feasible fields of business, feasible forms of business, industry competitiveness, and business risk. And the general business environment considers operational, market, national, and international business environments, PESTEL, Five Force Framework, SWOT analysis, Product-Market analysis, Portfolio analysis, Industry Life Cycle, etc.

Business plan is either prepared by the entrepreneur by him/herself in consultation with knowledgeable persons, or an internal team of an existing venture appointed by the entrepreneur in consultation with external professionals, or a professional firm contracted. Details of a feasibility plan depend on the scope and scale of the proposed venture. Prospective readers of a feasibility plan are executives. They look at three main characteristics of a feasibility plan: creativity worthiness, market worthiness, and financial viability. Also, among executives, "Five-minute

Reading" is a norm when reading a business plan. Executives initially rush to look at five points identified as FUQCO: Financial structure and soundness of the balance sheet, Unique feature of the venture, Quality of the entrepreneur, Characteristics of the venture, Overall soundness of the proposal.

Review Questions

1. Differentiate between feasibility planning and feasibility plan.
2. Elaborate the circumstances where the need for feasibility planning arises.
3. "Feasibility planning involves costs and benefits." Discuss this statement highlighting how they affect the corporate startups and small business startups.
4. Describe who prepares feasibility plans for whom, on what purpose, and under what planning premises.
5. Describe how useful is the PESTEL analysis in developing a feasibility plan.
6. "The Five-Force framework is helpful to identify the areas where competitiveness can be instilled for the proposed venture." Explain.
7. "SWOT analysis can guide entrepreneur to correctly formulate strategic position of the proposed venture." Discuss.
8. "The Product-Market Matrix helps entrepreneur to determine appropriate product and market strategies." Examine.
9. "BCG Matrix is more useful a tool for entrepreneurs who expand into new business projects and plan new product lines." Critically evaluate this statement.
10. Depict industry life cycle to ascertain advantages and disadvantages of the industry at the point of time when entrepreneur plans to enter the market.
11. What are the general business feasibilities searched by a business planner prior to preparation of the real feasibility plan?
12. Explain the factors that determine the soundness and completeness of a feasibility plan.
13. Is there a universally adopted standard format for a feasibility plan? If not, identify the components that should necessarily be included in a feasibility plan.

14. Provide the information required under the following components of a feasibility plan;

    Executive summary
    Business concept description
    Product and service plan
    Marketing plan
    Operations plan
    Human resource plan
    Financial plan
    Administration plan.

Additional Readings

1. Gartner, W.B., Carter, N.M., and Reynolds, P.D., 2004. Business start-up activities. In *Handbook of entrepreneurial dynamics: The process of business creation*, pp. 285–298.
2. Szpilko, D., Szydło, J., Glińska, E., Kobylińska, U., Rollnik-Sadowska, E., and Ryciuk, U., 2021. *Theoretical and practical aspects of business activity: Business planning*.
3. Badejo, O., and Ierapetritou, M., 2022. Integrating tactical planning, operational planning and scheduling using data-driven feasibility analysis. *Computers & Chemical Engineering*, *161*, p. 107759.
4. Ekanem, I., 2017. *Writing a business plan: A practical guide*. Routledge.
5. Chwolka, A., and Raith, M.G., 2012. The value of business planning before start-up—A decision-theoretical perspective. *Journal of Business Venturing*, *27*(3), pp. 385–399.
6. Narchal, R.M., Kittappa, K., and Bhattacharya, P., 1987. An environmental scanning system for business planning. *Long Range Planning*, *20*(6), pp. 96–105.
7. Lainos, I.A.S.O.N.A.S., 2011. *Red ocean vs blue ocean strategies* (Doctoral dissertation, University of Piraeus (Greece)).
8. Slater, S.F., and Narver, J.C., 1997. *Information search style and business performance in dynamic and stable environments: An exploratory study*. Cambridge, MA: Marketing Science Institute.

9. Kim, W.C., and Mauborgne, R.A., 2014. *Blue ocean strategy, expanded edition: How to create uncontested market space and make the competition irrelevant*. Harvard business review Press.
10. Aguilar, F.J., 1967. *Scanning the business environment*. New York: MacMillan Co.
11. Buye, R., 2021. Critical examination of the PESTEL analysis model. *Project: Action Research for Development*.
12. Porter, M.E., 1985. *The competitive advantage of nations*. New York: The Free Press—Simon & Shuster Inc.
13. Dobbs, M.E., 2014. Guidelines for applying Porter's five forces framework: A set of industry analysis templates. *Competitiveness Review, 24*(1), pp. 32–45.
14. Sammut-Bonnici, T., and Galea, D., 2015. SWOT analysis. *Wiley Encyclopedia of Management*, pp. 1–8.
15. Ansoff, I., 1957. Strategies for diversification. *Harvard Business Review, 35*(5), pp. 113–124.
16. Loredana, E.M., 2016. The use of Ansoff matrix in the field of business. In *MATEC Web of Conferences* (Vol. 44, p. 01006). Les Ulis, France: EDP Sciences.
17. Hax, A.C., and Majluf, N.S., 1983. The use of the growth-share matrix in strategic planning. *Interfaces, 13*(1), pp. 46–60.
18. Sabol, A., Šander, M., and Fučkan, D., 2013, June. The concept of industry life cycle and development of business strategies. In *International conference "Active Citizenship by Management, Knowledge Management & Innovation Knowledge and Learning", Zadar* (pp. 635–642).
19. Wyckham, R.G., and Wedley, W.C., 1990. Factors related to venture feasibility analysis and business plan preparation. *Journal of Small Business Management, 28*(4).
20. Covello, J., and Hazelgren, B., 2006. *The complete book of business plans: Simple steps to writing powerful business plans*. Sourcebooks, Inc.
21. Sutton, G., 2013. *Writing winning business plans: How to prepare a business plan that investors will want to read and invest in*. RDA Press, LLC.
22. Woerd, F.V.D., and Brink, T.V.D., 2004. Feasibility of a responsive business scorecard–a pilot study. *Journal of Business Ethics, 55*, pp. 173–186.

23. Ehmke, C., and Akridge, J., 2005. *The elements of a business plan: First steps for new entrepreneurs*. Purdue University, Purdue Extension.
24. Frese, M., 2000. Executive summary, conclusions, and policy implications. In *Success and failure of microbusiness owners in Africa: A psychological approach*, pp. 161–190.
25. Pinson, L., 2008. *Anatomy of a business plan: The step-by-step guide to building your business and securing your company's future*. Aka associates.
26. Silva, D.S., Ghezzi, A., Aguiar, R.B.D., Cortimiglia, M.N., and Caten, C.S., 2020. Lean startup, agile methodologies and customer development for business model innovation: A systematic review and research agenda. *International Journal of Entrepreneurial Behavior & Research, 26*(4), pp. 595–628.
27. Ian Stuart, F., and Tax, S.S., 1996. Planning for service quality: An integrative approach. *International Journal of Service Industry Management, 7*(4), pp. 58–77.
28. Bangs, D.H., 2002. *The market planning guide: Creating a plan to successfully market your business, product, or service*. Dearborn Financial.
29. Cohen, W.A., 2005. *The marketing plan*. John Wiley & Sons.
30. Silver, E.A., Pyke, D.F., and Peterson, R., 1998. *Inventory management and production planning and scheduling* (Vol. 3, p. 30). New York: Wiley.
31. Bhattacharyya, D.K., 2009. *Human resource planning*. Excel Books India.
32. Mengel, S., and Wouters, M., 2015. Financial planning and control in very small start-up companies: Antecedents and effects on company performance. *International Journal of Entrepreneurship and Small Business, 26*(2), pp. 191–216.
33. Davila, A., and Foster, G., 2007. Management control systems in early-stage startup companies. *The Accounting Review, 82*(4), pp. 907–937.

CHAPTER 10

Business Modeling and Venture Creation Process

Key Learning Points

- Introduction.
- Purposes of a business model.
- Business model as a unique business strategy.
- Business model and value creation.
- Types of business models.
- Business Model Matrix.
- Business model canvas.
- Major concerns of a business model.
- Production and marketing strategies.
- How to formulate strategies.
- What to produce strategies.
- Whom to sell strategies.
- How to sell strategies.
- Building business model.
- Business inception process.
- Identifying a suitable business form.
- Business registration process.
- Setting up Administrative System.
- Setting up Business Functions.
- Setting up Management Functions.

© The Author(s), under exclusive license to Springer Nature Singapore Pte Ltd. 2024

M. Rajaratne, *Concepts, Processes and Practice of Entrepreneurship*, Palgrave Studies in Global Entrepreneurship,
https://doi.org/10.1007/978-981-97-6180-7_10

Introduction

A business proven to be feasible in the feasibility analysis then requires an appropriate business model for its inception. Although the business model is briefly described in the feasibility plan under Product and Service Plan, Marketing Plan, and Operations Plan, such information is only sufficient for the purpose of introducing the business to interested parties prior to inception of the business. For actual commencement of a business, detailed business model is necessary to be developed for planning products, markets, and organization with the aim of profit, growth, and sustainability of the venture. Business success is a reward for business strategies that are formulated by unique business models.[1]

Business model, in that sense, is a uniquely designed business strategy based on product, market, and organizational strategies with the aim of satisfactorily addressing needs and wants of customers that the business anticipates. Some smalltime businesses hardly have any exceptional strategies except that they habitually operate businesses. Some other ventures seem to have already run out of business strategies. This is an indicator that there are ventures that do not have particular business models while some others have ineffective business models. However, most successful ventures operate on unique business models.[2] Business models can vary due to the nature of business and the changes taking place in the wider business environment along the time horizon. Single business model is not effective for all circumstances. Degree of profitability, growth, and sustainability are indicators of the effectiveness of a business model.[3]

Business Strategies

Business model is interpreted as business strategy and hence it varies across time horizons even for the same business according to the conditions of the external circumstances. Business model is not static and it evolves making new business models to exploit fresh business opportunities that arise from different circumstances. While business models must be set prior to start-up of a venture, already established businesses also find it worthwhile to update their business models to suit new trends experienced by the industry and the market they operate. Business model is not only an essential element of a business but also an attraction to prospective investors, directors, key managers, and job-hoppers who aspire to join the venture believing in the unique business strategy.[4]

Business model is the business core strategy that is comprised of three sub-strategies: (1) product innovation strategy, (2) market innovation strategy, and (3) organization innovation strategy. These sub-strategies are adopted to create three different values to customers. They respectively create, capture, and deliver values. So, as a whole, a business model aims at creating three different values to customers. These strategies are sometimes identified as sub-models of the principal business model: value creation model, revenue model, and operating model (Fig. 10.1). They are aimed at achieving profitability, growth, and sustainability of a venture.

Business model can also be comprehended as an overall strategic plan. So, it is a high-level plan that proposes values to customers and investors through specific and differentiated actions in contrast to those of the competitors. In addition to cost and revenue estimates, opportunities to partnering with established firms, long-term profitability, growth, and sustainability are the focus of a business model. Accordingly, a business model is a justifiable strategy to generate revenue and profit for

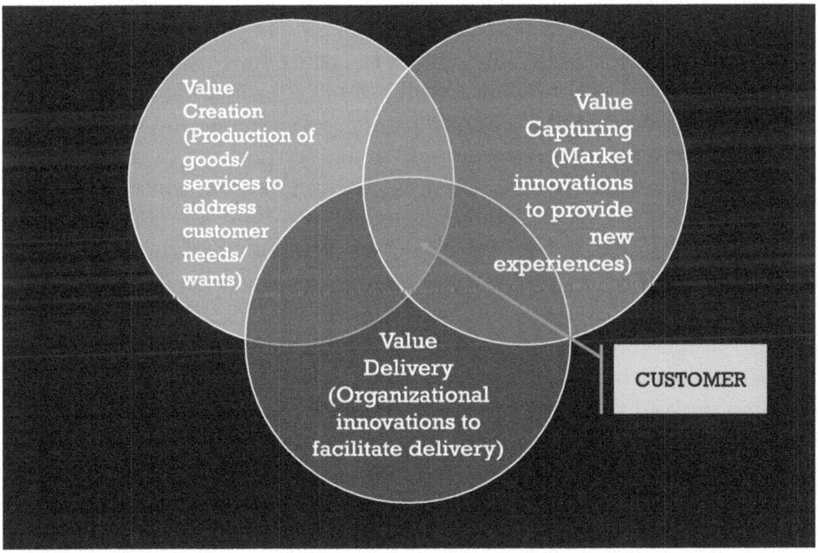

Fig. 10.1 Three circle business model (Author portrayal based on Grayfox Consulting Co. [2014][5])

the venture. A firm should seek revenues exceeding its costs; operating beyond the break-even point. Gross profit is an indicator of a good business model. For achieving this objective, the entrepreneur must bear in mind what is to be produced and then formulate the strategy how it should be produced and sold.[6]

Business Modeling

Business models have evolved ever since businesses were formed in the human history. In consequence, innumerous business models, with many major ones, are present today. The very reason for evolution of business models has been the need for different and effective strategies to make businesses successful. In essence, a business model is a set of strategies that focuses on (1) what to produce, (2) how to produce, (3) whom to sell, and (4) how to sell. For instance, the question what to produce is a question related to the innovation whereas how to produce is a question concerning production technology and strategy.[7] In manufacturing, hand-made, order-made, tailor-made, mass-made, license-made, and standardized products are optional answers for the question "how to make." These production strategies are concerns of a business model.[8]

Another instance can be illustrated referencing to the questions "where to sell and how to sell." Where to sell is a question related to the market strategy while how to sell is a question concerning marketing strategy. The answers to the question "where to sell" refers to the types of markets such as niche market, mass market, and market segmentation. But the question "how to sell" refers to the marketing strategies such as retail, wholesale, agency sale, authorized sale, franchise, department store shops, discount shops, seasonal bargain, credit card discounts, mail order sale, catalogue sale, personal sale, and mass market sale. These strategies compose the segment of marketing strategy of a business model.[9]

Business models are built upon a single strategy or a set of combined strategies derived from the functional areas of a business such as production, marketing, human resource, and finance. Product, production, and marketing strategies are major components of a business model. Thus, essentially, business models are constructed upon the strategies connected to the question of "what and how to produce and whom to and how to sell." All business functions thus, undergo all these strategies together or selectively.[10] While a business can have many business strategies, they all are not equally useful to build a business model. The day-to-day or ordinary production, marketing, or personnel strategies do not compose a business model, but they can be useful strategies under a certain business model. Examples of product, production, market, and marketing strategies connected to a business model are presented below.[11]

What to Produce-Strategies

- State-of-the-art technology-based production
- Best quality material-based production
- Approved material-based production
- Socially responsible production
- Environmentally responsible production
- Ethical production
- Authentic formula-based production
- Secret formula-based production
- Natural material-based production
- Social enterprising.

How to Produce Strategies

- Hand-made production
- Tailor-made production
- Order-made production
- Free size production
- Contracted production
- Putting-out mode of production
- Mass production
- Automated production
- Natural process of production
- Fast-track process of production
- Make-to-eye (food and drink) production
- Just-in-time production
- License-based production
- Franchise-based production
- Sub-contracting and outsourcing
- Service splitting (feed-in small airlines).

Whom to Sell Strategies

- Market segmentation
- Blue Ocean Market
- Niche market
- Personal market
- B2B market
- Regional market
- Open market
- Protected market
- World market
- Members' market
- Consumer club market
- Fan club market
- Premium member market
- Wholesale market
- Retail market
- Department store
- Supermarket.

How to Sell Strategies

- Bundling
- De-bundling
- Marketplace creation
- Personal sales
- Delivery to door step
- One dollar shop
- Discounting
- Razor-blade pricing
- Reverse razor-blade pricing
- Pay-as-you-go strategy
- Easy payments
- Brokerage
- Auction sales.

Entrepreneurs, in practice, combine production and marketing strategies to build effective business models, provided that suitable innovations are chosen. Production and marketing strategies are mutually inclusive, and thus, the production strategies help marketing strategies and, contrariwise, marketing strategies help production strategies. Entrepreneurs can capitalize on this interdependency for building successful business models. Against this backdrop, matrix relationship can be formulated relating to business model development combining production and marketing strategies.

Production-oriented business model is suitable for a venture that possesses strong production skills whereas marketing-oriented business model is suitable for a venture that possesses strong marketing skills. Yet, a perfect business model is feasible when a firm possesses higher order production and marketing competencies. Accordingly, a venture should seek for the best combination of competencies and develop the right business model suitable for different circumstances.

The Business Model Matrix depicted in Fig. 10.2 presents four different business models from which the right model can be chosen according to the contingent requirements.

1. High production orientation
2. High marketing orientation
3. Low production and marketing orientation
4. High production and marketing orientation.

High production orientation business model is common among the makers of components such as computer processors, memory chips, software, and precision goods. These industries face intense oligopolistic competition in technology. High marketing orientation is common among instant food makers, beverage makers, food supplement makers, fast-food chains, and supermarket chains as they operate in a market of near-perfect competition. Low production and low marketing orientation is the common business model of furniture makers, and bicycle makers whose products are more need satisfying than want satisfying. On the contrary, high production and high marketing-oriented business model is popular among the giant electronics and auto makers where the technology race and rivalries are intense.[12]

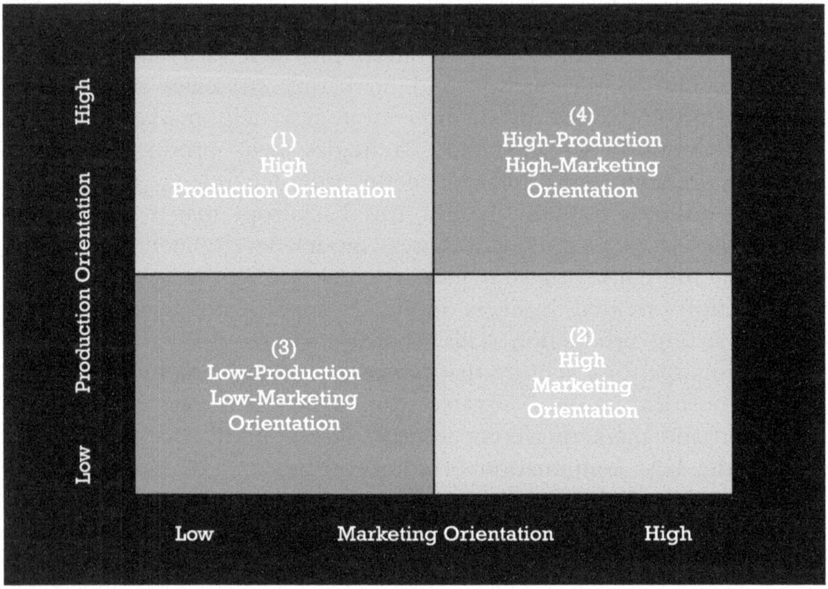

Fig. 10.2 Business model matrix (Author Portrayal)

Building Business Model

Building business model involves selecting a unique central strategy that helps achieve venture objectives. Business model building is a process in which major business strategies are determined. Major production and sales strategies in combination, after selecting the right innovation, thus formulates a business model. Common steps of building a business model are lined up below.[13]

1. Identify needs and wants that the prospective customers are struggling to fulfill. Customer needs and wants are the foundation stones of business model building. Needs are physiological and wants are psychological.
2. Recognize target markets based on customer needs and wants and the possibility for commercial intervention.
3. Recognize inventions suitable to address customer problems. Inventions create knowledge required to produce goods and services.

4. Finalize innovations (products) to satisfy customer needs and wants, i.e., to offer the right products that satisfy customer needs and wants.
5. Identify the most appropriate production strategies that guarantee lower cost and higher quality.
6. Determine the right marketing strategies that guarantee maximum sales and sale revenues.
7. Check whether the business model is capable of generating the expected revenues reviewing the innovation, production strategies, and marketing strategies.
8. Reengineer the business model, if weak, within its own premises to improve revenues.
9. Replace the failing business model with a new model to meet production- and marketing-related objectives with a new set of strategies.

Business Model Canvas

Gray Fox Consulting Co.[14] proposes a common canvas for building business model with nine components as given below. Seven of them are strategies and the other two are focus areas. The focus areas include the cost structure and the revenue streams. Business Model Canvas presents nine-step benchmark for business modeling.[15]

1. Customer Segments
2. Value Proposition
3. Communication Channels
4. Customer Relationships
5. Key Resources
6. Key Activities
7. Key Partnerships
8. Cost structure
9. Revenue streams.

Though a general business model proposes production and marketing strategies, an innovative business model captures a wider scope of a business to transform or reinvent it cutting across to all business functions for bringing in value proposition to the customers. Thus, an innovative business model aims at disrupting a market, instituting a defense against competitors, and making supernormal profits as an unchallengeable entity. Innovative business model can be adopted for a start-up or existing business. In order to create a formidable business entity, an innovative business model is essential.[16] Innovative business model creates smart, sturdy, and hegemonic ventures that can challenge market competition and set newer production methods, create markets, form organizational structures, and even competitiveness benchmarks.

Business Inception Process

Preceding chapters described the prerequisites for laying the foundation for a venture. After acceptance of the feasibility plan by the interested parties, the basic but most essential prerequisite for setting up of a venture is complete. At this point, the proposed venture requires a fully-fledged business model that sets its comprehensive business strategies. With completion of the business model, business inception process can be initiated. At this stage, every venture needs to determine the most suitable legal form for the venture prior to commencing business operations. Entrepreneur has options such as Proprietorship, Partnership, Private Limited Company, and Public Limited company to choose from. Each of these legal forms has its inherent merits and demerits. Registration process, administrative structure, accounting system, income tax, and audit procedures differ across the different organizational forms. Entrepreneurs, therefore, can select the most favorable legal form at the pre-start-up stage.[17]

Permits, licenses, and clearances are required to be obtained from the relevant authorities at the pre-start-up stage. Environmental clearance, export and import clearance, safety clearance, foreign exchange clearance, archaeology department clearance, forestry department clearance, import quota and permits, and license to drive a vehicle are examples of some of the prerequisites. Ventures, depending on differences of their business engagements, require different clearances, licenses, and permits. For instance, if the business belongs to the pharmaceutical industry, the firm is required to obtain clearance from the Food and Drug authority. If the firm is to import chemicals and materials for drug production, the firm is required to obtain importation clearance from Import Controller's Department. Further, if the output is to be exported, the firm has to obtain clearance from the Exports Controller's Department plus the food and drug agency of the importing country. In contrast, explosives- and firearms-related businesses are required a different set of clearances and permits.[18]

Different laws enforced by different countries and states over different times set varied requirements to be fulfilled. Mining, production, transportation, storage, exhibition, advertising, and selling organized in different countries are required to undergo intricate regulations. The laws relating to business differ across countries and time. Therefore, entrepreneurs must be aware of such requirements and fulfill them prior to commencing business operations. Failure to abide by the requirements set forth by public authorities will certainly involve legal actions and hence financial losses or banning of business, in extreme cases. Consumer Protection Authority, Environment Authority, local standard organizations, ISO, HCCP, OHSAS, GMP, SLSI, and SA8000 are major organizations that mandate operational standards.[19]

Though not required by law, at the pre-start-up stage, a firm needs to obtain Patents, Copyrights, Service, and Trademarks commonly known as Intellectual Property Rights. Obtaining Intellectual Property Rights is advantageous for the entrepreneur to protect formula, design, artwork, trade name, trademark, technology, processes, and unique or inherent knowledge from counterfeiting. To this end, entrepreneurs can apply for their rights from the office of the Intellectual Property Rights.[20] Once the firm has obtained Intellectual Property Rights, its rights are protected against unauthorized use of them by other persons or firms. An entrepreneur is required to fulfill some of these requirements at the time of producing the feasibility plan. Once the essential requirements at the pre-start-up stage are met, the entrepreneur can initiate registration of the business.

Registration of Business

A business can be registered as a proprietorship, partnership, private limited company, or public limited company according to how the venture is planned to be formed. Among all legal forms, registration of a proprietorship is the simplest. Proprietorship can exist with or without registration as long as it operates under the name of entrepreneur. Business registration is required if the owner chooses to operate the venture under a different name.[21]

In Sri Lanka, proprietorship can be registered at the Regional Council by submitting a designated application together with residence certificate obtained from the Village Officer and permissions, licenses, and approvals from other government departments or authorities as required. Regional Council acts as the agent of the relevant Provincial Council in handling the business registration affair. Licenses are required for certain businesses such as pharmacies, drug production, beauty parlors, mines, and quarries.

Business name registration procedure of a partnership is also quite similar to that of a proprietorship. The documents required for registration of a proprietorship are relevant to the registration of a partnership also. Designated application for business name registration of a partnership is obtained from the relevant Divisional Secretariat and the same, after filling in is submitted to the Divisional Secretary together with other documents and certificates required. A legally tenable document called Partnership Deed or Article of Partnership signed by the partners to agree upon the partnership name, business ownership, duties and responsibilities of the partners, and the matters related to administration and functioning of the partnership is required prior to business registration. If the application is satisfactory, Divisional Secretary issues the certificate of business registration.

Registration of a limited liability company requires much more effort than that of proprietorship or partnership. Limited liability company is required to be registered at the Company Registrar's Department by filling in a designated application and submitting a few legal documents also. They include the following: name of the company, name of the company secretary, Article of Association, Memorandum of Association, and the board of directors. The Companies Act No. 7 of 2007 of Sri Lanka stipulates the procedures of company registration as depicted in Fig. 10.3.[22]

If the submissions are satisfactory and in order, the Company Registrar initiates the company registration process. First, Company Identity Card (CID) and Certificate of Incorporation (CI) are issued to the company. With these two documents, private limited (Pvt. Ltd.) company is permitted to initiate its business operations. Yet, the procedures for registration of public limited company (PLC) involve a few more steps. Upon receipt of the Company ID and Certificate of Incorporation, the company is permitted to engage in the following activities: issuing shares to the public, entering into non-trade agreements, recruiting employees, and opening accounts and tax files. After completing these activities, the

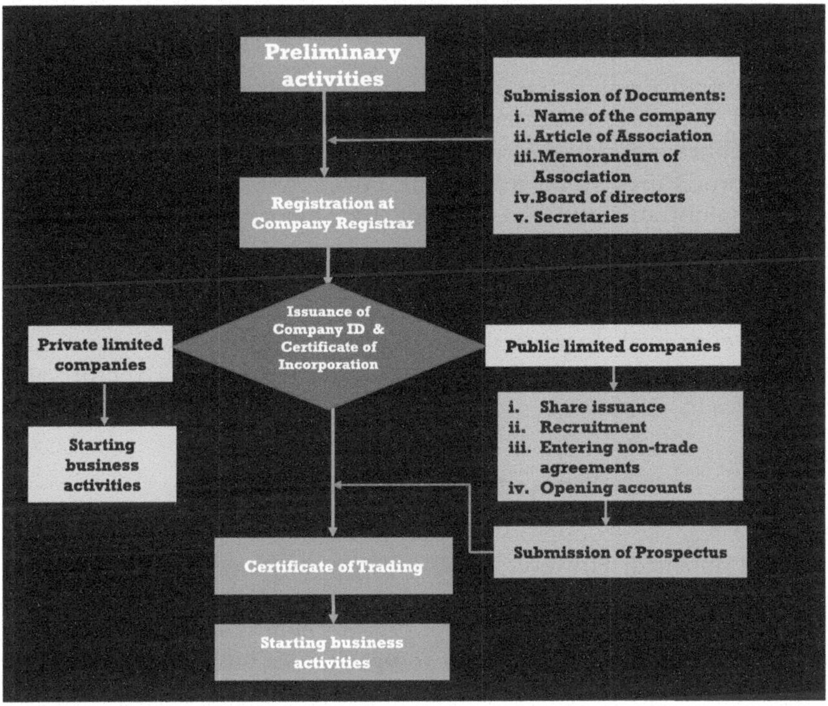

Fig. 10.3 Company registration process (Author Portrayal)

company submits the Business Prospectus to the Company Registrar and obtains the Certificate of Trading (CT) that permits commencement of business operations.

Setting Up Administration System

Administration consolidates venture as it lays down governing principles and practices. Administration is a system in which authority, responsibility, and accountability are hierarchically formed and delegated in order to consolidate the venture as an administrative entity. Administrative system, regardless of being simple or complex, is required for a venture to function. Administrative system constructs a business entity within a well-defined boundary. And it is the administrative system that keeps all activities of a venture within predetermined operational perimeters and parameters.[23]

Administrative system sets up operational guidelines in relation to organizational structure, positional hierarchy, positional powers, positional responsibilities, positional accountabilities, degree of positional freedom, policies, procedures, rules, regulations, ethics, and social responsibilities. When administrative system is present, the venture can initiate business functions and start routine operations. This bearing is equally applicable for virtual businesses also. In a micro enterprise, where single person carries out all business functions, an invisible micro administrative system is engrained. In general, and in conclusion, administrative system is the spine and the vein system that respectively erects a venture and coordinates its operations.

Setting Up Business Functions

In some cases, like proprietorship, a venture is first created and then registration is obtained. However, in all other instances, a venture is created after business registration is obtained. In whichever the case, once the venture is created and administrative or governing system is set up, business functions must be set up for it to operate as a business organization. Every business generally engages in five business functions: Production, Marketing, Finance, Human Resource, and Security. In fact, the security function was identified as a useful business function by Henri Fayol (1917) in his book *General and Industrial Management*. However, four functions except the security function are adopted as of today.[24]

Among all business functions, production is the foremost function because business emerges with commencement of production of goods or services. This implies that every firm has to produce goods or services as its major task. The goods and services are then marketed. Without marketing the output, a business cannot remain in business as its life blood is revenue. Production and marketing functions then require human resource as an input. For all of them, finance is required as a general input. Without finance, no business activity is feasible. Security function involves with the security of assets, transactions, resources, and intellectual properties. Figure 10.4 depicts how the production function is surrounded by the other business functions.

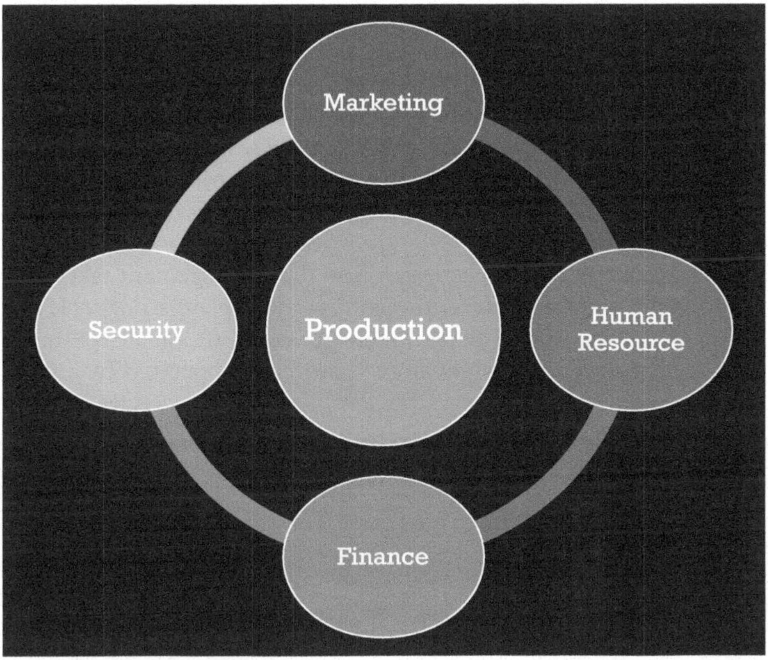

Fig. 10.4 Business functions (Author Portrayal)

Setting Up Management Functions

If the administrative system is the chassis and the business functions are the body, then the management functions are the four-cylinder combustion engine that runs the business organization. Business runs on planning, organizing, leading, and controlling functions. Based on the administrative system, management functions are set up to maneuver the venture to the destination recognized in the business vision. Therefore, achieving business mission through successful business strategies is the key responsibility left in the hands of management.

Business functions (Production, Marketing, Finance, Human Resource, and Security) are operationalized via management functions: Planning, Organizing, Leading, and Controlling. As described in Fig. 10.5, management is a process that starts with an organizational vision and mission. Management then identifies business functions and sets objectives relating to each business function, identifies resources required to achieve the objectives, prepares appropriate action plans, sets suitable strategies to carry out plans, prepares budgets for each plan, implements plans, monitors and measures actual performance, observes performance deviations, reviews or revises plans if necessary, and carries feedforward to reconsidering objectives. Management engages in strategic planning also if strategies are indispensable for achieving business objectives.

It is obvious from the above description that management takes charge of operations of ventures. Here, the entrepreneur plays a dual role as the entrepreneur as well as the general manager or CEO. Small ventures are operated by entrepreneurs while large ventures are operated by a team of

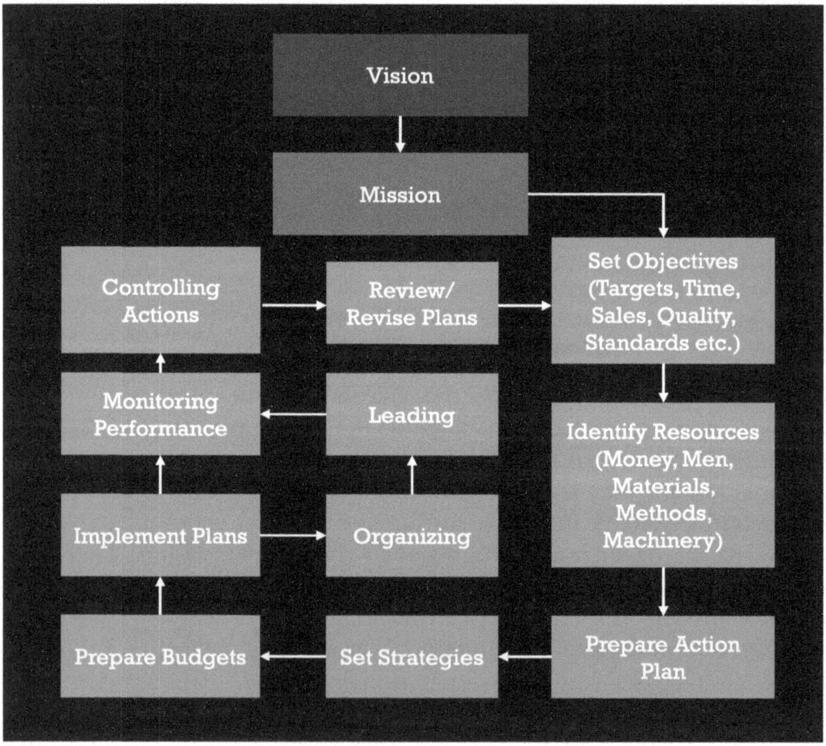

Fig. 10.5 The management process (Author Portrayal)

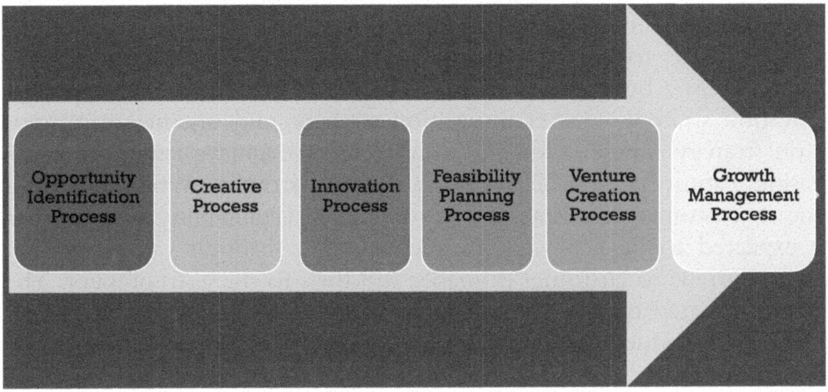

Fig. 10.6 Entrepreneurship process (Author Portrayal)

professional managers comprising of a chairman and a board of directors. With recruitment and deployment of a management team, a venture can inaugurate its start-up operations. In a small business, an entrepreneur quite often performs two other roles also. They are managerial role and technical role. The roles of a cashier, bookkeeper, waiter, and salesman are technical roles. This triple role (entrepreneurial, managerial, technical) cannot be avoided in case of small business. Yet, it is inappropriate for an entrepreneur to engage in non-entrepreneurial roles as managerial and technical skills can be hired for a salary. Entrepreneurial role is the most precious in a venture as it steers a venture. Figure 10.6 sequentially arranges all the five steps described in the preceding chapters plus the growth management component which will be described in the following chapter.

Chapter Summary

Feasibility plan introduces a brief business model as an introduction to the proposed business. Yet, a fully pledged business model that specifies products, markets, organizing for gaining profit, growth, and sustainability is required for commencement of a business. Business model is a uniquely designed business strategy that specifies production, marketing, and organizing of a venture. A business possesses a principal business model which is supported by three sub-models: value creation model, revenue model, and operating model. Business modeling is a strategy making process to fine-tune business ideas to suit to business circumstances. Thus, a business model is comprised of three strategies: product innovation strategy, market innovation strategy, and organization innovation strategy. These strategies are directed to achieve three purposes: creating, capturing, and delivering values to customers. While delivering value to customers, profitability, growth, and sustainability of a venture are expected to be achieved. Business model, through value creation, delivers surplus to customer primarily and then to the entrepreneur. The surplus imparted by a business is recognized by economists as consumer surplus and producer surplus.

Business model tries to find answers to four questions: what to produce, how to produce, whom to sell, and how to sell. Accordingly, these questions respectively focus on innovation strategy, production strategy, market strategy, and marketing strategy. Business models are developed on production-orientated strategies or marketing-orientated strategies or combination of both. These two strategies are interdependent and mostly complementary. Based on this relationship, Business Model Matrix is constructed and four business models are derived as follows: high production orientation, high marketing orientation, low production and marketing orientation, high production and marketing orientation. Gray Fox Consulting Co. proposes a common canvas for benchmarking business models. Out of the nine components of the Canvas, seven are strategies and the other two are focus areas; the latter focuses on the cost and revenue structure.

In venture creation, a suitable business form is required at the outset. Business forms are comprised of Proprietorship, Partnership, Private Limited Company, and Public Limited Company, Franchise, and Licensing. Each business form has its inherent merits and demerits. Business registration process, administrative structure, accounting system, income tax, and audit procedures differ across the different organizational forms. It is recommended that a firm obtains Patents, Copyrights, Service Marks, and Trademarks as appropriate, for protecting intellectual properties from counterfeiting. Permits, licenses, and clearances are also required prior to starting business operations. Environmental clearance, export and import clearance, safety clearance, foreign exchange clearance, archaeology department clearance, forestry department clearance, and import quota are examples of prerequisites. Finally, an application is required to be filed at local authorities or the company registrar's office to obtain approval and permit for business inception. After registration of a business, governing principles, procedures, authority, responsibility, and accountability must be set up to consolidate venture administration. Business functions and management functions are set up thereupon.

Review Questions

1. Differentiate between business modeling and business model.
2. Explain why an entrepreneur needs to be ready with a business model prior to starting up a venture?
3. Discuss the purpose of a business model and point out what a business model does.
4. Business model is designed to achieve (a) Value creation (b) Value capturing, and (c) Value delivering targets. Explain.
5. Identify and describe the major business modeling strategies.
6. "Business model is developed based on the answers to the following key questions." Discuss.

   a. What to produce
   b. How to produce
   c. Whom to sell
   d. How to sell.

7.

   a. What is Business Model Matrix?
   b. What are the four types of business orientations?
   c. How is the Business Model Matrix useful?

8. "Business model canvas is a common format for business modeling that suggests seven strategies and two focus areas." Comment.
9. "It is a prerequisite to select a suitable business form, after formulating a business model and before initiating the venture creation process." Explain why this need arises.
10. "Business registration process differs among nations due to different legal systems." Compare the easiness or difficulty of business registration in two countries.
11. Describe the steps and concerns involved in setting up of management functions for a new venture.
12. Explain how the business functions are determined and business objectives are set.

13. "With setting up of business functions and management functions, the venture creation process is complete and the business starts to operate." Elaborate this statement.

Additional Readings

1. DaSilva, C.M., and Trkman, P., 2014. Business model: What it is and what it is not. *Long Range Planning*, *47*(6), pp. 379–389.
2. Shafer, S.M., Smith, H.J., and Linder, J.C., 2005. The power of business models. *Business Horizons*, *48*(3), pp. 199–207.
3. Gordijn, J., and Akkermans, H., 2001. Designing and evaluating e-business models. *IEEE intelligent Systems*, *16*(4), pp. 11–17.
4. Geissdoerfer, M., Pieroni, M.P., Pigosso, D.C., and Soufani, K., 2020. Circular business models: A review. *Journal of Cleaner Production*, *277*, p. 123741.
5. https://www.gray-fox-consulting.com/en/.
6. Teece, D.J., 2010. Business models, business strategy and innovation. *Long Range Planning*, *43*(2–3), pp. 172–194.
7. Bridgeland, D.M., and Zahavi, R., 2008. *Business modeling: A practical guide to realizing business value*. Morgan Kaufmann.
8. Horkoff, J., Barone, D., et al., 2014. Strategic business modeling: Representation and reasoning. *Software & Systems Modeling*, *13*, pp. 1015–1041.
9. Mathur, S.S., and Kenyon, A., 1997. Our strategy is what we sell. *Long Range Planning*, *30*(3), pp. 455–458.
10. Vorhies, D.W., Morgan, R.E., and Autry, C.W., 2009. Product-market strategy and the marketing capabilities of the firm: Impact on market effectiveness and cash flow performance. *Strategic Management Journal*, *30*(12), pp. 1310–1334.
11. Zott, C., and Amit, R., 2008. The fit between product market strategy and business model: Implications for firm performance. *Strategic Management Journal*, *29*(1), pp. 1–26.
12. Chang, S.J., 2011. *Sony vs Samsung: The inside story of the electronics giants' battle for global supremacy*. John Wiley & Sons.
13. Wirtz, B., and Daiser, P., 2018. Business model innovation processes: A systematic literature review. *Journal of Business Models*, *6*(1), pp. 40–58.
14. https://www.gray-fox-consulting.com/en/.

15. Murray, A., and Scuotto, V., 2015. The business model canvas. *Symphonya. Emerging Issues in Management*, pp. 94–109.
16. Yashkova, E.V., Sineva, N.L., et al., 2016. Development of innovative business model of modern manager's qualities. *International Journal of Environmental and Science Education*, *11*(11), pp. 4650–4659.
17. Passaro, R., Quinto, I., Rippa, P., and Thomas, A., 2016. The start-up lifecycle: An interpretative framework proposal. *RSA AiIG*, pp. 1–25.
18. Castrogiovanni, G.J., 1996. Pre-startup planning and the survival of new small businesses: Theoretical linkages. *Journal of management*, *22*(6), pp. 801–822.
19. Tregear, R., 2014. Business process standardization. In *Handbook on business process management 2: Strategic alignment, governance, people and culture* (pp. 421–441). Berlin, Heidelberg: Springer Berlin Heidelberg.
20. Strathern, M., 2006. Intellectual property and rights. In *Handbook of material culture, 447*.
21. Dayan, Z., and Bolislis, W.R., 2017. Business registration pillars: Good regulatory practice for ASEAN.
22. https://simplebooks.com/srilanka/online-company-registration/.
23. Oliva, F.L., and Kotabe, M., 2019. Barriers, practices, methods and knowledge management tools in startups. *Journal of Knowledge Management*, *23*(9), pp. 1838–1856.
24. Keen, P.G., and Knapp, E.M., 1996. *Every manager's guide to business processes: A glossary of key terms and concepts for today's business leader*. Harvard Business School Press.

CHAPTER 11

Growth Management Process

Key Learning Points

- Introduction.
- Reasons for failure of startups.
- The "Valley of Death."
- Need for growth management.
- Perpetual growth.
- Venture growth and growth management.
- Growth as the source of funds.
- Arnold C. Cooper's growth model.
- Hayakawa's growth model.
- Credibility accumulation.
- Capital accumulation.
- Consideration accumulation.
- Capability accumulation.
- Clientele accumulation.
- The 5-C model.
- Balanced accumulation of 5-Cs.
- Unbalanced accumulation of 5-Cs.
- Venture classification by growth competency.
- Venture Growth Management Scheme.
- The "N" curve and growth management strategies.

© The Author(s), under exclusive license to Springer Nature Singapore Pte Ltd. 2024

M. Rajaratne, *Concepts, Processes and Practice of Entrepreneurship*, Palgrave Studies in Global Entrepreneurship,
https://doi.org/10.1007/978-981-97-6180-7_11

Introduction

Ventures are created to achieve growth objectives and thus all entrepreneurial activities are directed toward achievement of growth. However, the common experience of venture is that most of them do die at a very early stage or within a short period of time.[1] The Commerce Institute (2024)[2] announced its findings as only 80% of the startups survive the first year, 70% the second year, 50% the third year, and 30% the fifth year, 30% the 10th year, and 25% the fifteenth year. Table 11.1 summarizes the numerical findings of the Commerce Institute to highlight the gravity of business failures. Therefore, growth management is as important as venture creation. The steadier the venture growth, the higher will be its profit.[3] As venture growth is an inherent aspiration of entrepreneurs, they responsibly maneuver ventures for higher growth. Venture growth is presumably brought about by perpetual innovation. Perpetual innovation is an outcome of entrepreneurial competency. Yet, there is no generally accepted and preset formula for gaining venture growth. All ventures are not equally entrepreneurial and those ventures that engage in perpetual innovation acquire perpetual growth. The stagnating and declining ventures are signs of lack of entrepreneurial endowments and innovations.[4]

Because growth is the essential characteristic of entrepreneurship, management of growth is pivotal to venture success. Growth and growth management, therefore, are equally important concerns for an entrepreneur from the start-up stage. Growth is the means to channel

Table 11.1 Reasons for businesses failure

	Reason	*Weight (%)*
1	Absence of a market for products/services	42
2	Early running out of cash	29
3	Absence of a right team	23
4	Defeated to competitor	19
5	Pricing and costing issues	18
6	Poor product offering	17
7	Bad business model	17
8	Poor marketing	14
9	Poor customer relationship	14

Data: Commerce Institute (2024)[5]

funds required for current operations and investments in future expansions and technological advancements.[6] Thus, failure in achieving an adequate growth will hinder venture operations, expansions, and advancements. Innovation helps achievement of growth whereas management helps maintenance of growth. Therefore, poor growth and growth management adversely affect venture performance in the short run and then shorten the venture life.[7]

The Threat of Failure

It is common sense that ventures have a life span. Some startups, like Kongo Gumi of Japan, live centuries while most end up in the "Valley of Death" within the first few years since commencement of operations (Fig. 11.1). Ventures are supposed to pass through a few stages: Pre-start-up, product launch and commercialization, early growth, and later growth. Venture experiences negative net cash flow until it gains a significant growth in the early-growth stage. The negative cash flow elongates if the venture takes long in the second stage. The longer the venture takes in stage two, the venture intensifies to suffer from dehydration as cash dries up, as is the case of California Valley of Death, and eventually succumbs to death.[8] Some ventures survive but live short as early growth is not managed and still some fail before entering into the later-growth stage. So, it is obvious that a venture can go wrong anytime. Entrepreneurs thus, must try not to stay long in the Valley of Death but to move quickly to the early-growth stage and from there to focus on growth management.[9] Both innovation and management skills are essential to achieve and maintain growth; in absence of which the venture will wither and die even after walking out of the Valley of Death.

At the introductory or start-up stage, growth management basically attempts to consolidate the market position and financial strength required for its operations. At the early-growth stage, faster growth is expected. Yet, an unmanageable explosive growth will bring imminent danger as what happened to Osborne Computer Co., USA,[10] that was compelled to go out of business due to failing in managing growth during the early stage. Similarly, the majority of ventures set to die during the early stage failing to achieve adequate growth.[11] At early- and later-growth stages, saturation of growth can occur causing cash flows and profits to shrink inviting growth decline. Thus, at the maturity stage, venture reengineering through innovations and growth management are

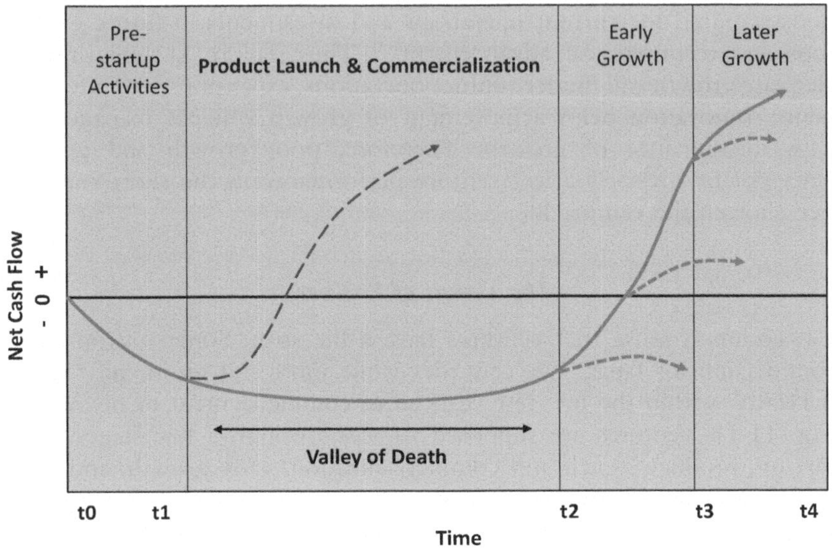

Fig. 11.1 Valley of Death (Author Portrayal)

indispensable to thwart imminent decline. Appropriate growth strategies can extend venture life through reinvigoration.

Need for Growth Management

Ventures that enter the decline stage, which can occur sooner or later in the venture life, require a different set of growth management strategies to avert and rescue from adverse impacts. If saturation and decline are experienced immediately after the start-up stage, innovation strategies are more useful than management strategies for picking up growth. However, if the venture experiences saturation and decline after a steady growth phase, both innovation and management strategies will be required for rescuing the venture. Product and market innovations can be helpful strategies, as proposed by Ansoff, to reinvigorate growth. This is possible for every time when a venture enters saturation or decline.[12]

In case the entrepreneurial capacity is inadequate to mend the issues, management strategies such as selling or closing down business lines, departments, and plants are being considered. Mergers and licensing are also options to keep up with operations. At the saturation stage, some entrepreneurs consider "going public," i.e., converting the business into a public limited company via public offering. This strategy will attract new investors, directors, and business experts who can revitalize the venture.[13] The entrepreneur, through this, can secure their share of wealth. Also, some entrepreneurs create successful ventures and sell them at the growth stage. Such entrepreneurs will never encounter latter stages of the venture life cycle because they keep creating and selling ventures. Such entrepreneurs treat ventures as goods that can be produced and sold.[14]

Perpetual Growth

Joseph Schumpeter (1934)[15] advocates that an entrepreneur not only desires to raise his consumption standard by earning handsome profits but aspires to find a private dynasty also. The term "dynasty" in this context refers absolutely to venture growth that can elevate a venture as an empire. Panasonic Corporation was marked by modest start but is now referred to as an electrical and electronic empire. Likewise, FedEx, Dell, Microsoft, and McDonald's are also corporate dynasties. Dynasty is not feasible in absence of spectacular growth. Robert Ronstadt (1984)[16] pointed out entrepreneurship as a dynamic process that creates incremental wealth. The ability to create incremental wealth certainly determines the degree of venture growth. Peter F. Drucker (1985)[17] explained that entrepreneurship occurs when resources are directed to progressive opportunities that bring about continuous growth. Karl Vesper (1980)[18] emphasized importance of venture growth by recognizing entrepreneurs as psychologically motivated achievers and adventurers. David Holt (2000)[19] stated that "vision for growth" is inherent in entrepreneurship.

Venture is created in response to entrepreneurial opportunity and venture growth is achieved through successive responses to subsequent entrepreneurial opportunities. The ventures that remain irresponsive to opportunities that come across in the entrepreneurial horizon will remain stagnant or small. Therefore, growth is an entrepreneurial phenomenon that occurs when ventures exploit chains of opportunities that ascend along the business "corridor".While opportunities are open for all ventures, the ventures that are competent in foreseeing and responding to them at the right time with right strategy will acquire growth.[20] Opportunities provide chances for innovation of goods and services and bringing about venture growth. Growth performance is an outcome of exploitation of opportunities and management of the growth process that involves managerial competencies also. Therefore, growth management, after creation of a venture, has become an indispensable responsibility of the entrepreneur. This chapter discusses several approaches to growth management.[21]

Cooper's Growth Model

Arnold C. Cooper (1982) advocates the notion that a business passes through four stages: Pre-start-up, Start-up, Early-growth, and Later-growth stages (Fig. 11.2). At the start-up stage, entrepreneur and their team strive to reach the planned sales targets, maintain projected costs and revenues, reach the initial growth targets, and position the products in the market. After achieving the start-up stage targets, the entrepreneur then dedicates to steer the venture to achieve continuous growth in the later stages.[22]

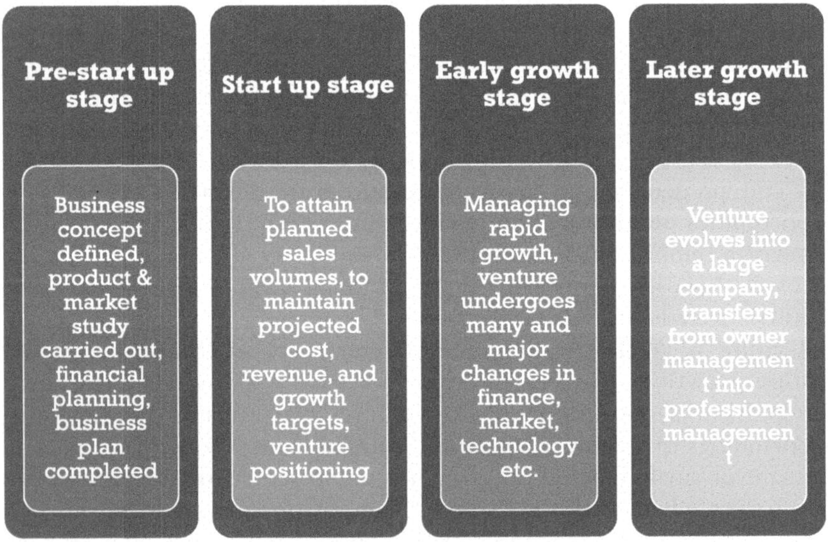

Fig. 11.2 Arnold Cooper—four-stage growth model (Author Portrayal)

In the early-growth stage, the venture may experience either slow growth or rapid growth. While slow growth is not normally preferable, rapid growth will be more challenging and riskier. Therefore, there is a need for managing growth. Absence of remedies to overcome slow growth will push the venture to premature saturation and early decline subsequently. Unexpected slow growth can be attributed to financial bottlenecks, weak marketing programs, drawbacks in innovation, defects in production due to man or machine, offensive rivalry from competitors, and adverse external factors. Entrepreneur should be aware of these possibilities and their impacts to device entrepreneurial and managerial solutions prior to the venture succumbing to adverse effects. Any delay in response would fail to retract growth.

On the other hand, rapid growth could also deliver hard times for a venture. If the products are unforeseeably popular and demanded for the reasons of newness, quality, competitive price, etc., the venture would encounter challenges such as supplying the quantities demanded, delivery to every location, granting sales credits, upscaling production, installing additional machinery and equipment, building inventories, hiring personnel, procuring space, warehousing, and logistics. In unanticipated growth situation, additional quick finances and resources need to be employed. If financing and resource procurement are weak production and supply fall, market share erodes, and growth withers. On the contrary, if the venture chooses to entertain increased demand through borrowing and extending credit facilities, as a means of growth management, liquidity problem could tremble the venture.

Osborne Computer Corporation that commenced operations in 1980 and soon became the most rapidly growing company in the USA but went bankrupt in 1985, coining also the term "Osborne effect," is perhaps the best example of failure in growth management at the early-growth stage. On the contrary, Akio Morita of Sony Corporation wisely managed a similar situation as an American radio seller placed an order to purchase 100,000 radios from Sony at its early-growth stage. Morita believed excessive orders would harm his company and resorted to manage order quantities by setting differential quantity price. He fixed a price for 5,000 units and from that point he set the price to decline for the next 5,000 units. From that point onward, he set incremental prices for every 10,000 units. Morita was concerned with the capacity of his factory that could comfortably produce only 10,000 radios annually. Thus, he pointed out that if the order size exceeds 10,000 units, his company had to bear unbearable additional costs. He confined to supply 10,000 units and his pricing strategy helped Sony to sustain growth.[23]

In fact, with successful management of the early-growth stage, a venture can enter the later-growth stage. Thus, a venture in the later-growth stage is a reward for the efforts of the entrepreneur and their management team. However, many ventures do not enter the later-growth stage due to weaknesses in innovation, finance, marketing, and technology experienced at the early-growth stage. The success at the later-growth stage pushes the venture into a big business or a corporate. In the later-growth stage, some ventures decide to go public through share issuance.

In such circumstances, venture ownership transfers from private ownership to public ownership where shareholders become owners. In parallel to this ownership change, venture control transfers from the entrepreneur to a director board. At this stage, the venture becomes a public entity and operating under different legal, political, and social circumstances. The founder can survive in the venture as long as a majority of shares are held in their ownership.

In the later-growth stage, the venture poses a number of new circumstances for the founder to undergo. In case of transforming the private venture into public venture, the Securities Exchange Commission stipulates the number of shares the founder can hold. Therefore, majority of shares will be held by others. Also, public trading of shares could lead to share ownership manipulation intended to overturn the board of directors. So, the founder may face the risk of their removal from the post of Chairman or CEO. In a corporate setup, the founder cannot exercise much authority as the company is now governed according to a new set of regulations, procedures, laws, and standards that the founder also has to abide by. Founder's views can be challenged and opposed by the board of directors which the governing authority is vested on. The founders who survived governance enmities remain as CEO, Chairman, President, or Senior President toward the end of the later-growth stage.

Churchill and Lewis Growth Model

Neil C. Churchill and Virginia L. Lewis (1983)[24] inquired into the growth of small businesses and found that small businesses pass through the below-mentioned five stages from their inception.

1. Existence stage
2. Survival stage
3. Success stage
4. Takeoff stage
5. Resource maturity stage.

The Five-Stage Growth Model presumes that a business grows from small to large as it passes from young through maturity phases. Interestingly, "evolution" of a business through these five stages is assigned to five types of "revolutions." An entrepreneur, thus, is expected to revolutionize their venture bringing in five different growth strategies as remedies for five probable crises that are encountered by ventures on their evolutionary process as depicted in Fig. 11.3. Although interchange between stages three and four is required for accurate understanding of the proposition, this model is useful for entrepreneurs to predict the crises that loom as the venture matures and to predetermine growth strategies for rescuing the venture from untimely crash.

The Five-Stage Growth Model is much extensive and thus, it does not only confine to merely recommending growth strategies. This model is

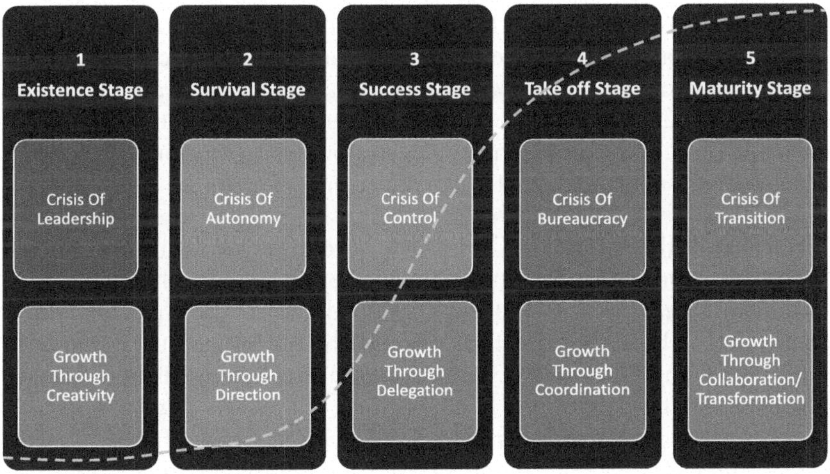

Fig. 11.3 Churchill and Lewis growth model (Author Portrayal based on Churchill and Lewis [1983])

based on five organizational factors such as management style, organizational complexity, management system, business strategy, and business ownership and it advocates the need for entrepreneur awareness of those factors over the five stages through which a venture evolves. So, this model is useful for entrepreneurs in formulating growth strategies taking into consideration the developments of each stage. The most prominent feature of this model is that it departs from the orthodoxy thought that growth stimulates from the principles of management: planning, organizing, leading, and controlling. In contrast, this model considers broad-based organizational challenges that could emanate along evolution of organization and recommends, in advance, growth strategies required for revolutionizing organizational evolution; instead of promoting reactionary strategies.

Hayakawa's Growth Principles

Persistent growth can transform a small business into a corporate venture. In contrast to a startup, a vast set of competencies is essential for a venture that prepares to enter into growth trajectory. In this connection, the growth principles of Tokuji Hayakawa (1970, 2005)[25] provide a useful framework for the entrepreneurs to adopt when seeking continuous growth. According to Hayakawa, opportunities are open for every entrepreneur but only very few capitalize on them and achieve venture growth. Hayakawa says "*opportunities elude while entrepreneurs remain unprepared.*" Thus, to be prepared, a venture must gradually accumulate five specific competencies throughout its operations. According to Hayakawa, venture growth can be achieved through five types of competencies.

Hayakawa, the founder of SHARP Corporation of Japan, introduced these growth principles first in 1970 and then in 2005, in his book titled *Watashino Kangaekata*. Hayakawa's model describes the types of venture competencies, how they are formed, and their relevance to and role in venture growth. This model proposes how a small enterprise can achieve growth and later become a large venture. Hayakawa's growth principles are constructed on accumulation of *Shinyo, Shihon, Houshi, Jinzai*, and *Torihikisaki*; which can respectively be translated into English as Credibility, Capital, Consideration, Capability, and Clientele (Fig. 11.4).

Hayakawa considers that venture growth is an absolute outcome of gradual accumulation of these five competencies. Although these

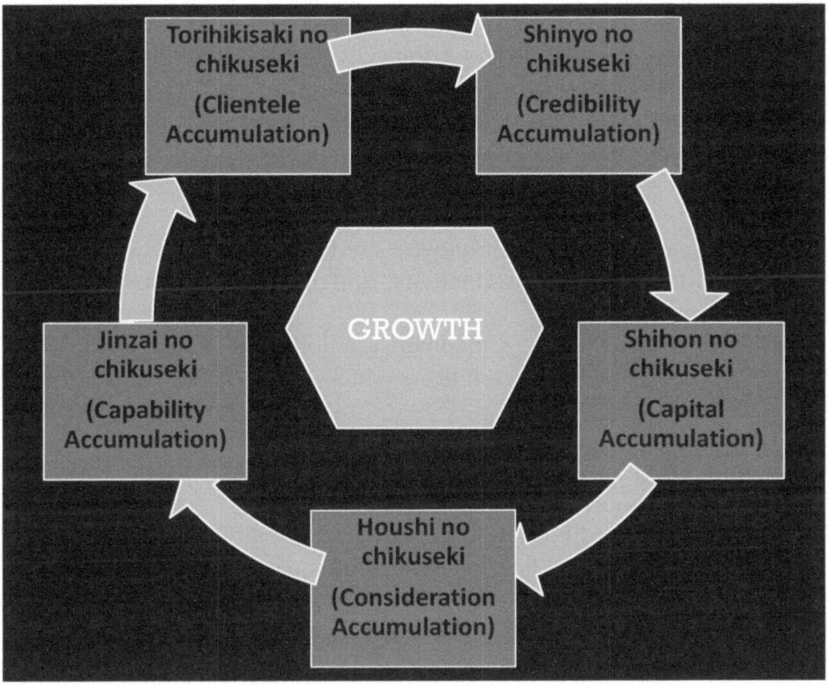

Fig. 11.4 Hayakawa growth principles (Author Portrayal)

competencies may effortlessly accumulate to a certain extent, Hayakawa advocates the need for organizational efforts for systematic accumulation of them from the initial stages of a venture. Gradual accumulation of these competencies will later build into an enormous power that is essential to capitalize on entrepreneurial opportunities that occur along the business horizon. Accumulation of the competencies advocated by Hayakawa will be helpful to accomplish vertical and horizontal integration also that Philip Wickham (1998) pointed out.

Credibility Accumulation

Hayakawa defines credibility as "sincere connections" that develop reliance between the venture and the stakeholders. He insists that credibility should solely exhibit sincerity and trust. This intangible competency cannot be accumulated instantly and thus, it should gradually accrue to conduct of the venture throughout the venture life. Credibility is an asset that cannot be procured or purchased. Credibility is not something that entrepreneur can impose on others but a consequence of their long-standing sincere behavior. Hayakawa specifies five sources that accumulate credibility.

a. Employee credibility—Employee credibility guarantees improved labor pooling, labor productivity, and industrial peace within the organization.
b. Customer credibility—Customer credibility guarantees turnover, market share, and sales cash flows which are essential for commercial operations.
c. Dealer and Supplier credibility—Dealer and supplier credibility builds sound business networks of sales and procurements which are useful for smooth operations.
d. Institutional credibility—Institutional credibility relates to credible dealings with banks, financial institutions, lawyers, accountants, and tax department, etc.
e. Social credibility—As the social acceptance of the venture determines the need for and the size of the venture, social credibility is needed for venture operations and its growth.

Capital Accumulation

Capital is pivotal for every business operation. Venture opportunities fade away while entrepreneurs are not ready with sufficient amount of capital to exploit them. Accordingly, capital is required from the pre-start-up stage through growth stages. Capital is accumulated by a venture in the forms of savings, retained earnings, stock offerings, and borrowings. Hayakawa suggests saving money (in reliable banks) is always a better option at the early stage of a venture. Continuous savings help building trustworthiness between the entrepreneur and the bank. This serves as a guarantee for the entrepreneur to borrow, at a later time, in excess of his outstanding savings at the bank. Also, entrepreneur's ability to repayment will improve their credit worthiness.

Capital comprises money and a few other physical assets. The primary form of capital is comprised of savings and deposits. The secondary form includes investments in stocks, machineries, premises, patents, and ongoing research. The primary form of capital carries highest level of liquidity. Ventures need liquidity for quick acquisitions, purchases, and procurements; failure of which disturbs smooth functioning of the venture. Thus, the money capital is a much important means of guaranteeing smooth operations. Strength of capital accumulation through primary source, in turn, is supportive to acquire capital through secondary sources such as issuance of shares and debentures. Venture's ability to accumulate capital through all these sources is helpful for the venture to improve its competency in capital that increases its financial capability; which is needed for expansion, acquisition, merger, and research and development.

Consideration Accumulation

The concept of consideration emanates from the knowledge of "lifelong borrowings and responsibility to payback" according to Hayakawa. The very meaning of this concept is that every venture obtains resources from the society and environment which is an act of dependency. Therefore, ventures have an obligation to "payback" to the society and environment by being considerate to the "lending" parties. Therefore, the principle of consideration specifies "service to others in compensation of their sacrifice." The service to others should not intend for any gains in return. The beneficiaries of consideration include customers, employees, shareholders, suppliers, dealers, pressure groups, society, natural environment, and the planet Earth in general. Seemingly, consideration relates to Corporate Social Responsibility also.

Consideration is pursued by way of producing quality products and making them available at affordable prices to customers, providing after-services such as repairs, guarantees, online instructions, technology that improves quality of life and saves the environment, providing improved work life to employees, generating work opportunities, paying dividends, giving discounts to dealers, offering attractive prices for suppliers, contributing to social welfare, saving natural environment, and caring corporate social responsibility. Hayakawa points out that consideration helps develop a lasting relationship between the beneficiary and benefactor. Manipulation of consideration in order to gain from beneficiaries, in return, violates the essence of this principle.

Capability Accumulation

Capability is defined as talents and skills of the human factor. Ventures find it difficult to always recruit personnel with right skills and talents that match the venture needs. Nevertheless, the venture can choose capacity building by way of training and development of human resources. The relentless changes taking place in the environmental and technological spheres require continuous adjustment to improve worker skills. The concept of capability development insists that the workers should be hired and developed not only to carry out mere routinely tasks but also to enhance cooperate work environment. The capability base of a venture comprises conceptual, technical, design, and human skills. Hayakawa insists that the entrepreneur himself must accumulate these capabilities before inculcating them in his team. Therefore, entrepreneurs ought to identify required capabilities and the avenues to develop human resources.

Capabilities finally appear as inventions, patent rights, copyrights, trademarks, management competences, research and development, technical and technological competences, trade and distribution networks, art of lobbying, power of influence, motivation, and ability to adjustments. The capability accumulation should begin from the start-up stage of a venture. Capability endows ventures with competition and growth competencies. Capability, thus, is an important input for current business operations and an integral component for the future growth. Especially, it is the strength of venture capability that elevates a venture.

Clientele Accumulation

This principle refers to the accumulation of customers and customer relations. Clientele of a venture, in a broader sense, comprises individual and corporate consumers, suppliers, dealers, and agents. Hayakawa emphasizes hunt for customers as a wrong practice. Customer hunting never helps develop customer relationships. Instead, the co-existence builds better relationships. The practice of changing suppliers often, delisting suppliers for small price differences, and severe bargaining with suppliers obviously harm client relations. Dealer relationship is essential for maintaining a distribution network to effectively dispatch products to the final customers. For the service they render, chances must be created for the dealers to earn satisfactory amount of profit. Through dealer satisfaction, sound relationship is built. Payments for consignments must be handled carefully so as not to damage the dealer relationship. Poor dealers at one time could become effective at another time. Therefore, frequent change of suppliers and dealers should be avoided.

With the final customers (consumers), an entrepreneur should always maintain a thankful and loyal relationship. Appreciation to customers can be expressed in several unique manners. They include giving due value for the price, providing comfort and friendly service, giving discounts, improving customer tastes and image, and ensuring all time satisfaction through after-sale service. These relationships build healthy co-existence with the customers. Customer loyalty is useful not only for their continued support but also for introduction of new customers which helps expansion of customer base. Expansion of the customer base and strengthening customer loyalty are key to growth of a venture.

The 5-C Growth Model

The 5-C Model (Rajaratne, 2011)[26] is an extension to Hayakawa's Growth Model. In contrast, the 5-C model considers the relevance of level and span of competency accumulation to venture growth. Competency accumulation is assumed to take low, moderate, and high intensities. And competency span is assumed to be either balanced or unbalanced; which is their parity. Based on the combinations of the level and span of competency accumulation, the 5-C model examines growth differentials of ventures. Sustaining a proper balance among competencies is imperative to effectively exploit venture opportunities. Any imbalance would obviously result in poor exploitation of venture opportunities. High accumulation of some competencies and low accumulation of others will cause growth bottlenecks. For instance, a situation with high accumulation of all competencies except capital will undoubtedly hinder venture growth due to shortage of finance to exploit opportunities.

One competency is complementary to another. Therefore, to achieve satisfactory growth of the venture, evenly spread competencies at higher level are imperative. Figure 11.5 presents low, medium, and high levels of competencies with even spans. Uneven span connected to any of these levels will create unfavorable condition for growth of the venture. This would cause hiccups in the growth engine and reduce its power uncompromisingly. Therefore, the entrepreneur should thoroughly check and make sure if all the five competencies are in the right condition. In the growth engine, the competencies operate as pistons. Any wear and tear of a piston will adversely affect the torque.

Figure 11.5 depicts the levels of competency in varying strengths such as low (L), medium (M), or high (H). While competencies can take either symmetrical or asymmetrical formation showing balanced or unbalanced spread, Fig. 11.5 depicts a balanced combination while Fig. 11.6 exhibits an instance of unbalanced combination. The balanced combination is always advantageous while an unbalanced combination is disadvantageous as it lacks certain competencies essential for growth. Moreover, it would even be risky trying exploitation of venture opportunities with an unbalanced combination of competencies.

In an unbalanced competency scenario, venturing is not only risky but also unproductive. For instance, a venture that attempts to increase production in absence of adequately accumulated clientele may end up

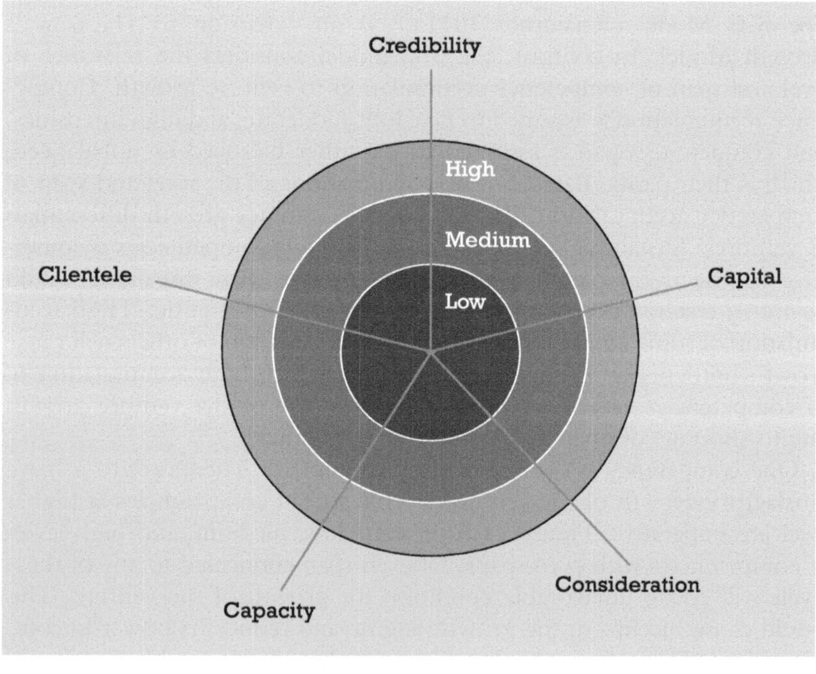

Fig. 11.5 Balanced accumulation of 5-C (Author Portrayal)

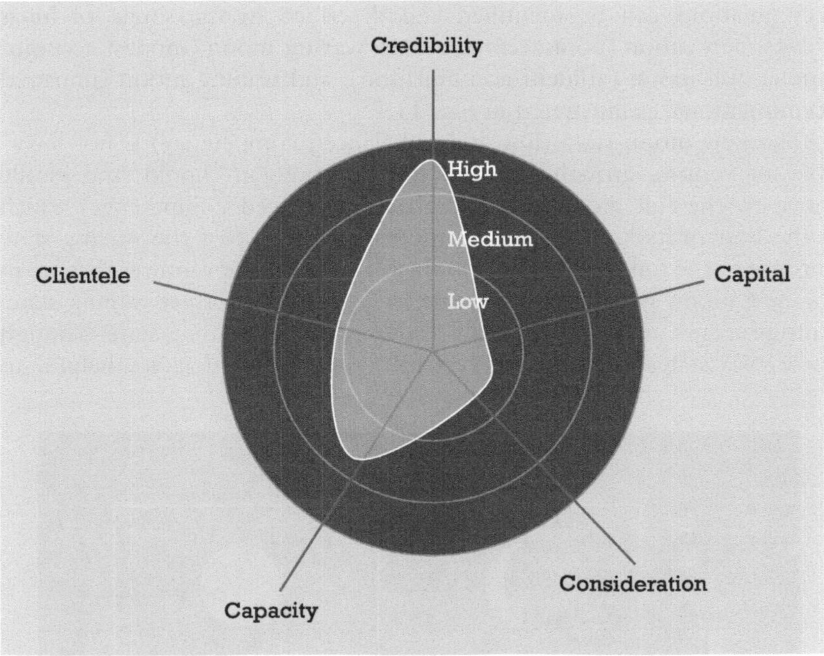

Fig. 11.6 Unbalanced accumulation of 5-C (Author Portrayal)

with poor sales. Therefore, entrepreneurs need to build and maintain balanced competency span at each level of strengths; L, M, and H according to the above portrayals. While the high competency level is the most preferred scenario for high growth, the low and medium level balanced competencies will respectively achieve low and medium growth. Accordingly, firms should only target suitable growth levels matching with competency levels.

The higher the strength and more balanced the competency span, the greater would be the capacity to exploit opportunities and achieve growth. Competency accumulation can be favorable or unfavorable. Favorable accumulation is a state in which competency strength is high and span is balanced. An unfavorable position represents a low and unbalanced competency. In another circumstance, competency accumulation can be low but balanced. Similarly, competency accumulation can be high but unbalanced. Accordingly, four basic states of competency accumulations can be identified and described in the simile of lunar phases; new moon (poor accumulation), waxing moon (modest accumulation), full moon (affluent accumulation), and waning moon (impaired accumulation), as illustrated in Fig. 11.7.

The new moon state (low and unbalanced competency) is not favorable for venture growth and thus the entrepreneur should strategically move to the full moon state (High and balanced competency) which is the best of its kind. However, the venture may pass the waxing state enroute to the full moon state. On the other hand, the ventures that are in the new moon state should struggle to regain their former waning state. Entrepreneurs must not be restful at the waxing or waning state. Though these two states demonstrate certain competencies that are helpful to

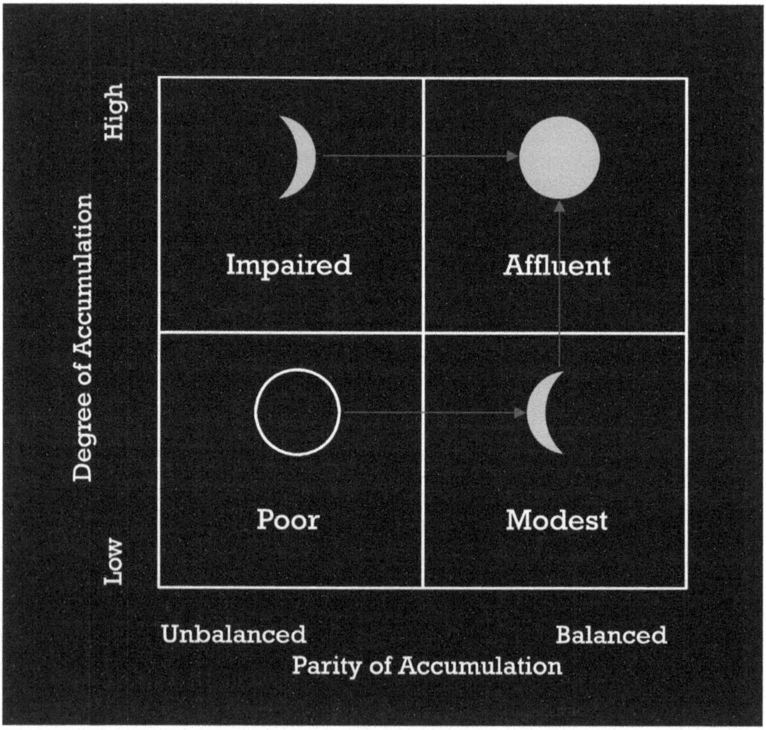

Fig. 11.7 Venture classification by competency (Author Portrayal)

exploit opportunities, they cannot bring about satisfactory growth. Therefore, the venture must aim at reaching the full moon state to exploit all potential opportunities with its fullest strength.

An inception of venture alone does not justify the very meaning of entrepreneurship unless it takes hold of growth. Although a single innovation may be sufficient for inception of a venture, many innovations are essential for acquiring growth thereafter. Opportunities for innovations avail for every venture regardless of its size and age. Yet, it is obvious that ventures react to opportunities differently and in consequence they experience dissimilar growth.

The 5-C model recommends that a venture must identify subcomponents of each competency and cultivate a balanced accumulation throughout the venture life. Different constitutions of these competencies determine differential venture growth. Ventures remain small as long as their competency base lacks power to adequately exploit entrepreneurial opportunities. Thus, a substantially balanced accumulation of the five competencies is required to achieve a significant venture growth. This model helps ascertain growth problem of ventures to competency accumulation problems that cause stagnation in venture growth and guides entrepreneurs in remedying ailments to stimulate growth.

Venture Growth Management Scheme

Venture growth is connected to the strength of entrepreneurial and management skills of a firm. Entrepreneurial skills relate to identifying venture opportunities, intervention, innovation, and commercialization. Managerial skills relate to venture formation and efficient operations. In small ventures, entrepreneur plays this dual role while in large organizations management teams are appointed to assist the entrepreneur. In this scenario, entrepreneurial skills are much related to venture growth whereas managerial skills contribute to sustainability. Both these skills are complementary to venture success but different combinations of the two bring about varying growth and venture sustainability. Therefore, there is no chance for the entrepreneur to choose between entrepreneurial skills and managerial skills but there is a choice for combining the two skills, as indicated in Fig. 11.8, in different situations the venture faces.

Figure 11.9 depicts venture growth combinations based on synchronization of entrepreneurial and managerial skills. Entrepreneurial sphere is demarcated in the BAD triangle and managerial sphere in the BCD

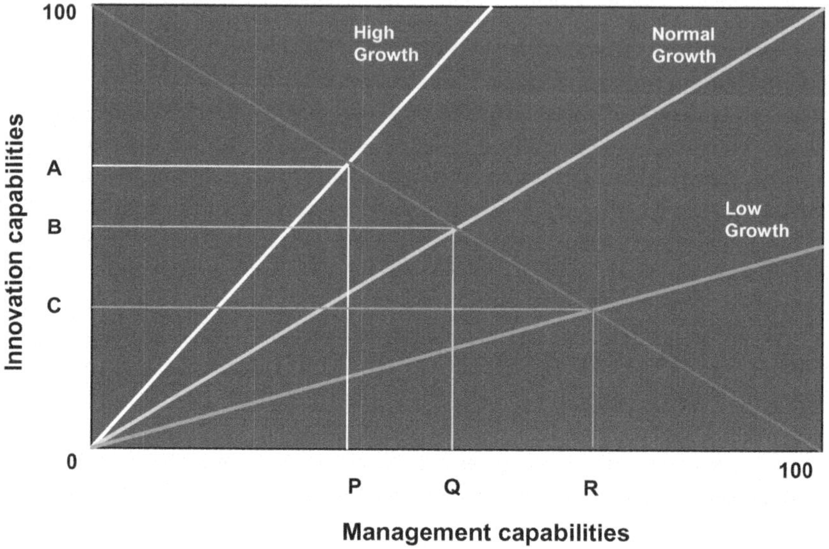

Fig. 11.8 Venture growth differentials (Author Portrayal)

triangle. Along the AC line, infinite combinations of entrepreneurial and managerial skill are indicated. Line BA associates higher entrepreneurial and lower managerial skill combinations. In contrast, the line BC indicates lower entrepreneurial and higher managerial skill combinations. Accordingly, point X represents a venture with higher entrepreneurial and lower managerial skills whereas point Y represents lower entrepreneurial and higher managerial skills. Point Z represents balanced combination of entrepreneurial and managerial skills.

Key to Fig. 11.9:
AC = Performance possibility frontier.
BD = Performance optimality path.
ZA = Innovation consolidation.
ZC = Management consolidation.
X = Innovation intensive *(p3)*.
Y = Management intensive *(p1)*.
T = Lower-level optimality *(p1)*.
U = Upper-level optimality *(p3)*.
Z = Medium level optimality *(p2)*.

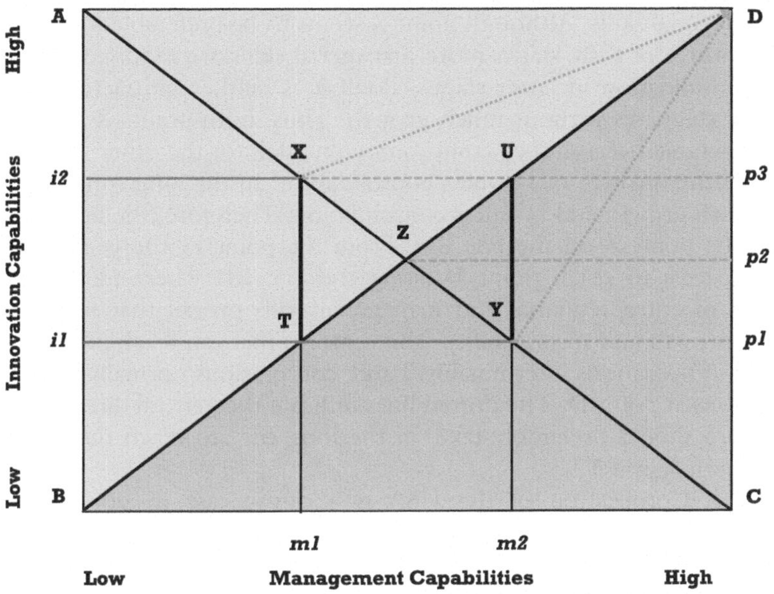

Fig. 11.9 Venture growth management scheme (Author Portrayal)

p1, p2, p3 = Performance level.
m1, m2 = Management Capability.
i1, i2 = Innovation Capability.
Choice of Strategy:
T→X = Innovation consolidation.
X→Z = Retrenchment from innovation to consolidate management.
Y→Z = Retrenchment from management to innovation consolidation.
Y→U = Innovation consolidation.
Z→U = Innovation and Management consolidation.
X→D = From Innovation to Management long term strategy.
Y→D = From Management to Innovation long term strategy.
T→Z→U→D = General optimality by Innovation and Management consolidation.

Accordingly, a venture operating at point X has higher growth potentials but lower sustainability as it depends more on entrepreneurial skills and less on managerial skills. In contrast, a venture operating at point Y has lower growth potentials but higher sustainability as it depends more on managerial skills. Although point X seems to be preferable for startups and ventures of early stage, more managerial skills are required for business consolidation in latter stages. Point Y is neither satisfactory as the venture stagnates without much growth. Thus, both points X and Y are not preferable because they compromise one skill for the other with sacrifice of either growth or business consolidation. In the long run, ventures need both growth and business consolidation. Therefore, the firm should reach the point Z on the line BD. From the point Z, the venture then should strive to reach point D along the line BD where ideal combinations of entrepreneurial and managerial skills prevail that help attain higher growth and sustainability. The ventures that can reach point D can remain in operations interminably. Large corporations normally represent operations at point D. The dotted lines indicate the general direction that a venture should preferably take, in the long run, to reach the point D from point X and Y.

Kodak Corporation of the USA is a classic case in point. Kodak encountered drying up innovations required to face the twenty-first-century digital photography challenges. Kodak was forced to go out of business as it had almost nothing at hand to sell in the modern digital market despite the fact that it had consolidated in the industry for many decades. Kodak was seen losing its position X and being reduced to operations at point T. Fuji Film Co. of Japan, the main rival of Kodak, on the other hand capitalized on its invention, innovation, and managerial skills and hurried to progress toward point D along the YD line. Agfa, another photography product giant, too, lost innovative skills. But capitalizing on managerial skills, it sold the personal imaging business unit on a management buyout agreement to Agfa-Photo GmbH which also filed bankruptcy sooner. These business stories showcase the importance of the proper combinations of entrepreneurial and managerial skills for a venture to be successful in the later stages of business.

Venture Growth Management Scheme advocates the importance of growth management and the notion that growth management is a combined phenomenon of both entrepreneurial and managerial skills. Also, it suggests that concentration on one skill at a time could derail the venture performance. Clever entrepreneurs thus maintain right combinations of both the skills for proper growth management. In particular, in start-up and early-growth stages, more of entrepreneurial skills are useful whereas for maturing and later-growth stages, more of managerial skills are useful. Ventures are created to remain in business in the long run and thus this objective can be only realized by adopting right combinations of entrepreneurial and managerial skills at each stage of the venture. Venture Growth Management Scheme thus advocates that venture success in the long run lies along the paths to point D.

Chapter Summary

Achieving and managing growth is pivotal for venture success. Growth management helps venture growth and sustainability. Therefore, from the start-up stage, growth and growth management are key concerns of an entrepreneur. Growth is an important source of funds required for current operations, future expansions, research and development, and technological advancements. Inadequate growth hinders all such actions and retard venture operations and prospects. For attainment of growth and growth management, innovative and managerial skills are equally essential. Innovation significantly contributes to achievement of growth whereas management especially helps maintenance of growth. Thus, weakness in innovation and management will adversely affect venture performance and shorten its life. Ventures have exclusive life spans from their startup. Some startups, like Kongo Gumi of Japan, have lived centuries while many others end up in the "Valley of Death" within the first few years of operations. Surviving ventures pass through introductory, growth, saturation, and decline stages. When a venture enters the saturation, measures are taken to infuse growth genes to prevent it from declining. Poor growth management results in stagnant and small ventures or drives ventures into the Valley of Death; as did Osborne Computer Corporation of the USA.

Growth management is an indispensable responsibility similar to daily operations of a venture. Similar to many other management practices, for growth management also, a few approaches are present. This chapter introduces them in detail. Arnold C. Cooper advocates that a venture passes through four stages: Pre-start-up, Start-up, Early-growth, and Later-growth stage. He extensively describes distinctive growth management techniques relevant to each stage. Tokuji Hayakawa, Chairman of Sharp Corporation of Japan, advocates five habits that a venture should adopt from the start-up stage to achieve and manage its growth systematically. He states these habits should never be compromised for short-term benefits. Any forgetfulness will damage the accumulation of growth competencies he proposed. Hayakawa says "*opportunities elude while entrepreneurs remain unprepared.*" So, he suggests a venture must gradually accumulate five types of competencies from the very outset of its inception. Hayakawa spells out the means to accumulate five growth competencies and through which how growth can be achieved and managed.

As an extension to Hayakawa's principles, the author proposes unique 5-C model of growth management. Accumulation of and competency in credibility, capital, consideration, capacity, and clientele are represented by 5-Cs. The 5-C model adds levels and spans (depth and width) to Hayakawa's proposition of competency accumulation and holds them as measures for growth management. Competency accumulation can take low, moderate, or high level while competency span can either be balanced or unbalanced. Based on the level and span of competency accumulation, the 5-C model examines growth differentials and growth management challenges of ventures. The Venture Growth Scheme, formulated by the author as a new approach to growth management, advocates the notion that growth management is determined by endowment of entrepreneurial and managerial skills of a venture. Accordingly, entrepreneurial skills relate to growth and managerial skills relate to growth management. Concentration on one skill and ignoring the other can derail venture performance and thus maintaining the right combinations of both is essential for growth management. The "N" curve proposed in this scheme suggests alternative directions of growth and growth management available to entrepreneurs.

Review Questions

1. Explain what growth management is and why growth needs to be managed.
2. Examine, providing relevant data, why most business startups fail during the first few years after commencement of business.
3. Describe, referring to cash flow bottlenecks also, the "Valley of Death" syndrome encountered by business startups.
4. "Growth Management is not only a concern of the slowly growing ventures but also of the fast-growing ventures." Discuss this statement with examples and referring to growth objectives.
5.

   a. What is perpetual growth?

b. Why perpetual growth is essential for a venture?
c. Why is perpetual growth needed?

6. "Venture growth is not only the growth of revenue but also the total progress of the venture." Discover the perspectives of venture growth.
7. Describe the propositions of Arnold C. Cooper's growth model and critically examine its recommendations.
8. What are the main business competencies that are supposed to bring about sustainable venture growth according to Hayakawa's Growth principles?
9. Explain how the following business competencies are accumulated in a venture;

   a. Credibility accumulation
   b. Capital Accumulation
   c. Consideration Accumulation
   d. Capability Accumulation
   e. Clientele Accumulation.

10. "The 5-C model is an extension of Hayakawa's Growth principles." Explain how the 5-C model differs from the original model.
11. Distinguish balanced accumulation from unbalanced accumulation of 5-Cs and describe how the competency accumulation parity and disparity cause venture growth differentials.
12. Discuss the relationship between the intensity of business competency accumulation and venture growth potentials.
13. "The parity and intensity of competency accumulation help classify ventures." Discuss the importance of classifying ventures according to these criteria.
14. Critically evaluate the arguments for and principles of the Venture Growth Management Scheme.
15. Comment on the curve "N" and the growth management strategies derived from the Growth Management Scheme.

Additional Readings

1. Chitkara, B., and Jamal Mahmood, S.M., 2019. An overview of the literature on startups failure: Trends and contributions. *Test Engineering and Management, 81.*

2. https://www.commerceinstitute.com/.
3. Roper, S., 1999. Modelling small business growth and profitability. *Small Business Economics*, *13*, pp. 235–252.
4. Sedláček, P., and Sterk, V., 2017. The growth potential of startups over the business cycle. *American Economic Review*, *107*(10), pp. 3182–3210.
5. https://www.commerceinstitute.com/.
6. Jo, G.S., and Jang, P., 2022. Innovation characteristics of high-growth startups: The Korean case startups. *Journal of Small Business & Entrepreneurship*, *34*(2), pp. 222–239.
7. Cantamessa, M., Gatteschi, V., Perboli, G., and Rosano, M., 2018. Startups' roads to failure. *Sustainability*, *10*(7), p. 2346.
8. Frank, C., Sink, C., Mynatt, L., Rogers, R., and Rappazzo, A., 1996. Surviving the "valley of death": A comparative analysis. *The Journal of Technology Transfer*, *21*, pp. 61–69.
9. Ellwood, P., Williams, C., and Egan, J., 2022. Crossing the valley of death: Five underlying innovation processes. *Technovation*, *109*, p. 102162.
10. https://www.xda-developers.com/40-years-ago-osborne-computer-bankruptcy/.
11. Sommers, W.P., and Koc, A., 1987. Why most new ventures fail (and how others don't). *Management Review*, *76*(9), p. 35.
12. Davidsson, P., Delmar, F., and Wiklund, J., 2017. Entrepreneurship as growth: Growth as entrepreneurship. In *Strategic entrepreneurship: Creating a new mindset* (pp. 328–342).
13. Baum, J.R., Locke, E.A., and Smith, K.G., 2001. A multidimensional model of venture growth. *Academy of Management Journal*, *44*(2), pp. 292–303.
14. Littunen, H., and Virtanen, M., 2009. Differentiating factors of venture growth: From statics to dynamics. *International Journal of Entrepreneurial Behavior & Research*, *15*(6), pp. 535–554.
15. Shumpeter, J.A., 1934. *The theory of economic development* (Schumpeter translated by R. Opie). Cambridge, MA: Harvard University Press.
16. Ronstadt, R., 1984. *Entrepreneurship: Text, cases and notes*. Virginia: Lord Publishing.
17. Drucker, P.F., 1985. Entrepreneurial strategies. California Management Review 1985/02, 27-2.

18. Vesper, K.H., 1980. *New venture strategies*. Englewood, Cliffs, NJ: Prentice-Hall.
19. Holt, D.H., 2000. *Entrepreneurship: New venture creation*. New Delhi: Prentice-Hall of India.
20. Kuratko, D.F., and Hornsby, J.S., 2020. *New venture management: The entrepreneur's roadmap for development, management, and growth*. Routledge.
21. Birley, S., and Stockley, S., 2017. Entrepreneurial teams and venture growth. In *The Blackwell handbook of entrepreneurship* (pp. 287–307).
22. Cooper, A.C. 1982, The entrepreneurship—Small business interface. In Kent, C.A., Sexton, D.L., and Vesper, K.H. (eds.), *Encyclopedia of entrepreneurship* (pp. 193–208). Englewood Cliffs, NJ: Prentice-Hall.
23. Morita, A., Reingold, E.M., and Shimomura, M., 1992. *Made in Japan: Akio Morita a Sony*. Pragma.
24. Lewis, V.L., and Churchill, N.C., 1983. The five stages of small business growth. *University of Illinois at Urbana-Champaign's Academy for Entrepreneurial Leadership Historical Research Reference in Entrepreneurship*.
25. Hayakawa, T., 2005. Watashino Kangaekata (2nd ed.). Osaka: Tosho Shuppan Namiwa Sha.
26. Parakramage, M.R.E., 2011. Entrepreneurship and venture growth: Revisiting the sharp model. *国際広報メディア・観光学ジャーナル*, *13*, pp. 51–62.

PART IV

Entrepreneurship in Practice

CHAPTER 12

Production and Service Ventures

Key Learning Points

- Orientation of production.
- Advantages of production venture.
- Approaches and orientations of production.
- Inventive approach.
- Extension approach.
- Duplication approach.
- Synthesis approach.
- Imitation approach.
- Identifying production opportunities.
- Sources of knowledge.
- Production orientations.
- Choice of production.
- Choice of technology.
- Features of high-tech products.
- Features of mid-tech products.
- Features of low-tech products.
- Concerns in product development.
- Product development process.
- Service ventures.
- Advantages of selecting service venture.

© The Author(s), under exclusive license to Springer Nature Singapore Pte Ltd. 2024

M. Rajaratne, *Concepts, Processes and Practice of Entrepreneurship*, Palgrave Studies in Global Entrepreneurship,
https://doi.org/10.1007/978-981-97-6180-7_12

- Determinants of demand for services.
- Psychological desires and the service sector opportunities.
- Characteristics of services.
- High-touch vs. High-tech.
- Service type and personal qualities.
- Organizing service ventures.
- Customer needs and type of services.
- Service quality and personal quality.

Introduction

Production is broadly classified into two types: production of goods and production of services. When planning a business, the entrepreneur ought to choose between the types of production at the outset. In fact, the feasibility plan not only proposes the type of venture but also the type of production. Entrepreneur has their liberty to select the type of production from a vast array of industries. The scope of production accommodates production of both goods and services.[1] Thus, production includes manufacturing, processing, assembly, agriculture, construction, information technology, food production, service, and many more.[2] Production of goods naturally contrasts with production of services. Therefore, there are two types of ventures: production ventures and service ventures.[3]

Production entrepreneurship is defined as the one that produces tangible products whereas service entrepreneurship is defined as producer of intangible products. In entrepreneurial sense, goods and services produced are supposed to be innovative and thus new[4] or better.[5] An entrepreneur who chooses to engage in manufacturing has the following approaches of production to choose from.

1. Inventive approach
2. Extension approach
3. Duplication approach
4. Synthesis approach
5. Imitation approach.

Inventive Approach

Inventive approach involves in production of entirely new goods based on inventions. New knowledge is required for production of new goods. Inventions bring about the knowledge required for this type of production. Literally, the inventive approach leads to production of inventive goods. Inventive goods are novel means to intervene in solving common problems.[6] Examples include the Computer, Calculator, Red Bull, Penicillin, Integrated Circuit, Transistor, Lithium-ion, Light Emitting Diode (LED), and millions of other products from industries like food, drug, electronics, and machinery.

New knowledge helps production of new goods but that knowledge obsoletes at a later time and thus, newer knowledge is needed to produce newer goods. Seemingly, at a time cross section, every market hosts new and newer goods. Considerably intensive research and intuition are required for generation of knowledge required for production of inventive goods. Knowledge is the foremost factor in inventive approach. For that reason, some prefer to call inventive goods as "knowledge goods" also.

Extension Approach

Extension approach involves production of improved or better goods. Improvement to existing goods brings about better goods. Research and development are required to produce improved goods. Improved goods are much similar to what used to exist in the market more popular than them. Laptop, ballpoint pen, digital camera, and electric car are a few examples of improved goods that are extensions of typewriter, fountain pen, SLR camera, and fossil fuel car respectively. These goods are not entirely new products. They are very similar to their earlier versions but perform better. Present products are mostly improved or extended to better satisfy needs and wants.[7] Certain goods like Marmite and gripe water are not extended but market share is maintained for a considerably long time by extending their markets only.[8]

Duplication Approach

Duplication approach involves production of goods with creative replication. Duplication is not mere imitation but ideation of products based on something presently existing. Therefore, new concepts are pivotal to duplication. And capital investment is a key feature of some duplication goods. Supermarkets and family restaurants are examples of duplication. The concept of a grocery shop or boutique is reformed into a supermarket and a normal restaurant is reformed into a family restaurant. Duplicated beach, zero-gravity chamber, virtual recreation (VR), Zoo, and aquarium are modern examples of duplications. These duplicates are identified as creative replicates.[9] Duplication is seen as brand imitation also in relation to branded and designer goods such as garments, sportswear, wristwatches, and handbags. Some of the duplicates are produced pirating intellectual property rights of original makers, which is an unlawful act.

Synthesis Approach

Synthesis approach advocates production of goods synchronizing numerous components into a single good. This sometimes features or is mistaken as assembling of goods. Assembling is different from synchronizing; automobile is a product after assembling but technologies such as Antilock Brake System (ABS) and Hill Assist are integrated and synchronized components in an automobile. Even if these synchronized features were removed, the vehicle can be functional and useful.

Unlike automobiles, smartphones and digital watches are classic examples of synchronized goods that will not properly function if some synchronized features are removed. Numerous goods produced at present are outcomes of synchronization of which integrated units cannot be removed without a loss to the product.[10] Smartphone is a synthesis of a telephone, camera, radio, television, audio recorder, video recorder, word processor, calculator, scanner, calendar, clock, health monitor, album, library, notepad, alarm clock, teleprompter, road map, road guide, and many more which are equivalent to a truck-load of conventional goods. Had not they been synthesized into the smartphone, the product would remain in the analog form.

Imitation Approach

Imitation is the most common form of goods. Imitations are inferior copies of authentic goods. Imitations are produced with light technologies, for short life cycles, and at incredibly low cost. Markets are flooded with a large number of imitated goods such as biscuits, carbonated drinks, garments, instant foods, and low-end electronics. Imitation sometimes does not infringe intellectual property rights because many original goods are not protected by intellectual property right laws. Some entrepreneurs find it easier to imitate than inventing, extending, synthesizing, or duplicating because the knowledge, skills, technology, and capital required for imitating is much insignificant.[11] Marketing of imitations is much easier in the markets where price sensitive customers dominate. Imitators not only copy formula and designs but trademarks also to benefit from the marketing programs of the original makers.

Identifying Production Opportunities

As elaborated in an earlier chapter, business opportunities are either explicit or implicit. Entrepreneurs can readily recognize explicit opportunities whereas implicit opportunities demand special entrepreneurial efforts.[12] Thus, in a situation where opportunities are implicit, the following techniques will be useful for an entrepreneur to identify venture opportunities.

- **Critical observations**: Observation of the extent to which the goods and the services available at the market at present can satisfy customer needs and wants. Any incapability of the present products provides opportunities for production of new or better products.
- **Customer sensitivity analysis**: Customer sensitivity to price, quality, quantity, performance, design, technology, prestige, functions, and convenience of the presently available products can derive opportunities for production of goods that can suit to customer budget, psychology, social status, etc.
- **Analysis of product drawbacks**: Any drawback detected in existing products creates opportunities for entrepreneurs to introduce enhancement or improvement to them via producing substitutes.
- **Search for inventions**: In order to better cater to customer needs and wants, there arise opportunities to bring about new products. When suitable inventions are available, entrepreneurs can engage in production of new products.
- **Mind Mapping**: Detailing out and focusing thoughts about prospective entrepreneurial engagement is done through mind mapping exercise. Mind mapping helps isolation of the right opportunity and production of the most viable goods.

- **Brainstorming**: Entrepreneur and his team can engage in brainstorming sessions to recognize an exact opportunity for a commercially viable product.
- **Intuition**: Opportunities sometimes occur only to intuition. Initially, intuition recognizes inventive ideas and then prospective markets. New ideas are then transformed into new or better products.
- **Resource Conversion**: Products are feasible with the materials or spaces that are familiar to entrepreneur or of easy access to him/her. Entrepreneurship Development Programs habitually promote production of goods out of the resources in close proximities.
- **Habit adoption**: Habit of masses is an important mark for an entrepreneur to innovate goods. Some habits continue amidst social and health concerns also. Chewing (something) has been an age-old habit of people in every corner of the world. Chewing gum is produced based on that habit.
- **Ritual adoption**: Every culture has longstanding rituals and they are mostly connected to religious practices. At temples, shrines, churches, and mosques, and any other religious place, prayers, sacrifices, offerings, and pooja are common. These rituals require certain products for offering or sacrifices. Also, in many cultures, ornaments represent ritualistic behavior of people. These goods are demanded in large quantities and opportunities arise for production of the same.

Sources of Knowledge

To produce the right goods, right knowledge about goods is essential. Knowledge is derived from external or/and internal sources.[13] Internal knowledge is primarily derived from invention process and that knowledge is then converted into goods through the innovation process. The knowledge of goods to be produced is derived from the following sources.

1. Research
2. Accidental occurrences
3. Challenging thoughts
4. Intuition
5. Development.

The knowledge required for innovating suitable products to address customer needs and wants is derived from designated research. Fundamental research creates knowledge that helps produce incredible goods, technologies, and processes. Integrated Circuit, Transistor, Remote sensing, and Artificial Intelligence are examples. Chemicals are also outcomes of fundamental research that have led to pharmaceuticals and many other products also. Accidental occurrences help create the knowledge required to produce useful goods. Unexpected findings led to Penicillin, Post-it, and McDonald's chain with no research but with some accidental happenings. Daring thoughts challenge incongruities or impossibilities.

Daring thoughts themselves provide knowledge to turn impossibilities into possibilities. Overnight parcel delivery in the USA was a onetime impossibility as the landmass is extensive. But UPS and FedEx devised a way out and succeeded. A radio that fits into a shirt pocket in the 1950s was an impossibility. Yet, Sony corporation introduced model TR-63 pocket radio in 1957 and overcame the impossibility. Intuition is inherent knowledge that can be directed to catch product ideas. Elephant Poo Papers and Red Bull energy brand are examples of the products emerged from intuition. Product development is a major source of production of new or better products. Ballpoint pen is an example of developed product which is a transformation of the quill pen.

Production Orientations

Production of different kinds of goods is related to types of production orientations also. Different entrepreneurs adopt different product orientations in the innovation process.[14] While there can be a large number of production orientations, the major types are described below.

- Imagination-based orientation—Products are innovated based on entrepreneur's imaginations (Air plane, Walkman, Pocket radio)
- Problem-solving orientation—Products are innovated to solve problems (Drugs, Online services, Calculator)
- Exploitation orientation—Products innovated to exploit short-term opportunities (Imitation, inferior goods, pilgrimage goods)
- Market gap orientation—Products innovated to tap market gaps (Three-wheeler, Flavored soya meat)

- Skill-based orientation—Products solely based on skills of the entrepreneur (Brass ware, steel and aluminum workshops, carpentry)
- Material-based orientation—Products innovated from materials or resources available in the proximity (Poo papers, Coconut shell products, pottery)
- Preference-based orientation—Products innovated in the preferred fields (Herbal products, Authentic food, Organic foods)
- Fashionable orientation—Products innovated to introduce fashions (Garments, Shoes, Ornaments)
- License orientation—Products that are manufactured under license of the original maker (Coke, Pepsi)
- Franchise orientation—Production under franchise agreements such as McDonald's, KFC, Pizza Hut operations)
- OEM, ODM orientation—Original Equipment Making and Original Design Making-based production. (Auto parts, and branded goods such as Nike, Gucci, Louis Vuitton).

Choice of Production

Production of goods can be appropriated to several sectors in the economy. Accordingly, production of goods comes from manufacturing, construction, processing, mining, and agriculture. Entrepreneurial opportunities are equally available in all these sectors. Relatively, manufacturing sector appears to be an opportunity rich sector as it is sensitively attuned to constant technological advancements. On the other hand, agricultural sector produces short-lived goods and thus, it creates extensive opportunities for production due to recurrence of needs.

Abundant opportunities prevail in the processing industry as the modern technology has invigorated the processing sector. Food processing, material processing, and assembly lines produce a vast array of goods. This phenomenon is internationally spread as Global Value Chain (GVC) at present. Mining has been revitalized due to the need for metal and mineral for industries generating lots of opportunities to be involved in that sector. The construction sector is rapidly expanding as housing, logistics, and city building play a vital role in human life. This brief backdrop reveals that opportunities are abundantly available for the entrepreneur to initiate ventures in all subsectors of production.

Entrepreneur's choice of a specific industrial sector is determined by two factors: personal factors and industry-specific factors. Personal factor includes personal attributes and preferences while industry-specific factor comprises advantages or disadvantages pertaining to the sector (Fig. 12.1). Personal attributes include entrepreneur's skills, experience, business connections, and knowledge in a field of production. A person who possesses production skills, sales skills, work experience, connections with business community, and knowledge in business operations finds it feasible to initiate a venture based on those attributes. Inception of soya meat production of Raigam Co.[15] was founded on unique homegrown recipe. Vendol[16] products are an outcome of the knowledge, skills, and experience of the company's chairman who is an Ayurvedic doctor. The elephant poo paper production was led by the intuitive knowledge of materials, paper production technique, and the uses of papers. Dingle brand mineral water company was founded on accessibility to mineral water resource and marketing network gained through past institutional experience of the Dingle CEO.[17]

Personal preference is also a determinant factor in choosing an area of production. Entrepreneur's likes or dislikes heavily matter in determining what to be produced. In this instance, attributes of the entrepreneur tend to downplay the decision-making. Preference is a reflection of personal attitudes. Attitudes are instilled in individuals by inculcation. A person who has long experience in or exposure to slaughtering animals may choose to produce animal foods instead of producing meat. Also, a person with banking skills may end up with plantation. Seemingly, personal preference is more powerful than personal attributes.

Even if a venture based on attributes could be successful, the entrepreneur may not want to engage in it due to his preference. For instance, poultry farming, goat farming, and meat processing could be more profitable than vegetable farming. But an entrepreneur may choose the low profit vegetable farming solely because they do not prefer animal husbandry. There are cases that some entrepreneurs prefer to confine to family business despite the fact that the business could be elevated as a quoted public company.

Inherent Advantages and Disadvantages

Every industry has its inherent advantages and disadvantages. Entrepreneurs preview them prior to selection of an industry. Compared

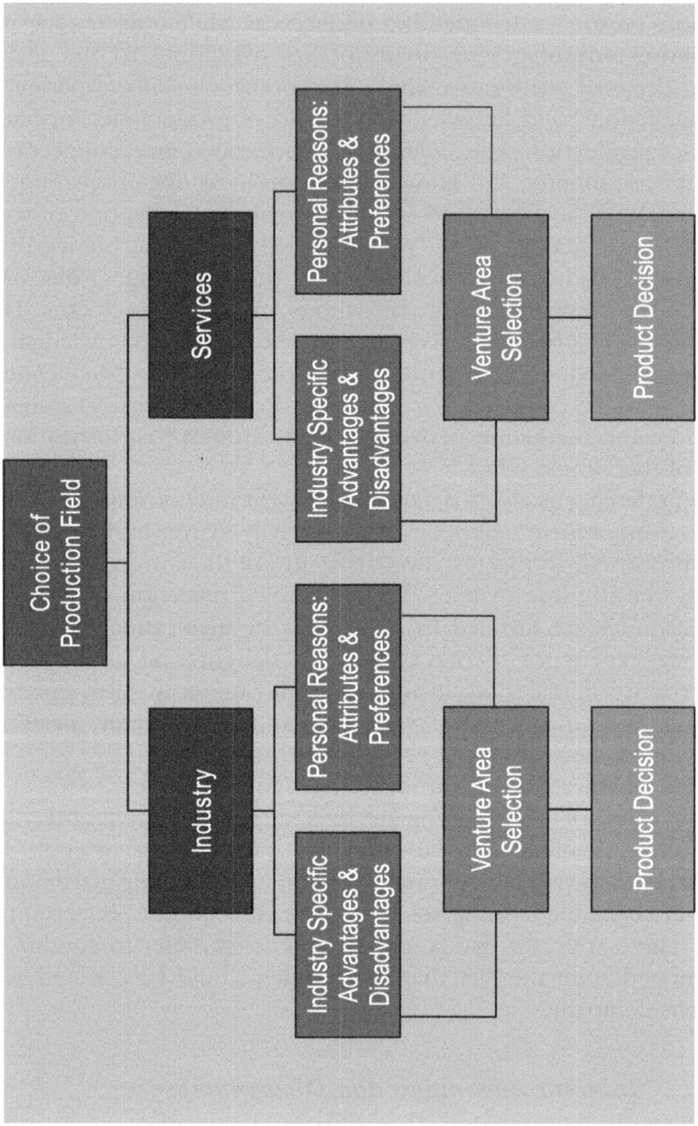

Fig. 12.1 Venture selection considerations (Author Portrayal)

to agriculture, fishing, forestry, and even construction, manufacturing has become a leading sector due to its own advantages and the relative disadvantages of the other sectors. Uncertainty, perishability, obsolescence, and legal restrains are common disadvantageous in the non-manufacturing sectors. Manufacturing sector advantages are summarized below in contrast to the agriculture sector.

- Value addition possibilities in the industry are more prevalent
- Profit margin in industry is normally high as price leadership can be retained
- Industry is less affected by weather and climatic changes
- Industry sometimes enjoys monopolistic advantage and thus price manipulation of industrial goods is possible
- Specialization and divisibility practices in the industrial sector is generally feasible
- Local or international sub-contracting and international transfer of production are feasible
- Ample possibilities prevail for introducing modifications to existing products
- Technological advancements help produce new goods.

Figure 12.2 depicts the value addition possibilities of a single material when processed under different techniques. Different processing techniques can bring about value differentials to a material. Wheat flour, in this instance, can be processed with bread making technology and at the innovation level Q which yields in N level of value addition. If cake processing technique is adopted, M amount of value is perceived at Q level of innovation. Further, under biscuit making technique, the highest level of value creation, at L, is feasible at Q level of innovation. It is clear that every innovation lies in a range of resource transformation. In this instance, innovation level is set at Q and value creation differentials are appropriated to three different products that use wheat flour as base material. This case in point explains that the properties of the base material help creating value differentials.

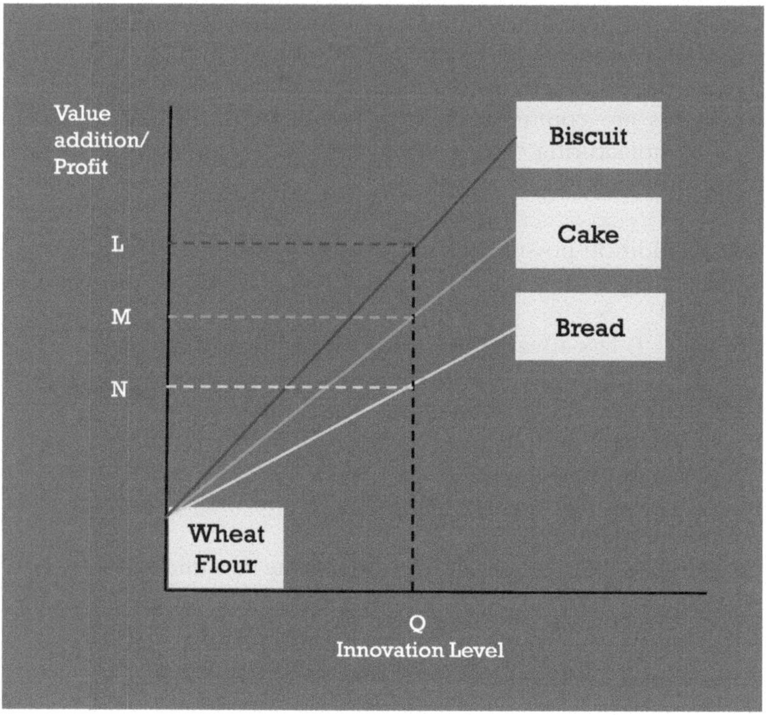

Fig. 12.2 Value addition differentials (Author Portrayal)

Choice of Technology

Technology plays a significant role in production of goods. Different technologies used in the production process determine the differences between products themselves. Product differences caused by technological differences can be observed in product quality, quantity of production, unit cost of production, and volume of supply of the product. In manufacturing, three different technology platforms can be observed. They are High-Tech, Mid-Tech, and Low-Tech. Among these different types of technologies, the right type should be selected considering its appropriateness to bring about expected quality, quantity, and unit cost of the product.

Features of High-Tech Products

High-Tech has its inherent attributes and the products manufactured based on High-Tech include precision goods such as powerful cameras, medical equipment, supercomputers, humanoid-robots, remote sensing products, space rockets, jets, and genetically modified food products.[18]

- Products based on High-Tech requires fundamental research and research for technology development. As research costs money, skills, time, and effort, only a few entrepreneurs can engage in High-Tech-based production.
- Technology obsoletes every moment as new technology is developed by the same venture or otherwise by the competitors. High-Tech ventures are therefore required to constantly engage in research and development. If new technology is not invented or developed, the venture will tend to lose its technological competitiveness.
- High-Tech-based production obligates the venture to maintain technology leadership. At any moment that the venture loses the grip of technology leadership, competitors will take over causing irrecoverable damage.
- High-Tech-based products necessitate the venture to obtain intellectual property rights, which is a tedious task, to protect technological inventions against infringements. If intellectual property rights are not obtained, competitors could infringe the technology as "free technology" at the cost of the inventor.
- The High-Tech-based products always can benefit from monopolistic advantage as they can maintain technological hegemony. This will result in market dominance and high profit margins.

Features of Mid-Tech Products

A vast array of goods is produced under Mid-Tech. The characteristics of this technology and the goods produced under it are described below. High-Tech usually turns into Mid-Tech after years are lapsed since its invention.[19] Personal computers, automobiles, electronic equipment, and devices are now identified as Mid-Tech products due to the technology generalization phenomenon. Main features of Mid-Tech are described below.

- Existing knowledge and technology are mostly sufficient for production and thus, the firm can avoid fundamental research.
- Technology development alone is sufficient for the product improvement.
- With less amount of capital, technology development can be accomplished.
- Mid-level technology can be easily purchased, contracted, licensed, or leased as it is prevalent and less expensive.
- Goods produced under Mid-Tech face severe competition as many competitors are present in the market due to easy access to the technology.
- Production under Mid-Tech is easy to be initiated and thus, the creation of ventures under this technology is less challenging.
- The products of this technological category are easy to be imitated and thus the venture shall have to face competition from the rivals in absence of commendable marketing strategy.

Features of Low-Tech Products

The Low-Tech character is vastly prevalent in common consumer goods market. Consumer goods such as pens, pencils, exercise books, processed foods, soap, detergents, garments, and some household apparatuses like furniture, electric fans, and plastic and lighting items are examples of Low-Tech products.[20] This technology is not protected through patent rights. Thus, these products are usually protected by trade names and trademarks to differentiate brand ownership. Main characteristics of Low-Tech are described below.

- Low-Tech is common and thus available free. No fee is needed to acquire this technology.
- Less capital and efforts are required for initiating a venture based on Low-Tech.
- Competitiveness is intense as many producers can easily adopt this technology.
- Product development is easy and inexpensive under this technology.
- Products are of short life cycles and of fashionable nature.
- Even minor innovative idea can make a significant breakthrough in the products.

- Product protection through intellectual property rights is difficult and not essential in most cases.
- This technology category is a good choice for small startups as production is easy.

Product Development Considerations

Before starting product development process, an entrepreneur needs to be aware of several important factors relating to a product and to consider adoption of several key features to the products. Entrepreneur considerations differ across different types of products. Although the product development literature frequently deals with environmental concerns, legal concerns, security concerns, cultural concerns, and ethical concerns, this section focuses on the overall and strategic features to be considered at the product planning stage.[21]

- **Design**—Every product must have a design. The design should be unique and attractive. Some goods sell themselves for the design itself. Therefore, the design must be an important concern when developing a product.
- **Durability**—Durability is an important concern of goods that are not frequently disposed. Some goods have short life cycles while some others live long. The durability thus is considered as essential aspect of the products with longer life cycles.
- **Quality**—Quality of a product is an intricate aspect. Performance and the usefulness of the product should be given importance in the product development process.
- **Reliability**—Reliability of a product is described in terms of performance and longevity. A product, after purchased, should guarantee customer satisfaction during the period the product lasts and thus, the product must last for a reasonable period of time.
- **Serviceability**—Serviceability is important for the goods that are made to last long. Some goods are produced to be used for several years and thus they need to be maintained through servicing until disposed. Therefore, the entrepreneur should give attention to serviceability of the product and commit to maintenance and supply of spare parts.

- **Movability**—Movability is an important aspect of every product. Shape, weight, and size are key factors of movability. Packaging matters for some goods. When designing a product, attention must be paid to transportation feasibility, possible damage, and suitable packaging.
- **Mobility**—Mobility is a key feature of many goods at present. Therefore, the mobility features are required to be instilled in goods that are expected to be mobile according to customer needs.
- **Conformity**—Goods cannot be produced as entrepreneur wishes. A large number of goods are required to be produced in conformity with technical, environmental, health, and safety standards. Conformity sometimes guarantees overall quality of the product also.
- **Continuity**—Continuity refers to ability to produce goods, once designed, for considerably long period of time. Ability to procurement of materials and develop essential components, and technological capability are an essential concern in guaranteeing continuity of a product.
- **Adaptability**—Adaptability of a good has technological, environmental, and market aspects. When a product continues for many years, it faces challenges from these factors. So, the entrepreneur must be able to adapt the goods to changing environments.
- **Disposability**—Goods are disposed after consumption, breakdown, obsolescence, or at the end of the product life. Therefore, the entrepreneur should consider the challenges of disposal and take measures to design and produce goods to be disposal friendly.
- **Affordability**—Affordability determines the demand of the goods. However, low price does not always guarantee high demand; nor does the high price bring low demand. High demand can be sustained due to overall quality also. Yet, some entrepreneurs compromise overall quality for maintaining lower price. In general, the pricing of the goods should be a major concern of the entrepreneur.

Figure 12.3 depicts considerations of entrepreneurs under two situations. The entrepreneur, under Situation-I, believes all the criteria of the product, except consumer affordability, are equally important and instills them into the product. Though the consumer affordability is low, in this instance, the product would sell successfully owing to its overall quality.

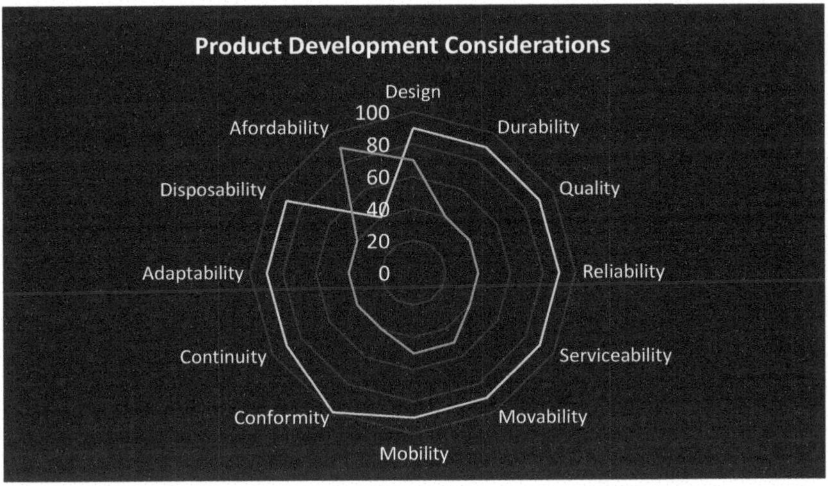

Fig. 12.3 Product development considerations (Author Portrayal)

Products of Apple Inc. and branded consumer goods belong to this category. On the other hand, the entrepreneur in Situation-II regards most of the criteria as less crucial except design and consumer affordability in the process of product development. Here, the entrepreneur is absolutely concerned with the design and the price. Imitations and fashionable goods belong to this type. Seemingly, entrepreneur gives importance to factors that they consider useful to establish commercial viabilities through product development.

Product Development Process

In the literature of product development, 15 sequential steps are identified as described below. For complex products, the development process is much rigorous while simple goods can be produced much easily. Products are developed from imaginations or existing things. For example, movies, songs, software, cartoons, fictions, telephone, vehicles, conveyor belt assemble system, lightbulb, and designer goods are products realized from imagination.[22] On the other hand, goods such as model cars, coffee table books, photographs, sculptures, and artificial flowers are examples of the goods produced based on existing things. Despite the fact that the

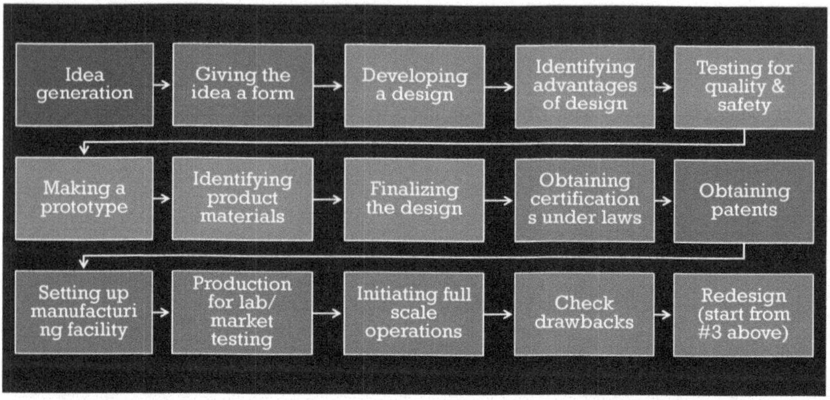

Fig. 12.4 Product development process (Author Portrayal)

products are developed on any of these two approaches, they are supposed to undergo the product development steps as sequentially indicated in Fig. 12.4.

1. Idea generation—An idea about a good to be produced. For example, the idea of two-way transmission of voice through copper rods/cables by Graham Bell or the two-way electric adopter by Konosuke Matsushita.
2. Giving the idea a form—General form of a good. For example, the shape of the telephone or the shape of the car and bus.
3. Developing a design—Developing the form into an attractive, ergonomic, and user-friendly design. Differentiation of models starts here.
4. Selecting the best design—After reviewing pros and cons, assessment of advantages, disadvantages, and flaws of each design, the most suitable design is selected.
5. Finalizing the design—With appraisals of design engineers, managers, customers, consultants, and stakeholders, the design is finalized.
6. Identifying product materials—Selection of the most suitable materials for the product.
7. Making a prototype—A sample product which has all attributes expected to be included in the final product.

8. Product testing for quality and safety—Standardized testing of the product to determine its market suitability and conformity.
9. Obtaining certification—Acquiring product certifications and approvals under various laws prior to release of the product.
10. Obtaining protection—Legal ownership of the product in the form of intellectual property rights for protecting the product from imitation.
11. Setting up manufacturing facility—Production plants, warehouse, etc.
12. Starting limited production—Making of actual products for laboratory and market testing.
13. Initiating full scale production—Actual production process at planned scale targeting the market.
14. Check drawbacks—Analysis of quality, performance, and standards of the product.
15. Redesign—If the product shows drawbacks, start the process from step three again.

Service Ventures

Domestic economy sequentially advances from agriculture to industry and to services. As an economy develops and the per capita income grows, demand for services steadily increases. This is due to constant search for comfort and convenience by people. Also, development of commerce of a country creates demand for services. When economies enter at least the lower middle-income category, significant increase in demand for services is observed. In consequence, large service sector is a prominent characteristic of advancing and advanced economies.[23]

Opportunities in the service sector are more implicit than those in the production sector. Clever entrepreneurs discover the needs of people for services and innovate service products to satisfy them. In some cases, even a very simple innovation is sufficient for creating a service venture; a home visit cleaning service is an example. The service sector has its inherent characteristics that are perhaps more attractive to entrepreneurs than those of the production sectors. This is a motivational factor for entrepreneurs to enter the service sector business. Micro-entrepreneurs, self-employing entrepreneurs, women entrepreneurs, and new entrants generally find starting service ventures are more rewarding compared to production ventures. However, the service sector has its inherent characteristics and pros and cons also. Following section describes the characteristics, advantages, and disadvantages of the service sector.[24]

Characteristics of Services

- Service lasts only until it is consumed. Same service cannot be consumed repeatedly. Once consumed, the service ceases to exist. Thus, once consumed, demand for the service is instantaneously created. This requires frequent production of services.
- Professional services cannot be mass produced and thus, there is no room for rise of monopolies. Services of lawyers, physicians, and accountants cannot be mass produced and this has led to creation of many firms to deliver those services.
- Services cannot be imitated as each service provider is unique. Therefore, many service enterprises can exist to provide services with a single trade like supermarket. Although supermarkets look alike, they provide competitive and unique service. Venture opportunities are open as long as unique services can be provided.
- Different customers need different services. Sometimes, even the same customer needs differentiated service at different occasions. Therefore, always, there is a demand for customized or personalized services. As services can be personalized, higher profit margins can be realized.
- As comfort of life is mainly brought about by services, an enormous portion of income generated in the agricultural and industrial sector is spent on purchasing services. This creates a constantly increasing demand for services.
- Many service enterprises can be initiated with small amount of capital. Some services can be produced by a single person and thus they individually can commence a service enterprise. Tailor shops, salons, consultancy firms, audit and accountancy firms are examples.
- Service sector has a natural market protection from imports. Services cannot normally be imported like goods. Competition from imported services is mostly absent (except for a few services such as banking, telecommunication, consultancies, etc.) and thus the local service enterprises are naturally protected from competition.
- Local entrepreneurs get opportunities to enter the service industry through obtaining foreign franchises. Fast-food restaurants such

as Pizza Hut, McDonald's, and KFC franchise their services to entrepreneurs worldwide. So, the local entrepreneurs can enter the same services by obtaining franchises.

- Service enterprise is less costly and much easier to operate as inventory, spare parts, repairs, and service points are not required. This encourages entrepreneurs to enter the service business.
- Maintenance is not required for the services like machinery, equipment, and software. Therefore, parallel maintenance service units need not be created for the service sector businesses.
- Many service enterprises do not require great volumes of capital and the state-of-the-art technology to commence business except services like telecommunication and banking.

High-Touch Vs. High-Tech

While technology is the most determinant factor for the product success, "human touch" is the most determinant factor for a successful service. Human touch, in other words, is the quality of the service ensured by the persons who produce and deliver. Goods makers and deliverers do not contact customers but the service makers and service providers always contact customers. Therefore, human contact is maintained at the highest capacity in the service business. When producing goods, high, medium, or low technology levels are adopted as appropriate. Obviously, yet, customers cannot be satisfied with services delivered with low or medium human touch. Thus, always, high level of human touch is essential for the service business. John Naisbitt (2001),[25] in his seminal work *High Tech High Touch*, highlighted the importance of the high-touch approach to the service business.

Manufacturing industry involves more science while service industry involves more arts. The service entrepreneurs should associate thoughtfulness, feelings, sentiments, and affections with the service they provide to the customers. Therefore, the "arts orientation" is the success factor of the service business.[26] In addition, like in the industrial ventures, service venture success also depends on perpetual innovations. Perpetual innovations are required to upgrade product quality. While innovations are needed for introducing different service products, "high human touch" of the entrepreneur and the team is indispensable for success of the service business. Moreover, services are performed in front of the customer. Thus, customer satisfaction is instantly determined by the service quality, customer relationship, and loyalty which are essential aspects of human touch.[27]

As much as innovations are, human touch is also a significant contributor to product success. In fact, to sell goods, number of services are required. In other words, a product travels from the factory to the hands of a customer via complementary services. Therefore, sale of goods is impossible without association of services. When human touch of the sales service is high, sales performance will also be high. Department stores, shopping malls, and airports particularly employ fleets of trained service personnel. In addition to the customer considerate service personnel, psycho-therapeutic infrastructure is also an element of high-touch service.[28] Every service requires a certain standard to be maintained to satisfy customers. Service standards then demand certain personal characteristics of the service provider.

Personal characteristics required for guaranteeing service business success differ across types of services. Reference of service type to personal qualities is given in Fig. 12.5. It is expected that the entrepreneur and their team should exert the personal qualities identified in respective of each type of service. As a whole, the service team should live up to high-touch standards to deliver every service. On the contrary, however, during the COVID-19 pandemic, high-touch services were highly challenged by the corona virus contamination threat. So, the service providers adopted high-tech to offer services. Services such as food, drugs, and commodity delivery, working from home, and mobile banking compromised high-touch of services.[29] However, the normalcy returned in the post-COVID-19 period which compelled the service sector to return to the high-touch services.

Organizing Service Ventures

Many concerns relevant and applicable to the production ventures are relevant to the service ventures also. However, due to special character of the services, additional concerns related to the human touch also are introduced when considering initiation of service ventures.[30] In organizing a service venture, the following steps are generally identified as relevant and useful.

1. Creation of the "service vision"—The exact purpose of the service.

SERVICE TYPE	• PERSONAL QUALITY
Professional services: Legal, Engineering, Accounting, Medical, & Designer.	•Professional and punctual
Personal services: Beauticians, tailors, barbers, babysitters, (medical, legal and design are also counted as personal services).	•Thoughtful and considerate
Merchandizing services: Supermarkets, personal trading, vending and selling.	•Humble, light-minded, •equality, friendliness
Delivery services: Parcels, mail, telegrams, newspapers, consumable goods, materials, machinery and equipment.	•Positive thinking, supportive, punctual, accurate
Maintenance Services: Maintenance of buildings, roads, utility services, machinery, equipment, vehicles, ship, aircraft, technologies, software.	•Positive thinking, supportive, accurate, punctual
Financial Services: Banking, leasing, financing, insurance, re-insurance, factoring, hedging, arbitration, pawning, venture capital.	•Honest, loyal, accurate
Hospitality services: Hotels, restaurants, lobbies, hospitals, nursing homes, homes for elderly, childcare services.	•Philosophical, supportive, kind, endurance, punctual
Educational services: Schools, universities, tuition, kindergartens, vocational schools, training centers.	•Creative, accurate, futuristic
Communication Services: Press, telecommunication, broadcasting services.	•Liberal minded
Recreational services: Amusement parks, sports, games and game centers, musical shows, entertainments, cinema, tourism, adventure.	•Philosophical and therapeutic

Fig. 12.5 Service type and personal quality (Author Portrayal)

2. Developing the mission—The ways and means to achieve the service purpose.
3. Vision realization—Getting the vision realized through the employees.
4. Effective hiring—Recruiting the right people to realize the vision.
5. Effective training—Providing appropriate training to recruits.
6. Reward system—Monetary and promotional reward system for the outstanding service of employees.

7. Teaching the "service vision"—Educating the team of the entrepreneur vision.
8. Sustainable motivation—Building work satisfaction.
9. Maintaining "art" of the service—Establishing service culture that pleases customers.
10. Developing service identities—Building unique service image via differentiation.
11. Protecting services—Developing a Service Mark that lasts generations.
12. Service expansion—Local and international expansion of the service business through franchise supported by the Service Mark.

Demand for services is generated by a variety of different service seekers. Therefore, each type of service demanded needs to be satisfied with specifically designed services and service delivery. Satisfaction derived of a service differs from person depending on social class, education, international exposure, and cultural values. Exclusive culinary practice of Japan to boil a crab alive or to cut a fish in front of the customer for making "sashimi" is impropriate for most of the people in the rest of the world. Therefore, it is mostly impracticable to maintain universal service standards. Services, thus need to be designed, personalized, or specialized according to the customer's need, age, mood, occasion, location, and circumstances under which the demand is exerted.[31]

The magical aspect of a service is that it is consumed while it is produced or delivered. So, the customer satisfaction can be observed concomitantly. Once spoiled, there is a remote chance for remedying the customer satisfaction. Therefore, the service provider must be prepared to deliver the right service with due care every time. Varying service quality, without improvement, on the same customer on different occasions is seen as substandard. Therefore, the service entrepreneurs must be extremely mindful of the customer expectations.[32] Figure 12.6 summarizes customer expectations and the types of services that need to be designed to satisfy them.

Consultancy services such as legal, accountancy, engineering, and medicine require professionals in the fields designated as lawyers, accountants, engineers, designers, and physicians. Professionals are supposed to possess diplomas, certificates, and memberships of professional bodies to qualify to deliver their service. Professional services are generally performed on individuals because they must be tailormade or customized

CUSTOMER EXPECTATION	•SERVICE TYPE
Professional solution	•Professional service
Fashion, Design, Styles	•Personalized service
Locational utility	•Distribution service
Traveling	•Transportation service
Problem fixing	•Maintenance service
Kind treatment	•Hospitality service
Knowledge & skill	•Educational service
Knowledge measurement	•Examination service
Information	•Communication service
Entertainment	•Recreational service

Fig. 12.6 Customer expectations and types of services (Author Portrayal)

to the needs of individuals. Individuals mostly seek differentiated, personalized, and tailormade services. For instance, fashions and styles are expressions of personal tastes and personalities that aim at defining, discriminating, and manifesting appearance and characters of individuals. Hair styles, garment designs, and dressing are a few examples of personalized services.[33]

Customers seek locational utility of goods. To endow locational utility, goods are required to be distributed to customers in the right quality and quantity at the proximity where customers need them. Delivery of fresh fish to markets or customers at a distance of hundreds of miles from the fishing harbor is an instance. Traveling is another need of people. The main concerns of traveling are punctual departure and safe arrival at destinations. Therefore, scheduled and reliable transportation services in the form of bus, train, airplane, and ferry are required to satisfy the customers.

Problem fixing is an everyday need of people and organizations. Problem fixing requires maintenance service. Maintenance services include maintenance of machinery, vehicle, equipment, utility, buildings, and premises. Other than repairs, routine maintenance of airports, harbors, airplanes, buildings, ships, trains, and playgrounds are essential maintenance services that require service professionals. For instance, exterior cleaning of skyscrapers is a highly professional job. Health care and hotel services, which are referred to as hospitality services, are expected to provide empathetic treatments. Qualified persons with kindness, consideration, and empathy are essential for providing hospitality services.

Education and training satisfy the demand for knowledge, learning, and skills. And examination service can satisfy the need for measurement and scaling of knowledge. Education service is prevalent at all levels and it carries out grading and scaling also. Still, there are some institutions, like the British Council, that provide examination services for those who want to grade their English skills. Information is a major product that is heavily demanded at present times. For gathering, processing, and broadcasting of information, services like radio and television are created. Furthermore, for information sharing, communication services such as telecommunication, video conferencing, Skype, and Facebook are developed. Additionally, entertainment is a human need that is satisfied via entertainment services such as Cinema, Opera, and amusement parks like Disney Land.

In order to guarantee high-touch service to the customer, service providers must take special care to maintain service providing personnel's quality.[34] The expected quality of a service can only be maintained through development of qualities of the employees who practically deliver the service. When a customer demands a service, they not only want to be satisfied by the service itself, but expect a satisfactory quality of that service. For instance, a patient not only wants to get treated for ailments but seeks kindness and empathy from the health workers when receiving the health service. Therefore, in the service venture, the entrepreneur ought to provide the demanded service with an additional pleasing action spelt out in Fig. 12.7.

It is obvious that delivery of service requires complementary actions to please customers in addition to providing the demanded service itself. A customer shopping at a supermarket expects the employees to provide the service cheerfully, thoughtfully, and supportively. An international traveler

SERVICE QUALITY	•PERSONAL QUALITY
Professional	•Professionalism
Consideration	•Thoughtfulness
Friendliness	•Humble, Endurance
Therapeutic	•Positive thinking
Hospitality	•Empathy, Kindness
Relationship	•Equality, Friendliness
Helpfulness& skill	•Supportive, Considerate
Loyalty	•Honesty
Improved service	•Creativity
Freedom	•Liberal mind
Enjoyment	•Philosophic, Considerate
Neatness	•Clarity, Simplicity

Fig. 12.7 Service quality and personal quality (Author Portrayal)

not only expects to reach the destination but also a punctual flight service, considerate, friendly, and supportive flight crew. Therefore, the quality of the aircraft and the number of crew are not sufficient to provide satisfactory flight service. High touch service of the crew is thus complementary to a quality flight service. Figure 12.7 summarizes the characteristics of the service quality and the required quality of the service personnel. According to the above figure, the service entrepreneur should provide the demanded service itself and exhibit certain qualities of the service personnel. Some of the qualities are professional qualities while many are human qualities. Personal qualities involved in and required for delivery of service quite often determine the success of service business. Therefore, it is not an exaggeration to point out that the personal qualities related to service delivery as success factors of the service ventures.

Services are required in both upstream supply chain and the downstream supply chain and thus, they connect most phases of the route that a product travels to the hands of a customer. Thus, it is obvious that opportunities for service business are abundant on supply chains. High human touch of the service deliverers is pivotal to successfully capitalize on the opportunities that arise from production-related activities also. Service business opportunities not only arise from the end user connected to personal needs but from various economic activities also. Service entrepreneur's responsibility is not only to start up service business but also to build it on high human touch.[35]

Chapter Summary

Production is broadly classified into production of goods and production of services. Entrepreneur chooses between the type of production at commencement of a venture. In advance, feasibility plan proposes the type of production; goods or services. Entrepreneur has the liberty to select the industry as well as the type of production. Producer entrepreneurship is defined as the one that produces goods and that is manufacturing. So, an entrepreneur who chooses to engage in manufacturing adopts from a few approaches to production: Inventive, Extension, Duplication, Synthesis, or Imitation. A producer entrepreneur recognizes opportunities for production through a few techniques: critical observation, customer sensitivity, product drawback, new invention, mind mapping, brainstorming, intuition, resource conversion, habit adoption, and ritual adoption. The knowledge required to produce goods is derived from one or more of the following sources: research, accidental occurrences, challenging thoughts, intuition, and development. Production is orientated on imagination, exploitation, skills, materials, preference, passion, design, market gap, problems, license, franchise, OEM, or ODM. Personal attributes and preferences of entrepreneur and the sector-specific advantages or disadvantages influence the choice of the type of production among the fields of production, agriculture, manufacturing, construction, and utility available to choose from.

Also, three types of technology platforms are available for a producer entrepreneur. They are High-Tech, Mid-Tech, and Low-Tech. High-Tech requires immense R&D expenditures and thus, is costly. Powerful cameras, medical equipment, supercomputers, humanoid-robots, space rockets, and their components are high-tech products. They are widely protected by intellectual property rights laws. Mid-Tech platform contains medium level technologies developed for specific products as well as the obsolete High-Tech after years of invention, but can be applied to production of Mid-Tech goods also. Household electronics, PCs, Laptops, and transportation equipment are Mid-Tech products. Intellectual property rights are heavily involved in this technology segment also. The Low-Tech is the platform for most consumer goods such as pens, pencils, exercise books, processed foods, soap, detergents, garments, furniture, electric fans, and common plastic products. Intellectual property rights are not generally obtained for most of the Low-Tech products. However, design rights are common in this category of technology. Among different technology platforms, an appropriate platform is selected by an entrepreneur to ensure quantity, quality, reliability, durability, serviceability, movability, mobility, conformity, continuity, adaptability, disposability, affordability, and unit cost of the selected product. Particularly, in manufacturing, product development process is involved and it passes through 15 sequential steps. Product development process of intricate products is rigorous whereas simple goods involve simple process.

Demand for services steadily increases along with economic growth and social modernization. Constant search for comfort and convenience is the reason behind this phenomenon. Development of commerce and auxiliary services support this trend. Services are required in both upstream supply chain and the downstream supply chain and thus, they connect most of the phases of the route that a product travels to the hands of a customer. So, it is obvious that entrepreneurs can trace abundant opportunities for service business on the supply chains. The service sector is predominant in the economies belonging to lower middle-income category and above.

Most lucrative opportunities in the service sector are implicit and subtle because they are often connected to psychological desires of people, only clever entrepreneurs make headway in the service sector. However, the service sector is rich in demand for simple innovations such as home visit cleaning, maintenance, culinary, and home delivery services. The inherent characteristics of the service sector that motivate entrepreneurs to enter the service sector are natural protection from import competition, lower capital requirement for many operations, ability for an individual to operate a service business, easiness to initiate and operate, absence of after service and maintenance, and a dozen other reasons. They are considered as motivators of the service sector. Micro-entrepreneurs, self-employing entrepreneurs, women entrepreneurs, and new entrants generally find starting a service venture is easier and more rewarding compared to production ventures. However, the service sector has its inherent disadvantages also.

In contrast to High-Tech in case of the producer venture, the determinant factor of a successful service venture is the concern for High-Touch. The persons who produce and deliver services are supposed to unleash human touch appropriate to the service to ensure and enhance the service quality. While producers of goods virtually have no physical contact with customers, service providers always have close contact with customers. Manufacturing involves more science in producing goods whereas service industry involves the art of customer relationship. Service entrepreneurs should possess a large number of personal qualities to uphold "arts orientation" as appropriate to the type of service provided.

The service entrepreneur thus should be punctual, considerate, humble, supportive, accurate, friendly, honest, loyal, kind, empathetical, and philosophical. As services are performed in front of the customer, their satisfaction is instantaneously felt and recognizable to the service provider. So, it provides instant feedback signaling improvements to the service quality through enhanced customer relationship and customer loyalty; an extra dose of human touch. The magical aspect of service is that service is consumed at the moment it is produced or delivered. Thus, once spoiled, there is a remote chance of remedying the customer satisfaction. Therefore, it is not an exaggeration to point out that the personal qualities related to service delivery as success factors of service ventures.

Review Questions

1. Distinguish production entrepreneurship from service entrepreneurship.
2. Elaborate on the following approaches to production;

    a. Inventive approach
    b. Extension approach
    c. Duplication approach
    d. Synthesis approach
    e. Imitation approach.

3. Describe the methods that are employed to identify opportunities for production.
4. "Production of right goods requires knowledge and knowledge is connected to a number of sources." Explain.

5. Describe the different types of orientations available for a production entrepreneur to choose from.
6. "Choice of production is determined based on the industry specific advantages and the personal preferences." Discuss.
7. What are the advantages inherent to the production sector that attract an entrepreneur?
8. Discuss the nature of the technology; High-tech, Mid-tech, and Low-tech, and their relevance to the choice of production.
9. Illustrate the major considerations of product development and the generally accepted steps of the product development process.
10. Interpret the characteristics inherent to the service sector ventures and discuss the advantages emanating from them in favor of service venture startups.
11. Describe the sources and nature of the demand for services and comment on the opportunities for service sector ventures.
12. "Service sector success is heavily determined by the quality of the service known as High-touch." Do you agree? Explain.
13. "Service types are connected to types of personal qualities." Discuss this statement connecting service providers and their services.
14. Identify the connection between customer needs and the types of the services, and explore opportunities for service production.

Additional Readings

1. Prajogo, D.I., 2006. The relationship between innovation and business performance—A comparative study between manufacturing and service firms. *Knowledge and Process Management*, *13*(3), pp. 218–225.
2. Wang, Q., Zhao, X., and Voss, C., 2016. Customer orientation and innovation: A comparative study of manufacturing and service firms. *International Journal of Production Economics*, *171*, pp. 221–230.
3. Ettlie, J.E., and Rosenthal, S.R., 2011. Service versus manufacturing innovation. *Journal of Product Innovation Management*, *28*(2), pp. 285–299.
4. Cooper, R.G., 1994. New products: The factors that drive success. *International Marketing Review*, *11*(1), pp. 60–76.

5. Vandenbosch, M., and Dawar, N., 2002. Beyond better products: Capturing value in customer interactions. *MIT Sloan Management Review*.
6. Yamashina, H., Ito, T., and Kawada, H., 2002. Innovative product development process by integrating QFD and TRIZ. *International Journal of Production Research*, *40*(5), pp. 1031–1050.
7. Thoben, K.D., Jagdev, H., and Eschenbächer, J., 2001, June. Extended products: Evolving traditional product concepts. In *Proceedings of the 7th International Conference on Concurrent Enterprising* (pp. 429–440). Bremen, Germany: Engineering the Knowledge Economy through Cooperation.
8. Bakker, C., Wang, F., Huisman, J., and Den Hollander, M., 2014. Products that go round: Exploring product life extension through design. *Journal of cleaner Production*, *69*, pp. 10–16.
9. Gabbott, M., and Hogg, G., 1999. Consumer involvement in services: A replication and extension. *Journal of Business Research*, *46*(2), pp. 159–166.
10. Seider, W.D., Lewin, D.R., Seader, J.D., Widagdo, S., Gani, R., and Ng, K.M., 2017. *Product and process design principles: Synthesis, analysis, and evaluation*. John Wiley & Sons.
11. Staake, T., Thiesse, F., and Fleisch, E., 2009. The emergence of counterfeit trade: A literature review. *European Journal of Marketing*, *43*(3/4), pp. 320–349.
12. Yang, M., Vladimirova, D., and Evans, S., 2017. Creating and capturing value through sustainability: The sustainable value analysis tool a new tool helps companies discover opportunities to create and capture value through sustainability. *Research-Technology Management*, *60*(3), pp. 30–39.
13. Svetina, A.C., and Prodan, I., 2008. How internal and external sources of knowledge contribute to firms' innovation performance. *Managing Global Transitions*, *6*(3), p. 277.
14. Flenskov, K., 2017. From production-orientation to customer-orientation–modules of a successful airline differentiation strategy. In *Strategic management in the aviation industry* (pp. 97–117). Routledge.
15. https://www.raigam.lk/.
16. https://lk.lakpura.com/pages/vendol-lanka-company-pvt-ltd.
17. http://www.dingleswater.epizy.com/?i=1.

18. Rosenzweig, E.D., and Roth, A.V., 2004. Towards a theory of competitive progression: Evidence from high-tech manufacturing. *Production and Operations Management*, *13*(4), pp. 354–368.
19. Santamaría, L., Nieto, M.J., and Barge-Gil, A., 2009. Beyond formal R&D: Taking advantage of other sources of innovation in low-and medium-technology industries. *Research Policy*, *38*(3), pp. 507–517.
20. Vyas, V., 2014. *Low-cost, low-tech innovation: New product development in the food industry*. Routledge.
21. Elverum, C.W., Welo, T., and Tronvoll, S., 2016. Prototyping in new product development: Strategy considerations. *Procedia CIRP*, *50*, pp. 117–122.
22. Schilling, M.A., and Hill, C.W., 1998. Managing the new product development process: Strategic imperatives. *Academy of Management Perspectives*, *12*(3), pp. 67–81.
23. Buera, F.J., and Kaboski, J.P., 2012. The rise of the service economy. *American Economic Review*, *102*(6), pp. 2540–2569.
24. Schmenner, R.W., 1986. How can service businesses survive and prosper. *Sloan Management Review*, *27*(3), pp. 21–32.
25. Naisbitt, J., and Philips, D., 2001. High tech high touch: Technology and our accelerated search for meaning.
26. Wünderlich, N.V., Wangenheim, F.V., and Bitner, M.J., 2013. High tech and high touch: A framework for understanding user attitudes and behaviors related to smart interactive services. *Journal of Service Research*, *16*(1), pp. 3–20.
27. Neuhofer, B., Buhalis, D., and Ladkin, A., 2013. High tech for high touch experiences: A case study from the hospitality industry. In *Information and communication technologies in tourism 2013: Proceedings of the international conference in Innsbruck, Austria, January 22–25, 2013* (pp. 290–301). Springer Berlin Heidelberg.
28. Ahearne, M., Jones, E., Rapp, A., and Mathieu, J., 2008. High touch through high tech: The impact of salesperson technology usage on sales performance via mediating mechanisms. *Management Science*, *54*(4), pp. 671–685.
29. Zeng, Z., Chen, P.J., and Lew, A.A., 2020. From high-touch to high-tech: COVID-19 drives robotics adoption. *Tourism Geographies*, *22*(3), pp. 724–734.
30. Rubalcaba, L., Michel, S., Sundbo, J., Brown, S.W., and Reynoso, J., 2012. Shaping, organizing, and rethinking service innovation:

A multidimensional framework. *Journal of Service Management*, *23*(5), pp. 696–715.

31. Johnston, R., 1995. The determinants of service quality: Satisfiers and dissatisfiers. *International Journal of Service Industry Management*, *6*(5), pp. 53–71.
32. Teas, R.K., 1993. Consumer expectations and the measurement of perceived service quality. *Journal of Professional Services Marketing*, *8*(2), pp. 33–54.
33. Ding, Y., and Keh, H.T., 2016. A Re-Examination of Service Standardization Versus Customization from the Consumer's Perspective. *Journal of Services Marketing*, *30*(1), pp. 16–28.
34. Lin, N.P., Chiu, H.C., and Hsieh, Y.C., 2001. Investigating the relationship between service providers' personality and customers' perceptions of service quality across gender. *Total Quality Management*, *12*(1), pp. 57–67.
35. Susskind, A.M., 2012. How to build service quality into your operation. In *The Cornell School of Hotel administration on hospitality: Cutting edge thinking and practice* (pp. 159–173).

CHAPTER 13

Acquisition and Merger, Franchising and Licensing

Key Learning Points

- Acquisition and Merger.
- Objectives and personal preferences of Acquisition and Merger.
- Opportunities of Acquisition and Merger.
- Business evaluation.
- Business valuation.
- Due Diligence evaluation.
- Methods of acquisition.
- Mergers and methods of merging.
- Franchising and licensing.
- Business Format Franchising (BFF).
- Product Distribution Franchise (PDF).
- Single or multiple franchisees.
- Advantages of franchising and licensing.
- Disadvantages of franchising and licensing.
- Choosing a suitable franchising and licensing.
- Acquisition and franchise as new avenues.
- Decision-making in acquisition.
- Purposes and types of business acquisitions.
- Considerations for acquisition.
- Acquisition and business integration.

© The Author(s), under exclusive license to Springer Nature Singapore Pte Ltd. 2024

M. Rajaratne, *Concepts, Processes and Practice of Entrepreneurship*, Palgrave Studies in Global Entrepreneurship,
https://doi.org/10.1007/978-981-97-6180-7_13

- Purposes and types of mergers.
- Types of franchising and licensing.
- Local and international franchising and licensing.
- The role of the franchisor and franchisee.
- Operational aspect of franchise and licensing.
- Privileges of a franchisee and licensee.

Introduction

In the venture creation process, there prevail alternative methods such as Merging, Acquisition, Franchising, and Licensing. Some entrepreneurs prefer buying out existing businesses or merging with another business to organize as a new entity. This method is known as acquisition and merger (sometimes merger and acquisition, or M&A).[1] In addition, there are opportunities for commencing ventures under franchise and licensing arrangements also. Acquisitions and mergers are feasible as some businesses go on sale after operations for some time. Still, some other businesses consider franchising or licensing their operations as a means to expansion. These business options are an intricate affair, entrepreneurs often seek consultant opinions before entering into these agreements. However, there are cases of buying out and merging of small ventures sans consultant opinions.[2]

Merging, Acquisition, Franchising, and Licensing are increasingly important international business phenomenon also. Businesses choose to sell divisions or the entire firm on restructuring programs. Some companies contemplate to acquire other firms to diversify, integrate, and expand as strategies to improve competitiveness. Also, some firms consider merging to seek synergetic and collaborative growth. The new world order allows international mobility of assets, capital, remittances, and even human resource.[3] Capitalizing on the liberal economic policies, firms show increasing acquisitions and mergers internationally also. In some other cases, certain products and services are either non-economical or impractical to export and import. In order to overcome these limitations, firms prefer international licensing and franchising. This has caused significant flow of foreign direct investment worldwide.[4] Figures 13.1 and 13.2 respectively indicate the value of mergers and acquisitions and the number of cases reported to the Institute of Merging, Acquisitions and Alliances.

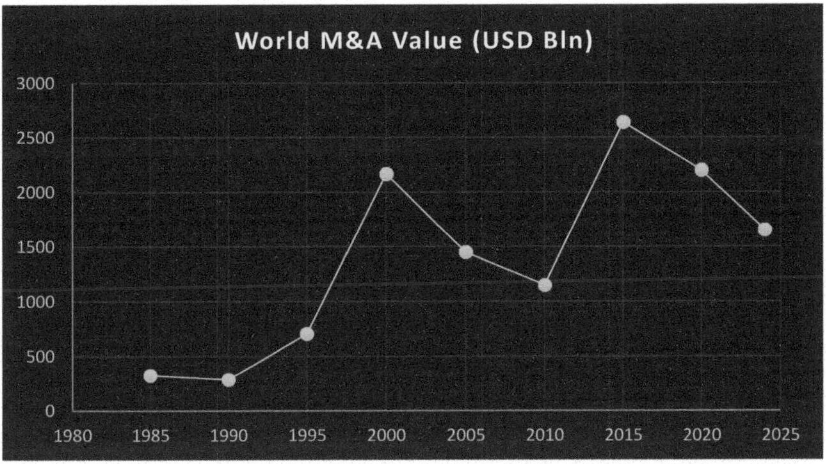

Fig. 13.1 World M&A—value (*Data* Institute for Mergers, Acquisitions and Alliances [2024][5])

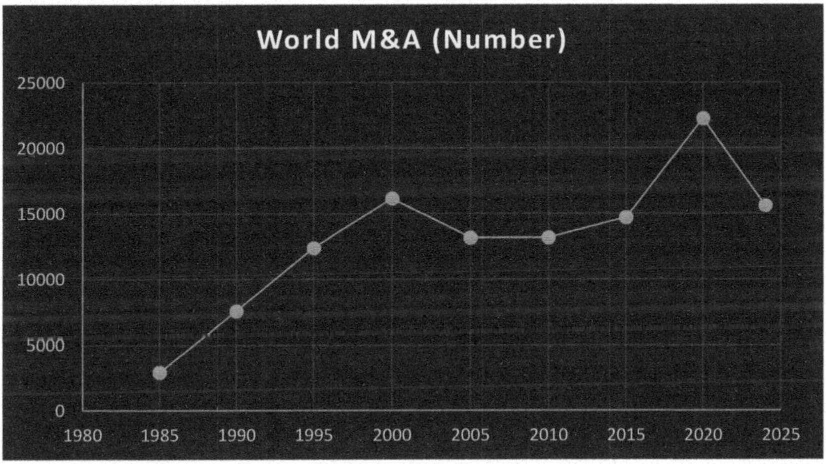

Fig. 13.2 World M&A—number (*Data* Institute for Mergers, Acquisitions and Alliances [2024][6])

Acquisition and Merger

Key Steps

In the buyer's attempt at merger and acquisition, ten key steps are followed to finalize a deal. For an acquisition and merger, there are two parties involved; buyer and seller. The following steps are identified as more appropriate to a buyer rather than a seller.[7] Both buyer and seller sides of aquation and merger are equally important in entrepreneurship as they create entrepreneurial opportunities for the two parties involved. While friendly acquisitions and mergers systematically follow the steps given below, a hostile acquisition and merger[8] may follow them much informally and often finalize a deal even without the consent of the Board of Directors of the target company; this is known as acquisition and merger by Tender Offer which is performed via acquisition of majority of shares.[9] Figure 13.3 elaborates on the normal and open merger and acquisition process.

Objectives

An entrepreneur who opts to acquire a business or merge with another business should act with a specific objective that can justify the acquisition or merger decision. Additionally, entrepreneurs must possess an action plan, upon acquisition and merger of a business, to achieve preset objectives. Logical and technical reasons, instead of subjective thoughts, must support the acquisition and merger decision. The objectives of buyout decision therefore should be rationally laid down. Upon a buyout, the business will be given a fresh entrepreneurial touch by the new owner.[10]

In many instances, acquisition takes place to append ventures to an existing business. In such cases, entrepreneur expects to gain economies of scale and economies of scope in the new business setup. Economies of scale are brought about by increasing output and expanding operational scale to acquire sizeable market share. In contrast, economies of scope are gained through increasing efficiencies and effectiveness of operations.[11] This, of course, is feasible if the acquisition is made within the same industry in which the entrepreneur has so far been operating. If acquisition took place in an entirely different industry, the acquisition objectives could have been different from what is mentioned above. Common objectives of business acquisition are mentioned below.

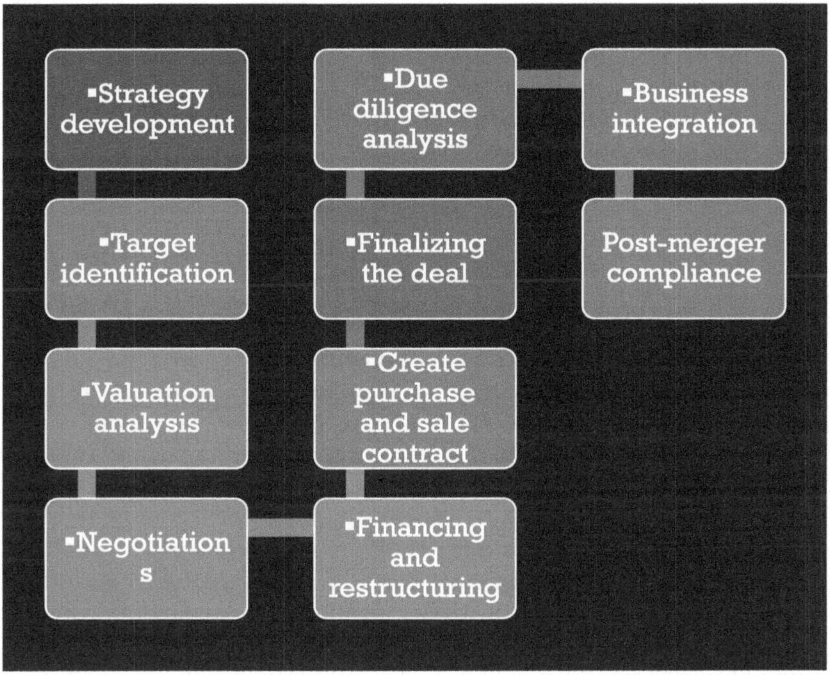

Fig. 13.3 Merging and acquisition process (Author Portrayal)

1. To introduce new product lines
2. To increase production volume
3. To reduce unit cost of production
4. To increase marginal profit
5. To modernize production facility
6. To introduce better production technologies
7. To establish effective management system
8. To increase customer base
9. To increase market share
10. To improve and develop distribution channels
11. To improve customer service
12. To maximize production capacity
13. To realign backward and forward integration
14. To improve inventory management system

15. To improve efficiency of utility consumption
16. To improve quality of products
17. To make use of idling resources
18. To make use of intellectual properties
19. To make use of business networks
20. To make use of goodwill

Personal Preference

Prospective entrepreneur selects to buy out a suitable business from what is available for sale mostly based on preference.[12] Ventures for sale can be in agriculture, manufacturing, services, of large, medium, or small scale, located locally or globally, startups or mature, or making profit or loss. In making an effective buying out decision, an entrepreneur's financial capacity, managerial capacity, business confidence, risk, intuition, skills, experience, interests, ego, values, ethics, and beliefs must be carefully considered. However, some smalltime entrepreneurs do not dare to acquire even very large businesses occasionally whereas some others do not hesitate to acquire loss-making ventures. Further, some consider acquisitions to diversify into unrelated ventures. Still, some who have strong internalization capacity opt to acquire foreign ventures. Vertical or horizontal integration or conglomeration strategy is another preference in business acquisitions.[13]

Opportunities

For buying out a business, entrepreneurs engage in thorough examination of reliable sources of acquisition opportunities.[14] Brokers are one of such sources. Brokers maintain database of businesses that are for sale. Goodwill, experience, and reliability are indicators of good brokers. Brokers are sometimes biased as they earn a commission from the seller and may influence the buyer to buy out businesses. Therefore, the buyer should avoid buying an unwanted or inappropriate business on the broker's influence. Advertisements are another useful source for the buyer to search for acquisition opportunities. Newspapers usually carry advertisements of businesses for sale (and merging opportunities).[15] In such cases, the buyer can contact the seller directly and avoid brokers. Trade sources such as trade associations, chambers of commerce, business networks, suppliers, distributors, and agents can also be helpful sources of acquisition opportunities. Professional sources are equally useful in searching acquisition opportunities. Professional sources comprise business consultants, attorneys, accountants, auditors, and company secretaries.[16]

PESTEL Considerations

When buying out decision is made, entrepreneur should investigate external factors that affect the future of the business under consideration. In this event, the PESTEL factors are taken into consideration in evaluating opportunities and threats encountered by the proposed buyout. PESTEL is the acronym for Political, Economic, Social, Technological, Environmental, and Legal factors. When making an acquisition decision, current and future trends of PESTEL factors and their impact on business in general and on a particular industry must be carefully screened to estimate the future of the business. Due to political animosity of countries, political risk increases and business prospect obscures. This is a matter of concern in acquiring a business in a country that is faced with hostility and sanctions.

In some instances, governments engage in nationalization of private business entities. So, it is unwise to purchase a business when the threat of nationalization is imminent. At times a society gears up for patriot movement in boycotting foreign products and promoting purchase of domestic goods only, acquisition of an importer firm will be risky. Also, buying out a business with outdated technology while the technology in the relevant industry is rapidly advancing would also be an unwise decision. At a time when environmental policy is revised and strict measures are implemented, buying out a plant that exceeds acceptable pollution levels would be risky.[17]

Business Evaluation

Business evaluation is the final step of the acquisition process. Entrepreneur enters the business evaluation step to make the final acquisition decision having completed the steps such as determining acquisition objectives, identifying opportunities, considering preferences, choosing a venture, and analyzing the PESTEL factors. In this final step, there are several factors that are relevant for the entrepreneur to consider in making the final decision in acquiring a business. A business offered for sale should be evaluated in terms of physical environment of the business, turnover, profits, financial and operating ratios, assets, liabilities, due diligence, research and technological strengths, intellectual property rights, personnel strength, management, location-specific strength, strategic advantages, etc.[18]

The business to be acquired should be assessed to determine whether it is feasible to continue usual operations at the present location without urge of relocation. Expiry of licenses and permits, need for renewal of such licenses and permits, depletion of raw materials at the present location, and new environmental regulations imposed by local governments determine the viability to continue normal operations or extended operations at the present location. The entrepreneur, therefore, should scan every detail relating to the possibility of continuation and its advantages. Further, it is necessary to examine the location related natural hazards such as flood, landslide, and bushfire before agreeing on a price for the business offered for sale. Insurability is also a major concern as some businesses may not qualify for insurance.[19]

Analysis of present operations is important because the price of the business is determined by its equity, debt, assets, liabilities, operational ratios, financial ratios, profit, or loss. Prospective entrepreneur should examine and review the past performance of the business in relation to its financial, marketing, and production performance. Historical data of a few years of production, sales, profits, and expenditure are required for an extensive analysis. Entrepreneurs should ask for these data from the seller of the business. Failure of providing important data, on the part of the seller, will pose difficulties in making the buyout decision. It is important for the buyer not to compromise analysis for emotional reasons. Analyses must be objective and technical. Past lawsuits encountered by the venture should also be taken into special consideration.[20]

When making the final acquisition decision, auditing of the assets and liabilities of the business is equally important. Entrepreneurs should compile an audit of all tangible and intangible assets. Tangible assets comprise lands, buildings, plants, machinery and tools, equipment, furniture and fixtures, accounts receivables, patent and copyrights, trademarks, investments, deposits, and cash.[21] Intangible assets include goodwill, reputation, clientele networks, and brand names. When analyzing assets, their value, volume, present condition, age, depreciation, outright or lease ownership, accounts receivables and their periods, remaining period of patents and copyrights, and hazardous incidents that tarnished goodwill should be examined. It is equally important to analyze existing liabilities also. Debts, accounts payable and their due dates, tax outstanding, salary, and provident fund payables are important aspects of liabilities.[22]

Due Diligence Evaluation

Business evaluation process mentioned above can be further reinforced with an evaluation of Due Diligence.[23] The Due Diligence evaluation supersedes common and orthodox business evaluation approaches and critically reviews every aspect of the business offered for sale. Here, the entrepreneur sets some important questions to review the below-mentioned critical aspects of the business.[24]

1. Why is the business offered for sale?
2. What is the physical state of the business?
3. How many key people are required to be employed after acquisition?
4. What is the competitiveness and competition of the business?
5. What are the underlying conditions and terms for leases and loans?
6. What are the collaterals against the assets?
7. What are the litigations encountered by the business?
8. Will the seller want to sign a covenant not to compete?
9. Are special licenses and permits required to run the business?
10. How much capital is needed for the acquisition?
11. How much would it cost for renovations and restructuring?
12. Will resources be available to operate the business?
13. What are the general obligations related to the location?
14. What formal and informal restrictions, and disturbances will surface?
15. What are the government's support schemes available for the business?

Business acquisition professionals who are consulted for large acquisitions customarily prepare Due Diligence Report which is a comprehensive document compiled under the following sections.[25]

1. Executive Summary (Company name, Products or services, Business concept, Key issues discovered by analysis, and financial summary).

2. Introduction to Business (The company, CEO, Date founded, Address, Company goals, Founders, Founders' share).
3. The Relevant Industry (Industry type, Competition, Primary competitor, Market share, Strongest and weakest firms in the industry, Next possible competitive move, Key factors of competitiveness).
4. Target Market and Customer Base (Size and scope of the target market, Company mission, Limitation for imitation, Rivalry firms, Growth of the market, and market share).
5. Real Operational Perspectives (Value addition, Management team, Business model, Business strategy, Marketing plan, Operations plan).
6. The SWOT Perspectives (Company strengths and Weaknesses, External opportunities and threats. Company strategies).
7. Financial Analysis (Ratio analysis, Cash flows, Valuation, Revenues, Profits, BreakEvens, Financial statements).
8. Other Considerations (Lawsuits, Restrictions, Special permissions, Supports, Freedom to operate, etc.).

It is important to evaluate the technological and locational strengths also of a business offered for sale. Technological perspective is an important concern of both manufacturing and service businesses. If the business is operating with an inappropriately high or low technology, then there will arise a need for adopting appropriate technology. This may include elevating or lowering the technology level to suit the market. Technology, in fact, determines the competitiveness of a business. Locational strength of the business is also extremely relevant in assessing a business. If the business offered for sale is a hotel, nature, tranquility, or city, amenities will be the major concerns to be reviewed. If a mining facility is offered for sale, then there comes the concern of availability of minerals in the mine and the license or freedom for mining and transporting. And if supermarkets, convenience store chains, and restaurant chains are the subject of the proposed sale, metropolitan atmosphere, supply chain, and logistics networks are strong locational aspects. In case of shifting a city to a new location (ex: from York to New York and Delhi to New Delhi), a shop located in the old city should be evaluated to weigh its new challenges.

Business Valuation

Business valuation is done by both the buyer and the seller involved in the transaction. Value of a business perceived by the seller is different from that of the buyer. The price differential is resulted from different values set by the seller and the buyer. This happens because the seller and the buyer consider different aspects of the business. The seller generally values the business high while the buyer valuates it low. In the final negotiation, the seller and the buyer will have to agree on a certain price to strike off a deal. However, price of the business will be determined by a few factors such as urgency of the sale, number of bidders, prospects of the business, and future of the industry also.[26]

In business valuation, generally, several factors are analyzed to assign value for each part of the business. History of the firm, nature of the market and market competition, market share, distribution, sales, production, plants and facilities, ownership, legal structure, management, employees, finance, are the factors that are commonly assessed. Several methods have been developed for business evaluation. Each method has its own merits and demerits and thus, some are popular while some are not.[27] A few commonly used business valuation methods at present are briefly introduced below.

1. Fixed price method—Business owner values the business and sets a price arbitrarily. A logical and systematic estimation method is not employed to assess the business but an arbitrary value is merely assigned by the owner.
2. The Book value (Balance sheet) methods—There are two versions of this method: tangible book value method and adjusted tangible book value method. Tangible book value is calculated as total assets minus total liabilities. Adjusted tangible book value is calculated by adjusting the tangible book value to the present market value.
3. Multiple of earnings method—Net income multiplied by the Price Earnings multiple. The P/E multiple is derived by dividing 100 by the Capitalization rate. The Capitalization rate is derived by dividing the net income by the market value of the asset.
4. Price Earnings Ratio method—The offered value of the business is divided by its earnings to derive P/E ratio. The lower the P/E ratio the higher the business value is. It is favorable for the buyer to consider a business with higher P/E ratio.

5. Discounted future earnings method—Valuation based on discounted future earnings of five to ten years. The discount rate is the average rate of future profit adjusted to inflation and to the business and industry-specific risks.
6. Return On Investment method—A simple and direct method used to value a business. The higher the ROI the higher the value of the business will be.
7. Replacement value method—Valuation of all assets assuming if they were to be replaced at present. Book values are adjusted then for the depreciation so far.
8. Liquidation value method—The value of a business if it were liquidated after bankruptcy. The net value of the business remaining for the shareholders after paying off all the liabilities is considered as the value of the business.
9. Excess earnings method—Normal earnings of tangible value at a certain fixed percentage are deducted from the Actual earnings to derive Excess earnings. Then Excess earnings are divided by the tax rate to derive the Intangible value of the firm. Total firm value is equal to Tangible value plus Intangible value.
10. Market value method—Arbitrarily assigned value considering comparative values of similar firms.

Methods of Acquisition

Methods of business acquisition are determined by the purposes of acquisition. Businesses are acquired for different purposes. After acquisition, the acquired business sometimes still remains under its original name. Japan's Sharp Corporation was recently acquired by Taiwan's Hon-Hai Corporation but the trade name Sharp was not changed. After acquisition, companies sometimes continue with the original trademarks and brand names also. Automobile brands such as Audi, Bentley, Bugatti, Lamborghini, and Porsche stand alone as independent brands though they have been acquired by Volkswagen Corp.[28]

On the contrary, China's Lenovo Corporation acquired the personal computer division of IBM together with its trademark but it soon dropped the IBM trademark to promote Lenovo brand. The business acquisition methods themselves are self-explanatory to the purposes of acquisition. Also, there are cases that the brand names are acquired to stop prospective operations under that brand. This helps eliminate market competition. The Celltel Lanka[29] company—the first mobile phone network in Sri Lanka—was acquired by Tigo.[30] And Tigo was acquired by Etisalat. Then, Etisalat Lanka[31] was acquired by Hutchison Group.[32] In this chain of acquisitions, every successor deserted the predecessor's brand name.

Three major business acquisition methods are described below.

1. **Horizontal Acquisition**—When one firm acquires another firm in the same industry or sector, that is identified as a Horizontal Acquisition. Facebook to acquire WhatsApp is a case in point. This is a common move to eradicate competitors and to dominate the market. In addition, this method is used to acquire technological and research capabilities and also to promote the existing brands of the buyer company as Lenovo did.
2. **Vertical Acquisition**—The acquisition of a company belonging to a supply chain or logistics system is referred to as Vertical Acquisition. The buyer gains advantages such as control over the supply and distribution chains through this acquisition type. The buyer chooses to bypass intermediaries in this way. This helps the buyer firm to gain monopolistic advantages.
3. **Conglomerate Acquisition**—Acquisition of a company in completely different field of business, industry, or sector is referred to as Conglomerate Acquisition. Business diversification is the motive of this type of acquisition. This move leads to create giant business conglomerates. Many Japanese corporates such as Mitsubishi and Asahi groups are examples of acquired conglomerates. Enormous and widespread business power is expected to be built and exercised through this type of acquisition.

In business acquisitions, both locally or internationally, a few modes of payment can be identified as follows.

1. **Leverage Buyout (LBO)**—a method that involves borrowings from other sources to finance the acquisition.
2. **Entrepreneurial Leverage Buyout (E-LBO)**—a method that involves more than 50% of equity purchase with managerial control

of the acquired firm. The remaining value is considered as borrowings or debt.

3. **Cash-flow Leverage Buyout (C-LBO)**—a financing method by loans and thus the buyer is heavily concerned with higher yield and steady cash flows.

Mergers and Methods of Merging

In contrast to acquisition, merger creates opportunity for consolidated joint operations of the merging parties as a company absorption does not take place. In case of a merger, company names are also merged. Examples include Suzuki-Maruti, Hero-Honda, and GlaxoSmithKline. There are five different types of business mergers as described below. Differences of mergers depend on the purpose of merger, nature of operations, and the relationship of the companies that choose to merge.

1. **Conglomerate merger**—A merger between companies of unrelated business activities. There are two sub types of conglomerate mergers: Pure and Mixed mergers. Pure mergers involve firms that have nothing common in their businesses whereas Mixed mergers have something common like product and market extension strategies.
2. **Horizontal merger**—A merger between competing companies in the same industry. Horizontal mergers are common in industries where a few oligopolistic firms operate. Horizontal mergers bring about synergy, greater market share, and competitive advantage.
3. **Vertical merger**—A merger between companies that are parts of the same supply chain. The vertical merger is sought for improving supplies, reducing costs, and controlling resources and components effectively.
4. **Market-extension merger**—A merger between companies that sell similar products in different markets. Through this merger, the companies get access to extended and wider market.
5. **Product-extension merger**—A merger between companies producing and selling related products or services in the same market. Technological collaboration, knowledge sharing, product development, production synergy, and market leadership are sought through this merger.

Franchising and Licensing

Franchising and licensing open avenues for initiating new ventures. In contrast to traditional ways of creating a venture, franchising and licensing provide new and unique opportunities for venture creation. Franchising and licensing provide opportunities for a firm to produce or sell goods and services of another firm at a royalty payment. An entrepreneur can look for a suitable opportunity from a vast array of franchising and licensing of local or international firms. A few factors are taken into consideration when selecting a suitable franchise or a license: type of business, nature of products, initial investment required, and conditions to be agreed. Generally, franchising and licensing provide chances for an entrepreneur to establish a venture at a much less cost.[33] Franchising and licensing provide the franchisee or licensee with established products together with brand names. Inexperienced entrepreneurs also can make use of franchise and licensing opportunities when prior business experience is not required to obtain a franchising or licensing opportunity. Additionally, the franchisor and licensor provide consultancies, promotional materials, funds, training, technical collaboration, business updates, and marketing strategies to the franchisee or licensee. The top-rated franchise brands and the costs required to become a franchisee are indicated in Table 13.1.

International Franchise Association (IFA) defines a franchise as "*a method of distributing products or services involving a franchisor, who establishes the brand's trademark or trade name and a business system where a franchisee pays a royalty and often an initial fee for the right to do business under the franchisor's name and system.*" Technically, a contract that binds two business parties is a franchise. In practice, the term franchise commonly refers to actual business that the franchisee operates. The practice of creating and distributing a brand in a franchise system is referred to as franchising. Franchises are licensed to a single or multiple franchisees locally or internationally. Once appointed, the franchisee can operate as an agent of specific product in designated geographical area.[35]

Types of Franchises

There are two different types of franchising. The most popular type is the Business Format Franchising (BFF). In this type, the franchisor provides the franchisee with not only the trade name, products, or services, but

Table 13.1 World top 10 franchise brands (Based on Revenue)

Name	*Category*	*Franchising from*	*Total units*	*Revenue US$ billion*	*Initial investment US$*
McDonald's	Fast food	1955	38,695	100.1	1.3 to 2.2 Mn
7-Eleven	Convenience store	1964	66,689	89.0	47,100 to 1.2 Mn
KFC	Fast food	1952	24,104	27.9	750,00 to 1.5 Mn
Burger King	Fast food	1954	15,000	22.9	350,000 to 1 Mn
Ace Hardware	Retail	1976	5312	17.0	286,000 to 1 Mn
Subway	Fast food	1974	40,869	16.1	100,000 to 250,000
Dominos	Fast food	1967	17,020	14.3	300,000 to 600,000
Pizza Hut	Fast food	1959	17,176	12.9	350,000 to 2 Mn
Chick-fill-A	Fast food	1946	2503	12.6	10,000
Circle K	Convenience store	1999	9392	12.4	171,000 to 190,000

Data Franchisesupermarket.com (2023)[34]

also the entire system of operation of the business under franchise agreement. The franchisor provides site selection and development support, operating manuals, training, standardization, quality control, marketing strategies, and advisory support to the franchisee. While Business Format Franchising involves both goods and services, it is more explicit to notice the service franchises such as McDonald's, KFC, Pizza Hut, Starbucks, and Hilton.[36]

The second type of franchising is identified as traditional franchise or Product Distribution Franchise (PDF). The franchise business of this type is more common than the former type and involves production and distribution activities. Franchisee obtains licenses to produce and distribute goods that belong to a franchisor. Licenses are provided to produce, use formula, use trademarks, and trade names. The production plant, production guidelines, quality control guidelines, and marketing strategies are also monitored by the franchisor. Coca-Cola and Pepsi are examples of production franchises and Mobil Oil, Shell, and Lanka IOC are examples of distribution franchises. Before entering into a franchise agreement, the entrepreneur must carefully weigh the pros and cons of each type of franchise and internal strength and weaknesses of the entrepreneur to operate the franchise. This type of franchise is identical to licensing also that designates authority to production and distribution.

Considerations for Franchise Contract

While franchising involves legal bond between the franchisor and franchisee, the core of franchise relates to the franchisor's brand value, franchisor support, franchisee's obligations in delivering goods and services, maintaining brand standards, and the health of the relationship between the franchisor and franchisee. Brand is the most valuable asset exerted on the customers by a firm. Customers are concerned with and loyal to the brand and the franchisee is insignificant to them. Therefore, a franchisor concentrates on developing customer loyalty and the brand image rather than promoting the franchisee's company name. If the franchise is of competitive nature rather than monopolistic nature, customer loyalty is the key to success of the franchise. Franchisors license the franchisee a single product or all his products. Some franchisors designate a single franchisee for a whole country while others designate multiple franchisees for a single country. The single franchisee enjoys monopolistic advantage while multiple franchisees are compelled to competition among the franchisees.[37]

The entrepreneurs who wish to obtain franchise can benefit from various supports from the franchisor. Some franchisors provide franchisees with business systems, machinery and tools, and other business support to enhance the franchisee's ability to maintain brand standards and to guarantee customer satisfaction. With this support, franchisees are supposed to enhance reputation of the brand within the area of his jurisdiction. Therefore, when selecting a franchise to license, the entrepreneur must evaluate the support provided and the responsibility and commitments entailed in the franchise license. As franchise is a system, the entrepreneur will have to operate it in a demanding and challenging manner. Franchising opportunities are attractive and widely available, and hence, the entrepreneur must carefully match their abilities with the franchise system they plan to operate.

Franchises are different from chain operations such as supermarket chain and convenience store chain. For examples, Walmart Inc. is operating its 10,566 shops as a shop chain, whereas McDonald's is operating its 40,031 restaurants under franchising. Franchise shops are not operated or managed by the franchisor but by the franchisee on a specific franchise license. Franchise licenses are not uniform across the world due to differences in legal systems. In some countries, franchise law can vary across states also. Therefore, entrepreneurs should be aware of the territorial operational limitation clause of franchise. Franchise fees too vary on the nature of license. Franchisee is usually required to pay one-time initial fee to enter into agreement and a continuing fee known as royalty for the use of franchisor's intellectual property rights such as trademark, trade name, and operating systems. The profit, loss, and risk are outcomes of the franchisee's ability to operate the franchise. Franchisee must be attentive to the franchisor's requirements also when continuing with the franchise.

Advantages of a Franchise

Major advantages of a franchise to a franchisee are listed below.

1. Franchise negotiations are a useful input for a feasibility plan to prove the strength of pre-start-up activities.
2. Franchise involves less financial risk than that of a proprietorship and partnership but provides business ownership to the franchisee.
3. Products are developed and passed to the franchisee so that they need not engage in research and development of products.
4. Business system, brand, trademark, trade name, and trading rights are passed to the franchisee for use.
5. Entrepreneur can avoid rigorous early steps of venture creation and concentrate on latter steps to make the franchise an early success.
6. Franchisee receives a support package from the franchisor that includes a proven business model. This relieves the franchisee from much of business model building efforts.

7. Franchise is considered as a "business for oneself, but not a business of oneself." Therefore, it requires less dedication than privately owned business.
8. Chance for business success is high because franchise appears to be a branch of an already successful business.
9. As franchisor spends time and money on franchise support package as a part of the franchise agreement, the franchisee is relieved from some burdens.
10. Some franchisors provide business mentor service for the franchisee to troubleshoot problems. This is a comfort for a franchisee entrepreneur.
11. As most franchise businesses are proven to be successful, franchisee can recover capital much easily compared to a traditional startup.
12. Franchisors possess sound relationships with various parties related to the business. These relationships can be advantageous to the franchisees also.
13. Because franchisor educates the business model and provides necessary training to the franchisee, they can run the business without much trouble. The guidance provided by the franchisor is like a help of a veteran.
14. A franchisor may prefer to offer a franchise to his employees also. This enables an employee to easily become an entrepreneur and they will be able to run the franchise successfully because of the familiarity with the products, brand, and the business model of the franchisor.

Disadvantages of a Franchise

There are several disadvantages also in operating a franchise. Therefore, the entrepreneur who seeks a franchise must consider the disadvantages connected to the franchise, also, before entering into an agreement.

1. Lucrative and well-established franchises are very expensive to be obtained. The high initial fee and annual royalty can be unbearable to an average entrepreneur.

2. Franchise is a pre-designed and highly standardized business model. This requires only standard operational styles doled out by the franchisor which deters creativity, experiments, and autonomy of the entrepreneur.
3. In most cases, franchisees are required to share financial information with the franchisors for decision-making and benchmarking purposes at the headquarters. While this practice is useful to the franchisee, it intrudes on the franchisee's privacy.
4. There can be operational mismatch between the franchisor and the franchisee due to cultural differences. In international franchising, culture will matter as different cultures have different paces of doing business. A local franchisee may find it difficult to keep pace with the franchisor's vigor.
5. Franchisor may add new conditions to the franchise agreement when the agreement is renewed. If the franchisee cannot meet the new condition, there is a possibility for loss of the franchise.
6. Political risk is involved in franchise business at times the franchisor and franchisee countries are in locked horns in bilateral relations. Bilateral animosities cause trade embargoes and moratoria that block operations of a franchise.
7. Political agitations erupt against franchisor country in the franchisee country can develop into attacks on franchise shops. Also, voluntary refrains from use of franchised products can harm sales.

Choosing the Right Franchise

There are a few factors that prospective entrepreneurs should consider before entering into a franchise or licensing agreement. This is required because once entered into an agreement, it will not be easy for the entrepreneur to exit. Also, an entrepreneur's choice to frequently change franchisor involves waste of money, time, and efforts. Therefore, the entrepreneur must do some research on the options about franchises and comparative advantages and disadvantages of different franchises. The following directions will be useful for an entrepreneur to choose the right franchise. The concerns of the prospective franchisee can be discussed and conditions be negotiated with the franchisor prior to entering into franchise agreement.[38]

1. Selection of suitable product, brand, or business model. This helps the entrepreneur not to get tired of unfamiliar franchise business models.
2. Fund requirements to run the franchise. A franchise usually requires initial fee, investment, and annual royalty fee and the costs involved in training, uniform, billboards, and premise upgrades.
3. Appropriate work style. In franchise, there are a few options of work styles. Some franchises can be operated from home enjoying much freedom while others are highly structured, competitive, dependent, rigorous, and demanding long work hours.
4. Market behavior. Demand and competition are important considerations when selecting a franchise. Thus, it is useful to conduct a survey on the market behavior in the area of operational focus.
5. Support extended by the franchisor. Supports extended by franchisors vary and some supports can involve hidden costs also. The adequacy, comfort, and effectiveness of the support are important aspects to be searched for.
6. Decision on own brand or franchised brand. Franchise is a type of business that does not guarantee complete operational freedom to the entrepreneur similar to own brand and business.
7. Franchise crowding effect. Success of a franchise invites more franchisees in a small territory causing a franchise crowding effect which ultimately contracts individual operators' market share.
8. Sustainability of the franchise. Sustainability of a franchise depends on the sustainability of the franchisor. It is of high risk if the franchisor abruptly discontinues the products or the business.
9. Training by franchisor. Franchisee should be aware of the extent of training and where it is provided. International traveling and expenses may also involve in this.
10. Mentoring and coaching. Franchisors sometimes offer business mentoring and coaching programs which are compulsory for the franchisee. The responsibility of bearing costs or fees is a concern.
11. Franchisor intervention. Intensiveness and rigor of monitoring the operations, business progress, and the intervention carried out by the franchisor are important concerns.
12. Frequency of franchisor updates. Marketing campaigns, materials, shop appearance and arrangement, products, and introduction of new products to be added by the franchisee and their impact on the business.

Entering into the Franchise/Licensing Business

Franchising and licensing business has two aspects; becoming a franchisor or licensor and becoming a franchisee or licensee. A venture that plans to expand its operations can consider the franchising or licensing strategy and become a franchisor or licensor. In contrast, an entrepreneur who contemplates to find strategic venture opportunity can enter into franchising or licensing agreement and become a franchisee or licensee. A prospective franchisor or licensor considers the following steps to elevate their business.

- Identify franchising/licensing advantages
- Recognize franchising/licensing opportunities
- Register intellectual property rights
- Prepare financial disclosure document (FDD)
- Draft franchising/licensing proposal
- Prepare operational manual
- Set standardization procedures
- Register financial disclosure document
- Set management strategy
- Advertise franchise offer.

Prospective entrepreneur searching for opportunities to operate as a franchisee or licensee, usually engages in a number of steps in the process of getting into franchising or licensing business. In the process of selecting an appropriate licensor, advantages and disadvantages of the license and the profile and prospect of the licensor are considered by licensee. Table 13.2 provides a list of the world top 10 licensors. The products that seek prominent world presence like Coca-Cola, Pepsi, Carlsberg, also look for promising local or foreign licensees.

- Evaluation of self-suitability
- Contact a franchise/licensing consultant
- Search for franchising/licensing options
- Compare available options
- Select the suitable option
- Identify the suitable operations location
- Secure funds and finances
- Sign the franchise/licensing agreement

Table 13.2 World top 10 licensors (Based on Revenue)

Rank	*Name*	*Revenue US$ Bn*
1	Walt Disney	61.7
2	Dotdash Meredith	31.5
3	Authentic Brand Group	24.1
4	Warner Bros. Discovery	15.8
5	Pokemon	11.6
6	Hasbro	11.5
7	NBC Universal	10.5
8	Mattel	8.0
9	Bluestar Alliance	7.5
10	WHP Global	6.7

Data statista.com (2023)[39]

- Obtain permits, licenses, clearances, and insurance
- Construct operations premises
- Hire staff and train them
- Open the franchise/licensing business.

Chapter Summary

Acquisition, Merging, Franchising, and Licensing are avenues for venture creation. Some prefer buying out existing businesses instead of conventionally starting up ventures. This method is known as acquisition and merger. Acquisition and merger are feasible as some businesses go on sale after operations for some time; small IT firms are a case in point. Opportunities for commencing ventures are created under franchise and licensing arrangements also. Some established businesses, as a means of expansion, offer franchise and licensing opportunities.

Acquisition is mostly aimed at appending ventures to an existing business for gaining from scale and scope economies. Acquisition decision is made on personal and industrial preferences. Acquisition begins with examination of acquisition opportunities. Broker firms are sources of information on acquisition opportunities. Buyout decision is made after careful analyses of external factors that affect business future. PESTEL and SWOT analysis are common tools used for this purpose. A business for sale is also evaluated in terms of geography, turnover, profit, assets, liabilities, due diligence, R&D and intellectual property rights, personnel strength, management, and strategic advantages. The value by the seller is higher than that of the buyer due to different valuation perceptions of the two. Business is professionally valued considering the factors such as business history, market, competition, market share, sales, production, plants and facilities, legal structure, management, employees, assets, liabilities, and finance.

The purpose of buyout determines the style such as horizontal integration, vertical integration, and conglomeration. Payments for acquisition are designated as Leverage buyout, Entrepreneurial leverage buyout, or Cash-flow leverage buyout. Merger creates opportunity for consolidated joint operation among the merging parties. In a merger, company names are also merged. There are five different types of mergers to select from among: Conglomerate, Horizontal, Vertical, Market-extension, and Product-extension. Differences of mergers depend on the purpose of merger, nature of operations, and the relationship of the merging companies.

Franchising and licensing provide new and unique opportunities for producing or selling goods and services of another firm at a royalty payment. Franchising and licensing opportunities are available from local or international firms. When selecting a suitable franchise or a license, the type of business, nature of products, initial investment, and conditions to be agreed are considered. Some franchisors and licensors do not require prior business experience of the franchisees and licensees. Generally, franchisors and licensors provide consultancies, promotional materials, funds, training, technical collaboration, business updates, and marketing strategies to the franchisee and licensee. The most popular type of franchising is Business Format Franchising (BFF).

Here, franchisor provides the franchisee with trade name, products or services, and the entire system of business operation. The second type of franchising is the Product Distribution Franchise (PDF). This type is more common and involves production and distribution activities. Here, Franchisee produces and distributes goods under license of a franchisor. License authorizes franchisee to produce and to sell goods under franchisor's formula, trademarks, and trade names. Franchisor provides production guidelines, quality control guidelines, and marketing strategies and monitors them. Entrepreneurs who choose to be franchisees should be mindful that it is costly to exit from a franchise or licensing agreement.

Review Questions

1. Define Acquisition and Merger and examine whether they are lucrative methods of entrepreneurship.
2. Discuss the purposes and objectives of entrepreneurs to engage in Acquisition and Merger.
3. "Acquisition and Merger decision is backed by personal preferences and prevalence of Acquisition and Merger opportunities." Critically examine.
4. Prepare a business evaluation format for the use of an entrepreneur who prepares to conclude an Acquisition or Merger.
5. a. What is Due Diligence evaluation?
   b. What are the criteria for Due Diligence evaluation?
   c. What are the components of a Due Diligence report?
6. Provide a comprehensive account of the methods of business valuation.
7. Describe the major methods of business acquisition and merger and identify their advantages and disadvantages.
8. Explain the possibilities of horizontal and vertical business integration via Acquisition and Merger.
9. Define Franchising and Licensing and examine whether they are lucrative methods of entrepreneurship.
10. What are the major types of Franchising and Licensing and the considerations of such agreements?
11. Discuss the advantages and disadvantages of Franchising and Licensing.
12. Explain the factors that need to be considered when entering into a Franchising and Licensing agreement.
13. "Franchising and Licensing opportunities are available both locally and internationally." Differentiate between the two types.
14. Compare and contrast the privileges of franchisor and franchisee, and licensor and licensee.

Additional Readings

1. Caiazza, R., and Volpe, T., 2015. M&A process: A literature review and research agenda. *Business Process Management Journal, 21*(1), pp. 205–220.

2. Ismail, T.H., Abdou, A.A., and Annis, R.M., 2011. *Review of literature linking corporate performance to mergers and acquisitions*. SSRN.
3. Buckley, P., and Ghauri, P.N., 2002. *International mergers and acquisitions: A reader*. Cengage.
4. Ghauri, P.N., and Buckley, P.J., 2003. International mergers and acquisitions: Past, present and future. In *Advances in mergers and acquisitions* (pp. 207–229). Emerald Group Publishing Limited.
5. https://imaa-institute.org/.
6. https://imaa-institute.org/.
7. Rouse, T., and Frame, T., 2009. The 10 steps to successful M&A integration. *Bain and Company Business Insights*.
8. Van Schaik, D., 2008. *M&A in Japan: An Analysis of Merger Waves and Hostile Takeovers* (No. EPS-2008-141-ORG).
9. Fleischer Jr, A., and Mundheim, R.H., 1966. Corporate Acquisition by Tender Offer. *University of Pennsylvania Law Review, 115*, p. 317.
10. Walter, G.A. and Barney, J.B., 1990. Research notes and communications management objectives in mergers and acquisitions. *Strategic Management Journal, 11*(1), pp. 79–86.
11. Ebner, S., 2012. *Essays on the Economics of Mergers and Acquisitions* (Doctoral dissertation, Universität Passau).
12. Jenter, D., and Lewellen, K., 2015. CEO preferences and acquisitions. *The Journal of Finance, 70*(6), pp. 2813–2852.
13. Rozen-Bakher, Z., 2018. Comparison of merger and acquisition (M&A) success in horizontal, vertical and conglomerate M&As: Industry sector vs. services sector. *The Service Industries Journal, 38*(7–8), pp. 492–518.
14. Hitt, M.A., King, D.R., Krishnan, H., Makri, M., Schijven, M., Shimizu, K., and Zhu, H., 2012. *Creating value through mergers and acquisitions: Challenges and opportunities*.
15. Benson, M.D., and Shippy, J.S., 2013. The M&A buy side process: An overview for acquiring companies. *Stout Journal*, pp. 1–8.
16. Benson, M.D., and Shippy, J.S., 2013. The M&A buy side process: An overview for acquiring companies. *Stout Journal*, pp. 1–8.
17. Weizhi, Y., 2011, January. A study on risks of cross-border merger and acquisition of SOES in China based on PEST model. In *MSIE 2011* (pp. 1260–1264). IEEE.

18. Hooke, J.C., 1997. *M&A: A practical guide to doing the deal* (Vol. 36). John Wiley & Sons.
19. Kearney, A.T., 2013. *M&A deal evaluation: Challenging metrics myths*. London: AT Kearney.
20. Ghauri, P., and Hassan, I. eds., 2014. *Evaluating companies for mergers and acquisitions*. Emerald Group Publishing.
21. Mehrotra, A., and Sahay, A., 2022. Financial performance of firms pre-and post-M&A: A study of selected Indian Acquirers. *Vision*, p. 09722629221087367.
22. Rozen-Bakher, Z., 2018. Could the pre-M&A performances predict integration risk in cross-border M&As? *International Journal of Organizational Analysis, 26*(4), pp. 652–668.
23. Howson, P., 2017. *Due diligence: The critical stage in mergers and acquisitions*. Routledge.
24. Burke, J., 2000. Due diligence in mergers & acquisitions. *Internal Auditor, 57*(5), pp. 37–37.
25. Harvey, M.G., and Lusch, R.F., 1995. Expanding the nature and scope of due diligence. *Journal of Business Venturing, 10*(1), pp. 5–21.
26. Aluko, B.T., and Amidu, A.R., 2005. Corporate business valuation for mergers and acquisitions. *International Journal of Strategic Property Management, 9*(3), pp. 173–189.
27. Saksonova, S., Abramishivi, N., and Papiashvili, T., 2020. Business valuation: Classical and advanced methods.
28. Chen, N., Lin, X., Luo, R. and Shao, G., 2021, July. Business Acquisition Analysis. In *2021 International Conference on Economic Development and Business Culture (ICEDBC 2021)* (pp. 231–235). Atlantis Press.
29. https://web.facebook.com/celltel/?_rdc=1&_rdr.
30. https://www.sundaytimes.lk/100103/BusinessTimes/bt26.html.
31. https://en.wikipedia.org/wiki/Etisalat_(Sri_Lanka).
32. https://hutch.lk/.
33. Gerhardt, S., Hazen, S., Lewis, S., and Hall, R., 2015. Entrepreneur options: "franchising" vs. "licensing" (McDonald's vs. Starbucks and Chick-Fil-A). *ASBBS E-Journal, 11*(1), p. 80.
34. https://www.franchisesupermarket.co.uk/franchising-in-2023-and-the-trends.

35. Brouthers, L.E., and McNicol, J.P., 2009. International franchising and licensing. *KOTABE, M.; HELSEN, K. The Sage handbook of international marketing*. London: Sage Publications, pp. 183–197.
36. Klein, B., 1995. The economics of franchise contracts. *Journal of Corporate Finance, 2*(1–2), pp. 9–37.
37. Lafontaine, F., and Blair, R.D., 2008. The evolution of franchising and franchise contracts: Evidence from the United States. *Entrepreneurial Bus. LJ, 3*, p. 381.
38. Baucus, D.A., Baucus, M.S., and Human, S.E., 1993. Choosing a franchise: How base fees and royalties relate to. *Journal of Small Business Management, 31*(2), p. 91.
39. https://www.statista.com/.

CHAPTER 14

Neo-entrepreneurship Models

Key Learning Points

- Introduction to neo-entrepreneurship models.
- Corporate entrepreneurship/Intrapreneurship.
- Entrepreneur and Intrapreneur.
- Intrapreneurship process.
- Intrapreneurship vs. Entrepreneurship.
- Intrapreneurship models: Enabler, Producer, Opportunist, Advocate.
- Social entrepreneurship.
- Reasons for and types of social entrepreneurship.
- Social enterprise and social business.
- Social entrepreneurship types.
- The purpose of social entrepreneurship.
- Women entrepreneurship.
- Importance of women entrepreneurship.
- Motives of women entrepreneurship.
- Support for women entrepreneurship.
- Organizational aspect.
- The issues of women entrepreneurship.
- Family business entrepreneurship.
- Determinants of family business.

© The Author(s), under exclusive license to Springer Nature Singapore Pte Ltd. 2024

M. Rajaratne, *Concepts, Processes and Practice of Entrepreneurship*, Palgrave Studies in Global Entrepreneurship,
https://doi.org/10.1007/978-981-97-6180-7_14

- Three Circle Model.
- Family business objectives.
- Advantages and disadvantages of family business.
- Limitation to family business.
- Hybrid entrepreneurship.
- Reasons for hybrid entrepreneurship.
- Prospects for Developing Countries and the need for promoting hybrid entrepreneurship

Introduction

The practice of entrepreneurship has developed a few newer approaches and models of entrepreneurship during the past decades. In the new entrepreneurship models also, the essential concepts and the core of entrepreneurship remain unchanged. Since the seventeenth century, when entrepreneurship had been defined as undertaking of contracts in war-related logistics, entrepreneurship has evolved in many directions. In contrast to conventional entrepreneurship, a few distinctive entrepreneurship models will be discussed in this chapter.[1]

1. Corporate entrepreneurship
2. Social entrepreneurship
3. Women entrepreneurship
4. Family business entrepreneurship
5. Hybrid entrepreneurship.

These entrepreneurship models exhibit distinctive and inherent characteristics and important reasons for them to ascend. Distinctive venture opportunities, venture purpose, organization style, organizational structure, operational structure, controls, and responsibility will be useful aspects to differentiate one method from another.[2]

Corporate Entrepreneurship

Corporate entrepreneurship, viz. intrapreneurship, is a relatively modern concept of business creation which has been recognized by large businesses. The term intrapreneurship was coined by Gifford and Elizabeth Pinchot, in 1978,[3] after amalgamating two words: “internal” (intra) and "entrepreneurship" and debuted in their paper *Intra-Corporate Entrepreneurship* at Tarrytown School for Entrepreneurs. Accordingly, an intrapreneurship originates when a large company provides its employees with an opportunity to work on a unique idea that leads to innovation of goods, services, projects, materials, and methods that can bear considerable impact on the company's business profile. Thus, intrapreneurship can be identified as a special arrangement of entrepreneurship by a corporate. Some scholars recognize this arrangement as Corporate Entrepreneurship because of its Intra-Corporate character.[4]

Extraordinarily innovative ideas are proposed by extra ordinarily motivated employees. Upon communication of such an idea to the company, the management investigates and deliberates it and, if found to be worthy, considers offering an opportunity to the employee and provides with financial and technical support to materialize his idea. A project initiated this way is called intrapreneurship and an employee of this kind is called an intrapreneur. So, the intrapreneur literally operates within the jurisdiction of their workplace and thus, does not face risk, nor can they make profit as typical entrepreneurs do. Thus, an intrapreneur leads special projects according to their own vision with patronage of the employer. However, an intrapreneur may later choose to resign from the workplace and start their own business on the same idea and become an entrepreneur. Intrapreneurship, thus, sometimes, is like a school for an employee to graduate from and become an entrepreneur.[5]

The Intrapreneur

There are major differences between the objectives of an intrapreneur and entrepreneur. An entrepreneur envisions creating an entirely new business from the scratch to produce goods and services to earn profit. In contrast, an intrapreneur eagerly works on innovations for a company and still earns monthly salary. Intrapreneur's vision may involve introducing sweeping changes to organizational culture, production process, products, and operational methods. Intrapreneur possesses directly applicable skills and work experience to instigate an envisioned change. Intrapreneur does not own a company and strives to uplift the company they are employed by making successful their project which is approved and supported by the company. Some intrapreneurs sacrifice their earnings and time on intrapreneurial projects and forgo personal wellbeing. Successful intrapreneur is rewarded by the company and he usually and equitably shares the rewards with his team.[6]

In the corporate sector, some executives perform intrapreneurial roles also in addition to carrying out their routine managerial responsibilities. Yet, some companies provide intrapreneurs with autonomy and freedom to devote to new projects and do not demand regular daily service requirements. This exception is granted for two qualities of an intrapreneur; primarily for the intrinsic motivation and then for the enterprising responsibility. Thus, an intrapreneur is not a mere idea factory but is one who turns an idea into business reality that can generate profit. Intrapreneurship fostering within a company is beneficial as it helps reengineer and reorient the company, reduce cost, and increase profitability. Successful intrapreneurs can benefit through career promotions also in addition to special monetary rewards.[7]

Intrapreneurs later destine themselves to creation of their own business and becoming entrepreneurs. Steve Jobs resigned from Apple Inc. and created his own venture Pixar Inc., Art Fry left 3M and created Post-It Inc., Ken Kutaragi quitted Nintendo Inc. and joined and got elevated as the Chairman of Sony Computer Entertainment for his innovation of PlayStation game portal. A company does not create intrapreneurs but identifies employee potentials as intrapreneurs based on their distinctive traits and characteristics. Intrapreneurial mindset of a company is conducive to recognizing employee potentials as intrapreneurs. Provided the right cooperative environment, employees will think out-of-the-box and demonstrate skills that help undertake innovative projects. New move of creating intrapreneurs from among outsiders has been initiated by Whirlpool Inc. as an exception.[8]

Intrapreneurship Process

Therefore, creation of intrapreneurial environment conducive for employees to demonstrate their entrepreneurial skills in their job role is useful for development of intrapreneurship.[9] Intrapreneurship appears not as mere action but as a process that involves six steps as indicated in Fig. 14.1.

1. An organization invites opinions from employees regarding a corporate issue or an objective.
2. Opinions are screened to match with organizational criteria.

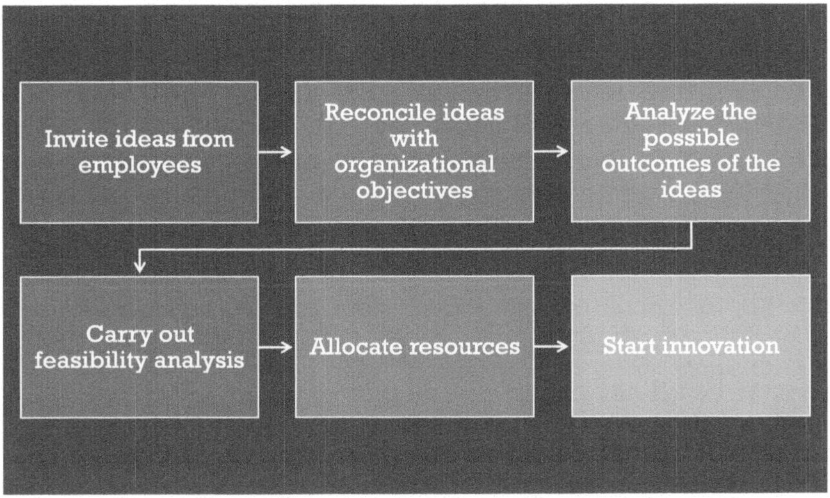

Fig. 14.1 Intrapreneurship process (Author Portrayal)

3. Opinions are assessed for determining entrepreneurial viability.
4. SWOT analysis is carried out to determine feasibility of selected opinions.
5. If the opinion is commercially feasible, the company acquires resources required for the project.
6. Selected opinion is put into action as a project.

The difference between intrapreneurship and entrepreneurship is determined by a few factors as presented in Fig. 14.2. In addition, intrapreneurship takes place in three distinctive levels as it is organized: (1) individual level, (2) team level, and (3) corporate level. Further, intrapreneurship can take place in private or public organizations, for-profit or not-for-profit organizations, and government organizations. Promotion of intrapreneurship is considered by many organizations as an alternative means to face increased market competition. Also, intrapreneurship is promoted in organizations motivating potential intrapreneurs among employees to capitalize on their unexploited skills in making the corporate innovative and profitable without extra remuneration.[10]

INTRAPRENEURSHIP	•ENTREPRENEURSHIP
Motive is corporate growth through entrepreneurial skills of employees	•Motive is to provide goods and services to the market through a new venture as its owner
Company culture poses challenges for employees to identify intrapreneurial opportunities	•Market and its competitiveness pose challenges to entrepreneurship
Resources, facilities, supports, and markets are arranged for intrapreneur by the company	•Procurement of resources, facilities, and access to markets are responsibilities of the entrepreneur
Intrapreneurial project belongs to the company and the intrapreneur is dependent on the company management	•Venture belongs to the entrepreneur and thus, they are independent in making decisions
Intrapreneur receives awards or promotions for the success of the project.	•Entrepreneur realizes profit or loss for business success or failure
Intrapreneurship does not impose commercial risk on the employee	•Entrepreneurship is risky and can lead to bankruptcy

Fig. 14.2 Intrapreneurship vs. entrepreneurship (Author Portrayal)

Intrapreneurship Models

Large corporates like multinational corporations, since recently, have been showing interest in intrapreneurship development for the reasons discussed in the previous section. For intrapreneurship development, corporates basically engage in four different roles such as Enabler, Producer, Opportunist, and Advocate which in turn are identified as intrapreneurship models.[11]

1. **Enabler**—Employees are encouraged to develop innovative opinions that would enhance company efficiency and performance. Google Inc. allows its engineers 20% of their time to work on their

own projects and to come up with suggestions. If suggestions are accepted by the higher management, they are implemented.

2. **Producer**—Companies educate employees on company's target operations and the connection of employee input with it. This is essentially a corporate training with an aim of enhancing business skills in employees to produce corporate intrapreneurs. Cargill Co. of the UK is recognized as an example of this model.
3. **Opportunist**—Company provides employees with opportunities to create mutually beneficial networks with other large companies. Through the networks created by this means, employees are expected to contribute more to their workplace and to build their career potentials also. Neo-classic automaker Zimmer (USA) is an example of opportunist model.
4. **Advocate**—Company gives freedom to employees for experimenting on minor but fundamental matters that can advocate greater impacts. Dupont corporation's support for its employees to develop designs for lighters and then to adopt the selected designs for production is an example.

Social Entrepreneurship

Social entrepreneurship, by definition, is the process that employs entrepreneurial principles and processes to recognize social problems and overcome them to induce social change. Diagnosis of a social problem, in contrast to diagnosis of a common problem in typical entrepreneurship, is of prime importance in case of social entrepreneurship. After diagnosis of a social problem, solution is designed to eliminate it and bring about a social change.[12] This requires setting up and managing an enterprise with lifetime commitment to the purpose. While social enterprise is designed to earn profit, its fundamental focus is formation of social capital. Like any other enterprise, social enterprise also requires monetary capital to obtain its objectives.[13]

Social Entrepreneurship Types

Social entrepreneurship is of two types: (1) social enterprise of profit-making objective and (2) social enterprise of non-profit-making objective. Social entrepreneurship includes ventures for environment protection, child rights, and women empowerment. Grameen Bank of Bangladesh for micro finance, Rang-De of India for online micro-credit platform, George Foundation of the USA for women empowerment, Ford Foundation of the USA for human welfare and education advancement, Carnegie Foundation of the USA for advancement of education, Amnesty International of UK for human rights, Bill & Melinda Gates Foundation of the USA for fighting poverty and disease, Otara Foundation of Sri Lanka for animal welfare are a few examples of social entrepreneurship organizations.[14]

The passion for social entrepreneurship is a relatively new phenomenon. At present, selfless motive of human beings has drawn many people to social entrepreneurship to satisfy their self-actualization needs as social entrepreneurs; the last need of a person according to Abraham Maslow. A social entrepreneur is thus, a person who takes on a social problem and devises innovative solutions to it. Profit-making is an auxiliary objective of social entrepreneurship and thus the social entrepreneur is intrinsically motivated in causing social change. Social entrepreneur promotes individuals to join onboard the social change bandwagon and to engage in the social change process; the key feature of social entrepreneurship.[15] Bill Drayton, America's top social entrepreneur, once said "*social entrepreneurs are not content just to give a fish or teach how to fish. They will not rest until they have revolutionized the entire fishing industry.*" This statement is self-explanatory to the scope of social entrepreneurship.

The Purpose of Social Entrepreneurship

The purpose of social entrepreneurship, in broad sense, is to uplift the social and natural environment. In the first place, economically and socially disadvantaged sectors are supposed to benefit from social entrepreneurship to improve livelihood. Social entrepreneurs care more for people's wellbeing than their productivity. Thus, workload, work-time flexibility, and work-from-home options are considered in social enterprises. Jobs are designed as full-time or part-time, for individuals or groups, for normal workers or disabled workers, on-site or working from home, and as putting-out or sub-contracting. Major purpose of social entrepreneurship is not mere wealth creation but wealth sharing among the participants. Accordingly, the internal stakeholders of social enterprise will finally become equity-holder community earning mostly an equitable income instead of a salary.[16]

Social entrepreneurs can easily obtain support from governments, charity organizations, and philanthropists because they engage in a social course. Thus, raising capital for social entrepreneurship is relatively easier. Due to the in-built social character, social enterprises can attract thoughtful employees at relatively lower salaries or even as volunteers. Social entrepreneurship excludes the principles of competition and competitiveness and thus, marketing perspective of social enterprise is different from other enterprises. Free or concessionary publicity, free shelf space of supermarkets, and customer networks can be secured as social entrepreneurship strives to gain effective social change instead of profit.[17] Large corporate enterprises and banks also extend assistance to the virtuous acts of social enterprise.

Accumulation of social capital is an important objective of social entrepreneurship. Social capital is defined as social contacts between and within groups. Social contact instills confidence and fosters relationships in the team and hence the team's effectiveness is improved. The World Bank regards social capital as an important factor for social and economic development. Social entrepreneurship develops and capitalizes on social capital for addressing social problem and uplifting affected communities. Although social capital is important for social change, there are barriers also to it emanating from the rigidity of social stratification. Ironically, breaking this barrier itself sometimes is an objective of social entrepreneurship.[18]

Social Entrepreneurship Models

Social entrepreneurs engage in two missions; economic mission and social mission of which the social mission is chief whereas the economic mission is complementary. Further, the economic mission procedures finances and other resources that are required for accomplishing objectives of the social mission. Accordingly, the economic mission is designed to generate profit or funds while the social mission is designed to deliver benefits. The economic mission either conceives for-profit-making or not-for-profit-making venture. On the other hand, the social mission targets internal beneficiaries or external beneficiaries. Internal beneficiaries are the team that involves in the economic mission whereas the external beneficiaries are outsiders (people, animal, environment, etc.) with no connection to the economic mission.

This four-factor scenario, depicted in Fig. 14.3, derives four social entrepreneurship models.

1. Social business model—Venture with profit-making objective and an organizational purpose of funding social missions aimed at internal beneficiaries.
2. Beneficent business model—Venture with profit-making objective and an organizational purpose of funding social missions aimed at external beneficiaries.
3. Benefactor business model—Venture with non-profit-making objective and an organizational purpose of funding social missions aimed at internal beneficiaries.
4. Social enterprise model—Venture with non-profit-making objective and an organizational purpose of funding social missions aimed at external beneficiaries.

Choice of Objective		SOCIAL MISSION	
		Internal Beneficiaries	External Beneficiaries
ECONOMIC MISSION	For-Profit Business	1 Social Business Model	2 Beneficent Business Model
	Not-For-Profit Business	3 Benefactor Business Model	4 Social Enterprise Model

Fig. 14.3 Social entrepreneurship models (Author Portrayal)

Social Enterprise and Social Business

Social enterprise and social business are not synonymous but they share some common values as if were siblings. Social enterprise is a project created for the purpose of tackling social problems, whereas social business is an entity created with the purpose of profit-making by and for socially marginalized groups. However, social business is generally misunderstood for and interchangeably used with social enterprise. The capital required for social enterprise is referred to as funds that can be raised as contributions and donations from philanthropists, governments, and societies. The funds required for social business are referred to as capital and raised by those groups who involve in initiating the business. In a broad sense, investments of a social business can comprise finance, skills, connections, entrepreneurial skills, and licenses. The investors can withdraw their contribution after the social course is completed or otherwise the organization deviates from its original purpose and objectives. In case of divestment of pioneers, the organization will have to either wind up operations or find new partners.[19]

Even though social businesses make profit, the profit-making objective is normally seen taking the back seat. Profit for sustainability is the theme for social business as members find it important to sustain the business to support livelihood. Any excess profit that is not shared is reinvested in the business itself. The success of social business is not measured in terms of profit but in terms of effectiveness of the positive social changes it causes. Therefore, it could be generalized that the very purpose of social business is not profit but social contribution through profit.[20] Thus, the social business is an alternate device to alleviate adverse market impact on an affected community. For example, the Grameen Bank of Bangladesh is a social business that devises alternative finance for social groups that are either affected by the market rates or have no access to mainstream financial system.[21]

Grameen Bank of Bangladesh

Muhammad Yunus, in founding the Grameen Bank, established seven principles to differentiate the Grameen Bank from common businesses. These principles are now known as the Principles of Social Business. They basically provide guidelines to define the purpose and modus operandi of social business.[22]

1. Business objective will be not to profit maximization but to overcome poverty or more problems such as low schooling, poor health, lack of shelter, access to technology, and environmental pollution that threatens people and society.
2. Financial and economic sustainability of disadvantaged people.
3. Investors get back their investment only. No dividend is given back beyond investment money when divested.
4. Even when total investment is paid back, profit remains with the company for operations, expansion, and improvement.
5. Gender sensitive and environmentally conscious.
6. Workforce gets market wage rate with better working conditions.
7. Do it with joy (joy by intrinsic motives rather than extrinsic motives).

Women Entrepreneurship

Women entrepreneurship is a branch of entrepreneurship that has caught limelight in the past few decades. Prior to discussing the reasons for and purposes and operations of women entrepreneurship, it is useful to recognize its essence at the outset. According to Joseph Schumpeter, "*Women entrepreneurs are those women who innovate, initiate or adopt a business activity.*" The government of India defines women entrepreneurship as *"an enterprise owned and controlled by a woman having a minimum financial interest up to 51 percent of the capital and giving at least 51 percent of the employment to women."* Therefore, the essence of women entrepreneurship is that the women, individually or in groups, organize and operate a business enterprise facing risks and handling economic uncertainty involved in it.[23]

Business endeavor has been predominantly an affair of men in the past. However, for various reasons, women also have made inroads to business increasingly during the past few decades and so, without any distinction, women enterprises have surged in all countries. It is estimated that in Canada, the USA, and India respectively 35%, 25%, and 10% of businesses are owned by women. Among many reasons for surge of women enterprises, the rights and liberties granted to women have paved ways for them to emerge as entrepreneurs and earn income. Education opportunities, cross-border exposure, and social networks also have effectively served women to enter the business field.[24]

Motives for Women Entrepreneurship

Feminist movements have advocated women independence; more specifically economic independence. This move has encouraged women primarily to find employment. However, the reasons such as sexual harassment, glass ceiling concern, demand for work experience, exposure, and networks, maternity leave, income loss after retirement, family attachment, and concerns have driven women to start own businesses. Among the psychological factors, freedom and mobility, social status, and dreams have predominantly influenced women to start business. Additionally, compulsion to make a living, need for additional income, absence of professional skills, displacements, and becoming a widow or breadwinner also have increasingly compelled women to the field of business. Women, generally in developing countries, are destined to a few incapacities (Fig. 14.4) that hinder advancement of their economic and social life. Women, thus, attempt to overcome such incapacities through engaging in business startups.[25]

Generally, the following factors have been identified as the major causes for women to enter micro entrepreneurship in India.

1. Inadequate income and poor living condition
2. Lack of resources to enhance life
3. Meager financial support from husband
4. Lack of education and training for employment
5. Need for wellbeing of a large family
6. General livelihood needs
7. Need for income security
8. Dire need for something than having nothing.

In contrast to male entrepreneurs, the field of business of women entrepreneurs is narrow and inauspicious. The reasons for women to engage in restricted areas of business include lack of training and education, aversion of high-risk and complex ventures, reluctance to engage in heavy industry, choice for small scale and easy management, choice of simple operations, and avoidance of high-tech business. In consequence, it is learned that women entrepreneurs choose traditional and simple industries like food, dairy, vegetable, fruit, pickles, cookies, cakes, weaving, hosiery, and garments. In line with social advancement, education, exposure, training, and social recognition for women, a trend of

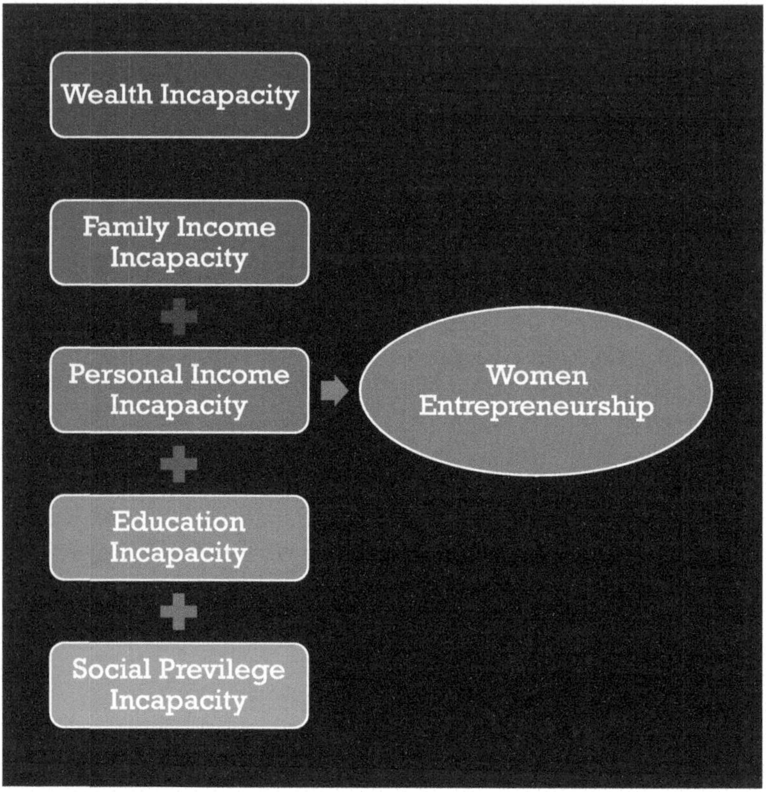

Fig. 14.4 Motives for women entrepreneurship (Author Portrayal)

women enterprise diversification into restaurant, flower, fashion, beauty salon, jewelry, handcraft, design, spa, and architecture has been witnessed presently.[26]

Support for Women Entrepreneurship

Women entrepreneurship is promoted by governments for several reasons. Economically disadvantaged women, minority women, widowed women with children, women with ill health, rural women, lowly educated women, and women of low caste are usually considered economically vulnerable. Governments, thus, pay special attention to empower them through various upward-bound support programs. Women entrepreneurship development is thus seen as a strategy for women empowerment.[27]

As important and effective as the women entrepreneurship, organizations such as governments, non-government organizations (NGOs), venture capital firms, micro-financiers, banks, and self-help funds extend their support to development of women entrepreneurship. This has resulted in financial support, training, education, skill development, market support, export orientation programs, and industrial motivational campaigns in support of women entrepreneurship development at present.[28] National and international organizations extend support to women entrepreneurs in regional, national, and international scale. Grameen Bank, a specialized micro finance bank of Bangladesh, initially was a women entrepreneurship development scheme.[29]

Capital with light collaterals, lower interest rates, seed capital loan projects, and repayment grace periods are the key features of favorable financial support. Further, the option of equity participation in the form of venture capital is also prevalent among financial supports for women entrepreneurs. Some banks in India have introduced Women Entrepreneur Section, a separate desk at the bank, to facilitate women entrepreneurship. In addition to financial support schemes, entrepreneurship orientation, business education, and training are also provided for both new and veteran women entrepreneurs. New venture areas such as manufacturing, electronics, printing, readymade garments, IT, and selected agricultural and horticultural crops are also promoted among the women who undergo the training.[30]

Organizational Aspect

Excitingly, in many countries, "Ladies Organizations" are formed to promote women entrepreneurship among themselves. Self-employed women associations, micro-credit women associations, councils of women entrepreneurs, designated industrial parks for women industrialists, and technology parks for women are a few examples that indicate the extent to which women entrepreneurship has become prevalent. Further, there are NGOs that prepare business proposals on behalf of the women who are illiterate and incapable of producing bankable documents. Cluster Development Program of India, though not confined to women, aims at forming clusters of similar enterprises. Cluster size usually is 100–300 enterprises. Cluster Coordination Office is set up to intervene in facilitation of operations.

Cluster Coordination Office intervenes clusters in two ways: soft intervention and hard intervention. The soft intervention involves capacity building through the following methods.

- Infrastructure and amenity coordination with government departments
- Diagnostic study of industry
- Forming associations for trust building and sector identity development
- Technical capacity and awareness building
- Managerial capacity building
- Organizing workshops and seminars
- Training, exposure visits, and tours
- Market development
- Design, quality, and productivity competitions
- Launch of websites and digital platforms
- Common procurement for the cluster
- Common sales and branding for the cluster
- Coordination of Entrepreneurship and Management Development Programs.

In contrast, the hard intervention methods include development of common fixed assets as individual entrepreneurs cannot afford to acquire expensive facilities by themselves. The facilities developed through hard intervention can be used by every member of the cluster free of charge or at a nominal fee. The hard intervention methods are as follows.

- Common meeting, seminar, and conference center
- Common tools and equipment depot
- Common design center
- Common testing laboratories
- Common incubator facilities
- Common training center
- Common R&D center
- Common inventory depot

- Common sales dispatch center
- Common display and exhibition center
- Stalls at international trade fairs

Issues Faced by Women Entrepreneurs

Although women entrepreneurship is imperative for poverty alleviation and social change, women often face many problems when entering into business. Women are largely economically disadvantaged and thus, they cannot provide collaterals for obtaining loans. As a result, the opportunity to obtain finance is scanty. Banks normally treat women as less creditworthy because of the notion that women could anytime leave business to bear children or to care for family responsibilities. The financial constraints for women enterprises are severe and thus, women entrepreneurs have limited access to finance. Loan Collaterals, financial risk, low creditworthiness, and inadequate funds are the key limiting factors for women entrepreneurship.[31]

Producer women entrepreneurs heavily depend on intermediaries for procurement and sales. Lack of marketing skills and constraints to frequent traveling compel women entrepreneurs to deal with intermediaries that eventually lead to draining of income. Women entrepreneurs, on the other hand, find it difficult to compete in the market due to the small size of their operations and lack of finance to advertise and promote their products. Additionally, women-made goods are generally believed to be inferior and thus this belief has bad leverage on sales.[32]

The goods such as baskets, mats, and coir and cane products are commonly made by women and the raw materials of which are obtained from natural sources. Extinction or depletion of the plants from which the materials are obtained, and the environmental, transportation, and inventory restrictions imposed on such materials also cause short supply of the natural inputs. Scarcity of materials and labor-intensive production methods push up the cost of production of the women enterprises. This has caused lower gains for the workers and entrepreneurs.

Doing business generally involves much traveling, lodging, networking, and entertaining of clients. Social restrictions and taboos for women to engage in such activities restrict women entrepreneurship. Also, due to restrictions, many women entrepreneurs tend to give up their ventures before long. After starting a business, women quite often struggle in balancing the responsibility between the business and the family. Many women, therefore, finally quit the business being reluctant to compromise family responsibilities. Women are often loaded with many family responsibilities like bearing and raising children, schooling them, house maintenance, cooking meals, and laundering which snatch time from women.[33]

In low-income countries, both formal education and technical education level of women are low due to lack of education opportunities for women. In consequence, women find it difficult to run a business as they lack the knowledge of management, marketing, and finance. This is a predominant character of women enterprise. Women tend to make a living with their business and thus, they do not bother to achieve higher business goals. This attitude severely curtails investments and expansions and hence inhibits growth of women enterprise. Gender discrimination and sexual harassment experienced at the pre-start-up stage of business also contribute to inhibiting women entrepreneurship.[34]

Family Entrepreneurship

Customarily, a business that descends from older generations of the same family is referred to as a family business. Accordingly, heredity is an important aspect of a family business. For this reason, startup of a business by a family is not recognized as a family business as it lacks the family lineage. Family business is distinguished from other businesses for three reasons: (1) ownership of business assets, (2) dominance in business control, and (3) the family inheritance. A family can dominate the business through owning most of the capital invested in the business. Capital investments, in turn, entitle them for management positions and hence the control of the business. Family inheritance is essential for a business to be recognized as a family business.[35]

In family business, the Chief Executive Officer and the Board of Directors are appointed by the family group itself. Thereby, the rights to strategic decision-making and the top-level responsibilities are retained within the family. Hence, the family interest in ownership and management of the business descends from generations at the will of the founders and the successors. Family, in a broad sense, is a group of people belonging to the same heredity, inheritance, biological ties, and kinships. The composition of a family includes the direct descendants and spouses also.[36]

Family business is guided by economic objectives set by the family members who assume different roles in the capacity of shareholder, manager, and worker. Each family business is unique due to infusion of inherent family values, management culture, business objectives, and strategies. These composites generate unique bonds and relationships among the director board members, managers, and workers. Family business can be categorized as small or large family business, young or old, and very old. Small family businesses exhibit impenetrable family ownership and tight management controls while large family businesses are organized more like corporates but retaining the top posts such as president, chairman, and CEO by way of share ownership.[37]

Three Circle Model

Tagiuri and Davis (1982 and 1996) proposed an approach to differentiate family business from other businesses taking three components into consideration: (1) family affiliation, (2) ownership of property, and (3) business management. They proposed "Three Circle Model" to identify family business characteristics. Figure 14.5 indicates each of these fundamentals and highlights their connections to determine the circumstances that create family business.

This model is constructed on three concepts as indicated in three circles: family connection (1), business ownership (3), and business/ management control (5). This relationship initially constructs three circumstances indicated as 2, 4, and 6. Circumstance 2 indicates a situation where a family owns a business but does not engage in management. Circumstance 4 indicates a situation where business ownership and management are not connected to the family. Circumstance 6 indicates a situation where family members manage the business without owning its shares as other members of the family own the business. Circumstances 2, 4, and 6 thus do not meet all the conditions required to germinate a family business. However, a fully pledged family business is created only in circumstance 7 where all the three conditions, i.e., family membership, family ownership, and control (directorship) are met. In circumstance 7, family owns and controls the business.

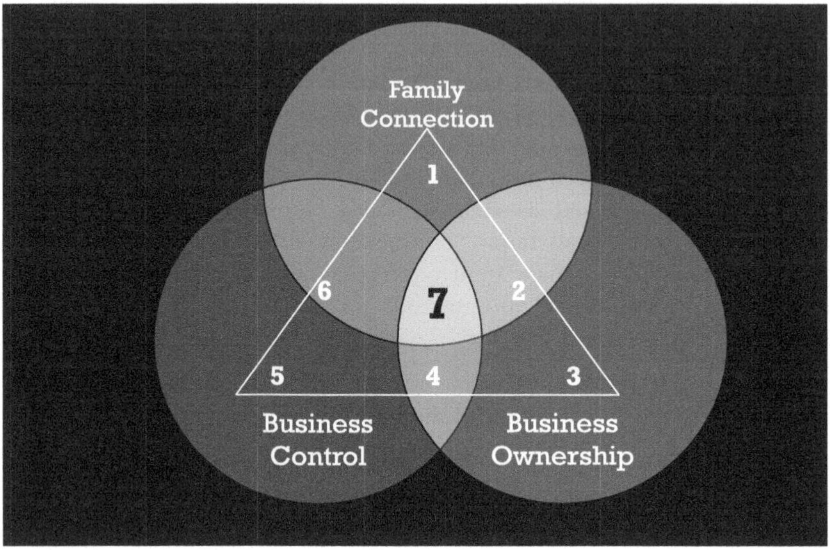

Fig. 14.5 The family business model (Author Portrayal based on Tagiuri and Davis [1996][38])

Family Business Objectives

Family business style is adopted in business to fulfill exclusive objectives. In addition to economic objectives, as of any other business, family businesses aim at specific non-economic objectives also. Economic wellbeing of the family is the main objective of a family business. The members who are involved in the business as owners, managers, or workers reasonably share any surplus among them considering the family intimacy; not the business logic. Another specific objective is long-run family wealth accumulation. Maintaining the trademark, in the long run, is also a quite significant objective. Members dedicate to business growth and benefit from the growth. Both at good times and bad times of the business, family wellbeing is considered as the prime objective of the business.[39]

Another objective of the family business is to maintain family inheritance. Some family businesses have been in operations for a few centuries. In each generation, a member of the family is chosen to lead the business. In Japan, some family businesses continue in the 55th generation of a family; Sudo Honke—sake (rice wine) maker—is an example. Protection and continuation of the family image in respect of the family predecessors is another important objective of the family business. Family operates as a clan and it endows unique skills and trades the others do not possess.[40]

Families of this sort regard it as family responsibility to continue ancestral trades and traditional production skills. In this circumstance, profit is not regarded as the main objective of the business. Instead, social and national recognition for the traditional craftsmanship, pride of generational operation, trustworthiness, and professionalism are considered as major returns. Maintaining family bond, unity, and goodwill are also non-economic objectives of a family business. Akio Morita, SONY co-founder, describes how hard it was for him to escape from the family business responsibility as the oldest son of the 15th generation Morita family to start Sony (Morita, 1992).[41] Akio barely escaped as his younger brother consented to take over the family business and the family agreed to it. The first son of a Japanese business family can never evade business responsibilities.

Inns, pubs, art and craft, construction, confectionary, and weaving are some of the trades that have been continuing through generations and centuries in Japan as family businesses. William Ohara (2003) published the history of the 100 oldest family businesses in the world (Table 14.1). The oldest among them is the Kongo Gumi, a construction family company, founded in AD 578 in Japan. Kongo Gumi has descended through 40 generations as of today. The second oldest is Nishiyama Onsen, a traditional Japanese inn, founded in AD 705. It is currently operated by the members of the 46th generation. Italy, France, Spain, Germany, Austria, and the UK host the majority of the oldest family businesses after Japan. Most of the oldest family businesses of the world have been founded after AD 1000. In 2008, Bank of Korea published a list of ventures that are more than 200 years old. It contains 5,586 ventures and out of which 3146 belong to Japan.

Although family business entrepreneurship is not as new as other models of entrepreneurships, family businesses possess unique entrepreneurship model which is useful for adapting to and facing challenges in the new business environment. This model thus, can promote family descendants for continuation of entrepreneurial operations in modern ways. Unlike corporates, family businesses possess unique characteristics, value systems, ethics, responsibilities, objectives, and visions. Therefore, management of the family business is quite different from regular businesses. Family businesses pose inherent advantages as well as

Table 14.1 Ten oldest family companies

Year (CE)	*Company*	*Country*	*Category*
578	Kongo Gumi	Japan	Construction
705	Nishiyama Onsen	Japan	Hotel (Inn)
717	Koman	Japan	Hotel (Inn)
718	Hoshi Ryokan	Japan	Hotel (Inn)
771	Genda Shigyo	Japan	Paper bags
803	Stiftskeller St. Peter	Austria	Restaurant
862	Staffelter Hof	Germany	Wine
885	Tanaka-Iga	Japan	Religious Goods
900	Sean's Bar	Ireland	Pub
953	The Bingley Arms	UK	Pub

Data William Ohara (2003)[42]

disadvantages which affect the successor's management and maneuverability. Although family business is not an open chance of entrepreneurship for everyone, it causes chances as well as challenges for the successors. Therefore, learning of the family business is useful for the younger generations to rise as successors.[43]

Advantages

- Family businesses are not fierce competitors. So, the competitiveness and technological challenges do not demand much from the entrepreneur.
- Family businesses have soft operational objectives and thus, the entrepreneurship is not a rigorous exercise. Therefore, entrepreneurs find adequate time to sacrifice for family matters also.
- Family businesses do not severely undergo market shocks and thus, the entrepreneur is not severely affected even during market shocks.
- Small family businesses do not undergo much shareholder pressure as shareholders are comprised of the family clan who bid loyalty and solidarity to the business.
- Family business investments are of long term and thus, it is guaranteed that capital shift will not occur frequently.
- Some family businesses are less professional and less competitive compared to corporate businesses. The descendants thus, will find it less risky and much easier to operate.

- Family businesses are usually stable during economic instability. So, there are better chances for them to wade off market fluctuations compared to other businesses.
- Family members attached to the business dedicated to save their ancestral business from failure. This is a relieving factor for the successive entrepreneurs.
- Small family businesses can be run with flexible and part-time work schedules. This practice helps entrepreneur to take care of personal affairs also while working.
- Family businesses do not normally unleash fierce competition. They operate much ethically, morally, and responsibly. This helps the entrepreneur obtain public and government support.
- Family businesses provide employment opportunities to economically disadvantaged local community and contract supplies from the locality. This helps boost goodwill that furnishes conducive environment for the successors to operate the business.
- Employees find it convenient to work for family business as advanced scientific work methods are not used. This serves as a motivational factor for the workers and thus, additional motivational budget may not be required.
- Wage rate is usually lower in family business. This helps maintain cost of production, wage bill, and the price of goods also low.
- Pressure from the external shareholders is negligible due to majority share ownership of the family members. Therefore, there is a rare chance of business takeover.
- Retaining earnings and reinvesting them is not much resisted by the family members as that helps growth of family wealth. This helps generate less expensive and less risky internal source of finance.
- Family businesses are far less bureaucratic and thus, entrepreneur enjoys greater flexibility to make decisions without bureaucratic restrictions and delays.
- Entrepreneur of a family business is a person who grows as a family member. This pre-exposure to and nurture of business functions and traditions are helpful for business operations.

Disadvantages

- Introduction of drastic changes to business as family businesses is difficult as they operate on strong and structured value systems, networks, and relationships.
- Management and ownership can be challenged by the siblings and cousins as rivalry might escalate among them after demise of parents.
- Business traditions, practices, and ownership can be challenged after a few generations as the extended family grows and the family values are drastically changed.
- There might occur conflicts in strategy synchronization due to generation gap of the active members and difference of their education, exposure, and expectations. Older generation might want to maintain the business as it is while the younger generation wants to revolutionize it.
- Key positions of the business are assigned to the family members and hence, qualified professionals from outside cannot be appointed.
- As family problems can spread to the workplace, the entrepreneur must take precautions to prevent them and must maintain an indifferent position as the chief.
- A disastrous event of the family will adversely affect business operations. The recovery of business will be connected to the speed of recovery from the family problem.
- Looming family problems, deaths of key members, congenital diseases, and lack of leadership skills among members can terminate a family business.

Limitations to Family Business

Family business is an easy entrance to the business world for the children of the business owner. The successors can benefit from the above-mentioned advantages and be aware of the disadvantages. Family members gain hands-on experience, training, and knowledge of doing business as a coherent aspect of the lives from their early age. From childhood, members get exposure to the business through seeing how business operations are carried out, handling increasingly responsible tasks, mingling with workers and managers, learning business secrets and formula, and quality standards. Business is, thus, not unfamiliar to the younger generations. This advantage is useful for them to lead the existing family business or extend its operations in new avenues integrating vertically and or horizontally.[44]

Notwithstanding all the favorable aspects of the family business, some or all children may not join the business for several reasons. Sue Birley (2002), in his article "Attitudes of Owner-Managers' Children toward Family and Business Issues" *observed* many reasons for children not to engage or take over family business.[45]

1. Parents' dissension to children's joining
2. Children's reluctance to work under parents
3. Having too many family members in the business
4. No interest in a particular business type
5. Too small a business/micro enterprise
6. No opportunities for talents in a business
7. Mismatch between business scope and skills
8. Lucrative earning opportunities elsewhere
9. No interest in business career

Hybrid Entrepreneurship

Hybrid entrepreneurship is a new concept that has emerged in Europe two decades ago and become a popular field of study with the pioneering seminal works of L. Kritskaya, L. Kolvereid, E. J. Isaksen, C. Demir,[46] A. Werner,[47] T. B. Folta, F. Delmar, and K. Wennberg.[48] Hybrid entrepreneurship is formed when salaried full-time employees engage in their own business that brings in an additional income in the form of profit. Hybrid entrepreneurship, thus, is a parallel engagement of making of profit which is different from waged part-time work or self-employment. After retirement from work, hybrid entrepreneurs continue their ventures as full-time engagement and so they become regular entrepreneurs.

Hybrid entrepreneurships can be recognized from the way they are operated. For instance, an employee starts up a venture while they are working as a full-time employee for an organization. Thus, their business is operated by the family members or subordinates (employees) while the owner is working full-time elsewhere. In hybrid entrepreneurship, the entrepreneur is mostly invisible but they play the entrepreneurial role behind the screen. The owner engages in the business primarily during evenings, weekends, or online. Owners of private medical clinics, schools, and consultation firms are a few examples. In contrast, some hybrid entrepreneurships are well organized as any other regular business by way of creating strong organizational structure. Online business has become a popular type of hybrid entrepreneurship since the recent past. Some hybrid entrepreneurships operate as family businesses where family members take care of the business while the entrepreneur is engaged in a full-time career.[49]

Reasons for Emergence of Hybrid Entrepreneurship

Hybrid entrepreneurship has been popular among many employees around the world for several reasons. The foremost reason is an employee's need for extra income, in the form of profit, in addition to the salary. This is purely an economic reason stemming from the need for better living standard. Another reason for creation of hybrid entrepreneurship emanates from passion of those employees who possess unique skills like music and dancing. In this type of hybrid entrepreneurship, profit is a secondary objective. Family obligation is another reason for hybrid entrepreneurship. Descendants may engage in hybrid business as a family obligation while working full-time elsewhere. There still are intrinsic and psychological reasons that push employees to hybrid entrepreneurship for seeking satisfaction that they cannot gain from employment. Another reason is that some employees initiate side businesses as a preparation for retirement.[50] Those who have creative skills but find no opportunities to make use of them at the workplace also tend to engage in hybrid entrepreneurship.

Hybrid entrepreneurship exhibits special characteristics in contrast to regular entrepreneurship. First, unique personal skills quite often serve as the basis of hybrid entrepreneurship. Second, the ventures organized as hybrid entrepreneurship remain small for the ease of operations. Some businesses of this type are open only during designated time of the day or week. Surveys in European countries have found that the employees enjoying high salary and autonomy, like university professors, do not tend to enter hybrid entrepreneurship. Therefore, lower income employee categories are present in hybrid entrepreneurship. Those who have work experience, expertise, professional qualification, and networking also take much interest in hybrid entrepreneurship. Employee learnings from technology transfer and sub-contracting arouse hybrid entrepreneurship attitudes in employees.

The employees who perceive uncertainty in their jobs tend to initiate hybrid entrepreneurship as a preparation for facing income displacement. Some who travel from countryside to workplace engage in trading commodities brought from the countryside. And they also carry goods from the city to the village regularly on the way back to village. Through these transactions, hybrid entrepreneurship is formed to gain from the price differentials yielded between the two locations. Hybrid entrepreneurs assume low risk and seek slow growth and thus their failure rate is lower than normal startups. Hybrid entrepreneurs do not strive for fast growth like other ventures because they enjoy a fixed monthly salary also. So, they tend to avoid high risk and settle with low profits. Another characteristic of hybrid entrepreneurs, in contrast to normal entrepreneurs, is their higher level of education and technical skills.[51]

Prospects for Developing Countries

A recent Norwegian study has shown that 25% of Norwegian employees are hybrid entrepreneurs. Almost 80% of them engage in various service businesses while the rest comprise construction, fishing, agriculture, and manufacturing. About 60% of hybrid entrepreneurs have obtained higher education. The women hybrid entrepreneurship ratio reaches 22%. However, though hybrid entrepreneurship is present in the Less Developed Countries (LDC) also to a certain extent, the phenomenon of hybrid entrepreneurship has not caught limelight in the LDCs.[52]

Employees of the LDCs are economically highly vulnerable and thus they face many economic issues such as low wage rates, low disposable family income, high taxes, weak social welfare, low purchasing power of earnings due to high inflation, lack of after-office-hour part-time jobs, and lack of decent source of second income. Hybrid entrepreneurship is a remote option for most of these employees. So, they often resort to accept bribes and engage in corruption to reconcile the money income and real income differentials. In most LDCs, bribery and corruption are quite a steady source of second income.

In Sri Lanka, low money income and real income have predominantly challenged the economic life of the full-time employees. This has led the employees to occupy shady alternative means to compensate for low income. This practice has become a workplace norm and caused widespread governance and social issues. In the first place, being the major employer, the government faces incessant pressure from the public sector trade unions to increase salaries and other benefits of the government sector employees. Strikes and other trade union actions are very common and loss of man-hours and general inefficiencies have pushed the public sector into disaster.

Wage increase causes economic repercussions like increase in money supply, high inflation, and high interest rates. This, in turn, deteriorates purchasing power, savings, and corporate investment. This then compels another round of wage increase. Alarmingly, this has caused a vicious circle in the public sector. It has not stopped there. Wide spread bribery and corruption in the public sector has become an inherent character as an alternative means to ease the income pressure. To end the public sector mayhem, there is only one sustainable alternative, i.e., the hybrid entrepreneurship option. With an entrepreneurship development drive, the public sector employees can be pushed to hybrid entrepreneurship capitalizing on their experience and networking.

Private sector is perhaps worse than the public sector in terms of wage rates. Salaries of the middle and lower-level private sector employees remain low. Private sector trade unions are weak and thus, their bargaining power also is weak. Unlike the public sector employees, the private sector has scant opportunities for bribery and corruption as the private sector services are not monopolistic. As a result, the private sector employees are economically more squeezed than the public sector employees. Therefore, the living standard of the private sector employees is relatively low in the LDCs. The lower wage rates provide impetus for the employees to consider additional sources of income. Technology transfer, learning, networking, and exposure are more prominent in the private sector and thus the private sector employees generally have more opportunities for hybrid entrepreneurship.

Hybrid entrepreneurship is useful as a sustainable national policy strategy in rescuing employees from the wage trap and the society from the bribery menace. The government can seek early retirement plans in combination with hybrid entrepreneurship programs for burdensome employees. This is a strategy for the government to manage its heavy wage bill. At present, general entrepreneurship development programs are conducted and facilitation is extended to promote full-time entrepreneurs. Similarly, the need prevails for the national policy of entrepreneurship development to extend its horizons incorporating the hybrid entrepreneurship also for addressing this intricate national problem. By this means, public and private sector employees could be promoted as hybrid entrepreneurs.

This is also helpful to enhance the supply of entrepreneurs in the country that works as an engine of economic growth and development. Hybrid entrepreneurship helps create surplus income through new avenues of value creation. Also, the spatial distribution of hybrid entrepreneurs helps alleviate regional income disparities via correction of income distribution through newly generated factor incomes through the demand for factors by the hybrid entrepreneurship. While hybrid entrepreneurship is useful for the employed individuals as a source of second income and a post-retirement project, it is an equally important means of public expenditure management, regional development, economic development, and social enhancement for the governments. More research is needed to explore benefits of hybrid entrepreneurship and the ways to develop hybrid entrepreneurship as an effective means to overcome national economic and social issues in the LDCs. Hybrid entrepreneurship requires more policy research because it is more than a phenomenon of individual entrepreneurship; it is significantly an economic development initiative.

Chapter Summary

The neo-entrepreneurship models introduced in this chapter include Corporate entrepreneurship, Social entrepreneurship, Women entrepreneurship, Family business entrepreneurship, and Hybrid entrepreneurship. Corporate entrepreneurship, known as Intrapreneurship also, begins as an employee proposes an extraordinarily innovative idea and the management considers it. The employee is provided with financial and technical support to materialize the idea. An employee who engages in own innovation while earning a salary is an intrapreneur. Intrapreneurs not only innovate products but production processes, operational methods, and organizational culture also. Corporates behave enabler, producer, opportunist, or advocate in supporting intrapreneurs.

Social entrepreneurship strives to recognize social problems, overcome them, and to induce social change thereby. This requires enterprise committed to the purpose lifetime. Social entrepreneurship is of two types: profit-making and non-profit-making. Social enterprise may earn profit but its fundamental focus is formation of social capital.

Economically and socially disadvantaged sector is the beneficiary of social entrepreneurship. Social entrepreneurship differs from social business though they share common values. Social enterprise is a project that tackles social problems whereas social business is a profit maker through and for socially marginalized groups.

Women entrepreneurship is promoted by feminist movements, governments, NGOs, micro-financiers, and self-help funds to economically empower women. Both employed and unemployed women seek entrepreneurship avenues. Sexual harassment, glass ceiling barriers, maternity leave issues, and family concerns push working women to entrepreneurship. Absence of skills, experience, exposure, and poverty drive unemployed women to entrepreneurship. Social, economic, psychological, educational, and displacement factors generally are the push factors. Women enterprises are largely seen in easy-to-do businesses.

Business descending from family for generations is a family business. New business lacks family lineage and thus is not a family business. Family business is ascertained by ownership of assets, business control, and inheritance. Tagiuri and Davis formulated the "Three Circle Model" to differentiate family business. Family business is guided by both business and family objectives. Some family businesses descend from generations; Sudo Honke (rice wine maker) of Japan that operates in its 55th generation is a case in point. Business leader is selected from each generation. Specialization in certain trade is common in family business. Compared to modern corporates, family businesses have unique vision, mission, value systems, and ethics.

Hybrid entrepreneurship is a new phenomenon emerged in northern Europe two decades ago. Hybrid entrepreneurship is formed when full-time employees start their own businesses. The reasons for creation of hybrid entrepreneurship are economic, passionate, unique skills, family obligation, intrinsic, psychological, and absence of opportunities to showcase skills at the workplace. Developing country employees face economic hardship, poor social welfare, low purchasing power, and lack of evening employment. As a result, bribery and corruption are widespread. Proliferation of Hybrid entrepreneurship thus, is a way out from this social evil. Hybrid entrepreneurship is a useful investment for the post-retirement economic life.

Review Questions

1. Compare conventional entrepreneurship models with neo-entrepreneurship models.
2. What are the types of entrepreneurships that are considered as neo-entrepreneurship models? Explain why.
3. What is corporate entrepreneurship, which is also referred to as intrapreneurship, and the difference between entrepreneur and intrapreneur?
4. Describe the intrapreneurship models such as Enabler, Producer, Opportunist, and Advocate highlighting their special features.
5. Illustrate the purposes and types of social entrepreneurship and explain what social entrepreneurs do to the society.
6. Differentiate between social enterprise and social business. Provide suitable examples to prove the differences.
7. Explain why women entrepreneurship is important giving reasons for and describing motives of women entrepreneurship.
8. "Women entrepreneurship is supported by many organizations." What are those organizations and their supports?
9. Examine the inherent issues of the women entrepreneurship in the developing countries and recommend solutions to them.
10. What is family business and family entrepreneurship? Explain how family business can be interpreted as a neo-business model.
11. Discuss whether the Three Circle Model is an appropriate tool to distinguish family entrepreneurship from conventional entrepreneurship.
12. List out both advantages and disadvantages and identify limitations of family entrepreneurship.
13. Define hybrid entrepreneurship and explain why people tend to start hybrid entrepreneurship.
14. "Hybrid entrepreneurship is equally useful for developing and developed countries." Explain why.

Additional Readings

1. Bodrožić, Z., and Adler, P.S., 2018. The evolution of management models: A neo-Schumpeterian theory. *Administrative Science Quarterly*, *63*(1), pp. 85–129.

2. Tíryakí, A., 2005. Theories of entrepreneurship: A critical overview. *Dumlupınar Üniversitesi Sosyal Bilimler Dergisi,* (13).
3. https://en.wikipedia.org/wiki/Gifford_Pinchot_III.
4. Antoncic, B., and Hisrich, R.D., 2003. Clarifying the intrapreneurship concept. *Journal of Small Business and Enterprise Development, 10*(1), pp. 7–24.
5. Cadar, O., and Badulescu, D., 2015. Entrepreneur, entrepreneurship and intrapreneurship. *A Literature Review.*
6. Huang, L.Y., Yang Lin, S.M., and Hsieh, Y.J., 2021. Cultivation of intrapreneurship: A framework and challenges. *Frontiers in Psychology, 12*, p. 731990.
7. Gawke, J.C., Gorgievski, M.J., and Bakker, A.B., 2018. Personal costs and benefits of employee intrapreneurship: Disentangling the employee intrapreneurship, well-being, and job performance relationship. *Journal of Occupational Health Psychology, 23*(4), p. 508.
8. Bager, T., Ottosson, H., and Schott, T., 2010. Intrapreneurs, entrepreneurs and spin-off entrepreneurs: Similarities and differences. *International Journal of Entrepreneurship and Small Business, 10*(3), pp. 339–358.
9. Janczak, S., and Boiteux, S., 2007. Understanding intrapreneurship: A process model for the logic of action used by intrapreneurs. *Journal of Business and Entrepreneurship, 19*(1), p. 1.
10. Deprez, J., Leroy, H., and Euwema, M., 2018. Three chronological steps toward encouraging intrapreneurship: Lessons from the Wehkamp case. *Business Horizons, 61*(1), pp. 135–145.
11. Lippitz, M.J., 2007. The four models of corporate entrepreneurship. *MIT Sloan Management Review.*
12. Praszkier, R., and Nowak, A., 2011. *Social entrepreneurship: Theory and practice.* Cambridge University Press.
13. Spear, R., 2006. Social entrepreneurship: A different model? *International Journal of Social Economics, 33*(5/6), pp. 399–410.
14. Smith, B.R., and Stevens, C.E., 2010. Different types of social entrepreneurship: The role of geography and embeddedness on the measurement and scaling of social value. *Entrepreneurship & Regional Development, 22*(6), pp. 575–598.
15. Sullivan Mort, G., Weerawardena, J., and Carnegie, K., 2003. Social entrepreneurship: Towards conceptualization. *International*

Journal of Nonprofit and Voluntary Sector Marketing, *8*(1), pp. 76–88.
16. Martin, R.L., and Osberg, S., 2015. *Getting beyond better: How social entrepreneurship works*. Harvard Business Review Press.
17. Santos, N.J., 2013. Social entrepreneurship that truly benefits the poor: An integrative justice approach. *Journal of Management for Global Sustainability*.
18. Hidalgo, G., Monticelli, J.M., and Vargas Bortolaso, I., 2024. Social capital as a driver of social entrepreneurship. *Journal of Social Entrepreneurship, 15*(1), pp. 182-205.
19. Barki, E., Comini, G., Cunliffe, A., Hart, S., and Rai, S., 2015. Social entrepreneurship and social business: Retrospective and prospective research. *Revista de Administração de Empresas, 55*, pp. 380–384.
20. Ridley-Duff, R., 2008. Social enterprise as a socially rational business. *International Journal of Entrepreneurial Behavior & Research, 14*(5), pp. 291–312.
21. Yunus, M., Moingeon, B., and Lehmann-Ortega, L., 2010. Building social business models: Lessons from the Grameen experience. *Long Range Planning, 43*(2–3), pp. 308–325.
22. Hossain, M., 1988. *Credit for alleviation of rural poverty: The Grameen Bank in Bangladesh* (Vol. 65). Intl Food Policy Res Inst.
23. Hossain, M., 1988. *Credit for alleviation of rural poverty: The Grameen Bank in Bangladesh* (Vol. 65). Intl Food Policy Res Inst.
24. Manolova, T.S., Brush, C.G., and Edelman, L.F., 2008. What do women entrepreneurs want? *Strategic Change, 17*(3-4), pp. 69–82.
25. Orhan, M., and Scott, D., 2001. Why women enter into entrepreneurship: An explanatory model. *Women in Management Review, 16*(5), pp. 232–247.
26. Pinkovetskaia, I.S., Kryukova, L.I., Campillo, D.F.A., and Rojas-Bahamon, M.J., 2019. Female entrepreneurship: Types of economic activity. *Journal of History Culture and Art Research, 8*(2), pp. 253–265.
27. Shingla, P., and Singh, M., 2015. Women empowerment through entrepreneurship development. *Studies on Home and Community Science, 9*(1), pp. 27–32.
28. Mukherjee, S., 2009. Women entrepreneurship development: The catalytic role of NGOs. *IUP Journal of Entrepreneurship Development, 6*(2), p. 21.

29. Mahmood, S., 2011. Microfinance and women entrepreneurs in Pakistan. *International Journal of Gender and Entrepreneurship, 3*(3), pp. 265–274.
30. Rani, B.S., 2015. Women entrepreneurship: Government and institutional support. *Clear International Journal of Research in Commerce & Management, 6*(11).
31. Showkat, S., 2013. Women entrepreneurship: Issues and challenges. *International Journal of Management Prudence, 5*(1), p. 14.
32. Kumbhar, V.M., 2013. Some critical issues of women entrepreneurship in rural India. *European Academic Research, 1*(2).
33. Kaushik, S., 2013. Challenges faced by women entrepreneurs in India. *Education, 35*(53), p. 53.
34. Minniti, M., 2009. Gender issues in entrepreneurship. *Foundations and Trends® in Entrepreneurship, 5*(7–8), pp. 497–621.
35. Debicki, B.J., Matherne III, C.F., Kellermanns, F.W., and Chrisman, J.J., 2009. Family business research in the new millennium: An overview of the who, the where, the what, and the why. *Family Business Review, 22*(2), pp. 151–166.
36. Davis, J.A., Hampton, M.M., and Lansberg, I., 1997. *Generation to generation: Life cycles of the family business*. Harvard Business Press.
37. Masulis, R.W., Pham, P.K., and Zein, J., 2011. Family business groups around the world: Financing advantages, control motivations, and organizational choices. *The Review of Financial Studies, 24*(11), pp. 3556–3600.
38. Tagiuri, R., and Davis, J.A., 1992. On the goals of successful family companies. *Family Business Review, 5*(1), pp. 43–62.
39. Westhead, P., 2003. Company performance and objectives reported by first and multi-generation family companies: A research note. *Journal of Small Business and Enterprise Development, 10*(1), pp. 93–105.
40. Romano, C.A., Tanewski, G.A., and Smyrnios, K.X., 2001. Capital structure decision making: A model for family business. *Journal of Business Venturing, 16*(3), pp. 285–310.
41. Morita, A., Reingold, E.M., and Shimomura, M., 1992. *Made in Japan: Akio Morita a Sony*. Pragma.

42. William T. O., 2003. *Centuries of Success, 1st Ed.* Avon, MA: Adams Media.
43. Au, K., Chiang, F.F., Birtch, T.A., and Ding, Z., 2013. Incubating the next generation to venture: The case of a family business in Hong Kong. *Asia Pacific Journal of Management, 30*, pp. 749–767.
44. Yeung, H.W.C., 2000. Limits to the growth of family-owned business? The case of Chinese transnational corporations from Hong Kong. *Family Business Review, 13*(1), pp. 55–70.
45. Birley, S., 2002. Attitudes of owner-managers' children towards family and business issues. *Entrepreneurship Theory and Practice, 26*(3), pp. 5–19.
46. Demir, C., et al. (2022). Hybrid entrepreneurship: A systematic literature review. *Journal of Small Business and Entrepreneurship, 34*(1).
47. Kriskaya, L., Kolvereid, L., and Isaksen, E.J. (2017). Hybrid entrepreneurs: Characteristics and achievements. *Entreprendre & Innover, 34*(3), p. 7. https://doi.org/10.3917/entin.034.0007
48. Folta, T.B., Delmar, F., and Wennberg, K. 2010. Hybrid entrepreneurship. *Management Science, 56*(2), pp. 253-269.
49. Solesvik, M.Z., 2017. Hybrid entrepreneurship: How and why entrepreneurs combine employment with self-employment. *Technology Innovation Management Review, 7*(3).
50. Tornikoski, E.T., Viljamaa, A., and Varamäki, E., 2015. Hybrid entrepreneurship during retirement: Comparison of motives and aspirations. In *Entrepreneurship, self-employment and retirement* (pp. 187–208). London: Palgrave Macmillan, UK.
51. Shepherd, D.A., Williams, T.A., and Zhao, E.Y., 2019. A framework for exploring the degree of hybridity in entrepreneurship. *Academy of Management Perspectives, 33*(4), pp. 491–512.
52. Luc, S., Chirita, G.M., Delvaux, E., and Kepnou, A.K., 2018. Hybrid Entrepreneurship: Employees Climbing the Entrepreneurial Ladder. *International Review of Entrepreneurship, 16*(1).

CHAPTER 15

Entrepreneurship Development Programs

Key Learning Points

- The need for entrepreneurship development.
- Purpose of entrepreneurship development.
- Target groups of EDPs.
- Aims and objectives of EDPs.
- The focus of EDPs.
- Approaches to EDPs.
- Governments and EDPs.
- General format of EDPs.
- Main approaches.
- Target groups.
- Entrepreneurship education.
- Participant motivation.
- Business feasibility.
- Venture formation.
- Venture support.
- Hands-on experience.
- The post-training stage.
- Developing countries and entrepreneurship development programs.
- EDP Support organizations of Sri Lanka.
- Financial institutions.

© The Author(s), under exclusive license to Springer Nature Singapore Pte Ltd. 2024

M. Rajaratne, *Concepts, Processes and Practice of Entrepreneurship*, Palgrave Studies in Global Entrepreneurship,
https://doi.org/10.1007/978-981-97-6180-7_15

- Department of Agriculture.
- Social welfare programs.
- NGOs and CSR projects.
- National Entrepreneurship Development Agency and its role.
- Industrial Development Board.
- National Apprentice and Industrial Training Authority and its Role.
- Export Development Board.
- Ministry of Youth and Sports.
- Other organizations.

Introduction

Entrepreneurship development programs (EDP) are very much universal as they are carried out in every country. Regardless of the per capita income levels, problems such as unemployment, inequality in income distribution, regional development disparity, and poor living standards of less-privileged social segments prevail in every country. However, the intensity of these issues is extremely high in the less developed countries. Therefore, governments, non-government organizations, and business corporates have made it a point to address these disparities.[1] Large corporates perceive this issue as a matter that falls within their social responsibility perimeters. Entrepreneurship development programs, thus have become a part of economic and social development endeavor of the world.[2]

Target Groups

Entrepreneurship development is an approach to inculcate entrepreneurial skills in persons. There are two target groups for entrepreneurship development programs; they are (1) prospective entrepreneurs (who are not in business) and (2) new entrepreneurs (startups). Short-supply of entrepreneurs is identified as a barrier to economic development. Thus, the underdeveloped countries have made it a policy to improve the supply of entrepreneurs via entrepreneurship development. And the developed countries engage in entrepreneurship development programs to alleviate unemployment and to improve earning power of selected social strata. Entrepreneurship development programs, in general, aim at improvement of living standards of economically and socially disadvantaged groups such as ethnic minorities, women, handicapped, low-caste communities, and unemployed youth.[3]

Aims and Objectives

Entrepreneurship development programs provide enthusiastic people with opportunities to acquire skills required for starting and running a business venture. EDPs, provide prospective entrepreneurs with entrepreneurial thoughts and essential entrepreneurial and managerial skills and new entrepreneurs with additional entrepreneurial, managerial, and organizational skills to enhance their ventures. EDPs initially target fresh entrepreneurs who have difficulties in identifying venture opportunities. EDPs then impart skills and knowledge required for initiating a new venture and making it successful. Thus, via EDPs, knowledge and skills of finance, organizing, marketing, and managing a business are imparted. In macroeconomic sense, EDPs aim at creating new entrepreneurs for increasing the supply of entrepreneurship in order to expand economic activities via increasing the demand for local capital, labor, land, and materials (Fig. 15.1). Both local and national governments aim at regional development, equitable development, alleviation of unemployment and poverty through entrepreneurship development.[4]

The Focus

EDPs usually focus on three constraints to entrepreneurship: (1) resources, (2) entrepreneurial activity, and (3) location. EDPs aim at educating and training prospective entrepreneurs to overcome these constraints. Availability of resources such as labor or materials and their relative opportunity costs are primarily identified. Thereafter, a potential venture activity that can use resources is figured out. And then the venture is matched with a suitable location to capitalize on the identified resources. The success of prospective ventures created this way depend on constant training and development provided to the entrepreneurs. Follow-up support services after completion of initial training have significant impact on the entrepreneurship development.[5]

It is a common practice that governments and other organizations provide incentives and facilities for people to initiate business. However, many end up with failure. Provision of technical assistance, machineries,

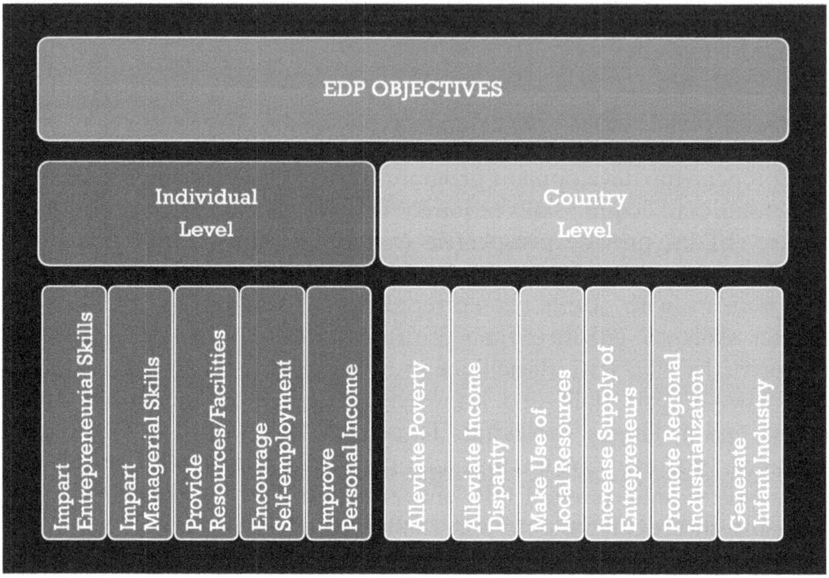

Fig. 15.1 Aims of ED programs (Author Portrayal)

finance, market information, industrial information, consultancy, and management training alone has proven impossibility to create successful entrepreneurs. Therefore, an effective EDP component is essential in every case of provision of other supports also. It is learned that an in-built entrepreneurship development component is essential in all entrepreneurship support programs that target creation of entrepreneurs.[6]

Approaches to EDPs

Formal entrepreneurship development program adopts four approaches to develop entrepreneurs, as mentioned below.

1. Building business interests and inculcating entrepreneurial abilities in persons
2. Guiding to recognize business opportunities and developing business plans
3. Developing operational and managerial capabilities

4. Guiding on or providing incentives and facilities initially required.

EDPs involve in human resource enhancement through education and training in entrepreneurship. Primarily, EDPs inculcate in minds of participants the importance and usefulness of entrepreneurship. This helps the participants to think entrepreneurially.[7] After creating entrepreneurial mindset, a set of specified skills required for an entrepreneur is imparted. Knowledge of entrepreneurial roles, responsibilities, ethics, and social responsibilities are also imparted by the EDPs. Further, participants are provided with knowledge of business management and administration required for running and developing a startup.[8] For this purpose, extensive teaching and training programs, industry exposure, brainstorming, mind mapping, hands-on-experience, and mock board meetings are lined up in EDPs.

Governments and EDPs

Governments aim to achieve several objectives through entrepreneurship development. Since long, it has been witnessed that economic growth is retarded by lack of entrepreneurship supply. This is true because entrepreneurship is a factor of production on one hand and on the other it is the factor that organizes all other factors of production. Therefore, governments now focus more on entrepreneurship than capital in planning economic growth. The power of entrepreneurship to organize all other factors of production helps a country to utilize idling capital, land, and labor and to create factor income. Entrepreneurship development thus helps overcome under-employment of factors of production. Increased supply of entrepreneurship thus, is a means to achieve development objective in the long run.[9]

Employment opportunity creation is another objective of the government. Entrepreneurship is believed to be a means of addressing unemployment and under-employment problem. Governments believe self-employment as a useful means to solve unemployment problem at a time when other sources of employment are dried up. Self-employment not only addresses unemployment problem but it generates incomes useful to increase family wealth also. Further, governments believe that self-employed micro-entrepreneurs ascend as large corporate entrepreneurs like multinational corporations in the future largely contributing to economic activities and growth of national wealth.[10]

Uneven distribution of income is a development problem. Disparity of income distribution causes regional income disparity and poverty. In the meantime, governments are aware of the regional factor endowment. Therefore, governments launch entrepreneurship development programs directed utilize such factors of production. Entrepreneurship development helps not only make use of the factors of production in geographical proximities but also to create factor income causing an upward shift in regional income. Therefore, governments entrust entrepreneurship development programs with an important role in enhancing regional development and alleviating regional development disparity.[11]

Industrial development is a key economic development strategy. It has been the practice of many governments to initiate heavy industries while leaving small and medium sized industries to the private entrepreneurs. As all sorts of industries are essential for industrial development, governments introduce various schemes to provide support and incentives for small and medium enterprises (SME) development under industrial development policy. Subsidized capital, tax reliefs, sub-contracts, buy-back offer of output, supply quota, industrial training, industrial incubators, laboratory facilities, export promotion facilities, trade fair, and common logistics hubs are a few means that governments employ to promote SMEs.[12]

Government Support

Government support for SMEs aims at creating employment opportunities and enhancing industrial output to achieve industrialization objectives. As an initial step, governments set up institutions such as Industrial Development Boards, Industrial Development Councils, and National Industrial Development Boards or Councils. These institutions provide entrepreneurs with technical and technological support, made-to-specifications machinery and tools, recommendation of lucrative industrial fields, and opportunities for building links between local authorities and entrepreneurs. These moves have a national focus to align industries to achieve national industrial goals.[13]

The scope of government cooperation for entrepreneurship development has gradually widened as governments believe entrepreneurship development as a means of many positive changes in a nation. In consequence, comprehensive and formal institutional setup for entrepreneurship development has emerged. Similarly, some public institutions like schools, universities, and administrative offices were assigned auxiliary responsibility of entrepreneurship development. Among the entrepreneurship support institutions, the following are common in many countries: Industrial Development Board, National Industrial Development Council, National Arts and Craft Council, Regional Industrial Development Centers, Export Development Board, Export Development Council, Human Resource Development Council, Regional Development Council, Regional Development Bank, Small and Medium Enterprise Development Board, and Industrial Incubation Centers (Fig. 15.2).

Through these institutions, governments launch total approach to entrepreneurship development via organizing training and education programs aimed at upbringing new entrepreneurs as well as uplifting present entrepreneurs. Some institutions, in particular, provide specialized

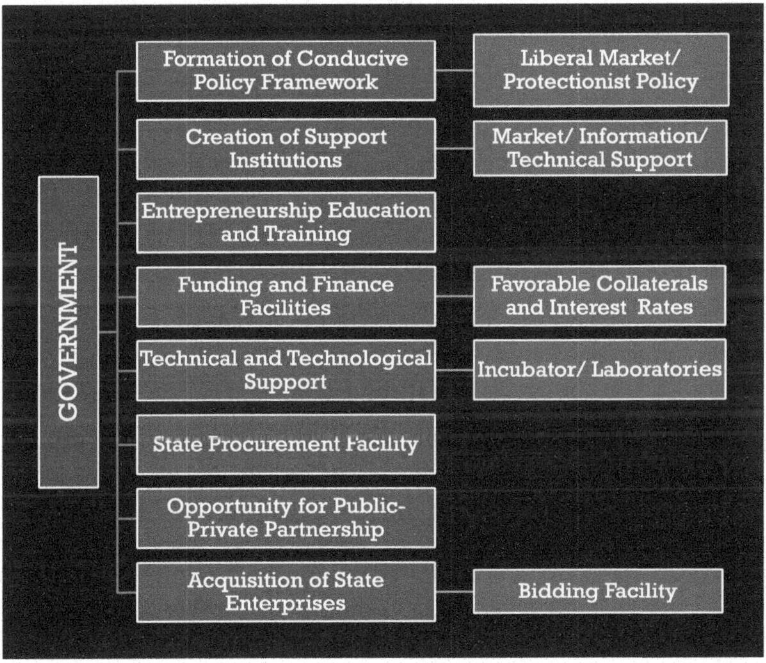

Fig. 15.2 Government's role in entrepreneurship development (Author Portrayal)

credit schemes to women entrepreneurs. Materials, machinery, technology, information, and production methods are provided by some institutions while others help with identification of markets and arranging markets for selected entrepreneurs. Information on export market opportunities, quality standards, and environmental compliance requirements. are also provided to exporter entrepreneurs by some of these institutions.[14]

General Format of EDPs

Entrepreneurship development programs are conducted by government institutions, non-government organizations, voluntary organizations, corporate social responsibility units, foreign agencies, and business development funds. Every entrepreneurship development program has its own approach and content, and thus are heterogenous. The integrated format of EDP described below aims at providing only a general view.[15]

Main Approaches

Entrepreneurship development authorities adopt three specific approaches to design and conduct an entrepreneurship development program: (1) Resource approach, (2) Finance approach, (3) Technical approach. The resource approach focuses on availability of resources such as labor and materials in a preferred proximity. The finance approach focuses on availability of finance for initiating venture.[16] The technical approach focuses on the technical aspect of production.[17] These approaches are constructed giving consideration to individual factors namely; resources, capital, and technology. In that accordance, entrepreneurship development is expected to be achieved through a selected factor among the three factors mentioned above.

Unlike the resource-based approach, the "Intervention approach" to entrepreneurship described in an earlier chapter is a useful alternative approach to entrepreneurship development also. The intervention approach views entrepreneurship as a process that starts with scanning common problems to identify entrepreneurial opportunities. This approach does not confine itself to predetermined factors of production available in the vicinity. Thus, "Intervention approach" is an open approach that recognizes entrepreneurial opportunities instead of resources. Opportunity triggers innovations and resources are used as inputs required for innovations. This new approach begins with identification of entrepreneurial opportunities and then innovating products suitable to intervene and resolve unresolved problems. Therefore, EDPs can adopt this approach to train prospective entrepreneurs to identify venture opportunities as the first and foremost step of venture creation.

Target Groups

Selection of target group of prospective entrepreneurs is an initial step of the EDP process. Different groups need different types of trainings, knowledge, and skills of entrepreneurship. These groups include prospective, new, and old entrepreneurs who need differentiated training and knowledge. Further, women entrepreneurs are treated as special group that requires different set of entrepreneurial skills and exposure.[18] Also, agricultural, manufacturing, and service entrepreneurs need differentiated knowledge and a set of specific skills. Export-oriented entrepreneurs constitute a distinctive segment which requires entirely different entrepreneurship training. Therefore, at the outset of planning an EDP, it is essential to classify participants based on their nature and involvement and then to design suitable and specialized training program to address their needs.[19]

Entrepreneurship Education

The selected groups of participants are educated on the importance, nature, scope, and limitations of entrepreneurship. This involves providing education and exposure of the real-world business to prospective entrepreneurs. The process of entrepreneurship and its sub-processes such as invention, innovation, and venture creation are the major components of this essential module. Relationship between innovation and profit, profit and risk, products and markets, venture creation and management, potentials for wealth creation, and achieving psychological objectives are explained to the selected groups at this level.[20]

Participant Motivation

Motivation of people to engage in entrepreneurship is a main objective of EDP. Therefore, every effort is made to inspire the participants of EDP. Success of an EDP program depends on the rate of participants becoming entrepreneurs and their long-term success as entrepreneurs. Motivational training helps change participant's mindset and psychological behavior. This is achieved through psychological games, goal setting exercises, and role plays. Exposure to entrepreneurial personalities, entrepreneurial roles, and entrepreneurial behavior are helpful means for psychologically transforming participants. EDPs inculcate in participants entrepreneurial value systems also to bring about positive attitudes in them toward entrepreneur, profit, risk, economic role, social role, wealth creation, etc.[21]

Venture Management

Management of a venture is an essential role of an entrepreneur and thus, imparting knowledge in management aspect of a firm is recognized as a core component of EDP. Among all skills required for an entrepreneur, innovation and management skills are of foremost importance. Under management skills, planning, organizing, coordination, and controlling skills are imparted. Participants are offered a learning component of business functions that includes production, marketing, human resource, and financial management. Learning of management environment that consists of internal and external stakeholders, controllable and uncontrollable factors, management styles, and problem-solving methods, is also equally important. Labor laws, production and sales laws, agency laws, tax laws, environmental laws, social responsibility, and business are also useful components of the management module of EDP.[22]

Business Feasibility

Estimation of business feasibility is of prime importance to a new venture. An entrepreneur needs to assess feasibility of a business they plan to start. It is risky to jump into venturing without a sound feasibility plan. Feasibility plan guides an entrepreneur in production, sales, finance, revenues, cost, break-even, technology, design, materials, labor, management, competition, and laws. Therefore, EDPs train participants in developing feasibility plan; which also is known as business plan. Feasibility plan identifies technical feasibility, financial feasibility, market feasibility, personnel feasibility, management feasibility, environmental feasibility, legal feasibility, and organizational feasibility. Feasibility plans are submitted to investors, lenders, financial institutions, professionals, and government organizations for consideration. EDPs train participants in developing feasibility plans or otherwise guide them to the consultants in the field.[23]

Venture Formation

An important milestone of EDPs is to guide participants to create venture. So, EDPs educate the process of venture creation that requires the participants to be familiar with different business models, types, and legal structures. A startup can take the form of micro, small, or medium in its size. Also, there are different legal forms to be considered when forming a business because specific legal requirements are applicable to certain businesses. EDPs guide advantages and disadvantages of the business size as well as the legal forms of ventures among which the entrepreneur could choose the most appropriate one. The legal forms of businesses include proprietorship, partnership, private limited company, public limited company, franchise, and agency. Participants are educated the pros and cons, advantages and disadvantages, risk and safety, management challenges, and sustainability of each business type.

Venture Support

EDPs present an array of venture supports at business startup and during the early growth. Main component of an EDP is provision of information to the participants on the institutions that support new ventures. Venture capital, financial facilities, credits, lease, tax concessions and incentives, market information, product and factory standardization, quality assurance, technical and market consultancies, management training, and worker training are major venture supports available through EDPs. These supports are equally useful at the pre-start-up, start-up, and early-growth stages of a venture.[24]

Hands-on Experience

EDPs provide opportunities for the prospective entrepreneurs to obtain hands-on experience via factory visits and in-plant training during the training period. Some participants may not have prior experience in even seeing how a production system operates or how a production process is organized. Visiting a factory helps participants to learn organization of production process, and to design their own operations system in a future event. Entrepreneurship trainees are exposed to entire business organization, production facilities, and the key personnel. Trainees will immensely benefit from this exposure and receive a chance to communicate with entrepreneurs. This experience is a significant motivation for the trainees to make up their minds to inculcate a passion for entrepreneurship. Similarly, this step is essential for completion of a successful entrepreneurship development program.

The Post-Training Stage

EDPs pass through pre-training, in-training, and post-training phases (Fig. 15.3). The post-training phase is identified as the follow-up phase. EDP organizers must maintain proper database of the past participants and communicate with them. The participants who have already completed the training start ventures at different times and thus, they need assistance from the EDP organizers. Business registration, document preparation, consultation on procurement process, plant layout, connection of utility services, obtaining subsidies, grants, incentives, management consultancies, troubleshooting, industry information, and advice on conducting market surveys are the major needs of the former participants. Therefore, the EDP organizers extend their support in these areas to achieve the final objective of EDPs, viz. successful creation of ventures.[25]

EDP Support Organizations of Sri Lanka

Financial Institutions

The institutional setup for entrepreneurship development and support in Sri Lanka includes several governmental institutions, non-governmental organizations, banks, and local and foreign voluntary programs. While there have been a few government programs to enhance small and traditional enterprises in the rural areas since the early 1960s, after implementation of the open market economic policies, in 1978, many more such programs, schemes, and institutions popped up in support of accelerated regional and national development.

Cooperative society established in 1911 was the first move that involved small enterprise development. At present, the Co-operative Rural

Fig. 15.3 Phases of entrepreneurship development (Author Portrayal)

Bank and the Federation of Thrift and Credit Co-operative Societies (SANASA)[26] are designated to provide support for small and micro enterprise development island-wide. The Development Finance Corporation of Ceylon (DFCC)[27] was created in 1955 on the recommendation of the first World Bank Mission to Sri Lanka with the objective to financially support the private sector businesses ranging from small entrepreneurships to very large corporates. People's Bank[28] and the Rural Bank[29] were set up in 1961 to support the small and medium scale rural and estate sector industry and commerce. National Development Bank (NDB)[30] was set up in 1979 to strengthen the corporate sector through finance and consultation. Regional and Rural Development Bank (RRDB), which was later renamed as Regional Development Bank (RDB),[31] was set up in 1985 in support of regional entrepreneurship development.

Sarvodaya movement, which was established in 1958, initiated Sarvodaya Economic Enterprise Development Services (SEEDS)[32] in 1986 to alleviate poverty by promoting economic empowerment through training in entrepreneurship, providing orientation to business activities, and consulting on preparation of project reports. SANASA (Pvt. Ltd.)[33] commenced in 1978 to support rural sector enterprises with micro-credit facilities. After two decades of successful operations, SANASA Development Bank[34] was established in 1997 to provide wider and effective service to the enterprise sector. In addition to the formal credit and consultancy services for enterprise development, several Micro Finance institutions, since the past two decades, have been active in providing credits and consultancy to micro entrepreneurs. Commercial banks like Hatton National Bank and Sampath Bank have introduced entrepreneurship development programs for the estate sector entrepreneurs and women entrepreneurs.

During the past few decades, financial facilities for new and existing entrepreneurs soared with steady growth of finance, micro finance, and leasing companies. Almost every commercial bank provides personalized loan programs and conducts entrepreneurship development and awareness programs for women and micro entrepreneurs. Leasing and finance companies also conduct educational and awareness programs for the entrepreneurs on the use of machinery and equipment. Also, they provide financial facilities with personalized payment schemes for acquisition of machineries. A large number of micro finance organizations scattered nation-wide customarily organize workshops for selected groups of people like women, widows, country men, and youth to educate on the entrepreneurship opportunities that can be exploited harnessing local materials and skills.

Department of Agriculture

Department of Agriculture of Sri Lanka, through its agriculture extension programs, world food program, and the programs to enhance food supply, conducts agribusiness programs to provide education on and exposure to scientific agricultural practices and feasibility of agribusiness. In addition, the Department of Agriculture provides training in food processing technologies aiming at transforming basic food materials into easy-to-use or instant food items and food preserving. Also, it conducts agricultural marketing and culinary programs also to provide knowledge on sorting, cleaning, displaying, food preparation, and sales. An exciting outcome of this sort is the Hela Bojun[35] eatery chain of the Department of Agriculture.

The Agriculture Department conducts a vast array of programs to promote entrepreneurship in spice cultivation, processing, packaging, and sales. Further, machineries are also introduced to the entrepreneurs for processing and transforming basic crops into value-added goods, preferably for exporting. The Department provides scientific knowledge for growing crops and technical knowledge for processing crops. In addition, the Department trains future entrepreneurs in mushroom growing, flower cultivation, horticulture, nursery, and organic manure production in the form of agribusiness. An extensive force of trainers, advisors, and consultants are deployed island-wide and a network of regional offices is operated to promote agribusiness as an avenue of entrepreneurship.

Social Welfare Programs

Janasaviya Program[36] (Poor People Empowerment Program) of the government of Sri Lanka which was later rebranded as Samurdhi Program (Prosperity Program), has a key component and objective of micro entrepreneurship development among the beneficiaries. The subsidy offered under the Janasaviya program consisted of rations and money. Rations were to be obtained from cooperative shops while the money was deposited in recipient savings accounts. Based on such deposits, members were given credit facility for business startups.

The Janasaviya Program was initiated in 1988 as a poverty alleviation program. It introduced investment and consumption package to the recipients. In 1990, the 100 million US dollar Janasaviya Trust Fund was established with the financial support of the World Bank and the International Development Association (IDA). Janasaviya Trust Fund adopted a "bottom-up approach" in business development with provision of credit for the members. Subsequent governments further enhanced this program through creation of the Samurdhi Bank[37] (membership micro finance institution) with an intensive entrepreneurship development approach. The beneficiaries are clients of the bank and they are eligible to obtain business loans. The bank helped financing micro business startups as a means of self-employment. The Samurdhi Program[38] presently conducts advisory and training programs on business also to the beneficiaries.

NGOs and CSR Projects

Non-government organizations (NGO), hundreds in number, engage in poverty alleviation, social development, women empowerment, and welfare improvement programs. Ethnic minorities and widowed women are prime beneficiaries of enterprise programs of NGOs. The mandate of the majority NGOs is to improve incomes of selected families and to be accountable for the funds received from foreign agencies. The major task of NGOs is skill development in identified trades and to make use of the learned skilled in earning money. NGOs thus involve in entrepreneurship development through skill development. Skills are generally developed in materials, designs, production, product quality, markets, distribution, sales, and customer relations. Usually, NGOs arrange trade fairs and exhibitions, shelves in supermarkets, and export avenues for the beneficiary entrepreneurs.

Universities and schools also engage in entrepreneurship development programs. The aim is to create entrepreneurs among students with assistance from Chamber of Commerce, Chamber of Young Lanka Entrepreneurs, and Industrial Development Authority. School entrepreneurship programs are active in urban schools while the Universities like Sri Jayewardenepura and Kelaniya have established Entrepreneurship Development Centers within campus premises. Some universities offer bachelor's degrees in entrepreneurship and almost all others teach courses in entrepreneurship. Also, some television channels occasionally conduct entrepreneurship development programs with participation of eminent entrepreneurs. These programs not only assess the feasibility of business ideas presented by entrepreneurs but also arrange investment through venture capital. In general, through these programs, companies perform Corporate Social Responsibility (CSR).

NEDA and Its Role

National Enterprise Development Authority (NEDA)[39] is a government institution established with the vision of enterprise development and a mission of facilitating and proactively supporting development, growth, and competitiveness of enterprises. NEDA's objectives include encouraging, promoting, and facilitating small and medium enterprise development, encouraging establishment and operations of enterprises abroad, empowerment of people through human capital development in the area of technical and entrepreneurial skills, and facilitating access to entrepreneurial finances.

NEDA has launched a few entrepreneurship development programs aiming at specific groups. The "Brain into Business Graduate Entrepreneurship Program" promotes micro, small, and medium enterprises among undergraduates in order to develop them as successful entrepreneurs by improving their capabilities and directing toward opportunities in the business world through Career Guidance Units established in universities. NEDA has been able to promote many graduates to initiate business with its support in business registration, access to finance, and access to business development services.

Research Commercialization is also a NEDA concept introduced to the universities through which collaboration between the universities and the industry is developed to establish the link between invention and innovation where the universities would invent knowledge and the industry would innovate products based on it. Individual researchers, universities, and research and development institutes invent ideas and knowledge worthy of producing goods and services but they lack entrepreneurial skills. In consequence, the knowledge developed by research is untapped for commercial purposes. The graduates of vocational training institutes who complete internship programs, and are incapable of procuring initial capital for purchasing new machinery and equipment, choose to find employment rather than starting business.

NEDA operates an Incubator Center with the aim of providing entrepreneurs with the required facilitates, knowledge on production, marketing, financial, and management. NEDA also operates a Business Research and Development (BREAD) center since 2017 in collaboration with University of Wayamba with the view of providing the state support for business development. The objectives are to promote new entrepreneurs, diversify existing enterprises, promote new technology, and promote new and value-added products. While NEDA supports startups in technical and product development, the BREAD center provides small entrepreneurs with total solution for food production and packaging which include technical assistance for food processing, business management services, and financial linkages. The machinery and equipment facilitation services include packing facilities, cooling facilities, extruder machine, dairy processing, bakery equipment, filling and mixing machines, grinding facilities and drying facilities focusing on food-related products and services such as dairy processing, bakery sweets, spices, processed fruit products, processed vegetable, and cereal products. The BREAD center also provides knowledge on food processing techniques, entrepreneurship, and business management.

NEDA provides entrepreneurs with the following machines for observation and trial for learning of and familiarizing with their uses.

1. Continuous Belt Sealing Machine
2. Semi-automatic Auger Filling Machine
3. Vacuum Packing machine
4. Semi-automatic Liquid Filling Machine
5. Shrink Wrapper Machine
6. Solid Ink Coding Machine
7. Semi-automatic Cap Sealing Machine
8. Food Canning Machine (Seaming)
9. High Pressure Canning Sterilizer
10. Sachet Packing Machine
11. Extruder Production Line
12. Pelletizer (Flat die feed pellet machine)
13. Heavy Duty Top Loading Scale
14. Mixing Machine (Ribbon Mixer)
15. Incubator Oven
16. Automated Yoghurt Filling Machine
17. Milk Homogenizer with Boiler
18. Ice Lolli Filling Machine
19. Milk Churner
20. Cheese Vat
21. Cheese Press Machine
22. Batch Milk Pasteurizer Machine
23. Homogenizer
24. Refrigerator
25. Cake Mixer (Spiral Mixer)
26. Cool Room
27. Incubator Room
28. Grinder - Hammer Mill (FCC disk mill)
29. Dough Mixer

NEDA conducts three Enterprise Forums: Regional Enterprise Forum (REF), District Enterprise Forum (DEF), and National Enterprise Forum

(NEF). The objective of the Enterprise Fora is to sustain a dialog among the relevant officials, NGOs, and business chambers relating to policy and regulations with the focus on creation and development of enterprise. The Regional Enterprise Forum (REF) is chaired by the Divisional Secretary. The District Enterprise Forum (DEF) is chaired by the District Secretary. And the National Enterprise Forum (NEF) is chaired by the Minister or the Ministerial Secretary. These forums help clarification and adoption of the government policies and regulations at the operational level and to carry feedback to the highest forum for policy making.

As a national authority, NEDA's mandate for enterprise development is wide. The activities summarized below are evidence of the scope of NEDA's programs. They include Market Linkage Programs, Trade Portal, Digital Platform for businesses to businesses (B2B), Businesses to customers (B2C) and customers to customers (C2C), regional, national, and international trade exhibitions, trade fair coordination through the Export Development Board, Chambers of Commerce and National Crafts Council, preparation of marketing plans, developing knowledge and skills on marketing strategies, assisting in conducting marketing feasibility studies for new or existing businesses, assisting in market research, conducting packaging programs, developing distribution methods, identifying and establishing links with exporters, providing knowledge on trade agreements, liaison with external organizations such as USAID, You Lead, ADB, UNDP, Chrysalis, Brandix, Keells, and Cargills supermarkets of Sri Lanka, and Social Ventures.

NEDA also conducts regional and national awarding ceremonies, regional Entrepreneurship Development Programs, Capacity Development and Training Programs, technology transfer and training, marketing and market linkages, business opportunity identification, business plan preparation, financial management education, accounting and bookkeeping training, human resource management, product innovations, women entrepreneurship development, product and service quality management, business cluster development programs in the identified clusters such as Batik, Incense sticks, Coconut shell products, Handicraft, Java Batik, Hair cutting, Beauty culture, Flower cultivation, Coir products, Kids garments, and Pottery.

Industrial Development Board

Industrial Development Board (IDB)[40] is another government institution that has long been providing wide-ranging assistance in research and development, machinery and tool making, and engineering. The IDB focuses on manufacturing industry where as many other fields of production and services. Therefore, there have been created several other government organizations to abridge this gap and serve the areas that fall outside the responsibility of the IDB.

NAITA and Its Role

National Apprentice and Industrial Training Authority (NAITA)[41] provides education, training, and skill development programs in a vast array of fields such as entrepreneurship, Human Resource Development, Human Resource Management, Finance and Accounting, Marketing, and Vocational training targeting the youth. Entrepreneurship Awareness programs, Entrepreneurship Development programs, Know About Business (KAB) training programs are the main programs of NAITA.

Export Development Board

The mandate of the Export Development Board (EDB)[42] is to promote Sri Lanka's exports and thus, it engages in many activities targeting production and export of goods. For production and exports, entrepreneurial skills are imparted by EDB. Further, expansion of exports is targeted through promotion of new producers and exporters also. Thus, the EDB provides prospective exporters with information on foreign buyers, information on new goods demanded, and product quality. EDB assists in marketing, technology, training, and entrepreneurship development also. Specialized women focus programs such as Women entrepreneurship development and "SheTrades" programs are also conducted by the EDB.

Ministry of Youth and Sports

Small Enterprises Development Division (SEDD)[43] under the Ministry of Youth and Sports provides an array of programs through five units of it: Entrepreneurship Development Unit (EDU), Financial and

Support Services Unit (FSSU), Market Development Unit (MDU), Technology and Innovation Unit (TIU), Research and Development Unit (RDU). The vision of the SEDD is "Entrepreneurship and Small Enterprises Development for sustainable growth." Its mission includes enhancement of entrepreneurial capabilities in youth and provision of supportive services for development of enterprises also. SEDD aims at creating "Local Entrepreneurial Culture" through the development of entrepreneurial capabilities in youth.

The activities performed by Entrepreneurship Development Unit include the following: entrepreneurship attitude development, entrepreneurship skills and knowledge development, management skills and knowledge development, business experience sharing, business opportunities identification support, guidance to select feasible business idea, business fora, and club development.

The Financial and Support Services Unit facilitates, supports, and strengthens mechanisms for easy and affordable access to finance, financial skills and literacy by providing skill development training. Main activities of this unit include development of financial skills and literacy for healthy financial management of SMEs, preparation of comprehensive business plan for SMEs, coordinating concessionary bank loan schemes for women and youth entrepreneurs, strengthening the capacity and skills of accountancy and bookkeeping of SMEs, strengthening the capacity and skills of IT base accountancy, support for enabling the suitable environment for SMEs, and arranging business clinics.

The Market Development Unit aims at improving packaging, branding, and providing market information to enable SMEs to access the local and global market. The main activities of this Unit are to enhance new market opportunities of SMEs to both local and international markets, to promote business linkages, to facilitate buyer–seller meetings and buy-back and sub-contracting with assured market for SMEs, to arrange regional, national, and international trade fairs and exhibitions to support SMEs to enter international market through trade fairs, exhibitions, and brand development, and to evaluate entrepreneurs for national awards.

The Technology and Innovation Unit aims at facilitating acquisition and adoption of state-of-the-art, modern, and clean technologies for SMEs to increase innovative and competitive products and to improving skills and knowledge of entrepreneurs. The objectives of the Unit include financial support for technological and professional training, improvement of IT-driven business knowledge of entrepreneurs, introducing new technology and machineries for SMEs with partnering institutes, promoting innovation and value-added products and services using local resource base, technological support to increase product quality with focusing innovation, productivity, and competitiveness.

The Research and Development Unit aims at providing information for decision-making regarding small and medium scale business development and entrepreneurship development through updated high quality and policy-oriented researches. Its objectives are to provide information for national level policy decisions related to SMEs and entrepreneurship development, undertake research and development, facilitate partnering with government and private organizations, and develop regional and national level plans for SMEs and entrepreneurship development.

Other Organizations

In addition to the Entrepreneurship Development Programs organized and conducted by the institutions described above, some other organizations periodically or occasionally conduct EDPs. Central Bank of Sri Lanka is one such institution that launches EDPs through its regional offices. Asian Development Bank occasionally provides expenses and expertise to conduct EDPs for target groups such as rural women and marginalized people as a livelihood enhancement alternative. Sri Lanka, as a member country, also receives ADB supports occasionally for entrepreneurship development programs. The World Bank allocates funds for poverty alleviation programs worldwide. Some fund allocations are available for EDPs and the member countries can benefit from them. Although the funds are not available for EDPs on regular basis, being a developing country, Sri Lanka receives financial and expert assistance to conduct EDPs. JAICA of Japan and KOICA of Korea too occasionally provide assistance for product development and technical skill development.

Chapter Summary

Entrepreneurship development programs (EDP) are directed to promote entrepreneurship among socially and economically backward segments and vulnerable women. Unemployment, income inequality, and poor living standards are the reasons for conducting EDPs. Governments,

NGOs, and large corporates are in the forefront of conducting EDPs. Both prospective entrepreneurs and new entrepreneurs (startups) are the target groups of EDPs.

Entrepreneurship is a growth engine and so, developing countries strive to improve supply of entrepreneurs via EDPs. Developed countries adopt EDPs to alleviate unemployment and to improve earnings of selected social strata. EDPs focus on improvement of living standards of ethnic minorities, women, handicapped, low-caste communities, and unemployed youth. EDPs, impart entrepreneurial thoughts, skills, and managerial skills. EDPs initially help identify venture opportunities and then impart skills and knowledge required for initiating and making successful venture. Entrepreneurship development increases supply of entrepreneurs who enlarge the volume of economic activities creating income for land, labor, capital, and materials.

EDPs aim at educating and training prospective entrepreneurs to overcome constraints to entrepreneurship and adopt four approaches to develop entrepreneurs: building business interests and abilities, guiding to business opportunities and developing business plans, developing operational and managerial capabilities, and guiding or providing incentives and facilities. EDPs develop entrepreneurial mindset and provides a set of specified skills to initiate and operate a venture and impart knowledge of entrepreneur responsibility, ethics, and social responsibilities. Teaching, training, industry exposure, brainstorming, mind mapping, hands-on-experience, and mock board meeting are major activities of EDPs.

EDPs are conducted through six phases: education phase, exposure phase, training phase, business planning phase, start-up phase, and follow-up phase. Entrepreneurship development authorities adopt three approaches in designing and conducting EDPs: Resource approach, Finance approach, Technical approach. "Intervention approach" described earlier in a chapter is an alternative approach. Entrepreneurship development is supported by numerous organizations in every country. Governments, ministries, banks, international organizations, and NGOs provide extensive support for entrepreneurship development.

Review Questions

1. Define entrepreneurship development programs (EDP) and ascertain their scope.

2. "Entrepreneurship Development is a need of all nations." Discuss the different needs for entrepreneurship development in different countries.
3. "Entrepreneurship development programs contemplate to create entrepreneurs." Discuss how successful are the EDPs in creating entrepreneurs.
4. Describe the following points in connection to entrepreneurship development programs;

   a. Target groups
   b. Aims and objectives
   c. The focus
   d. Approaches.

5. Elaborate on the general format of entrepreneur development programs describing their components also.
6. Discuss whether entrepreneurship development programs are more useful for the economically backward countries?
7. "There are entrepreneurship development support organizations in every country." Explain the role of the entrepreneurship development support organizations.
8. Compare the nature and role of the entrepreneurship development organizations between South Asia and East Asia highlighting the major differences.
9. "Entrepreneurship development programs sometimes take the nature of social welfare programs." Comment.
10. "Non-Government Organizations (NGOs) are keen in facilitating entrepreneurship development programs." Identify the reasons for the NGOs to do so.
11. Examine whether there is a connection between social entrepreneurship development projects and entrepreneurship development programs.
12. Compare the National Entrepreneurship Development Agency of Sri Lanka with a similar organization of another country and assess their effectiveness.
13. "Entrepreneurship development programs are not only helpful for prospective entrepreneurs but also for the existing entrepreneurs." Elaborate the scope and role of ED programs.
14. Evaluate the effects of entrepreneurship development programs in contrast to the notion "entrepreneurs are born not made."

Additional Readings

1. Sharma, S., 2021. *Entrepreneurship development*. PHI Learning Pvt. Ltd.
2. Ramachandran, K., 2008. *Entrepreneurship development*. New Delhi: Tata McGraw-Hill.
3. Melwani, R., 2018. Entrepreneurship development and economic development: A literature analysis. *Vol. XXIV Issue I*.
4. Gordon, E., Natarajan, K., and Arora, A., 2009. *Entrepreneurship development*. Mumbai, India: Himalaya publishing house.
5. Kasim, R.S.R., Zulkharnain, A., Hashim, Z., Ibrahim, W.N.W., and Yusof, S.E., 2014. Regenerating youth development through entrepreneurship. *Procedia-Social and Behavioral Sciences, 129*, pp. 322–327.
6. Kalita, P.C., 2019. Entrepreneurship Development Program: Its Role in creation of Entrepreneurs. *Think India Journal, 22*(14), pp. 15787–15804.
7. Lucky, E.O.I., 2011. Nurturing entrepreneurship development in the twenty-first century: The practical approaches. *International Journal of Humanities and Social Science, 1*(9), pp. 219–227.
8. Azim, M.T., 2020. Approaches to entrepreneurship development: A literature survey. *Entrepreneurship Review, 1*(1), pp. 22–48.
9. Obaji, N.O., and Olugu, M.U., 2014. The role of government policy in entrepreneurship development. *Science Journal of Business and Management, 2*(4), pp. 109–115.
10. Kulkarni, P.R., 2013. Entrepreneurship Development: Role of the Government and Institutional Agencies. *SEDME (Small Enterprises Development, Management & Extension Journal), 40*(1), pp. 13–21.
11. Galvão, A.R., Marques, C.S., Ferreira, J.J., and Braga, V., 2020. Stakeholders' role in entrepreneurship education and training programmes with impacts on regional development. *Journal of Rural Studies, 74*, pp. 169–179.
12. Blackburn, R.A., 2016. *Government, SMEs and entrepreneurship development: Policy, practice and challenges*. Routledge.
13. Kulkarni, P.R., 2013. Entrepreneurship Development: Role of the Government and Institutional Agencies. *SEDME (Small Enterprises Development, Management & Extension Journal), 40*(1), pp. 13–21.

14. Sraha, G., 2015. Public policy makers: Improving export promotion programs and entrepreneurial development in a lower emerging economy. *African Journal of Economic and Management Studies, 6*(1), pp. 55–71.
15. Azim, M.T., 2020. Approaches to entrepreneurship development: A literature survey. *Entrepreneurship Review, 1*(1), pp. 22–48.
16. Waithaka, T., Marangu, W.N., and N'gondu, C.N., 2014. Entrepreneurship Development by micro finance institutions effect on the growth of micro and small enterprises in Nairobi Central Business District: A case of Jitegemea Credit Scheme Nairobi. *European Journal of Business and Management, 6*(13), pp. 174–184.
17. Abdullah, S., 2008. *Technology entrepreneurship development in Malaysia: A case study of the national automotive industry* (Doctoral dissertation, University Malaya).
18. Abdul Mutalib, R., Arshad, R., Ismail, N.S.A., and Ahmad, Z., 2015. Women and entrepreneurship: An overview of women entrepreneurship programs in Malaysia. *Journal of Governance and Development, 11,* pp. 15–14.
19. Kolawole, O.D., and Ajila, K., 2015. Driving local community transformation through participatory rural entrepreneurship development. *World Journal of Entrepreneurship, Management and Sustainable Development, 11*(2), pp. 131–139.
20. Rasmussen, E.A., and Sørheim, R., 2006. Action-based entrepreneurship education. *Technovation, 26*(2), pp. 185–194.
21. Estay, C., Durrieu, F., and Akhter, M., 2013. Entrepreneurship: From motivation to start-up. *Journal of international Entrepreneurship, 11,* pp. 243–267.
22. Putta, S.S., 2014. Improving entrepreneur's management skills through entrepreneurship training. *Journal of Commerce and Management Thought, 5*(3), pp. 459–474.
23. Wheadon, J.D., and Duval-Couetil, N., 2014. Business plan development activities as a pedagogical tool in entrepreneurship education. *The Journal of Engineering Entrepreneurship, 5*(1), pp. 31–48.
24. Wheadon, J.D., and Duval-Couetil, N., 2014. Business plan development activities as a pedagogical tool in entrepreneurship education. *The Journal of Engineering Entrepreneurship, 5*(1), pp. 31–48.

25. Oghojafor, B.E.A., Okonji, P.S., and Olayemi, O.O., 2011. Fifty Years of Entrepreneurship Development in Nigeria: Challenges and Prospects.
26. https://sanasa.coop/.
27. https://www.dfcc.lk/.
28. https://www.peoplesbank.lk/.
29. https://rubank.lk/.
30. https://www.ndbbank.com/.
31. https://www.rdb.lk/.
32. https://www.sarvodaya.org/seeds/.
33. https://sanasainternational.lk/.
34. https://www.sdb.lk/en/.
35. https://www.agrimin.gov.lk/web/index.php/news-and-events/2091-28-04-2023-1e?lang=en.
36. https://en.wikipedia.org/wiki/Janasaviya.
37. https://ebank.samurdhi.gov.lk:8080/EASYBANK/login.action.
38. http://www.samurdhi.gov.lk/.
39. https://neda.gov.lk/.
40. https://idb.gov.lk/.
41. https://naita.gov.lk/.
42. https://www.srilankabusiness.com/.
43. http://www.sed.gov.lk/sedweb/en/.

PART V

New Topics of Entrepreneurship

CHAPTER 16

Comparative Entrepreneurship

Key Learning Points

- Policy differences.
- Major entrepreneurial cultures.
- Business culture of China.
- Business meetings, decision-making, and trust building.
- Protocols, foods, beverages, attire, and mannerism.
- Negotiation with government officials.
- The religious values.
- Entrepreneurship practices in Japan.
- Greetings and cultural values.
- Business meetings and decision-making.
- Business cards, socialization, and building trust.
- Loyalty to workplace.
- Entrepreneurship practices in India.
- Cultural, geographical, religious, political, and language diversity.
- Meetings, decision-making.
- Small talk, trust building, and gifts.
- Government and bureaucracy.
- Entrepreneurship practices in Arab.
- Culture, values, and business.
- Business meetings, negotiations, and trust building.

© The Author(s), under exclusive license to Springer Nature Singapore Pte Ltd. 2024

M. Rajaratne, *Concepts, Processes and Practice of Entrepreneurship*, Palgrave Studies in Global Entrepreneurship,
https://doi.org/10.1007/978-981-97-6180-7_16

- Holidays, appointments, delays.
- Entrepreneurship practices in the USA.
- Small talk, openness, friendliness.
- Punctuality, decision-making speed.
- Entrepreneurship practices in Europe.
- Diversity in language and geography.
- Political differences, punctuality, formality.

Introduction

Entrepreneurship is identified as the major force of economic growth and development. In fact, entrepreneurship is not only a business action but also a factor of production as distinguished by J. S. Mill. Entrepreneurship assumes the organizer role as it organizes all other factors of production; referred to as dormant factors of production by some scholars. Therefore, effectiveness of entrepreneurship unquestionably determines wealth of nations.[1] Countries accumulated wealth during the past decades through the market showcase their strength of national entrepreneurship. The World Bank classifies countries into different income groups and the top tier group enjoys extremely high per capita income compared to the bottom tier group. The Fortune 500 magazine (2022)[2] reports that the top 10 corporates contribute to one twentieth (or 5%) of the world GDP. The Global Entrepreneurship Index (2019) establishes strong correlation between per capita income differentials and the entrepreneurship capacity differentials of countries.[3]

The regression derived in Fig. 1.2 (Chapter 1) indicates that higher entrepreneurship capacity has leverage on greater potentials for earning higher per capita income.[4] The graph suggests that some countries are highly entrepreneurial while others are moderately or lowly entrepreneurial. In this backdrop it is presumable that practice of entrepreneurship is distinctive to each country and thus, the performance differentials are eminent.[5] This relationship encouraged us to make an inquiry into the practice of entrepreneurship in diverse countries, viz. comparative entrepreneurship. Inquiry of comparative entrepreneurship draws attention to culture, values, ethics, political, economic, and legal factors that determine nations' capacity to entrepreneurship.[6] In the world economy, there are countries that grow highly, moderately, and lowly. These growth differentials are a reflection of variety of factors that the country specific value creation capacity is constituted.

Policy Differences

Communist regimes in the past promoted public entrepreneurship and barred private entrepreneurship. Sri Lanka also experienced this phenomenon during the Pro-Soviet regime between 1970 and 1977. Perestroika (restructuring) program of the Soviet Union and stepwise economic liberalization of China helped regain private entrepreneurship in those countries which, in turn, led to experience thriving private sector before long.[7] However, the extremist Communist regimes like North Korea and Cuba are still promoting pro-public entrepreneurship and in consequence the state entrepreneurship has failed in value creation and boosting economic growth.[8] In pro-communist cultures, entrepreneurship is regarded as a skill that can be hired for a salary like any other human skill; against the notion of Francis A. Walker that entrepreneurship is more than an average skill.[9] The communist notion has been proven to be a mistake as entrepreneurial activities of these countries are far below the levels of pro-capitalist nations.

Western and the Far-Eastern countries are pro-entrepreneurial by culture for millennia, if not centuries. The culture of these countries values entrepreneurship and treats it as an essential social course. Therefore, these cultures well receive entrepreneurship and recognize the relevance of entrepreneur role for social progress.[10] In contrast, the South Asian nations are still struggling in figuring out the value of entrepreneurship as a valuable social course. On the other hand, there are many Central African countries with less advanced cultures where the value of entrepreneurship is apparently underestimated. The backward attitudes toward entrepreneurship have bearings on their low incomes also.[11]

Freedom for trade and travel contributes to advancement of entrepreneurship and thereby, growth in national income. Free trade and travel encouraged entrepreneurs to search for business opportunities and to exploit them. Then came the free-port, tax-free, duty-free, and entry-free regimes. Hong Kong[12] and Singapore[13] are classic examples of free-port and tax-free regimes during the second half of the twentieth century. Dubai became a center of duty-free trade a few decades ago.[14] European Union declared entry-free and common currency regime after lifting trade and travel barriers within the region. These policies and actions immensely impacted on liberalizing markets and market entry which are the most essential for advancement of entrepreneurial action. These countries rapidly advanced as new and capable entrepreneurs and soon entered the high-income category.[15]

Though this chapter does not intend to discuss the relationship between entrepreneurship and income among countries, it enquires into the entrepreneurial characteristics of a few major entrepreneurial nations to compare the differences. Comparative entrepreneurial culture is useful for learning of entrepreneurial character of different countries.[16] The low-entrepreneurial countries can benefit from the comparative entrepreneurship analysis for reengineering their entrepreneurial capacities for achieving higher economic growth and national income. Political belief of a culture is an important aspect that determines the destiny of private entrepreneurship. As an example, political attitudes toward private entrepreneurship in South Korea and North Korea are a case in point. Pro-private entrepreneurship attitudes play a significant role in the South, whereas pro-state entrepreneurship does so in the North. The income difference between the two is evidenced by the difference of their entrepreneurship policy.[17]

Major Entrepreneurial Cultures

The rest of this chapter enquires into major business cultures to identify their differences and similarities in doing business. Understanding of different business cultures is helpful for international entrepreneurs to successfully deal with their counterparts. Business culture of China, Japan, India, Arab, the USA, and the EU are recognized as major cultures not only due to their unique features but also for their volume of business. These countries and regions contribute to 70% of the word GDP of 101 trillion US$ in 2022. Besides, every country has unique business cultures due to spatial, cultural, legal, and historical identity. The South American nations, for instance, have some common features in business while the business culture of Argentina is different from that of Brazil. In South Asia, the business culture of India can be differentiated from that of Sri Lanka. Similarly, business culture of North African countries has distinctive features compared to that of South African nations while all African nations share some common business cultures also[18] (Table 16.1).

Recognition of similarities as well as dissimilarities in business cultures is not only useful for entrepreneurs to consider doing business in different

Table 16.1 Country profile

Criteria	*China*	*Japan*	*India*	*Arab World*	*USA*	*European Union*
Land Extent (Sq. Km. 1000)	9597	378	3287	13,132	9834	4233
Population (Billion)	1.426	0.123	1.44	0.465	0.342	0.449
Gross Domestic Product (US$ Trillion)	17.9	4.3	3.7	3.5	27.3	19.0
Per Capita Income (US$)	12,621	33,805	2612	11,700	81,623	42,440
Exports (US$ Trillion)	3.380	0.718	0.468	n.a	3.053	6.600
Imports (US$ Trillion)	2.560	0.784	0.720	n.a	2.100	7.100

Data Compiled from various sources for the period of 2022–2023

countries but also to be successful in different cultures. Knowledge of cultures is useful for the entrepreneurs who plan to engage in business or transactions with entrepreneurs from different cultures. Foreign counterparts must at least be familiar with languages and basic cultural practices of the partner country. In every culture, values, morals, ethics, taboos, rituals, and beliefs guide people and businesses. Religions and traditions provide inputs for a cultural system. Foreign business counterparts, when dealing with different cultures, will have to endure taboos, rituals, practices, and traditions. Lack of knowledge of them is disadvantageous while at least some knowledge will ease understanding and building trust between the involving parties. In essence, knowledge of culture will guide foreign counterparts what and how to do and what to avoid, for instance.[19]

Doing Business in China

Chinese culture is constructed upon Confucian, Taoist, and Buddhist morals. The business culture of China too is influenced by these religious teachings. When entering into agreements with Chinese business counterparts, entrepreneurs must be aware of the Chinese business culture and the behavior of the partner which is guided by the Chinese culture.[20] Confucianism is the foundation of Chinese culture. The Confucian principle *Guanxi* emphasizes that a relationship is indispensable for maintaining solidarity, loyalty, modesty, and courtesy of a person. Chinese society is constructed vertically with respect for seniority. Chinese do care for individual reputations and dignity. Because they are cautious of personal goodwill, they usually tend to avert risking their name. Decision-making takes a long process as all the relevant parties involve. Decisions are made after several rounds of meetings. Senior members of a team are supposed to express their opinions while subordinates usually do not express their opinions[21] (Map 16.1).

Decision-makers consider solutions to problems on a long-term social perspective. Chinese do not respect hasty decisions. The hierarchical structure is always important and thus, any move to circumvent it retards

Map 16.1 China (Photo Credit: Royalty free iStock Photo)

decision-making process. Chinese businessmen often seek long-term relationships and thus, strive to create relationships rather than striving for negotiating for short-lived benefits. Failure to cultivate a personal relationship with business counterparts can lead to failure in meeting the negotiation objectives. The negotiation process, that involves relationship building also, can take from several days to several months depending on the vastness and complexity of the business deal. This involves formal meetings, home visits, invitations to sport events, dinners, and drinks.

Because Chinese are reluctant to quickly build trust on strangers, meetings and discussions usually take place through a third-party mediation. This facilitates and helps building mutual trust to hold open discussions and exchange great deal of information between the partners at meetings. Punctuality is an important value in the Chinese society and thus, punctual attendance in business meetings is highly expected. Any delay in attending a meeting must be conveyed to the partner in advance and an apology should be tendered. When meeting with someone for the first time, use of some Chinese words will impress the counterpart. Light but long handshake of the Chinese counterpart is the norm of greeting at a meeting. Nodding and smiling are very common greetings too. Chinese business partners expect to be addressed by the professional title and the last name.[22]

Exchange of gifts between the partners is common at the beginning of a relationship. Gifts must be simple because too expensive gifts may carry hidden meanings, gifts should be well wrapped and not be more than a token of impression. Chinese culture does not allow hasty acceptance of gifts and thus, the gifts are initially dejected but accepted after a while. Gifts are given and accepted with both hands. Gifts are opened in front of the presenter and astonishing feelings are expressed to impress the giver. The dress code is formal for business meeting and the dress must reasonably reflect the partner's business success and thus good quality clothes, watches, and shoes serve as evidence of current success. Business cards are usually exchanged at business meetings. The card must be printed both in Chinese and English. Cards are exchanged with both hands. The surface of the card printed in Chinese must be turned to the Chinese counterpart allowing him to read the card without turning it around. The Chinese businessmen would read the card with attention and then treat it preciously. Writing on the cards in presence of the Chinese counterpart should be avoided[23] (Capture 16.1).

Capture 16.1 Meeting and Greeting (China) (Photo Credit: Royalty free iStock Photo)

Business meetings with Chinese usually take a long time and might take a few rounds to conclude. Chinese are typically indirect communicators. Even a disagreement on a matter will not be clearly expressed and thus, the listener must be familiar with the gestures and ambiguity of expressions to understand the correct message. It is not unusual for Chinese to obtain the service of an intermediary to deliver negative outcome of a meeting. Silence maintained during meetings is an integral part and thus, it is inappropriate to try to break silence. Speaker should not be disturbed by others when talking. Unlike the Westerners, Chinese use a very limited amount of body language. The team leader enters the meeting room first and sits in front of the host chairing the meeting and leading the negotiations. The team members will not express their opinions in the negotiation process unless the leader ask for it.[24]

Bargaining is an integral part of Chinese culture and thus, accepting without bargain is viewed as a sign of weakness. However, manipulation by exerting psychological pressure is not welcomed and appreciated. Harmonious relationship is treated as most important to strike off a deal. Even if you are actually triumphant after a successful meeting or striking off a deal, too much appreciation must be avoided. Kind words, politeness, or a faint smile would suffice to appreciate. Business meals are an important part of business relationship building. Seating arrangement is laid according to order of the rank of the participants. At the end of a meal, leaving some food on individuals' plates is an indication that you are full and the meal was sufficient. The host must pay for the meal and thus, invitees should not bother to pay the bill. When paying the bill, showing money in front of the guests is not admired.

At business proposal presentation, the partner is required to be well prepared for the task. The presentation must be specific, straightforward, and convincing. Chinese counterpart usually brings a large team to the meeting. So, the presenter should make more than a dozen prints of the presentation ready for distribution among the participants, if and when necessary. The presentations must not be multi-colored. Black and white slide-show is always preferred. Presentation is normally followed by a brief talk of the presenter. Emotions are viewed negatively and thus, the partner must maintain composure, calmness, but seriousness. With regard to deadlines, you must not pressurize the Chinese partner. Delays and follow-up meetings should be tolerated and patience be upheld. Hurrying to decision-making will cause negative impact.[25]

Chinese respect the order of importance of persons in a delegation and thus, the head of the delegation must enter the meeting room first and the rest must follow the order. The most favorable months of the year for business meeting are April to June, and September to October. When meetings are fixed, the office hours and the mid-day break must be respected. Business hours are 8:00 a.m. to 5:00 p.m. from Monday through Friday. The mid-day break falls between 12 p.m. to 2 p.m. During these hours, not only work the telephones and elevators are also halted. Greetings take the form of handshake and you must wait until the Chinese counterpart initiates it. Words like comrade and brother that represent sentiments must be avoided. In government business, gifts are considered as bribery and forbidden.[26]

At the beginning of conversations, the Chinese counterpart usually asks something like "*Have you eaten?*" or "*Where have you been?*" Those words are equivalent to "*How are you?*" in English. Therefore, the foreigner does not need to answer the questions in detail. Expressing "*yes*" or "*thank you*" or "*fine*" with a smile will be sufficient. It is also customary to utter a few Chinese words at the beginning of the meeting as greetings to reduce the cultural gap. Formal discussion is usually followed by a preliminary chat on popular topics like Chinese art, landmarks, climate, and geography. It will be worthy to share views and travel experiences in and outside China with positive impressions with the Chinese counterparts (Capture 16.2).

Political gossips or issues such as Tibet, Da-Lai-Lama, Taiwan, Hong Kong, and human rights must be avoided during the conversation. Chinese have concerns over hasty negations and strong negative impressions and thus, negative impressions, if any, must be conveyed softly, vaguely, and politely. Similarly, you must understand the exact meaning of what the Chinese counterpart means. Expression like "*Not a big issue*" is used in an instance of a big problem. The manners of body language and body movements are extremely important when negotiating business

Capture 16.2 Business card exchange (China) (Photo Credit: Royalty free iStock Photo)

in China. Stretch of arms, extreme facial expressions, dramatization, and gestures must be avoided or controlled. Body posture, attention, concentration, conduct, respectfulness, calmness, and exhibition of self-control are very important. After a meeting, foreigners are supposed to exit the meeting room prior to the Chinese counterpart.[27]

Bright colors are considered as inappropriate for the dress code. Black and white dresses and conservative dresses are preferred to fashionable dresses. Punctuality is highly appreciated and thus, delays of a partner connect to their downside. Business cards are exchanged almost with every participant before the meeting and thus, plenty of business cards will be required. Insufficiency of business cards is a bad sign of the partner. Business cards must be in Chinese and English languages and preferably in gold color prints to connote prosperity. Business card may carry additional information such as age and the size of the business. When giving business cards, the Chinese print must face the receiver. Business cards are exchanged using both hands and the receiver must patiently and enthusiastically read the card.

Usually, business meal is arranged after a business meeting. Seating arrangement is made according to protocol and thus, the foreign counterpart should wait until being guided to the appropriate seat. During the meal, business matters are not supposed to be discussed. Meals usually include liquor also. Chinese counterpart enjoys entertaining the foreign business partner. Some 20–30 dishes are served in a meal and the partner is expected to eat a bit of every dish. Scorpions, locusts, snake skin, dog meat, and snake or animal blood are also served in premium meals. The amounts and varieties eaten speak of the partner. Leaving an empty dish, after eating everything, means that foods ordered were not sufficient. On the other hand, eating no food is a disgrace and offensive to the Chinese partner.

During meal, the Chinese exhibit informal and light-minded behaviors and spend time leisurely. The foreign partners thus, should be patient and blend with them. Meals are meant not only for eating but also for cultural understanding and blending. Meal might end up with heavy drinking. Foreign partners are expected to fully enjoy the occasion. Exceptionally strong liquor may be offered to test the endurance and ability to handle alcohol. It is better to accept the challenge rather than refusing. In Chinese culture, alcohol is an auspicious good that represents well-wishing. Capacity to alcohol intake is a measure of stamina of a person.[28]

In Chinese culture, numerical numbers are assigned meanings and thus some numbers are auspicious and others are not. Therefore, some knowledge of numeric beliefs is essential when dealing with the Chinese counterparts. While number 7 is a lucky number in the West, number 8 is the lucky number in China. If a foreign partner receives eight of something from the Chinese counterpart, it is a gesture of good will and a sign of hopes. Number 6 is considered a blessing for smooth progress of the things planned. Number 4 is a taboo number because it sounds like the word "death" in Chinese and is considered unlucky. Similarly, number 73 sounds like "funeral" and number 84 sounds like "accidents." Therefore, the foreigner should avoid these unlucky numbers when fixing dates for meetings, appointing number of delegates, and offering something.

Mianzi is an important aspect of the Chinese society. This means gaining of one's face. In a collectivist society such as China, face reflects self-esteem, social recognition, and trustworthy interpersonal interactions of a person. Honor helps to gain face while embarrassment helps to lose face. This social conscience is useful in building lasting interpersonal connections and business relations. The concept of *Guanxi* (interpersonal connections) is also connected to *Mianzi* which together promote "psychological contract" between two persons or parties. *Guanxi*, in business settings, is instrumental to attain specific goal or desired outcome. *Guanxi* is maintained by means of mutual favors or returns. To maintain *Guanxi,* considerable time and effort into establishing, nourishing, and expanding network of relationships are needed. Communication is regarded as an art (*Yishu*) in China. Communication is essential for understanding and building lasting relationships. As art consumes time, communication too is expected to consume time. Interruptions and urgency in communication impede building good relationships with Chinese counterparts.

Foreign businessmen must take extra precautions in use of words by the Chinese counterpart. For example, the word "*yes*" suggests agreement and affirmation to Westerners while for the Chinese it generally means "*I am listening.*" Chinese communication practice is implicit, indirect, context-based, listening-centered, and face-oriented while the Western communication practice emphasizes meanings of words. Chinese believe that misfortune comes out of the mouth (*Huo Kong Kou Chu*) and thus they have control over the use of words. In Chinese business conversations honesty, truthfulness, and confidentiality are maintained. Nonverbal, facial, indirect, and signal-based communication of the Chinese counterpart requires second guessing to understand the exact outcome of the conversation. Modesty and humbleness are key personal characteristics and thus, boasting and claiming credit for others' work are looked down on. Chinese society is a construct of in-group and out-group spheres. In-group members receive preferential treatment. In-group relationships are collegial and cooperative. The in-group relationships prevail over company matters. The out-group relationships can be cold and restricted to business perimeters.[29]

Negotiation with Chinese partners is a difficult task for foreigners due to unfamiliarity of traditions. Chinese tend to use strong negotiation tactics like delaying, and reiteration, bargaining at the negotiation table. Chinese negotiators normally and initially pretend disinterest in foreign entrepreneur's offers. Chinese often use silence as a negotiating tactic. This encourages the foreign counterparts to misconceive that the negotiating process will breakdown. Foreigners, in fear of losing the opportunity, tend to offer hasty concessions and loosen conditions. Chinese may pretend that they are in negotiation with similar enterprises as a tactic to sway the negotiating party. The foreign businesspeople easily get frustrated due to this practice but the Chinese drag the negotiation for further rounds. Therefore, patience is an indispensable quality for foreign negotiators hoping to be successful in China. Chinese usually accompany large negotiating team and make a big presence in the meeting room. While the senior members speak, others will collect information and observe behavior of the counterpart. The decisions are not arrived at over the discussion table. The final decision is conveyed after deliberating with the in-house team at a later time.

Negotiation with the government organization is slow because of lengthy bureaucratic process. Negotiation with the government organizations involve many parties and thus, many rounds of meetings are required to obtain consensus of governmental departments. In the early stages of negotiation, a lawyer is not present. If a lawyer is present in the meeting, that is a sign that you are close to the deal. Although negotiations are concluded, the Chinese counterpart may request to change clauses in the contract that have already been finalized. Some other times, the Chinese will not make such requests, but arbitrarily change the terms already negotiated. Therefore, the foreign counterpart should be familiar with these moves of the Chinese. And it is advisable to employ a translator (preferably a foreigner) with business exposure to check the paperwork before striking off a deal (Capture 16.3).

Capture 16.3 Business meeting (China) (Photo Credit: Royalty free iStock Photo)

Because the Chinese culture has evolved through more than two millennia and is deeply rooted and widely stretched, Western businessmen find it challenging to understand Chinese entrepreneurial and managerial conduct. However, understanding of Chinese business ideology will guide the foreigner to limitless business opportunities. Chinese culture is constructed on three ideologies: Confucianism, Taoism, and Buddhism. Confucianism is the dominating force of the culture which has guided Chinese education philosophy since more than two millennia. Confucianism is behavioral and moral doctrine of human relationships, behavior, and work ethics. Confucianism emphasizes duty, sincerity, loyalty, honor, filial piety, respect for age and seniority. Among the most prominent legacies of the Confucian doctrine are the power distance and hierarchical relationship. In China, rank and seniority are extremely important in business relationships, especially when dealing with state-owned enterprises.

Taoism propagates the philosophy of nature. It demands letting things take their own course. Accordingly, the man follows the earth, the earth follows the heaven, heaven follows Tao, and Tao follows nature. Taoism maintains that heavy intervention in the affairs of other humans (or things) may produce opposite or negative outcomes. Thus, the people must observe fundamental principles while adapting to change when it is necessary. For example, a manager should lead by allowing his employees to do their work independently rather than micro-managing (or interfering in) their tasks. Chinese Communist Rule, however, has challenged Taoism and imposed political authority highly on the social and business affairs. Thus, in practice, Chinese managers usually adopt commandment to retain power at the higher levels without delegating the authority. Important decisions related to purchasing and pricing are taken by the higher-level management.[30]

Buddhism emphasizes that suffering can be eliminated through extinction of desires by way of advancement of wisdom. In China, "Wu" and "Yuan" are two basic concepts of Buddhism. The term "Wu" is translated as comprehension which means one's ability to comprehend an issue from its core. Chinese make use of this concept in business context to deeply understand people, their needs and wants, and situations. "Wu" is also a useful ability for a manager to understand people, situations, and to find solutions to problems. The concept Yuan is interpreted as predetermined cause-effect relationship, which is equivalent to Karma. Thus, they consider a chance to associate with a good person is precious and thus, is yuan. Therefore, Chinese attributes good business relationships to the concept of Yuan as a predetermined (heavenly) phenomenon. A failure in business cooperation is sometimes attributed to Yuan rather than to managerial woes.

Chinese traditions underwent hiccups in the post-Maoist era. Many traditional Chinese values were suppressed and replaced by communist values. When the "open-door" policy was implemented by President Deng Xiaoping, pragmatic methods were adopted for China's economic development. This led to materialistic overwhelming of the Chinese society which promoted evil and unethical business practices also. The "open-door" policy since 1978 allowed foreign concepts, cultures, and lifestyles into China. As a result, while China maintains its unique social stature, China underwent many changes such as adoption of capitalist flavor in the policy sphere, honoring international organizations such as World Trade Organization (WTO) and International Standards Organization (ISO), allowing Disneyland, and fast-food restaurant chains like McDonald's. This scenario has gradually but permanently changed the business landscape in China. This has infused competition, competitiveness, foreign values, trade relations, and foreign direct investments and thus, China is no longer a traditional and closed society relying solely on the power of *Guanxi* but a modern culture governed by business professionalism.[31]

Doing Business in Japan

Japan is sometimes referred to as "Japan Inc." due to her sophisticated business culture as a nation. This reference implies that Japan operates as a nation-corporate. In Japan, the history of business, family business, conglomerates, competition, business rivalry, sub-contracting, work culture, trade unions, innovations, and business attitudes are unique. Foreign entrepreneurs who plan to engage in business with Japanese counterparts thus require adequate understanding of the Japanese corporate culture. Cultural elements pose a profound impact on decision-making, business relations, and long-term business success. Japan's code of social conduct is very formal and it is almost like a law of the land. Concern for civility, grace, and consideration of others are also major elements of the Japanese culture. Knowledge of Japanese culture and Japanese language will be helpful for a foreign business counterpart to gain favorable impression and trust of the Japanese counterpart. Japanese business culture heavily comprises of business etiquette and trust[32] (Map 16.2).

It is important for the foreign counterparts to comprehend that doing business in Japan is not mere profession but a sacred affair. In Japanese entrepreneurship, customers are respected as if deities and called "*Okyaku-sama*" where the word "*sama*" is an honorific reference to deities and kings. Every entrepreneurial action is directed to "*Okyaku-sama no shiawase no tameini*" (to make customers pleased and fulfilled). Therefore, business practice is almost like a ritual for deities. Also, in Japanese entrepreneurship culture, it is believed that the god resides in every product. Therefore, the producers pay due attention to make products perfect and heavenly.[33]

Panasonic Chairman Konosuke Matsushita mentions that the goods produced by him (his company) are like his children. Once grown, children move out of home and reach the society. But the parents still inquire whether the children are doing well, admired by others, and well received by the society. Matsushita says entrepreneurs also, like parents,

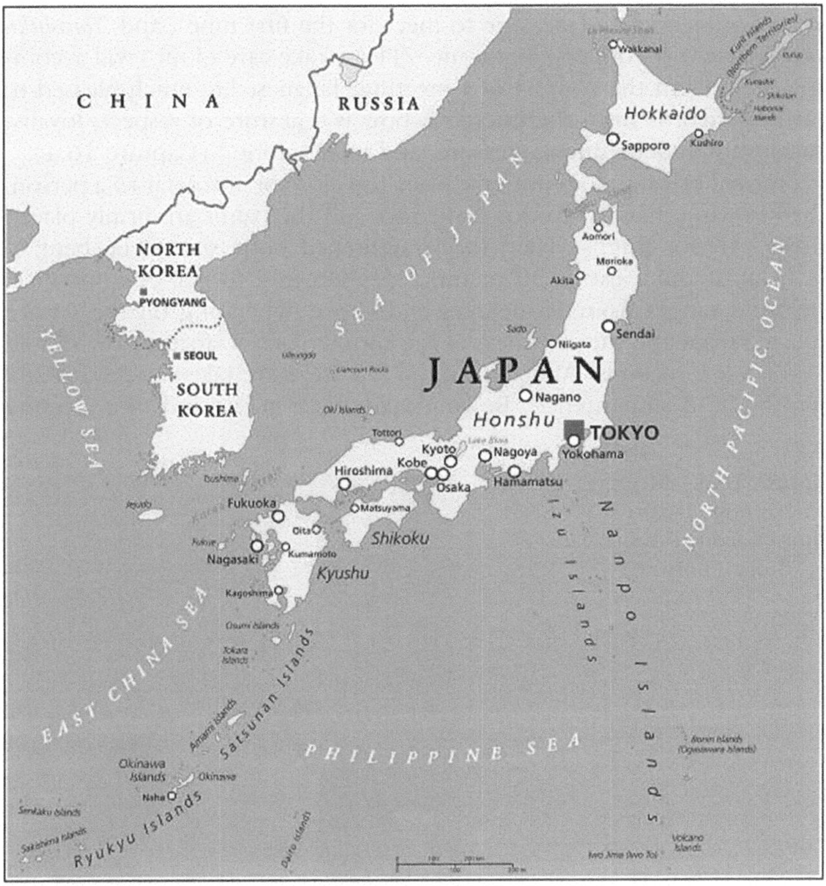

Map 16.2 Japan (Photo Credit: Royalty free iStock Photo)

must produce goods that are admirable, trustworthy, user friendly, and durable. Also, as parents make visits to children, entrepreneurs must meet the vendors, agents, and customers to get feedback on how the products are accepted and admired by and moving in the society.

Almost every Japanese action starts and ends with a bow; that is the generally accepted manner of greeting. Japanese not only bow to humans but everything that they find important, significant, worthy, respectful, and helpful. The words *Konnichi-wa* (wishing a good morning/good day), *Hajime mashite* (pleasure to meet for the first time), and *Yoroshiku onegaishimasu* (thank you in advance/Please take care of me) will accompany the bow in the context of a meeting. Japanese are much pleased to hear these words from the guests. A bow is a gesture of respect, loyalty, relationship, indebtedness, pleasure, and many more[34] (Capture 16.4).

A formal bowing does not take place too close or at too far to a person. When bowing, hands run down the legs and the palms are firmly placed on the exterior thighs. Then the straightened body should be bent to the front at the waist at 30 or more degrees in a formal circumstance. The bend ranges from 15 degrees and above depending on the service expected from and the greatness of the counterpart. A sincere bow should last for a few seconds. After bowing, a few steps are taken backward and then the head straightened. Bowing takes place at the end of a meeting

Capture 16.4 Meeting and greeting (Japan) (Photo Credit: Royalty free iStock Photo)

and departure also. Multiple bows are not uncommon especially at departures. Japanese counterparts read one's bow carefully to judge their ego and pride which can be counterproductive to a lasting relationship.

In the business setting, Japanese prefer less speaking or silence to over-speaking and exaggeration. Silence is linked to credibility as it is believed to represent wisdom and emotional self-control. Japanese culture is constructed on Confucianism, Taoism, Shintoism, and Buddhism. Self-control is a predominant feature of the Japanese culture taught by these traditions. At the beginning of a business relationship, more introverted and formal approach is likely to be received from the Japanese partners. One Japanese proverb is a case in point: "*The duck that quacks is the first to get shot.*" Therefore, it is always better to let the Japanese counterpart initiate the negotiations and to pick a clue from him/her for contributing to the ongoing negotiation. Japanese communicate more without words than uttering words. They communicate with indirect verbal expressions and pauses during discussions, but with less words and more body language and facial expressions.

At times of stress or difficulty in making a breakthrough of a meeting, Japanese usually resort to maintaining a pause and a silence. By this way, they try to release tension, provide some time to boost thinking and provoke intuition. At such times, it is unwise for the foreign counterpart to break the silence unless otherwise they have a brilliant idea that could make a breakthrough. This will help the foreign counterpart to outshine and exhibit wittiness. Business meeting could even be postponed amidst unresolvable issues. Japan is a group-oriented culture and thus, group solidarity is valued over individualism. A famous Japanese saying; "*a single arrow is easily broken, but not ten in a bundle*" implies the group construct of the Japanese society. Therefore, when dealing with the Japanese businessmen, individualism should not be considered as the norm. A group mentality will be always useful in a business deal.

Exchange of business cards (*Mei-shi*) is a norm in business meetings. A business card represents the identity of the partner and their company. The team members too must carry their business cards but should not hurry to exchange them until the team leader is done with card exchange. The team members should not hurry and haphazardly exchange business cards and should wait until it becomes proper for them to do so. Business card is convenient to the partner as it is a note of information that can be maintained in a card holder for future reference. Maintaining card pouch (holder) is also a Japanese custom. Business cards are given and accepted with both hands[35] (Capture 16.5).

Upon exchange, the cards are briefly read and placed on the table for reference during the meeting. Carrying business card in the back pocket or wallet is not appropriate. Therefore, business cards must be carried in a designated apparatus. When exchanged, the Japanese-printed side of the card must face the counterpart so that he can readily read without turning it around. Business cards must not be passed through others or tossed to the receiver. The card must be presented individually followed by other etiquette such as bowing and expressing a few courteous words such as "*Yoroshiku onegaishimasu.*" Business cards should never be exchanged single handed or while sitting.

In Japanese business culture, age is revered and seniority is respected in a business setting. Japanese CEOs are normally older than those of other countries with an average age of 62 years. Foreign business counterparts must, therefore, discriminately respect older executives with significant care against the younger members of a delegation. Business cards are

Capture 16.5 Business card exchange (Japan) (Photo Credit: Royalty free iStock Photo)

presented and greetings are conveyed according to the order of the age. In a business meeting, gentle and persuasive presentation that showcases the virtues of what is being proposed will be more accepted than trying a hard-sell approach by applying high pressure and confrontation.

It is unwise to drive too hard on decisions and deadlines. Japanese business decision-making is carried out by consensus and thus, any attempt to speed up the process will be counterproductive because hard-push is disrespectful and intolerable practice. Therefore, the foreign counterparts must build patience and contemplate opportunities to build trust and a lasting relationship. In Japan, trust and patience, and gentleness of handling affairs are highly revered. Hurried negotiations are always negative signs to Japanese counterparts.[36]

Japanese people are known as reserved and fond of privacy. Since early history, Japanese traditional dwellings have been fortified with tall wooden walls and later with thick live fences. Japanese tend to avoid strangers. A chat with a stranger will be usually limited to a few words. Asking many questions and personal details at the beginning is regarded a rude practice. But after building relationship, there can be almost nothing personal. Therefore, a foreign business partner should only gradually approach the Japanese counterpart. In Japan, things and practices are well-defined.

There is a Japanese saying "*maru shikaku*" which means absence of knowledge of right place for right activity; literally to know how to couple two things that match. For instance, the knowledge to choose the right ground for right game; soccer for square ground and baseball for circular grounds. Therefore, the foreigner must know what is right and what is wrong when dealing with the Japanese. For instance, although exchange of gifts is very common at business meetings, items such as lilies, lotus, and camellias do not suit to business meetings as they are used for funeral services. White flowers and pot-plants also carry negative superstitions. Number 4 is an unlucky number and hence, a set of four of anything deems to be unlucky. Number nine is also considered inauspicious.

Hot or cold damp towel (*oshibori*) provided at restaurants at the start of the meal must be used to clean your hands only. If there are no appropriate utensils provided for serving yourself from the common dishes, you are not supposed to use the end of your chopsticks which feed to mouth. However, the opposite end of the chopsticks can be used to pick up food to add to your plates. Chopsticks are not used to pierce food. The speed to catch up chopstick skill is a good indicator of your potentials to adjust to the Japanese way of doing. Also, eating authentic Japanese dishes like *Sashimi* (raw fish) and *Natto* (soybean-based dish) indicates your adaptation to the Japanese culture.

After a meeting, you are invited for meals at an authentic Japanese restaurant and thereafter to pubs; sometimes to a couple of pubs one after another. Authentic food includes raw and live fish also. Cutting and boiling fish alive is not uncommon in Japan. Eating pieces of living octopus is accepted as a brave and Japanized act. Eating all types of foods and drinking plenty of *Sake* (rice wine) and enjoying at pubs will make a good presentation of your stamina and attitudes to initiate good business relationship. Also, after finishing meals, leaving the chopsticks and earthenware neatly on the table is a good sign of food etiquette.

For business meetings, decent business suit is preferred. Women too are supposed to wear decent business dress with minimum of jewelry and accessories. Though women may wear high-heel shoes, their height should not be towering over the men in the teams. Height of women in the team should not overwhelm the height of men. Small detail of politeness makes a big deal of respect. Shoe-related etiquette is complicated in Japan. When entering a house, removal of the shoes, stepping into slippers provided by the householder, and again changing that pair of slippers to wear another pair of slippers for washrooms are important rules.

Also, leaving shoes or slippers when changing into another designated pair, the former pair has to be arranged so as to enter into them straightly. You should enter the *Tatami* floor (Japanese traditional floor made of paddy straws) bare foot or with socks only because the surface is gentle and can be damaged. If you have any doubt, it is wise to consult a Japanese team member always about the good practices of changing shoes. Learning is considered as a good personal attitude. Skill in shoe etiquette is an indicator of how quickly a foreigner adjusts to Japanese way of doing. Counter-wise steps are followed when leaving.

Punctuality is of prime importance in Japan. Participants must be on time for meetings and appointments. It is a good gesture to turn up a bit earlier to meetings. While all delays must be done away with, any unprecedented delay must be honestly apologized. While bowing is indispensable, shake-hand is acceptable at business meetings with foreigners. However, you must follow your Japanese counterpart in the greeting procedures to avoid mistakes. It is also a good practice to greet everyone in the team individually regardless of their positional importance at the meeting.[37]

When addressing the members of the Japanese counterpart, surname followed by appropriate title must always be used. Regardless of the gender, after someone's surname (family name), honorific word "*San*" (English equivalent of esquire) is used at every address. Depending on the honorific stature of the counterpart, the word "*Sama*" is used after one's surname. The word "*Sama*" is used as an honorific term to address deities and emperor. Yet, in Japanese business tradition, customers are called as "*Okyaku-sama*" (the word of highest honor).

Business card is a prominent feature of Japanese business and business meetings. Therefore, the business card must be treated respectfully by every partner. The way of handling your own and the ones that you receive from others is an indication of discipline, mannerism, and sentiment. Foreign counterparts should be ready with clean business cards of good condition that speak of the business and the person himself. Cards must be presented and received holding with their edges and not covering the print with fingers, facing the print to the receiver, and with a slight bow. While presenting and receiving a business card, the words "*Yoroshiku onegaishimasu*" are said to mean "please take care of me." After receiving a business card, a moment should be spent to read it with pleasure. Business cards should not be bent or inserted in the back pocket or wallet. The cards must be placed on the table in front of you during the meeting. And business card should not be used as a note pad to write on it. Simply, the business card also deserves the same respect that the counterpart deserves.

Prior to starting business meeting, a little socialization takes place for a while for warming up as a prerequisite for the meeting. Seating arrangement is made by the host according to the seniority of the members. The guests are offered a nearby seat to the host. In the event of no guidance to seating, it is appropriate to be seated closest to the entrance or furthest to the host to demonstrate humbleness. When large teams participate, each team sits facing the other across the table with the highest-ranking people sitting farthest from the entrance. Usually, brief welcome speech is delivered by the host at the beginning and tea may be served during the meeting. Refraining from drinking tea indicates disinterest in the meeting and disrespect for the host. When drinks are not served by hospitality personnel, you should wait until your neighbor fills your cup and in turn you should offer the same service to your neighbor next in the line and wait until the host starts drinking. In most cases Japanese style teas (Ocha) are offered instead of English style black tea.[38]

In Japan, it is extremely rude to use mobile phones during a business meeting. All mobile phones or any other electronic devices must be switched off or put on silent mode. It is common for there to be periods of silence during the meeting. Urge to break silence exhibits impatience; so it is regarded as interruption. Slow speaking, pausing between points, and allowing the Japanese counterpart to respond are some of the important manners at meetings. Japanese are fond of drawing, diagrams, and flowchart in explaining matters. Therefore, it is always useful to be ready with PowerPoint, Whiteboard, or printed materials of the presentation. Throughout the meeting, attention should be expressed by nodding the head. Usually, it takes long time for negotiation and arriving at consensus. The longer the meeting the more hopeful is the business deal. Therefore, patience is critical during negotiations (Capture 16.6).

In Japanese businesses culture, consensus is referred to as "*Nemawashi*"—the way to arrive at decisions. The literal meaning of "*Nemawashi*" is going around the roots of a plant by a gardener to dig it for replanting elsewhere. Business decisions are considered as the sum of all opinions and contribution of all. A business leader is not

Capture 16.6 Authentic food (Japan) (Photo Credit: Royalty free iStock Photo)

authoritative but facilitative of building consensus while maintaining group harmony. The decision-making thus is not an act of the leader but a process of bringing ideas together. This is called "*Matomeru*" in Japanese. Managerial hierarchy plays an important role in the process of "*Matomeru.*" Feedback and consensus of higher-ranked members are regarded important before announcement of the decision. In solving an issue, specific steps have to be followed rather than trying to solve it individually. The problem-solving process is often referred to as "*Horenso*"—an acronym of *Ho-koku* (report), *Ren-raku* (contact), and *So-dan* (consult). This concept guides employees to first report the problem to their superior who then contacts their boss to find a solution, and then the boss consults the subordinate with a solution.

In Japanese business culture, group is of prime importance and individuals in the group are only representatives of that group. This is derived from the collectivist principle of the Japanese society. Also, this collectivist mentality is based on a hierarchical structure that clearly defines the role of individuals and their relationship to the group. Thus, the group strives to achieve group goals with individual contribution to the best possible level. Harmonious relationship and respect for the hierarchy is indispensable. All accomplishments are considered by individuals as a group effort. Individuals are appreciated but not rewarded by a company.

Employment is generally lifetime and thus, loyalty and commitment to the company are very high among the employees. While the groups in an organization are harmonious, they also maintain light-hearted competitiveness among them. The training given since pre-school on competitiveness is later practiced at corporate level. This attitude is expected in business to perform tasks better than the competitors. The refinement, precision, continuous improvement (*Kaizen*), and perfection in artisanship (*Monozukuri*) in production, services, and presentation have been yielded to the notion of group competition.

Relationship is the foundation of Japanese business culture. For business success, it is believed that lasting cooperation, partnership, and relationship are essential. Therefore, when building a relationship, the Japanese counterpart wishes to know a great deal about the foreign partner and ask varied questions which may even be irrelevant to the business topic. Hobbies, foods, travels, liquor, and women, can be the topics of small talk. Socializing is also an important event after a business meeting. Socialization takes place at restaurants with dinners and drinks.

Socialization event takes a long time. Foreign partner is expected to eat and drink as much as possible. The greater the eating and drinking capability, the more reflective will be the masculinity. The maleness of a person (of a man or a woman) is highly appreciated in Japanese business culture. At a drink, many things are communicated. Thus, the drinking event is referred to as "*Nominication*" combining the Japanese word *Nomi* (drink) and English word "communication."

In a "*Kaisha*" (company), mutual consultancy and dependency are maintained. And strong relationship is maintained among colleagues and, in particular, among the senior members (veterans). This helps ease the "*Nemawashi*"—the Japanese style team decision-making process. Teamwork is regarded important for group harmony and quality improvement. Consideration is an essential mark of relationship and thus, bringing back "*Omiyage*" (souvenir) after making a trip is a habit. Failing to do so is seen as inconsiderate. Business relationships and personal relationships are not expected to conflict and thus, they are distinctive. Nepotism and favoritism are absent in business and thus, special privileges based on personal relationships too are absent. Gift giving is an important aspect of Japanese culture and of the business culture too. A gift like authentic food or handcraft from the home country with cultural value will be an important gift for the Japanese partner. Merchandize item of your company generally bears negative impression as it is considered a promotional item. The gift must be properly and professionally wrapped. The humble gesture of giving gift with both hands and with a slight bow are considered more valuable than the gift itself.

In place of a signature, "*Hanko*" (personal stamp) and "*Jitsu-in*" (registered seal) are used in Japan. Therefore, when signing documents or agreements, it is important even for the foreign partners to use registered seal to stamp them. There are cases that such a seal is required instead of a signature. Deadlines are strictly respected by the Japanese companies. Therefore, the foreign partners must place prime importance on meeting schedules and delivery on time to satisfy the Japanese counterpart. Foreign languages are not used in business and thus, service of an interpreter has to be obtained by either party. In Japanese "*Kaisha*," employee will not leave the workplace right after one's work is over but other colleagues are still working. Attending early and leaving late is a profound custom of Japanese workers. Working long hours without over-time payments is common in Japanese company. There are public holidays, counting to at least one in almost every month, and long festive seasons such as "*Bon*" and new year in Japan. The festive seasons should better be avoided by foreign business men in planning business visits because whole industry goes into a long sleep during vacation.

Japanese people avoid directly delivering refusals and negative responses. They often give vague responses to what they really do not agree or dislike. Sometimes, they response affirmatively to almost everything even if they do not really agree with. This is purposefully done for maintaining harmony with the partners. A foreigner may tend to misunderstand what the Japanese counterpart actually meant. Therefore, communication with Japanese requires special skill and attention to understand their body language. Also, a foreign business partner, without hastily concluding, will have to wait sometime until the Japanese counterpart confirms the final decisions. Long lasting silence or a chat of unrelated matters after the business meeting indicate that no further interest on the business matter prevails. An attempt to derive direct response from Japanese is seen offensive and rude.

Business attire for men is a suit in black, blue, or grey color preferably with a white long-sleeved shirt with a suitable pair of shoes and a neck tie. Women should dress in neutral colored business suit with the option of skirt or a pair of trousers. Tight-fit or sleeveless dresses are considered inappropriate for business. Shoes must be closed-toed with clean socks without holes in them. Easy-to-remove shoes are preferred because shoes are changed quite often in Japan depending on the premises entered. Tattoos, fancy haircut, and colored hair are considered disgrace at business meetings. Decent and appropriate handbags of both male and female, neat files and documents, and negotiation mannerism are also gestures of professionalism. Giving into every demand that is prompted by the Japanese counterpart is seen as a weak point. Instead, strong negotiation skills and cognition are appreciated as strong business skills.

Japanese businessmen are not concerned with short-term profits. The sustenance and the long-term profit are quite often speculated by the Japanese firms. Administrators and employees also sometimes own the company by way of shareholding. Retained earnings are often reinvested seeking growth of the company and sufficient protection for employees. Members of the director boards are comprised of heads of subsidiaries also. Values adopted by the company encourage long-term strategies and policies. Japanese investors also review a business from a long-term point of view. The short-term hardships are tolerated for the long-term gains. Japanese "*Kaisha*," prefers lifetime employment and thus, the employees are committed to long-term objectives of the firm. Salaries of the Japanese CEOs do not deviate much from the senior colleagues of the company except the allowances for accommodation, entertainment, and traveling. This equality fosters group sentiment among the co-workers and thus, they gratefully recognize their company as "*Uchi-no Kaisha*"—my home company.

Japanese are considered as tough negotiators. The Westerners call them "the knights of the round table." Japanese do not hurry to conclude deals without sufficient negotiations. Negotiations are normally slow and it takes long time to arrive at conclusions. Negotiations normally begin with the lower-level managers and then proceed to the high level for final negotiation and approval. Japanese often divide their members into a few groups in the process of negotiation. Interestingly, no single person holds responsibility of the overall process of negotiation. Opinions of all the groups are taken into consideration when arriving at final decision. All members contribute to decisions and agreements. Japanese businessmen are not bound by deadlines in negotiations and they take time until the most beneficial terms are being agreed. This process helps develop private relationships, trust, and understanding also. Because business is regarded as a set of reliable and mutual human relationships, mutual trust plays a critical role in establishment of business relationships.

Japanese businessmen highly value the "face" and thus, they do not like to resort to conflicts. Therefore, they communicate in an indirect manner to avoid bad temper. Once Japanese agree to a proposal and make their decision, it would be very difficult to change it. The top management alone would not change already concluded agreement which is an insult to the rest of the participants in the negotiation process. Content of an agreement with Japanese is usually simple because they expect the mutual trust to play integral role in contrast to the written content of an agreement. They sometimes satisfy with even verbal business agreements. For Japanese, a written agreement only serves as a reference when disputes arise. Japanese businessmen do not express their emotions on their faces and are diligent, down-to-earth, but less flexible. They contemplate trusted relationship, and undeceived business commitment from the foreign partner. For this reason, it is quite advantageous to meet Japanese counterparts through an introduction of a trustworthy person to them.

It is also very important for a foreign partner to have an understanding on the Japanese concept of "*Mottai-nai.*" The meaning of "*Mottai-nai*" is wasteful discard. This term is generally used to express alarming concern over unnecessary discarding. To the Japanese, everything is useful and valuable. Thus, they dislike wasting valuable things by individuals, firms, government, and even due to a natural process. Time, wealth, space, land, crop, natural beauty, or any other thing that comes your way without being adequately used by humans is a mark of "*Mottai-nai.*"

Foreign business partners, regardless how wealthy they and their companies are, must make it a point not to exhibit wasteful engagements to the Japanese counterparts. Japanese observe how many "*Mottai-nai*" things are happening around the foreign company. Japanese partners generally dislike lavishness. A foreign partner who is committing "*Mottai-nai*" affairs will not be attractive to the Japanese counterpart. Toyota Motor Corporation, a multi-billion-dollar company, once offered a tea-serving woman the best employee award for saving a few kilograms of tea during the year through sticking to "*Mottai-nai*" practice in tea making! Too much of luxuries, expenses, and waste of resources of the foreign partner will be counterproductive. Missing a chance to win a Japanese partner, on the contrary, is also a "*Mottai-nai*" affair.

Wearing uniform and company logo is an important culture of Japanese business. Company uniform is regarded as not only important for working but also to showcase the belongingness, togetherness, and solidarity among the employees. Uniforms are worn not only by the subordinates or lower ranking employees but equally by the company CEOs and Presidents also. Uniforms indicate equality among the company staff. In fact, responsibilities of the members differ but all are treated with equality and as members of a family. Presidents of companies adopt humble behaviors and thus, they not only mingle with employees but also eat meals served at company cafeteria with them. Employees take pride in wearing company badges on their shirts or suits even outside the company premises. After partnering with Japanese company, the Japanese partner would be happy to see the foreign partner also adopts those same practices.[39]

Employees are treated as lifetime family members in Japanese company. Thus, harmony, respect for seniority, mutual dependency, consultancy in company, and personal affairs are also built during the work life. Employees work not only to earn salary but also uphold the company. During hard times, some employees remain with the company and work even without a salary until the company gets back on track. They contribute to their company as much as they do for their family. They regard the failure of the company as their individual failure and thus, a shame. The company, on the other hand, treats the employees by way of rewarding annual or bi-annual bonus which is a lump sum of big monies. Also, some companies share company ownership with employees which yields dividends to them. Seemingly, the Japanese company is a family like entity engineered to share wealth.[40]

Doing Business in India

India has the most diverse geoclimatic and socio-cultural system. In India, as a whole, more than 1600 languages and dialects are spoken. Among them, 18 languages are widely spoken; including Hindi as the national language. English is prevalently used as the business language in India. Although Indians appreciate punctuality, they are found to be quite less punctual for appointments. In India, time is not quite objectively considered in planning and scheduling of work. Indians regard time as determined by order of other related matters. As a result, appointments, schedules, meetings, plans, and almost everything depends on things that are only remotely related or unrelated. Therefore, making business appointments should be done much in advance. Confirming, reconfirming, and reminding should precede to make a meeting happen[41] (Map 16.3).

Handling of affairs in the government sector is much different compared to the corporate sector. Making and keeping appointments with the government sector is extremely difficult. There is a greater likelihood that an appointment can be rescheduled at the last moment. Habitually, it can take long waiting hours before meetings. Therefore, foreign businessmen must be prepared for delays and disappointments. Also, for the foreign counterpart, it is always better to be early for appointments because of hectic road traffic. There is a possibility for another person to peg a casual appointment when the formal appointment is delayed. Finding an address in an Indian city is also very difficult because the numbering of buildings is pretty complicated. This has been aggravated by the frequent renaming of roads, streets, and renumbering of buildings. If Google Maps cannot help you, it is always good to seek someone's help to find places as a precaution against getting lost.

The work-week of India can vary from Monday to Friday or Monday to Saturday with five and a half working days. Work day can start at different hours like 8 a.m., 9 a.m. or 10 a.m. and the work day is 8 hours long. Some organizations are closed for the weekend while some others are closed from Saturday afternoon. The financial year starts in April and

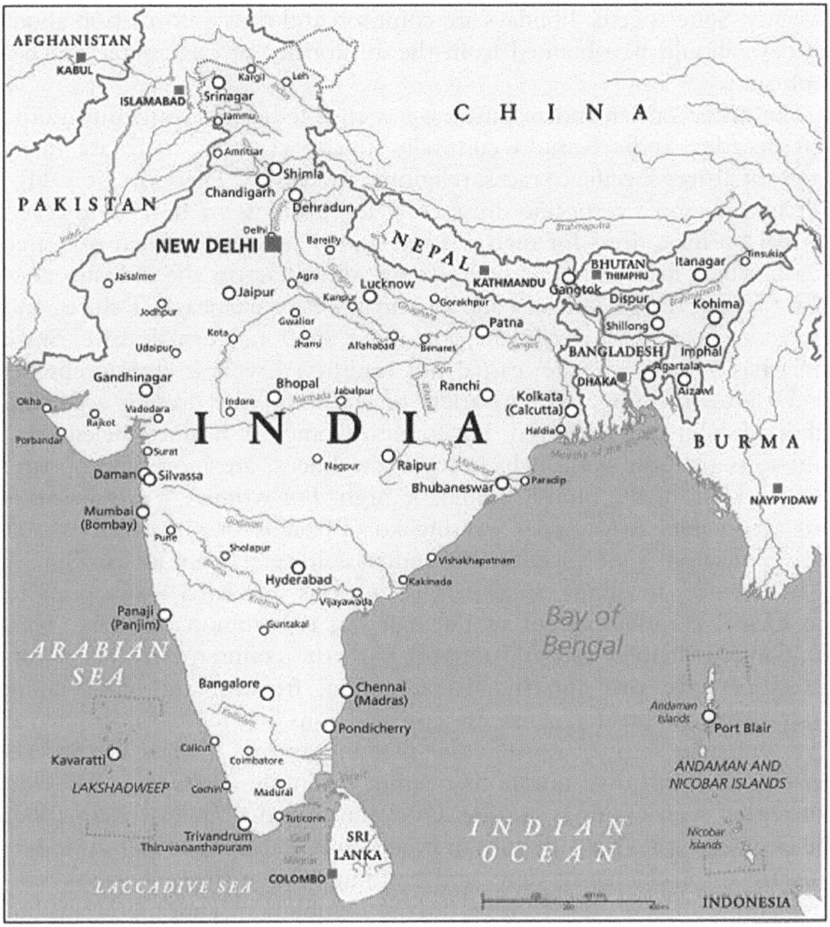

Map 16.3 India (Photo Credit: Royalty free iStock Photo)

ends in the following March. During March, government and the corporate sector organizations are extremely busy with closing of works for the financial year and thus, March is not favorable for business meetings. India has a long list of holidays which are mostly religious. Therefore, a foreigner must be aware of the holidays and ritual periods to avoid meetings. Regional disparity of holidays is present in India due to cultural diversity. State-specific holidays are common and thus, information about holidays should be obtained from the authorities of each state to avoid confusion.

The dress code in Indian business has changed significantly during the past decades. India being a culturally diverse country, there are many different attires specific to races, religions, and castes. Therefore, it is difficult to recognize a specific dress code for business in India. However, normal business dress for men is a suit and tie and for women is a saree or a business dress. Yet, the business suit differs across the industry also. In particular, the IT industry allows casual dresses like jeans, T-shirts, and sneakers while the government offices are strict on formal attire. Since India has a warm climate, casual but traditional wear is also acceptable for business meetings. While variety of colors for the dress is accepted, subdued colors are preferred. For foreign women in business delegation, pant-suits or long skirts, which cover the knees, are more appropriate. The neckline of the blouse should be high. For women, a salwar-suit is also acceptable. A foreigner wearing kurta-pajama or sari or salwar-suit are appreciated as a respect for the Indian culture[42] (Capture 16.7).

In business meetings, small talk on various unrelated issues prior to the formal commencement of the meeting is common in India. This, of course, is helpful to build rapport with the counterparts. The Westerners perceive that the Indians are open, friendly, and maintaining lesser sense of privacy. Business conversations, therefore, can start at even informal settings outside the meeting room. Indians usually ask personal and intrusive questions relating to family affairs also. They do not regard such inquiries as rude. Questions asked from an Indian about the family is treated as a gesture of friendliness. Business conversation sets a forum for exchange of views and building relationships. Western businesspeople observe that Indians heavily compliment and appreciate but seldom convey their disagreement in a direct manner. Direct expression of disagreement is interpreted as a sign of aggression to unfamiliar members of delegation. Disagreements are directly conveyed to those with whom a trusted relationship is already built. Mostly, disagreements are kept from being directly expressed and letting the other party realize it later.[43]

The welcome topics or small talk before starting business meetings include politics, cricket, movies, history, traditions, culture, and economic policies. Knowledge of some of these topics would be advantageous to foreign business counterparts in building relationship and gaining acceptance from the Indian party. Knowledge of personalities like Gandhi,

Capture 16.7 Meeting and greeting (India) (Photo Credit: Royalty free iStock Photo)

Nehru, film stars, musicians, and cricketers could amaze the Indian business counterparts. India has many regional political and social problems and thus, it is better to avoid expressing views on them if not known much. There can be members in the business meeting who come from the troubled regions who bear their own conflicting views to that of yours. In India, caste is a pivotal component of the social system. Therefore, it is advisable not to talk in favor or against any caste. The religious practices and diversity should not be compared but should be enthusiastically viewed without any bias to specific religion.

Indians are highly sensitive to regional political issues. India has its own stance on the geopolitics of the neighboring countries such as Pakistan, Afghanistan, Bangladesh, and Sri Lanka. Therefore, many Indians are biased and emotional on geopolitical issues. Thus, the counter arguments or views of the foreign party may be viewed as offensive to the national interest of India. So, the foreign business counterpart should take extra care to steer off such issues. Topics on inequity of income distribution and poverty are sensitive topics to Indians. The foreigners discussing on

India's poverty and social disparity can drive the Indians mad as they believe such conversations are impolite and will damage the country's good name. Indians have strong sentimental and spiritual bond to their motherland, Bharat, and thus they seek compliments from foreigners.[44]

Gift giving also takes place in Indian business meetings. Too expensive and too large gifts should be avoided as the receiver gets embarrassed. The gifts wrapped with black or white should be avoided as those colors are considered inauspicious. Indians do not open gifts in front of the giver. Yet, they want the foreigner to open the gifts received from the Indian counterpart. The enjoy hearing the admiration on the choice of the gift. Upon invitation to an Indian's home for dinner, taking a gift is acceptable and appreciated. When choosing a gift, being considerate of children and religion will be worthy. During festive seasons, gifting box of sweets will be admired. Indians believe numbers 11, 51, 101, and 501 are lucky and auspicious. When giving gifts, knowledge of these numbers would be helpful to a foreigner.

Authentic products, a photograph of the past memory with the Indian counterpart, would make it an important gift. When considering flowers as a gift, religious concerns connecting to flower must be considered because some flowers have religious connotations and are offered to gods, deities, and temples only. Thus, roses would be a safer choice among flowers. Alcohol is not much accepted in India. But those who appreciate liquor gifts would love to have branded liquor as a gift. Giving leather items as gifts needs precaution as India is rich in vegetarians and vegans and thus, they would not appreciate goods made out of animal skin. Giving gifts by men to women is viewed inappropriate. Yet, giving gifts to women delegates at a business meeting is not inappropriate. However, it is acceptable for a man to accept a gift from women.

Indian businesses are led by a few ethnic communities such as Parsi, Marwari, Gujarati, and Chettyar. Also, most of the businesses are operated as family businesses. While these businesses operate as modern firms, they are mostly governed according to certain cultural norms pertaining to the relevant communities. Thus, it will be an advantage for the foreign partners to have an understanding of the specific cultural practices of those communities. On the other hand, the public sector companies are much different from the private corporate sector because of their structured bureaucratic and hierarchical order. Yet, the modern ICT industry is more egalitarian and flexible than the two types mentioned above. Therefore, it is much easier for the foreign counterparts to deal with the liberal modern sector.[45]

Business etiquette differs regionally in India. The southern Indian companies are more conservative than those of the northern and the western part of India. In all parts of India, exchanging business cards is a common practice. Plenty of business cards will be necessary as business cards are exchanged even in non-business contexts also. When addressing the members of the Indian team, appropriate titles must be used with their last names. As English is mostly used in business meetings, it is not necessary to make the business cards translated into Indian languages. An interpreter would be needed only when the foreign counterpart does not speak English. Business brochures and promotional materials prepared in English can be used at the business meeting without hesitation. However, heavy accent and localized English terms are quite present in conversations which the foreigners find difficult to understand. It is not a mark of discourtesy if you ask to repeat what you did not understand.

Relationships are often built casually but they develop into trusted relationships rapidly with business transactions. India is a nation where innumerable business opportunities are present as the country has entered the rapid development phase. Also, tremendous disparities in the social sphere are a wealthy source of business opportunities. Therefore, lasting and productive relationship with Indian counterparts can help penetrate markets through innumerable goods and services. Indian culture is a construct of extended family, religion, caste, and community. Attachments to these social elements is stern and almost every personal activity, including business, is considerably influenced by them. As astrological, religious, and ritual aspect of business cannot be neglected when doing business with Indians, you have to tolerate them regardless how much a nonbeliever you are.

Being a patriarchal society, many businesses in India are organized in the form of family business in which the power vests at the top. In Indian family business, considerable family hierarchy is also maintained in the middle and lower levels of management. The business decision-making, therefore, is not much consultative or a teamwork. The top authority tends to make business decisions with intuition. Therefore, the foreign counterpart must be mindful of this organizational arrangement and should not rely on the lower level of the hierarchy but approach the top level itself. Further, this hierarchical mindset of the Indian business sector should not be ignored or down played by the foreign counterparts but respect this boss-subordinate construct at every level of the organizational structure. Business communication with Indians can be difficult to foreign counterparts as communication is indirect and has multiple interpretations. Body language and the tone of expressions play an important role in communication. Therefore, there is a hazard that foreigners hastily arrive at assumptions and conclusions in their favor which can be erroneous. Therefore, rechecking and reconfirming decisions will be a cautious approach helpful to foreigners[46] (Capture 16.8).

Although India appears as poverty driven misery to the outsiders, the society is highly variant in terms of wealth and attitudes across regions. In particular, the north Indians are flashier and more aggressive than the south Indians. Wealth and status are social and personal symbols of the north Indians. They are shrewd and skillful in business. The personal status of the south Indians is modest, humble, and friendly despite the wealthiness or social class. The eastern and western parts of India have century long profound history of merchandize trade with foreigners. As

Capture 16.8 Meeting with foreign counterparts (India) (Photo Credit: Royalty free iStock Photo)

a result, these coastal regions are more urban, liberal, and less conservative. From north to south, the class-consciousness, aggression, and flashy lifestyle fade away. Western Indians are described as punctual, soft, authority sharing, consultative, teamwork oriented, accountable, independent, taking initiatives, reliable, hardworking, less abstained, peaceful in the teams, honest, and soft spoken.

Bureaucracy prevails not only in the government offices but in the corporate sector also to a significant extent. Delays in processing, overload of paperwork, lack of confidence in the system, and general inefficiency are predominant signs of the bureaucracy in India. While bribery is common, if involved, it can cause damage to your reputation and would lead to legal consequences also. In some instances, certain transactions may not be feasible without bribing. This is an indicator for the foreign counterpart to learn limits to pursue business operations in India. In Indian business meetings, personal and awkward questions might be asked. Escaping from such questions is considered inappropriate. They often cross between business and personal topics during business conversations.

Shake-hand is accepted equally for men and women. Yet, it is more common in India to greet people with "*Namaste*" gesture with a slight frontward bent and the palms pressed together holding slightly below the chin, than offering a shake-hand. Indians use many gestures of body language and thus, the foreign counterparts face difficulties in comprehending the non-verbal communication. In distant communication, telephoning is quite essential to remind to read mail or email sent to Indian counterpart. Some casual media of communication like WhatsApp, SMS, and Viber are also common in business communication in India.

Indians give appointments to business meetings even if they are not interested. But, on a later date, they will cancel the appointment even without giving any reason and merely saying that they are busy. The word "busy" is mostly used to express disinterest. The last-minute cancelation of meetings is not unusual to Indian businessmen. Telephone calling during meetings is also common and thus, it is not regarded as a disrespect if you make a phone call while in a meeting. Because Indian community lives in many countries, a foreign entrepreneur planning to enter agreements with Indian business can meet the Indian community of his country to learn Indian culture, languages, norms, rituals, values, and ethics.

Indian community in those countries also holds annual cultural festivals. Cultural festivals are a good opportunity for a foreign entrepreneur to learn about the values, ethics, culture, food, products, and dresses. In India, guests are treated with respect and courtesy. Business entertainment is usually organized outside home. But there are occasions that you are invited to residences also. In case if the foreigner is inviting Indian counterpart, it is necessary to make sure whether there are vegetarians in the team. The nonvegetarian foreigners to consider offering vegetarian food to Indian counterpart will be a respectful gesture.[47]

Indian business culture is often comprised of the characteristics of delays, inefficiencies, subtleties, carelessness, casualness, and ignorance. This will bring disappointment and frustration to foreign counterparts initially. Feedback from meetings will often drag for a long time. Rigid organizational hierarchies and excessive management layers often limit exchange of views and open discussions. The Indian counterpart quite often maintains silence at times when opinions or critiques are invited over the table. Therefore, the foreign counterpart should be patient and prepared to understand the importance of hierarchy when dealing with Indian counterpart. If the CEO offers his personal telephone number, that is a clear sign of his further interest in close contact with you (Capture 16.9).

Personal relationships are very important in doing business in India. Therefore, follow-up visits and sending business delegation comprising of senior members are equally important to showcase commitment to doing business in India. This has indirect bearing that foreign CEO is sensitive to Indian culture which is pivotal for sustaining long-term relationship. Endurance of the foreign partner will be rewarded as it is a sign of understanding of Indian business culture. Being over-joyed at finalizing a business deal is not positively received by the Indian counterpart because such behavior indicates the success of the foreign counterpart which runs against the interests of the Indian counterpart.

Indian business community often looks to seize long-term success of partnering. Indians are clever bargainers also. They learn from their childhood how to bargain and select the right price for the right good. Therefore, the foreign counterpart must be aware of the bargaining skills of Indians to strike off a deal at the appropriate point of negotiation. It will be advantageous to foreigners if they could convince the Indian counterpart that the business relationship is long-term and it has prospects of wide scope. If Indian partner is taking much time and beating around the

Capture 16.9 Staff group photo (India) (Photo Credit: Royalty free iStock Photo)

bush rather than heading to the point of discussion, the foreign partner should be patient to understand the intention of such behavior. Hurrying or tempting to aggressively reach conclusion will be risky.

Pricing strategy in India has to be decided carefully without duplicating your home country pricing policies as most Indian customers have less capacity to pay. Appropriate pricing policy will help reach the mass market of India. Product policy also has to be designated to the Indian market rather than trying to sell the home country products in the Indian market. Indians are considered to be extremely value-conscious and thus, the foreign partner will be pressurized in terms of pricing. Global approach of marketing has mostly failed in India and thus, localization of products will bring business success. Although India appears to be an enormous market, it of course is a complex of small market segments comprised of cultural, ethnic, religious, geographic, and linguistic groups which require personalized product and marketing approach to each.[48]

Doing Business in the Arab World

Arabian countries began to prosper after the Organization of Petroleum Exporting Countries (OPEC) took initiatives to manipulate petroleum prices in the early 1970s. The wealth yielded to price manipulation was invested in business and infrastructure development and hence the Arabs rose from the sand to become a significant business destination before long. In particular, United Arab Emirates (UAE) emerged as a duty-free trading hub and an exciting tour destination (Map 16.4).

International business community found enormous opportunities in trade, travel, aviation, petroleum, construction, hospitality, and more in the region as a new destination to commence business operations. UAE became an international business hub before long with a significant foreign participation. In consequence, and as a long-term practice, a large portion of businesses in Arab is owned or operated by foreigners. And the workforce of Arab also consists of a large number of expatriates from around the world.

Though culturally monotonous, Arabian corporate and business culture is highly diverse due to entrepreneurs, CEOs, managers, and employees from around the world. Although the diversity in the corporate culture is advantageous, it poses challenges for business creation and operations also. Taboos, rituals, beliefs, values, ethics, attires, food, languages, body language, group behavior, group attitude, group responses, intercultural behaviors, intra-cultural behaviors, and many more make up the workforce and business landscape of Arab. It is learned that significant insight into cultural differences among employees help managers conduct business operations effectively. Business meetings are very challenging in Arab because an Arabian business delegation can comprise not only Arabs but foreigners also. In Arab a business meeting is mostly a cross-cultural meeting![49]

The Arabs often prefer face-to-face discussions to distance modes to get familiar with the counterparts. Communication is an important strategy in Arab for developing business relationships. Arab culture values group relationship. So, the Arabian managers prefer participative and consultative decision-making mechanisms. Frequent and face-to-face meetings are preferred for sharing and integrating ideas. They place much importance to building personal relationships in business meetings. In Arab, communication is seen indirect. Interruptions and annoyance of external environment are not regarded as disturbances and meetings

Map 16.4 Arab world (Photo Credit: Royalty free iStock Photo)

normally take place amidst such interruptions. Contained and non-verbal communication is common in Arabian business meetings but certain clues are gathered during meetings from its context. Often, the outcome of a business meeting is less predictable.

Arab's communalist and collectivist culture places much focus on relationships and intense loyalties. This provides opportunities for an entrepreneur to lay foundation for steady and long-lasting business relationships. Such relationships and loyalties sometimes overlap corporate bureaucracy. The Arabs equally rely on both formal and informal rules and procedures. The making of such procedures and practices are mostly subjected to the religious hegemony of Saudi Arabia. In the Arab culture, business meetings normally adhere to formalities but with less focus on linearity in decision-making; Arabs adopt circular and non-linear approach to reasoning[50] (Capture 16.10).

Arabian businessmen accept shake-hand and hugs. Prior to taking business matters, small talk is initiated on health of the participants and their families. Usually, tea is offered at the beginning of conversations. This first engagement takes much time in enjoying refreshment and talking about family wellbeing prior to penetrating into the core of the business talk. It is common to the Arabs not to directly step on to the task at hand but to loop around it. The warm-up social talk serves as an opening to enter into

Capture 16.10 Meeting and greeting (Arab) (Photo Credit: Royalty free iStock Photo)

the business matters. The Arabs do not consider spending time on social talks as a waste of time. Foreigners usually start to dislike this practice and then get frustrated and impatient as they believe time is scarce and ineffective use of time as a waste. For Westerners and Japanese, time is a resource that should be preciously used; it is a waste unless used thriftily.

Arabs consider building relationship is more than a matter of task and time. For them, time is abundant and flexible. The Western norm of punctuality and deadlines are not cared for in Arab. Waiting a long time for a scheduled meeting is common and thus, a foreigner must bear with it until the meeting is started. It is observed from the behavior of Arabs that there is no concept of time in the Middle East. Time for the Arabs is an open-ended flow having no strict starting or closing time. Meeting space is less defined and thus, open spaces are also chosen for meetings. During meetings, Arabs engage in personal chitchat with the members next to them. While this behavior is ridiculed by the Westerners, the Arabs primarily focus on interpersonal relationships and loyalty at business meetings. The Arab culture is highly patriarchal and thus, almost all business delegations are comprised of males.[51]

The business culture of Arab is a sub-culture of Islam and it gives prominence to family and hospitality. Organizational hierarchy is more vertical than horizontal with paternalistic relationship with subordinates. Higher management seeks inputs from stakeholders for the decision-making and they pass decisions downward along the hierarchy for implementation. Trustworthy relationships are sought by the Arabs at the expense of much time. As the family attachment is strong, the Arab businessmen rarely maintain clear distinction between business and family life. Oral and face-to-face discussions take the major form of business communication. Appointments are not fixed by secretaries but by the business leaders themselves. Normally, appointments are fixed two weeks prior to the meeting and usually confirmation is required a few days in advance. Business meetings are conceivable through a mutual contact (Capture 16.11).

In Arab, big businessmen declare "*Majlis*" meeting week which does not require prior appointments to meeting. For a foreign businessman, "*Majlis*" is much suitable to meet Arab businessmen and build contacts. Business contacts can also be created through Overseas Market Introduction Service (OMIS) and trade shows. The foreign counterpart should arrive on time for meetings and wait until he is invited to the meeting place/room. Friday is holiday in Arab and working hours of the private

Capture 16.11 A business deal (Arab) (Photo Credit: Royalty free iStock Photo)

sector is from Sunday through Thursday from 9 a.m. to 5 p.m. However, the public sector operates from Sunday through Thursday from 7:30 a.m. to 2:30 p.m. The Arabs worship five times a day at varying times every day. Thus, meetings are necessarily adjusted in accordance with prayer times. The weekend in Arab is Friday through Saturday.[52]

Arabic greetings at meetings go as "*Essalamu aleikum*" (may peace be with you). The re-greeting follows as "*wa aleikum essalam*" (and with you, peace). During Ramadan festive season, one greets by saying "*Ramadan Kareem*" (noble Ramadan) or "*Ramadan Mubarak*" (blessed Ramadan). However, foreigners may be greeted according to English custom. Shoes are supposed to be removed when entering the meeting room if a rug or a carpet is laid. Greeting takes place according to seniority of the members in the team with greeting of the senior most member first. Arabs shake hands for several minutes when greeting and thus, withdrawal of the hand abruptly is thought to be rude. In case of greeting a woman, the man only shakes hand if the woman offers her hand first. If not, shake-hand is not followed by greeting. In Arab, prolonged attention toward a female associate is regarded as indiscipline. In UAE, woman does not first offer hand but when a man offers, she accepts it as a gesture of greeting. As it is the case with European custom, right hand is offered always. Arabs like calling by first name followed by "*Sayed*" (Mr.) or "*Sayeda*" (Ms.).[53]

While gifts are not a custom, if received, Arabs appreciate it as a token of thoughtfulness. Gifts are exchanged with the right hand. The Arabs do not open gifts in public. When selecting a gift for an Arab business counterpart, gold jewelry, liquor, alcohol-based perfumes, pig leather goods, knives, objects representing dogs should be avoided. Upon receiving a gift, appreciation must be generously extended. Foreign delegates must avoid wearing Emiratis dresses and instead men and women should be dressed with decent business attire.

Business cards are a must and they must be on white surface with one side printed in English and preferably the other in Arabic. Instead of having both languages printed on one card, it is also acceptable to exchange business cards printed in each language. The business logo should appear on the top right-hand side of the card. Arabic language is read from right to left and thus, the Arab's eye is trained to read from the right most end. Business matters discussed at a meeting are followed by talking a bit about yourself, weather, and commuting. Foreign partners should inculcate patience and let relationship gradually build over a few rounds of meetings.

When presenting your case, you should focus the "*Sheikh*" (the decision leader) throughout your presentation. Private meetings are rare in the Arab culture. Because decision-making is a long process, any pressure from the foreign counterpart is viewed negatively. It is offensive to abruptly reject offers. Making telephone calls during a meeting is considered rude. Opinions on regional and religious conflicts, and monarchical issues are counterproductive. While in a meeting, crossing your legs one over another and showing the thumbs up gesture are unacceptable and offensive.[54]

It is always good for the foreign counterpart to wait rather than rushing for it until the Arab counterpart abides by the agreement. As communication is often indirect and exaggerations are too common, the foreign counterpart need not arrive at quick conclusions. Business meeting often takes place at cafes, restaurants, or hotels. Arabs are considerate and hospitable. So, they invite you to refreshments and meals at restaurants and would offer gifts. At a later time, treating them the same way is helpful to strengthen relationship.

Awareness of the right days and times for meetings is important when doing business in the Middle East. There are many religious holidays and festive periods during when the businesses are inoperative. Friday and Saturday should be avoided in contemplating business meetings because, in Arab, these two days are weekends. While all the Middle Eastern countries follow the Gregorian calendar, there are refinements included according to the Islamic lunar calendar for religious events. As holy activities follow the lunar movements, holidays and holy-times are different from one country to another in the region due to the time difference. Therefore, it is essential to update the personal calendar every time to ensure that you will not miss appointments. Arab is not only inhabited by the Muslims but by the Christian minorities also. In a country like Jordan, in addition to Islamic holidays, some Christian holidays are also in effect.

Telephone calls, fax, messages, and e-mails do not work much in business communication in Arab. Therefore, at any cost, the foreigners must prepare for face-to-face meetings. The Arabs place personal contact high because, for them, there is only a slight distinction between personal and business relationships. Doing business with a physically unseen party is generally avoided by the Arabs. Therefore, it is pivotal to arrange face-to-face meetings. The official language in the Middle East is Arabic. Yet, in a region like United Arab Emirates where the majority of the business people are expatriates, English is the business language (Capture 16.12).

Because the Arabs highly regard their mother tongue, it will be useful to have learned at least a few words of Arabic to bestow an impression on the Arab counterpart. If you are prepared to conduct business meetings in Arabic using an interpreter, the Arabs get impressed by your thoughtfulness of the language. Following expressions in Arabic would be very useful for the foreigner to have learned before meetings: "*Essalaam alaikum*" (Peace be upon you), "*Wa elaikum assalaam*" (And peace be upon you too), "*Marhaba*" (Hello), "*Shukran*" (Thank you), "*Keif al-haal?*" (How are you?), "*Al-hamdulillah*" (Thanks be to God), "*Min fadlak*" (Please - to a male), "*Min fadlik*" (Please - to a female), "*Insha-allah*" (with God's wish) "*Ma As-salama*" (goodbye).

Arabs do not have much distinction between family and business and thus prefer to look to you more as a friend than a business guest. So, they like to know the personal background of a foreigner at a meeting before initiating business talks. Questions about health, family details, home, and travel will be the first in the list that the Arabs would ask. They too like

Capture 16.12 A business deal (Arab) (Photo Credit: Royalty free iStock Photo)

the foreigner also to ask similar questions from them to get to trace each other's compatibility. However, sensitive and too many questions about the female members of the family would be not welcomed by Arabs.[55]

Introduction to or a connection with a highest-ranking person in a company is a prerequisite to establish contact with a company. Contacts can be established through a contact-sponsor or an intermediary to introduce you to the person you wish to meet. In the Middle East, this is called "*wasta/wasata*" (connection or clout or nepotism) which is accepted as a good practice. The idea behind this is to bar an unknown person from entering the socio-business system. Therefore, an influential contact is always essential to develop useful relationship.

Punctuality in the Western definition is quite not applicable in Arab. Therefore, you should be like an Arab while in Arab. The Arabs are usually late to meetings not because they are not interested but because they are used to. It is not surprising that they sometimes are a few hours late to meetings. The Arabs check their phones often and communicate with other people during meetings. But if you are really interested in their business, your presence on time and patience are essential. Also, preset agenda does not make much importance in a meeting. Multiple copies of your brochures, business plans, or proposals are essential to be handed over during the meeting because the decision-maker has to go through them at later time. Arab businessmen are identified as more traditional than professional and thus, they tend to engage in hard bargain in concluding deals. Bureaucratic red tapes are common and the negotiation process is slow in the Middle East. As they hardly meet paperwork deadlines, your patience is the most crucial in your business success in Arab.

In broader sense, Arab is a different world in entirety founded by Islamic laws and traditions. Islamic traditions are slightly different from one country to another in this region. Countries like Saudi Arabia and Iran are founded with extreme Islamic laws while the states of UAE and Lebanon are more liberal. Democracy, governance, judicial system, human rights, religious and fundamental rights practiced in the West and elsewhere in the modern world are hardly relevant to the Middle East as the Islamic law is the law of the land in this region. Food, liquor, women, sports, hobbies, rituals, customs, and ethics are heavily interpreted and guided by the Islamic laws. And the punishments connected to breaking laws are severe. The foreigners who are on business visits but unfamiliar with Arab social governance should do some homework to be familiar with the affairs of this region, with their territorial differences also, to avoid unexpected circumstances and to make the stay in Arab comfortable.[56]

Doing Business in the USA

Almost every businessman seeks to enter the USA to exploit not only markets but also technology, business network, business knowledge, management, operational, and prestige. By all means, the USA is the largest market and the world economic power. Doing business in the USA is a matter of pride to foreign entrepreneurs. For these and many other reasons such as political and economic freedom also, the USA has become an attractive business destination. Almost every large foreign corporate is operating a business office in the USA. The heavy presence of US businesses in most of the countries and their management hegemony have largely molded out business culture all over the world. Therefore, what many countries practice today in business is deeply rooted to the influence of US business. Thus, the businessmen around the world are familiar with the US business culture to a great extent. However, still, there are peculiarities that the foreign businessmen need to be familiar with when considering doing business in the USA[57] (Map 16.5).

Business meetings, in the USA, are punctual and the foreign participants must also be punctual. Lateness is an indicator of unprofessionalism and insult. A little early to meetings is accepted but very early to meetings is considered a poor habit. If a foreigner has much time before the meeting, they should better engage in some other thing and attend the meeting in time. Meetings normally start on time. Delaying the start of a meeting until some participants attend is regarded as an insult to those who are punctual. The person who is hosting and chairing the meeting must never be late. Unlike in many countries, business meetings in the USA can sometimes be casual. Americans create friendly atmosphere at meetings to encourage openness in discussions. Subtle humor plays an important role in developing friendly atmosphere. Yet, the Americans expect to maintain utmost professionalism in business negotiations.

Americans are light-minded and straightforward. They express their views directly and linearly. Business meetings are punctual and accorded with predetermined agenda. Discussions are immediately started without small talk and systematically pushed forward by the chairman. Meetings are often arranged over lunch, brunch, or dinner. Time is treated precious and the participant should be well prepared for the meetings with brochures, fliers, leaflet or documents to economize time. As Americans believe that track records and accomplishments are more important for business deals, it is a good idea to present the business credentials and success story also by the foreign counterpart to convince the viability of proposed business. Americans freely and transparently exchange ideas and opinions on the business deal at the very outset of the meeting. They expect the foreign delegates also to be transparent in negotiations.[58]

Age and seniority are not a priority in American business culture. Priority is given to useful ideas. Thus, anyone in the team is welcomed to present opinions at a meeting. Some big corporates have concerns over the hierarchy of the participants in decision-making, though. Silence during meetings makes American uncomfortable and thus, the participants must be shrewd to momentarily break silence. Disagreements are bluntly expressed and such act is not regarded rude in the USA. Decisions are made quickly and business meetings do not usually take many rounds.

Map 16.5 United States of America (Photo Credit: Royalty free iStock Photo)

Americans are clever and professional negotiators and their convincing power is enormous (Capture 16.13).

Negotiations are supposed to be based on the give-and-take principle. Verbal agreements are arrived at the end of a meeting and conveyed with a firm shake-hand. Yet, the foreign counterpart should not rush to believe it until everything is brought to papers later. If you need further clarification, you can inquire of the decision which is not rude in the USA. Unlike in the East, business cards are not heavily exchanged in the USA before a meeting. But after a meeting, for the purpose of later correspondence, business cards are exchanged without much formality.

Large corporate meetings are more formal and thus wearing business suits by both male and female participants is a norm. However, there can be informal meetings and in informal settings also. Unlike in the far-east, business suit is not a daily attire in the USA. Everyone is addressed by their first name. Nods and bodily expressions are prevalent in discussions.

Capture 16.13 Meeting and greeting (USA) (Photo Credit: Royalty free iStock Photo)

Signs and body language in the USA are different and thus, the participants must be cautious not to understand them in the same way as of their home culture.

Americans always contemplate to cultivate friendly business relationships. Thus, they adopt less formal and casual business environment to make the partners feel comfortable to share their opinions. Although the Americans are warm and welcoming, they do not mix personal affairs with business. Business is seen as a highly professional matter. Therefore, the foreign counterpart should be careful not to ask very personal questions and seek personal information even at a casual setting. Also, it is a good idea for the foreigners not to expose themselves unnecessarily.[59]

Individualist mentality of the employees is largely present in American business. Age, designation, and hierarchy are not as important as individual smartness. American business forgoes group and hierarchy mindset for knowledge culture and individual's work excellence. Loyalty and bond with the workplace are secondary to employee rewards and thus, the worker turnover is high in the US business sector. Managers closely and rigorously monitor employee productivity because American businesses are highly placed on metrics and management science. Thus, the employees are dedicated to individual and group productivity to claim financial rewards for their outstanding performance. It is important to note that the American employees are inspired by short-term benefits also.

The problem-solving culture in the American business is based on individualistic and objective approach. So, the disputes are dealt with privately isolating the problem from persons. The legal aspect of business agreements in the USA needs much attention because contracts are often laden with clauses that can pin liability on the other party. Therefore, the foreign counterpart must take caution not to be trapped into agreements. Many foreign businessmen know by their experience that the US litigation is cumbersome and frustrating. Thus, the agreements must be read with extra care to understand every minor detail also. Service of a legal consultant who is familiar with the US law is of extreme importance for a foreign counterpart. Also, it is a common practice of American companies to resort to lawsuits to settle disputes between partners. Further, it has been often reported that some American firms purposefully enter litigation to financially benefit from the business partners rather than doing truthful business for mutual benefits.

American market is vast and diverse and thus, selling in such a market is difficult without trustworthy sales agents. An affair like after sales service is quite challenging due to vastness of the country. Further, America adopts progressive standards relating not only to final products and services but to raw materials, technology, labor, environment, health, safety, production process also. Rigorous standards imposed by the US industrial culture will be quite challenging for a foreign businessman to enter the US market. This signals that only quality and price competitive products can enter the US market. Foreign businesses that can adapt to these standards can find their ways to the USA. Foreign businessmen may prevent from bribing for favors because the US public sector is perceived to be considerably clean (Capture 16.14).

Capture 16.14 Business card exchange (USA) (Photo Credit: Royalty free iStock Photo)

The way of greeting is a shake-hand indifferently for both male and female. Hugging, long shake-hand, and any other body contacts are avoided by the Americans. A distance about two feet should be maintained between the counterparts. In all circumstances, sitting or standing very closely is found to be uncomfortable for the Americans. Unlike in the East, using both hands when exchanging business cards, gifts, and brochures is not practiced in the USA. One hand is sufficient for the purpose. Also, it is observed that tossing things to another person is not a rude practice in America. The Spanish speaking people tend to use their mother tongue in many occasions where Spanish community is prevalent.[60]

Also, in many cases, some American terms can be confusing as they use slang and phrasal verbs to a great extent. Business card culture is not evolved much in the States and thus, they may not offer their business cards like the Japanese and Chinese do. They even put business cards in their wallet or back pocket of the trousers. If they want you to contact them later, they would offer their cards. The informal approach to most of the things will make the foreigners comfortable in the States. Despite that permission, inquisition of the price or value of one's own effects and sensitive personal matters, and intense comparison of persons should better be avoided when conversing with Americans.

Laughing and speaking with a high tone during meetings are usual among Americans. They not only talk with a sense of humor but welcome your jokes also. Sports make interesting topics to the business executives so that the foreigners may be prepared to toss sports topics also when talking. There are not many holidays in the States except long summer vacation. Saturday and Sunday comprise the weekend and many attend the church for prayers on Sunday. Sunday's breakfast is usually sacrificed to a Brunch (a combined breakfast with lunch). Eating while walking, driving, in casual meetings, and lectures is common. If you are invited to a meal, then you need not pay. But there are cases that you have to pay for your portion of the meal. Giving cash tips to waiters is an accepted practice in the USA. Inviting to one's home is not uncommon in the States. Acceptance or rejection of food and drink is an entire liberty of the guest and rejection of an offer is not regarded as offensive or rude.

Presenting a gift is pleasant but it is not expected. Even in case of presenting a gift, it usually happens at the end of a deal rather than at the first meeting. Gifts are opened publicly and shown to all immediately with much admiration. When visiting a home, it is not expected that you take a gift. However, you may take something like chocolate, flowers, or wine. Americans prefer non-personal gifts to personal gifts, and so, gifts like perfume and clothes must be avoided. Very formal dress and fancy hair styles are inappropriate for a business meeting though nobody gets irritated by them. Nor are the very casual dress and hair styles admired. American executives are opportunistic and willing to take even high risk if the business is a potential money machine. Executives will not hesitate to express their disagreement with you and thus, they do not maintain long silence during meetings to indirectly persuade their disagreement. Important character of American businessmen is that they are persistent, innovative, strategic, open, fast, and policy bound.

American business culture has been heavily influenced by Scientific Management and Entrepreneurship thoughts since early. As a result, US business sentiment is characterized by efficiency orientation and money making. Return On Investment is the fundamental concern of US business. In this context, time is perceived as the most precious resource of a person. Thus, quickness of working, methodical working, and hard-working became prominent characteristics of the US business culture. Age and hierarchical status of a person is less important but talents are more important in this scenario. This attitude is well reflected in US businesses having a large number of young CEOs compared to other countries. Decision-making is a well-defined quick process in the US business. Opportunities are given for everyone who participates in the decision-making process to express opinions regardless of the age or designation. The authority to make the final decision is vested on the person-in-charge of the decision-making team.

Personal relationship is secondary and business relationship is primary in the USA. This means the objectivity of the relationship is more important than subjectivity. Americans are more interested in the partner's project, technology, product quality, materials, cost, price, short, and long-term benefits than lasting personal relationships. They do not mind using email, Skype, video calls, and call conferencing in place of face-to-face meetings. Punctuality is highly respected while tardiness is regarded as disrespect and carelessness[61] (Capture 16.15).

For meetings, the foreigners must take special care in preparing for presentations with documents, evidence, statistics, and examples. If you could not cover everything you wanted in the presentation before the time-out, most probably, you will not get extra time or another opportunity to convey your message because meetings are started and concluded

Capture 16.15 Simple way (USA) (Photo Credit: Royalty free iStock Photo)

according to a schedule. While refreshment can be served after a meeting for socializing, it is very unusual that a meeting precedes to lunch or dinner.

Greeting can include a shake-hand, roughly of two feet distance, with direct eye contact and a smile. Hugging, kissing, patting, and touching are inappropriate gestures in the USA. Giving gift is not bad but the foreign partner must be aware of anti-bribery policies of the US counterpart. Even paying for your partner's meal may have bad consequences sometimes. Dress code is not static but senior executives in large companies usually wear business suit but this practice depends on the nature of the business and the duty of the employee. In IT companies, casual wear is accepted. However, for a business meeting first time, one should wear smartly. Business cards are rarely used and there is no defined protocol for business card exchange in the USA. So, the partners can exchange them at the beginning or end of a meeting. Presently, the US businessmen search Homepage and LinkedIn profiles of the counterparts and thus, they get to know about the foreign counterpart prior to meeting physically. Therefore, the company presence on the internet or other platforms will be useful for a foreign counterpart.[62]

Doing Business in Europe

Portuguese, Spanish, Dutch, French, and English were major international traders, voyagers, and conquerors across the seven seas since the sixteenth century. They initiated with trading and then moved to colonization, agriculture, and industry by the turn of the twentieth century. Most of the independent countries at present were colonies of the Europeans for a few centuries in the past. This was more than sufficient to instill European business culture in those former colonies. And hence, center–peripheral economic and political relationships prevail between the former European masters and the colonies. This legacy has left business links with the masters in plantations, mines, and industrial activities; some of which are still owned by the European masters[63] (Map 16.6).

The familiarity of languages, shared cultural values, and understanding between the former colony and the masters are beneficial for doing business between them at present. Therefore, the business dress, board meetings, decision-making process, organizational hierarchy setting, management practices, leadership, and problem-solving in most of these former colonies are very much of European style. Thus, the most foreign entrepreneurs from South America, Africa, and Asia find it easier to do business with the European countries[64] (Capture 16.16).

Europe is a large landmass that hosts more than two dozen of countries. While English is commonly spoken in business affairs, except in the UK, the other nations speak their own languages; German, French, Spanish, and several others. As these countries are non-native English speakers, foreign counterparts can easily communicate with them as they all speak international English; a simple language without phrasal verbs, idioms, and slang. Therefore, interpreter service is not much needed for business meetings with the European business partners.

During business meetings you should directly look into the eyes of the business partner; failure can be marked as lack of respect. Warm-up small talk would be useful at the beginning of a meeting to get to know each other. The topics on travel, nature and sightseeing, sports, and national events will be appropriate for the occasion. Topics of monarchies, politics, disputes, and the colonial rule seem negative. Special care should be taken

Map 16.6 Europe (Photo Credit: Royalty free iStock Photo)

when making humor as cultural differences may sometimes misinterpret meanings. It should not be forgotten that the European continent crams diverse cultures.

Business card is exchanged in Europe though it is not as prominent as in the Far-East. Business cards printed in English may be sufficient in most occasions. As the business card exchange culture is not so strict, cards can be exchanged at the beginning or at the end of a meeting. Some knowledge of Spanish, French, and German expressions would be useful to showcase your general knowledge. They are prominent languages in continental Europe. Business suit has to be almost always formal for both male and female with decent and dignified dress. The European cultures

Capture 16.16 Meeting and greeting (Europe) (Photo Credit: Royalty free iStock Photo)

respect personal freedom but they are not as much liberal as that of the USA (Capture 16.17).

Therefore, personal matters, jokes, informality, and certain humor can sometimes be costly to the foreign partners. Use of even academic titles before someone's name is common in Europe. In addition to titles such as Mr., Mrs., and Ms., academic titles such as Doctor, Professor are also commonly used. Keeping at least 2 feet distance between the counterparts is appropriate when greetings take place. Shake-hand is common in the European continent but hugging and kissing are also prevalent in a country like France. Therefore, the foreign counterparts must have a sense of appropriate greetings accepted in different countries in Europe. Overall, it is a polite practice that a man waits until a woman initiates a shake-hand.[65]

Some European nations wish to keep business and socialization separate. Business meetings are arranged in meeting rooms and socialization events are arranged after business meetings at different places. Serving

Capture 16.17 Business card exchange (Europe) (Photo Credit: Royalty free iStock Photo)

refreshments is found to be inappropriate by the British and Scandinavian negotiators during the meeting. Yet, the French like negotiation and socialization to happen at the same time. Negotiations over lunch or dinner is not a matter to be amazed at in France. The French likes to arrange business meetings at decent restaurants or hotels rather than in meeting rooms for the purpose of socialization also. The French, Spanish, Italian, and Greeks are less strict on schedules and thus, the meetings can drag after schedule. But the Britons, Germans, and Scandinavians are rather strict on schedules. These differences make some complications but the foreign counterparts must be familiar with the cultural differences when trying to strike off a business deal with each country.[66]

Bargaining is a practice in all European cultures. It should be understood by the foreign counterpart that lengthy bargaining as a good sign of finalizing a business deal. Foreigners should not take a deal for granted for the reason that they are invited for a business meeting. Therefore, impatience and rush will be counterproductive to a business agreement. A few rounds of business trips and deliberations may have to be made to strike off a deal. Some business partners like to engage in long-term business affairs where long-term relationships are also equally important (Capture 16.18).

A sound relationship will be beneficial for engaging with them in future endeavors also. Unlike Americans, Europeans are quite conservative. They are more patient and a lot calmer than the Americans. Thus, respectfulness, patience, and decency of the counterpart is always valued in Europe. Casual behaviors are not appreciated in Europe. They like lengthy and methodical negotiations that aim at weighing all details. The hierarchical foundation of the company is also represented in meetings. Final agreements are mostly made at internal corporate negotiations. Therefore, respectful behavior of the foreign counterpart during and when leaving a meeting will have positive bearing on the outcome on the final decision. It should not be that the European culture is similar to the American culture though the former speaks English at business meetings.[67]

Capture 16.18 Business deal (Europe) (Photo Credit: Royalty free iStock Photo)

Chapter Summary

Entrepreneurship determines wealth of nations and in turn, the wealth of nations showcases strength of their entrepreneurship. The Global Entrepreneurship Index (GEI) establishes strong correlation between per capita income differentials and the entrepreneurship capacity differentials of nations. It concludes that higher entrepreneurship capacity has leverage on higher per capita income. Some countries are highly entrepreneurial while others are moderately or lowly entrepreneurial. This is due to differentials in entrepreneurship capacity building. Culture, values, ethics, political, economic, and legal factors are the determinants of entrepreneurial capacity differentials. Knowledge of comparative entrepreneurial culture is useful for doing business overseas and enhancing entrepreneurial capacities. This chapter explores comparative entrepreneurship practices of major countries and regions that include China, Japan, India, Arab, the USA, and Europe.

Political economic ideology is a determinant factor of ownership of entrepreneurship. Capitalist ideology promotes private entrepreneurship whereas Communist ideology promotes state entrepreneurship. Change in political regimes between these ideologies creates extreme entrepreneurship environments. The political ideologies of South and North Koreas are a case in point where the South promotes pro-private entrepreneurship while the North promotes pro-state entrepreneurship. The Perestroika of the Soviet Union and economic reforms of China helped regain private entrepreneurship in those countries. Western and Far-Eastern cultures have been pro-entrepreneurial for millennia, if not centuries. They value entrepreneurship as an essential social course. South Asian countries, though had been colonized by the Westerners, are still struggling in figuring out an appropriate path of entrepreneurship. African nations have inherited French, English, German, Italian, Portuguese, Spanish, and Arabic entrepreneurial practices through colonialization. South American nations broadly practice European style entrepreneurship inherited from Spain.

Business culture of China, Japan, India, Arab, the USA, and Europe are recognized as major entrepreneurship cultures not only because unique features of their entrepreneurship styles but also for their volume of business in world production and trade. These countries and regions contribute to 70% of the word GDP. While there are some similarities in entrepreneurship practice among these nations, they clearly possess distinctive entrepreneurship cultures. Doing business cross border is a common phenomenon today and thus understanding of business cultures of different nations is pivotal for business success. Entrepreneurship culture is a composite of values, morals, ethics, taboos, rituals, practices, traditions, and beliefs. Foreign business counterparts find it foreign and strange, and challenging when dealing with different entrepreneurship cultures. This chapter elaborates main features of entrepreneurship culture and practice of the said nations highlighting the challenges that foreign business counterparts face. Procedures, norms, and mannerism are explored to find clues that could help in building trustworthy and lasting relationships for the long-term success.

Review Questions

1. "Comparative entrepreneurship advocates understanding of socio-cultural differences and their impacts on the cross-border business." Critically evaluate this statement.
2. Explain why the knowledge of comparative entrepreneurship culture is important for entrepreneurs.
3. What are the unique characteristics of the Chinese business culture with regard to decision-making and trust building between business counterparts?
4. "Familiarity with foods, drinks, attire, gifts, taboos, colors, choice of numbers, and meeting protocols is crucial for foreign entrepreneurs when dealing with Chinese counterparts." Elaborate.
5. Explain the differences, compared to private businesses, that foreign business counterparts should be familiar with when dealing with the Chinese government officials.
6. "Mannerism, values, attitudes, and customs are unique in Japan and thus the foreign business counterparts are required to take extra awareness of them." Describe giving examples and instances.
7. "Business meetings, decision-making, handling of business cards and gifts, socialization, and building trust are highly standardized in the Japanese entrepreneurial culture." Elaborate giving examples.
8. Explain how the ethnic, religious, language, and geographic diversity of India matter to the foreigners dealing with Indian business counterparts.

9. Discuss how foreign business counterparts should handle appointments, business meetings, punctuality, business deliberations, decision-making, and communication in the Indian business culture.
10. Comment on the bureaucracy and bureaucratic practices of India and the feasibility in concluding business deals with Indian government officials.
11. Identify the unique features of the Middle Eastern business culture.
12. Discuss the would be experiences in regard to punctuality, conducting meetings, negotiations, socialization, and trust building with the business counterparts of Arab.
13. "Small talk, humor, openness, friendliness, professionalism, punctuality, and speed of decision-making are major characteristics of the US business culture." Comment.
14. Describe the entrepreneurship culture in Europe taking into consideration the political differences, formality, punctuality, seriousness, language, and geographic diversity.

Additional Readings

1. van Stel, A.J., Carree, M.A., and Thurik, A.R., 2004. *The effect of entrepreneurship on national economic growth: An analysis using the GEM database* (No. 3404). Papers on Entrepreneurship, Growth and Public Policy.
2. https://fortune.com/ranking/global500/.
3. http://thegedi.org/global-entrepreneurship-and-development-index/.
4. Wennekers, S., 2006. *Entrepreneurship at country level: Economic and non-economic determinants* (No. 81).
5. Freytag, A., and Thurik, R., 2007. Entrepreneurship and its determinants in a cross-country setting. *Journal of evolutionary Economics, 17*, pp. 117–131.
6. Thomas, A.S., and Mueller, S.L., 2000. A case for comparative entrepreneurship: Assessing the relevance of culture. *Journal of International Business Studies, 31*, pp. 287–301.
7. Milanović, B., 1989. *Liberalization and entrepreneurship: Dynamics of Reform in Socialism and Capitalism.* ME Sharpe.

8. Freeman, J.R., 1982. State entrepreneurship and dependent development. *American Journal of Political Science*, pp. 90–112.
9. Walker, Francis A., 1888. *The Wages Question: A treatise on Wages and the Wages Class*, London: Macmillan and Co.
10. Morrison, A., 2000. Entrepreneurship: What triggers it? *International Journal of Entrepreneurial Behavior & Research*, *6*(2), pp. 59–71.
11. Elliot, E.A., Abban, R., and Cavazos, C., 2022. Entrepreneurship in a Developing Market: The Role of Socio-cultural and Environmental Hostilities. *Journal of Management Entrepreneurship.*
12. Yu, T.F.L., 1997. *Entrepreneurship and economic development in Hong Kong*. Routledge.
13. Pereira, A., 2007. Attitudes towards entrepreneurship in Singapore: The role of the state in cultural transition. *Asian Journal of Social Science, 35*(3), pp. 321–339.
14. Amponsah, C.T., and Ahmed, G., 2017. Factors affecting entrepreneurship in emerging economies: A case of Dubai. *Journal for International Business and Entrepreneurship Development, 10*(2), pp. 120–137.
15. Coulibaly, S.K., Erbao, C., and Mekongcho, T.M., 2018. Economic globalization, entrepreneurship, and development. *Technological Forecasting and Social Change, 127*, pp. 271–280.
16. Holt, D.H., 1997. A comparative study of values among Chinese and US entrepreneurs: Pragmatic convergence between contrasting cultures. *Journal of business venturing, 12*(6), pp. 483–505.
17. De Bruin, A., 2018. State entrepreneurship. In *Entrepreneurship: New Perspectives in a Global Age* (pp. 148–168). Routledge.
18. Suddle, K., Beugelsdijk, S., and Wennekers, S., 2009. Entrepreneurial culture and its effect on the rate of nascent entrepreneurship. In *Entrepreneurship and culture* (pp. 227–244). Berlin, Heidelberg: Springer Berlin Heidelberg.
19. Hayton, J.C., and Cacciotti, G., 2013. Is there an entrepreneurial culture? A review of empirical research. *Entrepreneurship & Regional Development, 25*(9–10), pp. 708–731.
20. Xin, S.Z., and R. Goodfellow (2005) China Business Culture: Strategies for Success, London: Thorogood Publishing Co.
21. Scott, D.S., 1999. Chinese business etiquette: A guide to protocol.
22. Lee, M., 2007. *How to Outsmart China: The complete guide to successful business in China*. Essex: Hampton Court Holdings Ltd.

23. Chance, G., 2022. *Doing business in China*. London: Routledge.
24. Ahlstrom, D., 2019. Understanding the rise of entrepreneurship in China. *Asia Pacific Journal of Management, 36*(3), pp. 631–657.
25. Baker & McKenzie, 2023. *Doing business in the United Arab Emirates*. Chicago: Baker & McKenzie.
26. Witzel, M., 2016. *Doing business in China*. Routledge.
27. Reuvid, J., and Yong, L. eds., 2006. *Doing business with China*. GMB Publishing Ltd.
28. Moser, M.J., and Yu, F. eds., 2014. *Doing business in China*. Juris Publishing, Inc.
29. Kriz, A., and Keating, B., 2009. Doing Business in China: Tips for an Outsider (Lǎowài).
30. Brahm, L.J., 2011. *Doing business in China: The Sun Tzu way*. Tuttle Publishing.
31. Tsang, E.W., 1998. Can guanxi be a source of sustained competitive advantage for doing business in China? *Academy of Management Perspectives, 12*(2), pp. 64–73.
32. Tsang, E.W., 1998. Can guanxi be a source of sustained competitive advantage for doing business in China? *Academy of Management Perspectives, 12*(2), pp. 64–73.
33. Davies, R.J., and Ikeno, O., 2011. *Japanese mind: Understanding contemporary Japanese culture*. Tuttle Publishing.
34. Feigenbaum, E.A., and Brunner, D.J., 2002. *The Japanese entrepreneur: Making the desert bloom*. Unpublished monograph, Stanford University.
35. Vardaman, J.M., and Vardaman, M., 2011. *Japanese etiquette today: A guide to business & social customs*. Tuttle Publishing.
36. Marriott, H., 1991. Etiquette in intercultural situations: A Japanese business luncheon. *Intercultural communication studies, 1*(1), pp. 69–94.
37. Tung, R.L., 1984. How to negotiate with the Japanese. *California Management Review, 26*(4), pp. 62–77.
38. Oikawa, N., and Tanner Jr, J.F., 1992. The Influence of Japanese Culture on Business Relationships and Negotiations. *Journal of Services Marketing, 6*(3), pp. 67–74.
39. Franklin, S., 2017. Japanese Business Culture: A Study on Foreigner Integration and Social Inclusion.

40. Orru, M., 1996. Practical and theoretical aspects of Japanese business networks. *DE GRUYTER STUDIES IN ORGANIZATION*, pp. 201–230.
41. Agarwal, A.K., 2022. *Doing Business in India: The PESTEL framework*. New York: Springer Link.
42. Shah, N., 2021. *Indian Etiquette: A glimpse into India's culture*. Chennai: Notion Press.
43. Desai, R., 2012. *Indian business culture*. Routledge.
44. Budhwar, P.S., and Varma, A. eds., 2010. *Doing business in India*. Routledge.
45. Gupta, S., and Bhaskar, A.U., 2016. Doing business in India: Cross-cultural issues in managing human resources. *Cross Cultural & Strategic Management, 23*(1), pp. 184–204.
46. Tenhunen, S., and Säävälä, M., 2012. *An introduction to changing India: Culture, politics and development*. Anthem Press.
47. Gesteland, R.R., and Gestel and, M.C., 2010. *India: Cross-cultural business behavior: For business people, expatriates and scholars*. Copenhagen Business School Press DK.
48. Kumar, R., and Sethi, A., 2016. *Doing business in India*. Springer.
49. Baker & McKenzie, 2023. *Doing business in the United Arab Emirates*. Chicago: Baker & McKenzie.
50. Berger, R., Silbiger, A., Herstein, R., and Barnes, B.R., 2015. Analyzing business-to-business relationships in an Arab context. *Journal of World Business, 50*(3), pp. 454–464.
51. Noack, S., 2009. *Business Guide: Doing Business in Dubai & the United Arab Emirates*. BoD–Books on Demand.
52. Baker & McKenzie, 2023. *Doing business in the United Arab Emirates*. Chicago: Baker & McKenzie.
53. Neto, F.M.N.B.D.A., 2021. *The dos and don'ts of doing business in the Middle East: GCC/United Arab Emirates* (Doctoral dissertation).
54. Moore, P.W., 1998. Doing business with the state: Explaining business lobbying in the Arab world.
55. Shoult, A., 2006. *Doing Business with Saudi Arabia*. GMB Publishing Ltd.
56. Gerald, J.O., 1991. Legal aspects of doing business in Kuwait. *Arab Law Quarterly, 6*(4), pp. 322–330.
57. Frankel, T., 2005. *Trust and honesty: America's business culture at a crossroad*. Oxford University Press.

58. Moreno, J., 2003. *Yankee don't go home: Mexican nationalism, American business culture, and the shaping of modern Mexico, 1920–1950*. UNC Press Books.
59. Datesman, M.K., Crandall, J., and Kearny, E.N., 2014. *American ways: An introduction to American culture*. Pearson.
60. Reynolds, P.D., 2007. *Entrepreneurship in the United States: The future is now* (Vol. 15). Springer Science & Business Media.
61. Bryers, H., 1997. *Doing business in America: Practical advice, useful information, and provocative views on the world's biggest market*. Mahon: Oak Tree Press.
62. Zhuplev, A., Stefl, M., and Rohm, A., 2018. *Doing business in the United States: A guide for small business entrepreneurs with a global mindset*. New York: Business Expert Press.
63. Luthans, F., Patrick, R.R., and Luthans, B.C., 1995. Doing business in Central and Eastern Europe: Political, economic, and cultural diversity. *Business Horizons, 38*(5), pp. 9–17.
64. Randlesome, C., and Brierley, W., 1993. *Business cultures in Europe*. Routledge.
65. Van Liedekerke, L., and Dubbink, W., 2008. Twenty years of European business ethics–past developments and future concerns. *Journal of Business Ethics, 82*, pp. 273–280.
66. Liñán, F., and Fernandez-Serrano, J., 2014. National culture, entrepreneurship and economic development: Different patterns across the European Union. *Small Business Economics, 42*, pp. 685–701.
67. Bishop, B., 2009. *European Union law for international business: An introduction*. Cambridge University Press.

CHAPTER 17

International Entrepreneurship

Key Learning Points

- Introduction.
- Principles of international entrepreneurship.
- Internalization and internationalization.
- Modes of international entrepreneurship.
- International entrepreneurship in numbers.
- Growth of international entrepreneurship
- Types of international entrepreneurship.
- Economic liberalization.
- Institutional infrastructure.
- Market competition.
- Franchising and Licensing.
- Seeking of advantages.
- The OLI factors.
- International destination-related factors.
- Challenges for international entrepreneurship.
- Measuring the degree of internationalization.
- Controllable factors.
- Uncontrollable factors.
- International Cultures.
- Culture Matrix and entrepreneurship.

© The Author(s), under exclusive license to Springer Nature Singapore Pte Ltd. 2024

M. Rajaratne, *Concepts, Processes and Practice of Entrepreneurship*, Palgrave Studies in Global Entrepreneurship,
https://doi.org/10.1007/978-981-97-6180-7_17

- International political systems.
- Political Freedom Matrix and entrepreneurship.
- International economic systems and entrepreneurship.
- Country selection and the Risk-Return Matrix.
- Determinant of international entry, exist, or exit (3Es).

Introduction

International entrepreneurship, by definition, is cross-border entrepreneurial operation. Although international entrepreneurship is presently a popular topic and a research area, it has been a prominent phenomenon throughout the past half a millennium. International entrepreneurship can be broadly defined as internationalization of domestic business. Internationalization creates multinational company. Every internationalized venture is not defined as multinational company because internationalization takes different administrative styles. Accordingly, multinational companies are identified as Multinational Corporation, International Corporation, Global Corporation, or Transnational Corporation. Despite this fact, all types of internationalized companies are popularly and generally referred to as Multinational Companies.[1]

The internationalization purpose of a venture is always strategic though the scope of strategic action can be macro or micro. The macro strategy of internationalization is to gain from economies of scale, economies of scope, backward and forward integration, access to resources, diversification of source of supplies, diversification of markets, and minimization of competitive risk caused by rivals. And the micro strategy of internationalization is to achieve specific venture objectives seeking resources, labor, markets, information, efficiency, strategic assets, strategic markets, technology, support industry, operations facility (EPZs, Industrial Parks, etc.), and government concessions. The micro-level strategies of internationalization will be further described later in this chapter.

Entrepreneurs engage in several modes of international operations to achieve both macro- and micro-level objectives of the firm. They include international merchandize trade, international service trade, international production, international sales points, international service points, international acquisition, international merger, international licensing, international franchise, greenfield investment, turn-key investment, build-own-operate (BOO) investment, build-operate-transfer (BOT) investment, public–private partnership (PPP), investment in equity, participation in international value chain, international logistics services, and global data storage farms.

Principles of International Entrepreneurship

Internalization Principle

Internationalization of entrepreneurship can be described in three principles developed in the literature of economics. Studies have been conducted to explore the reasons for entrepreneurs to engage in multi-plant operations. Ronald Coase (1937)[2] said markets are more imperfect than perfect and hence, the prices are unrealistic. Unrealistic prices cause higher costs of procurement of goods and services and thus, entrepreneurs choose to avoid "arms-length" transactions. Instead, they prefer to "internalize" as many operations as possible. This action of internalization results in integration of operations which were so far carried out at arms-length.

Organizing operations "in-house" rather than at "arms-length" can increase cost efficiency. This inquisition of Ronald Coase discovered the reason for a single-plant-firm to become a multi-pant-firm. It is usual that an entrepreneur who starts up a firm later moves to create more plants. Coase found the principle behind the entrepreneurial decision to opt for establishment of more connected plants or shops. He described this as the "internalization principle." Accordingly, entrepreneurs always strive to overcome unrealistic prices and to search realistic prices through internalization of every possible venture operation. Internalization sanctions entrepreneurs to integrate operations vertically and horizontally creating multi-plants under a single organizational and administrative umbrella.

Assume, an entrepreneur operating a garment factory procures materials from another maker. They later find the arms-length transaction takes place at an unrealistic price and hence, the input cost is high. After a cost analysis of material making process, the entrepreneur then realizes that the material maker earns a high profit margin. As the material maker's profit margin is attractive, the entrepreneur also chooses to start a material making plant to supply materials to the garment factory. With this backward integration, the entrepreneur now operates two plants: garment factory and material making plant. Now the entrepreneur can earn higher profits from the garment factory if the materials are transferred at the cost price. Otherwise, they can earn a profit from the material making plant also if the materials are transferred to the garment factory at a profit margin. Total profit of the entrepreneur has now increased.

Further, if the entrepreneur realizes that their garments are sold at a large profit margin at garment shop owned by another party, they would consider starting a garment shop also. Now they can sell the garment at their own shop and earn retail sales profit also. The entrepreneur has now integrated their business vertically both backward and forward. If the entrepreneur opts for starting several garment shops or to merge with and acquire other firms to increase sales, they will be engaging in horizontal integration also. In this manner, the entrepreneur now organizes multi-plant operations with vertical and horizontal integration. Although Coase confined his inquisition to domestic multi-plant operations of a firm, the principle he developed is capable of explaining internationalization of the firm as entrepreneurs internalize cross-border price inefficiencies also.

Ownership Advantage Principle

Stephen Hymer (1960 and 1976)[3] pointed out that every entrepreneur cannot internalize operations even if there were advantages of internalization. He argued that entrepreneurs who have accumulated ownerships in the current business only can internalize. According to Hymer, ownership asset is a prerequisite to internalization. Accordingly, the entrepreneurs who lack significant ownership assets cannot engage in internalization. He advocated ownership as an essential condition of internalization. According to Hymer, ownership assets of a firm include capital, intellectual properties, management, technology, employee skills, connections, experience, and networks. The stronger the ownership asset base the more intensive the tendency for internalization will be. Cross-border transfer of assets like direct investment, technology, and management under vertical and horizontal integration of business confirm Hymer's proposition.

Locational Advantage Principle

Raymond Vernon's (1966)[4] inquiry into international trade of the USA illuminated locational advantage as a principle of international entrepreneurship. Accordingly, a location can serve as advantageous or disadvantageous to an enterprise. As long as a location is advantageous, production will start and continue and the excess, after domestic consumption, is exported. However, the original location becomes less competitive due to rise of new competitive locations abroad. Firms losing locational advantages will choose to transfer their operations partially or fully to advantageous foreign location. If the technology of the product is static like that of garments, basic electronics, and even motor cars, operations will be shifted to foreign destinations to the tune of the locational competitiveness dynamics. Vernon's principle concludes that the entrepreneur will continue to domestically produce and export until the home country location becomes disadvantageous. When the home country is disadvantageous, operations are shifted to international locations where competitive advantage prevails.

The Eclectic Paradigm

The preceding discussion concludes that international entrepreneurship can be explained through three principles: (1) internalization, (2) ownership advantage, and (3) locational advantage. While these principles explain internationalization of the domestic firm, John Dunning (1977)[5] illustrated that these principles not individually but complementarily help explain internationalization of the firm. So, he proposed his eclectic paradigm integrating these three principles. Dunning observed that final action of an entrepreneur to integrate his operations is determined by internalization, ownership, and locational advantages. Later, these principles were heavily used to explain the phenomenon of internationalization of the firm.

This theoretical foundation helps explain the flow patterns of foreign direct investment (FDI), international production, global value chain, international trade, international auxiliary services, global income distribution, employment, and poverty alleviation. International entrepreneurship, therefore, is seen not only as the catalyst of international production and trade, but as world economic development also. Bruce Kogut (1983) developed a matrix to determine the choice for import or exports and

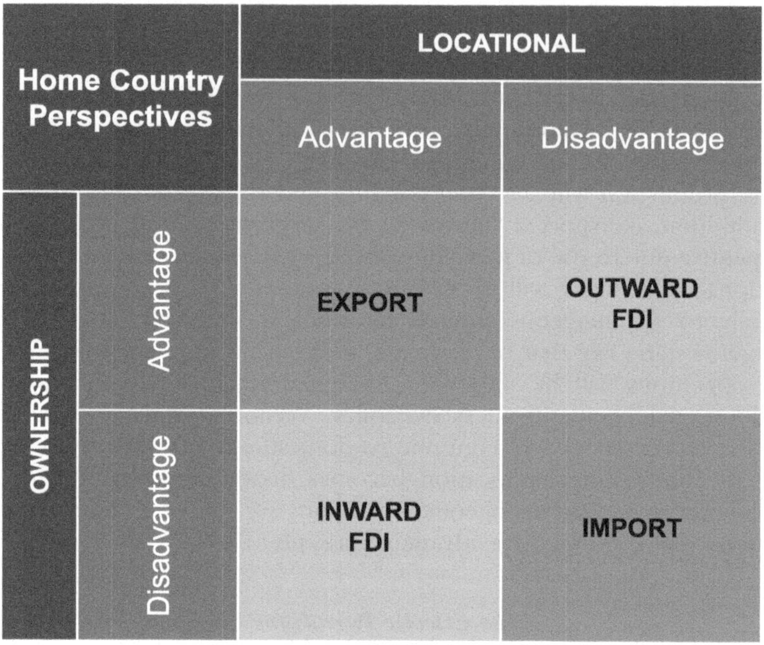

Fig. 17.1 Determinants of local and foreign production (Author portrayal based on Bruce Kogut [1983][6])

inward FDI or outward FDI (Fig. 17.1) based on the ownership and locational advantages.

International Entrepreneurship

The nature and impacts of international entrepreneurship are measured by the Global Entrepreneurship Index (GEI). This index examines the entrepreneurial skills, activities, and environment of each country. The GEI helps to compare entrepreneurial competencies of nations and to develop policies to improve country-specific entrepreneurship character. The countries such as the USA, Japan, the UK, and Germany rank the top in the index. The exciting and common feature of these high entrepreneurial countries is their extensive participation in international entrepreneurship. Key features of international entrepreneurship are

Table 17.1 Performance of top 100 non-financial multinationals

Variable	*2020*	*2021*	*2022*
Assets (US$ billion)			
Foreign	9765	10,428	10,065
Domestic	8489	8829	9139
Total	18,254	19,256	19,204
Foreign as a share of total (%)	53	54	52
Sales (US$ billion)			
Foreign	5203	6681	7413
Domestic	3999	4943	5552
Total	9203	11,624	12,965
Foreign as a share of total (%)	57	57	57
Employment (thousand)			
Foreign	9261	9051	9167
Domestic	10,132	11,053	10,833
Total	19,393	20,103	20,000
Foreign as a share of total (%)	48	45	46
Degree of internationalization			
Average Transnationality Index	62	62	62
Median Transnationality Index	62	63	62

Data World Investment Report (2023)[7]

analyzed in the World Investment Report (WIR) of the UNCTAD which was originally published by the UN Center for Transnational Corporation (UN-CTC) created in the 1990s.

The World Investment Report collects data of worldwide international entrepreneurship in terms of direct investment inflows and outflows, volume of international production and trade, new greenfield ventures, acquisitions and mergers, franchises, and royalties. Table 17.1 presents the operational dimensions of the non-financial multinationals. Also, the Global Entrepreneurship Monitor (GEM) provides extensive analyses on entrepreneurship strength of individual countries. The Global Entrepreneurship Development Report indicates the volume of operations of international entrepreneurs.

Growth of International Entrepreneurship

International entrepreneurship has been growing in immense volume during the past several decades in terms of the number of firms engaged in international operations, inward and outward foreign direct investment, international trade, scale of global value chain, intra-firm trade as witnessed by the above statistics. There are numerous external factors that have influenced or facilitated the domestic firms to internationalize their operations. Among external factors, technological advancement is of prime importance. The recent growth of technology in the sphere of ICT has, in particular, eased business operations remotely and at global scale. With technological advancement, entrepreneurs do not hesitate to internationalize their businesses because operations, controls, and management are not as difficult as they used to be in absence of advanced technology. Remote sensing, Artificial Intelligence, real-time controllability, 5-G remote operationality, global controllability of operations, and global standardization of mode of production have immensely influenced handling of entrepreneurial activities at global scale (Table 17.2).

Economic Liberalization

Economic liberalization that brought a domino effect caused the world to become an open market economy during the past several decades. Open market economy allows cross-border movements of capital, goods, resources, and people. Through this, they expect to improve exports,

Table 17.2 Global foreign direct investment flows

Region	*FDI Inflow (US$ Billion)*	*Share (%)*	*FDI outflow (US$ Billion)*	*Share (%)*
World	1295		1729	
Developed economies	378	29.2	1038	69.2
Europe	−107	−8.2	224	15.1
North America	338	26.1	452	30.4
Developing economies	916	70.8	459	30.8
Africa	45	3.5	6	0.4
Asia	662	51.1	396	26.6
Latin America	208	16.1	59	4.0

Data World Investment Report (2023)[8]

Table 17.3 Global greenfield projects

Region	*Projects (number)*	*Growth rate (%)*	*Project finance deals (number)*	*Growth rate (%)*
World	17,598	15	2564	8
Developed economies	10,790	4	1549	10
Europe	7382	−1	1038	19
North America	2469	19	331	2
Developing economies	6808	37	1015	5
Africa	766	39	157	15
Asia	4625	45	568	20
Latin America	1409	14	287	−18

Data World Investment Report (2023)[9]

and on the other hand, to acquire cost effective manufactured goods for domestic consumption via imports. This promotes interdependency and globalization which is achieved through international operations of domestic firms. The liberal policies constituted the world economy an oasis for the entrepreneurs to start their business worldwide. Widespread economic liberalization of the world reduced the political risk of investments and extended an invitation to entrepreneurs to initiate international production and trade with much freedom. Entrepreneurs capitalized on the openness of the world economy and penetrated into the world markets through internationalization of entrepreneurial activities. Global greenfield investment is an indicator of sound reaction to economic liberalization (Table 17.3).

Institutional Infrastructure

Entrepreneurs have noticed that institution and physical infrastructure are being developed to facilitate investment and trade by various countries. Institutions like the World Trade Organization (WTO), International Standards Organization (ISO), International Monetary Fund (IMF), international banking system, foreign exchange system, and international insurance firms are some of the institutions that either directly or indirectly support international entrepreneurship through finance, compensation, regulation, and laws. Additionally, support of host countries by way of setting up of Export Processing Zones, Industrial Parks, Free Trade Areas, International Trade Fairs, and Tax Havens encourages foreign entrepreneurs to operate in host countries. Entrepreneurs look for infrastructure facilities to easily start up their operations abroad and these infrastructure facilities serve as magnets to entrepreneurs.

Support industries play a pivotal role in attracting foreign entrepreneurs. Particularly, foreign entrepreneurs are reluctant to operate heavily abroad if the host countries do not possess useful support industries. Let us imagine an entrepreneur who makes automobiles wishes to internationalize the business through setting up of a production plant abroad. There, the entrepreneur looks for suppliers of components from the host country. If the host country possesses competitive support industries that manufacture goods such as tires, glass, electronics, paint, iron and steel, fabric, plastic, electricals and electronics, the entrepreneur prefers to shift the operations to that host country. During the past decades, many countries have developed their industries and thus the entrepreneurs have extensively benefited from starting operations capitalizing on such support industries.

Market Competition

With the international entrepreneurship, global competition has increased heavily. As a consequence, some host country locations later became too competitive due to industry crowd-out. This caused Red Ocean Markets in those countries and profits to fall drastically. In reaction, entrepreneurs then searched for less competitive Blue Ocean Markets. In this way, entrepreneurs relentlessly look for suitable locations for internationalization of their operations. Regional economic integration and bilateral and multilateral trade treaties also have stimulated entrepreneurs to go abroad as they provide them with special advantages such as tax benefits, tariff waivers, technological cooperation, public–private partnership (PPP) opportunities, status of the Most Favorite Nation (MFN) status, and flow of labor, materials, and money globally. The global greenfield projects in investment and number are rapidly growing across all industries indicating their reaction to market competition (Table 17.4).

There are many firm-specific internal factors that influence entrepreneurs to engage in international operations. Increased competitiveness of an industry urges entrepreneurs to look for foreign destinations that can install competitive edge. As explained by the Flying Wild Geese theory that was later refined by Kojima (2000)[11] and Ozawa (2016),[12] entrepreneurs decide to shift their manufacturing facilities abroad

Table 17.4 World greenfield projects by industry

Sector	*Value (US$ Billion)*	*Growth rate (%)*	*Number*	*Growth rate (%)*
Total	1213	64	17,598	15
Primary	97	618	118	1
Manufacturing	437	37	5790	24
Services	679	68	11,510	
Top ten industries				
Energy and gas supply	362	157	556	7
Electronics and electrical equipment	181	31	1167	6
Information and communication	120	14	5024	29
Extractive industries	95	718	89	51
Construction	62	27	211	−36
Automotive industry	59	53	694	−3
Transportation and storage	56	58	978	28
Metal and metal products	43	249	225	−1
Chemicals	26	12	474	4
Finance and insurance	22	46	1032	42

Data World Investment Report (2023)[10]

to recharge the lost competitiveness. For certain businesses, specific resources are pertinent. The choice of an entrepreneur to initiate business in the field of petroleum extraction, mineral extraction, extensive agriculture, etc., for instance, requires location of operations in that particular destination where the base resource is available. The construction entrepreneurs too will have to engage in operations at locations to which the construction is attached. An example of this type of cross-border operation is the bullet train project contracted to the Japanese Railway by the USA. Similarly, some entrepreneurs strive to gain monopolistic profits via controlling strategic resources. Oil wells and rare-earth materials are of strategic nature as the control of production of such resources helps gain monopolistic market advantage.

Merger and Acquisition and Franchising and Licensing

The decisions to increase global presence and market share at a selected destination requires engaging in business in those selected locations giving rise to internationalization of business. In some cases, it is costly

Table 17.5 World cross-border mergers and acquisitions

Sector/industry	*Value (US$ Billion)*	*Number*
Total	707	7763
Primary sector	122	389
Manufacturing sector	442	1406
Service sector	465	5968
Top ten industries		
Information and communication	166	1779
Extractive industries	121	216
Finance and insurance	88	602
Transportation and storage	41	297
Pharmaceuticals	36	169
Electronics and electricals	29	243
Trade	27	592
Professional services	23	730
Food, beverages, and tobacco	21	157
Real estate	20	336

Data World Investment Report (2023)[13]

to export certain goods and thus, the price of such goods tends to be too high in the foreign markets. Coke is a case in point. Bottling all Coke in Atlanta, USA and shipping worldwide is impractical and costly. Thus, Coca-Cola company licenses bottling internationally. McDonalds and KFC restaurants are examples of service businesses that seek increased global presence. They too authorize local operators to produce the same service under franchising license because fresh and warm foods cannot be exported worldwide from the USA. Also, cross-border merger and acquisitions have rapidly grown in seeking backward and forward integration as well as diversification seeking competitive advantage. Table 17.5 helps understand the significance of cross-border merger and acquisitions.

Advantage Seeking

Firms seek a large number of factors at international locations that are either essential or absolutely advantageous for operations. The cross-border investments that involve in international operations are thus identified as location-specific factor seekers. Accordingly, cross-border investments are identified as Labor seeking, expertise seeking, material seeking,

Table 17.6 Global value chain greenfield projects

Sector/industry	*2020*	*2021*	*2022*	*Growth 2021–2022 (%)*
Total				
Value (US$ Billion)	101	197	265	34
Number of projects	2796	3232	3402	5
Major sectors				
Electronics and electrical equipment				
Value (US$ Billion)	48	138	181	31
Number of projects	888	1100	1167	6
Automotive industry				
Value (US$ Billion)	35	39	59	53
Number of projects	578	718	694	−3
Machinery and equipment				
Value (US$ Billion)	7	8	12	52
Number of projects	670	650	727	12
Textile, clothing, and leather				
Value (US$ Billion)	11	13	127	−1
Number of projects	660	764	814	7

Data World Investment Report (2023)[14]

technology seeking, market seeking, efficiency seeking, strategic asset seeking, strategic market seeking, operations facility seeking, tax haven seeking, transfer price opportunity seeking, tariff gate seeking, and industrial hub seeking. With these objectives, entrepreneurs keep searching for lucrative locations that can provide what they seek. Once found what they have been looking for, entrepreneur will initiate entrepreneurial activities in those locations. International production is presently known as Global Value Chain. Global value chain is established based on the advantages that can be harnessed in the host countries. Global value chain greenfield projects, as indicated in Table 17.6, are evidence of seeking locational advantages.

The OLI Factors

International entrepreneurship is determined by the extent of entrepreneur's ownership assets also. As Hymer pointed out, the magnitude of international operations of firms are essentially determined by the ownership assets. Entrepreneurs who have accumulated ownership assets, choose to transfer them to international locations for starting up ventures. Further, the ownership assets are being used by entrepreneurs to acquire their emotional needs also; some entrepreneurs are fond of operating a business, or at least a business office, in some foreign locations. Owning a business office in New York, London, and Paris is sometimes only an emotional need unless such an office is imperative for regular operations.

International entrepreneurship is connected to the location-specific characteristics of foreign destinations. For doing business internationally, resources, facilities, government concessions, infrastructure, market proximity, legal and environmental advantages, skills, information, economic policy, urbanization, economic and political stability are considered by an entrepreneur. If he finds the factors that he looks for are available at a foreign destination, he will start operations in that country.

Hoteliers for instance, look for beaches, mountains, historical sites, and ski sites as ideal locations for setting up hotels. Farming companies look for land, water resources, and transportation routes. Complex manufacturing companies look for global value chains to join. And many entrepreneurs prefer industrial hubs and support industries. Likewise, a large number of location-specific concerns affect the entrepreneur's decision to internationalize operations. Seemingly, there are innumerous factors that inspire an entrepreneur to engage in international entrepreneurship as listed in Table 17.7.

Challenges for Internationalization

Measuring Internationalization

The above discussion provides an extensive account of reasons, opportunities, and extent of international entrepreneurship as of the present day. However, international entrepreneurship is not free from problems and limitations. While domestic entrepreneurship encounters a variety of problems and limitations, the international entrepreneurship faces multiplicative problems depending on the intensity of internationalization. The degree of international entrepreneurship can be viewed as Low, Medium or High because the entrepreneurs prefer to internationalize their business lowly, moderately, or highly. According to Daniels and Radebaugh (2011),[15] the degree of international operations is determined by the following criteria.

Table 17.7 International destination choice

#	*Factor*	#	*Factor*
1	Space, land mass and rent	21	Regional cooperation
2	Resource proximity	22	Political stability
3	Labor and wage rates	23	Economic stability
4	Access routes	24	Financial ranking
5	Market proximity	25	R&D facilities
6	Infrastructure proximity	26	Macroeconomic environment
7	Incentives	27	Tranquility
8	Environmental laws	28	Landscapes
9	Ethical concerns	29	Historical sites
10	Political systems	30	Air quality
11	Level of ICT facilities	31	Law and Order
12	Tax policy	32	Culture and language
13	Tariff policy	33	Operational sustainability
14	Financial facilities	34	Resource supply potentials
15	Industrial policy	35	Availability of supply chains
16	Support Industry	36	Cultural modernization
17	Exchange rate stability	37	Inflation and price levels
18	Supply of skilled labor	38	Urbanization
19	Industry information	39	Industrial hubs
20	Government attitude	40	Industrial Villages

Author Portrayal

A. Impetus for international operations
B. Internal handling (Internalization) of operations
C. Mode of international operations
D. Number of foreign countries involved
E. Similarity between domestic and foreign country

According to the degree of internationalization suggested by Daniels and Radebaugh, handling of international operations can be simple or complex. The intensity of internationalization invites different degrees of operational challenges. The challenges again depend on several factors that are direct outcomes of entrepreneur's determination to internationalize. With higher degree of internationalization, an entrepreneur faces greater number of challenges.

Controllable Factors

The factors listed below are manageable to the entrepreneur and thus, the entrepreneur determines the extent to which they control them. They include:

- Size of international investment compared to total investment
- Share and ratio of cross-border profit, fees, and royalty
- Share of global revenue to corporate revenue
- Share of equity capital, shares, and assets abroad
- Extent of global value chain
- Number of plants/facilities operated abroad
- Nationality of senior management
- Volume of intra-firm trade
- Ratio of intra-firm trade to arms-length trade
- Share of foreign workforce to total workforce
- Composition of foreign managers on board
- Amount of authority delegated to foreign management.

Uncontrollable Factors

International entrepreneur faces uncontrollable factors that they have to undergo in international operations. The major factors include international cultures, political systems, economic systems, and legal systems. Again, each factor consists of a large number of concerns; for instance, in international cultures, there are concerns such as religions, languages, values, taboos, customs, and morals. As far as economic systems are concerned, capitalist, socialist, or mixed economic policies, macroeconomic policies, public finance policies, monetary policies, trade policies, and foreign exchange policies pose challenges to international entrepreneurs. Large multinational entrepreneurs that operate in hundreds of countries face enormous and unimaginable count of challenges. One example is that Unilever operates in 190 countries and it has to deal with at least 190 languages, 190 cultures, 190 political systems, 190 legal systems, 190 economic systems! Challenges mentioned below are common for the international entrepreneurs while the intensity of them is determined by the intensity of internationalization.

1. Language barriers
2. Unfamiliar cultures and traditions
3. Unfamiliar laws, regulations, and procedures
4. Lack of information
5. Exchange rate complications and financial risk (exchange risk)
6. Hostile economic policies
7. Political risk through government change
8. Commercial risk through market failures
9. Requirement of capable management team
10. Leaving important affairs such as analytics and consultation to foreign intermediaries
11. Difficulty to monitor market movements.

International Cultures

For gaining entrepreneurial success, it is a prerequisite for the entrepreneur and their team to learn the cultural conduciveness for an intended venture in addition to economic conduciveness. Culture is social behavior shaped by thoughts distinctive to spatial or community identity that has evolved during centuries if not millenniums. Culture is a composite of beliefs, values, languages, traditions, customs, taboos, rituals, perception of right and wrong, perception of justice and injustice. Culture is predominantly perceived from its visible behaviors which are generally known as artifacts. It is a common mistake that artifacts are recognized as culture. Artifacts themselves are only signs or indicators of intricate behaviors that are governed by strict social values and rules that are connected to deeply rooted principal assumptions and beliefs. Therefore, artifacts are commonly described as the tip of an ice berg of which the ice mass is invisible as it lies below the surface of water. Thus, the construct of the culture has three layers. They are assumptions, values, and artifacts in the bottom-up order.[16]

Culture relates to business as a firm employs people, buys from and sells to society, and is owned by and regulated by people in a systematic form. Culture influences international entrepreneurship because international operations such as production, marketing, human resource management, and finance are carried out by people from various cultures. United Arab Emirates is a living example of multi-cultural international business setting. Learning to effectively deal with foreign cultures, adjusting to different cultures, and assessment of cultures is essential for the entrepreneurs to formulate suitable strategies to succeed in different cultural environments. Adjusting to culture ensures benefits while violation of it punishes.

Roaming cows in India is a chief artifact of Indian culture. One may tend to think that abundant supply of cows virtually without any cost is conducive for initiating a sustainable beef production venture in mega scale. But there is a cultural reason for the cows to roam in abundance in India. In Hindu culture, it is a taboo for the Hindus to consume beef. It is believed by the Hindus that the cow gives delight to the mankind and is associated with gods and thus, sacred. The sacred bull "Nandi" has much influence on Indian culture. "Nandi" is sacred because it is one of the many forms of the god Shiva. This belief, therefore, has influenced the Hindus not to consume beef. This value in turn, has caused cows to roam in India.

Cultural perspective of international entrepreneurship has been analyzed by Sundaram and Black (1996) using the matrix indicated in Fig. 17.2. This matrix considers two factors that determine cultural influence on business decisions. Differences of sharing and holding of a value in a society are proposed by this matrix. It measures the levels of sharing and holding of cultural value by a society. Certain values are extensively shared and deeply held by people while some other values are not treated the same way. Accordingly, in this matrix, four situations are depicted. This proposition is useful for entrepreneurs as it suggests different cultural settings that affect entrepreneurial decisions.

When a value is widely shared and deeply held, the entrepreneur must accord to the situation as there will not be a chance for him/her to alter it. Arabic culture will not allow pork shops by Arabs while nude beaches will not be allowed by Sri Lankans. The cultural perceptions in relation to these two scenarios are rock hard. Yet, a cultural scenario where value is widely shared but shallowly held, resistance to a business proposal by society will be minimal. For instance, it is widely shared that air pollution is unacceptable in Sri Lanka. But hardly anyone in Sri Lanka appears to hold to this idea deeply. Therefore, in Sri Lanka, ventures with considerable air pollution will be tolerated and thus, there will not be much resistance from the society to such ventures. Similarly, the values shared narrowly and held shallowly as well as those are shared narrowly and held deeply will not cast much resistance to most business proposals of local or national scale. But the entrepreneurs must scale the influence of cultures

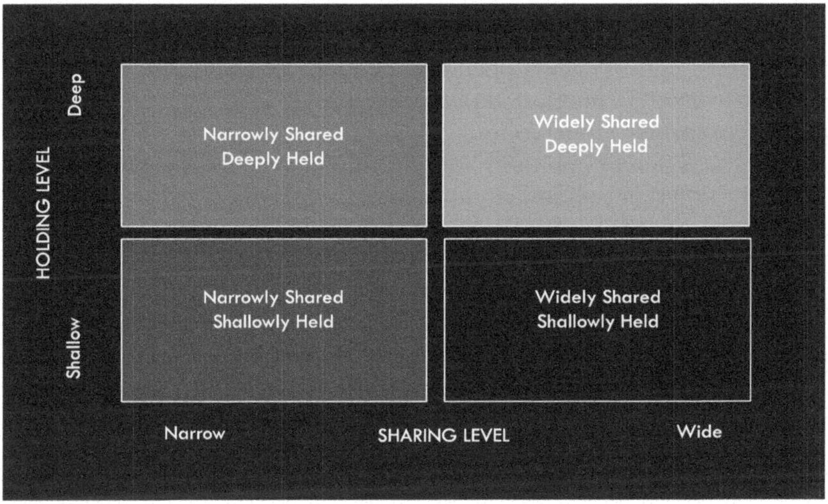

Fig. 17.2 Culture matrix (Author portrayal based on Sundaram and Black [1996][17])

and tactfully launch ventures to avoid or minimize the risk inflicted by cultural resistance.[18]

Entrepreneur chooses to react to cultural differences through polycentric, ethnocentric, or geocentric tactics. The polycentric policy advocates the need for adequate autonomy for the branches and subsidiaries to operate well adjusting to different international cultural settings. This approach is helpful to wade off location-specific cultural resistance and to guarantee smooth international operations. Ethnocentrism is a strict policy that believes that the home country culture is superior to those of foreign cultures and thus, the local culture can be ignored and overwhelmed. Giant corporates like Apple Inc. exercise this kind of attitude and are successful in global market. The geocentric approach adopts soft and in-between attitude toward locational differences. While giving adequate consideration to both home and host country values, in geocentric approach, cultural cohabitation attitude is adopted to succeed and sustain the venture in foreign soils.

International Political Systems

International entrepreneurs operating in single or multiple countries are bound to undergo political differences abroad in contrast to those of the entrepreneurs' home country. Political environments differ between countries as different countries adopt different political systems and they encounter different political circumstances due to differences in the political systems themselves and political relations. Therefore, international entrepreneurs need to have adequate knowledge of varying political systems and their influence on business in the host countries. Political systems, political stability, and political changes are connected to country-specific political risks. Sound assessment of political risk and security is beneficial for the entrepreneur to make three decisions: to entry, exist, and exit.

Politically conducive environment encourages entrepreneur to make decisions in relation to an entry into a host country, to determine length of existence, and to exit or not. As examples, the autocratic political system of the countries like Cuba and North Korea discourages the entry and existence decisions but encourages the decision to exit. In contrast, liberal and democratic countries are more favorable for the entry and exist decisions and thus, the international entrepreneurs are not politically compelled to exit from those countries. Political risks and security, therefore, certainly matter in making international venture decisions.[19]

Political systems represent political ideologies which are formulated by political ideas, theories, and objectives. It constitutes specific sociopolitical programs which are then glued to constitutions of the states. Constitutions create different political systems of countries that guide governance. Depending on the political systems, multi-party or single party governance system is determined. All political systems strive to hold the state sovereignty, hold the society together and thus, implement multifaceted policies to satisfy desires of various social groups. Depending on the belief of the majority population, or some other times by military coup, either democratic or autocratic regimes are established. As indicated in Fig. 17.3, radical, liberal, conservative, or reactionary governance styles can prevail under democratic system. On the other hand, fascist, communist, authoritarian, or military governance styles are maintained under autocratic system.[20]

International ventures encounter different business environments under different political systems. International entrepreneurs may find

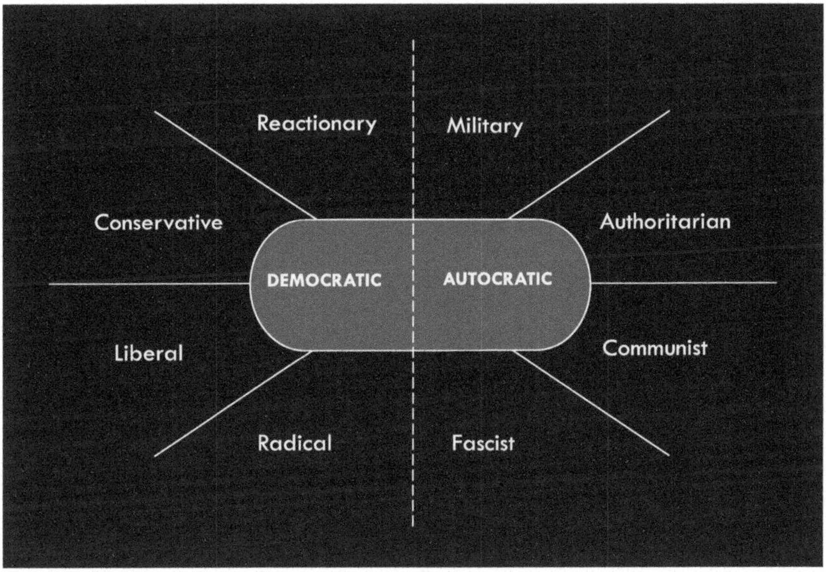

Fig. 17.3 Political systems (Author portrayal based on Sundaram and Black [1996])

venture opportunities in both democratic and undemocratic regimes. Sometimes, under undemocratic regimes, special political protection or guarantees may be granted for international ventures depending on the economic or strategic impact of the venture to the host country. It is observed that international entrepreneurs effectively operate in both democratic and undemocratic regimes. However, political risk is minimum in the democratic regimes and thus, most entrepreneurs prefer to operate in democratic political systems because democracies ensure a few freedoms through which political risk for international ventures is minimized.

Major freedoms with which the democracies are constituted include economic freedom, individual rights, corporate rights, and property rights among many other sociopolitical freedoms. In democratic regimes international ventures are granted the freedom to speak, debate, discussion, litigation, and opportunity to protect rights through international organizations such as WTO, UNO, and IPO. A classic comparison between democratic and autocratic regime can be made between North Korea and

South Korea; United Arab Emirates and Afghanistan; and former West and East Germany.

Figure 17.4 depicts basic freedoms that are useful for international entrepreneurs in carrying out venture operations. Some political regimes grant these freedoms while some others do not. The degree of these freedoms entitled to a society are important criteria for an entrepreneur for entry, exist, and exit decisions. The higher the value assigned on the freedom scale the more favorable is the host country for international entrepreneurs to do business with. So, this scale provides international entrepreneurs with a guideline that helps them make suitable locational decisions.

On the Political Freedom Assessment Matrix (Fig. 7.5), freedom values can be assigned for countries over a time cross section in the range of values from 10 to 100. These values then can be aggregated into a single value with reference to the country under observation and contrasted between other countries for selecting the most suitable location for international entry decision. Also changes in political freedom of countries can

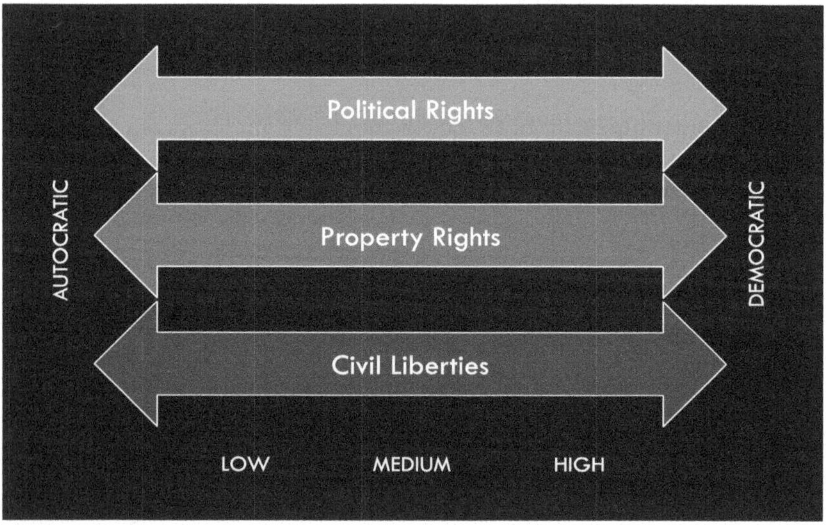

Fig. 17.4 Political freedom (Author portrayal based on Sundaram and Black [1996])

be measured with time series values and compared to examine improvements or declines in the medium or long term. The findings will be helpful to make the decisions either to exist with or to exit from a specific country. Also, if the decision is to exist, then the matrix can guide a further decision whether to expand or downsize operations at the present location (Fig. 17.5).

Political risk is an external risk related to location of operations and it can be divided into Micro and Macro political risks. Again, political risk is understood as individualistic or targeted for a single country or industry and communitarian or wide spread for all ventures in a foreign country. Political risk involves government takeovers, operational restrictions, and agitations against foreign ventures. Causes of political risk include hostile political leadership, civil disorder, animosity between investor and host country. Political risks can be categorized as micro and macro political risks. The political actions against specific foreign business or all ventures of a selected country considering the size and socioeconomic impact are defined as micro political risk. Macro political risk occurs when political actions affect broader spectrum of foreign ventures regardless of industry, nationality, or conduct of the business. In this background, international entrepreneurs are compelled to develop political strategies to overcome political risks.[21]

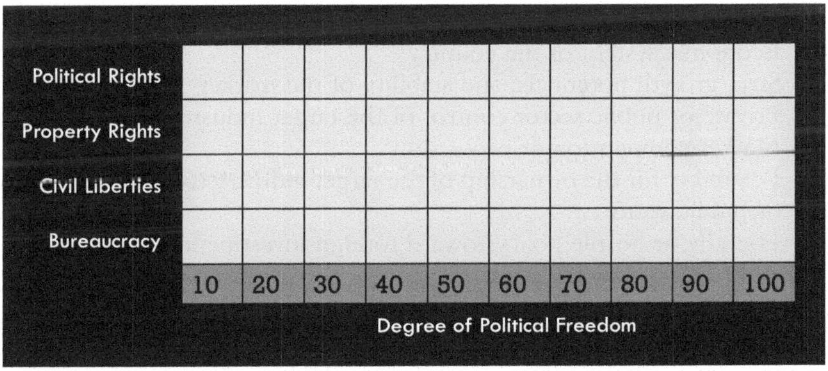

Fig. 17.5 Political freedom assessment matrix (Author Portrayal)

International Economic Systems

Internationalization decision is affected by the economic systems that prevail in host countries. Different economic systems are connected to different economic policies and thus, they pose different impacts on investment, trade, licensing, and franchising which are integral moves of international entrepreneurship. In foreign locations, international firms find resources and markets. The supply conditions of factors are determined by economic systems. Factor market and consumer market competitions are consequences of different economic systems. Economic policies are instruments of economic systems and economic policies there can be policies that provide either incentives or disincentives for international entrepreneurship. So, the knowledge of diverse economies is essential for the entrepreneurs to consider cost–benefit of international locations before country selection.[22]

The entrepreneurs preparing to operate cross-border must be aware of the kind of economic freedom emanating from varied policies. The economic freedom is determined by a number of factors such as trade policy, tariff policy, market intervention, foreign exchange rate policy, direct investment policy, financial sector policy, wage policy, price controls, property rights, and market regulations. Together with these policies, adequate knowledge of the following matters is also equally useful for an entrepreneur to operate internationally.[23]

- Economic system of the country
- Size, growth potentials, and stability of the market
- Private or public sector control of the target industry
- Market competition or protection
- Possibility for the ownership of the target industry to move to private or public sector
- Friendly or hostile policy toward foreign investments
- Role assigned to the private sector by the government.

Essentially, economic system is a mechanism for controlling the national economy according to political ideology of the government. Economic control determines resource ownership and allocation in an economy that in turn creates three different economic systems: Market, Command, and Mixed systems. An economic system can be specified by the ownership and control of the national product. Ownership has three different forms; state ownership, private ownership, and ownership of the state and private sector. The right to ownership of production exhibits the entrepreneurial freedom of an economy. Figure 17.6 indicates how an economic system is determined according to the ownership of production and the institutional arrangement for control of production.

Economic Systems Matrix guides entrepreneurs in selecting favorable economic systems for considering prospective operations. Accordingly, in this matrix, toward the country category A, countries enjoy the highest economic freedom in contrast to category I, where least economic freedom is allowed. If the entrepreneur prefers to operate in a country with much freedom, they should prepare to face competition and to engage in intensive marketing programs to position the products in the market. In an economic system where freedom is less, the entrepreneur can anticipate less market competition and easy market positioning. In mixed economic system like in country category E, entrepreneur will find opportunities not only in the private and in the public sector also. In this country category, there are opportunities for the foreign private sector to undertake state sector projects and to operate joint ventures in the form of Public Private Partnership (PPP). Because an economic system is

PUBLIC POLICY		OWNERSHIP OF PRODUCTION		
		Private	Combined	Public
CONTROL OF THE ECONOMY	Market	A	B	C
	Mixed	D	E	F
	Command	G	H	I

Fig. 17.6 Economic systems matrix (Author Portrayal)

connected to the political system, economic freedom should be viewed in political economic lens also.[24]

Country Selection

Political, economic, and cultural system are taken into careful consideration when selecting an international destination for business operations. All the political, economic, and cultural circumstances of individual countries that come under entrepreneur's examination are summarized into two factors viz. risk and return. The risk and return differentials are then compared and a suitable country is selected. In international entrepreneurship, firms seek appropriate cross-border production and marketing sites. This involves two questions; where to produce and where to sell. Services such as construction, hospitality, and retailing have to be located where the customers need them. Thus, in service industry, both production and marketing are connected to a single location. In contrast, manufacturing sites can be located almost at any place based on the site-specific advantages. The primary concern for selecting a production site is the cost advantage; inclusive of transport costs also.[25]

Sometimes, the whole product is produced at one location while some other times the product is divided into components and produced at different sites based on the production cost competitiveness of each component. Transport cost is considered in here as the goods produced need to be cost effectively dispatched to markets. Regional economic integration and the availability of facilities such as Industrial Hubs, Industrial Villages, Special Economic Zones, and Support Industry Bases are favorably considered in selecting a production site.[26] Entrepreneurs tend to capitalize on different international production sites base on cost advantages. Countries that are capable of providing natural resources, labor, technology, market, strategic assets, strategic markets, operations facilities, tax concessions, and transfer price opportunities are considered as locations that help improve firm competitiveness. Competitive production sites around the globe are interconnected to create Global Value Chains (GVC).[27]

For selection of a country for production and marketing, international entrepreneurs conduct surveys to identify the best possible production sites. Although a comprehensive analysis provides more precise guidance regarding business locations, too many details will complicate the decision-making process. Locational surveys are conducted to recognize specific opportunities and risks involved with each location. Market size, market growth, per capita income, economic growth rates, demographic characteristics, level of industrialization, size of the middle class, ease of operations, geographic proximities, similarity of legal systems, language, culture, market and economic conditions, technology, infrastructure, and availability of support industry, opportunity to ownership and remittance of profits, cost of labor, capital and land, R&D, physical and institutional infrastructure, transport cost differentials, and economic and political systems-related opportunities are considered as key opportunities for a venture to consider specific international business site.[28]

Risk-Return Concern

The types and sources of potential risks are assessed to determine the cost of international siting. Generally, three types of risks are identified: competitive risk, monetary risk, and political risk. The competitive risk is caused by the inability to be competitive in the market. This is a business risk of operations. The monetary risk is the inability to mitigate exchange rate risk. Exchange rate risk is related to loss in international transactions and asset depletion. The political risk is the inability to face micro and macro political risks connected to international locations which were described in an earlier section.[29]

Both analysis of risks and return specific to a certain location and comparison of them between locations are useful for the entrepreneurs in selecting a suitable location for production and marketing. International indexes are also constructed to measure certain economic, political, and social aspects of countries and these indexes are useful to figure out financial soundness, corruption, business friendliness, ease of business operations, economic growth, development state, and economic and political outlook. These statistics can be compared between countries as a preparation to identify the most appropriate production and marketing sites.

Figure 17.7 depicts five groups of countries based on their locational risks and returns. The international entrepreneur can select a location to operate from within these groups. There are locations with high or low risks and high or low returns according to this matrix. The combination of the two categorizes countries into five with different combinations of risks and returns. Countries with high risks and low returns are the least favored destinations, whereas low risk and high return countries are

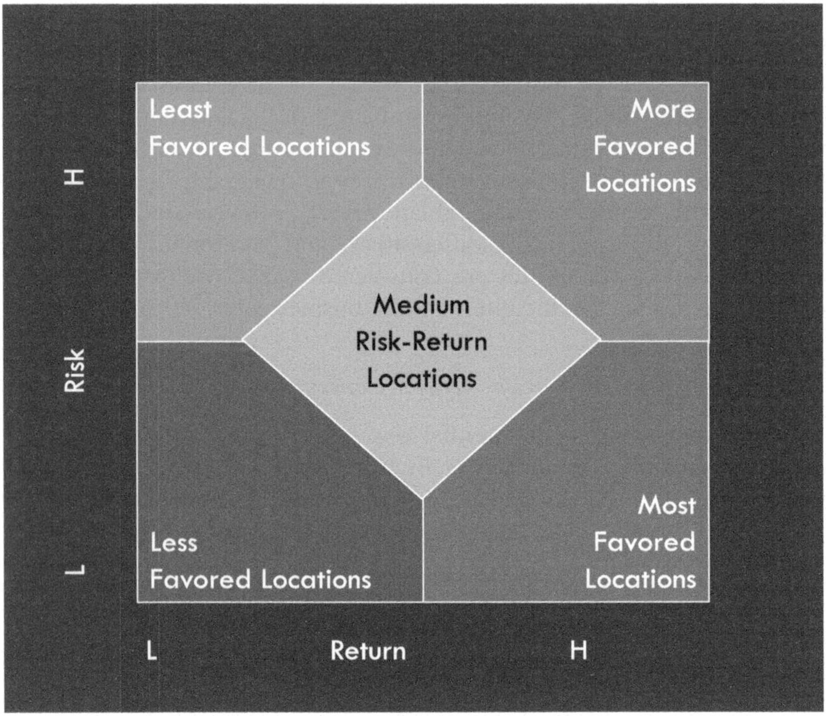

Fig. 17.7 The risk-return matrix (Author Portrayal)

the most favorite destinations. Similarly, low risk and low return destinations can also be favorable to some entrepreneurs who seek moderate growth. On the other hand, high risk and high return destinations are more popular among clever entrepreneurs because they can earn super normal profit from high risks businesses. However, some international entrepreneurs prefer medium risk-return destinations as they wish to avoid high risks but can be satisfied with moderate returns.

Entry, Exist, and Exit Decisions

As indicated in Fig. 17.8, strategies are activated in relation to the decisions of entry, exist, and exit. Foreign partnership, greenfield foreign direct investment, acquisition, merger, trading, licensed production, and

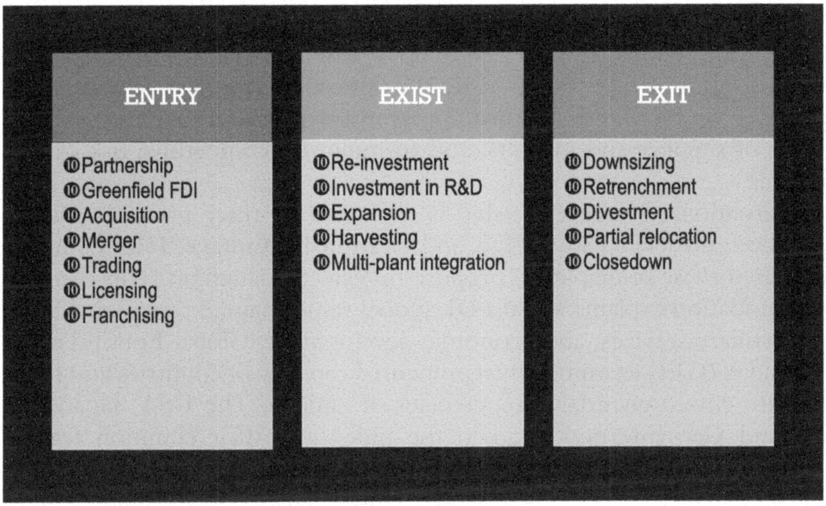

Fig. 17.8 Entry, exist, and exit decisions (Author Portrayal)

franchise operations are entry strategies.[30] Strategies such as reinvestment, investment in research and development, expansion of operations, harvesting, and backward and forward integration through multi-plant operations are selected in the decision to exist at a location. When the exit decision is made, strategies are available for gradual or abrupt exiting. Business downsizing, retrenchment, divestment, partial relocation, and closedown strategies are the strategic options for an exit. Interestingly, an exited firm may make a re-entry at a later time when location specific conditions are improved.[31]

Chapter Summary

International entrepreneurship occurs when domestic businesses internationalize their operations; in other words, organize business cross border. Production, service, merchandizing, value chain, sales and service point, acquisition, merger, licensing and franchising, greenfield investment, turn-key investment, build-own-operate (BOO) investment, build-operate-transfer (BOT) investment, public–private partnership (PPP), investment in equity, supply chain, logistics, and data storage farms are the major forms of cross-border operations and they are carried out mainly by organizations such as Multinational Corporation, International Corporation, Global Corporation, and Transnational Corporation. Internationalization is the strategy to gain from economies of scale and scope, achieve backward and forward integration, access resources, diversify source of supplies and markets, and to minimize competitive risk caused by rivals.

International entrepreneurship is explained by three principles: internalization, ownership advantage, and locational advantage. John Dunning integrated these principles to propose his eclectic paradigm. This theoretical foundation explains world FDI, global value chain, international trade and auxiliary services, and economic development. Global Entrepreneurship Index (GEI) examines entrepreneurial capacity of countries and helps compare entrepreneurial competencies of nations. The USA, Japan, the UK, and Germany rank high in the index and their common feature is the extensive internationalization. Global Entrepreneurship Monitor (GEM) also provides extensive analyses on international entrepreneurship. World Investment Report is a major source of FDI-related international entrepreneurial operations.

Numerous factors have influenced internationalization of entrepreneurial operations: technological advancement, economic liberalization, institutional and physical infrastructure, support industries, lost competitiveness, monopolistic gains, and resource controlling. The degree of internationalization of a firm is viewed as low, medium, and high. According to Daniels and Radebaugh, the degree of internationalization is measured against five criteria: impetus for international operations, internalization of operations, mode of international operations, number of foreign countries involved, and similarity between domestic and foreign countries. International entrepreneur faces uncontrollable factors such as international cultures, political systems, economic systems, and legal systems and they are carefully assessed by entrepreneurs when selecting an international location for operations. Risks and returns are key considerations of locations. The Risk-Return Matrix introduced here helps compare risk-return differentials of countries and make decisions relating to entry, exist, or exit (3Ex).

Review Questions

1. Define and trace the boundaries of international entrepreneurship.

2. "International 'internalization' causes international entrepreneurship." Explain referring to the proposition of Ronald Coase.
3. Discuss how ownership advantages and locational advantages collectively determine opportunities for international entrepreneurship.
4. "Ownership, Locational, and Internalization (OLI) factors were combined by John Dunning to construct the Eclectic paradigm; a formula that explain international entrepreneurship." Discuss.
5. Analyze the recent data of the World Investment Report and highlight the nature and magnitudes of international entrepreneurship.
6. Describe the factors that have promoted the growth of international entrepreneurship in the recent past.
7. "Franchising and Licensing are a major field of international entrepreneurship at present." Examine this statement with relevant data.
8. What do the international entrepreneurs commonly seek to access in foreign destinations when making internationalization decision?
9. "Multinational Corporations are a significant indicator of international entrepreneurship." Numerically elaborate the dimensions of the multinational firm.
10. Examine the major administrative models of international business and describe their operational practices.
11. "The degree of internationalization of entrepreneurship is measured using five criteria." Workout an example.
12. Describe the scope of international entrepreneurship opportunities that can be appropriated to the Culture Matrix.
13. "The Political Freedom Matrix measures the political impact on international entrepreneurship." Explain.
14. Assess the impact of international economic systems as an influential factor of determining international entrepreneurship.
15. "Selection of a country for entrepreneurial operations is guided by the Risk-Return Matrix." Discuss how the Risk-Return Matrix guides entrepreneurs in making Entry, Exist, or Exit (3Es) decisions.

Additional Readings

1. Bennet, R., 2003. *International business*. Singapore: Pearson Education Pte.
2. Coase, R.H., 1937. The nature of the firm. *Economica, 4*(16).

3. Hymer, S.H., 1960. *The international operations of national firms, a study of direct foreign investment.* Massachusetts: MIT Press.
4. Vernon, R., 1966. International investment and international trade in the product cycle. *The Quarterly Journal of Economics,* (80).
5. Dunning, J.H., 1977. Trade, location of economic activity and the MNE: A search for an eclectic approach. In *The international allocation of economic activity: Proceedings of a Nobel Symposium held at Stockholm* (pp. 395–418). London: Palgrave Macmillan UK.
6. Kogut, B., 1983. Foreign direct investment as a sequential process. *The multinational corporation in the 1980s*, pp. 38–56.
7. https://unctad.org/publication/world-investment-report-2023.
8. https://unctad.org/publication/world-investment-report-2023.
9. https://unctad.org/publication/world-investment-report-2023.
10. https://unctad.org/publication/world-investment-report-2023.
11. Kojima, K., 2000. The "flying geese" model of Asian economic development: Origin, theoretical extensions, and regional policy implications. *Journal of Asian Economics, 11*(4), pp. 375–401.
12. Ozawa, T., 2007. *Institutions, industrial upgrading, and economic performance in Japan: The flying-geese paradigm of catch-up growth.* Edward Elgar Publishing.
13. https://unctad.org/publication/world-investment-report-2023.
14. https://unctad.org/publication/world-investment-report-2023.
15. Daniels, J.D., Radebaugh, L.H., and Sullivan, D.P., 2019. *International business: Environments and operations.* Pearson.
16. Leung, K., Bhagat, R.S., Buchan, N.R., Erez, M., and Gibson, C.B., 2005. Culture and international business: Recent advances and their implications for future research. *Journal of International Business Studies, 36*, pp. 357–378.
17. Sundaram, A.K., and Black, J.S., 1996. *The International Business Environment: Text and Cases.* New Delhi: Pentice Hall of India.
18. Nowak, W., 2018. Doing business in the fastest growing least developed countries. *Economic and Social Development: Book of Proceedings*, pp. 537–543.
19. Daniels, J.D., Radebaugh, L.H., and Sullivan, D.P., 2019. *International business: Environments and operations.* Pearson.
20. Boddewyn, J.J., and Brewer, T.L., 1994. International-business political behavior: New theoretical directions. *Academy of Management Review, 19*(1), pp. 119–143.

21. Almond, G.A., 1956. Comparative political systems. *The Journal of Politics, 18*(3), pp. 391–409.
22. Hoekman, B.M., and Kostecki, M.M., 2009. *The political economy of the world trading system: The WTO and beyond*. Oxford University Press.
23. Frey, B.S., 1984. International political economy. *Oxford1984*.
24. Frieden, J., and Martin, L.L., 2002. International political economy: Global and domestic interactions. *Political science: The State of the Discipline*, pp. 118–146.
25. Kim, J.U., and Aguilera, R.V., 2016. Foreign location choice: Review and extensions. *International Journal of Management Reviews, 18*(2), pp. 133–159.
26. Van der Marel, E., 2015. Positioning on the global value chain map: Where do you want to be? *Journal of World Trade, 49*(6).
27. Antràs, P., and De Gortari, A., 2020. On the geography of global value chains. *Econometrica, 88*(4), pp. 1553–1598.
28. Dunning, J.H., and Norman, G., 1987. The location choice of offices of international companies. *Environment and Planning A, 19*(5), pp. 613–631.
29. Wheeler, D., and Mody, A., 1992. International investment location decisions: The case of US firms. *Journal of international economics, 33*(1–2), pp. 57–76.
30. Hill, C.W., Hwang, P., and Kim, W.C., 1990. An eclectic theory of the choice of international entry mode. *Strategic Management Journal, 11*(2), pp. 117–128.
31. Vissak, T., Francioni, B., and Freeman, S., 2020. Foreign market entries, exits and re-entries: The role of knowledge, network relationships and decision-making logic. *International Business Review, 29*(1), p. 101592.

CHAPTER 18

The Political Economy of Entrepreneurship

Key Learning Points

- Introduction.
- State and the government.
- Government and entrepreneurship.
- Public policy of entrepreneurship.
- Government's role in entrepreneurship.
- Political economic ideology of the state and entrepreneurship environment of nations.
- Public policy objectives.
- Political economy of entrepreneurship as a new field of research.
- State and private sector entrepreneurship.
- Nationalization and privatization of enterprises.
- Annual Budget, Parliamentary Acts, and Ordinances as policy indicators.
- Analytical approaches of political economy.
- Sri Lanka as a case of political economy of entrepreneurship.
- Colonial policy regime.
- Policy Regime of 1948–1978.
- Policy Regime since 1978.
- General overview.

© The Author(s), under exclusive license to Springer Nature Singapore Pte Ltd. 2024

M. Rajaratne, *Concepts, Processes and Practice of Entrepreneurship*, Palgrave Studies in Global Entrepreneurship,
https://doi.org/10.1007/978-981-97-6180-7_18

Introduction

Political economy is a discourse of political systems of public institutions and public policy measures that influence and impact the political choice of nations. French philosophers like Jean Rousseau, Francois Quesnay, and Jacques Turgot originated the political economic views as early as the seventeenth century. The French political economic discourse was then pushed to the fore and improved by classical economists such as Adam Smith, David Ricardo, J. S. Mill, and Carl Marx; whose contribution widened the scope of political economic discourse.[1]

At present, political economic analyses encompass numerous policy spheres such as market policy, macroeconomic policy, monetary policy, fiscal policy, development policy, entrepreneurship development policy, poverty alleviation policy, technology development policy, exports and imports policy, industrial policy, agricultural policy, education policy, health policy, social service policy, environmental policy and many more. All these policies either directly or indirectly impact on entrepreneurship practices of nations. And hence, entrepreneurship differences among nations are much a reflection of the policy sphere.[2]

State and the Government

The concept and practice of political economy emerged as communities rose and transformed as nation states which empowered with governing authority known as the government or polity.[3] Government coordinates and controls economic activities via macroeconomic, fiscal, and development policies. In contrast, in a feudal system, economic activities are not coordinated by a central mechanism but only organized by individuals or organizations. The nation state aligning to its polity, produces national currency and then establishes national bank (Central Bank) and national treasury as a devise for monetary controls. With this setup, the nation state initially formulates general policies such as monetary policy, fiscal policy, exchange rate policy, and macroeconomic policy related to control of the economy.[4] Successively, varied policies and institutions are formulated to guide and oversee wider national activities. Then, a governance system is formulated to glue all the activities carried out by the state and the private sector within the jurisdiction of the nation state according to the political ideologies of the government (Fig. 18.1).[5]

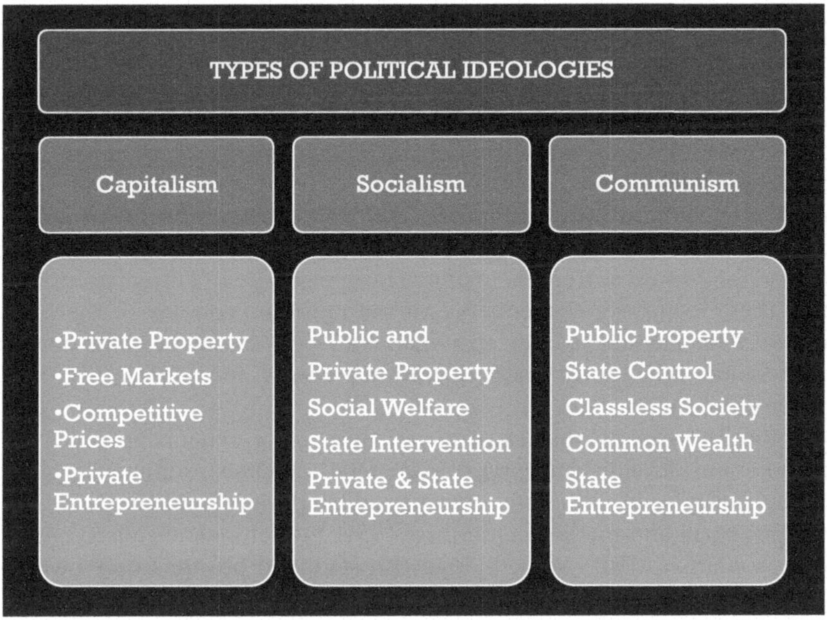

Fig. 18.1 Political ideologies (Author Portrayal)

Public Policy

Policy sphere is the determinant factor of the strength and scope of the institutional setup that maintains the governance system. The Central Bank is vested powers to handle monetary and exchange rate policies, whereas other institutions handle rest of the policies to the tune of political economic ideology of the government. State chooses its political economic sentiment basically from capitalist or socialist ideology. Variations to these two are social market ideology and communist ideology.[6]

Nation state is given public mandate to choose an economic ideology and to formulate policies, institutional systems, and to run it. Single economic ideology does not prevail all time in a nation state and switching to different ideologies at different times is not uncommon. The choice of governance is selected from the spectrum of political economic ideologies that span between laissez-faire and controlled regime. Accordingly, political economic ideologies lead to different policy regimes that determine the depth and width of the state's role in the economy. The discourse on this affair is wholly parceled in the concept of political economy.[7]

Among the factors of production, entrepreneurship is the dynamic factor that possesses organizing ability of other dormant factors: capital, land, and labor. Thus, entrepreneurship is instrumental to organizing of economic activities in a nation. Entrepreneurship may appear as state entrepreneurship, private entrepreneurship, or public–private partnership (PPP). The private entrepreneurship is again categorized as local private and foreign private entrepreneurship. The appearance of entrepreneurship in all these forms is a consequence of the political economy of the state because it is the state policy that mandates business ownership, operational scope, operational scale, operational liberty, income earning, and mode of production.[8]

Among numerous policies of governance, entrepreneurship policy to promote and develop enterprises, in general, deserves prominence place in the policy spheres. State entrepreneurship development programs (SEDP), small and medium enterprise (SME) development, micro enterprise programs (MEP), self-employment, state and private sector ownership of enterprises, privatization, nationalization, public–private partnerships (PPP), international merger and acquisition (IM&A), international licensing and franchising (IL&F), foreign direct investment (FDI), offshore companies, and foreign joint ventures (FJV) are artifacts of the political economic ideology of entrepreneurship. Numerous policies, programs, systems, and state institutions are set up for achieving entrepreneurship development objectives. The institutional and policy framework and its conduct and impact encompass the political economy of entrepreneurship.[9]

Policy Objectives

The political economy of entrepreneurship is relevant as government heavily interacts and interferes in entrepreneurship. State generally strives to accomplish the following key objectives through manipulating entrepreneurship policy.[10]

1. Higher economic growth
2. National wealth creation
3. Wealth ownership management
4. Affiliating to political blocs

5. Foreign exchange earnings
6. Income disparity and poverty alleviation
7. Regional development
8. Addressing unemployment problem
9. Industrial development
10. Technological advancement

For accomplishment of these objectives, state formulates policies in favor of certain entrepreneurships and against some others. The entrepreneurship that appears to be in line with the government's political ideology are promoted while others are either ignored or suppressed. Policy instruments and institutional setups are altered and fine-tuned and thus, they are not constant in the long run. Inquiry into the economic policy regimes is the foundation of political economic analysis of entrepreneurship. The state entrepreneurship policy, policy objectives, change of policies and policy objectives, institutional setup, policy implementation mechanisms, policy outcomes, and economics of entrepreneurship are the components of political economic analysis of entrepreneurship.[11]

Analytical Approaches

The political economy of entrepreneurship can be viewed as a matter specific to a nation state. But because policy regime of a state is not constant, evolution of the political economy of entrepreneurship also becomes a topic of inquiry. As entrepreneurship policy regimes can change in a state over time, comparative political economy of entrepreneurship also is a valid topic of investigation. Furthermore, comparative studies between two or more countries will furnish an important topic of examination to determine effectiveness of entrepreneurship policy regimes. Effective policy regime of one country is advantageous for learning and adoption of the same for remaking of the political economy of entrepreneurship in other countries.[12]

There is a dearth in study of the political economy of entrepreneurship in the literature. Unlike the classical economists who generally propagated the laissez-faire and free market policy for achieving efficiency and general equilibrium, Joseph Schumpeter (1934)[13] advocated the notion that the government has a role to play in harnessing entrepreneurship to bring about innovations (destructive innovation, in particular) useful for economic development. Yet, Schumpeterian notion is only a single aspect of the political economy of entrepreneurship.

Although political economic analyses are popular in the fields like socio-economy, public finance, and economic development policy, the political economic discourse of entrepreneurship is a topic that has not caught limelight. A few authors, however, have recently contributed to the subject showing new directions and dimensions. Works of Magnus Henrekson and Robin Douhan (2008)[14] are the most significant contributors to the literature of political economy of entrepreneurship.[15] Figure 18.2 presents the approach of the political economic analysis.

They constructed their analysis on three pillars; (1) seeing entrepreneurship as an engine of growth and the need for favorable public policy, (2) property rights policy that promotes ownership of assets between private and public sector and protection from rent-seeking predatory entrepreneurs, and (3) political power and market power balancing issue. lvar Jonsson (2016)[16] advocates three levels of innovations; (1) macro-level (the impact of innovation activity on economic growth and production systems), (2) meso-level (relations between firms, research institutes and governmental role in innovation), (3) micro-level (dynamics of innovations within firms and organizations). He

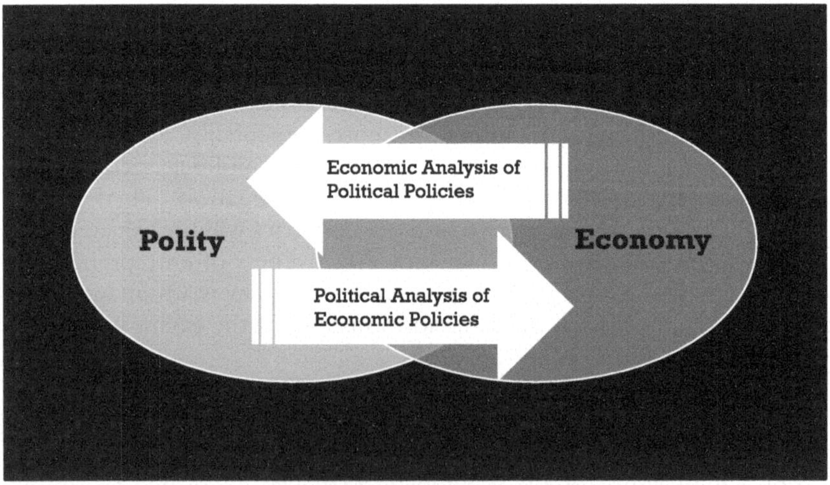

Fig. 18.2 Political economic analytical method (Author Portrayal)

advances the collective entrepreneurship concept as a practice for social construction through collaboration of a group of individuals engaging in entrepreneurship sharing resources, skills, expertise, etc. Amidst this awakening, a few other scholars also have investigated various political economic issues of entrepreneurship. Following are some of the political economic issues illuminated by later studies.

1. Governments create limited opportunities for innovations and entrepreneurial success
2. Policy sanctions on institutional governance and control of predatory entrepreneurship grant monopolistic power for licensed entrepreneurs
3. Governments manipulate regulations for quick personal benefits.
4. Governments believe the state as the best entrepreneur
5. Heavy market intervention of the state
6. Inadequate recognition of private property rights
7. Government's attitude on use of the private assets
8. Control of private assets and entrepreneurial endeavor by heavy income tax
9. Burden of progressive tax (instead of proportionate tax)
10. Opportunities for tax evasion and lack of contribution to economic growth
11. Reluctance to investment due to weak and unsteady property rights laws and practices
12. Lack of reinvestment due to weak property rights laws
13. Insecurity of future earnings due to volatile tax policy
14. Loss compensation and negative taxes on public ventures
15. Provision of subsidies to startups and breeding rivals for existing new firms
16. Loan guarantees of the state as a cause for poor performance
17. Crowding out of personal savings of entrepreneurs due to subsidies
18. Crowding out of venture capital and cut back of support by venture capitalists amidst prevalence of subsidies and loans
19. Investor perception retarded by privatization policy
20. Externalities of small firms in contrast to corporates
21. Government choice for state entrepreneurship to counter private entrepreneurs exiting due to detrimental policy
22. Poor performance of heavily granted enterprises
23. Use of political play in securing entrepreneurship opportunities

24. Political power and rent-seeking opportunities.

Sri Lanka as a Case

Background

Like in any other country, entrepreneurship persisted in Sri Lanka since the early BCE times. Yet, coordinated policy or institutional arrangements cannot be detected until recently. Entrepreneurship has prevailed as feudal economic activities in the past. Ancient governments had implemented tax policy indiscriminately on entrepreneurial and household incomes. With that only, significant political economic connection cannot be traced to entrepreneurship. Tax revenues were spent on the public projects such as irrigation systems. In the Polonnaruwa reign, elephant trading floor was operated by the government where imports, trading, and exports of elephants were carried out and taxes were collected. Historical records show the government's interests on the elephant trading floor but not on other businesses. Tax revenue was partly spent on agriculture but it is still hard to trace evidence that the government had set up a coordinated policy and institutional framework for business which is a sign of absence of political economy of entrepreneurship.[17]

Colonial Policy Regime

In the mediaeval times, when the Portuguese organized the liquor industry, there has been a proper licensing and taxing system related to that industry (Kumari Jayawardene, 2000).[18] The Dutch East India Trading Company, after the Portuguese rule ended, organized and coordinated coffee garden cultivation system on the coastal belt and initiated coffee processing plants as state entrepreneurship. Thereafter, large cinnamon plantations were started as the state projects (Vanden Driesen, 1963).[19] More than any other crop, cinnamon business was heavily coordinated and controlled by the state rising as the sole owner of the crop by enacting the cinnamon law also (Rajaratne, 2008).[20] Other crops and trading articles also were controlled to a great extent by the Dutch government and the taxes collected from trades were invested in road and canal construction and setting up of the civil administrative system. A remarkable shift in the political economy of entrepreneurship was noted during the British rule, particularly after the Colebrook-Cameron

Reforms introduced in 1832.[21] Although a laissez-faire system had been recommended, land alienation, plantation permission, and taxation rights were held by the government showing that there was a central control of entrepreneurial activities.

The end of the coffee era in the 1870s marked the end of the laissez-faire regime recommended by Colebrook and Cameron. Since then, the government engaged in more formal coordination and control of business activities. Lack of steady income caused troubles to colonial administration and additionally, Ceylon had the obligation to contribute to her Master -the British empire. Tea and rubber took the lead of plantation crops and the government took control of many facets of the plantation business except engaging in cultivation and exports.[22] Coordination and control of the plantation industry were pivotal to the government as it was the means to earn tax incomes to run the colony.[23]

Construction of roads, ports, railway, telephone system, setting up of banking and financial system, authorized collector and trader dealership system, research and development, land alienation, and many other aspects of the plantation industry were assumed by the government as its responsibilities. Government managed to collect enormous income from fees and taxes and invested the income in infrastructure development, peasant agriculture sector, public health and education, public administration, food subsidy, and many more. In later years of the colonial administration, ordinances on commercial, industrial, labor, safety, and merchandising were introduced to control and coordinate the entrepreneurial activities. Toward the end of the colonial rule, state led corporations were initiated to achieve self-sufficiency in goods otherwise had to be imported.[24]

Policy Regime of 1948–1978

After gaining independence from the British rule in 1948, Sri Lanka took a drastic turn in the political economy of everything and thus, entrepreneurship was no exception. Private entrepreneurship was regarded as an essential activity while the state also assumed significant role in entrepreneurship. Since independence, it is evident that there is a duality in entrepreneurship in Sri Lanka; the state sector entrepreneurship and the private sector entrepreneurship. Large projects and heavy industries were initiated by the state for two reasons; first, absence of private entrepreneurs, and second, the government's attitude to control crucial utility industries such as water, gas, and electricity. In the early years since independence, both private and state sector entrepreneurship enjoyed an environment conducive for co-existence. However, the duality in entrepreneurship has produced discriminatory outcomes.[25]

The periodic change in governments led to drastic changes in the entrepreneurship policy of the also. An era of state sector entrepreneurship emerged giving birth to more than two dozens of state corporations since the early 1960s. The idea was to take crucial industries into the hands of government according to its industrial development policy. Industrial Development Board, Small and Medium Industry initiatives, handcraft development departments, Tourist Board, Hotel corporation, state banks, insurance corporation, and many more were created at the outset.[26] Then began the nationalization of foreign enterprises. Petroleum companies, airport, harbor, manufacturing industries, and service industries were first targets. Unites State, conflicted with Sri Lanka (then Ceylon) conflicted against nationalization of their corporates by imposing Hickenlooper Amendment Law[27] and slashed all corporate relations. And then plantations, hotels, and almost every business of foreign ownership and some local ownership fell into the hands of government by the mid-1970s. As a result, during this period, entrepreneurial activities were lying low and GDP remained largely stagnant as indicated in Fig. 18.3.

Entrepreneurial opportunities left for the private sector were meager. Business Undertakings Acquisitions Act of 1971[29] and Land Reforms Act of 1972[30] capped the opportunities for the private sector entrepreneurship. Public revenues were channeled to the state corporations (Vidanapathirana, 1985)[31] which were producing under-capacity and making loss, despite they enjoyed monopolistic privileges. Investments and reinvestments were discouraged in the private sector. However, smalltime domestic producers popped up to cater to the market gap caused by import shortages.

Policy Regime Since 1978

Economic growth was slowed down due to poor performance and inefficiencies of the state sector monopolies by the year 1977.[32] As a remedy, market liberalization policies came into effect in Sri Lanka after that year. Entrepreneurship liberalization, market liberalization, financial

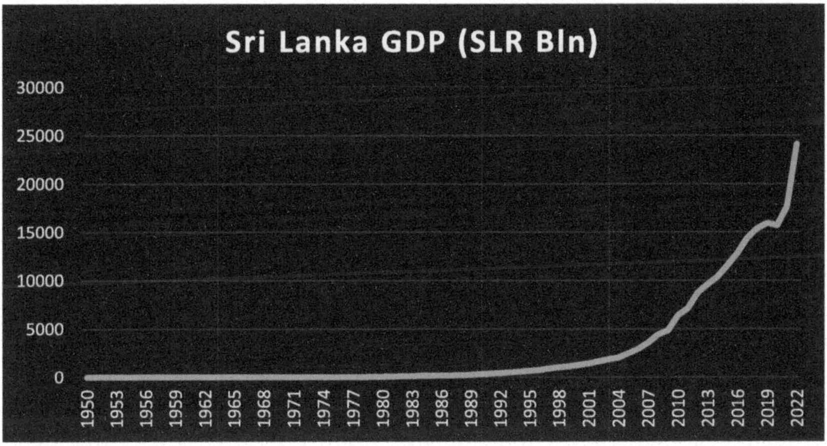

Fig. 18.3 Sri Lanka GDP (1950–2022) (*Data* Central Bank of Sri Lanka [2023][28])

liberalization, export–import liberalization, and foreign exchange liberalization were the principal instruments of the liberalization regime. A large number of legislations and institutions also were furnished to support the liberalization program. In addition, abolishing and repealing of restrictive laws, and amending existing Acts and enactment of new laws also are significant in the reforms. The local private sector was encouraged to play a significant role as the engine of growth.[33]

Amidst the facilitation extended to the local private entrepreneurship, the foreign private investors also were invited to invest in industries under special incentives provided by the Greater Colombo Economic Commission; which was later named as the Board of Investment. Foreign Direct Investment (FDI)-driven export promotion industrialization policy was a key economic development strategy. The policy of the government was to end the state monopoly of industry and thus, measures were taken to privatize state sector corporations and to enhance their performance. However, the government was reluctant to privatize some key enterprises such as electricity, gas, water, transportation, telecommunication, and aviation.[34]

In order to alleviate regional income disparity and to enhance regional development, regional factory installation project was introduced in the early 1990s. A significant change in the political economy of entrepreneurship occurred in the early 1990s as the Public Enterprise Reforms Commission (PERC) was introduced. The state-run telecom, airline, gas, plantations, and a few other state corporations came under privatization on the recommendation of the PERC after 1994.[35]

In the recent past, again, new state enterprises were introduced after re-nationalization of the previously privatized enterprises such as aviation, insurance, and gas. The Revival of Underperforming Enterprises or Underutilized Assets Act, no. 43 of 2011[36] was passed targeting nationalization of already privatized but underutilized enterprises. A mix approach to the policy of entrepreneurship was noticed during the past two decades as politicians heavily entered business. This move has a direct relationship between accumulation of political power and expenses of election campaign of individual politicians. The electoral and governance systems formulated an environment conducive for the politician to enter business. Monopolistic and license-based entrepreneurship opportunities were mostly reserved for the politicians. This makes a turnaround in the policy of entrepreneurship in the country in the recent past.

Foreign participation of business also was expanded through infrastructure development such as Colombo Port City, Hambantota port, and jetties of Colombo Harbor in addition to foreign direct investment in other trades. Setting up of the Board of Investment (BOI) in 1992 liberalizing the GCEC regulations to include the whole country to government concessions scheme to every foreign investment project is a significant step of the policy to get foreign participation in business. The BOI is now considering large projects to be approved on the basis of Build Own Operate (BOO), and Build Operate Transfer (BOT) as new greenfield ventures. In response, both local and foreign participation in export trade expanded after 1978 as it is evident from Fig. 18.4.[37]

Small and Medium Enterprise Development, Entrepreneurship Development, Micro finance, and Women enterprise development have been considered and institutionalized to boost the national income, to alleviate poverty and regional income disparity. Tourism industry has been considered as a key sector of regional and national economic development and thus, financing, training, human resource development, and tourism promotion are imparted through the Tourist Board. At present, with the looming economic crisis, the government seeks ways to privatize several state-run enterprises which are a burden for the national budget. The proposed privatization will invite local and foreign entrepreneurs and will

Fig. 18.4 Sri Lanka Export Earnings (1950–2022) (*Data* Central Bank of Sri Lanka [2023][38])

help make a home-run to the entrepreneurship policy that existed before the 1960s.[39]

The policies and institutional framework of the government of Sri Lanka concerning entrepreneurship have been inconstant during the past several decades. Political ideologies of different governments have considerably affected the political economy of entrepreneurship in the country. Every government has upheld micro enterprise and small and medium industry development despite the poly framework adopted has been different. Domestic entrepreneurship and industry protection policy was a key feature of the close market policy. However, the open market policy aimed at improving competitiveness of the domestic private entrepreneurs as well as the state enterprises instead of protection. This confirms that different policy instruments have been adopted to suit to different policy frameworks. However, the formation of entrepreneurial culture takes long time. Any disturbance suppresses the entrepreneurial vigor of a country. Sri Lanka's long experience of entrepreneurship hostile policies have thwarted progressing entrepreneurship as indicated in Fig. 18.5.

Since 1978, the political economy of Sri Lanka was entrepreneur-friendly and as a result entrepreneurial activities rapidly expanded with foreign direct investment projects under Board of Investment giving rise to the per capita income as indicated in Fig. 18.6. However, significant

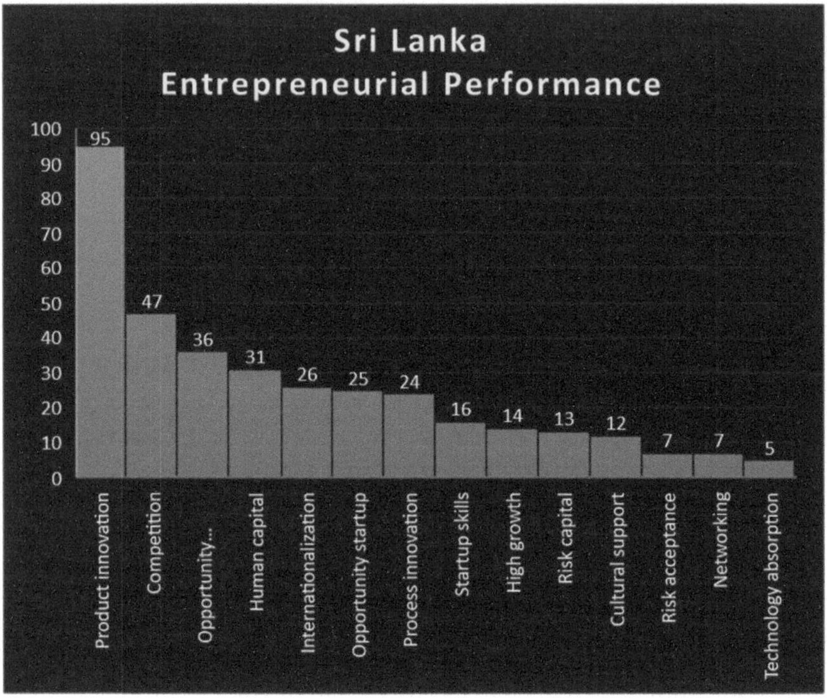

Fig. 18.5 Sri Lanka entrepreneurial performance (*Data* Global Entrepreneurship Development Report [2019][40])

growth of per capita income is only realized after the year 2000 and then after 2009 as the civil war ended and entrepreneurial activities expanded. Per capita income has been massaged by the income from tourism also which does not have much connection to innovation process. Due to decline in tourist arrival since 2018 and then during the COVID-19 pandemic and the economic crisis followed by, the per capita income has sharply declined.[41]

A General Overview

An inquiry into institutional setup of the governments in the past several decades reveals that every government has committed to development of domestic industries. These initiatives have two aspects; one is private

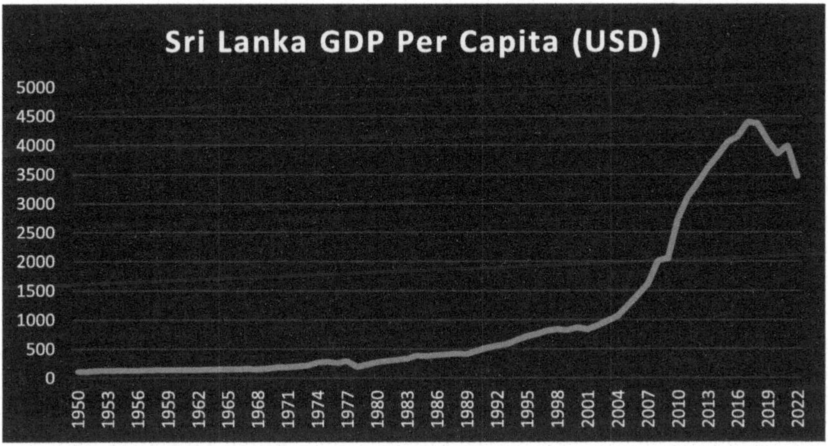

Fig. 18.6 Sri Lanka per capita income (1950–2022) (*Data* Central Bank of Sri Lanka [2023][42])

sector enterprise development and the other is the state sector enterprise development. Sri Lanka invariably attempted to maintain "a balance" between public and private enterprises under both closed and open market policy regimes. This stance led to serious crowd-out in the private sector entrepreneurship; particularly in large enterprises. But governments found that the state sector enterprises were instrumental for the governments to intervene in markets and to promote political ideologies against market economy.[43]

Change in the tax policy, subsidies to entrepreneurs, concessions for the foreign investors, nationalization, and privatization of the same enterprise back and forth are some of the signs of different public initiatives to enterprise development. Initially, in 1952, World Bank mission recognized the role of small enterprises (popularly identified as Cottage and Small-Scale Industries = CSSI) in economic development in Sri Lanka. As an initiative to small enterprise development, in 1957, the Department of Rural Development and Cottage Industry Development was established. In 1964, Laksala was established for the purpose of empowerment of handcraft industry. The Department of CSSI was restructured to establish the Department of Rural Development and Small Industries in 1968. Handloom, pottery, and woodworks were the major rural industries that were promoted under this department. Establishment of

Ministry of Industries and Industrial Development Board were milestones of political economy of entrepreneurship in Sri Lanka.[44]

Under closed market policies, a large number of public enterprises were established in the form of public Departments, Corporations, Boards, and Authorities. Under open market policies since 1978, Sri Lanka entered a new sphere of industrial development that heavily promoted domestic and foreign entrepreneurship and privatization of public enterprises. Implementation of Foreign Investments Advisory Committee, Board of Investment, Export Processing Zones are main features of foreign entrepreneurship promotion in the country. Also, provincial enterprise development programs, regional and rural banking for enterprise development, export promotion, invention promotion, standard and packaging development, technology development, banking and credit facility enhancement, rural development, and women empowerment are examples for broader initiatives of the government.

Efficiencies, inefficiencies, encouragement to investment, discouragement to investment, loss of private assets, limitation to operations in certain fields of business, retardment of innovation, barriers to technological advancement, support for innovation and technological development, local entrepreneurship development and so forth are the topics of the political economy of entrepreneurship in Sri Lanka. Major information sources of these topics are national budget speeches, public policy documents, Public Ordinances and Acts, Government Gazettes, and the Hansard Reports. These primary sources exhibit the historical formation and different facets of the political economy of entrepreneurship in Sri Lanka. Table 18.1 provides general indicators that help estimating the entrepreneurial state of Sri Lanka. Apparently, Sri Lanka is rated highly undesirable entrepreneurship location which can only be overturned with favorable policy regime.[45]

Chapter Summary

Political economy encompasses numerous policy spheres including market policy, macroeconomic policy, monetary policy, fiscal policy, development policy, entrepreneurship development policy, poverty alleviation policy, exports and imports policy, industrial policy, and many more. The concept and practice of political economy emerged as communities rose and transformed as nation states which were empowered with governing authority known as government or polity. Government coordinates and controls the

Table 18.1 Sri Lanka's entrepreneurial position

Data source and criteria	*Value/rank*	*Note*
Global Entrepreneurship Index (Value)	22	Out of 100 points (2019)
Global Entrepreneurship Index (Rank)	90	Among 137 countries (2019)
Ease of Doing Business (Rank)	99	Among 190 countries (2020)
Global Entrepreneurship Monitor (Value)	19.9	Out of 100 points (2021)
Global Innovation Index (Value)	23.3	Out of 100 points (2022)
Global Innovation Index (Rank)	85	Among 132 countries (2022)
Economic Complexity Index (Rank)	80	Most complex economy out of 133 countries (2021)
Global Competitiveness Index (Rank)	69	Out of 140 countries (2021)
Corruption Perception Index (Rank)	94	Out of 140 countries (2021)

Data Compiled from various sources as indicated in the table

socio-economy through a wide institutional setup to the tune of political economic ideology of the government. All these policies either directly or indirectly impact on entrepreneurship opportunities, practices, success, and sustainability. Therefore, degree and strength of entrepreneurship of nations are much a reflection of their policy spheres.

Entrepreneurship policy to promote and develop enterprises, among numerous policies of governance, deserves prominence in the policy sphere at present. Entrepreneurship policy sometimes is not advocated in its name but in numerous programs proposed in the Government Annual Budget under ministerial allocations, Parliamentary Acts, or Ordinances. Public policy and programs are designed either in favor of state entrepreneurship or private entrepreneurship; nationalization and privatization of ventures are the outcomes. Some programs are designed to enhance entrepreneurial atmosphere via economic liberalization and open market policy regimes whereas some other programs enhance entrepreneurs by way of providing financial or other assistance. Micro entrepreneurship development programs provide direct support to entrepreneurs.

State entrepreneurship development programs (SEDP), small and medium enterprise (SME) development, micro enterprise programs

(MEP), self-employment micro entrepreneurship programs, privatization of state ventures, nationalization of private ventures, public–private partnerships (PPP), international merger and acquisition (IM&A), international licensing and franchising (IL&F), foreign direct investment (FDI), offshore companies, and foreign joint ventures (FJV) reflect the political economic ideology of a country in relation to entrepreneurship. Industry support schemes, infant industry protection schemes, free trade zones, and tax havens are also favorable signs of entrepreneurship friendly environment.

Examination of the economic policy regimes lays foundation for political economic analysis of entrepreneurship. The state entrepreneurship policy, policy objectives, policy implementation support systems, policy shift, policy outcomes, and economics of entrepreneurship are the key concerns of the political economic analysis of entrepreneurship. Although political economic analyses are popular in the fields like socio-economy, public finance, underdevelopment, and development, the political economic discourse of entrepreneurship is a topic that has not caught much limelight. A few authors, however, have recently shown new directions and dimensions of analyses in this field. Works of Magnus Henrekson and Robin Douhan significantly contribute to the literature of the political economy of entrepreneurship. Entrepreneurship is as worthy as an engine of economic development. But, in the literature, entrepreneurship policy analyses, country cases, and comparative studies are hardly traceable. This chapter introduces a bit of flavor of a case study of Sri Lanka.

Review Questions

1. Define political economy of entrepreneurship.
2. Discuss the relationship among the government, public policy, and entrepreneurship opportunities.
3. "Governments assume an important role in entrepreneurship via regulating and creating state enterprises." Explain why governments intervene in entrepreneurship.
4. "Political economic ideology of the state determines entrepreneurship environment of nations." Discuss referring to diverse political ideologies.

5. Evaluate political economy of entrepreneurship as a new field as it suggests vast potential for the prospective researchers to investigate the role of the state.
6. Differentiate between the state entrepreneurship and the private entrepreneurship highlighting the differences of their objectives and practices.
7. Assess the impact of nationalization and privatization policies of governments on the private sector entrepreneurial spirit providing specific examples.
8. "Annual Budgets, Parliamentary Acts, and Ordinances are important sources of public policy on entrepreneurship." Explain how they are useful for researchers.
9. Describe the entrepreneurial experience of Sri Lanka as a case of political economy of entrepreneurship comparing with another country of your choice.
10. "The East Asian nations adopted private entrepreneurship friendly policies as early as 1960s and became high entrepreneurial and high-income countries after two decades." Express your views on this statement.
11. "China's stepwise economic liberalization led to massive entrepreneurship development since mid-1970s." Explain the political economy of entrepreneurship of China.
12. "South Asia is a latecomer in liberalization of entrepreneurship and now gaining momentum of entrepreneurship power in the region." Comment.
13. "Sri Lanka's political economy of entrepreneurship sharply contrasts between two periods: 1948–1978 and post 1978 period." Contrast the public policies of the two political economic regimes.
14. Explain how the colonial policy regimes converted non-entrepreneurial nations into entrepreneurial nations during the colonial administration. Give examples from the experience of Africa, Asia, and South America.

Additional Readings

1. Magnus, H., Wallenberg, J. et al. Eds., 2008. *The political economy of entrepreneurship*. Gloucestershire: Edward Elgar Publishing.

2. Henrikson, M., and Douhan, R., 2008. *The political economy of entrepreneurship* (Vol II). Cheltenham: Edward Elgar Publishing.
3. Brown, S., 1984. The world polity and the nation-state system: An updated analysis. *International Journal, 39*(3), pp. 509–528.
4. Fuerlinger, G., Fandl, U., and Funke, T., 2015. The role of the state in the entrepreneurship ecosystem: Insights from Germany. *Triple Helix, 2*(1), pp. 1–26.
5. Bennett, D.L., Boudreaux, C., and Nikolaev, B., 2021. Populist Discourse and Entrepreneurial Action: The Role of Political Ideology and Institutions. In *Academy of Management Proceedings* (Vol. 2021, No. 1, p. 15795). Briarcliff Manor, NY 10510: Academy of Management.
6. Douhan, R., and Henrekson, M., 2008. Productive and destructive entrepreneurship in a political economy framework.
7. Link, A.N., and Link, J.R., 2009. *Government as entrepreneur*. Oxford University Press.
8. Milanović, B., 1989. *Liberalization and entrepreneurship: Dynamics of Reform in Socialism and Capitalism*. ME Sharpe.
9. Sharma, S., 2021. *Entrepreneurship development*. PHI Learning Pvt. Ltd.
10. Yahya, S., and Kingsman, B., 2002. Modelling a multi-objective allocation problem in a government sponsored entrepreneur development program. *European Journal of Operational Research, 136*(2), pp. 430–448.
11. Ebner, A., 2005. Entrepreneurship and economic development: From classical political economy to economic sociology. *Journal of Economic Studies, 32*(3), pp. 256–274.
12. Goel, R.K., and Nelson, M.A., 2023. Which political regimes foster entrepreneurship? An international examination. *The Journal of Technology Transfer, 48*(1), pp. 126–146.
13. Schumpeter, J.A., and Swedberg, R., 2021. *The theory of economic development*. Routledge.
14. Henrekson, M., and Douhan, R., 2008. *The political economy of Entrepreneurship*. Edward Elgar Publishing.
15. Krishna, K.V.S.M., 2011. Magnus Henrekson and Robin Douhan (eds), The political economy of entrepreneurship (Vol. II). Cheltenham: Edward Elgar Publishing, 2008, 534 pp. *The Journal of Entrepreneurship, 20*(1), pp. 147–151.

16. Jonsson, I., 2016. *The political economy of innovation and entrepreneurship: From theories to practice*. Routledge.
17. Mendis, G.C., 1996. *The Early History of Ceylon and Its Relations with India and Other Foreign Countries*. Asian Educational Services.
18. Jayawardena, K., 2000. *Nobodies to Somebodies—The rise of the colonial bourgeoisie*. Colombo: Social Scientist Association.
19. Driesen, I.H.V., 1963. *The economic history of Ceylon in the nineteenth century—The plantation industry, land, and capital*. Maharagama: Saman Publishers.
20. Rajaratne, M., 2008. Historical facets of the direct investment policy of Sri Lanka—The plantation era. In Dayaratne-Banda et al. (eds.), *Sri Lanka Aarthikaya: Nirbadhikaranaya haa Sanvardhanaya*. Colombo: Pathfinder Foundation.
21. https://www.britannica.com/topic/Colebrook-Cameron-Commission.
22. Craig, J.E., 2013. Ceylon. In *Tropical development* (pp. 221–249). Routledge.
23. Wickramasinghe, D.A., and Cameron, D.C., 2004. British capital, Ceylonese land, Indian labour: The imperialism and colonialism of evolution of tea plantations in Sri Lanka. *University of Sri Jayewardenepura*.
24. Snodgrass, D.R., 1966. *Ceylon: An export economy in transition*. Irwin Publishing.
25. Fernando, T., 1982. Political and economic development in Sri Lanka. *Current History, 81*(475), pp. 211–228.
26. Gamage, A.S., 2003. Small and medium enterprise development in Sri Lanka: A review. *Meijo Review, 3*(4), pp. 133 150.
27. https://www.sciencedirect.com/science/article/abs/pii/-0007681368900888.
28. https://www.cbsl.gov.lk/en/publications/economic-and-financial-reports/annual-reports.
29. http://www.commonlii.org/lk/legis/num_act/bua35o1971424/.
30. http://www.commonlii.org/lk/legis/consol_act/lr297160.pdf.
31. Vidanapathirana, U., 1986. Patterns of industrialization: Strategies and responses. In Rasaputra W., et al. (eds), *Facets of development in independent Sri Lanka*. Colombo: Ministry of Finance and Planning.

32. Shastri, A., 1997. Transitions to a free market: Economic liberalization in Sri Lanka. *The Round Table, 86*(344), pp. 485–511.
33. Athukorala, P.C., and Rajapatirana, S., 2000. Liberalization and industrial transformation: Lessons from the Sri Lankan experience. *Economic Development and Cultural Change, 48*(3), pp. 543–572.
34. Dunham, D., and Kelegama, S., 1994. Economic liberalization and structural reforms: The experience of Sri Lanka, 1977–93. *ISS Working Paper Series/General Series, 163*, pp. 1–37.
35. Balasooriya, A.F., Alam, Q., and Coghill, K., 2007. Ownership, competition and regulation under privatization policy: The Sri Lankan experience. *International Review of Administrative Sciences, 73*(4), pp. 611–628.
36. https://www.treasury.gov.lk/web/laws-regulations-and-reforms/section/revival%20of%20underperforming%20enterprises%20or%20underutilized%20assets.
37. Sultanuzzaman, M.R., Fan, H., Akash, M., Wang, B., and Shakij, U.S.M., 2018. The role of FDI inflows and export on economic growth in Sri Lanka: An ARDL approach. *Cogent Economics & Finance, 6*(1), p. 1518116.
38. https://www.cbsl.gov.lk/en/publications/economic-and-financial-reports/annual-reports.
39. Rajapakshe, W., 2018. An evaluation of four-decade experience of industrial policy in Sri Lanka: 1977–2017. *International Journal of Academic Research in Business and Social Sciences, 8*(12).
40. https://www.gemconsortium.org/report/gem-2019-2020-global-report.
41. Ravindra, D.M., 2011. Information communication technology (ICT) policy of Sri Lanka and its impacts to socioeconomic development: A review of Sri Lankan experience. *Journal of Education and Vocational Research, 1*(2), pp. 53–59.
42. https://www.cbsl.gov.lk/en/publications/economic-and-financial-reports/annual-reports.
43. Sally, R., 2006, November. Sri Lanka: The political economy of failure. In *Conference on Globalization and Economic Success: Policy Options for Sri Lanka*.
44. Rajapatirana, S., 2004. Industrial policy. *Economic Policy in Sri Lanka: Issues and Debates*, pp. 213–236.

45. Wignaraja, G., 2002. Trade and industrial policies and experience in Sri Lanka. In *Trade Policy and Industrialization in Turbulent Times* (pp. 407–438). Routledge.

CHAPTER 19

Entrepreneur Social Responsibility and Ethics

Key Learning Points

- Introduction.
- Individual's and corporate responsibility.
- Corporate ethics.
- Ethical Principles.
- Corporate Social Responsibility.
- Views of Andrew Carnegie.
- Views of Keith Davis and William Frederick.
- Views of Milton Friedman.
- Views of Tim Stobiersky.
- Views of Zadek.
- Levels of Corporate Social Responsibility.
- Corporate Ethics.
- Debate on Corporate Social Responsibility.
- Corporate Citizen.
- Entrepreneurship and social responsibility.
- Entrepreneurship and ethics.
- Society as a watchdog of business activities.
- Need for socially responsible and ethical organizations.
- Conflict between Entrepreneurial goals and social goals.
- Costs and benefits of social responsibility and ethics.

© The Author(s), under exclusive license to Springer Nature Singapore Pte Ltd. 2024

M. Rajaratne, *Concepts, Processes and Practice of Entrepreneurship*, Palgrave Studies in Global Entrepreneurship,
https://doi.org/10.1007/978-981-97-6180-7_19

- The discourse of social responsibility and ethics.
- Socially friendly entrepreneurial practices.

Introduction

The evolution of cultures through millenniums has rewarded individuals, clans, households, and organizations with laws, rules, responsibilities, values, morals, and ethics. Thus, both individuals and organizations are supposed to conduct themselves in a way acceptable to the society at large.[1] Legal restrictions curtail or standardize behaviors; and breach of the laws is retributive according to the provisions of the law itself. But social responsibility, values, morals, and ethics are subjective and thus, they cannot set uniform behaviors in a society. Also, responsibilities, values, morals, and ethics are specific to persons and organizations and hence, personal and organizational behaviors are also different.[2] Perhaps an organization promotes responsibilities and values within its administration, but the individuals may rather behave on their beliefs and judgments than on the organizational standards.

Ethics involve personal judgments of good and bad, right and wrong, pleasant and unpleasant, nice and not nice, should and shouldn't. This connects to what should be sought or avoided. For business, ethics is an additional concern to management and principles of administration. Social responsibility, values, ethics, and morals guide business decisions and their applications. It is believed that ethical behavior of organizations always leads to benefits such as higher quality, higher profit, customer loyalty, and sustainability. On the contrary, some believe that unethical businesses bring more success compared to ethical businesses and that unethical behaviors carry high costs. Generally, however, integrity and accountability are considered as guiding principles of business.[3]

Social Responsibility of Individuals and Corporates

Corporate social responsibility is greater than that of individuals as corporates are more indebted to the society than individuals. Tokuji Hayakawa, the founder of Sharp Corporation, in his book "*Watashino Kangae Kata*"[4] mentioned that corporates have unrelinquishable indebtedness to the society. If the society or the market demands socially responsible corporate behavior, then the corporates must adopt responsibility practices. When the society has no concern of corporate's behavior, the entrepreneurs are free to carry out their operations without much worries. On the contrary, extreme competition to eliminate rivals might promote social agony against large firms. Therefore, some corporates resort to implementing social marketing programs to earn good faith of the society.[5]

It is within this context that entrepreneur social responsibility and ethics are considered as an important topic. Corporates have been increasingly compromising their responsibilities and ethics to fraud customers and the society for gaining unfair profit and market hegemony. So, the notion "corporate responsibility and ethics" emerged in the academic circles to guide the corporates and correct their irresponsible and unethical conduct. Entrepreneur is the person who builds and runs business organizations at a small or corporate scale. Therefore, entrepreneur engages in business decisions that may be counterproductive to the customers, markets, and society at large. Therefore, in entrepreneurship, due consideration needs to be given to entrepreneurial decision-making for constituting responsible and ethical organizational base and to highly commit to build an organization to pursue sustained advantages.[6]

Corporate Ethical Principles

For the question whether good ethics means good business, the answer is yes because the firms with good ethical conduct have generally achieved higher performance and sustainability. The increasing and extensive role of corporates has aroused social concerns over corporate social interaction, environmental impact, appropriateness of the use of resources to achieve corporate goals. In this background, the society values businesses not only in economic and legal terms but also in moral and ethical terms. Although ventures are created to achieve profitability goals, certain other concerns such as social norms, morality, social responsibility, and conduct also have to be considered in present day business.[7]

Now, unlike in the past several decades, entrepreneurs cannot ignore morality but concentrate only on venture growth and profit. Every entrepreneurial decision, thus, is tightly connected to responsibility and morality that are mirrored in the social and ethical conduct of the venture. So, the entrepreneur cannot evade from his responsibilities. Business ethics is believed to be a set of social responsibilities that are connected to morality and norms of the entrepreneur.[8] Some recognize entrepreneurship ethics as an invisible force that influences the entrepreneur in making business decisions ethically. Business decisions finally are seen as a regulator of the relationship between the business and the society which helps building harmony in that relationship.

The following ethical principles are commonly accepted and recommended for adoption in contemporary businesses.[9]

1. A business must not only develop and deliver products or services but also moral values
2. Businesses must direct their funds and profits toward socially important goals
3. Agenda on reconciling challenges must be given priority.

These principles advocate and support moral maturity of a business which in turn determines the ethical state of a business. An entrepreneur should not be hypersensitive to financial indicators in the short run but adopt core ethical values in him to guide his venture from the beginning. Well-defined ethical statements of a venture can differentiate it from rest of the ventures. In elevating ethical state of a business, the entrepreneur should do away with the following practices.[10]

- Production of low-quality goods
- Hiding information from authorities
- Price manipulation
- Product manipulation
- Collusive practices
- Fraudulent negotiations
- Cheating operational standards
- Personal gains from business
- Shady transactions
- Greediness and quick gains
- Cheating customer.

Corporate Social Responsibility

Corporate social responsibility requires the firm to designate specific actions for the benefit of the society in which it operates. This costs money and needs efforts and hence is sometimes believed to be counterproductive to profit maximization of the firm. So, it should be understood that the profit maximization objective needs to be achieved subject to responsibilities of the firm. Thus, the cost and revenue formula of the firm are affected by the social pressure for upholding corporate social responsibility and ethical behavior. In this sense, business profit is required to be justified by the firm's dedication to its social responsibility and ethics. The required scope of social responsibility practice of a firm thus corresponds to the degree of its impact on the society. The lower the corporate impact on the society, the lower will be its commitment to social responsibility. Therefore, the entrepreneurs who unleash much social impact through their businesses are obliged to bear responsibility to reconcile the impact.[11] The Triple Bottom Line principle (Fig. 19.1) is the most recent guideline that advocates people and planet friendly corporate performance.[12]

Views of Andrew Carnegie

The pioneering views of corporate social responsibility emerged from the book "*Gospel of Wealth*" of Andrew Carnegie (1899).[13] However, the literature of corporate social responsibility caught limelight after publication of the seminal book "*Social Responsibilities of the Businessman*" (Howard Bowen, 1953).[14] Bowen points out that businessmen are not free to operate at any cost to the society and thus, they are responsible for the social impact of their business actions. Robert Ackerman's book "*The Social Challenge to Business*" published in 1975[15] discusses the dilemmas of large corporations as they are caught in the cross-currents of the increasing public expectations regarding social issues. Ackerman raises the concerns such as pollution control, consumer safety, minority hiring, and the job placements and promotions for women on the corporate administration hierarchy. He recommends the large corporations to adapt to the new and demanding social climate adopting policies of social responsiveness, for their broader success, instead of reacting to social pressure.[16]

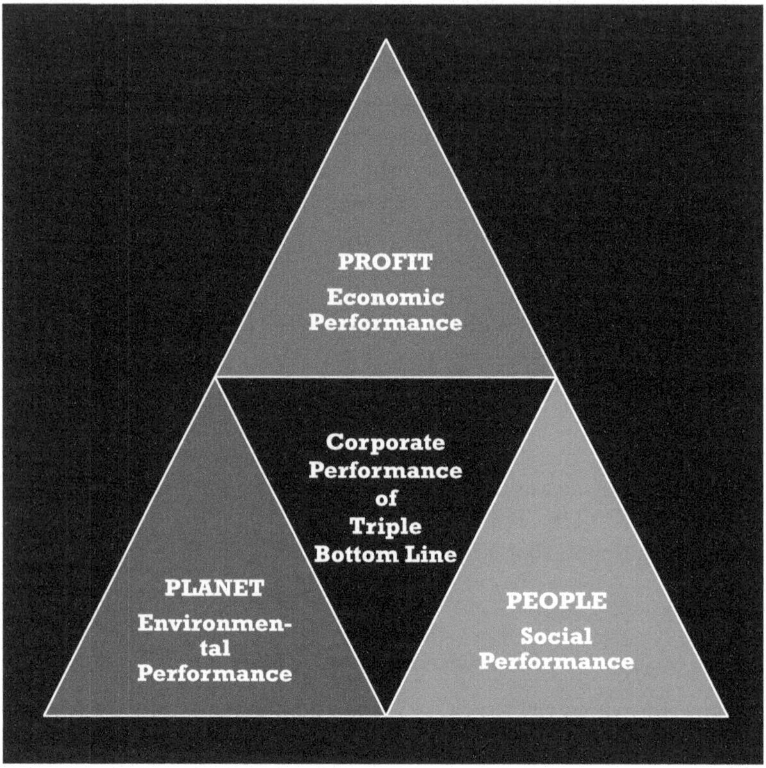

Fig. 19.1 The triple bottom line of CSR (Author Portrayal)

Views of Keith Davis and William Frederick

Keith Davis[17] and William Frederick[18] propagated Ackerman's views and established the notion "Corporate Social Responsiveness" as a means to build reconciliation between corporates and society.[19] Furthermore, recent studies propagate the notion that the corporate plan itself should carry objectives to uplift the society, and the corporate mission should employ designated actions to achieve such objectives. Some advocate the notion that corporate social responsibility should not be a mere reaction to issues but a pro-action to forecast the social impact of business activities and to avoid, control, or repair social damage.[20]

Views of Milton Friedman

Milton Friedman opposes to the views that suggest that the corporates should spend their resources in the interest of social responsibility. He points out that the sacrifice of corporate resources for non-entrepreneurial activities is counterproductive to achievement of chief corporate objective, i.e., profit maximization. His strong opinion is that anything that hinders profit maximization is a mark of loss of productivity which is a waste. Friedman iterated that waste causes social cost and thus, profit maximization itself is an action of cherishing social responsibility. In Friedman's view, the chief responsibility of the entrepreneur is to increase corporate profit and to operate as an agent of wealth creation.[21]

Views of Tim Stobiersky

Tim Stobiersky points out four types of corporate social responsibilities of a firm.[22] They are Environmental responsibility, Ethical responsibility, Philanthropic responsibility, and Economic responsibility. Environmental responsibility refers to corporate actions such as reducing harmful practices, controlling energy consumption, and offsetting negative environmental impact. The ethical responsibility is concerned with ethical business practices such as fairtrade and fair wage policy, child labor prohibition rule, prevention from aiding terrorism, crime, and apartheid. The philanthropic responsibility involves the corporate practices such as generating charitable funds and sacrificing a portion of earnings to support the socially and economically disadvantaged groups of population. Food aid, medical aid, education, training, and shelter are examples of charity actions. Economic responsibility, according to Stobiersky, is to aim at achieving economic and financial objectives of the firm with the purpose of achieving also the responsibilities to make the world peaceful, fair, and livable rather than concentrating only on profit maximization.

Views of Zadek

Zadek pointed out that corporates execute responsibilities in five stages.[23] They are Defensive, Compliance, Managerial, Strategic, and Civil in ascending order. The defensive action involves defending of criticism, through rejection, escalated against the firm by the society. At the next stage, the firm complies with the social critiques and does something casual only to satisfy the pressure groups. Managerial involvement comes next if the issue still remains and needs the firm to admit to it and take measures to rectify it. Strategic stage refers to the corporate strategic action that helps reap long-term gains via abiding by social responsibility. Social responsibility is embodied in corporate strategic plan at this stage. Finally, at the civil stage, corporate sets itself a moral example and leads socially friendly industry standards where the rivals are encouraged to follow the standards.

Levels of Corporate Social Responsibility

Corporate social responsibility is believed to be present at four levels: owner's level, organizational level, functional level, and social level. At each level, the entrepreneur is bestowed with specific responsibilities to be fulfilled. Firstly, at the owner's level, expectations of the investors and the members of the director board, (as internal stakeholders) must be attended.[24] Secondly, at the organizational level, expectations of the managers and workers (as internal stakeholders) must be fulfilled. Thirdly, at the functional level, the expectations of the stakeholders pertaining to the functional network (external stakeholders) of the organization need to be fulfilled. Fourthly, the social level consists of general public with varied expectations to be fulfilled by the corporates.[25]

Corporate Ethics

Most social issues that prevail today are believed to be caused by businesses and the majority of the issues are emanated from ignorance of ethics. Therefore, it is suggested that corporate behavior should be assigned with ethics to dress corporates as ethical entities.[26] Four types of corporate ethics are identified and recommended in the literature. They include Social-level ethics, Stakeholder-level ethics, Policy-level ethics, and Personal-level ethics. The social-level ethics suggest a business not to involve in practices that help promote racist, apartheid, and extremist social systems. Stakeholder-level ethics is concerned with the justice to be bidden for the internal and external stakeholders who are connected to or affected by the business. The policy-level ethics involves ethical and just and equal treatment for the employees in case of promotion and punishment, employee rights and contracts. The personal-level ethics refers to the interpersonal ethical relationship among the people within and outside the organization.[27]

Corporate ethics are described in four different terms which are interconnected: Values, Rights, Duties, Moral rules. All these ethics are required to be integrated into business policies and programs to give them due recognition within the corporate. This requires establishment of procedures, rules, by-laws, committees, ombudsman office, training, and education of ethical practices. Finally, it is recommended that corporates should conduct a Social Audit to learn the extent to which social responsibility and ethics are being practiced, the areas of less attention, drawbacks, and the remedial measures need to be undertaken.[28] Figure 19.2 indicates generally accepted corporate ethics.

Debate on Corporate Social Responsibility

An ongoing debate is seen in the corporate social responsibility literature. Some scholars are supportive while others are against the corporates' concern of social responsibility. Therefore, there are two sets of arguments for and against corporate social responsibility.[29] The common experience has been that the corporates do not much care about the social and environment impact of their own business activities and thus, governments have been imposing laws and standards for the corporates to comply with to protect consumers, employees, and natural environment. The non-commitment of businesses to principal responsibilities sometimes encourages the government to intervene in getting corporates to comply with them by regulation.[30] The debate on corporate social responsibility is summarized in Figs. 19.3 and 19.4 respectively presenting arguments for and against corporate social responsibility.

Views of Andrew Carnegie

The notion of social responsibility of business firms was first introduced by Andrew Carnegie (1899) in his book *The Gospel of Wealth*.[33] He described social responsibility of firms via two principles. They are; Charity principle and Stewardship principle. The charity principle identifies two groups of people in a society; one is affluent and the other is poor or needy. So, it is a responsibility of the affluent persons to help the disadvantaged (needy) persons. Businesses are considered as affluent whereas, unemployed, handicapped, sick, and elderly are considered as

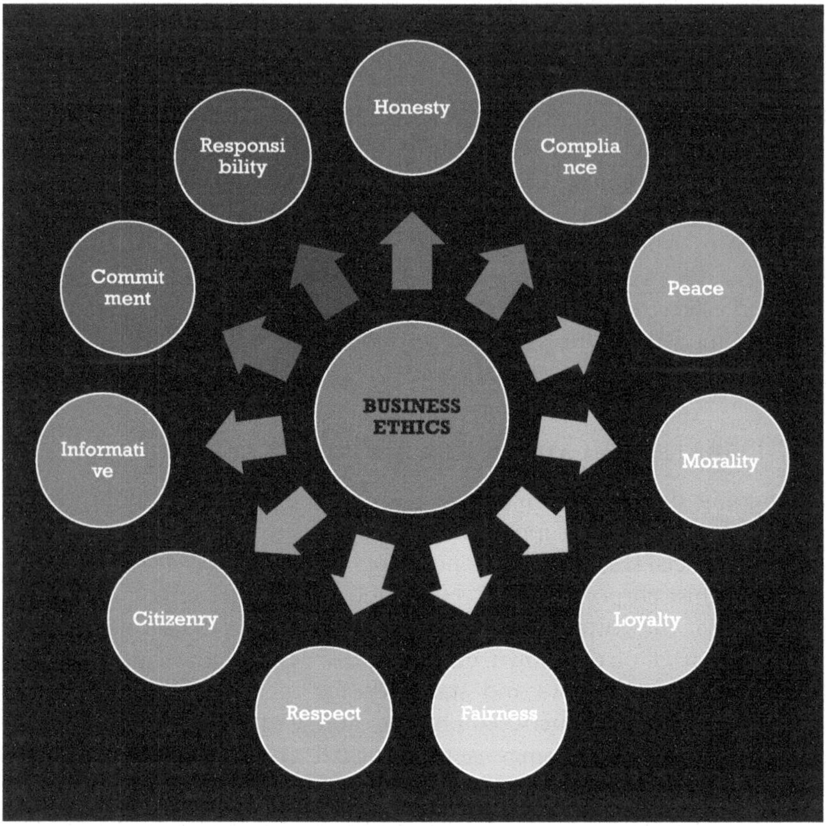

Fig. 19.2 Components of corporate ethics (Author Portrayal)

disadvantaged. The charity principle, thus, advocates that the former should directly or indirectly help the latter. According to the stewardship principle, businesses are considered as the trustees of wealth of nation. Businesses own enormous amounts of national wealth and the businesses should spend that wealth for the social wellbeing when needs arise in the society. Carnegie emphasizes that businesses should voluntarily perform this mission as a duty rather than as a response to legal compulsion.

ARGUMENTS FOR SOCIAL CARE OF BUSINESS

1. Business receives charter from the society and thus, has to positively respond to the needs of the society
2. Creation of better environment is beneficial to business as it in turn provides better employees, consumers, and suppliers
3. Social involvement rewards the business with government support
4. Businesses enjoys enormous amount of power and thus, they should accompany equal amount of responsibility.
5. Business activities are interdependent and corporate concern for external environment is indispensable
6. Stockholders may approve social involvement
7. Social involvement creates favorable public image
8. Businesses always have solutions to problems faced or caused by other institutions
9. Businesses can proactively engage in addressing social problems
10. Businesses have abundant resources and some of which can be sacrificed to social needs.

Fig. 19.3 Arguments for corporate social care (Author portrayal based on Weihrich, H. and Harold Koontz [1993][31])

Views of Milton Friedman

Milton Friedman, well known economist, maintained the notion that every business is given a social responsibility to efficiently use its resources and to maximize its profit.[34] He further mentions that managers are neither delegated authority nor do they have rights to spend any of the business assets on social needs. The care for social responsibility only helps

ARGUMENTS AGAINST SOCIAL CARE OF BUSINESS

1. Social involvement can reduce economic efficiency and profit of business
2. If committed resources for social action, the cost of production increases and the society ultimately pays the price
3. Businesses spending for social wellbeing may be less competitive than those who do not bear such expenses and the competitive issue might weaken balance of payment and national currency
4. Social involvement can further increase the power of businesses which already prevails at a high level
5. Training and skills gathered by businesses are for economic activities and thus, they may not be much useful to social activities
6. Lack of business accountability has caused some social problems and increase of accountability itself can bring down social problems
7. Conflicting views among the director board members will lead to confusion in selecting between business goals and social goals

Fig. 19.4 Arguments against corporate social care (Author portrayal based on Weihrich, H. and Harold Koontz [1993][32])

uplift social wellbeing but compromises the principal mission of achieving internal stakeholder objectives. So, he emphasized that corporate enthusiasm on social responsibility can harm the business and the stakeholder interests. Accordingly, Friedman mentioned that the managers are trustees of corporates and thus, they should engage in fulfilling the responsibilities assigned to them by the corporate owners through exerting corporate mission they are delegated but not in any outside responsibilities. He further stressed that corporate interest should confine to efficient production, distribution, and sales of goods and services and to let governments and other voluntary organizations carry out social works.

Views of Keith Davis

In the article, "*social responsibility is inevitable*," published in California Management Review, Keith Davis (1976)[35] argued that corporates must behave with enlightened self-interest to care for the society. Although businesses can operate without much consideration of the society in the short run, they should take the social issues into consideration as social acceptance and recognition are essential for the long-term survival. When a business spends some of its earnings for the benefit of the society, the society in turn helps to protect the business from hostile moves of governments and pressure groups. Additionally, the enlightened self-interest can be upheld through the corporate actions such as fair trade, loyalty, and environmentally friendly production processes.

Views of Robert Ackerman

Robert Ackerman (1976)[36] advocated the notion Corporate Social Responsiveness. Accordingly, corporates should adopt a mechanism to recognize social problems and devise suitable responses to help overcome them. This notion establishes the importance of viewing corporate involvement in social problems as a process of response rather than as a responsibility. Ackerman pointed out social response of business as a cyclical process in which recognizing, studying, identifying solutions, and remedying social issues are essential components. Ackerman's model calls for the corporate focus on internal policies and their relevance to social responsibilities. He proposes six strategies that a corporate could adopt: (1) rejection strategy, (2) adversary strategy, (3) resistance strategy, (4) compliance strategy, (5) accommodation strategy, and (6) proactive strategy.

Views of Archie Carroll

Archie Carroll (1979)[37] suggests that Corporate Social Performance is a more appropriate approach to deal with social responsibility. This approach emphasizes that a social contract is built with the corporates that comply with legal, ethical, and economic principles. So, the corporates should take measures to establish mechanism in business policies to uphold this social contract. Carroll suggests four types of social performances. First, reactive performance that invites businesses to react to the social pressure. Second, defensive performance to avert and to protect from social pressure. Third, accommodative performance to perform in accordance with legal and social guidance. Fourth, proactive performance to act in advance to recognize social problems and to prepare the corporate to face them. These responses correspond to Carroll's pyramid of CSR.[38] Accordingly, a business to be socially responsible should meet economic, legal, ethical, and philanthropic expectations assigned to it by the society. The expectations rise in a pyramid like formation down from economic responsibilities (profitable), legal responsibilities (legitimate), ethical responsibilities (moral), and to philanthropic responsibilities (corporate citizenry).

New Trends

Despite the fact that there are profound arguments for and against corporate social responsibility, there has been a wide acceptance among corporates to achieve some social responsibility targets during the past couple of decades. Regardless of the scale of the business, commitment to social responsibility has become a usual practice at present. Social impact of irresponsible and unethical business practices is a heavier concern for large corporates as they operate in wider markets and international scale. The entrepreneurs, therefore, are compelled to design their businesses to mitigate the social impact on one hand and to compensate damage on the other. Also, entrepreneur's social responsibility attitudes are examined in their business proposals by the interested parties such as government agencies, bankers, investors, and professional managers. The entrepreneurs who exhibit favorable attitudes toward social responsibility are more likely to receive favorable responses from the prospective stakeholders.[39]

Small startups usually do not bother about the social responsibilities that are concerns of the scale described above. However, for small businesses, moral and ethical practices are more relevant than social responsibility. In other words, the larger the business the more relevant the corporate social responsibility. This, however, does not rule out that the small businesses are free from social responsibility. It is always useful for businesses, regardless of their scale, to be concerned with social responsibilities and ethics as Tokuji Hayakawa, the founder of Sharp Corporation, pointed out in his "eternal indebtedness" concept. Therefore, it is always a sensible practice for all the types of businesses to be concerned with social responsibility and ethics. Thus, an entrepreneur who is looking for business opportunities should be mindful to understand the social impact of his business move to intervene in fulfilling social needs and wants.[40]

In a business proposal, an entrepreneur should include his concerns for the social impact of the business and his commitment to social responsibility and ethical practices through venture operations. The social responsibility and ethical concerns will be helpful to improve the goodness of a feasibility plan.[41] It will not be challenging for the entrepreneur to work with different layers of the organization to build commitment to social responsibility and ethics because objectives are already included in the business proposal. Also, the entrepreneurs should be mindful of the fact that social pressure escalates against the business as it grows and the operations are more diversified. At growth and maturity stages, entrepreneurs should be mindful and strategic to adopt social responsibility and ethics in the form of Corporate Social Contract and thereupon, Corporate Social Reporting to maintain social friendly operations.[42]

Corporate Citizen

The commitment to corporate social responsibility finally will qualify firms to be designated as Corporate Citizens (Howard Bowen, 2013).[43] At present, corporates can gain public recognition through good corporate governance practices and designation as corporate citizens.[44] Corporate governance and corporate citizenship emphasize the commitment to build responsible, ethical, and accountable businesses. Accordingly, corporate citizens (broadly the business, founders, and leaders) are recognized by every government. As an example, Japanese Emperor's award, "The Order of the Rising Sun,"[45] is endowed to noble Japanese entrepreneurs on behalf of their good corporate practices. Further, foreign governments and international organizations also recognize corporate citizens. Konosuke Matsushita of Panasonic corporation and Akio Morita of Sony corporation were given a large number of such foreign awards to recognize their contribution as the founder entrepreneurs. Becoming a distinctive corporate citizen is not only a personal pride for the entrepreneur but also an

Table 19.1 World top 10 corporate citizens

Rank	*Company*	*Score*
1	Owens Corning	91.88
2	PepsiCo Inc.	91.01
3	Apple Inc.	90.65
4	HP Inc.	89.95
5	Sisco Systems Inc.	88.79
6	Merc & Co. Inc.	87.41
7	Microsoft Corp.	86.95
8	PSEG Inc.	86.69
9	Ford Motor Co.	86.54
10	Intel Corp.	85.30

Data 3BL Media LLC (2022)[47]

indicator of building a corporate that contributes to the wellbeing of all its stakeholders being a high-trust, high-commitment, and high-performance entity (Beer, 2009),[46] which is the ultimate goal of all entrepreneurs; a good corporate citizen with corporate sustainability. Table 19.1 identifies the world top 10 corporate citizens.

Chapter Summary

Entrepreneurship is a wider social course of action that affects the society both favorably and unfavorably. It is the entrepreneurs who organize operations of the supply chain that involve production and trade which comprise 100 trillion currently as world GDP. Society is keen on the entrepreneurial actions and their impacts on the people's lives. As a result, social responsibility and ethics of business have become a critical concern. Corporates tend to commit fraud to both internal and external stakeholders for gaining market hegemony and undue profit. Accumulation of wealth, waste, uneconomical use of resources, discrimination, conspiracy, and subversive acts are also social concerns emanating from entrepreneurial actions. More importantly, yet, pollution is also an acute related concern.

The notion Corporate Social Responsibility (CSR) and Ethics thus, has emerged from the society and the academia as a social pressure to set the right direction for entrepreneurial actions. The aim of which is to create socially responsible and ethical organizations. Society values businesses not only as economic entities but also as moral and ethical entities. Although ventures are created to achieve profitability goals, present day businesses are monitored for conduct also. Because organizational behaviors vary, their social responsibility, values, morals, and ethics also vary across organizations. Ethics involve personal judgments on good and bad, right and wrong, pleasant and unpleasant, nice and not nice, should and shouldn't, etc. Social responsibility and ethics are beneficial as they guide businesses to good governance. It is proven that good governance brings higher profit, customer loyalty, and venture sustainability. Dissenting views are also present against the notion of corporate social responsibility. Milton Friedman's early views encouraged a discourse to challenge the pro-responsibility views propagating the notion that businesses' care about social responsibility are not cost effective as their funds deviate from the corporate mission.

A few ethical principles are commonly accepted and recommended for adoption in contemporary businesses. They are a business must not only develop and deliver products or services but also moral values, businesses must direct their funds and profits toward socially important goals, and agenda on reconciling challenges must be given priority. Corporate social responsibility requires the firm to designate specific actions for the benefit of the society in which it operates. This costs money and needs efforts and hence is sometimes believed to be counterproductive to profit maximization. Therefore, it is believed that profit maximization objective also can be achieved while caring for social responsibility. More importantly, it is expected that the entrepreneurs who unleash social impact through their business operations are obliged to bear its responsibility and must reconcile the impact. This chapter reviews the views of Andrew Carnegie, Howard Bowen, Robert Ackerman, Keith Davis and William Frederick, Archie Carroll, Milton Friedman, and Tim Stobiersky who have contributed largely to the subject area.

Review Questions

1. Explain what is meant by "entrepreneur social responsibility and ethics."
2. Discuss whether entrepreneur social responsibility and ethics are complementary to public laws or a public duty of organizations.
3. Describe the nature, principles, and practice of entrepreneur responsibility and ethics.

4. Discuss how corporate social responsibility and ethics have been proliferated by the major thoughts.
5. "Corporate Social Responsibility (CSR) is constructed at different levels." Identify the levels of CSR and describe the responsibilities pertaining to each level.
6. "Corporate ethics are a set of different principles compared to CSR and they are more related to attitudes than obligations." Critically evaluate.
7. Define Corporate Citizen and identify the responsibilities of a Corporate Citizen. Explain why an entrepreneur is expected to become a good Corporate Citizen.
8. "Society is a watchdog of business activities and thus the entrepreneurs must constantly adopt social friendly operations." Critically evaluate this statement.
9. "Entrepreneurial goals and social goals are conflicting." Comment.
10. "Commitment to social responsibility and ethics incur costs and yield benefits to entrepreneurs." Discuss whether the benefits can trade off the costs.
11. Examine the major views for and against the corporate social responsibility and ethics quoting major thought leaders.
12. What are the socially friendly entrepreneurship practices in contrast to socially hostile practices?
13. Suggest essential principles and practices for an entrepreneur to become a good Corporate Citizen.

Additional Readings

1. Bowen, H.R., 1953. *Social responsibility of the businessman*. New York: Harper & Row.
2. Hartman, L., 2003. *Perspective in business ethics*. New Delhi: Tata McGraw-Hill.
3. Ackerman, R.W., 1975. *The social challenge to business*. Berlin: De Gruyter.
4. Hayakawa, T., 2005. *Watashino Kangaekata* (2nd Ed.). Osaka: Tosho Shuppan Namiwa Sha.
5. Stobiersky, T., 2022. Types of corporate social responsibility to be aware of. *Harvard Business Review*.

6. Beer, M., 2009. *High commitment, high performance: How to build an organization capable of sustained advantage*. San Francisco: Jossey-Bass.
7. Donaldson, J., and Fafaliou, I., 2003. Business ethics, corporate social responsibility and corporate governance: A review and summary critique.
8. Joyner, B.E., and Payne, D., 2002. Evolution and implementation: A study of values, business ethics and corporate social responsibility. *Journal of Business Ethics, 41*, pp. 297–311.
9. Velasquez, M.G., 2018. *Business ethics: Concepts and cases*. Pearson.
10. Clegg, S., Kornberger, M., and Rhodes, C., 2007. Business ethics as practice. *British Journal of Management, 18*(2), pp. 107–122.
11. Carroll, A.B., 1979. A three-dimensional conceptual model of corporate performance. *The Academy of Management Review, 4*(4), pp. 497–505. https://doi.org/10.2307/257850.
12. Painter-Morland, M., 2006. Triple bottom-line reporting as social grammar: Integrating corporate social responsibility and corporate codes of conduct. *Business Ethics: A European Review, 15*(4), pp. 352–364.
13. Carnegie, A., 1889. The gospel of wealth and other timely essays. In *North American Review, CXLVIII*.
14. Bowen, H.R., 1953. *Social responsibility of the businessman*. New York: Harper & Row.
15. Ackerman, R.W. (1975). *The social challenge to business*. Berlin: De Gruyter.
16. Jamali, D., and Mirshak, R., 2007. Corporate social responsibility (CSR): Theory and practice in a developing country context. *Journal of Business Ethics, 72*, pp. 243–262.
17. Davis, K., 1960. Can business afford to ignore social responsibilities? *California Management Review, 2*(3), pp. 70–76.
18. Frederick, W.C., 1960. The growing concern over business responsibility. *California Management Review, 2*(4), pp. 54–61.
19. Davis, K., 1973. The case for and against business assumption of social responsibilities. *Academy of Management Journal, 16*(2), pp. 312–322.
20. Chang, C.H., 2015. Proactive and reactive corporate social responsibility: Antecedent and consequence. *Management Decision, 53*(2), pp. 451–468.

21. Friedman, M., 2007. The social responsibility of business is to increase its profits. In *Corporate ethics and corporate governance* (pp. 173–178). Berlin, Heidelberg: Springer Berlin Heidelberg.
22. Stobiersky, T., 2022. Types of corporate social responsibility to be aware of. *Harvard Business Review.*
23. Zadek, S. (2004). The path to corporate responsibility. In *Harvard Business Review*, 190–207. http://dx.doi.org/10.2307/1880689
24. Idowu, S.O., and Vertigans, S., 2016. *Stages of corporate social responsibility*. Springer.
25. Weber, M., 2008. The business case for corporate social responsibility: A company-level measurement approach for CSR. *European Management Journal, 26*(4), pp. 247–261.
26. Freeman, R.E., and Gilbert, D.R., 1988. *Corporate strategy and the search for ethics* (Vol. 1). Englewood Cliffs, NJ: Prentice Hall.
27. Babri, M., Davidson, B., and Helin, S., 2021. An updated inquiry into the study of corporate codes of ethics: 2005–2016. *Journal of Business Ethics, 168*, pp. 71–108.
28. Morimoto, R., Ash, J., and Hope, C., 2005. Corporate social responsibility audit: From theory to practice. *Journal of Business Ethics, 62*, pp. 315–325.
29. May, S.K., Cheney, G., and Roper, J., eds., 2007. *The debate over corporate social responsibility*. Oxford University Press.
30. Rahim, M.M., 2013. Legal regulation of corporate social responsibility. *CSR, Sustaina Eility, Ethics & Governance. DOI, 10*, pp. 978-3.
31. Weihrich, H., and Koontz, H., 1993. *Management: A global perspective*. New York: McGrow-Hill.
32. Weihrich, H., and Koontz, H., 1993. *Management: A global perspective*. New York: McGrow-Hill.
33. Carnegie, A., 1889. The gospel of wealth and other timely essays. In *North American Review, CXLVIII*.
34. Friedman, M., 2007. The social responsibility of business is to increase its profits. In *Corporate ethics and corporate governance* (pp. 173–178). Berlin, Heidelberg: Springer Berlin Heidelberg.
35. Davis, K., 1976. Social responsibility is inevitable. *California Management Review, 19*(1), pp. 14–20.
36. Ackerman, R.W., and Bauer, R.A., 1976. Corporate social responsiveness: The modern dilemma [sic]. *(No Title).*

37. Carroll, A.B., 1979. A three-dimensional conceptual model of corporate performance. *The Academy of Management Review, 4*(4), pp. 497–505. https://doi.org/10.2307/257850.
38. Carroll, A.B., 2016. Carroll's pyramid of CSR: Taking another look. *International Journal of Corporate Social Responsibility, 1*, pp. 1–8.
39. Morsing, M., and Schultz, M., 2006. Corporate social responsibility communication: Stakeholder information, response and involvement strategies. *Business Ethics: A European Review, 15*(4), pp. 323–338.
40. Morsing, M. and Schultz, M., 2006. Corporate social responsibility communication: Stakeholder information, response and involvement strategies. *Business Ethics: A European Review, 15*(4), pp. 323–338.
41. Yuan, W., Bao, Y., and Verbeke, A., 2011. Integrating CSR initiatives in business: An organizing framework. *Journal of Business Ethics, 101*, pp. 75–92.
42. Gray, R., Owen, D., and Maunders, K., 1988. Corporate social reporting: Emerging trends in accountability and the social contract. *Accounting, Auditing & Accountability Journal, 1*(1), pp. 6–20.
43. Bowen, H.R., 2013. *Social responsibilities of the businessman*. University of Iowa Press.
44. Carroll, A.B., 1998. The four faces of corporate citizenship. *Business and Society Review, 100*(1), pp. 1–7.
45. https://www.britannica.com/topic/Order-of-the-Rising-Sun.
46. Beer, M., 2009. *High commitment, high performance: How to build an organization capable of sustained advantage*. San Francisco: Jossey-Bass.
47. https://www.bloomberg.com/profile/company/0207305D:US.

Index

© The Editor(s) (if applicable) and The Author(s), under exclusive license to Springer Nature Singapore Pte Ltd. 2024
M. Rajaratne, *Concepts, Processes and Practice of Entrepreneurship*, Palgrave Studies in Global Entrepreneurship,
https://doi.org/10.1007/978-981-97-6180-7

SPRINGER NATURE

GPSR Compliance

The European Union's (EU) General Product Safety Regulation (GPSR) is a set of rules that requires consumer products to be safe and our obligations to ensure this.

If you have any concerns about our products, you can contact us on ProductSafety@springernature.com

In case Publisher is established outside the EU, the EU authorized representative is:

Springer Nature Customer Service Center GmbH
Europaplatz 3
69115 Heidelberg, Germany

The manufacturer's authorised representative in the EU is Springer Nature Customer Service Centre GmbH, Europaplatz 3, 69115 Heidelberg, Germany. If you have any concerns regarding our products, please contact ProductSafety@springernature.com

Printed and bound by CPI Group (UK) Ltd, Croydon, CR0 4YY
01/10/2026
02225854-0019